A TEXT BOOK OF

HYDRAULICS AND PNEUMATICS

For
T.E. SEMESTER – I

THIRD YEAR DEGREE COURSES IN
MECHANICAL ENGINEERING

As Per New Revised Syllabus of UoP, 2014

(Also useful for Production Engineering)

Dr. ANAND K. BEWOOR
Professor
Deptt. of Mech. Engg.
Cummins College of Engg. for Women's
Karvenagar, Pune.

Late SK PONDE
Formerly Professor and Head
Mechanical Engg. Dept.
Army Institute of Technology,
Dighi, Pune.

N 3170

HYDRAULICS AND PNEUMATICS (T.E, MECH)   **ISBN 978-93-5164-134-6**

Second Edition : August 2014

© : **Authors**

The text of this publication, or any part thereof, should not be reproduced or transmitted in any form or stored in any computer storage system or device for distribution including photocopy, recording, taping or information retrieval system or reproduced on any disc, tape, perforated media or other information storage device etc., without the written permission of Authors with whom the rights are reserved. Breach of this condition is liable for legal action.

Every effort has been made to avoid errors or omissions in this publication. In spite of this, errors may have crept in. Any mistake, error or discrepancy so noted and shall be brought to our notice shall be taken care of in the next edition. It is notified that neither the publisher nor the authors or seller shall be responsible for any damage or loss of action to any one, of any kind, in any manner, therefrom.

Published By :   **Printed By :**
NIRALI PRAKASHAN   **REPRO INDIA LTD,**
Abhyudaya Pragati, 1312, Shivaji Nagar,   **Mumbai**
Off J.M. Road, PUNE - 411005
Tel - (020) 25512336/37/39, Fax - (020) 25511379
Email : niralipune@pragationline.com

DISTRIBUTION CENTRES

PUNE

Nirali Prakashan   *Nirali Prakashan*
119, Budhwar Peth, Jogeshwari Mandir Lane   S. No. 28/25, Dhyari,
Pune 411002, Maharashtra   Near Pari Company, Pune 411041
Tel : (020) 2445 2044, 66022708, Fax : (020) 2445 1538   Tel : (022) 24690204 Fax : (020) 24690316
Email : bookorder@pragationline.com   Email : dhyari@pragationline.com
                                                                                       bookorder@pragationline.com

MUMBAI

Nirali Prakashan
385, S.V.P. Road, Rasdhara Co-op. Hsg. Society Ltd.,
Girgaum, Mumbai 400004, Maharashtra
Tel : (022) 2385 6339 / 2386 9976, Fax : (022) 2386 9976
Email : niralimumbai@pragationline.com

DISTRIBUTION BRANCHES

NAGPUR   **JALGAON**
Pratibha Book Distributors   *Nirali Prakashan*
Above Maratha Mandir, Shop No. 3, First Floor,   34, V. V. Golani Market, Navi Peth, Jalgaon 425001,
Rani Jhansi Square, Sitabuldi, Nagpur 440012,   Maharashtra, Tel : (0257) 222 0395
Maharashtra, Tel : (0712) 254 7129   Mob : 94234 91860

BENGALURU   **KOLHAPUR**
Pragati Book House   *Nirali Prakashan*
House No. 1, Sanjeevappa Lane, Avenue Road Cross,   New Mahadvar Road,
Opp. Rice Church, Bengaluru - 560002.   Kedar Plaza, 1st Floor Opp. IDBI Bank
Tel : (080) 64513344, 64513355,   Kolhapur 416 012, Maharashtra. Mob :
Mob : 9880582331, 9845021552   9855046155
Email:bharatsavla@yahoo.com

CHENNAI
Pragati Books
9/1, Montieth Road, Behind Taas Mahal, Egmore,
Chennai 600008 Tamil Nadu, Tel : (044) 6518 3535,
Mob : 94440 01782 / 98450 21552 / 98805 82331, Email : bharatsavla@yahoo.com

RETAIL OUTLETS

PUNE

Pragati Book Centre   *Pragati Book Centre*
157, Budhwar Peth, Opp. Ratan Talkies,   676/B, Budhwar Peth, Opp. Jogeshwari Mandir,
Pune 411002, Maharashtra   Pune 411002, Maharashtra
Tel : (020) 2445 8887 / 6602 2707, Fax : (020) 2445 8887   Tel : (020) 6601 7784 / 6602 0855
Pragati Book Centre   *PBC Book Sellers & Stationers*
Amber Chamber, 28/A, Budhwar Peth,   152, Budhwar Peth, Pune 411002, Maharashtra
Appa Balwant Chowk, Pune : 411002, Maharashtra,   Tel : (020) 2445 2254 / 6609 2463
Tel : (020) 20240335 / 66281669
Email : pbcpune@pragationline.com

MUMBAI
Pragati Book Corner
Indira Niwas, 111 - A, Bhavani Shankar Road, Dadar (W), Mumbai 400028, Maharashtra
Tel : (022) 2422 3526 / 6662 5254, Email : pbcmumbai@pragationline.com

PREFACE ......

It gives us immense pleasure to present this book **'Hydraulics and Pneumatic'** to the students of Third year Mechanical Engineering and Production Engineering of the University of Pune.

Many different machines and processes use a fluid for developing a force to move or hold an object or for controlling an action for higher accuracy in speed, force and position control. Scope of hydraulic and pneumatics is very vast. Countless applications can be cited. These revolutionary changes happening in the field of Fluid Power Technology are due to the integration of electronics as a control medium for hydraulic components and system.

Hydraulic system, which could generate high power and accuracy are now extensively used in machine tools, material handling devices, transport and other mobile equipments. And application of compressed air, pneumatic system, which is a cheap but very effective method of (low cost and speedy) automation technique and has found extensive use all over the world.

In this context, the first unit of the book deals with basic fluid power principles, components and applications. And also, types of hydraulic fluids and its conditioning. The second unit discusses. Various types of pumps and accumulator. The third unit explains and pneumatic circuits, various types of pressure, flow and directional control valves.

The Third unit focuses on discussion of actuators and its design aspects. Also, some important industrial circuits are discussed. The fifth unit enables us to understand principles, components and applications of pneumatics. The last (sixth) unit deals with design of hydraulic/pneumatic circuit of practical applications along with selection of different systems component.

The primary purpose of this book is to have the clear insite into the subject and make it understanding to the students. We advice the students to carefully to through the objectives of the Unit and keep in mind while reading. The authors will feel satisfied, if the book serves the cause of the students for whom this is intended, in that case they are thankful to all their friends, colleagues and admires.

As per New Revised Examination Scheme which has been implemented from this academic year, In-semester assessment carries 30 Marks, over first three units and End Semester Examination carries 70 Marks over entire syllabus of which First Three Units will carry 20 Marks and Units 4, 5, 6 will carry 50 Marks.

Publication of this book in such a short period required a very dedicated and active co-operation of the publisher. We gratefully acknowledge this co-operation from Shri Dineshbhai Furia, Shri Jignesh Furia and Shri M. P. Munde and team Mrs. Deepa Lachake, Mrs. Roshan Shaikh, Mrs. Shilpa Kale.

Our special thanks to our family members, students, and all those who directly or indirectly supported us in this project.

The frontiers of knowledge are boundless and fathomless. Any suggestions and feedback shall be appreciated and acknowledged.

Pune   **Authors**

SYLLABUS ......

Unit - I Introduction to Hydraulics and Pneumatics (08 hrs)

Introduction to oil hydraulics and pneumatics, their structure, advantages and limitations. Properties of fluids, Fluids for hydraulic systems, governing laws. Distribution of fluid power, ISO symbols, energy losses in hydraulic systems.

Unit - II Pumps (08 hrs)

Types, classification, principle of working and constructional details of vane pumps, gear pumps, radial and axial plunger pumps, screw pumps, power and efficiency calculations, characteristics curves, selection of pumps for hydraulic Power transmission.

Power units and accessories: Types of power units, reservoir assembly, constructional details, pressure switches, temperature switches.

Accumulators: Types, selection/ design procedure, applications of accumulators. Types of Intensifiers, Pressure switches /sensors, Temperature switches/sensors, Level sensors.

Unit - III Hydraulic Actuators (08 hrs)

(i) Linear and Rotary. (ii) Hydraulic motors - Types- Vane, Gear, Piston types, radial piston. (iii)Methods of control of acceleration, deceleration. (iv) Types of cylinders and mountings. (v) Calculation of piston velocity, thrust under static and dynamic applications, considering friction, inertia loads. (vi) Design considerations for cylinders. Cushioning of cylinders. (Numerical treatment).

Unit - IV Industrial Circuits (08 hrs)

Simple reciprocating, Regenerative, Speed control (Meter in, Meter out and bleed off), Sequencing, Synchronization, transverse and feed, circuit for riveting machine, automatic reciprocating, fail safe circuit, counter balance circuit, actuator locking, circuit for hydraulic press, unloading circuit (Numerical treatment), motor breaking circuit.

Unit - V Pneumatics (08 hrs)

Principle of Pneumatics: (i) Laws of compression, types of compressors, selection of compressors. (ii) Comparison of Pneumatics with Hydraulic power transmissions. (iii) Types of filters, regulators, lubricators, mufflers, dryers. (iv) Pressure regulating valves, (v) Direction control valves, two way, three way, four way valves. Solenoid operated valves, push button, lever control valves. (vi) Speed regulating Methods used in Pneumatics. (vii) Pneumatic actuators-rotary, reciprocating.(viii) Air motors- radial piston, vane, axial piston (ix) Basic pneumatic circuit, selection of components, (x) Application of pneumatics in low cost automation and in industrial automation.

Introduction to vacuum and vacuum measurement, Vacuum pumps, types, introduction to vacuum sensors and valves. Industrial application of vacuum.

Unit - VI System Design (08 hrs)

Design of hydraulic/pneumatic circuit for practical application, Selection of different components such as reservoir, various valves, actuators, filters, pumps based on design. (Students are advised to refer manufacturers catalogues)

CONTENTS ......

Unit I : Introduction of Hydraulic and Pneumatic   1.1-1.66

1.1 Introduction to Hydraulics and Pneumatics   1.1
     1.1.1 History   1.1
     1.1.2 Applications of Fluid Power   1.2
1.2 Structure of Hydraulic and Pneumatic Systems   1.6
1.3 Advantages of Fluid (Hydraulic and Pneumatic) Power Over Mechanical Power   1.8
1.4 Governing Laws and Properties of Fluids   1.9
     1.4.1 Introduction   1.9
     1.4.2 Pascal's law   1.9
     1.4.3 Bramah's Press   1.10
     1.4.4 Law of Conservation of Energy   1.10
     1.4.5 Law of Conservation of Mass and Equation of Continuity   1.10
     1.4.6 Newton's Second Law of Motion   1.11
     1.4.7 Principle of Angular Momentum   1.11
     1.4.8 Momentum Equation in a Differential Form   1.12
     1.4.9 Euler's Equation   1.12
     1.4.10 Energy Equation   1.12
1.5 Fluid Properties   1.12
     1.5.1 Viscosity   1.12
     1.5.2 Surface Tension   1.12
     1.5.3 Capillarity   1.13
     1.5.4 Bulk Modulus and Compressibility   1.13
     1.5.5 Reynold's Number 'Re'   1.14
     1.5.6 Types of Fluid Flow   1.14
     1.5.7 Boundary Layer   1.15
1.6 Fluid Pressure   1.15
1.7 Fluid Friction   1.16
1.8 Si System of Units   1.17
1.9 Fluids for Hydraulic Systems   1.18
     1.9.1 Introduction   1.18
     1.9.2 Functions of a Hydraulic Fluid   1.18
     1.9.3 Types of Hydraulic Fluids   1.19
         1.9.3.1 Mineral Oils   1.19
         1.9.3.2 Oil-in-Water Emulsion   1.19
         1.9.3.3 Water-in-Oil Emulsion   1.19
         1.9.3.4 Water Glycol Fluids   1.20
         1.9.3.5 Phosphate Esters   1.20
     1.9.4 Desirable Properties of Hydraulic Fluids   1.20

		1.9.4.1 Specific Gravity	1.20
		1.9.4.2 Viscosity	1.20
	1.9.5	Stability in Shear	1.23
	1.9.6	Foaming Characteristics	1.23
	1.9.7	Cloud Point and Pour Point	1.24
	1.9.8	Oil Compressibility and Bulk Modulus	1.24
	1.9.9	Coefficient of Thermal Expansion	1.24
	1.9.10	Wettability	1.24
	1.9.11	Flammability	1.24
	1.9.12	Chemical Status	1.25
	1.9.13	Affinity for Moisture	1.25
	1.9.14	Gumming Tendency	1.25
	1.9.15	Oxidation Tendency	1.25
	1.9.16	Corrosion Resistance	1.25
	1.9.17	Wear Resistance	1.25
	1.9.18	Compatibility with System Materials	1.25
	1.9.19	Heat Dissipation Property	1.25
	1.9.20	Non-toxic, easy to handle and available	1.27
1.10	Additives to Hydraulic Fluids		1.27
1.11	Factors Influencing the Selection of a Fluid		1.27
1.12	Some Commonly Used Hydraulic Fluids		1.28
	1.12.1	Petroleum Oils	1.28
	1.12.2	Water	1.29
	1.12.3	High Water Based Fluids	1.29
	1.12.4	Fire Resistant Fluids	1.30
1.13	Distribution of Fluid Power		1.30
	1.13.1	Introduction to Seals	1.30
		1.13.1.1 Classification of Seals	1.31
	1.13.2	Factors Influencing the Selection of Seals	1.33
	1.13.3	Desirable Properties of an Ideal Material for Seals	1.33
	1.13.4	Seal Materials	1.34
1.14	Compatibility of Seal with Fludis		1.35
1.15	Types of Seals		1.37
1.16	Wiper Ring		1.38
1.17	Seal Friction		1.39
1.18	Causes for Seal Failure		1.40
1.19	Introduction to Pipers and Hoses		1.40
1.20	Metallic Pipes		1.41
1.21	Schedule Number of Standard Pipe		1.42
1.22	Hydraulic Hoses		1.42

		1.22.1	Advantages and Limitations of Hoses	1.43
		1.22.2	Hose Materials	1.43
		1.22.3	Construction of Hoses	1.44
		1.22.4	Reinforcement for Hoses	1.45
		1.22.5	Protective Covers and other Devices	1.46
		1.22.6	Sizing of Tubings, and Hoses	1.46
		1.22.7	Factors Influencing the Selection of Hoses	1.47
	1.23	Hose Fittings and Connectors		1.47
		1.23.1	Types of Hose Fittings	1.48
			1.23.1.1 Quick Couplings	1.48
		1.23.2	Flared and Compression Fitting	1.49
	1.24	ISO Symboles		1.51
		1.24.1	Introduction	1.51
		1.24.2	Pumps	1.52
		1.24.3	Motors	1.52
		1.24.4	Cylinders	1.53
		1.24.5	Valves	1.53
		1.24.6	Flow Control Valves	1.54
		1.24.7	Directional Control Valves	1.54
		1.24.8	Energy Transmission and Accessories	1.55
	1.25	Energy Losses in Hydraulic Systems		1.61
		1.25.1	Introduction to Energy Losses in Hydraulics	1.61
		1.25.2	Losses in Pipeline Components	1.62
•		Exercise		1.67
Unit II : Pumps				**2.1-2.100**
	2.1	Introduction to Hydraulic Pumps		2.1
	2.2	Classification of Hydraulic Pumps		2.2
		2.2.1	Principle and Salient Features of Non-positive (Hydro-dynamic) Displacement Pumps	2.3
		2.2.2	Centrifugal Pumps	2.4
	2.3	Principle and Advantages of Hydrostatic/Positive Displacement Pumps		2.6
	2.4	Vane Pumps		2.6
		2.4.1	Construction and Principle of Operation	2.6
		2.4.2	Side Thrust on the Shaft	2.7
		2.4.3	Balanced Vane Pump	2.8
		2.4.4	Variable Displacement Vane Pump	2.8
		2.4.5	Pressure Compensated Vane Pump	2.9
		2.4.6	Performance Characteristics of Vane Pumps	2.10
	2.5	Gear Pumps		2.11
		2.5.1	Introduction	2.11

	2.5.2	Construction and Principle of Working	2.11
	2.5.3	Performance Characteristics of a Gear Pump	2.13
	2.5.4	Pressure Balancing in a Gear Pump	2.16
	2.5.5	Wear Plates	2.16
	2.5.6	Internal Gear Pump	2.17
	2.5.7	Herring-bone Gear Pump	2.18
	2.5.8	Gerotor Pump	2.18
2.6	Lobe Pumps		2.19
2.7	Piston Pumps		2.20
	2.7.1	Radial Piston Pumps (Radial Plunger Pump)	2.21
	2.7.2	Axial Piston Pumps	2.22
	2.7.3	In Line Axial Piston Pump (Parallel Piston Pump)	2.22
	2.7.4	Bent Axis Axial Piston Pumps	2.26
	2.7.5	Performance of Axial Piston Pump	2.27
	2.7.6	In-line Crank-shaft Driven Pumps	2.28
2.8	Difference Between Positive Displacement Pumps and Non-Positive Displacement Pumps		2.29
2.9	Selection of Pumps		2.30
2.10	Expected Life to Hydraulic Pumps		2.31
2.11	Noise from Hydraulic Pumps		2.32
2.12	Summary of Formulae for Pump Displacement		2.33
2.13	Introduction to Reservoir		2.47
	2.13.1	Functions of Reservoir	2.47
	2.13.2	Types of Reservoirs	2.47
	2.13.3	Reservoir Sizing	2.48
	2.13.4	Reservoir Shapes	2.48
	2.13.5	Design of Reservoir Surface for Heat Dissipation	2.49
	2.13.6	Reservoir Construction and Design Features	2.49
	2.13.7	Accessories to the Reservoir	2.51
2.14	Filtration		2.52
	2.14.1	Terminologies in Filtration	2.52
	2.14.2	Design Considerations of a Filter	2.52
	2.14.3	Types of Filters	2.53
	2.14.4	Technology of Filtration	2.55
	2.14.5	Indicators of Filter-Condition	2.57
	2.14.6	Construction of Filters	2.58
	2.14.7	Location of a Filter	2.60
	2.14.8	Sizing of Filters	2.62
2.15	Pressure Switches		2.64
2.16	Temperature Switches		2.64

2.17	Introduction to Accumulator	2.65
	2.17.1 Dead Weight or Gravity Type	2.66
	2.17.2 Spring Loaded Accumulator	2.66
	2.17.3 Gas Loaded/Charged accumulators	2.67
	2.17.4 Comparison of Various Types of Gas Filled Accumulators	2.71
	2.17.5 Significance of nitrogen for gas filled accumulator	2.72
	2.17.6 Applications of Hydraulic Accumulators	2.72
	2.17.7 Calculation Of Demand Volume Of An Accumulator	2.76
	2.17.8 Comparison Of Various Types Of Gas Filled Accumulators	2.78
	2.17.9 Efficiency Of An Accumulator Circuit	2.78
2.18	Intensifier	2.78
	2.18.1 Hydraulic Intensifier	2.79
	2.18.2 Construction of an intensifier	2.82
	2.18.3 Principle of operation	2.83
•	Exercise	2.97

Unit - III : Hydraulic Actuators   3.1-3.46

3.1	Introduction	3.1
3.2	Rotary Actuators (Hydraulic Motors)	3.2
3.3	Vane Motors	3.2
3.4	Gear Motors	3.4
3.5	Piston Motors	3.6
	3.5.1 Axial Piston Motors	3.6
	3.5.2 Radial Piston Motors	3.7
3.6	Semi-Rotary (or Limited Rotation) Actuators	3.8
	3.6.1 Vane Type Semi-Rotary Actuators	3.9
	3.6.2 Piston Type Semi-Rotary Actuator	3.10
	3.6.3 Chain and Sprocket Actuator	3.11
	3.6.4 Helical Screw Actuator	3.11
	3.6.5 Control of Semi-Rotary Actuators	3.12
3.7	Deceleration Type Flow Control Valve	3.12
3.8	Linear Actuators (Hydraulic Cylinders)	3.13
3.9	Constructional Features	3.17
3.10	Mountings of Hydraulic Cylinders	3.17
3.11	Methods of Installation	3.18
3.12	Estimation of Cylinder Force, Acceleration and Losses	3.19
	3.12.1 Estimation of Friction Force and Cylinder Losses	3.21
	3.12.2 Effective Useful Cylinder Force	3.22
	3.12.3 Estimation of Pressure Drop in Cylinder	3.22
	3.12.4 Determination of Piston Rod Diameter and Length	3.22
	3.12.5 Loading on the Piston Rod	3.23

		3.12.6	Determination of Cylinder Forces	3.23
		3.12.7	Estimation of Flow Velocities	3.23
		3.12.8	Design of Piston Rod	3.24
		3.12.9	Maximum Piston-speeds	3.25
	3.13	Efficiency of Cylinder		3.26
	3.14	Determination of Cylinder Wall Thickness		3.27
	3.15	Permissible Operating Temperature		3.28
	3.16	Determination of Speed of a Double Acting Cylinder		3.28
	3.17	Determination of Cylinder Thrust		3.30
	3.18	Acceleration and Deceleration of Cylinder Loads		3.30
	3.19	Cylinder Cushioning (A Method of Achieve Pistion Deceleration Towards the End of Stroke)		3.31
	•	Exercise		3.45

Unit IV : Industrial Circuits — 4.1-4.78

4.1	Necessity of Fluid Control			4.1
	4.1.1	Need of Direction Control		4.1
	4.1.2	Need of Pressure Control		4.1
	4.1.3	Need of Flow Control		4.1
4.2	Pressure Control Valves			4.2
4.2.1	Types of Pressure Control Valves			4.2
	4.2.2	Pressure Relief Valves		4.2
	4.2.3	Pressure Control Valve Characteristic		4.4
	4.2.4	Pilot Operated Relief Valve		4.5
	4.2.5	Dual Pressure Relief Valves		4.6
	4.2.6	Selection of Relief Valve and Choice of Pressure Setting		4.6
4.3	Safety Valves			4.7
4.4	Pressure Sequencing Valves			4.7
4.5	Unloaded Valves			4.8
4.6	Pressure Reducing Valves			4.9
4.7	Counter Balance Valves			4.10
4.8	Hydraulic Fuse			4.12
4.9	Flow Control Valves			4.16
	4.9.1	Basic Principle of a Flow Control		4.16
	4.9.2	Flow Phenomena Across a Throttling Aperture		4.18
	4.9.3	Coefficient of Resistance 'ξ' (Signifies Energy Loss in Bends, Tees, Valves etc.		4.19
	4.9.4	Determination of Flow Rate		4.19
	4.9.5	Forms of Throttle		4.19
	4.9.6	Performance of Throttle Valve		4.23
4.10	Estimation of Flow Rate Through an Orifice			4.24

4.11	Types of Flow Control Valves	4.25
	4.11.1 Pressure Compensated Flow Control Valve	4.25
	4.11.2 Temperature or Viscosity Compensated Flow Control Valves	4.27
	4.11.3 Deceleration Type Flow Control Valve	4.27
4.12	Regerative Circuit of a Hydraulic Cylinder	4.28
4.13	Industrial Hydraulic Circuits	4.29
4.14	Control of a Single Acting Sprin Return Hydraulic Cylinder (Simple Reciprocating Circuit)	4.30
4.15	Control of Double Acting Hydraulic Cylinder	4.31
4.16	Regenerative Circuit for Fast Extending of a Double Acting Cylinder	4.32
4.17	Speed Control	4.33
4.18	Sequencing Circuit	4.37
4.19	Hydraulic Circuit For Synchronization Of Cylinders	4.39
	4.19.1 Synchronizing with Flow Control Valves	4.39
	4.19.2 Synchronizing with Flow Dividing Motors	4.40
4.20	Transverse and Feed	4.41
4.21	Circuit for Riveting Machine	4.43
4.22	Hydraulic Circuit for Automatic Reciprocation of a Hydraulic Cylinder	4.44
4.23	Hydraulic Circuit With Fail – Safe Feature	4.45
4.24	Hydraulic Circuit Using Counter Balance Valve	4.47
4.25	Hydraulic Circuit for Hydraulic Press	4.50
4.26	Hydraulic Circuit for Unloading of Pump	4.50
4.27	Hydraulic Circuit for Braking of Hydraulic Motor	4.50
•	Exercise	4.70
Unit – V : Pneumatics		**5.1-5.128**
5.1	Introduction	5.1
5.2	Principles of Pneumatics	5.1
	5.2.1 Properties of Air	5.2
	5.2.2 The Gas Laws	5.2
	5.2.3 Types of Expansion and Compression	5.3
	5.2.4 Expansion of Air	5.4
	5.2.5 Compression of Air	5.5
5.3	Basic Pneumatic System	5.6
	5.3.1 Flow through Pipes and Pressure Drop	5.6
5.4	Compressor Plant Layout	5.7
	5.4.1 Piping and Line Installation	5.8
	5.4.2 Installation of Pipings	5.11
5.5	Introduction to Compressors	5.14
5.6	Classification of Compressors	5.14
	5.6.1 Single Acting Compressors	5.15

	5.6.2	Double Acting Compressors	5.15
5.7	Reciprocating Compressors	5.15
	5.7.1	Construction	5.15
5.8	P-V Diagram for the Compressor	5.17
	5.8.1	Work Done in One Cycle of Compression	5.18
	5.8.2	Volumetric Efficiency of Compressor	5.18
	5.8.3	Mean Effective Pressure	5.18
	5.8.4	Selection Criteria for Compressors	5.18
5.9	Rotary Vane Compressor	5.19
5.10	Liquid Ring Compressor	5.20
5.11	Lobe Compressor	5.21
5.12	Screw Compressor	5.21
5.13	Centrifugal Compressors	5.22
5.14	Air Receiver	5.22
5.15	Factors Influencing Selection of Air Compressors	5.24
5.16	Comparison of Pneumatic and Hydraulic Systems	5.29
	5.16.1	Introduction to Air Treatment	5.30
5.17	Service Unit or F-R-L Unit	5.32
	5.17.1	Air Filter	5.32
	5.17.2	Construction and Working of Air Filter	5.32
	5.17.3	Pressure Regulator	5.34
	5.17.4	Lubricator	5.35
5.18	Drying of Compressed Air	5.37
5.19	After Cooler	5.43
5.20	Muffler (Pneumatic Silencer)	5.44
5.21	Pressure Regulating Valve	5.44
5.22	Pneumatic Valves	5.46
5.23	Direction Control Valves	5.46
	5.23.1	Poppet and Ball Seat Valves and Sliding Spool Valves	5.48
5.24	Non-Return Valves	5.61
5.25	Speed Control Valves	5.64
5.26	Pneumatic Actuators	5.65
5.27	Pneumatic Cylinders	5.65
	5.27.1	Single Acting Single Rod Cylinders	5.65
	5.27.2	Diaphragm Cylinders	5.66
	5.27.3	Double Acting Cylinders	5.67
	5.27.4	Special Type Cylinders	5.68
	5.27.5	Cushioning of Standard Double Acting Cylinder	5.73
	5.27.6	Cylinder Sizing	5.74
5.28	Pneumatic Motors (Rotary Actuators)	5.78

	5.28.1 Vane Motors	5.79
	5.28.2 Piston Motors (Radial and Axial)	5.80
	5.28.3 Gear Motors	5.80
	5.28.4 Air Motor Efficiencies	5.81
5.29	Basic Pneumatic Circuits	5.82
	5.29.1 Control of Single Acting Cylinder	5.82
5.30	Control of Double Acting Cylinders	5.84
5.31	Speed Control of Pneumatic Cylinders	5.85
5.32	Safety Circuit	5.87
5.33	Cylinder Cycle Timing System	5.88
5.34	Use of Start-Up Interlock	5.89
5.35	Air Motor Control Circuit	5.91
5.36	Air Cushioning of Cylinders in Both Stroke Ends	5.91
5.37	Sequence Circuits	5.91
5.38	Applications of Pneumatics in low cost Automation and Industrial Automation	5.95
5.39	Instruction for selection of Pneumatic Components	5.99
	5.39.1 General instruction for selection of Pneumatic components	5.99
	5.39.2 Product Selection Instructions	5.99
	5.39.3 Product Assembly and Installation Instructions	5.100
	5.39.4 Cylinder and Accessories Selection	5.101
5.40	Vacuum Measurement	5.115
	5.40.1 McLeod Gage	5.116
	5.40.2 Pirani Gage	5.117
	5.40.3 Ionization Gage	5.117
5.41	Vacuum Pumps	5.118
5.41.1	Rotary Pump	5.118
	5.41.2 Other Mechanical Pumps	5.121
5.42 Vacuum Sensors		5.122
•	Exercise	5.125
Unit - VI : System Design		**6.1-6-50**
6.1	Introduction	6.1
6.2	Design Considerations	6.1
6.3	Information Required for Design	6.2
6.4	Design Study	6.2
•	Exercise	6.49
Appendix		**A.1-A.12**

Unit I

INTRODUCTION TO HYDRAULICS AND PNEUMATICS

1.1 INTRODUCTION TO HYDRAULICS AND PNEUMATICS

Fluid power technology as the name suggests, is the system that uses fluid for generation of power for performing a variety of tasks. The technology also deals with control and transmission of power. The fluid to which pressure is given, can be a liquid or a gas. The tasks of machines, machine tools and various other devices that consist of pushing, pulling, regulating and driving various units are now efficiently undertaken by more and more increasing use of fluid power technology. In every walk of life we find applications like brakes in automobiles, launching of aircrafts, moving of earth, cutting, harvesting crops, taking out coals from mines, driving machine tools, processing of food etc. that use the fluid power technology.

Systems using liquid as fluid are known as Hydraulic systems. They use liquids such as petroleum oils, water, synthetic oils.

Systems using gas as medium are pneumatic systems. Pneumatic systems use air as gas medium. Air is abundant and can be exhausted into the atmosphere after the work is complete.

Fluid power systems, are meant for performing some work while fluid transport systems have entirely different objectives like pumping water, gas to homes etc.

In fluid power systems, work is obtained by pressurised fluid bearing directly on a fluid cylinder or motor. The fluid cylinder produces force and linear motion while the motor produces torque and rotary motion.

1.1.1 History

Earlier water was used as a fluid medium with watermills and propel ships were driven with air windmills. These are low pressure high flow applications.

Following is a brief history of events and developments in the field of fluid power.

Table 1.1

Year	Event/Development happened
1650	Pascal's law.
1750	Bernoulli's developed law of conservation of energy.
1850	Industrial revolution in European countries.
1870	Electrical energy replaced hydraulic systems for driving cranes, presses, winches, extruding machines, jacks, riveting machines etc. Till 1906 there was total dominance of electrical systems.
1906	Hydraulic system was developed for replacing electrical system for application of elevating and controlling guns on a battleship, USS Virginia. Use of oil as medium.
1926	Development of packaged hydraulic system having pump, controls and actuators. Thereafter ever increasing use in the naval industry, cargo handling, winches, submarine control system, aerospace technology and so on.

1.1.2 Applications of Fluid Power   (Dec. 08, May 10)

Fluid Power Applications (Broad Classification):

- **Mobile:** Here fluid power is used to transport, excavate and lift materials as well as control or power mobile equipment. The end use industries include construction, agriculture, marine and the military. Applications include backhoes, graders, tractors, truck brakes and suspensions, spreaders and highway maintenance vehicles.

- **Industrial:** Here the fluid power is used to provide power transmission and motion control for the machines of the industry. End use industries range from plastics working to paper production. Applications include metal working equipment, controllers, automated manipulators, material handling and assembly equipment.

- **Aerospace:** Fluid power is used for both commercial and military aircraft, spacecraft and related support equipments. Applications include landing gear, brakes, flight controls, motor controls and cargo loading equipment.

Fluid Power Products :

Fluid power products are sold as individual components or as systems for the original equipment manufacturing, maintenance, repair and replacement markets.

1. Use of Fluid Power in Machine Tools, Processes and Automation :

Oil and air systems are widely used to serve various purposes in machine tools and automation systems. The tasks of clamping work pieces, moving materials from station to station, actual performance of operations like punching, welding, drilling, loading and unloading machines, safety to operators and many other such functions are now accomplished by using fluid power systems in machine tools, transfer machines, special purpose machines, NC/CNC machines and flexible manufacturing systems.

Some examples are given below.

- A 17 spindle, automatic indexing machine produces nine different part sizes in three different part configurations. Pneumatic and hydraulic systems are used to give production rates of 80 parts per hour to 170 parts per hour.

- In a typical die casting machine used for casting of aluminium filled electric motor rotors, extensive hydraulic system is used. Interlocks are also provided unless the door is closed or machine does not start. A large accumulator is provided to assist the hydraulic pump at peak pressure requirements. Petroleum fluids and fire resistant fluids are used in such systems.

- In many automobiles or other components like connecting rods or crankcases of compressors, special purpose machines are employed for drilling or boring operations. The production rate is high, i.e between 800 to 1000 parts per hour. All operations such as clamping of parts, movement of two slides simultaneously for feeding, indexing, are performed by hydraulic systems.

Air operated chucks and tailstocks are used on high speed production lathes.

- In a three axis milling machines, NC controlled or CNC controlled or machining centres in todays world, command signals are generated through programmes and are given to the hydraulic control actuators to get the motion and force required for performing operations. Rapid response, ease of control, precision and accuracy, variable speed and amplification of force are important features of such machines.

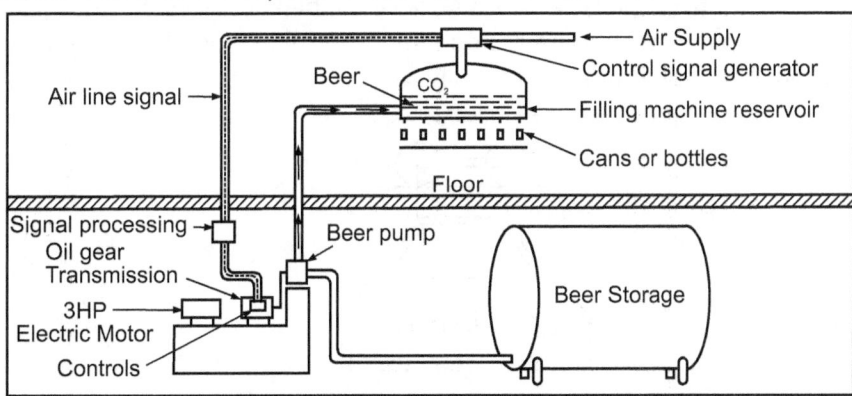

Fig. 1.1: Stabilizing beer filling level

- Fig. 1.1 shows the use of fluid power in making beverages. Gentle handling of bottles, accurate level filling of quantity (because speedily filling creates foam) in bottles become important considerations. Fluid power provides the solution. Beer is pumped from storage tanks to the bottle or can filling machine reservoirs on the floor above. For controlling liquid level low pressure CO_2 signal is used. It is pressure signal CO_2 signal is relayed to controls of transmission, which control the beer pumps.

- In Fig. 1.2 the use of hydraulic system for positioning and holding parts while welding is done is illustrated. Here it is required to hold the part first and then welding should start. This is achieved by the use of sequence valve.

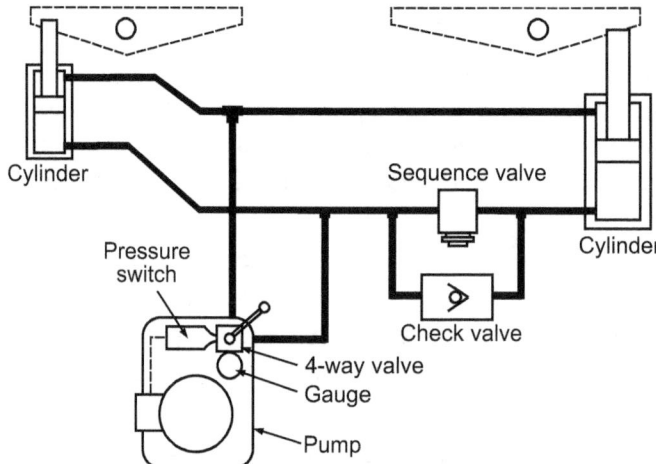

Fig. 1.2: Hydraulic circuit for welding application

2. Fluid Power Used for High Wire Overhead Tram :

In a unique 22 passenger, 12000 lb hydraulically powered and controlled sky-tram is shown in Fig. 1.3. The pump supplies fluid to 4 motors to drive two friction drive wheels. Here the tram moves instead of the cable (which otherwise happens in usual electrical cable moved cars) and hence operation can start stop and reverse independently. Different torque requirements are met with a suitable system here.

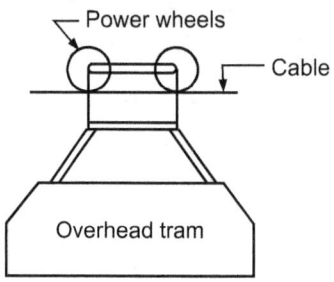

Fig. 1.3

3. Agriculture Industry :

Fluid power is used to solve problems dealing with harvesting of food crops for obtaining a high rate of production. Cutting, separation of husks and moving grains to trailers are the tasks required to be done. These are handled by conveyors and other machines that are hydraulically driven.

4. Power Brushes for Cleaning :

For cleaning roads, floors etc. in industries and other places, power driven brushes are required. The sweep-scrub brushes are placed at the underside of the vehicle which are directly driven by compact hydraulic motors.

5. Material Movement in Industry :

Material handling is a crucial function in any industry. Various equipments are required to move materials from one place to another including conveyors, fork lifts, robots and other equipments. A fork lift may have to lift a load of 5000 lb and raising, lowering, tilting are required so that the products are kept in the proper place. All this can be achieved by using a hydraulic system.

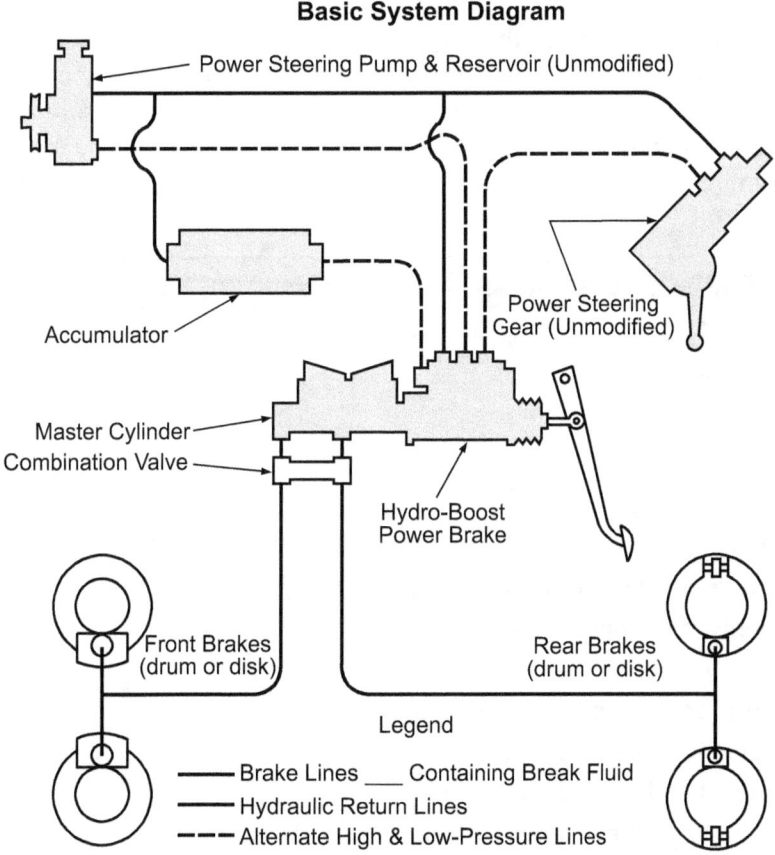

Fig. 1.4: Bendix Hydro-Boost power brake system

6. Earth Moving and Coal Mining Industry :

Front end loaders filling earth in dump trucks use hydraulic powdered buckets for scooping up the soil. With lower effort the operator can control all complex actions. Several hydraulic cylinders and jacks are used for digging and loading coal from mines at a very high rate e.g. 2 tons per minute. The hydraulic controls can be actuated from one location to operate the machine. Fluid power thus gives better, safer and more efficient methods in mining coal.

7. Use in Injection Moulding Machines :

Plastic parts produced in large quantities are widely used in industry and in domestic uses. Products like, tooth brush handles, combs, tubes, buckets, thermoware parts are made in injection moulding machines. The entire system of opening and closing moulds, feeding and injection of plastic into them, part removal and safety features are accomplished using hydraulic systems.

8. Use of Fluid Power in Automobiles :

Fluid power offers safe and dependable power source for vehicle steering and braking systems. The pump is powered by the engine and supplies fluid to the system. Refer Fig. 1.4. Special valves are provided for braking and steering functions. The accumulator (that is a device for storage of pressure energy) is also kept charged. Pressure is supplied for assistance in steering and to dual master cylinder braking system finally to actuate discs or drum for braking. The system is compact and comfortable for automobile drivers.

1.2 STRUCTURE OF HYDRAULIC AND PNEUMATIC SYSTEMS

Basic components of a hydraulic system are:
- Tank (reservoir),
- Pump,
- Electric motor to drive the pump,
- Valves to control fluid flow.
- Actuator to convert hydraulic energy into mechanical force or torque.
- Connections and pipings to transport fluid in the system.

Basic components of the pneumatic system are :
- Air tank to store the compressed air.
- Compressor: For obtaining the pressured air.
- Electric motor to drive the compressor.
- Valves to direct and control the air flow.
- Actuators similar to the hydraulic system.
- Piping to carry the air.

In actual practice, two fluids are most commonly used viz. oil and compressed air. A fluid system that uses oil is called a "hydraulic system". And a fluid system that uses compressed air is called a "pneumatic system".

(a) Hydraulic System Components: (May 12)

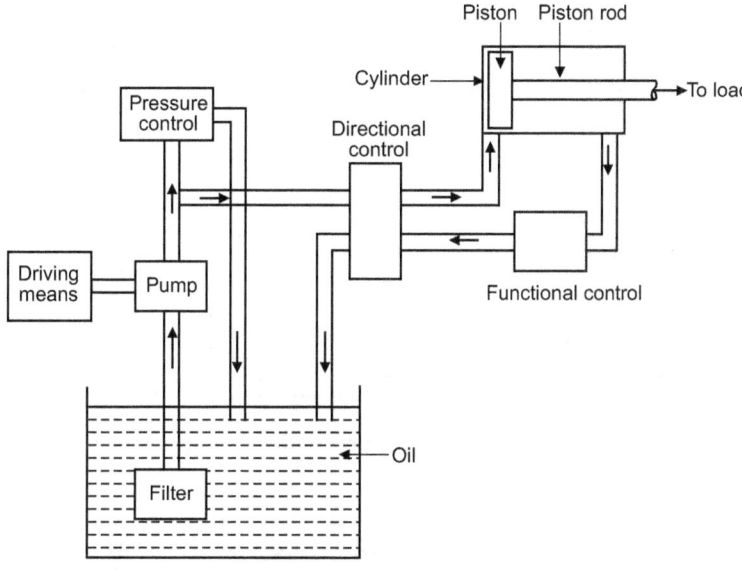

Fig. 1.5 : Typical hydraulic system

Refer Fig. 1.5 which represents simple hydraulic system. It consists of oil which flows from the tank or the reservoir through a hose tube or a pipe into a pump. The pump can be driven by an electric motor/gas turbine/I.C. engine. This pump increases the oil pressure. This high-pressure oil flows through the control (direction/flow/ pressure) valve. Relief valve is used to protect the system by setting it at a desired safe maximum pressure to prevent damage to either the system or the surroundings. Then the pressured oil enters into the cylinder and exerts pressure on the piston; this action over the area of the piston develops a force on the piston rod, which can be used to move a load a device. Then oil from the cylinder returns to the reservoir. When oil passes through the filter, dirt and foreign matter are removed from the oil.

(b) Pneumatic System Components: This system uses compressed air as a fluid. Fig. 1.2 explains the pneumatic system. Compressor compresses the air taken from the atmosphere and increases the pressure of air. It is run by either an electric motor or an I.C. engine. A filter unit in the system removes the dirt from this compressed air and the lubricator in the circuit adds some oil to the air passing through it which in turn lubricates any sliding surfaces viz. the piston and cylinder surfaces. This filtered, lubricated compressed air develops a force on the piston in turn piston rod for moving a device or rod in a straight line. A relief valve unit in the circuit is situated at the compressor's discharge side, which is used to avoid dangerously high pressure.

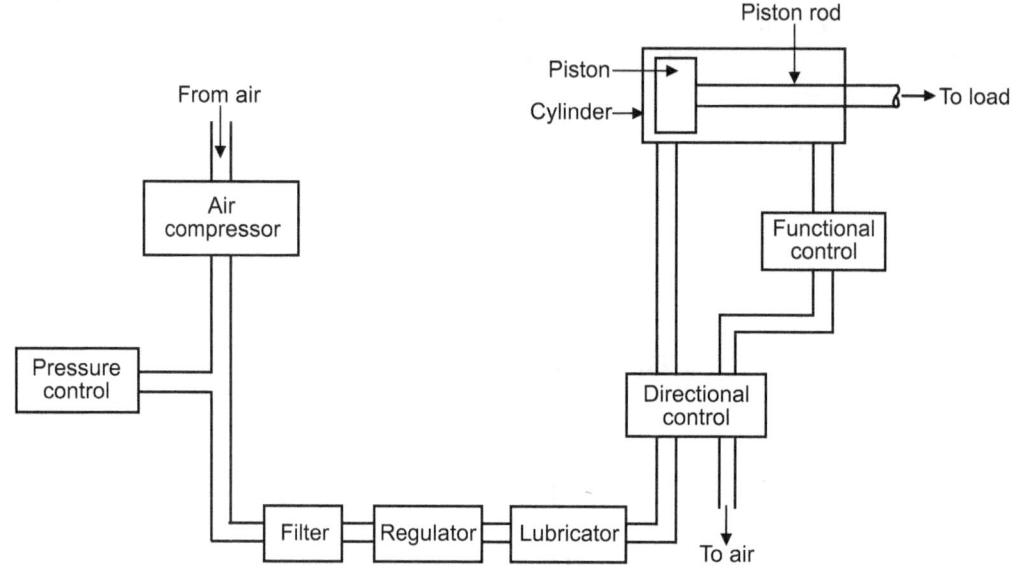

Fig. 1.6: Typical pneumatic system

1.3 Advantages of Fluid (Hydraulic and Pneumatic) Power Over Mechanical Power

Fluid power systems provide many benefits to users including:

- **Multiplication and variation of force:** Linear or rotary force can be multiplied from a fraction of an ounce to several hundred tons of output.

- **Easy, accurate control:** You can start, stop, accelerate, decelerate, reverse or position large forces with great accuracy. Both analog (infinitely variable) and digital (on/off) controls are possible. Instant reversible motion - within less than half a revolution can be achieved.

- **Multi-function control:** A single hydraulic pump or air compressor can provide power and control for numerous machines or machine functions when combined with fluid power manifolds and valves.

- **High horsepower, low weight ratio:** Pneumatic components are compact and light-weight. You can hold a five horsepower hydraulic motor in the palm of your hand.

- **Low speed torque:** Unlike electric motors, air or hydraulic motors can produce large amounts of torque (twisting force) while operating at low speeds. Some hydraulic and air motors can even maintain torque at zero speed without overheating.

- **Constant force or torque:** This is a unique fluid power attribute.

- **Safety in hazardous environments:** Fluid power can be used in mines, chemical plants, near explosives and in paint applications because it is inherently spark-free and can tolerate high temperatures.

- **Established standards and engineering:** The fluid power industry has established design and performance standards for hydraulic and pneumatic products through NFPA, the National Fluid Power Association and ISO, the International Organization for Standardization.

1.4 GOVERNING LAWS AND PROPERTIES OF FLUIDS

1.4.1 Introduction

For better understanding of the subject of Industrial Fluid Power, a review of hydraulic principles is worthwhile. Hydraulics are concerned with the characteristics and usage of liquids. Man has been using the basics of hydraulics since ages e.g. floating down a river astride a leg of wood, producing power using water wheels.

In 17th century, the science of hydraulics was introduced, by a French scientist Pascal.

1.4.2 Pascal's law

This law states that pressure applied on a confined fluid is transmitted equally in all directions.

A glass bottle full of liquid breaks when a stopper is forced into it. The liquid being incompressible, develops a very high pressure due to the force on the stopper. This pressure is equally transmitted in all directions thereby causing the bottle to break. Fig. 1.7 illustrates the concept.

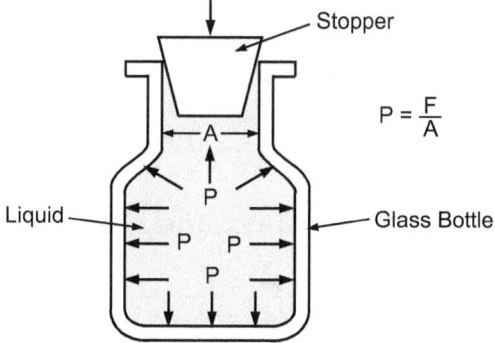

Fig. 1.7 : Pressure is transmitted equally in directions in a confined fluid

1.4.3 Bramah's Press

It was a British mechanic Bramah who utilised the Pascal's law to produce a large force while applying a small force on a small area as shown in Fig. 1.8.

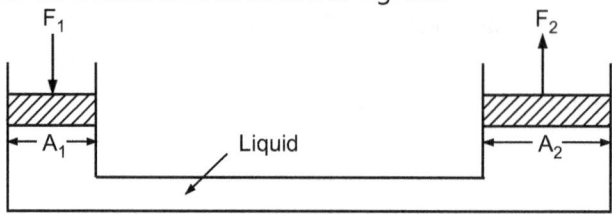

Fig. 1.8: Bramah's press

$$p = \frac{F_1}{A_1} \qquad \text{hence } F_2 = p \times A_2$$

Thus $\quad \dfrac{F_1}{A_1} = \dfrac{F_2}{A_2} \qquad \therefore \quad F_2 = F_1 \times \dfrac{A_2}{A_1}$

1.4.4 Law of Conservation of Energy

This law states that energy can neither be created nor can it be destroyed i.e. total energy in the universe remains constant.

Bernoulli's Theorem: The application of the law of conservation of energy applied to a steady flow of fluid, through a pipe leads to the Bernoulli's theorem.

This theorem states that in a steady flow of fluid, the sum of the potential head (datum head), velocity head and pressure head remains constant throughout.

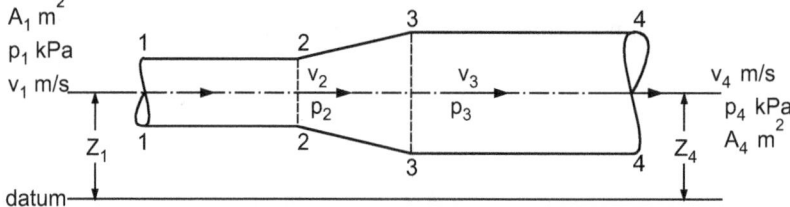

Fig. 1.9: Steady flow of fluid through a pipe

Neglecting the losses, it can be written as

$$\frac{p_1}{eg} + \frac{v_1^2}{zg} + z_1 = \frac{p_2}{eg} + \frac{v_2^2}{zg} + z_2 \ldots = \frac{p_4}{eg} + \frac{v_4^2}{zg} + z_2 \text{ m}$$

1.4.5 Law of Conservation of Mass and Equation of Continuity

The law of conservation of mass states that mass can neither be created nor destroyed i.e. total mass in the universe remains constant.

The application of the law of conservation of mass to a steady flow of fluid through a pipe line leads to the equation of continuity.

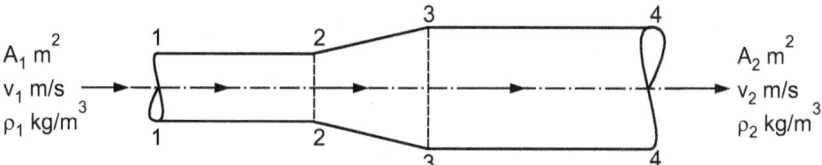

Fig. 1.10: Steady flow of fluid through a pipe line

For any steady flow system,

$$\therefore \quad \Delta m_{system} = 0$$

$\therefore$ Total mass entering the system/s = Total mass leaving the system/s
= Total mass flow crossing any intermediate section/s

$$\therefore \quad \rho_1 A_1 v_1 = \rho_2 A_2 v_2 = \rho_3 A_3 v_3 = \rho_4 A_4 v_4 \text{ kg/s} \qquad \ldots (1.1)$$

Equation (1.1) is known as the equation of continuity for a compressible fluid flow.

In case of a steady flow of liquids which are regarded incompressible for all practical purposes (i.e. having constant density throughout), the continuity equation assumes a still single form.

$$A_1 v_1 = A_2 v_2 = A_3 v_3 = A_4 v_4 \text{ m}^3/\text{s} \qquad \ldots (1.2)$$

$$\therefore \rho = \text{constant} \ldots\ldots$$

1.4.6 Newton's Second Law of Motion

This law states that force 'F' is proportional to the rate of change of momentum 'M'.

Thus
$$F \propto \frac{dM}{dt} \propto \frac{d}{dt}(mV)$$

$$= K \times m \frac{dV}{dt} \quad \text{when mass 'm' is constant.}$$

- **Fluid:** Anything that can flow is a fluid. Hydraulic systems employ incompressible fluids while pneumatic systems use compressible fluids like gas as a working medium.

  A fluid deforms continuously under the application of a shear (tangential) stress.

- **Ideal Fluid:** It is defined as an incompressible fluid having zero viscosity.
- **Newtonian Fluid:** It is defined as the fluid in which the shear stress is directly proportional to the rate of deformation.
- **Non-Newtonian Fluid:** These are fluids in which the shear stress is not directly proportional to the rate of deformation.

1.4.7 Principle of Angular Momentum

This principle states that the rate of change of angular momentum is equal to the sum of all the torques acting on the system.

$$T = \frac{dH}{dt} \text{ N-m} \qquad \ldots (1.3)$$

where H = Angular momentum of the system.

HYDRAULICS AND PNEUMATICS

1.4.8 Momentum Equation in a Differential Form

The equation for Newton's second law of motion is also known as the momentum equation. It can be written in a differential form

$$F = K \frac{dM}{dt} \quad \text{where } M = \int v\, dm \quad \text{... (1.4)}$$

$$\therefore \quad dF = K \times m \frac{dV}{dt} \quad \text{if } m = \text{constant.}$$

1.4.9 Euler's Equation

The equation of motion for frictionless flow of a fluid is known as Euler's equation. In a single vector form, it is given by

$$\rho g - \nabla p = \rho \frac{dV}{dt} \quad \text{... (1.5)}$$

1.4.10 Energy Equation

This equation is based on the law of conservation of energy.

For a steady flow of incompressible fluid through a pipe line without any work transfer and shear stress, the energy equation is

$$Q = \dot{m}(u_2 - u_1) + \dot{m}\left(\frac{p_2 - p_1}{\rho}\right) + \dot{m}g(z_2 - z_1) + \int_{A_2} \frac{v^2}{2} \rho v_2\, dA_2 - \int_{A_1} \frac{v_1^2}{2} \rho v_1\, dA_1 \quad \text{... (1.6)}$$

1.5 FLUID PROPERTIES

1.5.1 Viscosity

It is an important property of a fluid. It is the measure of internal resistance of a fluid for flow.

For a Newtonian fluid -

$$J \propto \frac{du}{dy} = \mu \frac{du}{dy} \quad \text{... (1.7)}$$

where μ = Constant of proportionality known as absolute or dynamic viscosity

$$\therefore \quad \mu = \frac{J}{du/dy} \quad \text{... (1.8 a)}$$

$$\text{Kinematic viscosity 'v'} = \frac{\text{Dynamic viscosity}}{\text{Density of fluid}} = \frac{\mu}{\rho} \text{ stoke} \quad \text{... (1.8 b)}$$

1.5.2 Surface Tension

Liquids exhibit a free and leveled surface. However, when the liquid is put inside a container, the free surface of the liquid displays either a rise or a depression near the wall of the container.

Similarly, formation of soap bubbles, water droplets trickling from a leaking tap, a liquid drop under equilibrium on a dry solid surface, all these phenomena are due to the property of a liquid known as *surface tension*.

Surface tension is caused by a cohesive force and adhesive force. The surface tension coefficient 'σ' is defined as the force per unit length of any line on the free surface of a liquid necessary to hold the surface together at that line. The value of 'σ' for a given liquid depends upon the temperature, pressure and the substance with which it is in contact. It is expressed in mN/m (milli Newton per meter). Surface tension decreases linearly with temperature. Most organic compounds have a surface tension coefficient in the range of 25 - 40 mN/m. The surface tension coefficient of water at 70°C is 73 mN/m. Liquid metals have a value in the range of 300 - 600 mN/m and liquid mercury has 'σ' of 450 mN/m at 70°C.

1.5.3 Capillarity

When a capillary tube is immersed in a bath of liquid, the level of the liquid inside the tube rises above the free surface for a wetting fluid. In case of a non-wetting fluid, a depression of level inside the tube is observed. This behaviour of the liquid is known as *capillarity*. The phenomenon is shown in Fig. 1.11 (a) and 1.11 (b).

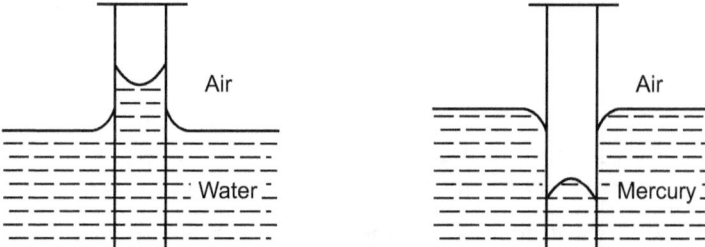

(a) Capillary tube in a wetting fluid   (b) Capillary tube in a non-wetting fluid

Fig. 1.11

1.5.4 Bulk Modulus and Compressibility

Coefficient of compressibility 'β' is defined as the ratio of change of volume per unit volume with change of applied pressure at a given temperature. Thus

$$\beta = -\frac{1}{v}\left(\frac{\partial v}{\partial p}\right)_{T=C} \qquad \ldots (1.9)$$

The isothermal bulk modulus or bulk modulus of elasticity 'K' is defined as the reciprocal of isothermal compressibility 'β'.

$$K = \frac{1}{\beta} = -v\left(\frac{\partial p}{\partial v}\right)_{T=C} \qquad \ldots (1.10)$$

1.5.5 Reynold's Number 'Re'

It is a dimensionless number referred to a compressible or incompressible fluid flow. It was postulated by a British engineer **Osborne Reynolds.** The Reynold's number sets a criteria by which the flow regime may be distinguished. The Reynold's number 'R_e' is given by

$$R_e = \frac{\rho v D}{\mu}$$

where
- ρ = Density of fluid, kg/m³
- v = Velocity of fluid, m/s
- D = Diameter of the pipe, m
- μ = Absolute or dynamic viscosity, Pa - s or ms/m²

1.5.6 Types of Fluid Flow

Based on the range of Reynold's number, the flow of fluid is classified as laminar flow, transition flow and turbulent flow.

- **Laminar Flow:** In the laminar flow region, the flow structure is characterised by the smooth motion of the laminae or layers. When there is no macroscopic mixing of adjacent fluid layers for the flow in the laminar regime, the Reynold number is less than 2000.

- **Turbulent Flow:** In the turbulent flow, the flow structure is characterised by a random motion of fluid particles in three dimensions in addition to mean motion. There is a considerable macroscopic mixing of adjacent fluid layers and significant velocity fluctuations. For the turbulent flow, the Reynolds number is greater than 4000.

- **Transition Flow:** In the transition regime of flow, the flow is in transition between the laminar and turbulent flow. The Reynold's number lies between 2000 and 4000.

The flow of fluids are often classified as (i) One dimensional flow, (ii) Two dimensional flow, and (iii) Three dimensional flow depending upon the number of space co-ordinates necessary to specify the velocity field.

- **One Dimensional Flow:** In this flow, the flow parameters vary only along the direction of forward flow and the flow parameters along the transverse direction of flow are constant.

- **Two Dimensional Flow:** In this flow, the flow parameters vary in X-X and Y-Y directions only while these are constant in Z-Z direction.

- **Three Dimensional Flow:** In this flow, the flow parameters vary in all three directions.

- **Inviscid Flow:** The flow in which the effect of viscosity is negligible is termed as inviscid flow. In an inviscid flow, the absolute or dynamic viscosity 'μ' of the fluid is assumed to be zero. In reality, fluids having zero viscosity do not exist. In many real-life problems, the analysis is simplified when viscous forces are neglected.

1.5.7 Boundary Layer

The concept of 'boundary layer' was evolved by the Germal Physicist Ludwig Prandtl in 1904. The concept of boundary layer helped to clarify several complex phenomena of fluid mechanics.

When a fluid flow passes over a stationary solid surface, the velocity of fluid particles at the surface of the solid is zero due to the viscosity of the fluid. There would be a velocity gradient in the normal direction to the flow owing to the shearing action of one fluid layer over the adjacent fluid layer moving at a higher velocity.

Prandtl suggested that in the region close to the solid surface, the effects of viscosity cannot be neglected. This region is known as the 'boundary layer.' The boundary layer ends where the velocity of flow is 0.99 times the free stream velocity. The laws of perfect fluid flow are applicable outside the boundary layer. The velocity profile in the laminar and turbulent boundary layer are shown in Fig. 1.12 (a) and 1.12 (b).

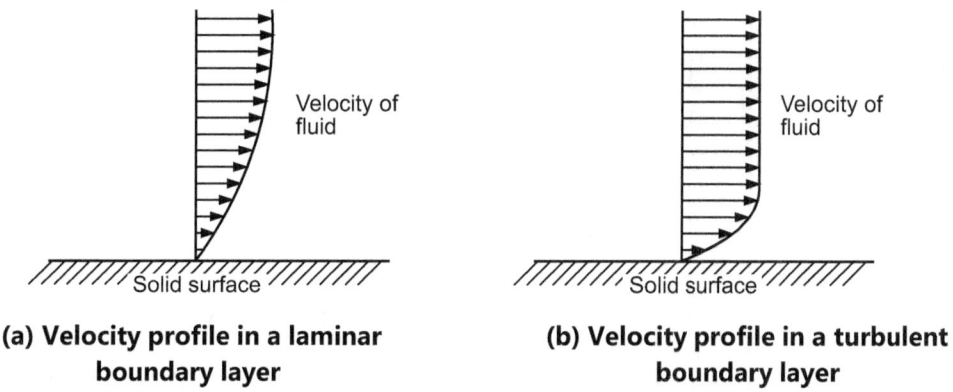

(a) Velocity profile in a laminar boundary layer

(b) Velocity profile in a turbulent boundary layer

Fig. 1.12

1.6 FLUID PRESSURE

It is denoted by the symbol 'p'. It is the ratio of force divided by the area i.e.

$$p = \frac{F}{A} \text{ Pa or N/m}^2$$

where   F = Force on the fluid, N

A = Area, m².

In a fluid column of specific weight 'γ' N/m³, height 'h' m and gravitational acceleration 'g' m/s², the intensity of pressure due to the fluid column standing above the level under consideration, is given by

$$p = \gamma \times h \text{ Pa}$$

$$= \frac{\rho g}{g_c} \times h \text{ Pa} \qquad \ldots (1.11)$$

The fluid pressure is expressed basically in Pascal. (1 Pa = 1 N/m²). The other units adopted for expressing the pressure are

$$1 \text{ kPa} = 10^3 \text{ Pa}, \quad 1 \text{ bar} = 10^2 \text{ KPa} = 10^5 \text{ Pa}$$

In a fluid system, it is often convenient to express the pressure in terms of height of the fluid column.

Rearranging the equation (1.11), it may be written as

$$h = \frac{p}{eg} \text{ m of fluid column} \qquad \ldots (1.12)$$

The common units for expressing the fluid pressure are cm of mercury, m of water etc.

Fig. 1.13 illustrates the concept of fluid pressure. The fluid pressure increases as the depth of the column increases below the free surface.

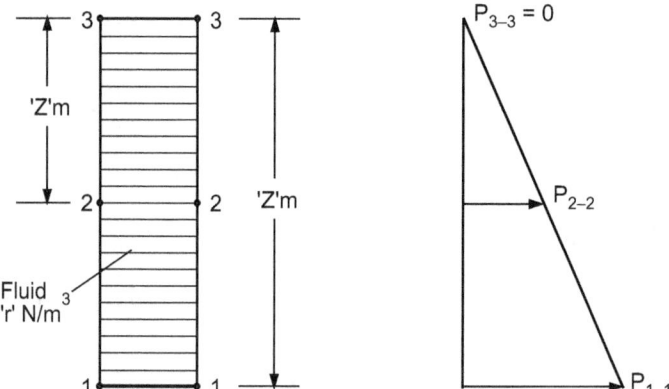

Fig. 1.13: Fluid pressure and its variation with depth of fluid column

It may be noted that the intensity of fluid pressure at a given level below the free surface depends only on the height of the fluid column and is independent of the area of cross-section of the column.

1.7 FLUID FRICTION

Whenever a fluid flows in a system, it has to overcome the frictional resistance offered by the surface of the passage. Friction generates heat so that part of energy of the fluid is lost in the form of heat.

Friction cannot be completely eliminated. However, it can be minimised. Frictional loss of energy is found to be influenced by the velocity of flow, length of the passage, diameter of the passage, surface roughness etc.

Friction affects the pressure of the fluid. The viscosity of fluid reduces due to the heat generated. This promotes undesirable leakage which in turn reduces the pressure.

Darcy-Weisback Equation: This equation is useful to evaluate the loss of head due to friction in a pipe of diameter 'D' m, length 'l' m and coefficient of pipe friction 'f' carrying the flow of fluid with a velocity 'v' m/s and flow rate 'Q' m³/s.

$$h_f = \frac{4 f l v^2}{2gD} \text{ m} \qquad \ldots (1.13)$$

$$= \frac{f l Q^2}{12 \, gD^5} \text{ m} \qquad \ldots (1.14)$$

The friction factor f' is equal to 4 f.

For laminar flow, $\quad f = \dfrac{64}{R_e}$ ... (1.15)

and for turbulent flow, $\quad f = \dfrac{0.1364}{0.25}$ ... (1.16)

where R_e = Reynolds number.

1.8 SI SYSTEM OF UNITS

Most of the countries in the world, including India adopt the SI system of units.. The basic and derived units for various parameters are listed below.

SI System of Units:

Basic units: The six basic units are:

Parameter	SI unit	Symbol
1. Length	metre	m
2. Mass	kilogram	kg
3. Time	second	s
4. Electric current	ampere	A
5. Thermodynamic temperature	Kelvin	K
6. Luminous intensity	Candela	cd

The symbols of unit do not take a plural form (e.g. 1 kg, 5 kg, 1 N, 100 N etc.)

Supplementary Units:		
1. Plane angle	radian	rad
2. Solid angle	steradian	sr

Derived Units :

Area	- m^2	Viscosity	-	dynamic/absolute - Ns/m^2
Volume	- m^3			kinematic - m^2/s
Frequency	- Hz - cycles/s	Work	-	Nm
Density	- kg/m^3	Heat	-	Joule, J
Velocity	- linear - m/s, angular - rad/s	Power	-	W (J/s)
Acceleration	- linear - m/s^2, angular - rad/s^2	Temperature	-	degree Celsius, °C
		Specific heat	-	J/kg-K
Force	- N	Specific weight	-	γ, N/m^3
Pressure	- N/m^2 or Pa	Specific volume	-	m^3/kg

Definitions :

- **Length:** The unit of length called the metre is 1650763.73 wavelengths of the orange-red emission line corresponding to the transition between the energy levels 2 p_{10} and 5 d_5 of the Krypton-86 atom in vacuum.
- **Mass:** The unit of mass, called the kilogram, is the mass of the international prototype of a platinum-iridium cylinder kept in S'evres in Paris.
- **Time:** The unit of time, called the second is the duration of 9192631770 periods of the radiation corresponding to the transition between the two hyperfine levels of the ground state of the Caesium - 133 atom.

1.9 FLUIDS FOR HYDRAULIC SYSTEMS

1.9.1 Introduction

A hydraulic fluid is used as a media for transmission and control of energy in a system. Incompressible fluids like oils are used in hydraulic systems. Energy is added to the hydraulic fluid by pumps while this energy is converted into the useful work by hydraulic cylinders or actuators.

The transmission of energy from the pump to the actuator is effected by the flow of the hydraulic fluid through metal tubes or elastomeric hoses. The control of fluid power is achieved with the use of various types of valves. The functions of a hydraulic fluid in a system are as follows.

1.9.2 Functions of a Hydraulic Fluid

- It should receive, transmit, convert and control energy in a system.
- It should lubricate the moving components of the system while in operation.
- It should be compatible with the materials of the system components, seals, gaskets, packings, hoses etc.

- It should help to dissipate the heat energy generated within the system.
- It should resist corrosion to enhance the life of the system.
- It should flush impurities and contamination.
- It should repel moisture.

1.9.3 Types of Hydraulic Fluids (Dec. 11)

Several types of hydraulic fluids are in use at present. The various types of hydraulic fluids are as follows.

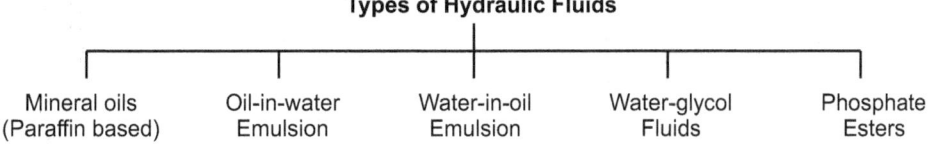

1.9.3.1 Mineral Oils

These oils are most extensively used. They are cheaper, easily available, have a range of viscosity, have good lubricating ability and are corrosion resistant. They are chemically stable below 40°C and decompose above 40°C, forming acids, varnishes, resins and sludge, thereby losing their lubricating property. However, these drawbacks can be controlled with the use of additives.

The major drawbacks of mineral oils are flammability and increase of viscosity at high pressure. Therefore, these oils are not recommended for use in hazardous areas like injection moulding, plastic moulding machines, coal mines and furnace regions. Their use is restricted to applications below 1000 bar. These oils are compatible with most of the sealing materials except butyl rubber.

1.9.3.2 Oil-in-Water Emulsion

This is an emulsion formed by fine oil droplets dispersed in water. It is typically 2% oil blended in water. The emulsion has properties like that of pure water. It is fire resistance, incompressible and dissipates heat quickly out of the system. It is however, a poor lubricant. Also its low viscosity results in greater leakage losses. It is used in large systems such as mining systems and is suitable for hazardous areas.

1.9.3.3 Water-in-Oil Emulsion

These emulsions are fire resistant and are prepared by dispersing fine water droplets in oil. Their properties are more like those of oil with reduced lubricating ability. A typical blend may have 40% water blended with 60% oil. They are suitable upto 25°C for continuous use and upto 50°C for intermittent use. Above 50°C, evaporation of water leads to poor fire resistance. Also the emulsion is highly prone to cavitation. The close control of suction pressure drop at the pump inlet is necessary. It is preferable to operate the pump with a suction head rather than a suction lift.

These emulsions are not compatible with cadmium, magnesium, cork etc. Also use of butyl rubber seals should be avoided.

1.9.3.4 Water Glycol Fluids

These fluids due to their non-flammability are often used in air-crafts. Water content however, restricts their use for low temperature systems only. Compared to mineral oils, these fluids have poor lubricity. Aqueous contents in the fluid make them more corrosion prone. These fluids are found to adversely affect zinc, magnesium, cadmium, aluminium components and also attack paints. They have good shear resistance and their low freezing point makes them suitable for low temperature applications.

1.9.3.5 Phosphate Esters

These fluids have extremely good fire resistance. Hence, these fluids are used in high fire-risk situations like plastic moulding, die-casting etc. They possess almost the same lubricity as that of mineral oils and are compatible with silicon polymers and butyl rubber. However, these fluids are found to attack some metals like aluminium and paints.

The environmental and health hazard of these fluids restrict their usage inspite of their otherwise good performance characteristics.

1.9.4 Desirable Properties of Hydraulic Fluids
(May 2007, 2008; Dec. 2010, 11)

An ideal hydraulic fluid is expected to have following desirable properties to fulfil its duty requirements.

1.9.4.1 Specific Gravity

It is an important property of a hydraulic fluid for design of the pump, reservoir, piping sizing and for calculation of pressure at pump inlet. The specific gravity of mineral oil is about 0.90 while that of synthetic fluid exceeds 1.0.

1.9.4.2 Viscosity

It is yet another important property of a hydraulic fluid. It is a measure of internal fluid friction for flow. It is an important factor for selection of a fluid for a given application. The hydraulic fluid must separate and lubricate surfaces to minimize friction and wear. The fluid should have enough viscosity for the system to be sealed and to control leakage. Yet it should be low enough for easy flowability.

1.9.4.2.1 Measurement of Viscosity

Dynamic viscosity 'μ' is measured by using an instrument called viscometer. It is expressed in SI units as Ns/m^2 or poise.

In each of the above case, viscosity is measured by a specially designed viscometer.

In an Engler viscometer, the time of flow of 200 g of oil at its working temperature is measured while passing through a 4 mm diameter aperture of a container. Similarly, equal amount of distilled water at 20°C is passed through the aperture and time is measured.

$$°E = \frac{\text{time (in s) to pass 200 g of oil at its temperature}}{\text{time (in s) to pass 200 g of distilled water at 20°C}}$$

In the Redwood viscometer, the time required to pass 50 cc of oil at its working temperature through a standard aperture is measured in seconds.

Dynamic viscosity 'μ' is expressed in Ns/m² or poise while kinematic viscosity 'υ' is expressed in m²/s or stoke. The following formula may be used for conversion of °E to m²/s.

$$\upsilon = \left(7.32° \, E - \frac{6.31}{°E}\right) \times 10^{-6} \, m^2/s$$

Interconversion of various units of viscosity can be more readily done using Nomograms [Refer Appendix].

1.9.4.2.2 Viscosity Index (May 09, Dec. 09)

Viscosity of all oils decreases with the increase of temperature. Viscosity Index (VI) is a measure of change in viscosity with the change of temperature. A high viscosity index signifies relatively small change in viscosity with a given change of temperature. Viscosity index of 80 and above is said to be high, that ranging between 40 and 80 is regarded as medium while viscosity index below 40 is taken as a low value.

Viscosity index can be improved by some additives to the oil. Fig. 1.14 shows the variation of kinematic viscosity with temperature for oils having different viscosity index.

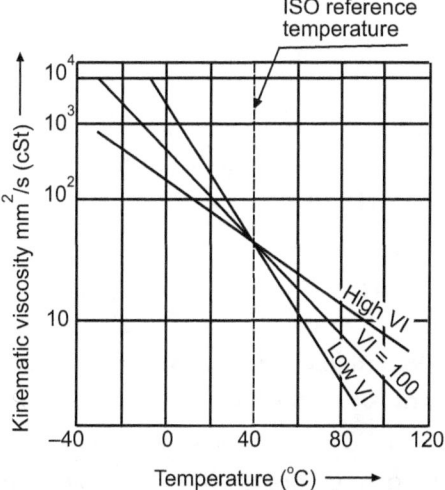

Fig. 1.14: Viscosity index and Temperature - Viscosity

1.9.4.2.3 Viscosity - Pressure Relationship   (May 09, Dec. 09)

Viscosity of many oils is found to increase with the increase of pressure of hydraulic oils. Modern hydraulic systems employ very high operating pressures often exceeding 1000 bar. At extremely high pressures, the viscosity of oil increases considerably and eventually the oil may turn solid. Fig. 1.15 illustrates variation of kinematic viscosity with temperature and pressure.

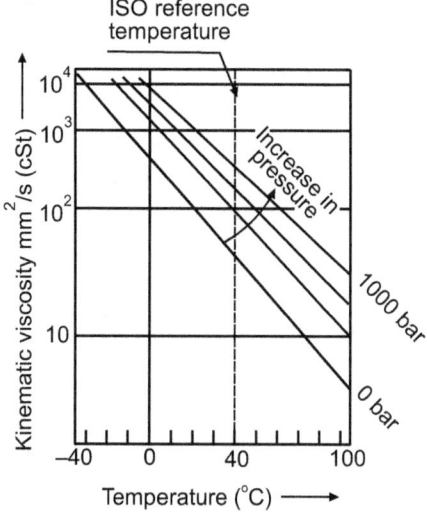

Fig. 1.15: Pressure and Temperature - Viscosity

1.9.4.2.4 Effect of Viscosity on Power Loss   (May 09)

As viscosity increases, the internal fluid friction for flow increases resulting in a loss of power for circulation of fluid through the system. Fig. 1.16 shows the variation of power loss with dynamic viscosity.

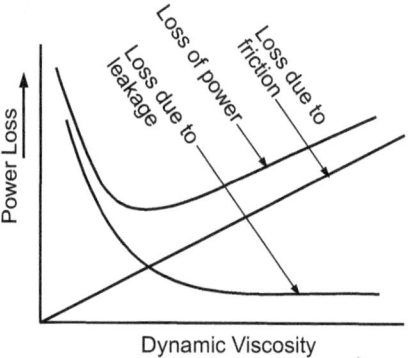

Fig. 1.16: Variation of power loss with dynamic viscosity

1.9.4.2.5 Effect of Viscosity on Overall Efficiency

With the increase of viscosity, fluid friction increases which in turn increases the power for circulation of the fluid. Also due to greater friction, fluids get heated thereby reducing viscosity and promoting leakage.

Fig. 1.17 illustrates variation of the overall efficiency of the system against pressure loss with dynamic viscosity as a parameter.

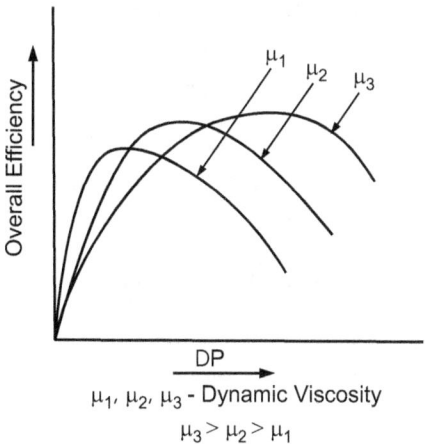

μ_1, μ_2, μ_3 - Dynamic Viscosity
$\mu_3 > \mu_2 > \mu_1$

Fig. 1.17: Variation of overall efficiency with pressure loss

1.9.4.2.6 Identification of Oils Based on Viscosity

As viscosity of oils is the most critical property in lubrication, automotive engine oils have been standardised by the society of Automotive engineers, USA, based on viscosity only. Standardisation of industrial lubricants has been done by the International Organisation for Standardisation (ISO). This classification spans 18 grades of viscosity between 2 cSt and 1500 cSt at 40°C.

1.9.5 Stability in Shear

In many hydraulic systems, oil is subjected to a high rate of shear at some region. At such sections, its viscosity reduces abruptly. But as soon as it leaves such a region, the oil regains its viscosity. For such regions, the performance of oil has to be closely monitored.

1.9.6 Foaming Characteristics

All oils contain dissolved air for their given temperature and pressure. A mineral oil may contain air upto 10 % by volume. With increase in temperature and/or reduction in pressure, the dissolved air is separated leading to cavitation.

Entrained air differs from dissolved air. The entrained air exists as discrete tiny bubbles. It makes the fluid compressible and spongy and leads to cavitation of the pump which in turn lowers the efficiency and promotes wear.

Entrainment of air is caused by improper design of the reservoir, leakage in the pump suction line and from seals. The oil with entrained air, causes foaming when it returns to the reservoir. The accumulation of foam is undesirable. The foaming tendency of an oil can be arrested by adding foam depressant additives, which help rapid breakdown of the foam.

1.9.7 Cloud Point and Pour Point

The pour point of an oil is the temperature at which it ceases to flow and turns semisolid, while the cloud point indicates the temperature at which the oil starts crystallising and forming clouds. The cloud point temperature is higher than the pour point temperature.

The operating temperature of oil in the system should be above its cloud point temperature. In case, it is below the cloud point temperature, oil becomes more viscous, increasing the fluid friction, power consumption of pump and pressure drop across the filter.

1.9.8 Oil Compressibility and Bulk Modulus

Oils have relatively small compressibility as compared to that of gases. For mineral oils, for every 100 bar increase of pressure, their volume reduces by about 0.7 %. Oil containing entrained air has greater compressibility.

The bulk modulus 'β' of an oil is defined as the ratio of stress to volumetric strain thus

$$\beta = \frac{\Delta p}{\Delta CV/V}$$

It thus represents the change in pressure needed per unit volumetric strain. It varies from fluid to fluid. For water it is 20,000 bar. Severe decompression shocks are generated when the high pressure of a large volume of fluid in a container is rapidly lowered. Ideal fluid should have minimum compressibility or high bulk modulus.

1.9.9 Coefficient of Thermal Expansion

Fluids undergo volumetric expansion with increase in its temperature. Typically 0.7% increase of volume per 10°C rise of temperature is common. The change of climatic conditions or the operating temperature of oil in a closed loop system affects its volume. Proper provision in the system design is necessary to accommodate this change in coefficient of thermal expansion.

1.9.10 Wettability

It signifies the ability of an oil to wet the surface by its adherence. A good wettability of oil is necessary to obtain effective lubrication performance. The wettability can be improved by the use of additives to oil.

1.9.11 Flammability

An ideal fluid must be non-flammable. It should have a high flash point and a high fire point, much above its operating temperature to avoid fire hazard. Mineral oils have low flash point temperature compared to synthetic oils.

1.9.12 Chemical Status

Oil should be preferably neutral with a pH value of 7. It should be chemically inert i.e. it should not adversely affect the surfaces and components of the system.

1.9.13 Affinity for Moisture

An ideal oil should preferably be non-hygroscopic to maintain its viscosity and corrosion resistance. Polydiester oils are highly hygroscopic.

1.9.14 Gumming Tendency

Certain oils when used at high temperature form gum on the surfaces. The accumulated layer of gum enhances friction, reduces flow area of the pipes and needs skilled maintenance. Oil used for hydraulic systems should have minimum gumming tendency.

1.9.15 Oxidation Tendency

Oil when exposed to ambient conditions tends to oxidise. Oxidation alters the characteristics of oil and reduces its operational life. Hence oils with minimum oxidation tendency are preferable.

1.9.16 Corrosion Resistance

A high resistance to corrosion is necessary to get a longer life of the system. The corrosion resistance characteristic of the hydraulic oil can be improved by additives.

1.9.17 Wear Resistance

Oil should have high resistance for wear to enhance the life of the system and to reduce leakage. Some additives can be used to reduce wear and scuffing under boundary lubrication conditions.

1.9.18 Compatibility with System Materials

Oil should be compatible with the materials of the system. The system may malfunction and lose its efficiency if oil attacks the materials, dissolving some component.

1.9.19 Heat Dissipation Property

An ideal oil should help to dissipate the heat faster from the system. Fluid friction generates heat.

Table 1.2 summarises the salient properties of various hydraulic fluids and should be used only as a guideline.

Table 1.2: Salient properties of various hydraulic fluids

Properties	Mineral oil	Water-Glycol	Invert Emulsion	HWBF	Phosphate Ester
Density	0.85 to 0.9	1.05	0.95	1.00	1.2
Viscosity	Very low to very high			1 cSt	Very low to very high
Typical viscosity at 40°C (cSt)	30 - 70	45	65	1	60
Viscosity index range	50 - 200	140 - 275	150 - 210		< 0 - 200
Average viscosity index	100	150	160		15
Vapour pressure	Low	High	High	High	Low
Corrosion resistance					Good
liquid phase	Good	Good	Good	Good	Good (unless contaminated by water)
vapour phase	Fair	Fair-Poor	Fair-Poor	Fair-Poor	
Stability	Excellent	Good	Poor	Poor	Good
Lubricity	Excellent	Limited	Limited	Limited	Excellent
Bulk fluid temperature (°C)	– 30 to 65	– 30 to 65	– 10 to 65	– 10 to 65	20 to 150
Optimum operation temperature (°C)	40	25	25	25	65
Fire resistance	None	Good	Good	Excellent	Excellent
Compatibility with:					
Seals	Neoprene, Nitrile (Buna N), Viton, not butyl	As for mineral oil, not leather	As for mineral oil, not leather	As for mineral oil, not butyl, ethyl-propylene, silicon	Butyl, Viton, Teflon

Cont….

metals		not zinc, cadmium magnesium aluminium	not magnesium cadmium	not copper aluminium	Can be problems with aluminium
paints		Attacks most paints			Attacks most paints
other materials	not cork, leather, paper	not leather, cork, asbestos, paper			
Special precautions and problems		Down rate systems to 40%	Down rate systems to 50%	70 bar max. 1500 rpm max. Good filtration required. High leakage pump inlet conditions are critical.	Down rate to 80 - 85% Toxic Too high viscosity at low temperatures

1.9.20 Non-toxic, Easy to Handle and Available

These characteristics refer to the interaction of the fluid with people who repair, handle, use or pay for the hydraulic system or hydraulic fluid. Obviously, it is desirable that the fluid be simple to handle, available and as cheap as possible.

1.10 ADDITIVES TO HYDRAULIC FLUIDS (May 08)

The performance of hydraulic fluids can to some extent be improved by using additives to improve their properties. The various additives are classified based on the property of oil that they improve such as:

- Pour point depressant
- Viscosity index improvers
- De-foamers
- Oxidation inhibitors
- Corrosion inhibitors
- Anti wear agents

1.11 FACTORS INFLUENCING THE SELECTION OF A FLUID
(Dec. 07, May 09, Dec. 09)

The selection of a hydraulic fluid for a given system is governed by the following factors.
- Environmental conditions such as normal, extreme, fire prone
- Operating pressure
- Operating temperature and its variation if any.
- Component materials for compatibility with oil.
- Speed of operation
- Availability of replacement fluid
- Cost of transmission lines
- Contamination possibilities
- Lubricity
- Safety to operators
- Expected service life.

1.12 SOME COMMONLY USED HYDRAULIC FLUIDS (May 07, Dec. 10)

In the present era of industrial automation, hydraulic circuits are being extensively used. Several hydraulic fluids are used now a days. In what follows hereafter, such commonly used fluids are discussed.

1.12.1 Petroleum Oils (May 07, 09, 11, 12; Dec. 11)

The properties of petroleum oils depend on :
- the origin and type of crude oil used.
- the method and degree of refining.
- chemical treatment given if any.

These oils have advantages like :
- rust protection.
- good sealing characteristics.
- better heat dissipation.
- easy for maintenance.
- excellent lubricating property.
- these oils can be cleaned easily by mechanical filtration and gravity separation.

The main drawback of these oils is their high flammability.

1.12.2 Water   (May 12)

Water offers several advantages in comparison with oil as listed below :
- Low viscosity and high viscosity index.
- Cheap and available in plenty.
- Non-flammability
- Chemically stable for long life.
- Leakage does not make the floor slippery.
- Excellent fire resistance.

But due to its following prominent drawbacks, it is being replaced fast.
- Limited range of operating temperatures.
- Poor lubricity.
- Highly corrosion and promotes rusting.

1.12.3 High Water Based Fluids   (May 07, 12; Dec. 11)

The spiralling cost of petroleum products since the early 70's led to the development of high water based fluids having better wear resistance. The American National Standards Institute (ANSI) named these fluids as High Water Content Fluids (HWCF).

Based on the water content, these fluids are referred as 95/5 or 90/10 fluids i.e. 95% or 90% water and the remaining oil. These fluids have low viscosity, are leakage prone and rust prone. These fluids are likely to dominate several applications in the future owing to their low cost.

Some note worthy **advantages of HWCF** are :
- Fire resistant due to high flash point of about 150°C.
- Lower system operating temperature due to good heat dissipation.
- Additives to HWCF are biodegradable and environment friendly.
- Cleaner operation of the system.
- High viscosity index of HWCF, operating speed and circulation flow rate remains unaffected.
- Low cost.
- Low transportation cost as users have to procure only concentrate.
- Compact storage and space saving as only HWCF in concentrate has to be stored.

Drawbacks of HWCF:
- Greater contamination due to higher density of fluids.
- Faster corrosion due to oxidation.
- Greater aeration and foaming tendency.

- Higher evaporation loss.
- Greater maintenance of fluid condition to maintain pH value of 7.5 to 9.0. Acidic nature of the fluid promotes bacterial growth and filtration difficulties.
- Non-compatibility with paints

Additives to HWCF:

The performance of HWCF can be further improved by adding various additives listed below.

- Anti wear additives.
- Anti foaming additives
- Corrosion inhibitor additives.
- Biocides for inhibiting growth of water-borne bacteria.
- Emulsifying agents.
- Lubricity improvers like oiliness agents, EP agents.
- Anti-bacterial agents.
- Flocculation promoter additives.
- Deionization agents.
- Oxidation inhibitors
- Anti-vaporising agents.

1.12.4 Fire Resistant Fluids (May 09, 11)

These fluids are designated as HF-A, HF-B, HF-C and HF-D.

HF-A — These are high water content fluids (over 80% water) e.g. Oil-water emulsion.

HF-B — This is a water in oil emulsion containing petroleum oil, water.

HF-C — This is a solution of water and glycols.

HF-D — This is a synthetic fluid e.g. Phosphates or phosphate petroleum oil blend.

1.13 DISTRIBUTION OF FLUID POWER

1.13.1 Introduction to Seals

Successful performance of a hydraulic system depends upon the effective control of leakage. Leakage can be external or internal. The measures of leakage control are provided at the design stage of the system.

Complete elimination of leakage is seldom possible. Seals plays an important role in the fluid power system. Though it is a tiny part in a giant machine but it is such a critical element that for want of it the complete machine may remain inoperative increasing its idle time.

Functions of Seals:

The main functions of seals are:

- Control of external and internal leakage of fluid to or from the system.
- Prevention of contaminants entering the system.
- Maintenance of system pressure.
- Control of fluid loss.
- Enhancing the system life and reliability of system performance.

1.13.1.1 Classification of Seals (May 07)

Seals are classified according to various criteria as explained below:

- According to the method of sealing: Positive sealing (prevents minute leakage) and non-positive sealing. (Allows small leakage for lubrication).
- According to their location in a system such as static seals and dynamic seals. (Refer Fig. 1.18). Static seals are used when no relative movement occurs between mating parts, while dynamic seals are used between surfaces of hydraulic parts where movement occurs and controls both leakage and lubrication.

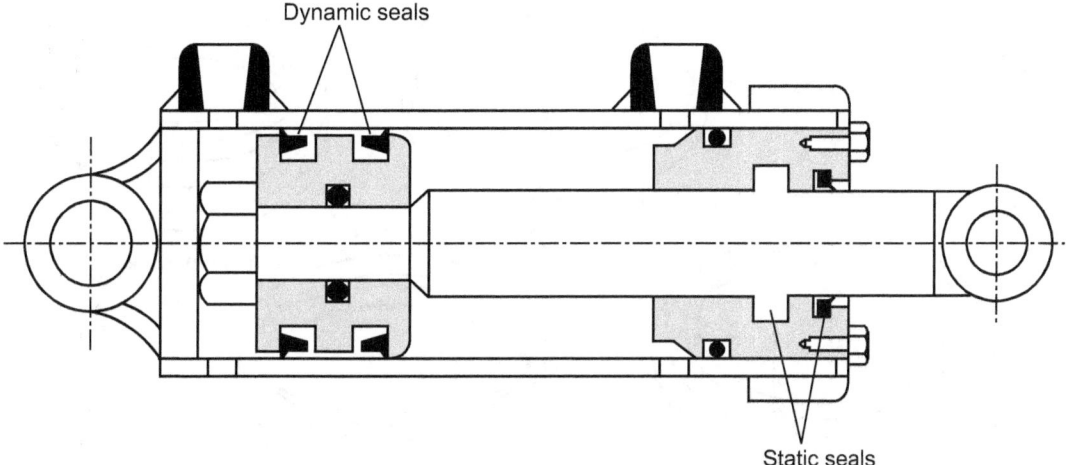

Fig. 1.18: Static and dynamic seals

- According to geometric shape or configuration during their fabrication such as: U-cup ring, hat ring, T-ring, Quad-ring, O-ring, V-ring. These are shown in Fig. 1.21 (a) and (b). All the forms of seals stated may be used both as static and dynamic seals. They can also be used singly or in combination.

- According to sealing action: Internal seals control leakage between areas of differential pressure. The leakage between the contact surface of the seal and the mating part leads to loss of volumetric efficiency, loss of system power, poor control and poor sensitivity of system response, system malfunctioning and excessive heat generation.

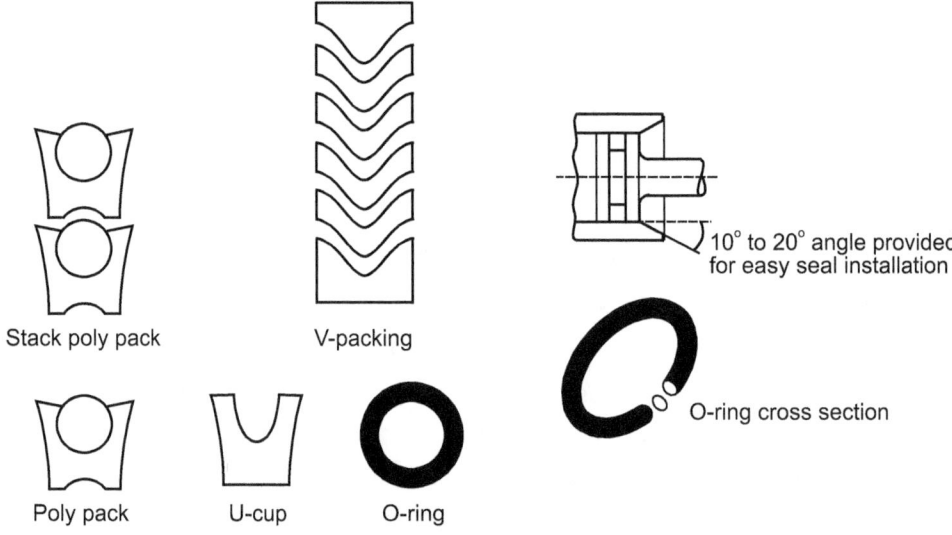

Fig. 1.19 (a): Shapes and cross-section of seals

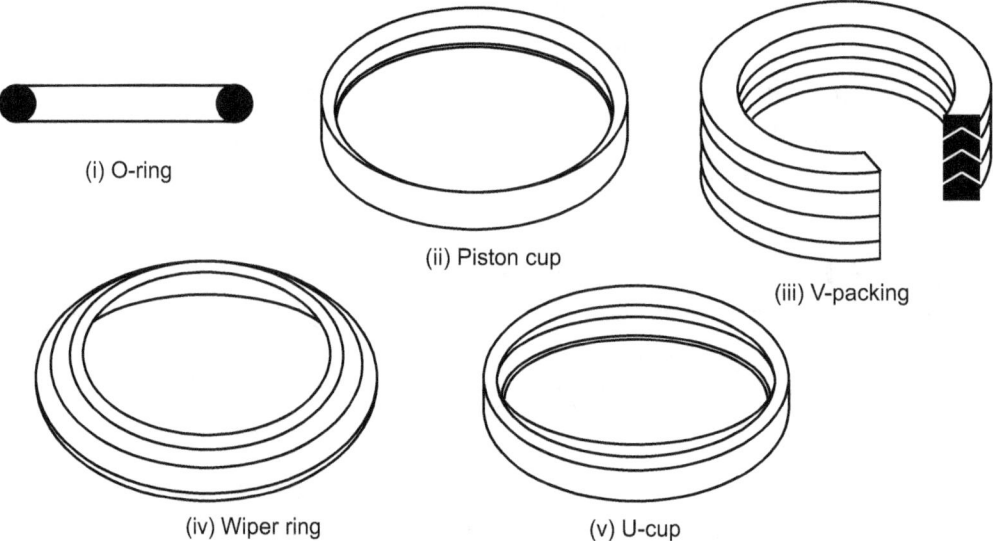

Fig. 1.19 (b): Classification of seals as per their geometric shape

External seals control leakage against system pressure, outside ambient pressure and lubrication control of seal and bearing support.

- According to seal material: The seals are often classified based on their materials, such as leather seals, metal seals, polymers, elastomers and plastic seals, asbestos, nylon seals etc.

1.13.2 Factors Influencing the Selection of Seals (May 07, Dec. 08)

The selection of seals and seal material is influenced by the physical characteristics of system such as:

(i) operating pressure and its variation.

(ii) ambient conditions.

(iii) operating temperature of the system.

(iv) working fluid.

(v) application of seal such as static or dynamic.

(vi) operational reliability expected.

(vii) expected life of the system.

1.13.3 Desirable Properties of an Ideal Material for Seals

An ideal material for a seal should have several properties as discussed below:

(a) **Hardness:** The seal material should be softer (low hardness) for low pressure systems and harder (high hardness) for high pressure systems. Softer and harder seals wear more rapidly.

The hardness of elastomer material is measured using "share A" scale ranging between 0° and 100°.

(b) **Change of Volume:** The seal material is found to undergo a change of volume causing swelling or shrinkage when it is in contact with the system fluid.

A small amount of swelling is usually desirable to compensate for seal wear. Excessive swelling is not tolerable in dynamic seals. For dynamic 'O'-rings, swell upto 20% is tolerable while for fixed seals, swell upto 40% to 50% can be permissible.

(c) **Compression Set:** Elastometers lose their resilience. The compression set is defined as the ratio of loss in thickness of an elastomer after it deforms to its original thickness. It is alternately defined as the permanent distortion of an elastomer after compression at a specified temperature for a specified time.

Compression set increases with increase in temperature while it decreases with increase of the 'O' ring size.

(d) **Tensile Strength:** The seal performance is influenced by tensile strength, tear strength, elongation as the seals stretch, wear and tear, abrasion due to relative motion. Polymer compounds have good tensile strength.

The ultimate elongation of a seal is defined as the maximum length an elastomer attains before failure and is expressed as a percentage of its original length.

(e) **Permanent Set:** It is the permanent distortion of an elastomer after elongation.

(f) **Adhesion:** It is the ability of rubber to stick to a surface in contact.

(g) **Aniline Point:** It is the temperature at which fresh aniline reacts with oil. Higher the aniline point temperature, lower is the swell of the rubber.

(h) **Squeeze:** It is the diametral compression of the 'O' ring between the two mating surfaces of the gland.

Final squeeze = Initial squeeze + Swell − Compression set

1.13.4 Seal Materials (May 2007, 12; Dec. 2008, 11)

Seals are made of various metallic and non-metallic materials.

(i) **Metals:** The metals are non-resilient and are suitable for high pressure and high temperature applications and even for cryogenic applications. These are preferred for static sealing only. Their main advantage is that they are inert to most hydraulic fluids. The metal seals are well suited for radioactive situations.

(ii) **Leather:** The chrome tanned polyurethene impregnated leather is widely used as a seal material for static and dynamic seals. It is readily available, has low coefficient of friction, good lubricity and excellent wear and abrasion characteristics. It is suitable for a temperature range of − 50°C to + 100°C.

(iii) **Asbestos:** It is used for static and dynamic seals and is temperature resistant. However, in view of health and hygenic issues, its usage is severely restricted.

(iv) **Rubber, Elastomers and Plastics:** These are most extensively used sealing materials due to their good resilience, ready availability, ease of fabrication and wide temperature range. The ingredients of rubber are:

1. Carbon black for reinforcement
2. Fillers
3. Activators
4. Plasticizers
5. Sulphur for vulcanizing or curing
6. Antioxidants
7. Accelerators

Various additives can be used to form different compounds of rubber having specific properties. Common elastomeric sealing materials and compounds are:

1. Butyl
2. Ethylene propylene
3. Flurocarbon
4. Isoprene
5. Flurosilicone
6. Neoprene
7. Buna S
8. Natural rubber
9. Plastics
10. Nylon
11. Silicone
12. Polyurethane
13. Polysulphide
14. Polyethylene
15. Teflon (PTFE)

1.14 COMPATIBILITY OF SEAL WITH FLUDIS

In many hydraulic oils quite a number of chemical additives are used for various purposes viz. antioxidant, corrosion inhibitors, detergents, rust inhibitors, VI improvers antiform agent, E.P. agent, flash point and pour point agents etc. Many of these additives are mostly essential and hence cannot be avoided. In modern oils, multipurpose additives are also used e.g. polymethacrylate.

In some group of these additives, full valcanising material which works at high temperature and thus further hardness of the rubber seal material reduces its resilience and increase its brittleness and breaks up subsequently.

The influence of the contact fluid on the elastomer does not limit only to volume change (i.e. swelling). Apart from this, the tearing creep failure due to factors like stretching, torsion, hardening, reduction of resilience and tensile strength, cracks may also take place.

Amongst the physically active additives, isobutalence and methacrylate polymer and VI improper and flash point reducer are common as far as physically active additives are concerned because of their high molecular weight.

Anti-foam agents, dye and perfume material are used in very significant amount and hence need not be considered for any effect on the rubber seal material like the elastomer.

It is very important to keep the fluids free from contaminants. This is because metallic and other solid contaminants present in the oil may damage the elastomeric seals used in the system through abrasion.

The seal, apart from losing its sealing ability may be a source of contaminants of elastomeric materials which ultimately may form gummy material in the oil chamber in association with other oxidised materials.

Table 1.5 : Summary of salient features of seal materials

Sr. No.	Seal material	Positive point	Limitation	General range of working temperature in °C	Shore hardness at room temperature
1.	Butyl rubber	Better compatibility with synthetic oil	Poor shear strength	−50 to 100	−
2.	Neoprene rubber	Better weather resistance in exposed condition	High friction if not reinforced with fabrics	−50 to 180	−
3.	Ethylene propylene rubber	Good weathering	Permeable to higher pressure Not to be exposed to petroleum based oils	−50 to 150	80 to 90 A
4.	Fluorocarbon rubber (Viton)	Better heat resistance	Slow memory and high mould shrinkage	−50 to 200	75 A
5.	Leather (Chrome tan polyurethane impregnated)	Low friction, high abrasion resistance, slight polishing action in bore	Useable for low temperature range and for simple seal configuration only	−50 to 80	−
6.	Nitrile rubber (Buna N)	Good general purpose use	Prone to damage due to weathering	−50 to 150	70 to 90 A
7.	PTFE (Teflon)	Very wide fluid and material compatibility, less friction	Slow memory	−250 to 400	−
8.	Polyurethane	High abrasion resistance, low friction. Most suitable for high pressure, shock load and abrasion contamination	Poor compatibility with synthetics and hot water	−50 to 150	95 to 105 A
9.	Polyurethane	Resistance to abrasion and extrusion	Poor resistance to synthetics and hot water	−20 to 100	−
10.	Silicone	Excellent heat resistance	−	−115 to 370	70 A

Table 1.4 : Hydraulic fluids of seal materials compatibility chart

Sealing material	Fluid compatibility
Natural rubber (NR)	Water-base fluids
Leather (Treated)	Petroleum-base fluids
(Impregnated with thick oil)	Some synthetics and phosphate ester
Butyl rubber	Petroleum-base fluids
(Buna-N) (Hycar)	Water-base fluids and some synthetics
Silicone rubbers	Water-base fluids: Fair with petroleum base; good with some synthetics
Fluoro-plastics (Teflon) (Kel-F)	Good with almost all fluids used
Fluoro-elastomers (Viton A)	Good with water-base, petroleum-base, and most synthetic fluids

1.15 TYPES OF SEALS   (Dec. 07; May 08, 09; Dec. 10)

Various cross-sections and geometric shapes used for hydraulic seals and packings are shown in the figures below:

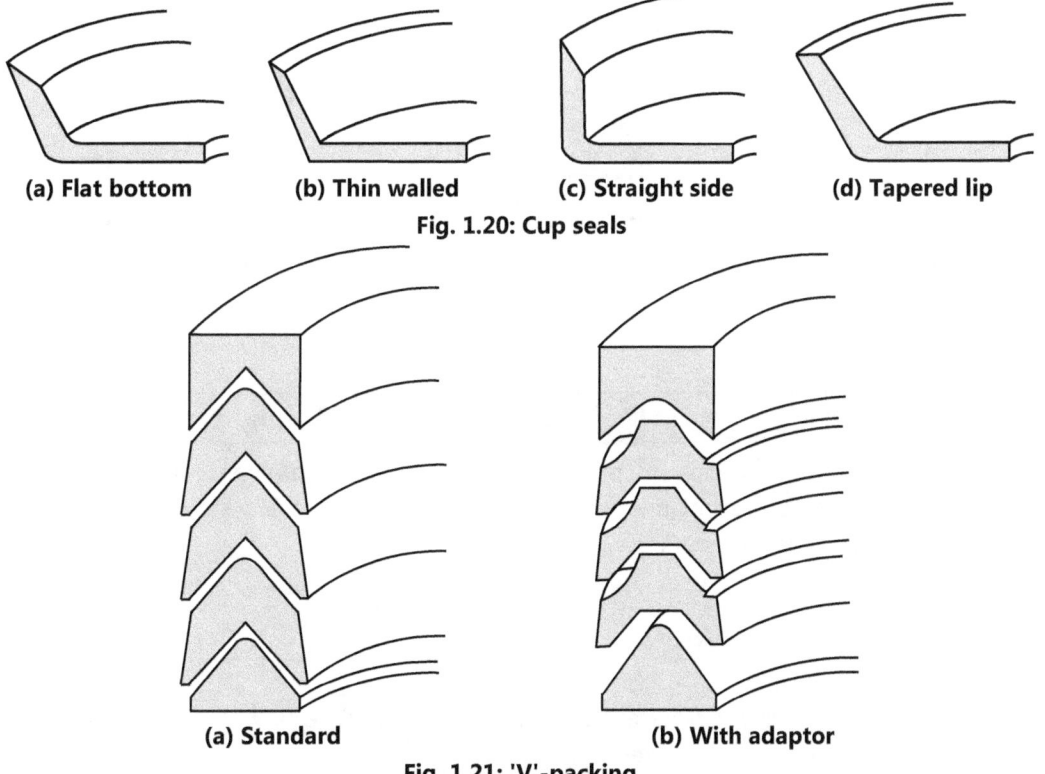

(a) Flat bottom   (b) Thin walled   (c) Straight side   (d) Tapered lip

Fig. 1.20: Cup seals

(a) Standard   (b) With adaptor

Fig. 1.21: 'V'-packing

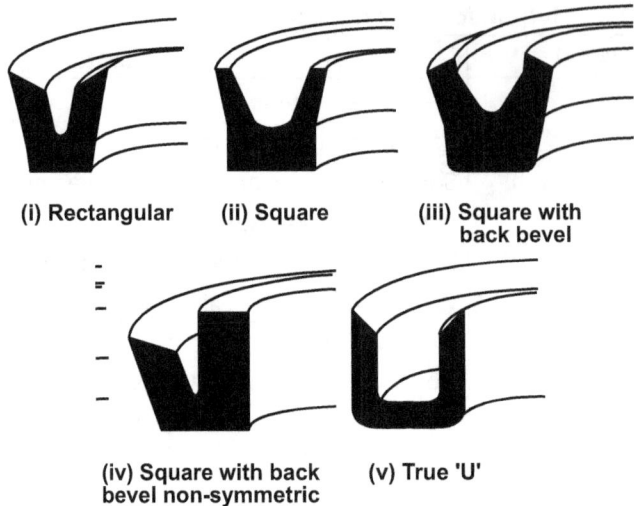

(i) Rectangular (ii) Square (iii) Square with back bevel

(iv) Square with back bevel non-symmetric (v) True 'U'

Fig. 1.22: 'U'-packing seal

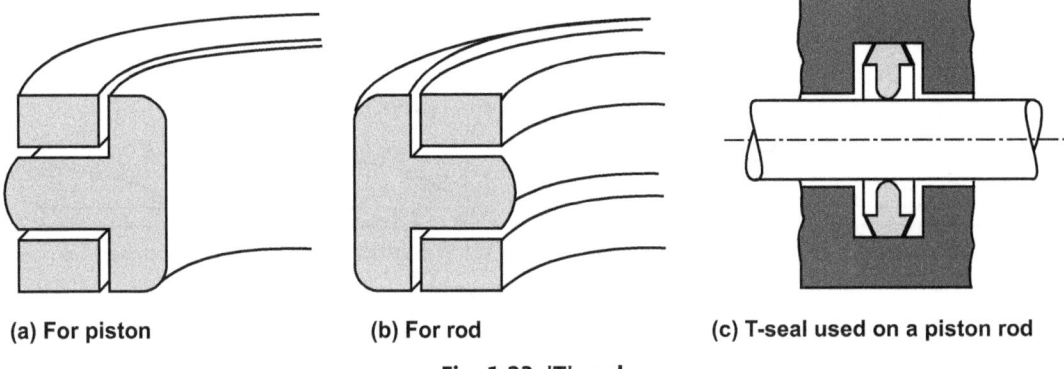

(a) For piston (b) For rod (c) T-seal used on a piston rod

Fig. 1.23: 'T' seal

1.16 Wiper Rings

Piston rod is the main component promoting ingress of contaminants into the cylinder. Wiper seals are used to prevent the entry of contaminants into the system. Wiper seals are also known as wipers or scrappers.

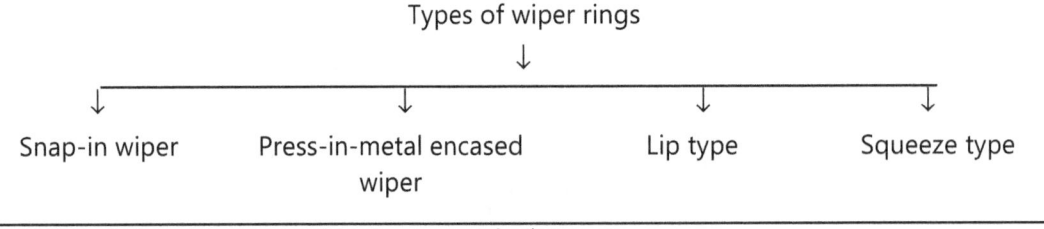

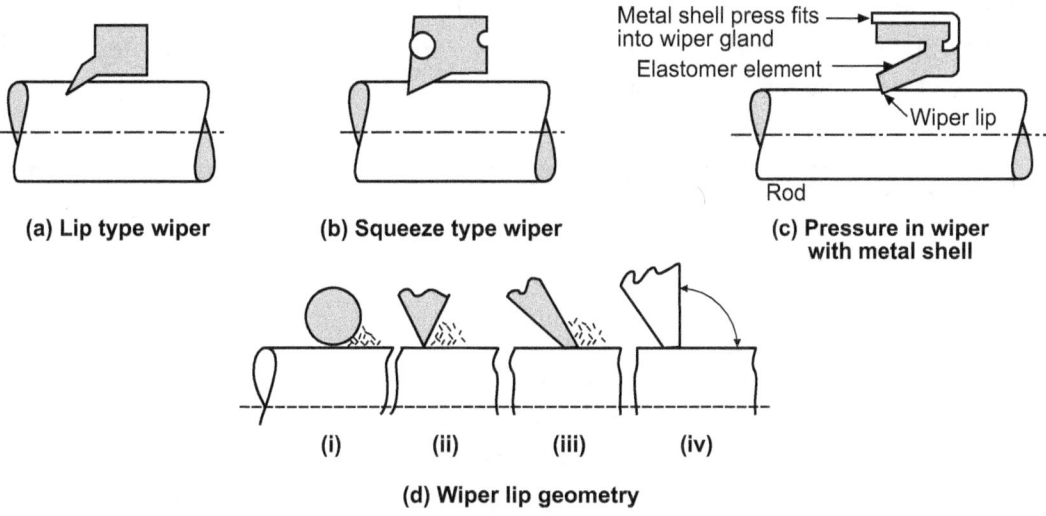

Fig. 1.24: Types of wiper rings

1.17 SEAL FRICTION

When dynamic seals are placed in position, they offer frictional resistance of linear or rotary motion. For a given geometry of seals, the friction force is found to depend upon:
(i) the pressure, and (ii) the sliding speed or peripheral speed.

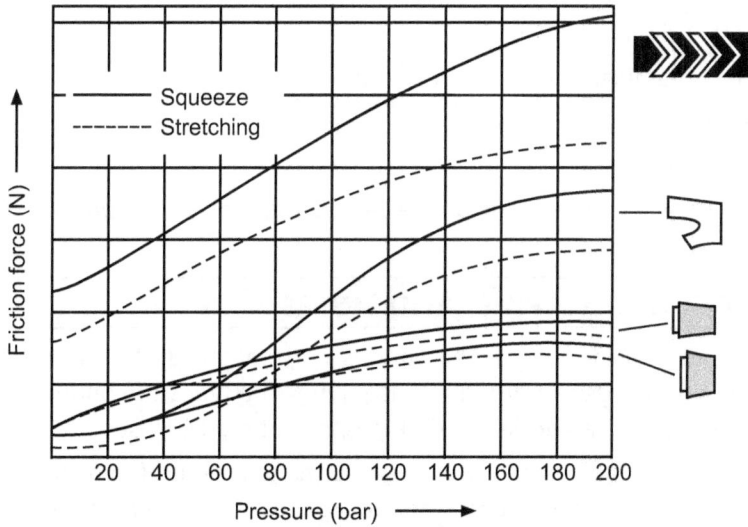

Fig. 1.25 : Effect of pressure on seal friction

Fig. 1.25 (a) illustrates the variation of friction force for various operating pressures and different geometry of the seal during squeezing and stretching.

Fig. 1.25 (b) shows the variation of friction force for various sliding speeds for different geometry of seals under squeezing and stretching.

1.18 CAUSES FOR SEAL FAILURE

The various causes of seal failure are:
1. Incorrect installation
2. Worn out shafts
3. Incompatibility of seal material and oil.
4. Vibrations generated due to bent shaft, imbalance of rotating components, broken vane, misaligned bearing, detective coupling etc.
5. In reciprocating situations, excessive side loads, wobbling of piston rod etc.
6. Excessive radial movement of soft seals.
7. Extremely high or low operating temperatures.
8. Neglected oil leakage.
9. Improper speed of piston stroke
10. Squeeze
11. Improper lubrication
12. Exposure to excessive pressure difference.
13. Incorrect D/d ratio of 'O' rings.
14. Gum or contaminant deposits on the surface.
15. Severe side loads.
16. Missing back-up ring.

By minimizing the presence of the above causes, the seal life can be extended.

1.19 INTRODUCTION TO PIPES AND HOSES

Hydraulic fluid is conveyed through the various parts of the system through a system of conducting lines which is generally termed as piping. The types of conducting lines may be identified in three general categories as: (i) Pipes, (ii) Tubes, (iii) Hoses.

Pipes are rigid conducting lines and provide a permanent type of connection and are least expensive. Tubings and hoses are flexible and make more convenient forms of connections.

In hydraulic and pneumatic systems, pipes, hoses and tubings play a great role in conveying a fluid from one component to the next, under pressure. These conducting elements are connected to various components using a variety of connectors. The control of leakage of a fluid from the system is particularly critical in hydraulic systems operating under considerable pressure. Control of leakage is incorporated using seals, packings, 'O' rings, and gaskets at appropriate locations.

1.20 METALLIC PIPES

Iron pipes are economical and are suitable for low pressure applications. Their major drawbacks are inability to sustain pressure surges, their high wall thickness and lack of toughness. Pipes need threading for connectivity.

Tubings are advantageous in that they can bend easily, are available in several sizes and materials and need few fittings. Tubes are simple to cut and assemble at site.

Pipes are usually specified by their ID (NB), though the actual ID may vary for its specified size. Therefore, it is necessary to mention nominal ID (NB) and the pipe schedule number which is indicative of its wall thickness.

Cast iron pipes are restricted for use on return line only due to their limited burst pressure. The common material for pipes and tubes is steel. Other metals include stainless steel and cuprons nickel, zinc coated advanced iron, copper-based pipes are suitable for low pressure system requiring small bore sizes. Copper and zinc coated G.I. tubes promote chemical degradation of some oils.

Steel tubes are made of annealed m.s. or soft ductile carbon steel. They are made with superior outer finish and closer tolerance on ID and OD. Seamless cold drawn tubes are preferred due to their smooth and polished inner surface over the electric resistance welded (ERW) tubes. Other advantages of seamless tubes are high wall thickness, high tensile strength and better bending characteristics. The tolerance on OD for various sizes of seamless tubes are tabulated below.

Table 1.5: Tolerance on OD for seamless tubes

Nominal OD mm	Tolerance, mm
4 – 30	± 0.10
30 – 38	± 0.15
Above 38	± 0.20

Finished steel tubes are given phosphating treatment for corrosion resistance or are painted with anti-corrosive paints compatible with oil.

Weight/m and maximum working pressure for different factors of safety, for various sizes of cold draw seamless carbon steel tubes as per DIN 2391/C. [Refer Appendix]

Steel tubes are expensive, Copper tubes are unsuitable with petroleum oils as they accelerate oxidation. Zinc, magnesium and cadmium tubings are rapidly corrected when used with water-glycol fluids and G.I. pipe surface flakes off into the hydraulic fluid.

The choice of proper wall thickness of tubes depends upon the factor of safety which in turn is governed by the operating pressure of the system. Table 1.6 gives the factor of safety preferable for various operating pressures.

Table 1.6: Factor of safety for tubes at various operating pressures

Operating pressure range, bar	Factor of safety
30 – 70	8 : 1
70 – 130	6 : 1
Above 160	4 : 1

1.21 SCHEDULE NUMBER OF STANDARD PIPE   (Dec. 10, May 12)

Many years ago piping was designed as standard, extra heavy and double extra heavy. There was no provision for walled pipes and no intervening standard thickness between the three schedules, which covers too large a spread to be economical without intermediate weights. In order to overcome this difficulty the American National Standard Institute had established a method of designing the pipes by their schedule numbers, which are calculated by using the formula,

$$\text{Schedule number} = \frac{100 \times P}{SE}$$

where,

P = Operating pressure

SE = Allowable stress range multiplied by the joint efficiency

These numbers are rounded in steps of 10 and a scale was established from 10 to 160. On this scale 40 corresponds to a standard pipe, 80 extra heavy pipe and the remaining covers the pipes with the greatest wall thickness under this system. The old double heavy classification is slightly thicker than schedule 160. Currently, this system is being used for designing the hydraulic pipes. As the schedule increases the pipe wall thickness and hence the busting pressure increases.

1.22 HYDRAULIC HOSES

In many hydraulic systems, flexible synthetic hoses are often used particularly for their flexibility. Various synthetic materials are used for the manufacture of hoses. Hoses are reinforced with steel wire mesh for high pressure systems.

1.22.1 Advantages and Limitations of Hoses

The **prominent advantages of rubber and plastic hoses** are :
- They are flexible.
- Their ability to sustain shock and vibration is even better than metal tubes.
- They are easy to assemble and disassemble.
- They can be manufactured in large lengths.
- They can be adopted for high pressure applications.

However their **salient limitations** are :
- Their abrasion resistance is poor.
- They have high initial cost.
- They offer poor weather resistance.
- They have shorter life due to abrasive wear and incompatibility with oil.

1.22.2 Hose Materials

The hoses are made of various materials as given in Table 1.7.

Table 1.7: Hose materials

Category	Material	Salient features
Plastic	Nylon	Good abrasion and impact resistance, suitable upto 15 bar pressure and temperature range 75°C – 105°C.
	Braided nylon hose	Suitable for medium to high pressure, has long life, lighter weight, low cost, high bulk modulus.
	Polyvinyl chloride	Suitable for low pressure pneumatic systems, greater flexibility, limited operating temperature range (–10 to +40°C), poor abrasion and corrosion resistance, short working life.
	Textile braided hoses	Cotton braded hoses suitable for pressures upto 35 bar.
	Thermoplastic	Suitable for operating temperature range of – 40°C to 110°C. Compatible with phosphate esters, petroleum, water-based oils.
	Teflon	Polytetrafluroethylene (PTFE) suitable for temperature range – 50°C – 204°C, available in bending radius of 38 – 400 nm, working pressure of 10 – 105 bar. Steel braded hoses suitable for vibrations, pulsating forces, chemically inert, non-flammable, low coefficient of friction.

Cont...

	Hypalon (Chloro sulphonated polyethylene)	Good tensile strength and abrasion resistance, good compatibility with water-glycol emulsion.
	Ethylene propylene diene (EPDn)	Good weather and heat resistance, poor compatibility with petroleum oils, water-oil emulsions, poor resistance to flame.
	Chlorinated polyethylene	Good compatibility with petroleum based water glycol, water-oil emulsion and phosphate ester, good permeability and ozone resistance.
Synthetic Rubber	Buna N	Known as Nitrile rubber, operating temperature range – 50°C to + 150°C, compatible with petroleum based oils, not suitable with phosphate based esters. Poor abrasion resistance, swelling resistance.
	Neoprene	Known as chloroprene, Not compatible with aromatic hydrocarbons, Good abrasion resistance.
	Natural rubber	Compatible with water-glycol fluids, swells by 20 % while working with petroleum fluids, good abrasion resistance.
	Butyl	Suitable for temperature range –50°C to + 150°C, poor oil resistance, rapid degradation when used with petroleum fluids, good compatibility with phosphate ester oils.

1.22.3 Construction of Hoses

Fig. 1.26 shows the constructional features of a typical hose. Hoses are fabricated in layers of elastomers and braided fabric or braided wires thus strengthening them for high pressure applications. The hose may have a minimum of three layers including one braided layer or can have several layers to sustain the higher operating pressures.

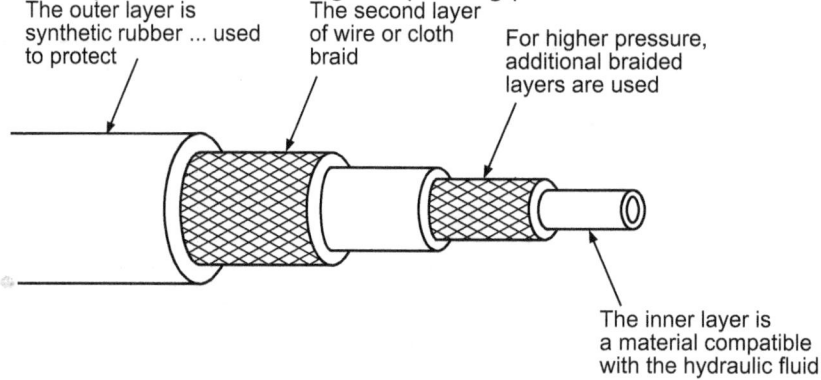

Fig. 1.26

The steel wires may have spiral weave or cross weave. Spiral reinforced hoses have high strength and require fittings to be supplied by the manufacturer. The cross woven braids are re-usable and are easy to assemble. The inner tube material of a hose should be compatible with the fluid.

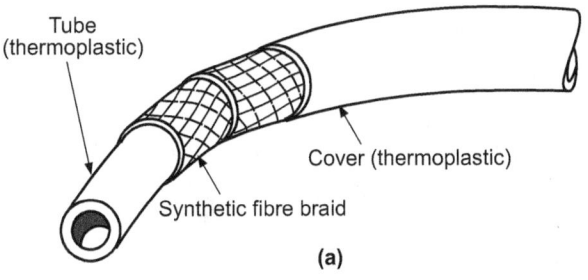

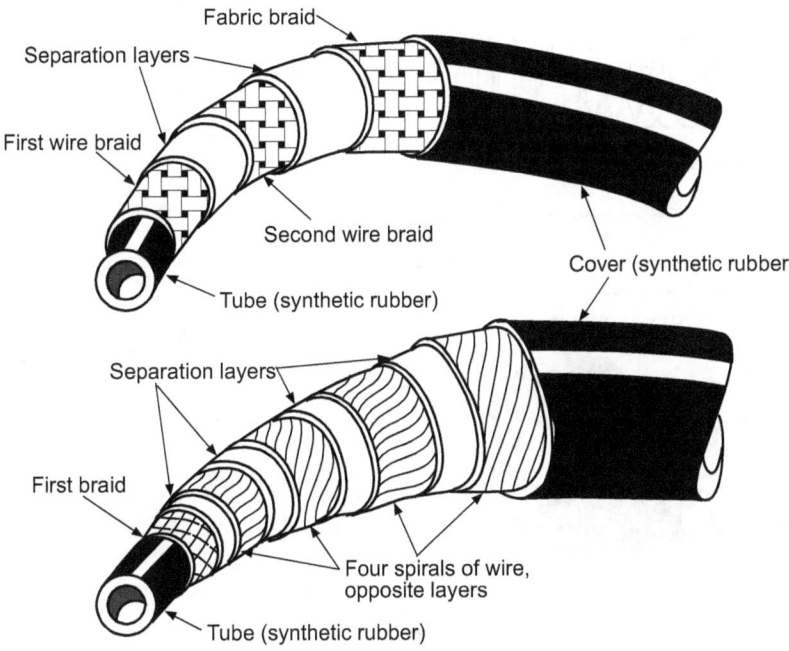

Fig. 1.27

Fig. 1.27 (a) shows a thermoplastic hose and Fig. 1.27 (b) shows a synthetic rubber hose with different weave pattern.

1.22.4 Reinforcement for Hoses

The strengthening of the inner tube needs reinforcement by adding additional layers. These layers are made up of various materials like:

- Nylon
- Cotton or textile
- Rayon
- Synthetic elastometer
- Steel wires
- Synthetic yarn

Each of the above materials has its own characteristics and suitability of a specific pressure range.

1.22.5 Protective Covers and other Devices

The reinforcement of a hose need protection from corrosion, abrasion and other external sources of damages. The outer cover provides such a protection. The outer covers are made of Neoprene or synthetic rubber. Fig. 1.28 shows some protective devices.

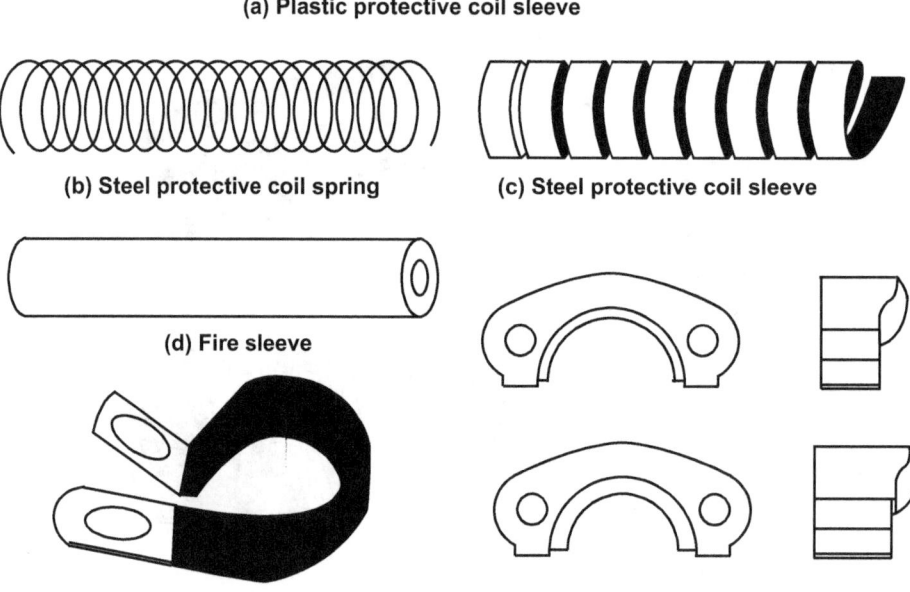

(a) Plastic protective coil sleeve

(b) Steel protective coil spring

(c) Steel protective coil sleeve

(d) Fire sleeve

(e) Support clamp

(f) Spit flanges

Fig. 1.28

1.22.6 Sizing of Tubings, and Hoses

The proper sizing of a tubing or a hose is very vital as it indirectly influences efficiency of power transmission, which in turn depends upon the fluid pressure and the flow rate.

For a given operating pressure, greater power can be transmitted using higher flow rates. However, the flow velocities in various fluid lines are usually restricted as given below:

Recommended fluid velocity:
  (a) Suction lines and return lines – 0.5 to 1.2 m/s.
  (b) Pressure lines – 2 to 4.5 m/s.

Greater flow velocities result in turbulent flow loss of pressure and more heat generation and poor efficiency. Large diameter of tubes and hoses is thus desirable. Smaller diameter tubes and hoses are low cost and compact in size.

The sizing of the hose can be done by the following equation

$$d = 1.127\sqrt{\frac{Q}{v}} \quad \ldots(1.17)$$

where
- d = Diameter of hose, m
- Q = Flow rate, m³/s
- v = Velocity, m/s

Estimation of Pressure Drop:

The design of a hydraulic pipe includes estimation of pressure drop of fluid while it flows through the circuit. The estimation of pressure drop in a straight pipe can be easily done either by manual calculations or by use of a nomogram.

1.22.7 Factors Influencing the Selection of Hoses

The selection of hoses is influenced by several factors listed below:
- Working pressure of the system.
- Pressure surge if any during operation.
- Operating temperature of the system
- Ambient temperature variations if any.
- Flow carrying capacity.
- Length of the hose for avoiding sag or stretching.
- Type of end fitting, other fittings for determination of equivalent length.
- Vibrations and shocks present in the system.
- Flexibility.
- Resistance to external and internal abrasion.
- External mechanical loads like flexing twist, kinking, tensile loads etc.
- Factor of safety - For normal operation it is 4 : 1 while 2.5 : 1 when shock loads are to be sustained.

1.23 HOSE FITTINGS AND CONNECTORS

Careful design and fabrication of end fittings is important, as improper design, incorrect crimping and bad swaging result in hose failure. An ideal hose assembly should have the following features:
- It should provide positive locking with adequate reinforcement.
- It should establish leak-proof connection with the system components.
- It should not corrode in the surrounding atmosphere.
- It should be able.

1.23.1 Types of Hose Fittings

Fig. 1.29 shows various types of hose fittings.

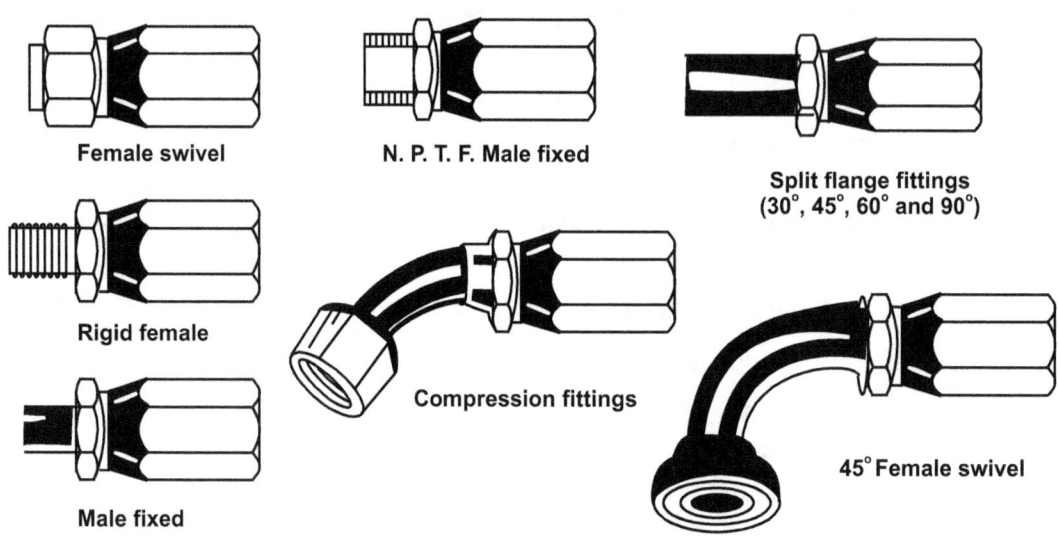

Fig. 1.29: Types of hose fittings

1.23.1.1 Quick Couplings   (May 11)

These are highly precision components of the hydraulic system, manufactured with close tolerance. These couplings enable easy and quick connection and disconnection with the system components, without any necessity of hand tools and skills. Quick coupling consists of a male nipple and a female coupler. Fig. 1.29 shows various types of quick couplings. This type of fitting permits assembly and disassembly in a matter of a second or two. There are three basic designs which are:

1. **One-way Shutoff Design:** This design locates the shutoff of the fluid source connections but leaves the actuators unblocked. In this system, contamination due to the entrance of dirt in the open end of the fitting can be a problem.

2. **Two-way Shutoff Design:** This design enables shutoff of both ends of the pressurized lines when disconnected. In this case there is no chance of premature flow or waste due to a partial connection.

3. **Straight Through Design:** This design enables minimum restriction to flow but does not prevent fluid loss from the system when the coupling is disconnected.

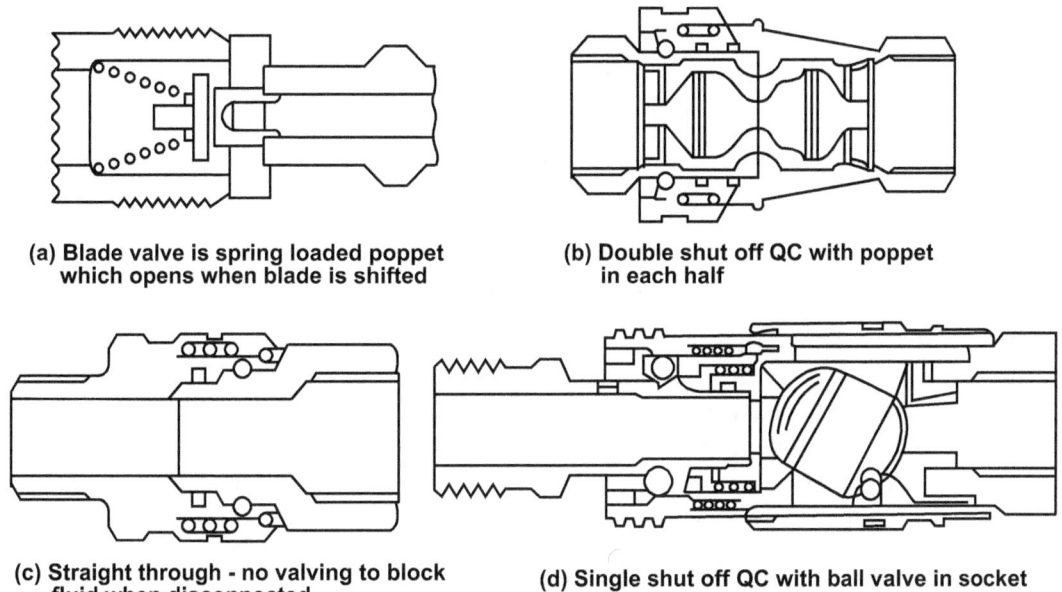

(a) Blade valve is spring loaded poppet which opens when blade is shifted

(b) Double shut off QC with poppet in each half

(c) Straight through - no valving to block fluid when disconnected

(d) Single shut off QC with ball valve in socket

Fig. 1.30 : Types of quick couplings

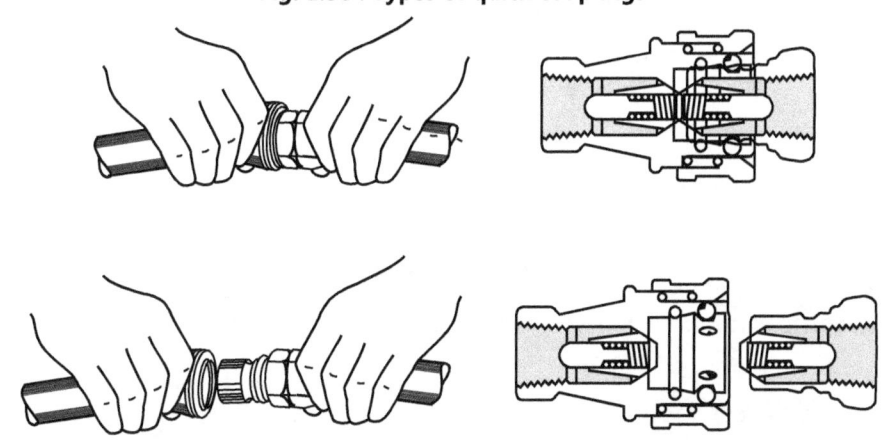

Fig. 1.31: Quick-disconnect coupling

1.23.2 Flared and Compression Fitting (May 08; Dec. 10, 11)

These fittings are generally used for fitting of pipings as they cannot be threaded and hence threaded connections are not possible.

Flared Fitting: In case of flared fitting the sealing is achieved by squeezing the flared end of the tube against the seal using a flaring tool when the compression nut is tightened. The flaring is done generally at 37° angle and for high pressure applications a 45° flaring can also be done. Flaring fitting can be done on pipes upto 50 mm. This type of fitting is comparatively reasonable. It is shown in Fig. 1.32.

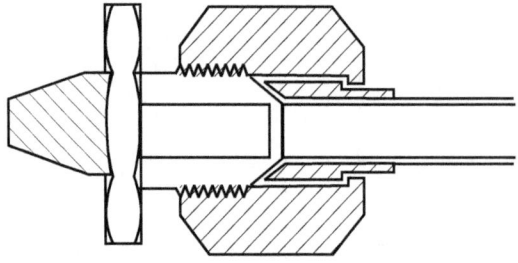

Fig. 1.32 : Flared fittings

Compression Fitting: This type of fitting is used when flaring cannot be done or flaring is to be avoided. Generally, compression fitting can be used with a ferrule, O-ring or sleeves. It is done on the forming tool and is fitted on the pipe. A ferrule is fitted on the piping for giving the sealing. When a coupling nut is tightened, the ferrule will cut its own seat on the pipe wall. O-ring compression fittings are used when a high degree of sealing is required. The seal becomes tighter as pressure increases. It is shown in Fig. 1.33.

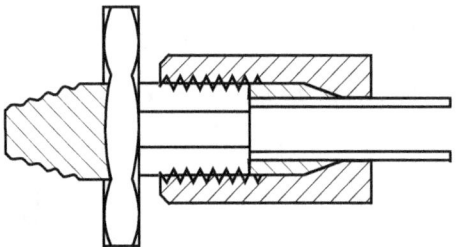

Fig. 1.33: Compression fittings

SOLVED EXAMPLES

Example 1.1: *The following data refers to a certain hydraulic system.*

  Specific weight of oil = 0.95

  Kinematic viscosity oil = 50 cSt

  Flow rate = 45 l.p.m.

  Nominal bore of pipe = 30 mm

  Length of pipe = 5 m

Determine the pressure drop per meter length of the pipe.

Solution: Refer the nomogram shown Appendix.

Draw the line joining given viscosity of 50 cst and specific weight of 0.95.

This line intersects the reference line 1 at point 'A'. Now join point 'A' to the given flow rate point at 45 l.p.m. This line intersects the reference line 2 at point 'B'.

Then join point 'B' by a line to the nominal bore point at 30 mm. This line intersects the pressure drop line at 0.018 kg/cm² which is the estimated pressure drop, per meter length of the pipe.

Therefore, total pressure drop = 5 × 0.018 = 0.09 kg/cm²

(for 5 m pipe)

Example 1.2: *A certain static O-ring has a diameter of 10 mm and is given an initial squeeze of 12 %. The swell of the seal is equal to 20 % increase in squeeze while the compression set is 10 %. Calculate the final squeeze percentage of the seal.*

Solution: Final squeeze = Initial squeeze + Swell − Compression set

$$= 10 \times \frac{12}{100} + 10 \times \frac{20}{100} - 10 \times \frac{10}{100}$$

$$= 10\,(0.12 + 0.20 - 0.10)$$

$$= 2.2 \text{ mm}$$

∴ % final squeeze = $\frac{2.2}{10} \times 100$ = **22%** ... **Ans.**

1.24 ISO Symboles

1.24.1 Introduction

The representation of hydraulic and pneumatic circuits having several components can be conveniently done using standard symbols.

Various standardisation institutes like ANSI (American National Standards Institute), ISO (International Standards Organisation), UNI etc. have standardised graphic symbols for various components of a hydraulic and pneumatic circuit.

OSHA Standard: OSHA is the abbreviation used for "Occupational Safety and Health Administration". It is enforced by, the Government of India under the department of labour to be displayed at the place of employment. These standards are related to safe practices for avoiding hazards, harmful to personnel at work.

These standards are divided into various subparts concerning occupational health and environmental control, compressed gas and air equipment, material handling and storage, machinery and machinery guarding etc. Some of the aspects covered in these parts can be enumerated as - safety of floors and working surfaces, wall openings, access and exit requirement, sanitation, fire and emergency protection, machine guards, operational techniques, safety devices, mounting, anchoring, grounding, ignitable toxic materials, safe storage and handling of combustible liquids, medical first aid services, personal protection devices, special training required, electrical pneumatic hydraulic steam power source hazards, welding, brazing, abrasive blasting, spray painting, saw mills, administrative regulations etc.

It is obligatory for the employer to display an OSHA document stating the rights and obligations of the employer and employees at the place of employment and keep a record of all accidents, injuries, illnesses etc.

Table 1.8 lists the hydraulic symbols according to UNI - ISO standards.

Table 1.9 (a) lists ISO symbols for fluid circuits and Table 1.9 (b) for the pneumatic circuit components.

1.24.2 Pumps

Table 1.8: Hydraulic symbols according to UNI - ISO Standards

Graphical Symbol		Item	Description
(a)	(b)	Fixed displacement pump	One flow direction (a) Two flow directions (b)
(a)	(b)	Variable displacement pump	One flow direction (a) Two flow directions (b)
		Hand pump	Lever pumping

1.24.3 Motors

Graphical Symbol		Item	Description
(a)	(b)	Fixed displacement motor	One rotation sense (a) Two rotation senses (b)
(a)	(b)	Variable displacement motor	One rotation sense (a) Two rotation senses (b)
		Rotary motor	Hydraulic motor with limited angle of rotation

1.24.4 Cylinders

Graphical Symbol	Item	Description
	Single acting cylinder	Return stroke by external force
		Return stroke through a spring
	Double acting cylinder	Single rod
		Double rod
	Cylinder with fixed stroke end cushioning	Cushioning on one side
		Cushioning on both sides
	Cylinder with adjustable stroke end cushioning	Cushioning on one side
		Cushioning on both sides
	Telescopic cylinder	Cushioning on one side
		Cushioning on both sides

1.24.5 Valves

Pressure Relief Valve		Sequence Valve	
Direct operated	Pilot operated	Direct operated	Pilot operated

Pressure relief valve		Counter pressure valve
Direct operated	Pilot operated	

1.24.6 Flow Control Valves

Variable throttling valve		Compensated flow valve	
Two way	With check	Two way	With check

1.24.7 Directional Control Valves

Check Valves			
Standard	Calibrated	Pilot operated	Piloted with drainage

Directional Valves			
2 ways-2 positions	3 ways - 2 positions	4 ways - 2 positions	4 ways–3 positions

Controls for directional valves			
Mechanical	Push button	Lever	Pedal
Spring	Cam	Electric (solenoid)	Electro-hydraulic
Pneumatic	Hydraulic	Electric (proportional)	Electro-hydraulic (proportional)

1.24.8 Energy Transmission and Accessories

Graphic symbol	Item	Description	Graphic symbol	Item	Description
(M)=	Motor	Electric	⊔	Reservoir	Pipings above level
▭=		Engine	⊔		Pipings under level
───	Pipings and connections	Main	⊝		Pressurised reservoir
------		Pilot	⊤	Air bleed	
....		Drain	⊖	Hydraulic accumulator	
⌣		Flexible hose	◇	Filter	
┼		Connection point	◈	Heat Exchanger	Heater
┼		Crossing	◈		Cooler
──⤬	Branching	Closed	◈		Liquid operated cooler
⤬←		With connected piping	Ø	Pressure gauge	
→•←	Coupling	Fast coupling	⊣•⌒⟋⋁⋁	Pressure switch	
─◇•◇─		With check valves	⊬	Rotating shaft	1 - direction
			⊬		2 - directions

Table 1.9 (a): ISO symbols for fluid circuits

Energy Conversion		Control Valve	
	Uni-directional air-compressor	**Direction control valve**	2/2 Directional control valve (normally closed)
	Vacuum pump		
	Hydro pump		2/2 Directional control valve (normally open)
Air Motor			3/2 D.C. valve (normally closed)
	Pneumatic motor uni-directional		
	Pneumatic motor two-directional		3/2 D.C. valve (normally open)
	Oscillating motor		
Cylinder			3/3 D.C. valve-zero positions all ports closed
	Single acting cylinder return by external force		
	Single acting cylinder return by spring		4/2 D.C. valve
	Double acting cylinder		4/3 D.C. valve - zero positions all ports closed
	Double acting cylinder with through rod		5/2 D.C. valve

		Check Valve	
	D.A. cylinder with adjustable cushioning at both ends		Non-return valve
			Shuttle valve
	Cylinder with built-on control		Non-return valve control valve
	Cylinder with built-on control valve and hydraulic check valve		Quick exhaust valve
			Twin pressure sequence valve
		Nomenclature	
	Pressure Intensifier	Working port	– A, B, C
		Pressure port	– P
		Exhaust port	– R, S, T
	Pressure medium changer	Drain port	– L
		Pilot port	– X, Y, Z
		Pneumatic	– Δ
		Hydraulic	– $\Delta \pi$

Pressure Control Valve		Flow Valve	
	Pressure relief valve		Flow control general symbol
	Sequence valve		Flow control (insignificant influence of viscosity)
	Pressure regulator		Adjustable flow control
	Pressure regulator with self relieving		Flow control valve controlled mechanically with spring
			Pressure compensated flow control valve
Exhaust		**Energy Transmission**	
	Unthreaded air exhaust port		Main supply pressure
			Working return and feed line
	Threaded air exhaust port		Control line
	Hydraulic tank		Drain line
Shut-off valve			Assembly line
	Shut-off valve		Electrical line
Power take off			Flexible line
	Plugging		Line junction
	With take off line		Crossing line

Quick Release Coupling		Rotary Connections	
→│←	Coupled without check valve	⊖	One line flow
—◊—│—◊—	Coupled with check valve	≡⊖≡	Three lines flow
—→ │	Half of quick release coupling without valve		Silencer
—◊ │	Half of quick release coupling with closed valve	—⊂═⊃—	Accumulator
Actuations			
Mechanical Components		**Control Methods**	
⇥ ⇤	One direction of rotation or two respectively of shaft	**Manual Control**	**Mechanical Control**
—∨—	Detent	⊢ General symbol	⊣ Plunger
▯	Locking Device	⊢ Push button	⊣ Roller
═══→	Over centre device	⊢ Lever	⊣ Roller trip
═∨═		⊢ Pedal	⊣ Spring

	Linkages	Electrical Control	Pressure Control
	Simple	Electro magnet	By applying pressure
	with linkages	By solenoid and servo valve	By releasing pressure
	with fixed fulcrum		By differential pressure
Servicing			
	Filter		Service unit (Detailed symbol)
	Water trap manual drain		
	Water trap- automatic draining		Service unit (Simple symbol)
	Filter with water trap and drain		Cooler without flow lines
	Desiccator air dry by chemicals		Cooler with flow lines
	Lubricator		

Table 1.9 (b): Electrical symbols used in pneumatic circuits

Symbol	Description	Symbol	Description
c	Contactor switch	d	N.O. contact delayed closing
d	Auxiliary switch	a	Single throw contact N.O.
	Solenoid	b	Double throw contact
d	Time relay	e	Pressure switch
	N.O. contact	e — Fuse	
	N.C. contact		
b	N.O. contact delayed opening	h	Indicator lamp
b	N.O. contact delayed opening	m	Transformer
b	N.O. contact limit operated	b	Manual controlled switch
b	N.O. contact limit operated	70	Electro mechanic element with AC motor

1.25 ENERGY LOSSES IN HYDRAULIC SYSTEMS

1.25.1 Introduction to Energy Losses in Hydraulics

In general one can state that hydraulics is used for generation, control and transmission of power using pressurized liquids. However, since the entire hydraulic system is composed out of tubes, valves, obstacles, filters, tanks actuators etc., the flow of liquid is not possible without some energy losses related to:

- Friction
- Pressure drops
- Leakages

Energy losses in hydraulics have always been a popular field for research since hydraulic systems provide great solutions for power generation, control and transmition. Determining the losses of energy in such systems is not that straightforward as it may seem. The most common approach is to break down the entire hydraulic system to component level and calculate the losses for each component individually. The total energy loss is the sum of the individual components. The amount of hydraulic losses Δh is being computed separately for straight periods of tubes or hoses and for the other local sources of flow resistance (e.g. all types of connections, tanks, valves, filters, diameter changes etc.). In most cases where energy losses are related to friction, the total loss is significantly larger compared to systemsconnected with local obstacles. Hence, friction losses are sometimes grouped under the term major losses. On the other hand, it is not that seldom to encounter a system where energy losses from the local flow resistance sources will outnumber the friction losses. These losses are also known as minor losses and relate to energy consumption from local flow resistance sources.

1.25.2 Losses in pipeline components

1. Linear Losses (Major Losses)

When a fluid flows through a pipe the internal roughness of the pipe wall can create eddycurrents1 within the fluid adding a resistance to flow of the fluid. Pipes with smooth wallssuch as glass, copper, brass and polyethylene have only a small effect on the frictionalresistance in contrast with walls make of concrete, cast iron or steel which will create largereddy currents. Rough pipes can have a significant effect on the frictional resistance. Thevelocity profile in a pipe will show that the fluid at the center of the stream will move morequickly than the fluid towards the edge of the stream (figure).

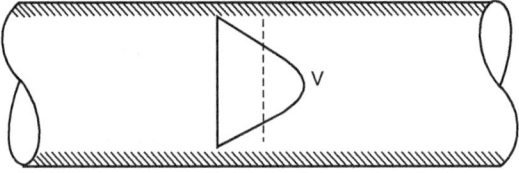

Fig. 1.34 : Speed profile of the fluid in a straight tube

Therefore friction will occurbetween layers within the fluid. Fluids with a high viscosity will flow more slowly and willgenerally not support eddy currents and therefore the internal roughness of the pipe willhave no effect on the frictional resistance. This condition is known as laminar flow. Lossescorresponding to the general flow in a rectilinear conduit are often called linear losses. Theyare also called major losses since they are directly related to few factors connected to boththe fluid and the tube shape and properties, those factors are:

- Tube length
- Hydraulic diameter
- Average flow velocity

Moreover these losses can be characterized by a linear resistance coefficient which can be established via several methods and in general relate to the conditions describing the fluid flow through the tubes.

2 Local Losses (Minor Losses)

Local losses or sometimes called minor losses origin from all sorts of obstacles2. In most cases, local losses are dependent on the average velocity behind the obstacle and the local resistance coefficient which is related to the type of obstacle and the Reynolds number. If the Reynolds number exceeds 104, the local resistance coefficient no longer is dependent on the Reynolds number. The most commonly encountered local flow resistant sources are summed up below. More detailed information can be found in Reservoir outlet, Reservoir inlet, Sudden decrease in diameter, Sudden increase in diameter, Knee, Bolt valve, Butterfly valve, Gas tap, Poppet valve.

The minor losses may raised by: 1. Pipe entrance or exit, 2. Sudden expansion or contraction, 3. Bends, elbows, tees, and other fittings, 4. Valves,open or partially closed, 5. Gradual expansions or contractions.

$$h_L = \frac{\Delta p}{\rho g} = K_L \frac{v^2}{2g}$$

where K_L means (local) loss coefficient. Although K_L is dimensionless, it is not correlated in the literature with the Reynolds number and roughness ratio but rather simply with the raw size of the pipe. Almost all data are reported for turbulent-flow conditions.

Loss Coefficients for Pipe Components $\left(h_L = K_L \frac{v^2}{2g}\right)$

Component	K_L
(a) Elbows	
Regular 90°, flanged	0.3
Regular 90°, threaded	1.5
Long radius 90°, flanged	0.2
Long radius 90°, threaded	0.7
Long radius 45°, flanged	0.2
Regular 45°, thread	0.4
(b) 180° return bends	
180° return bends, flanged	0.2
180° return bends, threaded	1.5
(c) Tees	
Lines flow, flanged	0.2
Line flow, threaded	0.9
Branch flow, flanged	1.0
Branch flow, threaded	2.0
(d) union, threaded	0.08

Cont...

(e) Valves

Globe, fully open	10
Angle fully open	2
Gate, fully open	0.15
Gate ¼ closed	0.26
Gate ½ closed	2.1
Gate ¾ closed	17
Swing check, forward flow	2
Swing check, backward flow	∞
Ball valve, fully open	0.05
Ball valve 1/3 closed	5.5
Ball valve 2/3 closed	210

3. Modeling Approach

There are several different methods for modeling the energy losses in hydraulic systems. As the basic phenomena and contributing factors are known, few variables need to be estimated during the modeling process. Important factors during hydraulic system modeling are:

- Density and specific weight of fluid
- Viscosity of fluid
- Fluid flow rate

Another important assumption during hydraulic system modeling is that changes of state of hydraulic system are only present in discrete time periods and that fluid flow rate is not changing between two periods. This assumption is called the condition of steady state hydraulics. A common approach to simulate the dynamic behavior of hydraulic systems is based on combining models of steady state for each period of time. This procedure is known as the hydraulic step with updating the system state at the beginning of each step (EPS-extended period simulation). The different modeling approaches show different methods of estimating necessary parameters for calculating energy losses in hydraulic systems.

Our intension here is generalized the one-dimensional Bernoulli equation for viscous flow. When the viscosity of the fluid is taken into account total energy head H.

$$H = \frac{v^2}{2g} + \frac{p}{\rho g} + z$$

is no longerconstant along the pipe. In direction of flow, due to friction cause by viscosity of the fluid we have

$$\frac{v_1^2}{2g} + \frac{p_1}{\rho g} + z_1 > \frac{v_2^2}{2g} + \frac{p_2}{\rho g} + z_2$$

So to restore the equality we must add some scalar quantity to the right side of this inequality.

$$\frac{v_1^2}{2g} + \frac{p_1}{\rho g} + z_1 > \frac{v_2^2}{2g} + \frac{p_2}{\rho g} + z_2 + \Delta h_{ls}$$

This scalar quantity Δ_{ls} is called as hydraulic loss. The hydraulic loss between two different crosssection along the pipe is equal to the difference of total energy for this cross section:

$$\Delta h_{ls} = H_1 - H_2$$

Head loss is express by Darcy-Weisbach equation:

$$h_L = f \frac{L}{D} \frac{v^2}{2g}$$

(a) Energy Losses in Hydraulic Cylinders

A hydraulic cylinder (also called linear hydraulic motor) is a mechanical actuator that is used to give a unidirectional force through a unidirectional stroke. A typical hydraulic cylinder is composed of several elements. The main parts are: Cylinder barrel, Cylinder bottom or cap, Cylinder head, Piston, Piston rod, Rod gland.

Other parts are: cylinder bottom connection, cushion, seals, etc. The most common cylinders are the single and double acting cylinders. In order to properly model the friction inside a hydraulic cylinder, all aspects should be taken into account. Friction force can be modeled as a function of the relative velocity and pressure. The three most dominant friction phenomena are: Stribeck friction, Coulomb friction, Viscous friction. The final friction for should be the sum of the three above components. To simulate the energy losses in hydraulic cylinders, all the previously mentioned friction components are combined to finally arrive at following equations

$$F = F_c \cdot (1 + K_{brk} - 1) \cdot e^{-c_v \cdot |v|} \cdot \sin(v) + f_{vfr} \cdot v$$

$$F_c = F_{pr} + f_{cfr} \cdot (p_a + p_b)$$

with
- F : friction force
- F_c : Coulomb friction
- F_{pr} : preload force
- f_{cfr} : coulomb friction coefficient
- p_a, p_b : pressures in cylinder chambers
- K_{brk} : Breakaway friction force increase coefficient
- C_y : transition coefficient
- v : relative velocity in the contact
- f_{vfr} : viscous friction coefficient

(b) Energy Losses in Hydraulic Pumps

Hydraulic pumps are one of the most crucial components of the hydraulic system because they are the source of fluid flow and pressure, responsible for the entire hydraulic system characteristics. However it is impossible to construct an ideal machine therefore we need to consider pumps' efficiencies. Modern pumps manufacturers put a high priority towards lowering energy losses as much as possible. Nowadays modern pumps can operate with efficiencies over 90% for overall efficiency. Generally, hydraulic pumps can be split up into two major categories namely: positive displacement pumps and kinetic pumps. During the designing and modeling phase of a particular hydraulic system, several characteristic features can provide information about the overall efficiency of a hydraulic pump. The overall pump efficiency is the product of the mechanical efficiency $\eta_{mechanical}$ and the volumetric efficiency $\eta_{volumetric}$. The mechanical efficiency is important when considering energy losses caused by friction and the volumetric efficiency is based on the hydraulic fluid leakages between the pumps. The degree of the perfection of the conversion process between the mechanical work supplied and the energy of the fluid is called the pump efficiency. The mechanical and volumetric efficiencies are used to calculate the overall efficiency. (refer unit 2 for pump efficiency calculations).

(c) Leakages

It is almost inevitable that leakages occur in a hydraulic system; therefore it is strongly advised to introduce some leakages factors into the complete model. This is even more important when the model will be used to estimate the energy losses. Two types of leakages can be distinguished namely: internal and external leakages.

Internal (non-positive) must be built into hydraulic components to lubricate valve spools, shafts, pistons, bearings, pumping mechanisms, and other moving parts. In some hydraulic valves, pumps and motor compensator controls, leakage paths are incorporated to provide precise control and to avoid hunting (oscillation) of spools and pistons. Oil is not lost in internal leakage; it returns to a reservoir through return lines or specially provided drain passages.

External leakage can be hazardous, expensive, and unsightly. Faulty installation and poor maintenance are the prime causes of external leakage. Joints may leak because they were not assembled properly or because shock and vibration in the lines shook them loose. Adding supports to the lines prevents this. If assembled and installed correctly, components seldom leak. However, failure to connect drain lines, excessive pressures, or contamination can cause seals to blow or be damaged, resulting in external leakage from the components. The leakage problem can also be a combined case of internal and external leakage.

EXERCISE

1. What are the important advantages of fluid power? **(May 01, Dec. 02)**
2. Compare the characteristics and applications of hydraulic and pneumatic drive. **(May 01, Dec. 02)**
3. Draw a simple hydraulic circuit, showing all its essential components. State the functions of each components. **(Dec. 01, May 02, Dec. 04)**
4. Enumerate the advantages and disadvantages of hydraulic and pneumatic systems. **(May 02)**
5. What are the functions of a hydraulic fluid? **(May 2001)**
6. Explain the terms (i) Bulk modulus, (ii) Viscosity index. **(May 2001, Dec. 2002)**
7. Under what conditions should fire resistance fluid be used? **(May 2001)**
8. What are the different fluids used in the hydraulic circuit? State the suitable fluid for the following operations: **(Dec. 2002)**
   (i) Operation of a heavy door of a furnace.
   (ii) Accurate positioning of a machine tool slide. **(Dec. 2001)**
9. What precautions are to be taken to save oil from contamination? **(Dec. 2001)**
10. Draw a neat sketch and explain the working of (1) Pilot operated check valve, (2) 5 way, 2 way position DCV. **(Dec. 2001)**
11. Classify the types of hydraulic fluids? What are the desirable proportion of hydraulic fluids? **(May 2002)**
12. Why are "additives and inhibitors" used in hydraulic fluids? **(Dec. 03, 04, May 02)**
13. Write a short note on fluid conditions. **(May 02, Dec. 03, 04)**
14. Compare petroleum, oil and water as a hydraulic fluid. **(May 03)**
15. What are the merits and demerits of High Water Content Fluids (HWCF)? **(May 03)**
16. Explain the desirable properties of hydraulic fluid. **(Dec. 03, May 04)**
17. If viscosity is two high, what can happen to the system? **(May 2004)**
18. What is the difference between a static and a dynamic seal? Name four types of materials used for seal. **(May 01, 04)**
19. What are the materials used for manufacturing a seal when water is used as a working fluid? Give reasons for the selection. **(May 01, 02)**
20. Classify the types of seals and define them. **(May 02, Dec. 02)**
21. What are the factors which affect the performance of seals? **(May 02)**

22. Discuss the seal material composition, specification, application and design or shape. **(May 02)**
23. Explain the types of seals used in a hydraulic system. Mention various materials of seals. **(May 03, Dec. 04)**
24. Compare hoses with pipe connections. **(May 01)**
25. Explain the purpose and construction of a quick connecting fitting with a neat sketch. **(Dec. 02)**
26. Why it is important to select properly the size of a pipe, valve and fittings in a hydraulic system. **(Dec. 02)**
27. Write short notes on:
    (i) Schedule number of standard pipe. **(May 03)**
    (ii) Hydraulic conductors and fittings. **(Dec. 03)**
28. How pipe is classified? **(May 03)**
29. What is meant by schedule number of pipe? **(May 03)**
30. What is the difference between flared fitting and a compression fitting?
    (May 03, Dec. 03)
31. Under what conditions would flexible hoses be used in a hydraulic system? **(May 03)**
32. What variables determine the wall thickness and safety factor of a conductor for a particulate operating pressure? **(Dec. 03)**

Unit II

PUMPS

2.1 INTRODUCTION TO HYDRAULIC PUMPS

A Hydraulic pump is essentially the heart of a hydraulic system. It converts mechanical energy into hydraulic energy. The pump is supplied with mechanical energy from the prime mover, usually an electric motor. The pumps do not pump pressure, they only generate fluid flow. The discharge pressure is determined by the resistance to this flow offered by the hydraulic system.

The two main categories of the pump are:

(1) Non-positive displacement pumps, and

(2) Positive displacement pumps.

1. Non-positive Displacement Pumps:

The working principle of these pumps is explained in the subsequent article 5.1.1.

These pumps are generally used for low pressure, high volume flow applications. As these pumps are incapable of withstanding high pressures, they are seldom used in the fluid power circuits. Their maximum pressure is limited to 15 bar to 20 bar. These pumps are mainly used for fluid transportation, circulation etc.

Its advantages are as follows.

Advantages of non-positive displacement pumps:

- Low initial cost
- Low maintenance cost
- Quiet operation
- Operational simplicity
- Capability of handling contaminated and heterogeneous fluids like paper pulp, slurry, molasses, sewage etc.
- Greater reliability.

2. Positive Displacement Pumps:

The working principle of these pumps is explained in the subsequent article 5.3.

These pumps are widely used in fluid power circuits. As implied in the name, these pumps delivers a fixed volume of fluid per revolution, into the hydraulic system. These pumps are capable of overcoming the pressure due to mechanical loading on the system and also the pressure due to fluid friction.

The positive displacement pumps offer several advantages over the non-positive displacement pumps such as :

- High pressure capability, upto 600 bar or higher.
- Small, compact size with high power to weight ratio.
- High volumetric efficiency.
- Small variation of efficiency through the operating pressure range.
- Wide flexibility of performance under varying speed and pressure range.

The positive displacement pumps are of (i) Fixed displacement type, and (ii) Variable displacement type.

Fixed displacement pumps are those in which fluid discharge per revolution cannot be varied. While in a variable displacement pump, a variable rate of discharge of fluid can be obtained by change of physical inter-relationship of various pump components, though the pump speed is constant.

A positive displacement pump does not pump pressure but only produces fluid flow. The discharge pressure is governed by the resistance to the flow offered by the hydraulic system. e.g. when a positive displacement pump operates with discharge line open to the atmosphere, it discharges the flow of fluid at atmospheric pressure, as there is no resistance to flow. But when the discharge line is blocked, the resistance to flow is very high. The discharged fluid has no place to go. The fluid being incompressible, any further fluid discharged develops very high pressures, enough to damage the components. Therefore, this pump is provided with a pressure relief valve, for safety against excessive pressure built-up.

Some positive displacement pumps are designed for variable displacement, pressure compensation capability. When the system pressure increases, these pumps produce less flow; and at pre-set maximum pressure, the flow rate drops to zero due to zero displacement. This arrests any further built up of pressure. Thus pressure relief valves are not necessary for these pumps.

2.2 CLASSIFICATION OF HYDRAULIC PUMPS

Fig. 2.1 shows the classification of hydraulic pumps. (Non-positive and non-positive displacements)

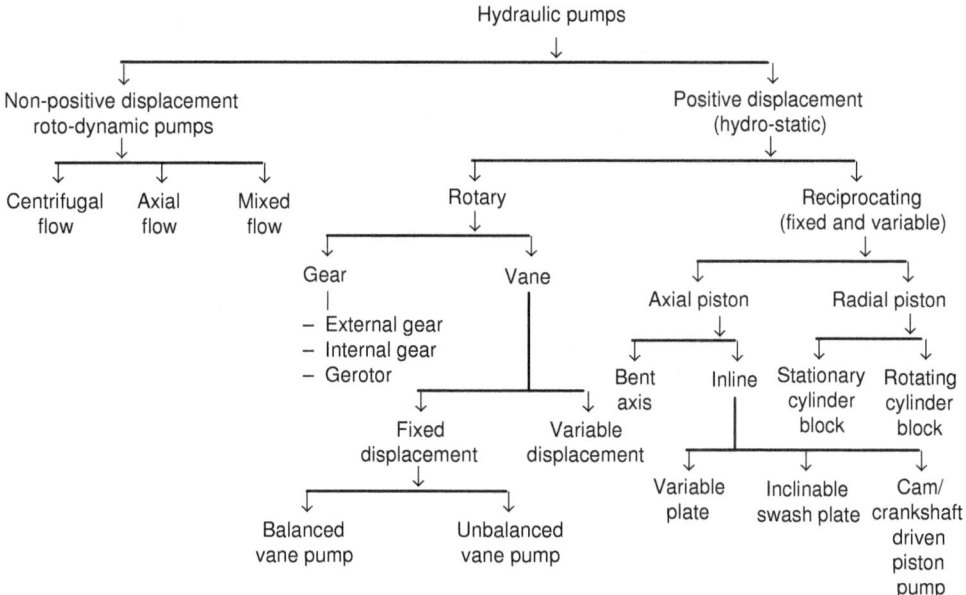

Fig. 2.1

2.2.1 Principle and Salient Features of Non-positive (Hydro-dynamic) Displacement Pumps

The typical types of these pumps are centrifugal (impeller) and axial (propeller) flow pumps, as shown in Fig. 2.2 (a) and Fig. 2.2 (b).

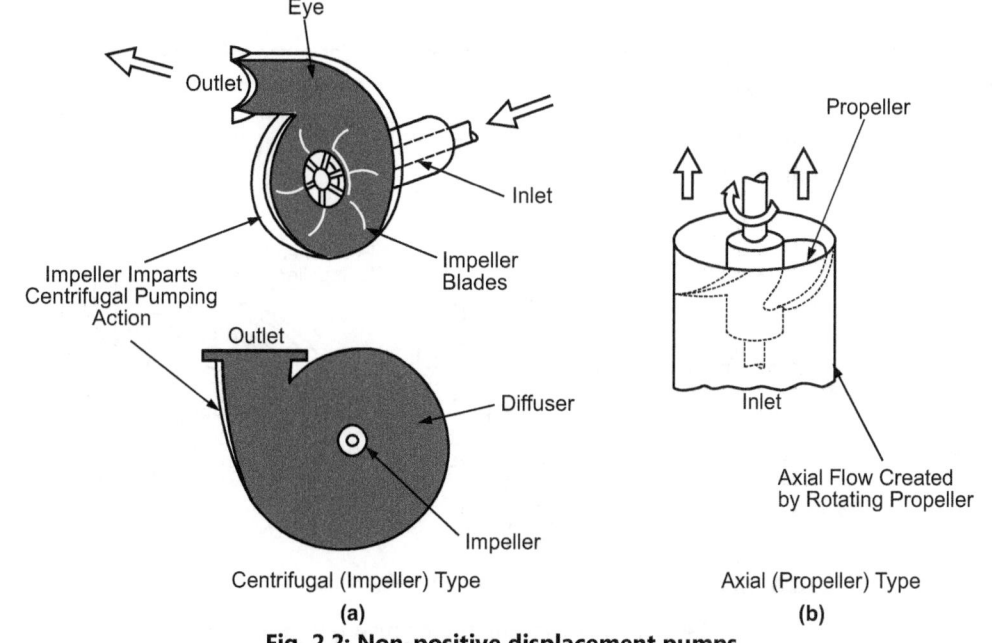

Fig. 2.2: Non-positive displacement pumps

These pumps provide continuous discharge. But the flow rate reduces with the increase of system resistance. These pumps are suitable for low pressure, high volume flow systems.

Due to considerable clearance between the stationary and rotating elements, these pumps are not self priming. The displacement between the suction and discharge is not positive. The flow rate of the pump depends upon the rotational speed of the pump as well as the external resistance of the system.

With increase of external resistance, some fluid slips back from the discharge side to the suction side thereby reducing the discharge into the system. The slippage is attributed to the principle that fluid follows the path of least resistance. When the external resistance is infinite (when the delivery value is closed), the pump will not produce axial flow and the volumetric efficiency reduces to zero.

As external resistance reduces with the opening of the delivery valve, the flow increases at the cost of reduced pressure. The maximum pressure when the delivery valve is shut off is known as shut-off head.

Fig. 2.3 shows the delivery pressure versus the discharge characteristic for a typical centrifugal pump.

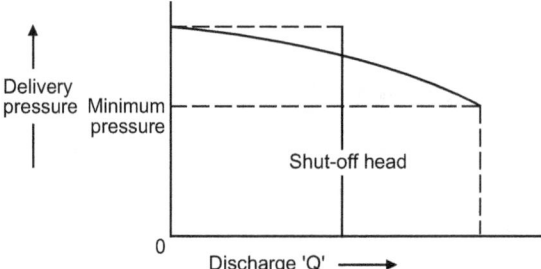

Fig. 2.3: Delivery pressure versus discharge curve for a centrifugal pump

2.2.2 Centrifugal Pumps

These pumps are non-positive displacement type hydrodynamic pumps. These pumps are suitable for high volume low pressure applications.

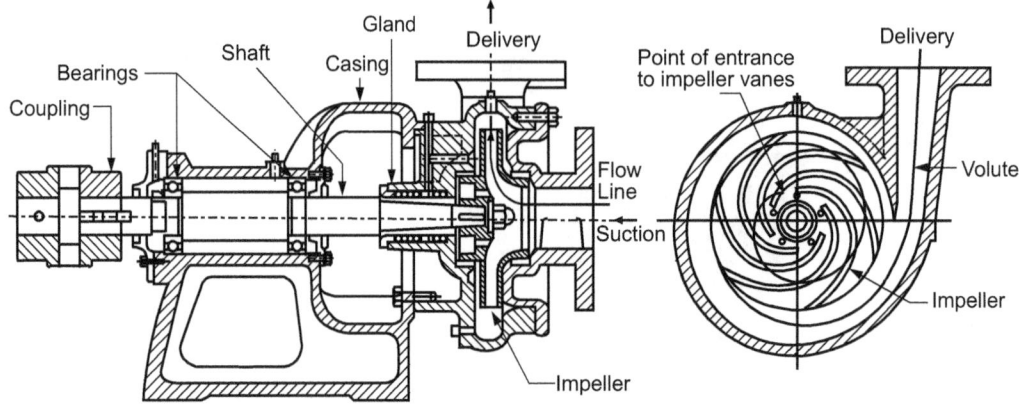

Fig. 2.4 (a): Construction of a centrifugal pump

Fig. 2.4 (a) shows the construction of a centrifugal pump which typically consists of:
1. Shaft with bearings
2. Impellar with curved vanes
3. Diffuser casing
4. Suction inlet
5. Delivery diffuser
6. Delivery valve
7. Reflux (non-return) valve
8. Suction pipe with foot valve/strainer

The variation of the velocity of the fluid through the centrifugal pump is shown in Fig. 2.4 (b).

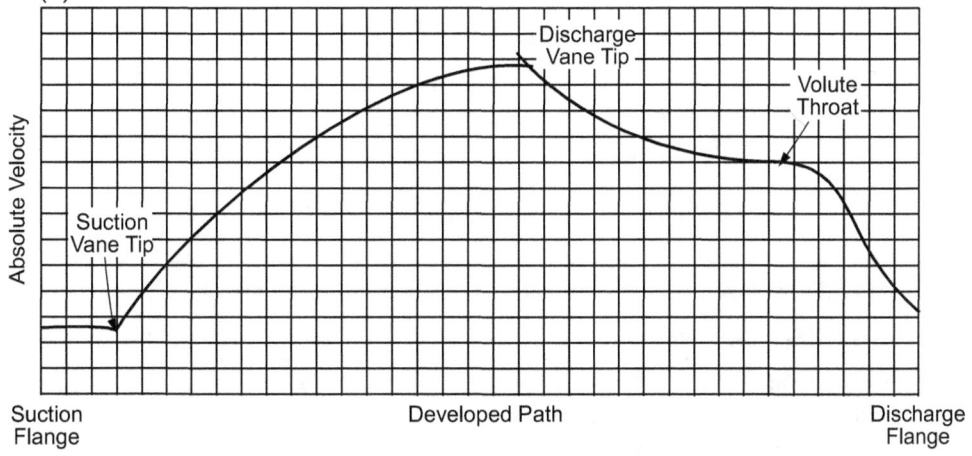

Fig. 2.4 (b): Variation of velocity of fluid through the centrifugal pump

Fig. 2.5 illustrates the typical layout of a centrifugal pump installation.

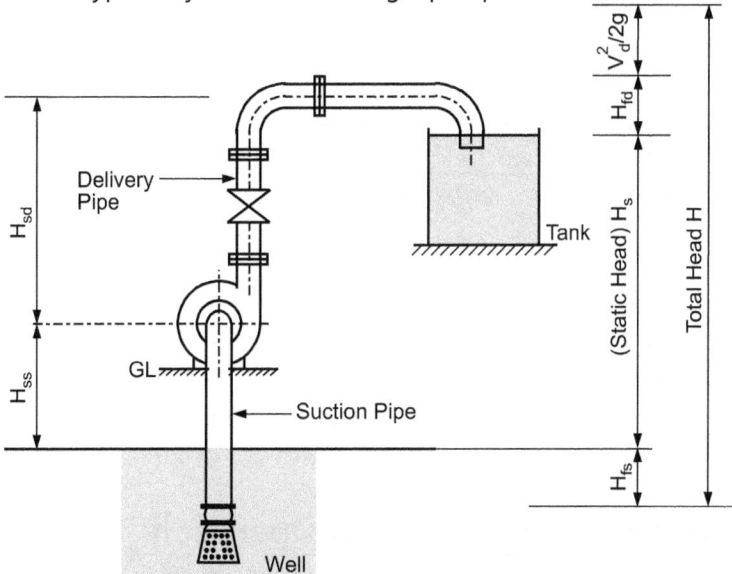

Fig. 2.5: Typical layout of a centrifugal pump

Fig. 2.6 illustrates the operating characteristics of a centrifugal pump operating at constant speed.

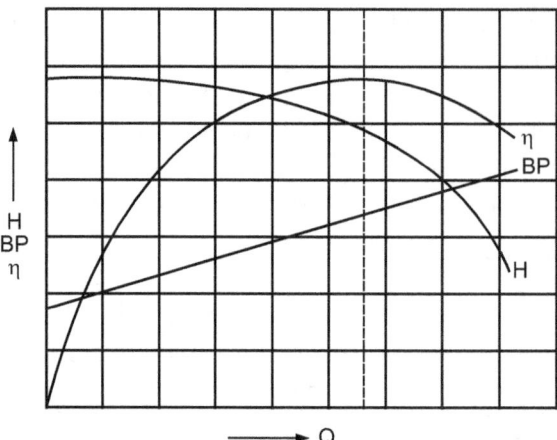

Fig. 2.6: Operating characteristics of a centrifugal pump

2.3 Principle and Advantages of Hydrostatic/Positive Displacement Pumps

This type of pump discharges a fixed quantity of fluid per revolution i.e. delivers a constant flow rate, neglecting internal leakage. These pumps are well suited for fluid power systems. However, proper protection against excessive pressure built-up must be provided when external resistance to flow becomes very large or infinite. A positive displacement pump continues its discharge of fluid even though the fluid has no place to go, leading to extremely fast pressure built up. A pressure relief valve for protecting the pump against excessive pressure by diverting the flow back to the reservoir, is used.

2.4 Vane Pumps

Vane pumps are widely used in various hydraulic systems. Vane pumps are classified as follows:

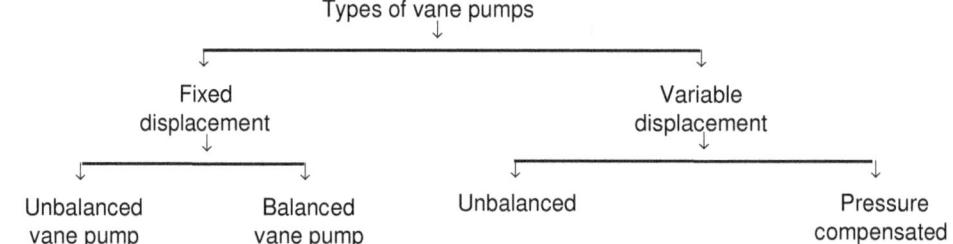

2.4.1 Construction and Principle of Operation   (May 2011)

The construction of a fixed displacement unbalanced vane pump is shown in Fig. 2.7.

It consists of a rotor with radial slots mounted on the shaft. The rotor is housed in the pump casing with an offset. The rotor houses several sliding vanes in its radial slots. It rotates inside a cam ring. Each vane tip contacts with the surface of the cam ring. During one half rotation of the rotor, the volume increases between the rotor and the cam ring. This volume expansion develops a vacuum to draw in the fluid through the inlet port to fill in the void. As the rotation of the rotor continues, through the latter half of the rotation, the surface of the cam ring forces the vanes back into their slots thereby reducing the trapped volume of the fluid. This pushes the trapped fluid positively through the discharge port.

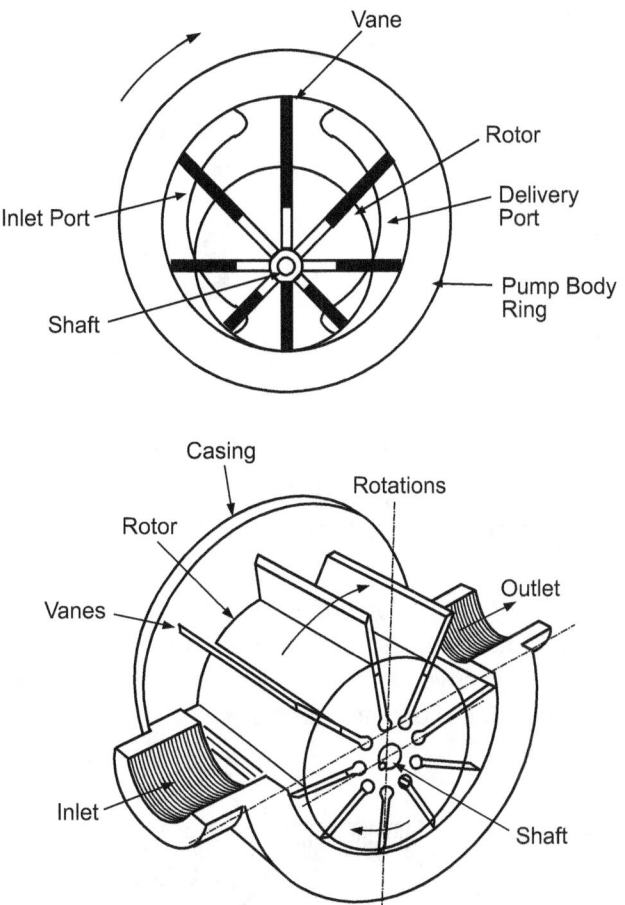

Fig. 2.7: Vane pump (Fixed displacement type)

2.4.2 Side Thrust on the Shaft

While the pump is in operation, there is high pressure at the pump discharge side and vacuum pressure at the pump section. This pressure differential generates an unwanted side thrust on the rotor shaft. This unbalanced side thrust damages the pump components and shortens the pump life.

Therefore, vane pumps with eccentrically mounted circular ring are rarely used. A balanced vane pumps with elliptically contoured cam ring is now-a-days used.

2.4.3 Balanced Vane Pump

It has two suction and two discharge ports placed diametrically opposite each other (Refer Fig. 2.8). Thus the pressure ports are also opposite to each other. This establishes a pressure balance and eliminates the side thrust on the shaft.

A major limitation of a balanced vane pump is that it cannot be designed for variable displacement. This pump uses an elliptical housing instead of a circular ring.

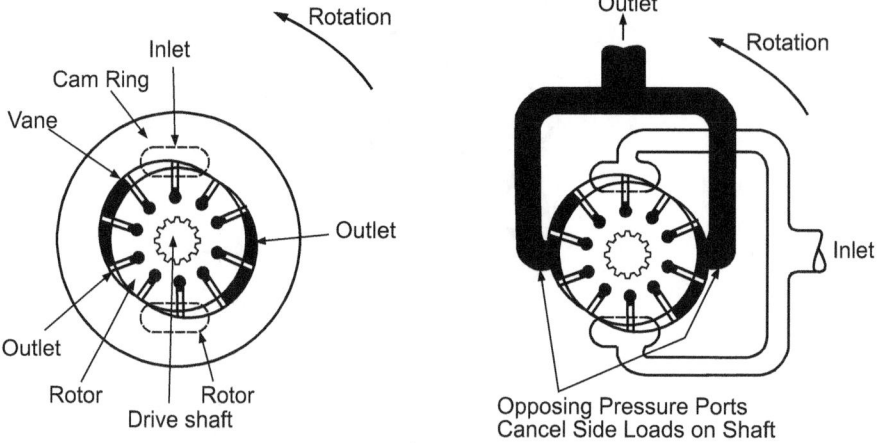

Fig. 2.8

2.4.4 Variable Displacement Vane Pump   (May 12)

Some vane pumps are provided with a mechanism for varying the eccentricity between the rotor and the cam ring or housing. Such vane pumps have variable displacement and is shown in Fig. 2.9. A hand wheel or a pressure compensator is used to move the cam ring for changing the eccentricity. The movement of the cam ring on either side of the rotor can be used for reversing the direction of flow through the pump.

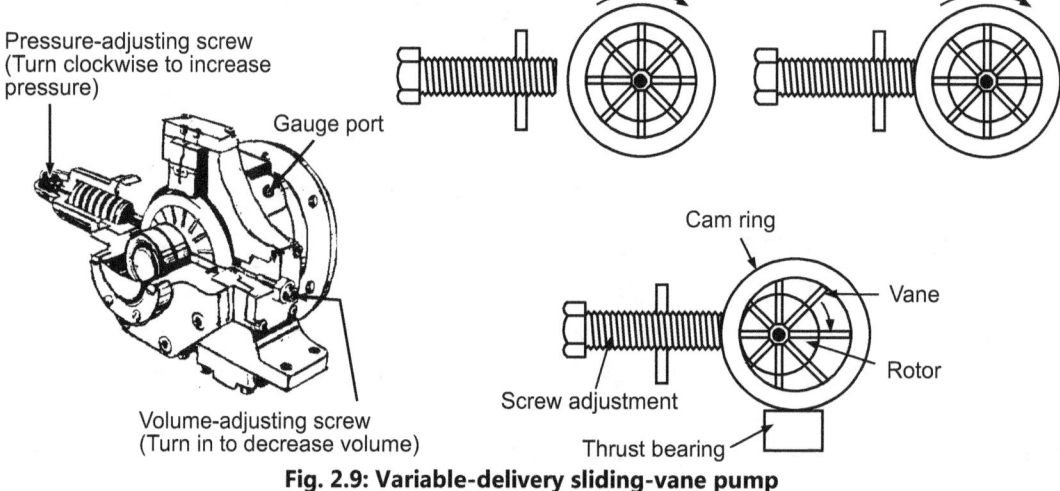

Fig. 2.9: Variable-delivery sliding-vane pump

2.4.5 Pressure Compensated Vane Pump

The vane pump shown in Fig. 2.10 is of a pressure compensated type. In this pump, the system pressure is made to act directly on the cam ring through a hydraulic piston on the right side. This forces the cam ring against the compensator spring-loaded piston on the left of the cam ring. When the discharge pressure is high, it overcomes the compensator spring force and displaces the cam ring to the left. This in turn reduces the eccentricity. The eccentricity is maximum when the discharge pressure is zero. With high discharge pressure, eccentricity is zero, thus reducing the pump discharge to zero.

This pump has a built-in protection against excessive pressure built-up. When the discharge pressure reaches the cut-out pressure, the compensator spring force equals the hydraulic piston force. Any further increase of pressure compresses the compensator spring to reduce the eccentricity to zero. The corresponding maximum pressure attained is known as dead head pressure. This pressure compensation in addition to protection against excessive pressure built-up, averts fluid heating.

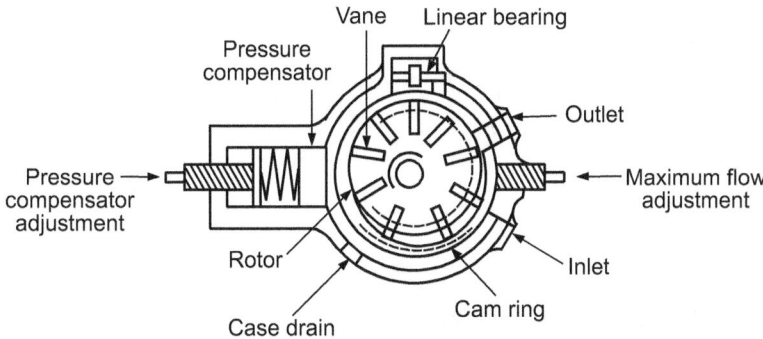

Fig. 2.10 (a): Pressure compensated vane pump with straight vane

Fig. 2.10 (b): Cutaway photograph of pressure-compensated vane pump

2.4.6 Performance Characteristics of Vane Pumps

The performance analysis of vane pumps is explained as under:

Let,
- D_C = Diameter of cam ring, m
- D_R = Diameter of rotor, m
- L = Width of rotor, m
- N = Speed of rotor, r.p.m.
- V_D = Volumetric displacement of pump, m³
- e = Eccentricity, m
- e_{max} = Maximum possible eccentricity, m
- $V_{D_{max}}$ = Maximum possible volumetric displacement, m³

It is evident from the pump geometry that

Maximum possible eccentricity, $e_{max} = \dfrac{D_C - D_R}{2}$

and maximum volumetric displacement.

$$V_{D_{max}} = \dfrac{\pi}{4}[(D_C^2 - D_R^2)L] \text{ m}^3 = \dfrac{\pi}{4}[(D_C + D_R)(D_C - D_R)L] \text{ m}^3$$

$$= \left[\dfrac{\pi}{4}(D_C + D_R) \times 2\, e_{max} \times L\right] \text{ m}^3$$

Similarly, for any eccentricity 'e',

Actual volumetric displacement $V_D = \left[\dfrac{\pi}{2}(D_C + D_R) \times e \times L\right] \text{ m}^3$

The performance characteristics showing the variation of percentage flow rate, percentage power input required and percentage efficiency against discharge pressure for a constant speed driven vane pump are illustrated in Fig. 2.11.

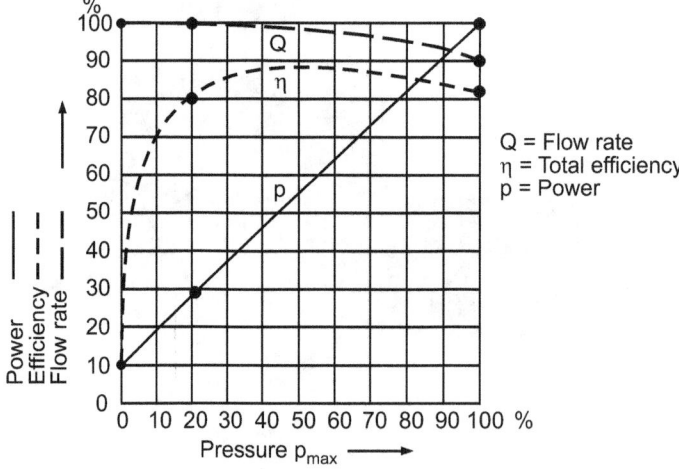

Fig. 2.11: Characteristic of a vane pump at constant speed

For a pressure-compensated vane pump, the flow rate discharge pressure characteristic is shown in Fig. 2.12.

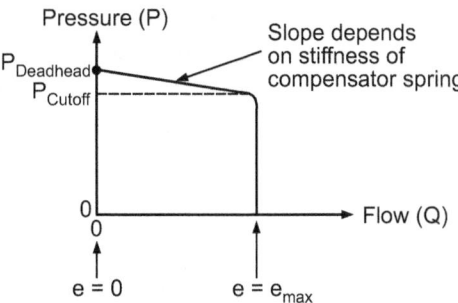

Fig. 2.12: Variation of flow rate against discharge pressure of a pressure compensated vane pump

2.5 GEAR PUMPS (Dec. 07)

These are positive displacement type rotary pumps and are suitable for high pressure low volume discharge applications.

2.5.1 Introduction

In the arena of pumps, in addition to the traditional pumps, a large variety of other positive displacement pumps are used for diverse applications.

The gear pumps are basically rotary pumps consisting of two gears. However, its action is not dynamic, like that of a centrifugal pump. It merely displaces the liquid from the suction side to the delivery side. The flow rate of the liquid is uniform and continuous without any change of velocity and acceleration.

2.5.2 Construction and Principle of Working

The gear pumps can further be categorised as:
   (i) External gear pump and
   (ii) Internal gear pump

A typical external gear pump is shown in Fig. 2.13. It consists of two spur gears mounted on their respective shafts. The shafts are supported between the bearings. The assembly is contained in a housing or casing. The casing is made of cast iron while the gearing and the shafts of alloy steel. The gears are heat treated and hardened for wear resistance. The gears are finished with fine tolerances and smooth surface finish. The assembly is made with great precision and fine radial and axial clearances. The pump is externally driven by an electric motor or a diesel engine. One of the gears is driven from the prime mover while the other is driven from the driver gear.

For the direction of rotation of the gears shown in the figure, the liquid fills up the interstitial gaps between the meshing gears. This entrapped liquid is carried forward as the gears rotate and is discharged towards the delivery side having high pressure. Most of the liquid carried is discharged towards the delivery side while a small quantity of liquid returns back to the suction side. The delivery side remains separated from the suction side through the flanks of the meshing teeth and the outer casing of the pump. Smaller the clearances, minimum is the leakage of liquid.

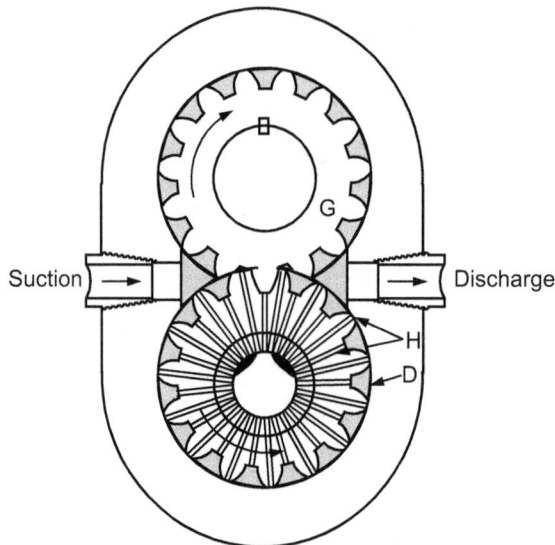

Fig. 2.13: External gear pump

During the meshing of the gear teeth, a small closed space or a squeeze room is formed between them. This squeeze room attains minimum volume (ideally zero volume in the absence of any play). The liquid trapped in this space can attain abnormally high pressures to damage the pump.

It is therefore, necessary to provide a way out to this entrapped liquid. This is done by providing the distance of the edge of the meeting line of the two teeths from the line joining the two centres. Often radial holes are provided which open at the centre and which bypass the entrapped liquid from the squeeze room.

Each gear teeth functions like a tiny piston to push the liquid positively forward. The gear pumps are thus positive displacement pumps.

The manufacture and assembly of a gear pump requires good surface finish, precise dimension control and very fine clearances. Low viscosity fluids need smaller play and minimum clearances otherwise internal leakage is large. On the other hand, high viscosity fluids need bigger play and greater clearance to control excessive friction and power consumption. Clear fluids with low viscosity need small gaps between the gears and the casing.

These pump use bush bearings or roller bearings which are lubricated by the oil flow itself or they are placed outside the casing and external lubrication is provided. For very high viscosity fluids, the casing is equipped with a heater jacket to reduce the viscosity of the fluids. These pumps are normally used to develop small heads. However, these pumps are often used for high discharge pressures upto 300 bar.

The gear pump is provided with a protection against excessive pressure built-up with a built-up pressure relief valve or an internal bypass as shown in Fig. 2.14.

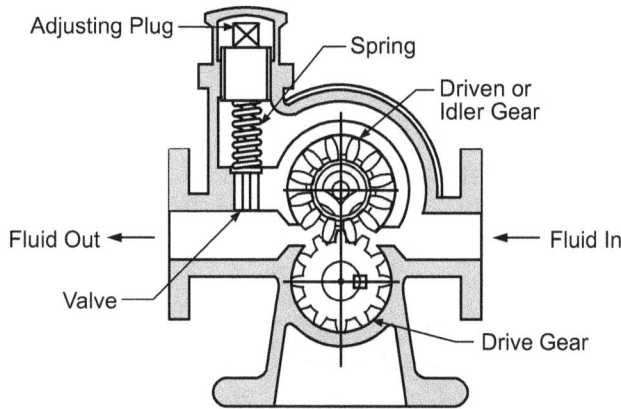

Fig. 2.14: Gear pump with internal bypass

2.5.3 Performance Characteristics of a Gear Pump (May 09, Dec. 11)

The theoretical discharge per revolution can be estimated from the volume of liquid contained in the teeth gaps of both the gears. Irregular teeth passage however, make it difficult to arrive at a general equation for the discharge.

The empirical relation for estimation of theoretical discharge proposed by Hagen is

$$Q_{th} = \frac{m^2 \times \pi bN}{60} \left[2n + \left(1 + \frac{n}{n'}\right)\left(1 - \frac{\pi^2 \cos^2 \alpha}{48}\right) \right] \times 10^{-6} \text{ l.p.s.} \qquad \ldots (2.1)$$

where m = Module, mm
 b = Width of gear, mm
 N = Speed of the pump, rpm
 n = Number of teeth of the driving gear
 n' = Number of teeth of the driven gear
 α = Pressure angle

Equation (2.1) is based on the assumption that there is no flank clearance. When the flank clearance is to be considered, the equation is modified as

$$Q_{th} = \frac{\pi m^2 b M}{60}\left[2n + \left(1 + \frac{n}{n'}\right)\left(1 - \frac{\pi^2 \cos^2 \alpha}{12}\right)\right] \times 10^{-6} \text{ l.p.s.} \quad \text{... (2.2)}$$

For both spur gear wheels, having equal number of teeth, Molly proposed the following equation for theoretical discharge as

$$Q_{th} = \frac{\pi}{2}\left(D_k^2 - c^2 - D_b^2 \frac{\pi^2}{32^2}\right) b\, n$$

Were, D_k = Diameter of the outer circle, cm

           c = Distance between the axes, cm

           D_b = Diameter on the base circle, cm

The actual discharge is usually less than the theoretical as some flow returns along the casing and from the entrapped space flows back to the suction. The volumetric efficiency of the gear pump is defined as the ratio of actual discharge to the theoretical discharge. It depends upon the viscosity of the liquid, the clearances provided and the surface finish of the pump.

$$\text{Volumetric efficiency} = \frac{\text{Actual discharge/s}}{\text{Theoretical discharge/s}} \times 100 \quad \text{... (2.3)}$$

A simple equation for theoretical discharge is

$$Q_{th} = \frac{2 \times a \times b \times n \times N}{60} \times 10^{-3} \text{ l.p.s.} \quad \text{... (2.4)}$$

where a = Area enclosed between two successive teeth, cm^2

           b = Width of gear, cm

           n = Number of teeth

           N = Speed

The power output (utilized) of the pump is given by

$$\text{Power output} = \rho \times Q_{act} \times g \times \Delta H \times 10^{-3} \text{ kW} \quad \text{... (2.5)}$$

where ρ = Density of the oil, kg/m^3

           Q = Actual discharge, m^3/s

           ΔH = Pressure head developed by the pump, m of oil

Thus, the overall efficiency is obtained as:

$$\text{Overall } \eta = \frac{\text{Power output}}{\text{Power input to pump}} \quad \text{... (2.6)}$$

The overall efficiency accounts for the volumetric (leakage) losses of the discharge and the mechanical frictional losses.

The performance characteristics of a gear pump are shown in Fig. 2.15 (a, b, c, d and e).

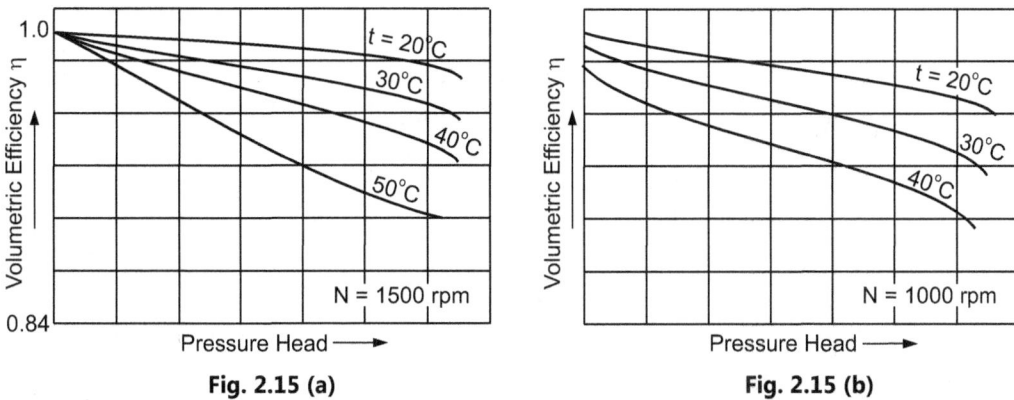

Fig. 2.15 (a) Fig. 2.15 (b)

It is seen from Fig. 2.15 (a) as the pressure head developed by the pump increases, the volumetric efficiency for a given temperature decreases. The drop in volumetric efficiency is more at higher temperatures than at lower temperatures due to low viscosity and more internal leakage.

Fig. 2.15 (b) shows the variation of volumetric efficiency versus pressure head at 1000 r.p.m. At lower speed, volumetric efficiency is somewhat less.

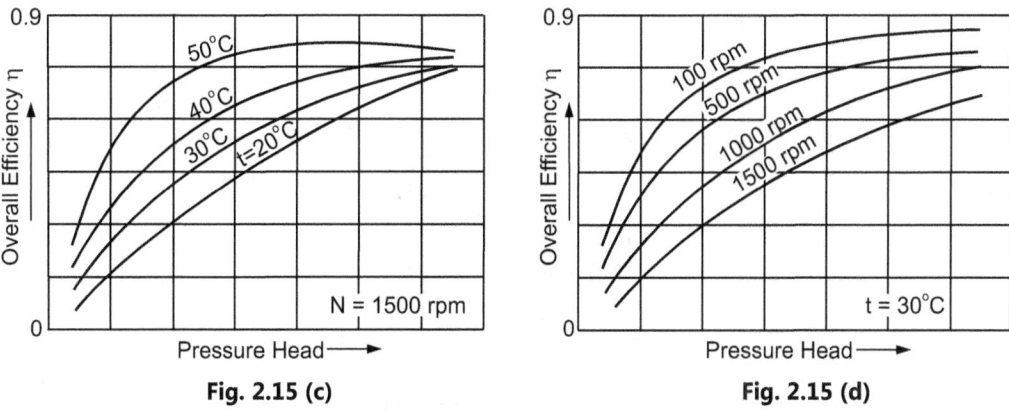

Fig. 2.15 (c) Fig. 2.15 (d)

The variation of overall efficiency versus pressure head is illustrated in Fig. 2.15 (c) for a constant speed of 1500 rpm. For a given pressure head, overall efficiency is greater at higher temperature than at lower temperature.

Fig. 2.15 (d) depicts the variation of overall efficiency versus pressure head for a given temperature and various speeds. For a given pressure head, the overall efficiency is low at higher speed.

Similarly, the variation of discharge and power consumption are plotted against the discharge pressure in Fig. 2.15 (e). For a constant discharge pressure, the discharge and power consumption is greater at high speed than at low speed.

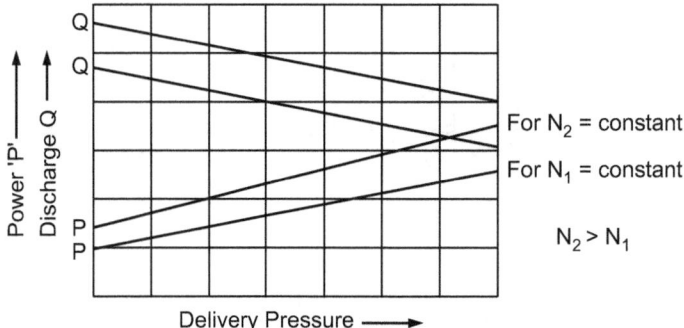

Fig. 2.15 (e): Variation of discharge and power against delivery pressure

2.5.4 Pressure Balancing in a Gear Pump

During the operation of a gear pump, fluid flows from a low pressure (vacuum) suction region to a high pressure discharge region. This results in a pressure gradient around the perimeter of the gear inside the casing. Owing to this undesirable pressure gradient, the surfaces tend to distort, especially under high pressure gradient. The distortion is attributed to the unbalance pressure force. It can be avoided by pressure balancing.

One method of pressure balancing as seen from Fig. 2.13 is by connecting the ducts. Ducts are tiny passages drilled through each teeth. This method is not only difficult for manufacture but is also found to increase leakage.

2.5.5 Wear Plates

Wear plates are placed on each side of the gear and the casing plates. The wear plates provide contact surface of superior bearing quality. These are made of bronze.

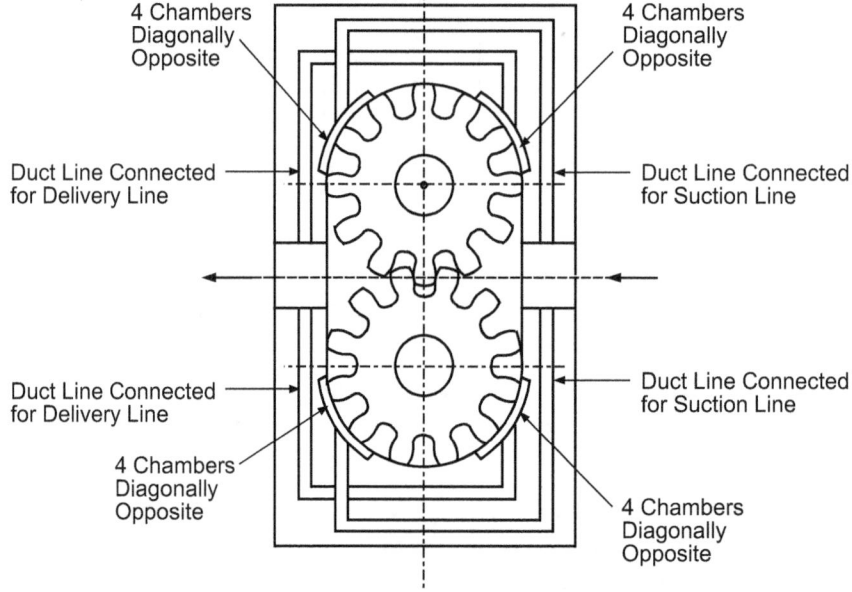

Fig. 2.16: Pressure balancing of gear pump

Oil makes its way between the wear plate and the casing plate. This oil exerts pressure against the wear plates. The wear plates have a pressure balance near the discharge region. But near the suction region, wear plates are subjected to a large pressure differential. The unbalanced force deflects the plate against the gear. The gear teeth mill away the surface of wearing plates, increasing the clearance and adversely affecting the performance of the gear pump.

The deflection of wear plates under the unbalanced pressure can be eliminated by pressure balancing as shown in Fig. 2.16.

2.5.6 Internal Gear Pump

Fig. 2.17 (a) shows an internal gear pump and Fig. 2.17 (b) illustrates an internal gear pump with a built-in pressure relief valve.

It typically consists of an internal gear, a regular spur gear, a crescent shaped seal and an external housing. As the power is supplied to any one of the gears, the motion of the gears draws in fluid from the reservoir. In Fig. 2.18 the internal gear drives the external gear. Near the inlet port teeth unmesh, the cavity volume decreases and the suction occurs. The fluid is forced around both the sides of the crescent seal which isolates the suction and discharge openings. When the teeth mesh on the opposite side to that of the crescent seal, the volume reduces and the fluid is forced to the discharge port of the pump. Fig. 2.18 illustrates the working of an internal gear pump.

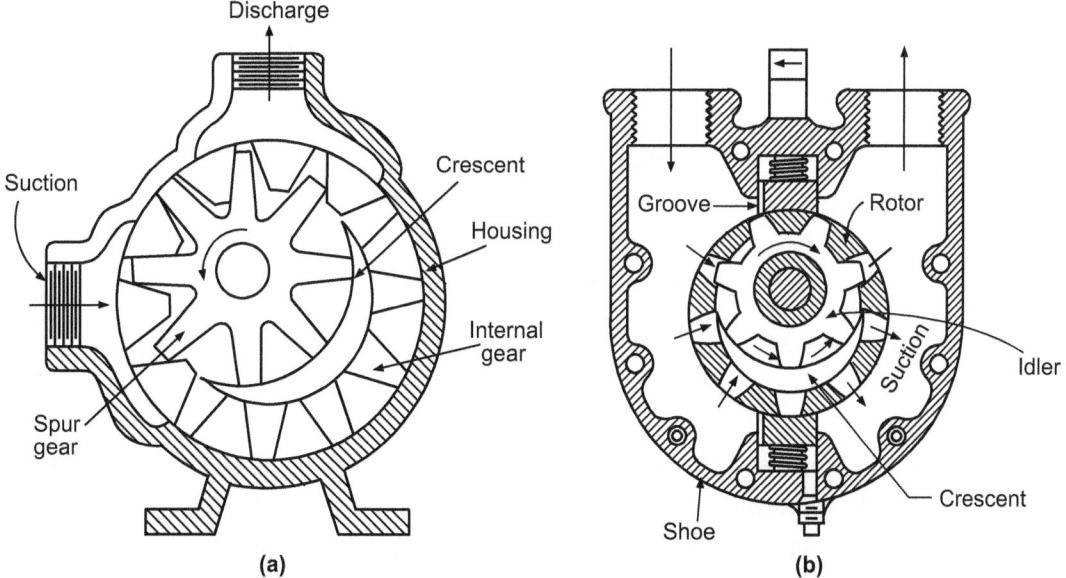

Fig. 2.17: Internal gear pump with pressure relief valve

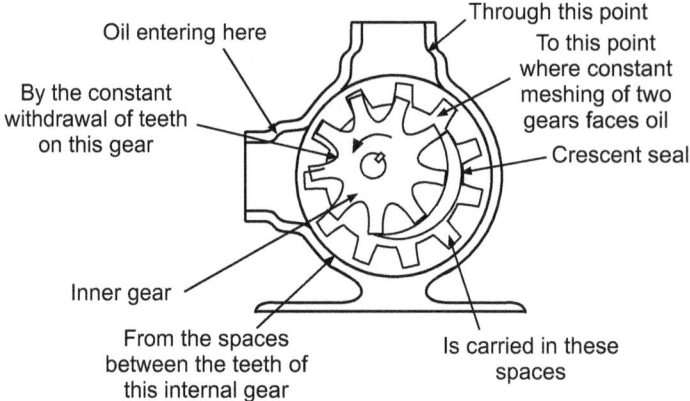

Fig. 2.18: Internal gear pump

2.5.7 Herring-bone Gear Pump

This gear pump consists of two helix gear teeth cut in opposite direction.

Most spur or helical gear pumps are reversible whereas a herringbone gear pump is unidirectional. The main advantage of this gear pump is the low noise and no axial thrust. These pumps deliver large volumes of oil at high pressure.

2.5.8 Gerotor Pump

The operation of this pump is similar to that of an internal gear pump. The construction of a gerotor pump is shown in Fig. 2.19.

It consists of an outer-ring, an outer gerotor and an inner gerotor. The outer gerotor is idler while the inner gerotor is the driver. The inner gerotor has always one tooth less than that of the outer gerotor. The axis of the inner and the outer gerotor are offset.

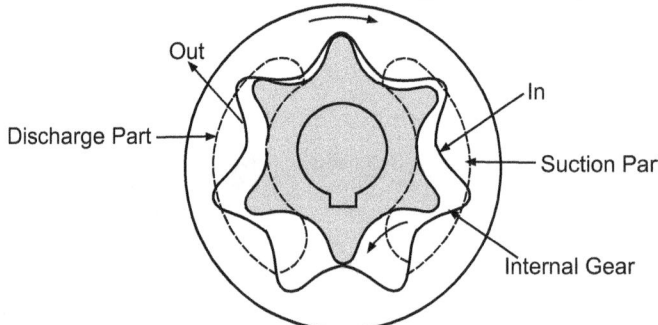

Fig. 2.19: Gerotor pump

When the number of teeth on the inner and outer gerotor are 4 and 5 respectively, for every revolution of the inner gerotor, the outer gerotor completes 4/5 or 0.8 revolution only.

The inner gerotor draws the outer gerotor around while they mesh. This develops inlet and discharge pumping chambers between the gerotor lobes. The tips of both the gerotors establish contact to seal the pumping chambers to avoid leakage. The volumetric displacement is dependent upon the space formed by the extra teeth in the outer gerotor. The operation of the gerotor pump is shown in Fig. 2.20.

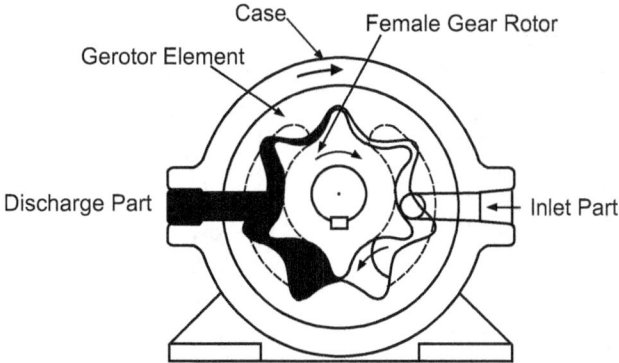

Fig. 2.20: Working of a gerotor pump

2.6 LOBE PUMPS

There are several designs of lobe pumps. The pump has two or three lobes. The construction of a twin lobe pump and a three lobe pump is shown in Fig. 2.21 (a) and Fig. 2.21 (b).

These lobes operate like gears. One of the rotors is driven by the motor while the other is driven through twinning gears. As the rotors rotate, the fluid is trapped between each lobe and the wall of the pump housing and is carried along from the suction side to discharge side.

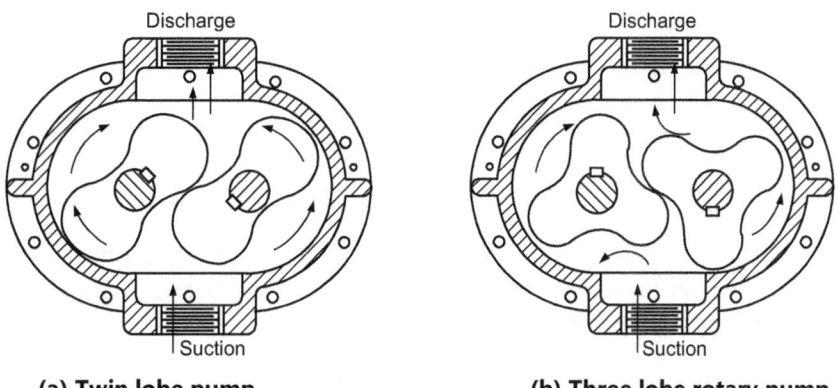

(a) Twin lobe pump   **(b) Three lobe rotary pump**

Fig. 2.21

The discharge from these pumps is quite pulsating since only few lobes are adopted. The line of contact between the meshing lobes and between the lobe and casing establishes leak-proof seal separating high pressure discharge side from the low pressure suction side. These pumps require extreme precision machining, finish of the lobe profile and an accurate control of radial and axial clearances. These pumps are suitable for low viscosity and uncontaminated fluids only. They are used for low pressure, high volume flow applications.

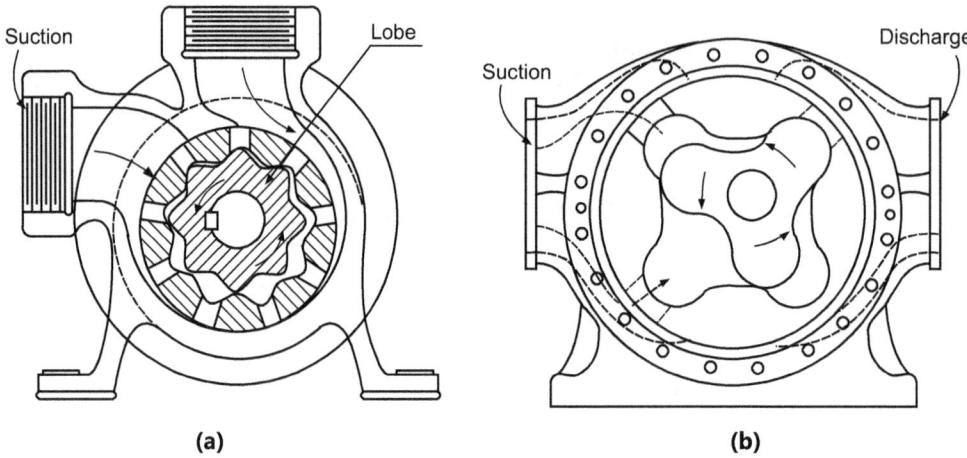

Fig. 2.22: Internal lobe pumps

In this pump, the number of lobes on the male rotor is one less than that in the female rotor.

2.7 Piston Pumps

In this pump, pumping action is produced by the reciprocating piston in a precision cylinder. The retracting piston draws in fluid in the cylinder while its forward travel expels the fluid towards the discharge port.

Piston pumps are further classified as -

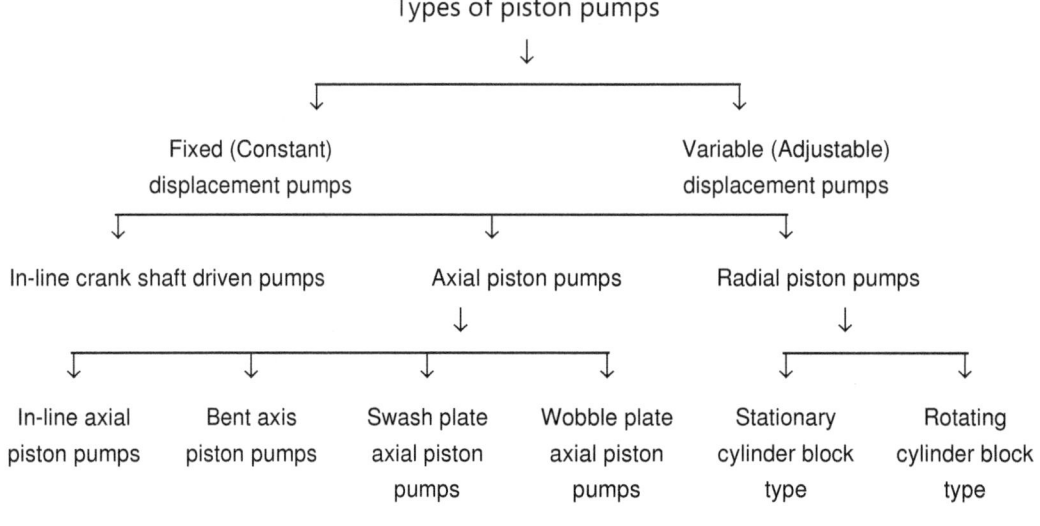

2.7.1 Radial Piston Pumps (Radial Plunger Pump)

(Dec. 07, 10; May 08, 10, 12)

The two basic types of radial piston pumps are:

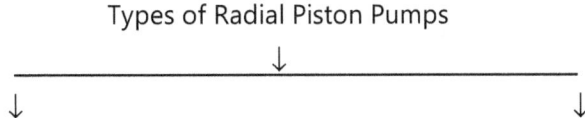

In stationary cylinder block type radial piston pumps, the cylinder block is stationary while the pistons reciprocate by the actuation from a rotating cam. The cylinder head of each cylinder is connected to the inlet and discharge check valves.

In the rotating cylinder block type radial piston pump, the rotating cylinder block is driven from the pump shaft. The outer ring may be fixed or rotating with the cylinder block.

The cylinder block and the outer ring are eccentrically placed. The pistons are actuated outwards due to centrifugal action and are pushed back due to eccentricity between the rotor ring and cylinder block.

Fig. 2.23 shows the construction and working of a radial piston pump.

The pintle directs the fluid into or out of the cylinders. A cylinder barrel with pistons revolves around the pintle (stationary). The piston heads press against a reaction ring housed in the rotor. The centre of the reaction ring is offset with the centre of the pintle or the shaft. Because of the rotation of the cylinder barrel, the pistons on one side are displaced outwards. This sucks in the fluid as each cylinder passes the suction ports of the pintle. After the pistons pass the point of maximum eccentricity, the pistons are forced inward by the reaction ring. This forces the fluid to be discharged to the discharge port of the pintle.

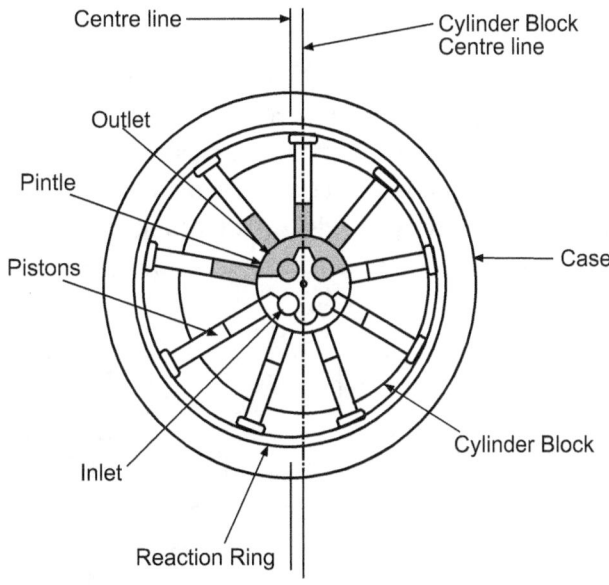

Fig. 2.23 (a): Working of a radial piston pump

The piston displacement and the flow rate of fluid discharged can be varied by varying the eccentricity. Performance characteristics of these are shown in Fig. 2.23 (b).

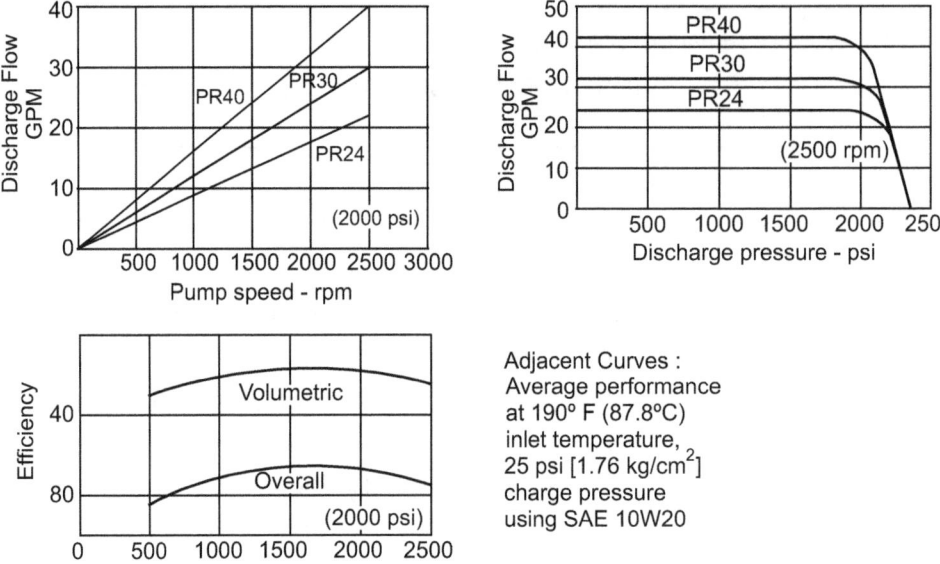

Fig. 2.23 (b): Performance curves of radial piston pumps

2.7.2 Axial Piston Pumps (May 08; Dec. 08)

The axial piston pumps are divided into two categories as: (i) In-line axial piston pumps, and (ii) Bent axis piston pumps.

2.7.3 In-line axial piston pump (Parallel piston pump) (Dec. 11)

In this pump, the axis of all pistons are parallel to each other. Depending upon the method of actuating the pistons, these pumps are further divided into two groups as: (1) swash plate axial piston pumps, and (2) wobble plate axial piston pumps.

(i) Swash plate type axial piston pump:

Fig. 2.24 shows the schematic of a swash plate type axial piston pump.

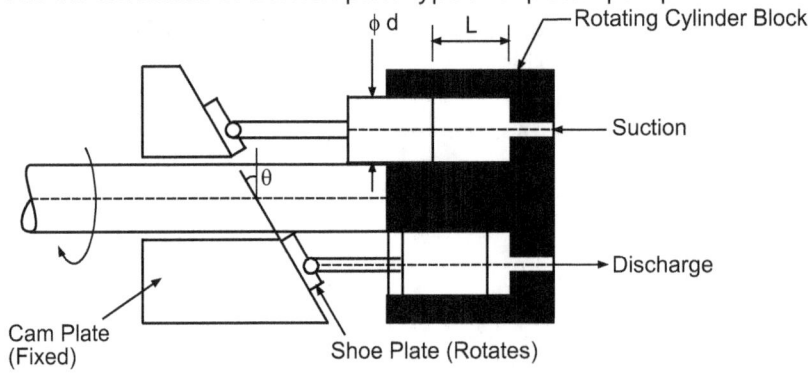

Fig. 2.24: Swash plate type axial piston pump

It consists of a rotating cylinder block which houses several cylinders. It is mounted on the shaft driven by the motor. A stationary cam (swash) plate supported on the shaft, houses several shoe plates each connected to the piston through the piston rod. As the cylinder block rotates, the piston shoe follows the surface of the swash plate. As the swash plate is at an angle, the piston has to reciprocate within the cylinder bore.

A stationary plate having suction and discharge port behind the rotating cylinder block, admits fluid into those cylinders having retracting pistons and collects the discharge of fluid from those cylinders having pistons moving rightwards.

The flow rate varies directly with the driving speed of the shaft for a fixed angle of inclination of the swash plate with the vertical. And for a fixed speed of rotation of the shaft, the greater the angle of inclination of the swash plate with the vertical, the greater the flow rate from the pump due to greater stroke travel of each piston.

The theoretical discharge from the pump is dependent upon (a) number of cylinders, n (b) speed of the pump, N (c) diameter of the cylinder, d (d) stroke length of the piston, 'L' which in turn depends upon the angle of inclination of the swash plate with the vertical.

The fixed capacity axial piston pump has the swash plate inclined at 60° with the vertical. The theoretical discharge 'Q_T' is given by

$$Q_T = n \times N \times \frac{\pi}{4} \times d^2 \times L \text{ cc/min.}$$

(ii) Wobble plate type axial piston pump:

In this pump, the cylinder block is stationary while the swash plate is driven by the shaft. The rotating swash plate is called as the wobble plate. The shoe plate is prevented from rotating. The swash plate rotating on the surface of shoe plate generates reciprocating motion of the pistons. The swash plates are also known as cam plates when stationary.

A typical wobble plate axial piston pump is shown in Fig. 2.25 (a).

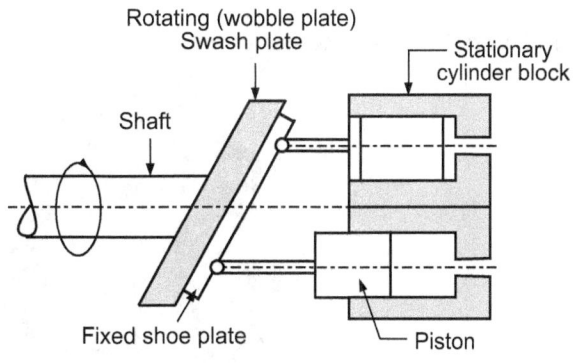

(a) Wobble plate axial piston pump

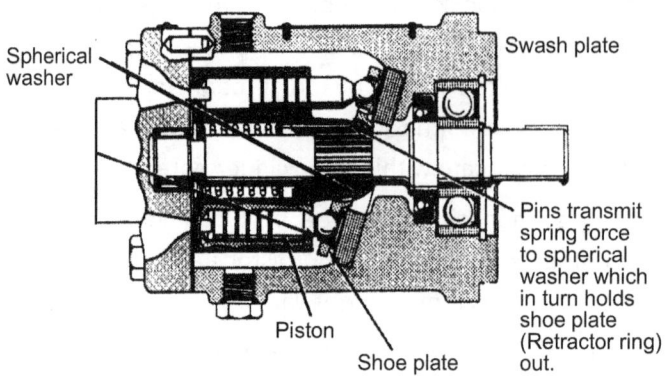

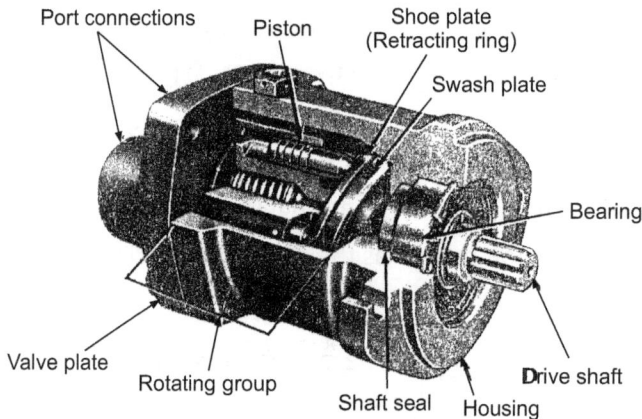

(b) In-line design piston pump

Fig. 2.25

(iii) Variable displacement swash plate axial piston pump: (May 2007)

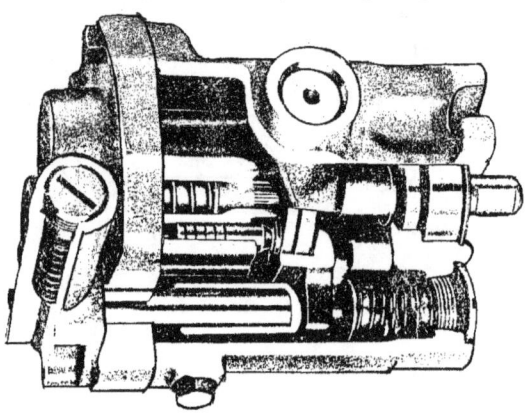

(a) Variable displacement axial piston pump

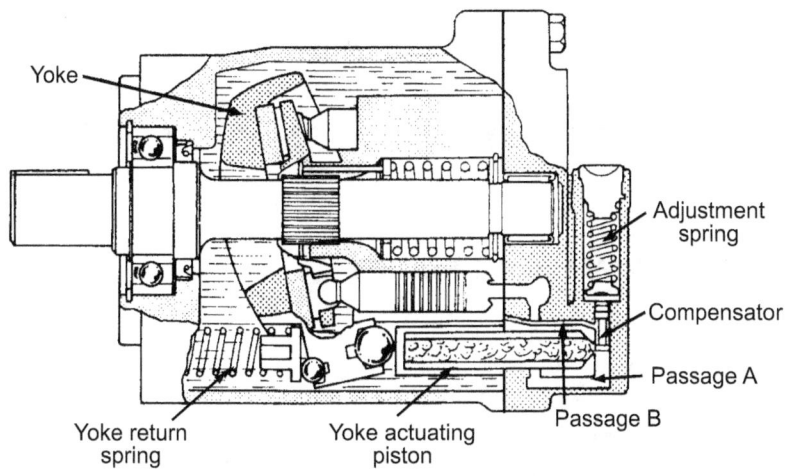

(b) Variable displacement swash plate pump

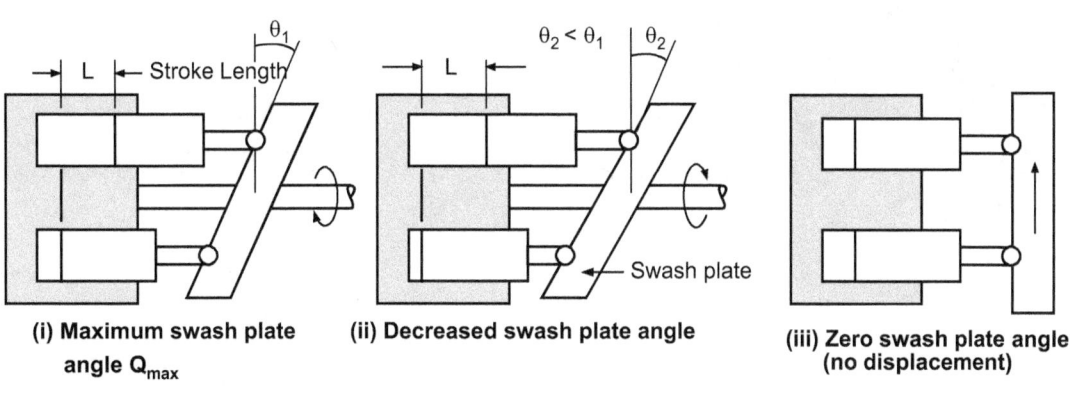

(i) Maximum swash plate angle Q_{max}

(ii) Decreased swash plate angle

(iii) Zero swash plate angle (no displacement)

(c)

Fig. 2.26

It is clear from the explanation in the preceding paragraph that the stroke of a piston, is governed by the angle of inclination of the swash plate with the vertical. When the swash plate is vertical, the stroke length of the piston is zero. Fig. 2.26 illustrates the point.

Therefore, the volume flow rate from the pump can be varied by charging the swash plate angle. This can be done mechanically or by the action of a yoke actuating piston operated by the pressure compensating valve. Refer Fig. 2.26 (a). It illustrates a pump with pressure compensator valve. When pressure in the compensator line exceeds the compensator setting, the compensator valve is positioned to allow the pressure oil in the delivery line to enter the control cylinder behind the piston which, in turn, overcomes the control spring force and delivery until the pressure in the delivery line holds at the compensator setting. When pressure in the delivery line is below the compensator setting the control cylinder is connected to a drain and the control spring pushes the swash plate for full delivery.

The maximum inclination of the swash plate with the vertical is usually restricted to 71.5°. Thus a stepless variation of flow rate is possible between the angle of inclination of 0° to 71.5°.

2.7.4 Bent Axis Axial Piston Pumps

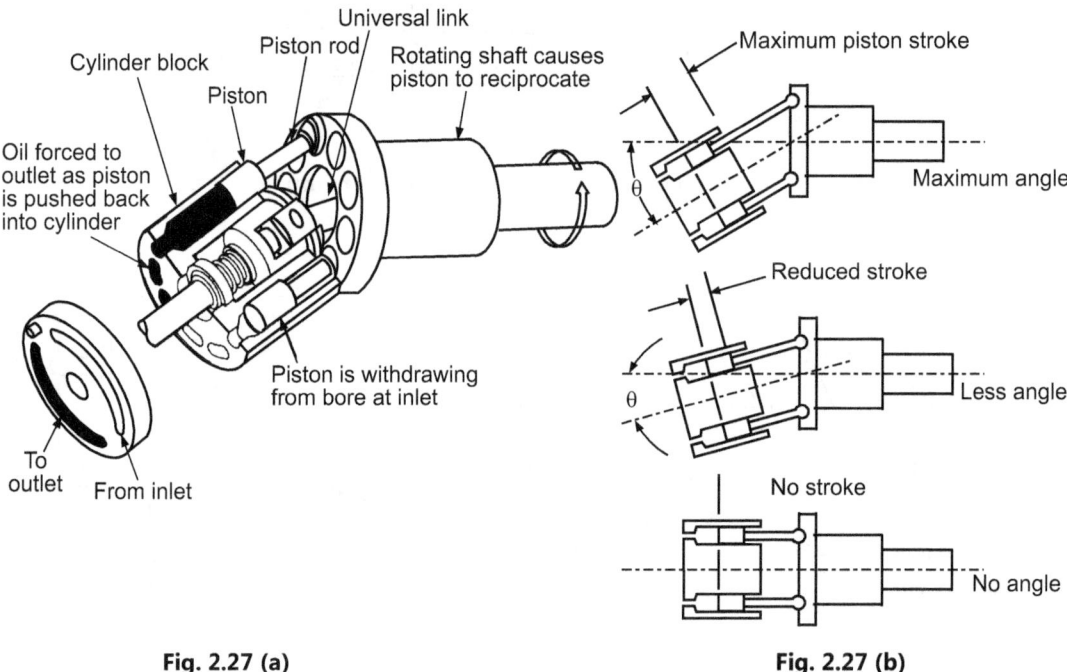

Fig. 2.27 (a) **Fig. 2.27 (b)**

In this pump, the axis of the pistons is inclined to the axis of the driving shaft. The cylinder block rotates with the driving shaft. The piston rods are connected to the drive shaft flange by ball and socket joints. The pistons are actuated in and out of their bores as the distance between the drive shaft flange and cylinder block changes. A universal joint connects the block to the driving shaft. Refer Fig. 2.27 (a).

The volumetric displacement of the pump varies with the offset angle θ as shown in Fig. 2.27 (b). The other performance curves are shown in Fig. 2.27 (c).

When the offset angle is zero, there is no flow. The offset angle 'θ' usually can be varied between 0° and 30°. The fixed displacement bent axis axial piston pumps usually adopt offset angle of 23° to 30°.

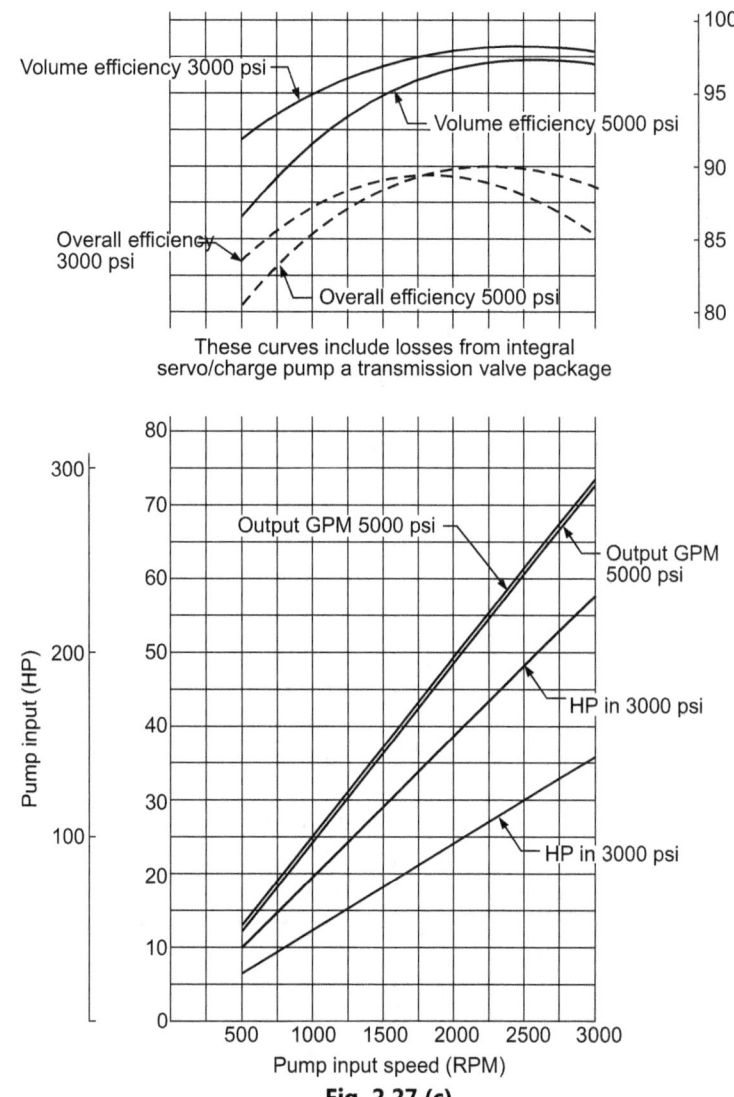

Fig. 2.27 (c)

The offset angle can be altered to vary the flow rate, with the help of a yoke and external control.

2.7.5 Performance of Axial Piston Pump

The performance of axial piston pump can be analyzed as follows:

Let
- θ = Off-set angle, degrees
- L = Stroke length of piston, m
- D = Diameter of piston-circle, m
- n = Number of pistons
- A = Area of cross-section of piston, m^2

Then $\tan\theta = \dfrac{L}{D}$

∴ $L = D\tan\theta$

Total theoretical displacement / revolution

$V_D = n \times A \times L = n \times A \times D \tan\theta$ m³/min.

∴ Theoretical discharge Q_T m³/min.

Q_T = Theoretical displacement/rev. × Speed, m³/min.

$= n\,A\,D\tan\theta \times N$ m³/min.

2.7.6 In-line Crank-shaft Driven Pumps

A single cylinder piston pump is shown in Fig. 2.28. It consists of a plunger (piston) and a precision machined cylinder (barrel). The piston is driven by the electric motor and a cam. The suction and discharge ports are controlled by ball valves allowing the flow only in one direction.

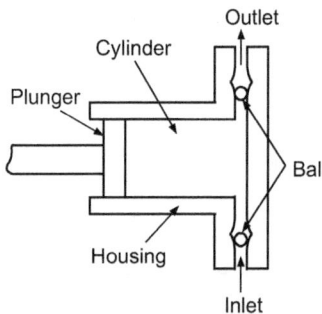

Fig. 2.28: Piston pump

As the piston retracts outwards, the creation of vacuum in the cylinder draws in the fluid, filling the cylinder. As the piston returns subsequently, the inlet port is closed by the ball while the ball in the discharge port unseats allowing the fluid to be discharged out of the cylinder.

The cyclic working of the pump provides a pulsating flow characteristic as depicted in Fig. 2.29.

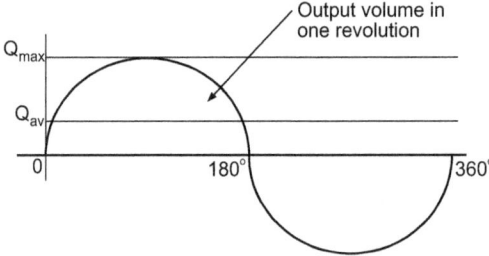

Fig. 2.29: Flow characteristics in a single piston pump

The pulsating flow characteristics of a single piston pump are highly undesirable.

The flow pulsation can be smoothened and the discharge (flow rate) from a pump can be increased by using several cylinders and pistons in parallel and operated by a common crank shaft, in an out of phase manner.

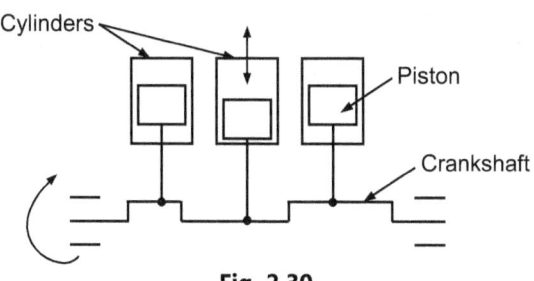

Fig. 2.30

The schematic of a typical three cylinder piston pump having a phase difference of 120° is shown in Fig. 2.30.

2.8 Difference Between Positive Displacement Pumps and Non-Positive Displacement Pumps (May 12)

	Positive Displacement Pump		Non-positive Displacement Pumps
1.	It works on the principle of increasing the pressure on the fluid by pumping action by displacement of a constant amount of fluid per revolution of pump shaft.	1.	In this case, pumping action is developed by transferring the fluid by inertia principle.
2.	Movement of fluid is done by varying the physical size of pumping chamber.	2.	Fluid velocity is varied by the action of centrifugal force.
3.	Irrespective of system resistance, pump output flow is constant as constant volume is pumped per cycle.	3.	As external resistance increases slip flow increases which ultimately reduces the pump output flow.
4.	High and low pressure sections of pumping chamber are separate which avoids the inner circulation of fluid.	4.	As inlet and outlet sections are connected therefore circulation of fluid in the chamber is possible.
5.	Pressure relief valve is necessary to protect the pump from failure due to excessively high pressure created by complete closure of the delivery valve.	5.	Due to 100% slip phenomenon, which allows internal circulation (even when delivery valve is completely closed) releases the necessity of pressure relief valve of non-positive displacement pumps.
6.	Due to very small clearances, these pumps are self primed.	6.	These pumps require external priming due to large clearances.
7.	Volumetric efficiency is constant over the design pressure range.	7.	Volumetric efficiency varies from zero to about 60%.
8.	Small, compact and costly installation.	8.	Bulky, robust and comparatively low cost installation.
9.	Suitable for high pressure (700 bar) and low volume requirements. e.g. = Industrial hydraulic system.	9.	Suitable for high volume and low pressure requirements. e.g. = Irrigation.
10.	**Examples:** Vane pump, gear pump, piston pump.	10.	**Examples:** Centrifugal pump, axial flow pump.

2.9 SELECTION OF PUMPS (Dec. 08, 11; May 11, 12)

The factors influencing the selection of the type of pump for a particular application are:
- Maximum operating pressure
- Maximum flow rate required
- Pump driving speed
- Type of fluid
- Tolerable pump noise level
- Type of pump control desirable
- Availability and interchangeability
- Pump contamination tolerance
- Cost constraints
- Maintenance/Spares, etc.

Table 2.1: Salient features of hydraulic pumps

Pump Type	Operating Pressure (continuous) (bar)		Flow Range maximum (litres/min.)	
	Maximum	Normal	From	To
Precision Gear	300	170	0.25	760
Internal Gear				
Single stage	210	100		
Multi stage	300	200	0.6	740
Balanced vane	175	100	2	620
Pressure compensated vane	175	100	6	360
Cam rotor	175	120	1	1400
Axial piston swash plate				
Port plates	350	200	0.7	600
seated valves	700	350	1	760
variable displacement	350	200	1	1450
Axial piston bent axis	350	300	7.5	3500
variable displacement	350	210	17	3500
Radial piston	1720	300	0.3	1000
variable displacement	350	175	1	580
Plunger in-line	1000	400	0.1	600

(a) **Maximum Operating Pressure:** Higher the operating pressure, lesser the flow rate required for a system power. This leads to a compact pump, smaller pipe sizes and small components. However, at high pressures, the compressibility of the fluid adversely affects the load control. Table 2.1 lists the pressure and flow rate ranges for various types of hydraulic pumps.

(b) **Maximum Flow Rate/Variation of Flow Rate:** The pump should meet the maximum flow rate and also the variation of flow rate required, if any, by the system. Accordingly, a constant displacement type pump can be chosen. The flow rate is affected by the temperature and viscosity of the fluid. A reduced viscosity or a higher pressure promotes leakage.

(c) **Pump Driving Speed:** The flow rate is dependent upon the driving speed. Higher the speed, more the pump wear and pump life is shortened.

(d) **Type of Fluid:** Pumps are designed for a particular type of fluid. Synthetic fluid and water based oils reduce pump life.

(e) **Tolerable Pump Noise Level:** The operating noise level for a given type of pump varies with the workmanship. Higher operating pressures and speed generate more noise.

(f) **Type Of Pump Control Desirable:** It depends upon the requirements of the system.

(g) **Availability And Interchangeability:** Various manufacturers of pumps have adopted international standards for interchangeability of components.

(h) **Pump Contamination Tolerance:** Precision pumps with fine clearances are prone to contamination. Some gear pumps, lobe pumps, etc. can tolerate dirt. Pump suction line must have a filter fitted.

(i) **Cost Constraint:** Gear pumps and vane pumps are cheaper than piston pumps. Capital cost is of secondary concern compared to the maintenance and operating cost.

(j) **Maintenance / Spares:** Gear pumps when worn-out are replaced while in vane pumps, all wearing parts are replaced as a set.

2.10 EXPECTED LIFE TO HYDRAULIC PUMPS

Usually, 20,000 working hours life is expected and a volumetric efficiency of about 97% is desirable, from internal gear pumps.

Table 2.2: Weight: Power Ratio Of Hydraulic Pumps

Types Of Hydraulic Pump	Weight: Power Ratio
External gear	1.5
Single stage vane	5.0
Varial displacement axial piston	6.0
Bent axis piston	10.0
Radial piston	20

Radial piston pumps fetch long life and are suitable for high pressure systems. Axial piston pumps offer a long life of about 40000 working hours under the operating pressure of 200 - 250 bar. The life reduces drastically when operated at high pressure.

Table 2.2 lists the weight to power ratio of various hydraulic pumps.

2.11 NOISE FROM HYDRAULIC PUMPS

Noise level generated by the hydraulic pumps depends upon the type of pump, its material, mounting vibration control methods used, rigidity of mounting, manufacturing precision, flow rate, operating pressure and speed.

A noise level beyond 90 dB (A) is treated as a load while that below 60 dB (A) is regarded as quiet running. Table 2.3 gives the noise level of various hydraulic pumps.

Table 2.3: Noise level of hydraulic pumps (at 100 bar, 1500 rpm, 50°C and flow rate 20 cc/rev.

Type Of Pump	Noise Level Db (A)
Swash plate	68
Bent Axis	65
Vane	63
Internal Gear	60
External Gear	65

Fig. 2.31 shows the variation of noise level with speed, pressure and displacement.

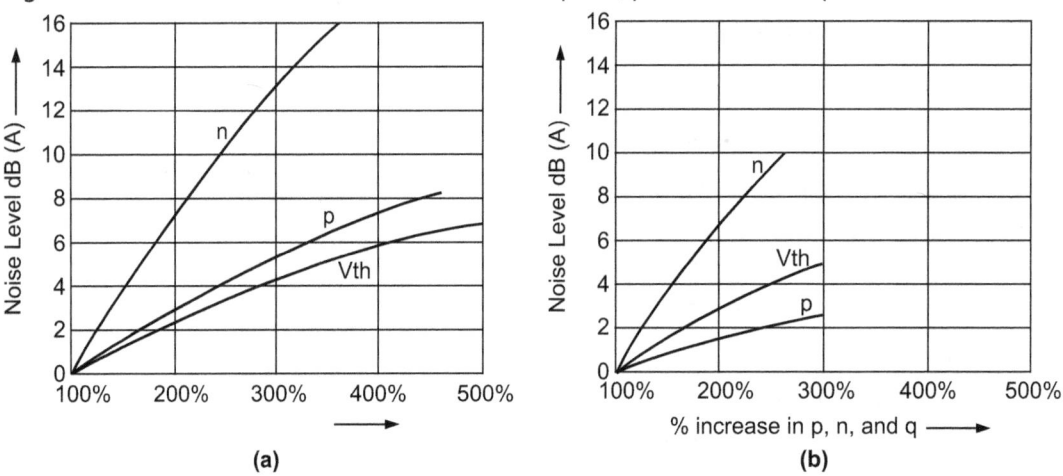

Fig. 2.31: Variation of pump noise with speed, pressure and displacement

2.12 SUMMARY OF FORMULAE FOR PUMP DISPLACEMENT (M-08)

The following Table 2.4 gives the summary of formulae for determination of displacement of various pumps, power and efficiencies.

Table 2.4: Summary of formulae for displacement of pumps, power and efficiencies

Type Of Pumps	Formulae for calculation of theoretical pump displacement 'q_t' cc/rev.	Nomenclature
1. External gear pump-two gear	$q_t = 2\pi D_p b \times m$	D_p = gear pitch circle diameter = mZ, cm m = gear module, cm b = width of gear, cm
2. Screw pump - two spindles	$q_t = \left\{ \dfrac{\pi}{4}(d_o^2 - d_i^2) - \left(\dfrac{d_o^2}{4}\right) - \dfrac{\pi\theta}{(180 - \sin\theta)} \right\} h$ cc $\cos\theta/2 = \dfrac{a}{d_o}$	d_i = core diameter of screw, cm d_o = outer diameter of screw, cm h = pitch of screw, cm a = distance between two screw centre lines, cm
3. Variable vane pump- single cell	$q_t = 2eb(\pi D - SZ)$	e = eccentricity of vane rotor and casing, cm b = width of vanes D = vane rotor diameter, cm S = vane thickness, cm Z = number of vanes
4. Balanced vane pump-two cell	$q_t = \dfrac{2\pi}{b(D+1)}$	b = width of vanes, cm D = vane rotor diameter
5. Radial piston pump	$q_t = \dfrac{\pi}{2} \times d^2 eZ$	d = diameter of piston, cm e = eccentricity of rotor piston cylinder block, cm Z = number of pistons

Cont......

6.	Bent axis piston pump	$q_t = \dfrac{\pi}{4} d^2 Z D_C \sin \alpha$	d = diameter of piston, cm Z = number of pistons D_C = centre distance between pistons in a cylinder block, cm α = off-set angle, degrees
7.	Swash plate axial piston pump	$q_t = \dfrac{\pi}{4} a^2 Z D_C \tan \alpha$	d = diameter of piston, cm Z = number of pistons D_C = centre distance between pistons in a cylinder block, cm α = offset angle of swash plate, degrees
8.	Input power	$p_i = \dfrac{P_t}{\eta_m} = \dfrac{pQ}{612 \times \eta_V \eta_m}$ $= \dfrac{pQ}{612 \eta_o}$	P_i = input power, kW p = pressure, bar Q = actual flow rate, l.p.m. η_m = mechanical efficiency, % η_o = overall efficiency, % η_V = volumetric efficiency
9.	Hydraulic power	$P = \dfrac{pQ}{612}$	p = pressure, bar Q = actual flow rate, l.p.m.
10.	Theoretical hydraulic power	$P_t = \dfrac{pQ_t}{612} = \dfrac{pQ}{612 \times \eta_V}$	p = pressure bar, Q_t = theoretical flow rate, l.p.m. η_V = volumetric efficiency % a = actual flow rate, l.m.p.
11.	Volumetric efficiency	$\eta_V = \dfrac{Q}{Q_t} \times 100$	Q = actual flow rate, l.p.m. Q_t = theoretical flow rate l.p.m.
12.	Overall efficiency	$\eta_o = \dfrac{P}{P_t}$	P = pump output power, kW P_t = theoretical power, kW
13.	Theoretical pump discharge (displacement)	$Q_t = \dfrac{q_t \times n}{1000}$	n = speed, r.p.m. q_t = theoretical pump displacement, cc/rev.

SOLVED EXAMPLES

Example 2.1: *A gear pump has an outside diameter of 7.62 cm and an inside diameter of 5.08 cm. The width of the gears is 2.54 cm. If the actual flow rate of the pump at 1800 r.p.m. and rated pressure is 126 l.p.m. calculate the volumetric efficiency of the pump.*

Solution: Displacement volume/revolution

$$= \frac{\pi}{4}\{D_o^2 - D_i^2\} \times b = \frac{\pi}{4}\{7.62^2 - 5.08^2\} \times 2.5$$

$$= 81.935 \text{ cm}^3/\text{rev.}$$

∴ Theoretical flow rate, Q_t = Displacement volume/rev. × N × 10^{-3} litres/min.

$$= 81.935 \times 1800 \times 10^{-3} = 147.48 \text{ l.p.m.}$$

∴ Volumetric efficiency = $\dfrac{\text{Actual flow rate}}{\text{Theoretical flow rate}} \times 100$

$$= \frac{126}{147.48} \times 100 = \mathbf{85.43\%} \qquad \text{... Ans.}$$

Example 2.2: *A gear pump has 75 mm outside diameter, 50 mm inside diameter and 25 mm width. If its volumetric efficiency at rated pressure is 95%, calculate the actual flow rate from this pump. The pump speed is 1440 r.p.m.*

Solution: The pump displacement volume/rev.

$$V_D = \frac{\pi}{4}\{0.075^2 - 0.050^2\} \times 0.025$$

$$= 0.0000614 \text{ m}^3/\text{rev.} = 0.0614 \text{ litre/rev.}$$

∴ Theoretical flow rate, Q_t = 0.0614 × N = 0.00614 × 1440 litre/min.

$$= 88.416 \text{ litre/min.}$$

∴ Actual flow rate/min. = Theoretical flow rate × Volume η

$$= \mathbf{83.995 \text{ litre/min.}} \qquad \text{... Ans.}$$

Example 2.3: *A vane pump has a volumetric displacement of 80 cm³/rev. It has a rotor diameter of 5 cm, a cam ring diameter of 7.5 cm and a vane width of 5.0 cm. What is the eccentricity of this pump?*

Solution: Eccentricity $\varepsilon = \dfrac{2 V_D}{\pi \{D_C + D_R\} L}$

$$= \frac{2 \times 80}{\pi \{5 + 7.5\} \times 5} = \mathbf{0.8149 \text{ cm}} \qquad \text{... Ans.}$$

HYDRAULICS AND PNEUMATICS — PUMPS

Example 2.4: *A vane pump has a rotor diameter of 50 mm, a cam-ring diameter of 75 mm and width of vane 50 mm. If it has an eccentricity of 8 mm determine the theoretical flow rate of the pump running at 1000 r.p.m.*

Solution: Theoretical displacement/rev.

$$V_D = \frac{\pi}{2}\{D_C + D_R\}\, b \times e \text{ cc/rev.}$$

$$= \frac{\pi}{2}\{0.050 + 0.075\}\, 0.008 \times 0.050 \times 10^{-6} \text{ m}^3/\text{rev.}$$

$$= 0.0000785 \text{ m}^3/\text{rev.}$$

∴ Q_t = Theoretical flow rate = 0.0000785×1000

$$= 0.0785 \text{ m}^3/\text{min.} = \mathbf{78.50 \text{ l.p.m.}} \quad \text{... Ans.}$$

Example 2.5: *Calculate the offset angle for an axial piston pump which delivers 72 litres per minute while running at 3000 r.p.m. The piston has 12.5 mm diameter and a total of 9 pistons placed on a 127 mm pitch circle diameter.*

Solution:

$$\tan\theta = \frac{Q}{DANY} = \frac{72 \times 10^{-3}}{0.127 \times \frac{\pi}{4}(0.0125)^2 \times 3000 \times 9} = 0.1711$$

∴ $\theta = \mathbf{9.71°}$ ... Ans.

Example 2.6: *An axial piston pump runs at 2000 r.p.m. The pump has total 10 pistons of 15 mm diameter arranged on a 125 mm pitch circle diameter. The off-set angle is set at 12°. Determine the theoretical flow rate in litre/s.*

Solution: Theoretical flow rate/min.

$$Q_t = DANY \tan\theta$$

$$= 0.125 \times \frac{\pi}{4} \times 0.015^2 \times 2000 \times (\tan 12°) \times \text{ m}^3/\text{min.}$$

$$= \mathbf{84.51 \text{ litres/min.}} \quad \text{... Ans.}$$

Example 2.7: *A pump has a displacement of 80 cm³/rev. It delivers 77 litres/min when operated at 1000 r.p.m. and 70 bar. If the input torque of the prime mover is 100 N-m,*
  (a) *What is the overall efficiency of the pump?*
  (b) *What is the theoretical torque required to operate the pump?*

Solution: Theoretical flow rate

$$Q_t = V_D \times N = 80 \times 1000 \text{ cc/min.} = 80 \text{ litres/min.}$$

$$\text{Volumetric efficiency} = \frac{\text{Actual flow rate}}{\text{Theoretical flow rate}} = \frac{77}{80} \times 100$$

HYDRAULICS AND PNEUMATICS   PUMPS

$$\eta_{vol.} = 96.25\%$$

Now, theoretical power input $= \dfrac{2\pi N}{60} \times T = \dfrac{2\pi \times 1000}{60} \times \dfrac{100}{1000} = 10.472 \text{ kW}$

Hydraulic power $= \dfrac{P \times Q_t}{60} = \dfrac{70 \times 10^2 \times 80 \times 10^{-3}}{60}$ kW $= 9.333$ kW

∴ Mechanical efficiency $= \dfrac{9.333}{10.472} \times 100$

$\eta_{mechanical} = 89.127\%$

∴ Overall efficiency $= \eta_{mech.} \times \eta_{vol.} = 0.9625 \times 89.127 = \mathbf{85.78\%}$ ... Ans.

Theoretical torque required $=$ Actual torque input $\times \eta_{vol.}$

$= 100 \times 0.8578 = \mathbf{85.78 \text{ N-m}}$ ... Ans.

Example 2.8: *A pump having a displacement volume of 14 cm³/rev. runs at 2000 r.p.m. It operates against a maximum system pressure of 150 bar. The volumetric and overall efficiency of the pump are 0.90 and 0.80 respectively. Determine:*

(i) Actual flow rate delivered in litre/min.

(ii) Input power required to drive the pump

(iii) The drive torque at the pump shaft.

Solution: Actual flow rate $Q_d = $ Volumetric efficiency $\times V_D \times N$

$= 0.9 \times 14 \times 10^{-3} \times 2000$ litres/min.

$= \mathbf{25.2 \text{ litre/min.}}$ ... Ans.

Input power required $= \dfrac{\text{Hydraulic power}}{\text{Overall efficiency}}$

$= \dfrac{p \times Q_a}{0.80} = \dfrac{150 \times 10^2 \times 25.2 \times 10^{-3}}{60 \times 0.80}$

$= \mathbf{7.875 \text{ kW}}$ ... Ans.

Now, mechanical (or torque) efficiency $= \dfrac{\text{Overall efficiency}}{\text{Volumetric efficiency}}$

$\eta_{mech.} = \dfrac{0.80}{0.90} = 0.89$

Torque at the pump shaft $= \dfrac{\text{Hydraulic power}}{\dfrac{2\pi N}{60} \times \eta_{mech.}} = \dfrac{150 \times 10^2 \times 25.2 \times 10^{-3}}{60 \times \dfrac{2\pi \times 2000}{60} \times 0.89}$

$= \mathbf{33.8 \text{ N-m}}$ ... Ans.

HYDRAULICS AND PNEUMATICS   PUMPS

Example 2.9: *A pump has displacement of volume of 98.4 cm³. It delivers 0.00152 m³/s of oil at 1000 rpm and 70 bar pressure. If the prime mover input torque is 124.3 N-m, what is the theoretical torque required to operate the pump? What is the overall efficiency of the pump?*

(May 2003)

Solution: Part A: Calculation for Mechanical Efficiency: As per given data, displacement volume/geometric volume $= 98.4 \text{ cm}^3 = 98.4 \times 10^{-6} \text{ m}^3 = V_g$

Theoretical displacement $= V_g \times$ Speed

$$V_D = \frac{98.4 \times 10^{-6} \times 1000}{60} = 1.64 \times 10^{-3} \text{ m}^3/\text{sec}$$

Pressure on the oil i.e. pressure delivered by pump (given) =

$$70 \text{ bar} = 70 \times 10^5 \text{ Pa} = \Delta p$$

Pump discharge (given) $= 0.0152 \text{ m}^3/\text{s}$

$$Q = 1.52 \times 10^{-3} \text{ m}^3/\text{sec}$$

∴ Theoretical power required $= Q \times \Delta P$

$$= (1.52 \times 10^{-3}) \times (70 \times 10^5 \times 10^{-3})$$

$$= 10.64 \text{ kW}$$

Now, to find theoretical torque required to run the pump, we know that,

$$\text{Power} = \frac{2\pi NT}{60}$$

$$10.64 \times 10^3 = \frac{2\pi \times 1000 \times T}{60}$$

$$T = \frac{60 \times 10.64 \times 10^3}{2\pi \times 1000}$$

Torque at pump shaft $= 101.6 \text{ Nm}$

And prime mover input torque (given) is 124.3 Nm. But the pump gives an output corresponding to 101.6 Nm.

∴ Mechanical efficiency $= \dfrac{\text{Output torque}}{\text{Input torque}}$

$$\eta_{mechanical} = \frac{101.6}{124.3} = 81.24\%$$

Part B: Calculations for volumetric efficiency:

Theoretical flow rate $= V_D \times$ Speed

$$= \frac{(98.4 \times 10^{-4}) \times 1000}{60}$$

Unit II | 2.38

HYDRAULICS AND PNEUMATICS   PUMPS

$$= 1.64 \times 10^{-3} \text{ m}^3/\text{sec}$$

But, actual discharge $= 1.52 \times 10^{-3} \text{ m}^3/\text{sec}$

∴ Volumetric efficiency $= \dfrac{1.52 \times 10^{-3}}{1.62 \times 10^{-3}} = 92.68\%$

Overall efficiency $= \eta_{\text{mechanical}} \times \eta_{\text{volumetric}}$

$\eta_{\text{overall}} = 75.76\%$

Example 2.10: *In a hydraulically powered machine, the cylinder moves rapidly during the first 500 mm of stroke without any flow control against a load of 9 kV. The speed during the remaining stroke of 250 mm is to be 100 mm per second against a load of 20 kN. The rapid return is against a load of 1.2 kN. The other particular are as follows:*

(A) *Actuator: Piston diameter = 56.4 mm, Piston rod diameter = 40 mm,*
  Total stroke = 750 mm.

(B) *Pump: Capacity = 833 cc/sec, Maximum pressure = 150 bar.*

Find:
(i) *What is the flow rate of oil through each component during the feed?*
(ii) *Determine the pressure of the cylinder.*
(iii) *What is the efficiency of the system, if the overall efficiency of the pump is 90%?*
A meter out circuit is to be used for motion control. Draw the circuit. **(May 2003)**

Solution: Pump capacity (given) $= 833$ cc/sec

$$= 0.833 \times 10^{-3} \text{ m}^3/\text{sec}$$

From given data (d $= 56.4$ mm $= 56.4 \times 10^{-3}$ m)

∴ Piston area $= \dfrac{\pi}{4} (56.4 \times 10^{-3})^2$

∴ Rod area $= \dfrac{\pi}{4} (40 \times 10^{-3})^2$

Velocity of feed (given) $= 100$ mm/sec

Now, Discharge during feed $= A_v$

$$= \dfrac{\pi}{4} (56.4 \times 10^{-3})^2 \times (100 \times 10^{-3})$$

$$= 0.25 \times 10^{-3} \text{ m}^3/\text{sec}$$

(ii) Force required during feed $= 20 \times 10^3$ N   ... (given)

∴ Pressure during feed $= \dfrac{F}{A} = \dfrac{20 \times 10^3 \text{ N}}{\dfrac{\pi}{4}(56.4 \times 10^{-3})^2}$

$$= 80 \text{ bar}$$

And, Power required during feed $= \begin{pmatrix} \text{Discharge during} \\ \text{feed} \end{pmatrix} \times \begin{pmatrix} \text{Pressure during} \\ \text{feed} \end{pmatrix}$

$$= (0.25 \times 10^{-3}) \times (80 \times 10^5)$$
$$= 2000 \text{ W}$$

(iii) Now, consider the case where the given pump capacity is 833×10^6 m³/sec, maximum pressure is 150×10^5 Pa and efficiency is 90% then to calculate overall efficiency of the system, first calculate

$$\text{Pump output power} = (833 \times 10^{-6}) \times (150 \times 10^5) \times (0.9)$$
$$= 11.24 \text{ kW}$$

Now, $\quad \text{Overall efficiency} = \left(\dfrac{2}{11.24}\right) \times 100$

$$\eta_{overall} = 17.78\%$$

Example 2.11: *A hydraulic motor has a displacement of 164 cm³ and operates with a pressure of 70 bar and a speed of 200 rpm. If the actual flow rate consumed by the motor is 0.006 m³/s and the actual torque delivered by the motor is 170 N.m, find:*
  (i) *Volumetric efficiency,*
  (ii) *Mechanical efficiency,*
  (iii) *Overall efficiency and*
  (iv) *The actual kW delivered by the motor.* **(Dec. 08, May 12)**

Solution:

$$\text{Theoretical flow rate} = \dfrac{\text{Displacement / Revolution} \times \text{RPM}}{60}$$

$$= \dfrac{164 \times 10^{-6} \times 2000}{60} = 5.467 \times 10^{-3} \text{ m}^3/\text{s}$$

$$\text{Volumetric efficiency} = \dfrac{\text{Theoretical flow rate}}{\text{Actual flow rate}} = \dfrac{5.467 \times 10^{-3}}{6 \times 10^{-3}} = \mathbf{91.1\%} \quad \text{... Ans.}$$

Theoretical torque delivered by the motor

$$= \dfrac{\text{Supply pressure} \times \text{Displacement volume / revolution}}{2\pi}$$

$$= \dfrac{70 \times 164 \times 10^{-6} \times 10^5}{2\pi} = 182.7 \text{ N.m}$$

$$\text{Mechanical efficiency} = \dfrac{\text{Actual torque}}{\text{Theoretical torque}}$$

$$= \dfrac{170}{182.7} = \mathbf{93.05\%} \quad \text{... Ans.}$$

$$\text{Overall efficiency} = \text{Mechanical efficiency} \times \text{Volumetric efficiency}$$
$$= 0.9305 \times 0.911 = \mathbf{0.8476} \quad \text{... Ans.}$$

Actual power delivered by the motor

$$= \frac{2\pi \times \text{Speed} \times \text{Actual torque}}{60}$$

$$= \frac{2\pi \times 2000 \times 170}{60 \times 1000} = \textbf{35.6 kW} \quad \text{... Ans.}$$

Example 2.12: *A pump has a displacement volume of 98.4 cm³. It delivers 0.0152 m³/s of oil at 1000 rpm and 70 bar. If the prime mover input torque is 124.3 N.m,*
  (i) What is the overall efficiency of the pump?
  (ii) What is the theoretical torque required to operate the pump? **(Dec. 2008)**

Solution: Given: Displacement volume = V_D = 98.4 cm³
Actual flow rate = Q_A = 0.0152 m³/sec
Speed = N = 1000 r.p.m.
Pressure = P = 70 bar
Actual torque = T_A = 124.3 N.m
Find (i) $\eta_{overall}$ = ?, (ii) T_T = ?

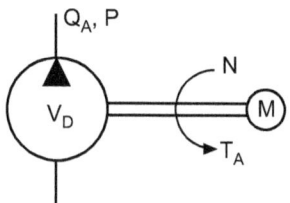

Fig. 2.32

Theoretical flow rate,

$$Q_T = \frac{V_D N}{60} = \frac{(98.4 \times 10^{-6})(1000)}{60} = 1.64 \times 10^{-3} \text{ m}^3/\text{sec}$$

Volumetric efficiency,

$$\eta_V = \frac{Q_A}{A_T} = \frac{0.00152}{1.64 \times 10^{-3}} = 0.9268 \text{ or } 92.68\%$$

Mechanical efficiency,

$$\eta_m = \frac{P \times Q_T \times 60}{2\pi NT} = \frac{(70 \times 10^5)(1.64 \times 10^{-3}) \times 60}{2\pi \times 1000 \times 124.3}$$

$$= 0.8819 = 88.19\%$$

The overall efficiency,

$$\eta_{overall} = \eta_V \eta_m = 0.9268 \times 0.8819 = 0.8173$$

$$\eta_o = \textbf{81.73\%} \quad \text{... Ans.}$$

Theoretical torque,

$$T_T = \eta_m \times T_A = 0.8819 \times 124.3$$

$$T_T = \textbf{109.62 N.m} \quad \text{... Ans.}$$

Example 2.13: *The double pump system is as shown in Fig. 2.40. What should be the pressure settings of the unloading valve and pressure relief valve under the following conditions:*
   (a) Sheet metal punching operation requires a force of 8000 N.
   (b) Hydraulic cylinder has a 3.75 cm diameter piston and a 1.25 cm diameter rod.
   (c) During rapid extension of the cylinder, a frictional pressure loss of 675 kPa occurs in the line from the high flow pump to the blank end of the cylinder. During the same time, a 350 kPa pressure loss occurs in the return line from the rod end of the cylinder to the oil tank. Frictional pressure losses in these lines are negligibly small during the punching operation.
   (d) Assume that the unloading valve and relief valve pressure settings (for their full pump flow requirements) should be 50% higher than the pressure required to overcome frictional pressure losses and the cylinder punching load respectively.

(May 2009)

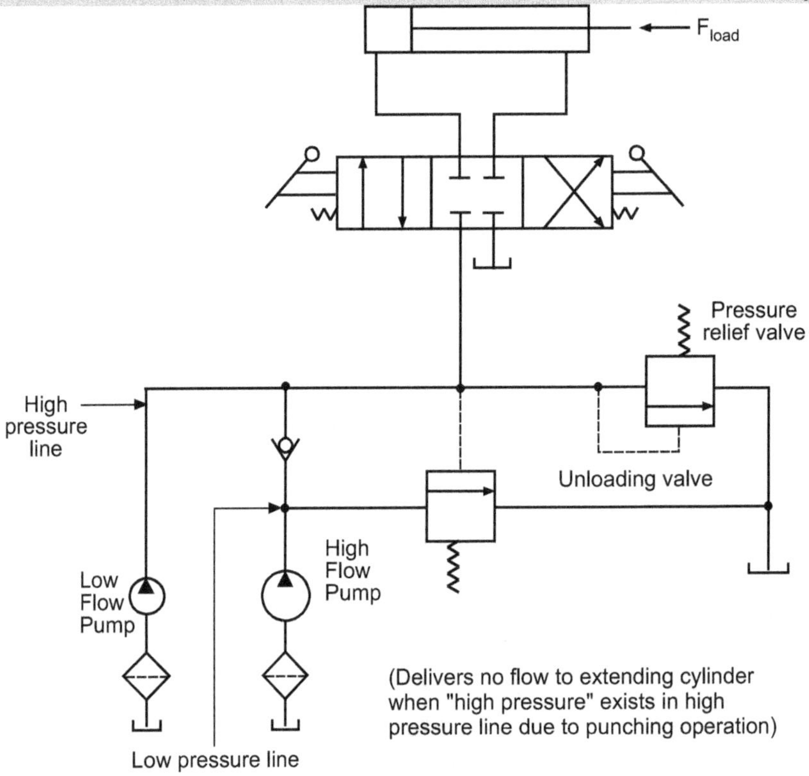

Fig. 2.33 (a)

Solution: Actual pressure required in the blind end of the cylinder

$$= \frac{8000}{\frac{\pi}{4}(0.0375)^2} = 7243318.299 \text{ N/m}^2$$

$$= \mathbf{72.43 \text{ bar}} \qquad \text{... Ans.}$$

Pressure loss in the pipelines due to friction

$$= 675 + 350 = 1025 \text{ kPa}$$
$$= 10.25 \text{ bar} \qquad \text{... Ans.}$$

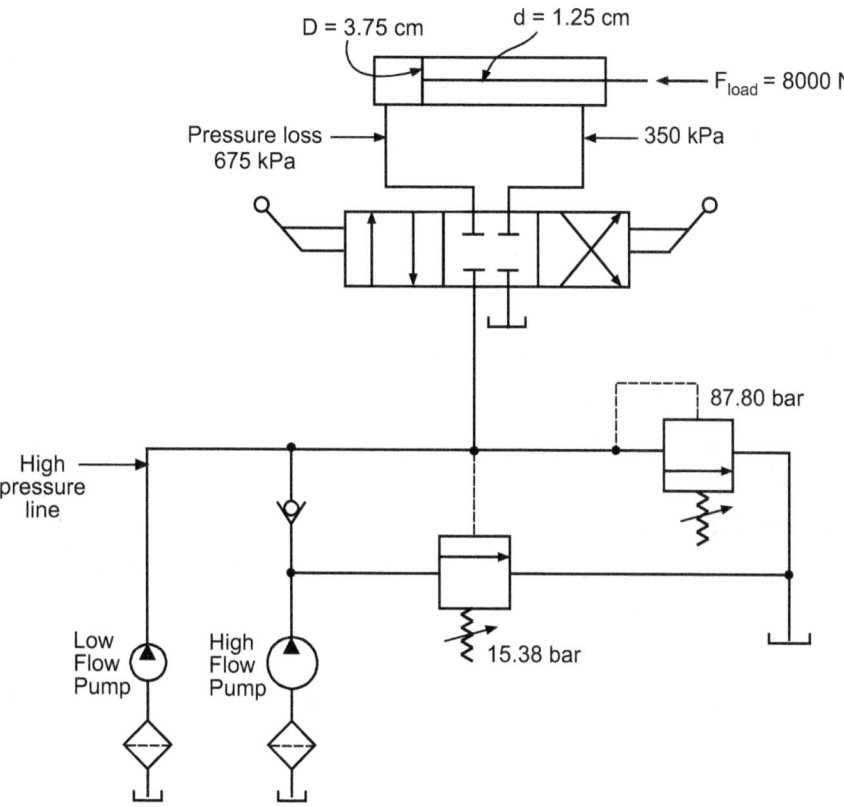

Fig. 2.33 (b)

Pressure of oil required at the outlet of the pump

$$= 72.43 + 10.25$$
$$= 82.68 \text{ bar} \qquad \text{... Ans.}$$

Now, Pressure setting for unloading valve

$$= 10.25 + 0.5 \times 10.25$$
$$= 15.375 \text{ bar} \qquad \text{... Ans.}$$

Pressure setting for pressure relief valve

$$= 82.68 + 0.5 \times 10.25$$
$$= 87.80 \text{ bar} \qquad \text{... Ans.}$$

HYDRAULICS AND PNEUMATICS — PUMPS

Example 2.14: *Obtain the probable specification details of high-low pumps required for the following output of a double acting cylinder: Cylinder bore 40 mm, piston to advance initially at 0.8 m/s and at 0.25 m/s at full load (corresponding to 60 bar pressure on the piston). Assume volumetric efficiency of pump to be 90% and running at 1000 rev/min. Make suitable assumptions and suggest pressure ratings of the relief valve and pilot operated unloading valve.*
(May 2010)

Solution: Given data: D = 40 mm = 0.04 m

$$V_{ext} = 0.8 \text{ m/s and } 0.25 \text{ m/s at full load}$$

P = 60 bar, η_v = 90%, N = 1000 rpm

Assume 10% of the pressure loss in the pipeline due to friction = (60 × 0.1) = 6 bar

The pressure due to friction = 6 bar

Pressure of oil required at outlet of the pump = 60 + 6 = 66 bar

Pressure setting for unloading valve:

Assuming pressure settings 50% higher than the pressure required to overcome frictional resistance = (6 × 0.5) + 6 = 9 bar

Pressure settings for relief valve:

Assuming pressure settings 50% higher than the pressure required to overcome frictional resistance = 66 + (0.5 × 6) = 66 + 3 = 69 bar

Selection of pumps:

Actual flow required to get the velocity of extension as 0.8 m/s during rapid advancement.

$$Q_{act} = A \times V_{ext}$$

$$= \frac{3.14}{4} \times (0.04)^2 \times 0.8 = 1.004 \times 10^{-3} \text{ m}^3/\text{sec} = 1 \text{ l.p.m.}$$

But, η_v = 90%

$$\eta_v = \frac{Q_{act}}{Q_{th}}$$

$$Q_{th} = \frac{Q_{act}}{0.9} = \frac{1}{0.9} = 1.11 \text{ l.p.m.} \qquad \text{... Ans.}$$

Flow required at full load:

$$Q_{act} = A \times V_{ext} = \frac{3.14}{4} \times (0.04)^2 \times 0.25$$

$$= 3.14 \times 10^{-4} \text{ m}^3/\text{sec} = 0.314 \text{ l.p.m.}$$

HYDRAULICS AND PNEUMATICS — PUMPS

$$\eta_v = \frac{Q_{act}}{Q_{th}}$$

$$Q_{th} = \frac{0.314}{0.9} = 0.33 \text{ l.p.m.} \quad \text{... Ans.}$$

Example 2.15: *A press requires a flow rate of 200 litres/min for high speed opening and closing of the dies at a maximum pressure of 30 bars. The work stroke needs a maximum pressure of 400 bars, but a flow rate between 12 and 20 litres/min will be acceptable. The circuit uses a dual pump and an unloading valve. Draw the circuit. Calculate the discharges required for high pressure, low volume pump and high volume, low pressure pump.*

(Dec. 2010)

Solution: Also calculate the power required and power saved instead of an equivalent single pump.

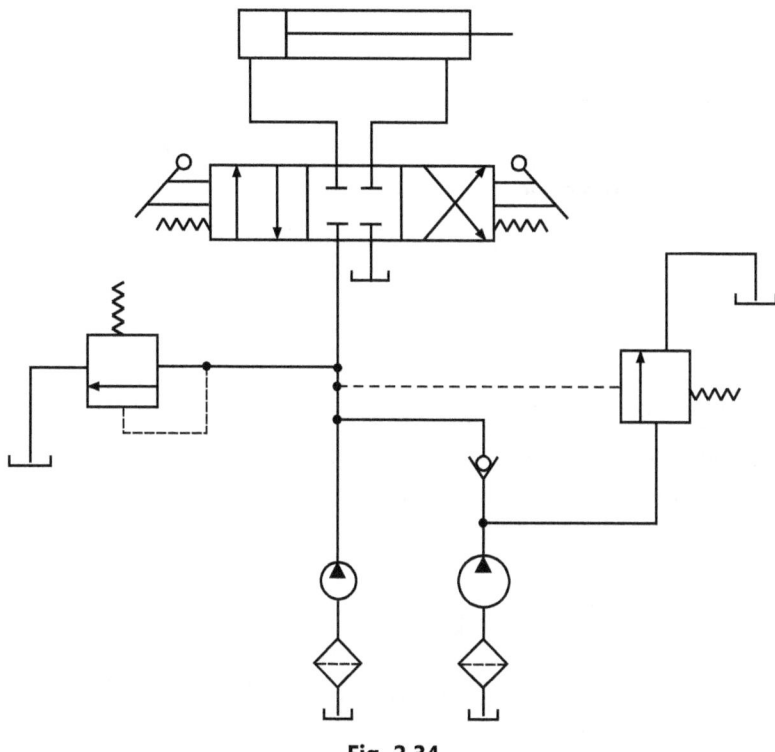

Fig. 2.34

High Pressure Low Volume Pump: A pump with pressure 400 bar and 20 lit/min volume flow rate can be selected as high pressure, low volume flow rate pump. Power required to operate the pump can be calculated by knowing the pump efficiency.

Assume pump efficiency as 80%.

$$\eta = \frac{\text{Output power}}{\text{Input power}}$$

$$0.80 = \frac{\text{Output power}}{\text{Input power}}$$

$$\text{Input power} = \frac{\text{Output power}}{0.80}$$

Output power of pump = $P \times Q$

$$P \times Q = 400 \times 10^5 \times \frac{20 \times 10^{-3}}{60}$$

$$= 13.33 \text{ kW}$$

$$\text{Input power} = \frac{13.33}{0.80}$$

$$= 16.66 \text{ kW}$$

Power required to operate the pump = 16.66 kW

High volume low pressure pump: A pump with pressure 30 bar and flow rate 180 lit/min can be selected for the operation.

$$\text{Output power of pump} = P \times Q = 30 \times 10^5 \times \frac{180 \times 10^{-3}}{60} = 9 \text{ kW}$$

$$\text{Input power} = \frac{9}{0.80}$$

Power required to operate the pump = 11.25 kW

Instead of two separate pumps, if a single pump with 400 bar pressure and 200 lit/min capacity is used then the power required to operate the pump becomes

$$\text{Output power of pump} = P \times Q = 400 \times 10^5 \times \frac{200 \times 10^{-3}}{60}$$

$$= 133.33 \text{ kW}$$

$$\text{Input power} = \frac{133.33}{0.80} = 166.66 \text{ kW}$$

Total power required when two separate pumps are used is,

$$= 16.66 + 11.25 = 27.91 \text{ kW}$$

Instead of using a single pump if two separate pumps are used then the power saved becomes

$$= 16.66 - 27.91 = \textbf{138.75 kW} \qquad \textbf{... Ans.}$$

2.13 INTRODUCTION TO RESERVOIR

In case of industrial hydraulic systems, fluid used must be kept within the system and protected from contaminations. The tank or container which is used to store hydraulic fluid are called reservoirs. It plays an important role in proper functioning of the system and various components as well as maintaining the various working parameters to a reasonably desired level. Though, the reservoir is relatively simple in construction, it serves several functions besides that of storing the fluid like dissipation of heat, trapping of foreign matter, separation of air bubble from the fluid etc. in the interest of the overall functioning of the system. Along with above mentioned, the other functions to be performed by the reservoir are summarized as follows:

2.13.1 Functions of Reservoir   (May 07, Dec. 10, May 11, Dec. 11)

(a) **Oil storage:** The reservoir provides sufficient volume to store oil for the complete system.

(b) **Heat dissipation from oil:** The reservoir helps to dissipate heat from the heated oil returning from the system, by providing a large surface.

(c) **Thermal expansion of fluid:** The reservoir provides space for accommodating thermal expansion of the fluid due to temperature variation.

(d) **Separation of various contaminants:** The reservoir allows setting and separation of contaminants from the oil. It enables entrained and entrapped air to be released into the atmosphere. Thus it assists in de-aeration of the oil.

(e) **Access and filling point:** The reservoir provides access for drainage of the contaminated and 'burnt' oil and to refill it by fresh oil

(f) **Leakage compensation:** The reservoir makes up the oil into the hydraulic circuit for compensating leakage of oil.

(g) **Absorption of flow functions:** The reservoir absorbs the fluctuations of flow during the operating cycle of the hydraulic circuit.

2.13.2 Types of Reservoirs   (May 08, Dec. 08)

There are many types of reservoirs in use.

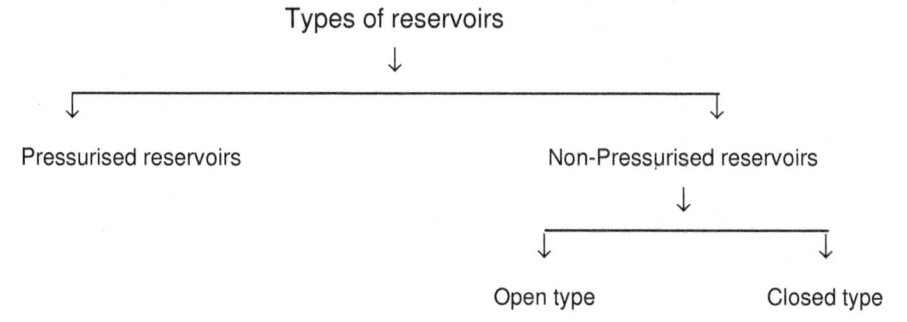

Pressurised reservoirs: These reservoirs operate at higher pressure than that of the surrounding atmosphere. These are used in aviation and other special systems. The operating pressure is usually 0.35 - 1.4 bar and are equipped with pressure control. The main advantages of pressurised reservoirs are to provide boost pressure to main pump and to eliminate ingress of the atmospheric contaminants.

Non-pressurised reservoirs: These reservoirs operate at atmospheric pressure. These are extensively used in several industrial systems, machine tools etc.

Open type reservoirs are open to atmosphere. As such they are prone to air-borne contaminants. Hence these are not commonly used.

Closed type reservoirs are enclosed and are isolated from the atmosphere. Thus ingress of air-borne contaminants into the oil is greatly avoided.

The non-pressurised reservoirs are covered under ANSI standards.

2.13.3 Reservoir Sizing

The storage capacity of the reservoir should be sufficient to accommodate the fluctuations of fluid volume within the system. It should provide adequate surface area for heat dissipation from the oil. However, an oversized reservoir results in a high initial cost, greater space required and long warm-up period particularly during cold start-up. The sizing of the reservoir usually follow empirical guide lines based on practice.

(i) The minimum capacity of the reservoir should never be less than twice the pump delivery per minute. This is however, the absolute minimum capacity and may be inadequate to accommodate the fluid volume changes in the system.

(ii) Usually the reservoir capacity of 3 - 4 times the pump discharge/min. is provided. This often make them unsuitable for mobile application.

(iii) Another guide line suggests the capacity to be 2 – 15 litre per installed horse power. This often leads to very bulky reservoirs.

2.13.4 Reservoir Shapes

Various considerations influence the shapes of reservoir, as enumerated below.

(i) **Heat Dissipation:** Square and rectangular shape promote heat transfer. A tall and narrow cylindrical shape is unsuitable for de-aeration of oil due to inadequate surface area. A shallow cylindrical shape does not utilise the complete surface for rapid heat dissipation. Compact sized reservoirs are suitable when the outside ambient is cold, or when a separate oil cooler is incorporated or when cycling is intermittent.

(ii) **Pump Cavitation:** The capacity of the reservoir should be such so as to eliminate the occurrence of cavitation.

(iii) Setting of Contaminants: The reservoir shape should be such so as to facilitate rapid settlement of the contaminants. Shallow shaped reservoirs are preferable in this respect.

2.13.5 Design of Reservoir Surface for Heat Dissipation

For reservoirs primarily performing as heat exchangers, the estimation of heat transfer surface for rapid heat dissipation is of great significance.

Let
- H = heat transferred, watts
- h = overall heat transfer coefficient, w/m² - °C
- A = surface area, m²
- Δt = temperature differential, °C

$\therefore \quad H = hA\, \Delta t \times 3.6$ watts ... (2.7)

For a vertical plate of height 'L'

$$h = 1.42 \left(\frac{\Delta t}{L}\right)^{1/4} \text{ W/m}^2 \text{ - °C} \quad \text{... (2.8)}$$

and for a horizontal plate of width 'W',

$$h = 1.32 \left(\frac{\Delta t}{W}\right)^{1/4} \text{ W/m}^2 \text{ - °C} \quad \text{... (2.9)}$$

These formulae apply to natural radiation. Reservoirs of minimum height and maximum length have maximum heat radiation. (Fig. 2.35 a, b).

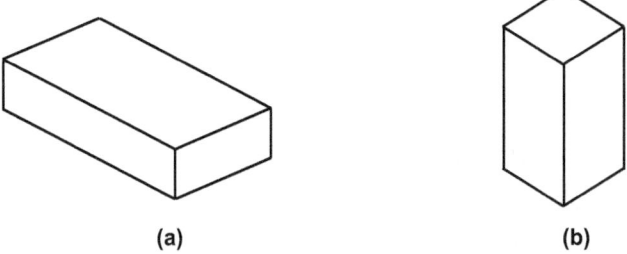

(a) (b)

Fig. 2.35: Reservoir shapes

There should be no horizontal lips or angles on the vertical surface as it affects natural air convection. Heat transfer can be augmented by providing vertical (and not horizontal) fins. To avail the bottom surface of the reservoir for heat dissipation, the reservoir should be mounted clear of the ground, raised on legs.

2.13.6 Reservoir Construction and Design Features

(May 07; Dec. 09, 11)

An ideal reservoir for a hydraulic system should have several good design features. Fig. 2.36 shows a reservoir incorporating these features.

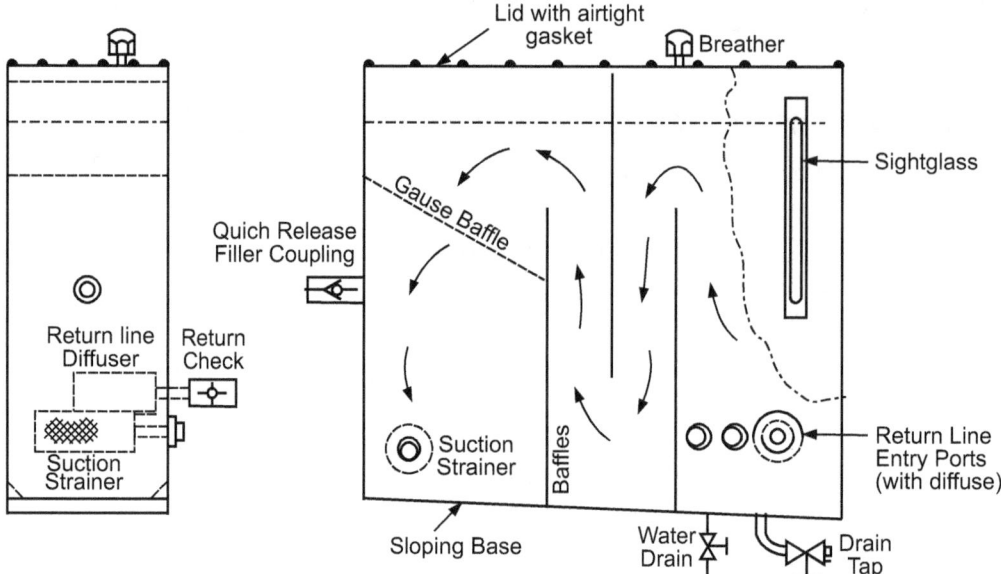

Fig. 2.36: Ideal reservoir with good design features

(a) Good Design Features are:

- Structural rigidity for strength and isolation of vibrations
- Adequate surface area for heat dissipation.
- Filling point with breather and strainer.
- Conveniently located drain plug.
- Well placed baffles.
- Baffles to minimise turbulence.
- Sloping base for rapid drainage.
- Gause baffle for proper de-aeration.
- Proper locations of return line part and suction part.
- Proper location of man hole for good accessibility.
- Material and point compatibility with oil
- Provision of accessories like temperature/level indicators

(b) Reservoir Mounting: The reservoir should be mounted with a ground clearance of at least 15 cm for easy drainage, easy servicing and proper air circulation.

Quite often, the pump with its prime mover, hydraulic components are placed on the top-plate of the reservoir, thereby transmitting the vibrations to the reservoir as shown in Fig. 2.37 (a).

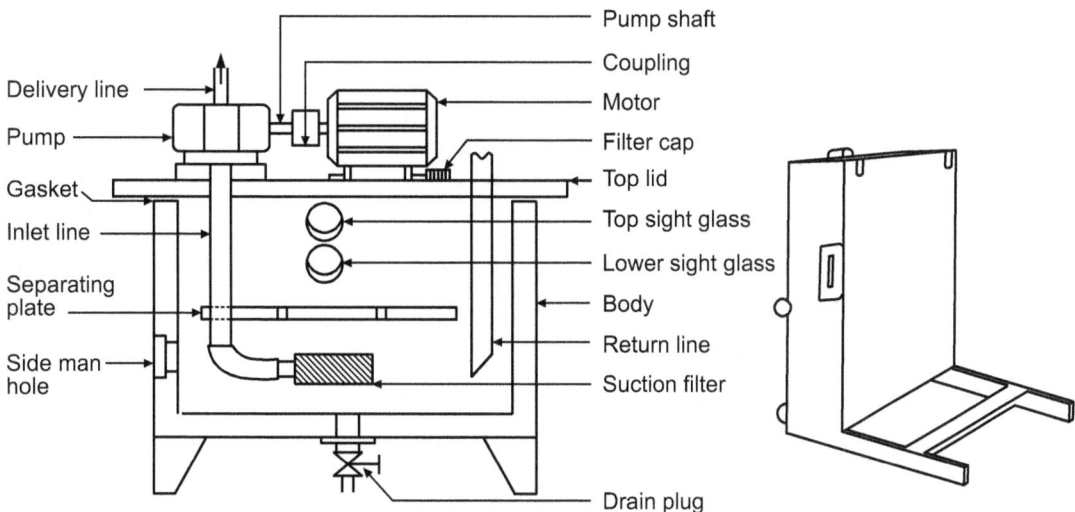

Fig. 2.37 (a): Basic design of a hydraulic reservoir   **Fig. 2.37 (b): L-shaped oil reservoir**

Sometimes, a 'L' shaped reservoir is used (Refer 2.36). It allows gravity feeding of oil to the pump inlet thus avoiding occurrence of cavitation. Further, servicing and maintenance of the reservoir can be done without disturbing the pump unit. It however needs greater floor space.

(c) Reservoir Construction: It is usually fabricated from mild steel plates of 3 mm or greater thickness and has short height with long length and breadth. The lid is placed at the top, with a gasket to seal the ingress of contaminants.

The filler opening has built-in strainer having a 100 micron mesh. The filler opening cap usually has a breather also. The reservoir should store oil only upto a specified level marked on the sight glass.

The pump unit, when placed on the top lid is mounted with the vibration isolating pads. The return pipe inlet is away from pump suction inlet by a separator plate to avoid the migration of contaminants. The pipe ends are cut at 45°.

A reservoir is provided with a man hole for easy cleaning. The man-hole cover is so made so as to facilitate easy removal and refitting by a single person, as seen from Fig. 2.37 (b).

Various pipes enter the reservoir vertically. The interior surface is blasted to eliminate scale and corrosion. The welded joints are made leak proof.

2.13.7 Accessories to the Reservoir

The reservoir is often provided with the following accessories serving various functions such as:

- Indicator of oil level - level indicators, sight glass.
- Indicator of oil temperature - Temperature gauge.

- Removal of metallic and particulate contaminants - magnetic trappers, filters.
- Separation of the return line inlet and pump-inlet-baffles, separators.
- De-aeration of entrapped air-diffusers at the return line inlet, gauge baffle.

2.14 FILTRATION

Filters have a vital role in a hydraulic system. It filters the oil and removes the particulate contaminants. The correct rating of a filter is very necessary to :

- Increase the life of the filter, system components and fluid.
- Arrest migration of undesirable contaminants along with the fluid.
- Simplify maintenance and reduce frequency of preventive maintenance.
- Minimise system failures and improve operational efficiency.
- Minimise chemical degradation and ensure lubricity of the fluid.
- Minimise effects of pressure, flow and temperature variation of the filter functioning.

2.14.1 Terminologies in Filtration

The following terminology referred in filtration is now explained.

(i) **Mesh Number:** A mesh number or sieve number is a measure of the number of openings in a filter element per unit area. The higher the sieve number, the finer the screen. This method of filter sizing is not used now-a-days.

(ii) **Filter and Strainer:** Both the devices retain particulate contaminants. A strainer is a coarse filter.

(iii) **Sieve Number And Equivalent Size In Micron:** The sieve number signifies the number of openings per square inch of the filter surface.

(iv) **Particle Count:** The dirt particulate in a 100 ml oil sample is classified based on size, counted and arranged in a cleanliness class. The particle count indicates the type, number and quality of particulate in an oil sample.

(v) **Silt index:** It is a measure of the number of particles below 5 micron in an oil sample.

2.14.2 Design Considerations of a Filter

The choice of type and size of a filter for a given hydraulic system is governed by many factors listed below for obtaining optimum filtration efficiency.

(a) Recommended Values of Filtration Rating: The filteration rating should be appropriate to match the requirements of the system components. Table 2.5 lists the component wise cleanliness class and the corresponding filtration recommended.

Table 2.5: Recommended filtration rating for fluid power components

System component	ISO cleanliness class	Absolute filtration rating recommended (μm)
1. Cylinder:	19/15	20
Servo cylinder	17/13	5
2. Pumps:		
Gear	19/15	20
Vane	18/14	10
Piston	18/14	10
3. Valves:		
D.C. valve	19/15	20
4. Flow control valve	19/15	20
5. Pressure relief valve	19/15	20
6. Pressure valve	18/14	10
7. Proportional valve	18/14	10
8. Servo valve	17/13	5

(b) **Pressure drop across the filter at normal viscosity and clean element:** For pressure line filter, recommended pressure drops are given below.
- without by pass valve – 1.0 bar
- with by pass valve – 0.5 bar
- Return line filter – 0.3 to 0.5 bar

(c) **Flow rate through the filter:** The flow rate required to pass through the filter is decided by the filtration area and the pore size. The flow rate is however, dependent upon the location of the filter.

For design of filter characteristics further important points are :
- Filter material compatibility with the fluid.
- Filter housing - It should be able to sustain fatigue and fluid shocks.
- Operating temperature - The viscosity and viscosity index of fluid helps in filter sizing.
- Filter types - Filters are available in a great variety such as with/without indicators, by pass valves, clogging indicators of visual, electric and electronic types.

The overall filtration performance is dependent on these aspects.

2.14.3 Types of Filters   (May 07, Dec. 08, May 11)

The filters are classified according to the distance that the fluid is required to travel across a filtering element: (i) Surface filter, (ii) Depth filter.

Surface Filters: These are essentially screens which clean oil passing through their pores. The screen has a very small thickness. Contaminant particles are collected on the upstream face of the screen.

Depth Filter: These are thick walled elements. The separation capacity of these filters is higher than that of a surface filter. Fig. 2.38 illustrates the dirt holding capacity of a surface filter and depth filter for various particulate sizes.

Filters are sometimes classified as: **(May 12)**

(i) Full flow filter, (ii) By-pass filter.

(i) **Full Flow Filter:** In this filter, the entire flow rate of oil from that part of the circuit is passed through the filter. The filter size is selected so as to accommodate full flow rate.

(ii) **By-pass Filter:** At times, the entire flow of fluid does not require filtration. In that case, only a part of the oil flow is routed through the filter while the remaining is passed without filtration through a separate passage.

The by-pass filter offers several advantages as follows:

- Filtration does not depend upon the status of the system whether in operation or shut down.
- Filter element replacement is possible without the shut-down of the system.
- Less down time of system.
- Cheaper filter element.
- Less maintenance.
- Greater capacity of dirt retention on account of low and steady flow rate of oil.

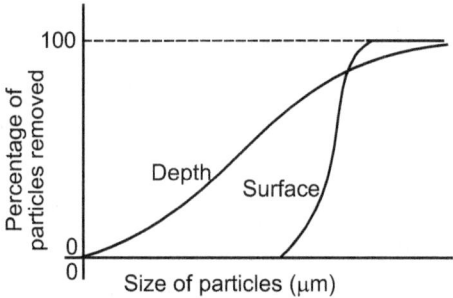

Fig. 2.38: Dirt holding capacity of surface and depth filter

Surface type filters can be easily cleaned by back-flushing while depth-type filter elements cannot be cleaned and are replaced when dirty.

- **Magnetic Separators:** These are used to separate large ferrous particles. They consist of magnetic plates fitted into the fluid reservoir or magnetic plugs housed in the filter body. Only Ferro-magnetic particles above the silt size can be separated by this method.
- **Electrostatic Filtration:** Fluid gets contaminated by static electricity. But the principle is used for oil purification. Two electrodes are immersed into the oil and an electric current

is passed across the electrodes through the fluid. The particulate in the fluid get electrically charged and attach themselves on a collector plate placed between the electrodes. Particles of sizes upto 0.05 micron can be separated by this method. The main drawback of this method is the possibility of removal of additives from the oil.

2.14.4 Technology of Filtration

- Some technological aspects of filtration are explained below.
- **Filter Capacity:** The contamination capacity of a filter is as an indication of the mass of contaminants the filter can hold under a given pressure drop under specified conditions.
- The flow rate through a filter depends upon the pressure drop across the elements. Surface type elements have a large percentage of open area (usually about 30 %) resulting in a low pressure drop for a given flow rate as compared with a depth type filter. The filter capacity does not indicate the life of a filter element in a circuit, as the life depends upon the cleanliness of the fluid and the environmental conditions.
- **Filter Rating:** The filter rating is expressed in different ways. **(Dec. 11, May 12)**
- **Nominal Rating:** This is a micrometer rating indicated by the manufacturer. This rating is seldom used now-a-days.
- **Absolute Rating:** This rating specifies the diameter of the largest hard spherical particle which will pass through the filter under specified test conditions. It thus indicates, the largest opening in the filter element.
- **Mean Pore Size or Mean Filtration Rating:** This is a measure of the average size of pores in the element.
- **Beta Rating:** The beta ratio is an indication of the efficiency of contaminant removal from the fluid flowing through the filter element. **(May 12)**

$$\text{Filtration ratio, } \beta_x = \frac{\text{Number of upstream particles larger than x } \mu m}{\text{Number of downstream particles larger than x } \mu m}$$

$$\text{Efficiency of filtration } (E_x) = \frac{\beta_x - 1}{\beta_x} \times 100$$

Thus, the β rating is a measure of the filter performance indicating to what extent the particles greater than the micron rating of the filter in the incoming fluid are removed by the filter. A higher value of β indicates that more particles above the specified size are trapped by the filter. The β rating is designated as;

$$\beta_x = y$$

where, x indicates the minimum particle size in microns trapped by the filter and y indicates the value of the ratio of upstream particle count to the downstream particle count.

Now consider the following example.

If the number of upstream particles larger than 10 μm = 15,000

and the number of downstream particles larger than 10 μm = 200

Then, $\beta_{10} = \dfrac{15000}{200} = 75$

and Efficiency $= \dfrac{75-1}{75} \times 100 = 98.5\%$

This means the filter can stop 98.5% of particles of size 10 μm or greater from going to the system.

Similarly, a filter having β_{10} ratio of 3 will only stop 66.66 % of the particles of 10 μm and greater. Therefore, higher the 'β' ratio, greater the efficiency of the filter element.

Similarly, consider the specification $\beta_{20} = 50$ which is illustrated as follows:

- This is β rating of the filter.
- Now consider n_1 = number of particles of size greater than 'x' upstream of the filter and n_2 = number of particles of size greater than 'x' downstream of the filter, then

$$\beta_x = \dfrac{n_1}{n_0}, \text{ in example considered } \beta_{20} = 50 \text{ that means the ratio}$$

of the number of particles is 50 and β efficiency is defined as,

$$E_x = \dfrac{\beta_x - 1}{\beta_x} = \dfrac{50 - 1}{50}$$

∴ Beta efficiency = 98%

The β ratio is estimated by conducting an ISO multipass test using artificial contaminant of known consistent particle shape and size distribution.

The filtration efficiency is found to be affected by filter housing construction, cyclic flow, differential pressure, by pass leakage and fire resistant fluids.

The micron size at which $\beta_x = 75$ is said to be equivalent to the absolute rating of a filter.

Example 2.16: *Determine the beta ratio of a filter when, during test operation, 30,000 particles greater than 20 μm enter the filter and 1050 of these particles pass through the filter. What is beta efficiency?* **(Dec. 2001)**

Solution: Beta ratio $= \dfrac{\text{Particle count upstream}}{\text{Particle count downstream}}$

$$= \frac{30{,}000}{1050} = 28.57$$

$$\text{Beta efficiency} = \frac{\text{Particle count upstream} - \text{Particle count down stream}}{\text{Particle count upstream}}$$

$$= \frac{30{,}000 - 1050}{30{,}000} = 96.5\%$$

Collapse Pressure of Filter Element:

The filter elements are designed to withstand a maximum pressure drop across the element, of 10 bar. This however does not limit the circuit operating pressure. These filters can be used in circuits having high pressure, say 500 bar. So long as the pressure drop across the element is upto 10 bar, the element with remain intact.

Disposal elements with special reinforcement can withstand a differential pressure of 210 bar and are used in housing without a bypass valve. When the element gets dirty or clogged, the pressure drop increases, blocking the fluid flow. Hence, they are often referred to as 'dirt fuse'. The major drawback is a large reduction in the output power and excessive heating of the fluid occurs when the element gets very dirty. They are 3 - 4 times costly as compared to the low pressure elements. A pressure drop of 7 bar is regarded. Recleanable sintered metal elements have a high burst pressure and a high collapse pressure. They are known as 'last chance' filters.

Provision of By-pass Valves:

The maximum permissible pressure drop across a filter element under contaminated condition is known as 'terminal pressure'. A By-pass valve is often provided for on-line replacement of a clogged filter element. It also allows the same fluid to by-pass the filter and to go further into the system without filtration. This reduces the loading on the filter.

By-pass valves are available in three types -

- A check valve built into the housing head-when the filter is blocked, pressure drop across the element approaches the spring load on the check valve and the check valve opens bypassing the filter element.
- A check valve can be built into the filter element.
- The filter element can also be spring loaded. When the pressure drop across the element increases, the element is displaced until it clears an opening, allowing a part of flow to be by-passed.

2.14.5 Indicators of Filter-Condition

It is necessary to know the condition of a filter element during the operation of a circuit. This would indicate whether the element needs cleaning, replacement etc. The various types of indicators provided are :

- In the filter element part, a pressure gauge is placed. The reading of the pressure gauge is recorded when the element is new and is working under normal conditions. Further, the pressure at which the element needs replacement is also marked. This method is suitable for low pressure systems only.
- A mechanical device operates a by-pass valve. When the by-pass valves opens on clogging of the filter element, a mechanical link operates an an external pointer thereby indicating the condition of the filter.
- A differential pressure switch monitors the pressure drop across the filter element. This can be a mechanical visual indicator or an electrical pressure switch.

For critical applications, a dual indicator may be provided. One indicates a warning that the element needs replacement and the other operating at a slightly higher pressure, closes down the system before by-pass valve opens, in case, the earlier warning is ignored.

When filters without indicators are used, it is necessary to replace the element at regular intervals. Fatigue failure of the filter may occur when subjected to cyclic pressure changes. When the element is ruptured, the indicators will indicate a clean element. It is therefore, safer to replace the element at regular intervals even if no indication is given.

2.14.6 Construction of Filters

Fig. 2.39 shows the construction of a typical pressure line filter with by-pass valve incorporated.

It consists of a housing to which a bowl is connected through the threading. The bowl houses the filter element. The inlet and outlet passages for the fluid are provided in the housing only. The housing also houses a spring loaded by-pass valve. The fluid enters the element through the annular space, gets filtered and leaves the element from the inner passage. The spring load on the by-pass valve keeps it normally closed. In the event of the element getting heavily clogged, the upstream pressure rises. When it exceeds the spring pressure, the by-pass valve opens and allows the flow directly to the system, by-passing the filter. The construction of housing depends upon the location of the filter in the circuit. When the housing is subjected to high pressures, it is made from steel forging or casting. For low pressure locations like the return line and the suction line of a pump, pressed steel castings are preferred to save costs.

In addition to a by-pass valve, filters usually incorporate differential pressure indicators to measure the pressure drop.

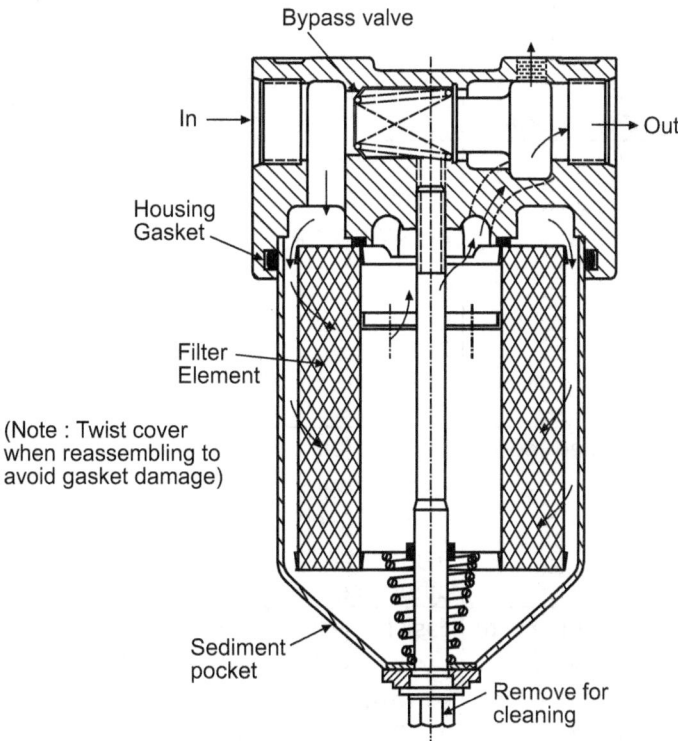

Fig. 2.39

Type of Filter Media:

There are several types of filter media to choose from. The filter media can be either fixed pore or non-fixed pore type. Fixed pore media offers several advantages over the non-fixed pore media.

Table 2.6 lists some fixed pore type and non-fixed pore type media.

Table 2.6: Fixed pore vs Non-fixed pore

Fixed Pore	Non-Fixed Pore
• Woven mesh	• Fibre, glass, unbounded
• Sintered powder	• Cotton wound
• Membrane (Mixed ester and polymeric)	• Sand beds
	• Diatomaceous earth,
• Resin impregnated fibre matrix.	• Fullers earth
	• Poorly bonded paper
	• Waste (Shredded Newsprint, Rags, Wood chips)

Table 2.7 enumerates materials for surface filters, their construction, advantages, disadvantages and fit field of applications.

Table 2.7: Surface filter

Material	Construction	Advantages	Disadvantages	Application
1. Square mesh stainless steel galvanised iron and phosphor bronze	Wire mesh	Easy to clean elements. Low pressure drop	Low filtration rating (< 10 μm), different small free filter area.	Lubricating oil filters, coarse filters, suction filter etc. May be used for filtering water, resistant fluids etc.
2. Wire gauges, stainless steel gauges.	Braided mesh	Easy to clean. Low pressure drop and very high pressure difference	Multipass not possible	Coarse filters protection filters.
3. Stainless steel	Split tube with triangular section, wire wound around at different pitch angles	Easy to clean, can be used for corrosive media, water, fire resistant fluids etc.	High filtration rating (> 50 μm), small free filter area	Suitable for back flushing or as coarse filter

Dirt Capacity and Service Life:

Dirt capacity is defined as the amount of dirt which can be allowed to the filter test system till the terminal pressure drop is reached.

Service life is defined as the length of time a filter can last in an actual system before the terminal pressure drop is reached.

The dirt capacity and the service life of a filter is dependent upon flow rate of the fluid, ingress-rate of the contaminants, generation rate, terminal pressure drop, particle size distribution etc.

2.14.7 Location of a Filter (Dec. 09)

A filter can be located at various places in a hydraulic circuit. Ideally on the upstream of each critical component in a system, a suitable filter is necessary. This is however not practical. Usually one or two filters suffice. The various locations of a filter in a system are discussed hereafter. (Refer Fig. 2.40)

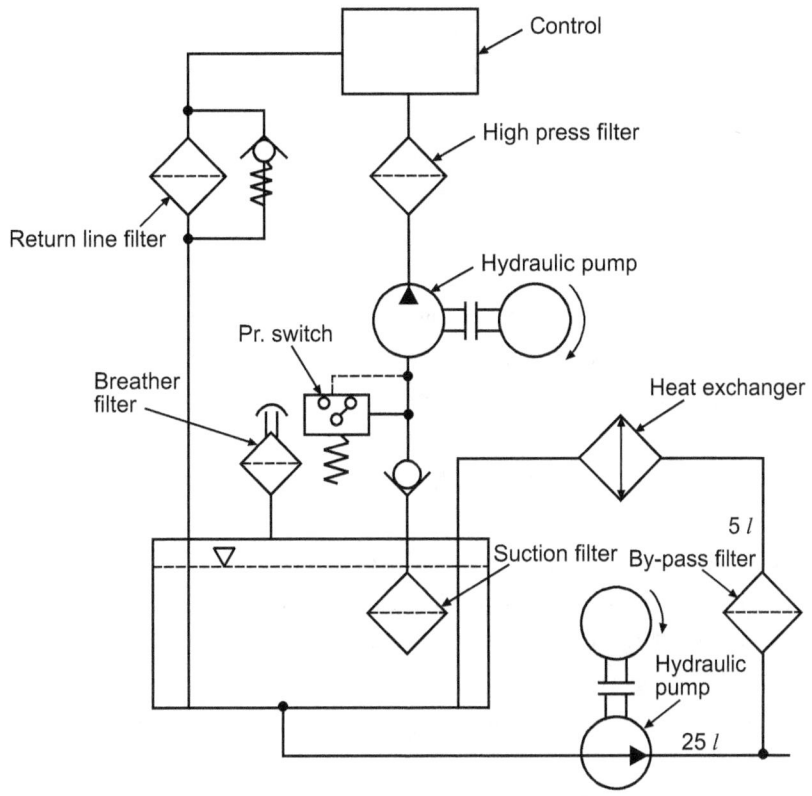

Fig. 2.40

(i) **Suction Line Filter:** The filter is placed in the pump suction line. This filter has to have very low pressure drop to avoid cavitation and low pressure (0.1 bar) bypass value is necessary. Elements of absolute rating between 25 - 125 micron are desirable. The housing is of light metal pressing. The suction strainer is a much coarse filter of mesh 125 - 250 microns and does not have a bypass.

(ii) **Pressure Line Filter (May 07, 12; Dec. 11):** Here the filter is placed on the pump discharge line before the relief valve. This way, the filter protects all the components in the system ahead. The filter is unprotected from pressure surges when the filter is located after relief valve.

The filter uses depth type disposable element. With this filter location, fine filtration is possible.

(iii) **Return Line Filter (May 09):** This filter is placed in the main return line collecting flow from all prominent components. The location of the filter must ensure unrestricted drain lines to prevent set up of a high back pressure. The fluid returned from the drain line is usually unfiltered. This location of the filter does not avoid migration of contaminants ingress into the reservoir and generated in the pump.

(iv) **Relief-valve Filter:** This is also a return-line filter operating at low pressure. Since the pressure drop across this filter is not critical very fine filtration down to 3 micron can be provided. The fluctuating value over the relief value, subjects the filter to flow surges which in turn degrades the filter media. This filter cleans only a fraction of the total flow, which is not a constant fraction.

(v) **Bypass and Bleed-off Filter:** Partial flow filtration is opted for when the cost of a full flow filter is high. This method cleans up small quantities of fluid at a time. This method is unsuitable for systems involving sensitive components.

Bypass type filter is placed in a pressure line. This filter has a built-in venturi which allows a partial flow through the filter, by-passing the remaining flow. Progressive blocking of the filter element, increases the flow rate of the fluid by-passed.

The bleed-off filter is a return line filter. A flow control valve bleeds off some flow through the filter to the tank.

(vi) **Servo-valve Filter or Component Filter:** These are basically pressure line filters placed so as to protect the special components having precision clearances. This filter has an absolute rating of 3 microns or better ($\beta_x \geq 75$)

(vii) **Reverse flow filters:** These filters have a special valve arrangement allowing the flow to pass through the element in one direction and to by-pass the element in case of a reverse flow.

Air breather filter: This filter cleans the air by eliminating contaminants, while it enters the reservoir. The blockage of this filter results in very low pressure at the pump suction and consequent cavitation. The low pressure is likely to damage the reservoir. The reservoir need be protected by a pressure/vacuum relief valve.

(viii) **Clean-up loop filter:** In large systems, a secondary pump-filter circuit is often used. The flow rate across the loop filter should be at least 10 % of the flow through the main circuit. These are quite useful for initial charging of the fluid, and for system flushing. Such loop filters can also be added with additional conditioning measures such as oil coolers, dewatering units etc.

2.14.8 Sizing of Filters

The proper sizing of a filter for a given system is a very complicated task. The sizing of a filter includes specifying (i) micrometer rating, (ii) target cleanliness levels requirement, (iii) flow capacity, (iv) permissible pressure drop, (v) estimation of surface area of element.

(i) **Micrometer Rating:** It depends upon several factors like
- Operating pressure and temperature.
- Duty cycle of the system.
- Sensitivity of system components to contaminants.

- Reliability required.
- Environmental conditions
- Expected life
- Safety requirements

(ii) Target cleanliness levels required. It is dependent upon the clearances provided in the components to be protected.

Table 2.8 gives representative clearances normally adopted for various components of the system.

Table 2.8: Typical critical clearance fluid system components

Item	Typical clearance Microns
Gear Pump (Pressure Loaded)	
Gear to side plate	1/2 - 5
Gear tip to case	1/2 - 5
Vane Pump	
Tip of vane	1/2 = 1*
Sides of vane	5 - 13
Piston Pumps	
Piston to bore**	5 - 40
Valve plate to cylinder	1/2 - 5
Servo valve	
Orifice	130 - 450
Flapper wall	18 - 63
Spool sleeve (R)**	1 - 4
Control valve	
Orifice	130 - 10000
Spool sleeve (R)**	1 - 23
Disc type	1/2 - 1*
Poppet type	13 - 40
Actuators	50 - 250
Hydrostatic bearings	1 - 25
Antifriction bearings	* 1/2-
Slide bearings	*1/2 -

* Estimate for thin lubricant film, ** Radial clearance.

2.15 PRESSURE SWITCHES (May 2007)

This switch is actuated by fluid pressure. The switch converts the pressure signal into an electric signal by closing the contacts in an electric circuit. The current flowing through the electric circuit is then used to perform the same function as in the hydraulic circuit like starting or stopping of a pump, opening or closing of a valve. The conversion of pressure signal into an electric signal is effected using a small piston, bourdon's tube, bellow.

The pressure switches are extensively used to sense an increasing or decreasing pressure. They are used in accumulator circuits, in filtering and cleaning circuits etc. The pressure switch needs damping in the wake of pressure surges. Several damping devices are available to provide damping.

There are two types of switching elements viz. normally open (NO) and normally close (NC).

In case of normally open configuration, no current can flow through the switching element until the switch is actuated. An in case of normally closed switch, current flows through the switching element until the switch is actuated.

These pressure switches have three electrical terminals identified: C [common], NC [normally closed], and NO [normally open]. When wining in a switch, only two terminals are used. The common terminal is always used, plus a second terminal, either NC or NO depending on whether the switch is to operate as a normally open or normally closed switch is used.

- **Symbol for Pressure Switches:**

Fig. 2.41

2.16 TEMPERATURE SWITCHES

Temperature switches is an instrument that automatically senses a change in temperature and opens or closes an electrical switching element when a predetermined temperature point is reached. At the top end of the temperature switches there is one adjustment screw which is generally used to change the actuation point. This switch has a rated accuracy of ± °F maximum. A particular temperature switch incorporates a compensating device to cancel out the adverse effect of ambient fluctuations.

As in case of pressure switches, temperature switches can be wired either normally open (NO) or normally closed (NC). The capillary tube and bulb construction permit remote temperature sensing. Hence, the actual temperature switch can be located at a substantial distance from the oil whose temperature is to be sensed.

These temperature switches are used to protect a fluid power system from serious damage when a system component such as a pump, strainer or cooler begins to malfunction. This will result in excessive oil temperature rise, which is sensed by the temperature switch, which shuts off the entire system. This allows troubleshooting of the system to repair or replace the faulty component.

The symbol for temperature switch is shown in Fig. 2.42.

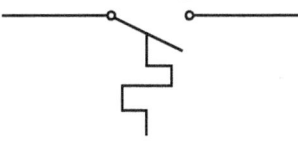

Fig. 2.42

2.17 INTRODUCTION TO ACCUMULATOR   (Dec. 07; May 08; Dec. 08, 10)

A hydraulic accumulator is a device which stores the potential energy of an compressible fluid held under pressure by an external source against some dynamic force from sources like gravity, mechanical spring, and compressed gases. The potential energy is stored when the demand of energy by the system is less than that available from the prime mover and is released to the system during its period of peak demand of energy which the prime mover alone cannot meet. Its function is analogus to that of a flywheel in a mechanical system and a capacitor in an electrical circuit.

The acccumulator is particularly useful for applications having a variable demand of energy during its operating cycle. The addition of accumulator in such systems reduces the capacity of the prime mover required.   **(Dec. 2007, May 2008, Dec. 2008, Dec. 2010, Dec. 11)**

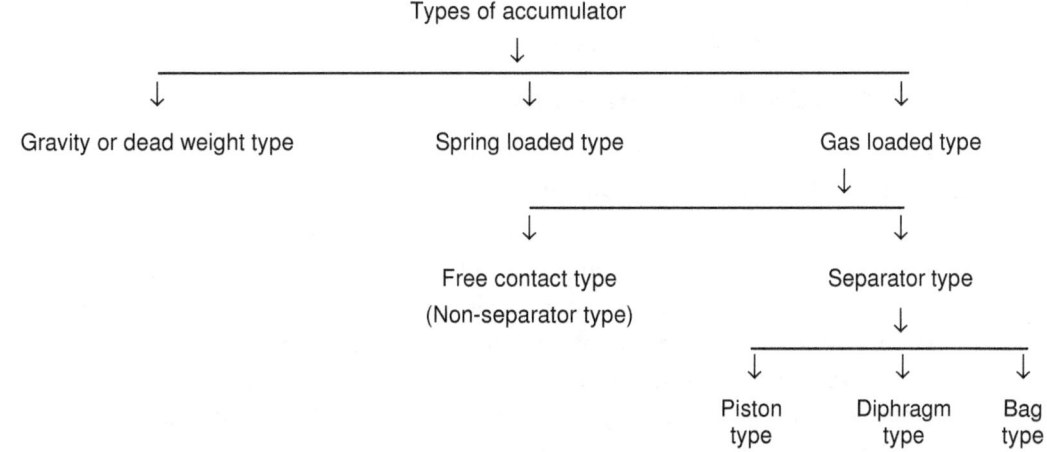

2.17.1 Dead Weight or Gravity Type

Fig. 2.43 (a) shows a typical dead weight type accumulator. It is the oldest type in use. It consists of a vertical, thick-walled steel cylinder housing a piston with packing inside to prevent leakage. The piston rod extending out of the cylinder supports the dead weight, by raising the piston on admitting high pressure fluid.

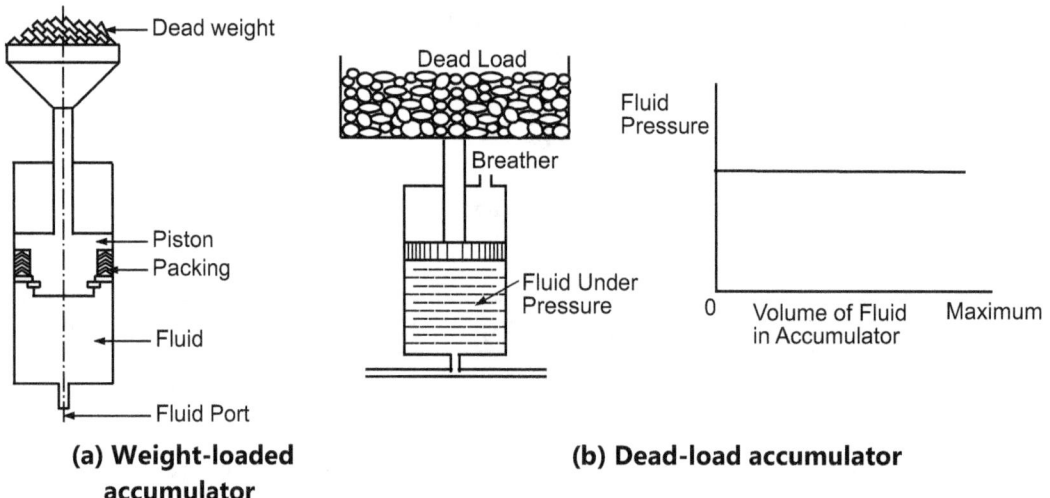

(a) Weight-loaded accumulator

(b) Dead-load accumulator

Fig. 2.43

The force of gravity of the dead weight is used to store potential energy. This accumulator generates a constant pressure of fluid through the full volume output of fluid independent of rate and quantity of the energy supply from the prime mover. On the contrary, in other types of accumulators, the fluid output pressure decreases as a function of the flow rate output of the accumulator Fig. 2.43 (b) shows the pressure vs. volume of fluid in the accumulator characteristic.

The main drawback of this type of accumulator is its very large size and heavy weight which renders it unsuitable for mobile applications.

2.17.2 Spring Loaded Accumulator   (May 2011)

It is similar to a dead weight type except that the piston is preloaded with a spring compression. Fig. 2.44 (a) shows the constructional features.

The spring is a source of energy acting against the piston. The pressure created by this type of accumulator depends upon the stiffness and pre-loading of spring. Further the pressure exerted on the fluid is not constant. It typically delivers a low flow rate of oil at low pressures. Hence for high pressure situations, these accumulators are somewhat heavy. This type of accumulator is not suitable for applications demanding high cycle rates as the spring may fail in fatigue and lose its elasticity. This in turn will make the accumulator inoperative.

HYDRAULICS AND PNEUMATICS   PUMPS

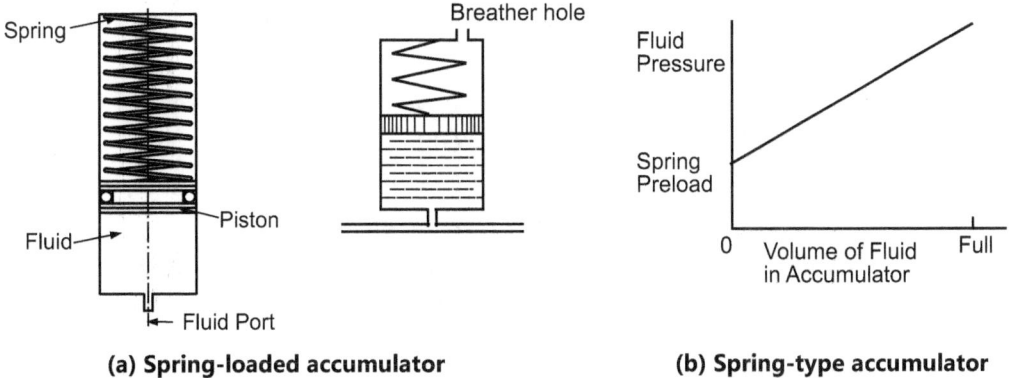

(a) Spring-loaded accumulator   (b) Spring-type accumulator

Fig. 2.44

Fig. 2.44 (b) shows the variation of fluid pressure with the volume of fluid in the accumulator.

2.17.3 Gas Loaded/Charged Accumulators   (May 2011, Dec. 11)

These are also known as hydro-pneumatic accumulators. These accumulators are more practical than the dead weight and spring loaded type.

The gas loaded accumulators work on the principles of the Boyle's law of ideal gases. The storage of potential energy is due to the compressibility of gases. The expansion of gas forces the oil out of the accumulator.

The gas loaded accumulators are further classified as:

(1) Non-separator type (2) separator type.

(1) Non separator or Free Contact Type:

The non-separator type consists of an enclosed cylindrical shell having one oil part at the bottom and a gas charging part on the top as shown in Fig. 2.45 (a). The oil below is in free contact with the gas above without any separator.

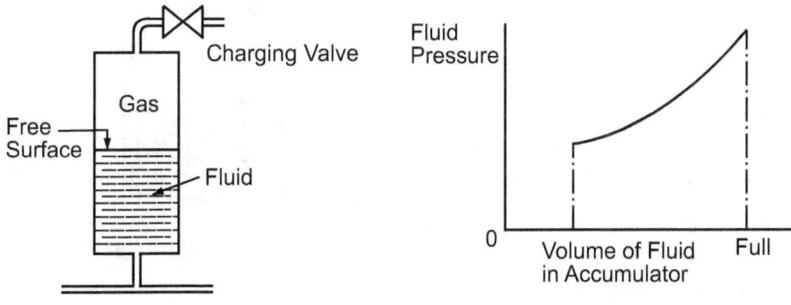

(a) Free-contact gas-loaded accumulator   (b) p-v characteristic

Fig. 2.45

The prominent advantage of this accumulator is that it can handle high volumes of oil. While its major drawback is ingress of gas into oil by absorption. This type of accumulator is not suitable for systems using high speed pumps as the entrapped gas in the oil promotes cavitation resulting in pump damage. Fig. 2.45 (b) shows the variation of oil pressure versus volume of oil in the accumulator.

The pressure-volume characteristic of a gas is governed by the speed of the gas compression/ expansion and can be any of the following:

- **(a) Isothermal:** When the expansion/compression of the gas is extremely slow, the process is isothermal following the relation PV = constant.
- **(b) Isentropic (Adiabatic):** This is a process which occurs at such a fast speed that there is no flow of heat into or out of the accumulator. The process follows the law PV^γ = constant where $\gamma = C_p/C_w = 1.4$.
- **(c) Polytropic:** In this process, the speed of its occurrence is neither too fast nor too slow. The process follows the law pV^n = constant where $\gamma > n > 1$.

(2) Separator type Accumulator:

This is the most commonly used type of accumulator. In this type there is a physical partition between the gas and the oil. This partition or separator allows effective utilization of the compressibility of the gas. The separator type of accumulators are further divided into three types such as: (i) Piston type, (ii) Diaphragm type, and (iii) Bladder (or Bag) type.

(i) Piston Type Accumulator: Fig. 2.46 shows a typical piston type accumulator. It consists of a cylinder housing a freely floating piston. The piston separates the gas and oil. Their major disadvantages is high cost of manufacture and size restriction. The friction between the piston and seals may adversely affect the working of particularly low pressure systems. Leakage past the piston is yet another problem requiring frequent precharging.

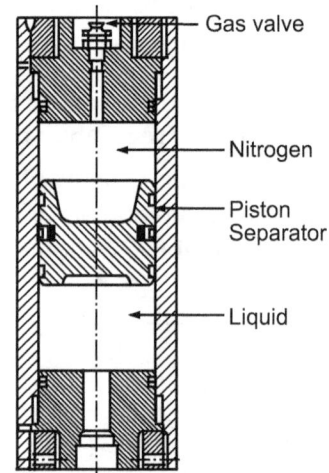

Due to greater inertia and seal friction, these accumulators are unsuitable for damping, pressure pulsation or shock absorption. Their main advantage is that they can handle very high or very low temperature fluids from the system.

Fig. 2.46: Piston-type gas-loaded accumulator

These accumulators are often incorporated with built-in safety devices like the safety seal. When the pressure exceeds the safe limits, end cap O-rings lose their pressure seal.

The variation of gas pressure with volume of oil in the accumulator is similar to that in case of free contact type as shown in Fig. 2.45 (b).

(ii) Diaphragm Type Accumulator: Fig. 2.47 shows the construction of a diaphragm type accumulator. It consists of a diaphragm attached to the shell. The diaphragm acts like a flexible partition between the oil and gas. At the base of the diaphragm, a shut-off button is secured. The button covers the inlet of the line connection when the diaphragm is fully stretched. This avoids the diaphragm from being pressed into the opening during the pre-charge period. A screw plug on the gas side enables control of the gas pressure and also the gas charging.

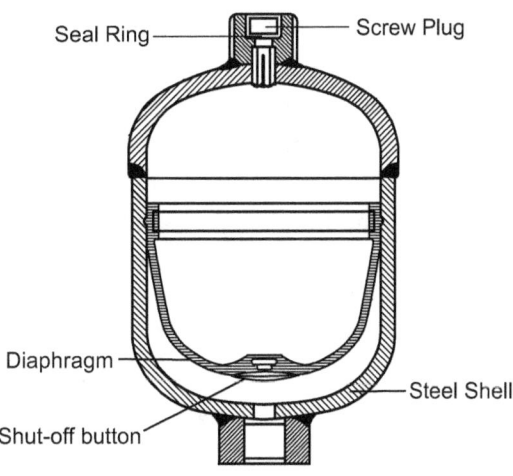

Fig. 2.47: Diaphragm type accumulator

Fig. 2.48 illustrates the operation of a diaphragm type accumulator, showing the diaphragm in various stages of accumulator charging and discharging. The main advantage of this accumulator is its small weight to volume ratio.

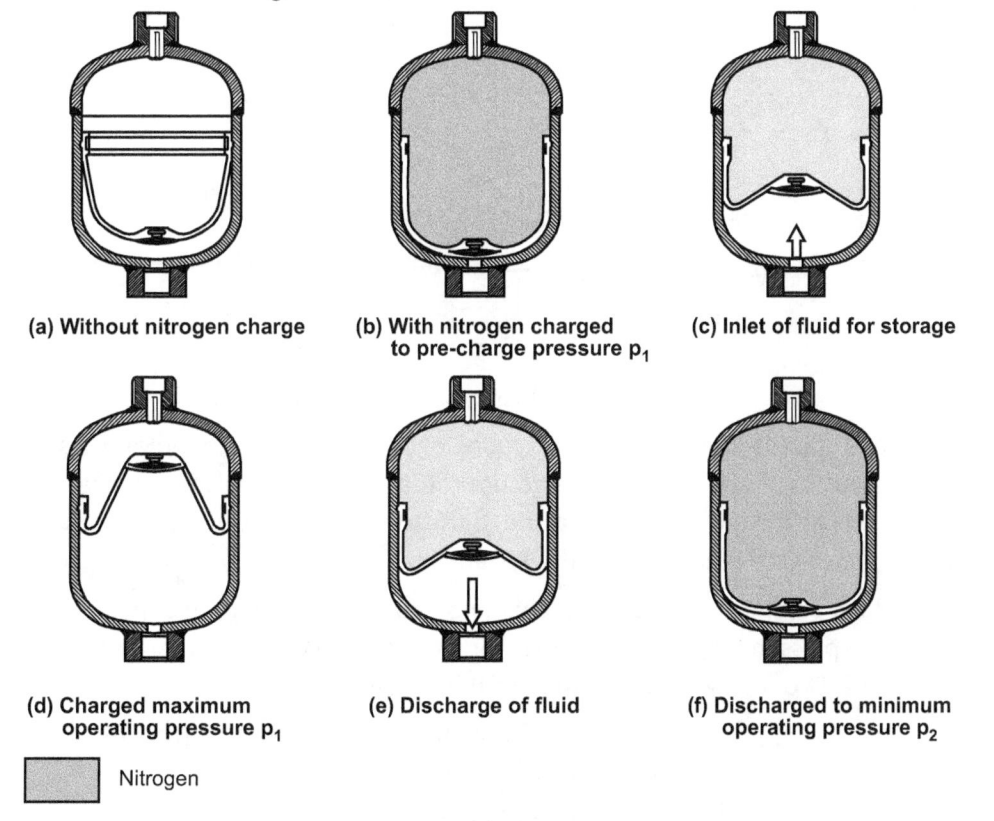

(a) Without nitrogen charge

(b) With nitrogen charged to pre-charge pressure p_1

(c) Inlet of fluid for storage

(d) Charged maximum operating pressure p_1

(e) Discharge of fluid

(f) Discharged to minimum operating pressure p_2

Nitrogen

Fig. 2.48: Operation of a diaphragm type accumulator

(iii) Bladder (or Bag) type accumulator: The construction of the accumulator is shown in Fig. 2.49. It contains a synthetic polymer rubber bladder made of chloroprene nitrile etc. inside a metal shell. The bladder separates the oil and gas. The bladder is fitted in the accumulator by means of a vulcanized gas-valve element and can be easily placed or removed through the shell opening at the poppet valve. The poppet valve closes the inlet when the bladder is fully expanded. Thus the pressing of the bladder into the opening is prevented. The main advantages of this accumulator are positive sealing between gas and oil and quick response to system demands. But its major disadvantage is the possibility of bladder failure.

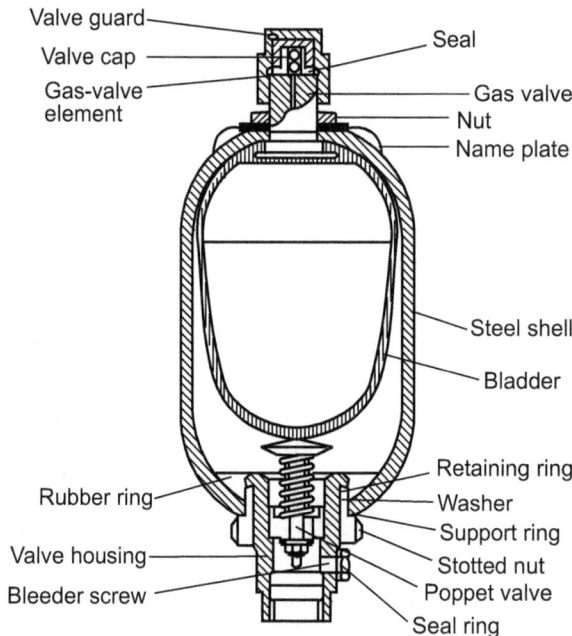

Fig. 2.49: Bladder-type accumulator

Fig. 2.50 shows the bladder in various positions of accumulator charging and discharging. The air delivered by the pump into the accumulator deforms the bladder while increasing the gas pressure as the gas gets compressed, thus storing energy. During discharging of the accumulator, the oil is discharged into the system to meet the additional oil demand.

The gas charged accumulator needs pre-charging of gas when its empty of hydraulic oil. The gas pre-charge pressure depends upon the working pressure of the system. It is always upto a minimum of 25% of the working pressure of the system.

Let,
p_1 = Gas pre-charge pressure in the bladder or gas chamber during operation, kPa

p_2 = Minimum operating pressure, kPa

p_3 = Maximum operating pressure, kPa

The usual practice dictates that $p_1 = 0.9\ p_2$ and $p_3 \leq 3\ p_2$

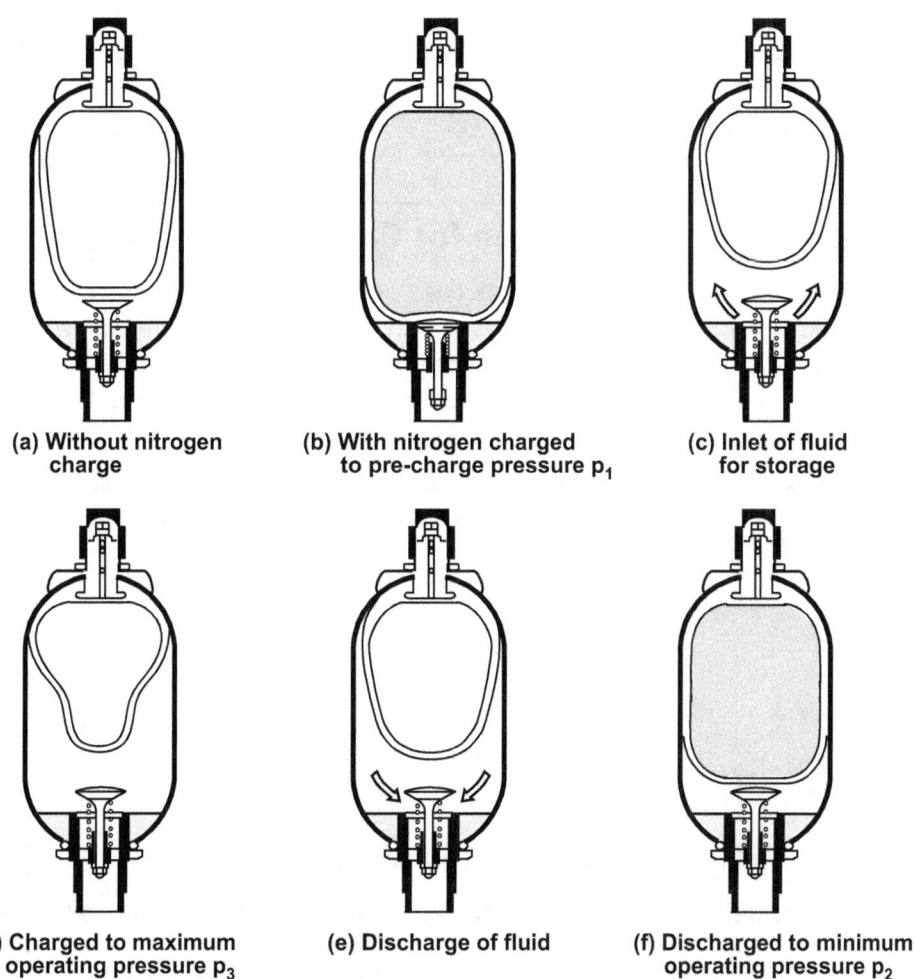

(a) Without nitrogen charge

(b) With nitrogen charged to pre-charge pressure p_1

(c) Inlet of fluid for storage

(d) Charged to maximum operating pressure p_3

(e) Discharge of fluid

(f) Discharged to minimum operating pressure p_2

Fig. 2.50: Operation of a bladder-type accumulator

The maximum pressure 'p_3' is restricted upto a maximum equal to $3\ p_2$. It should not exceed $3\ p_2$ else temperature rises very fast due to rapid compression which may damage or deform bladder or diaphragm.

The gas filled accumulators should be preferably installed vertical.

2.17.4 Comparison of Various Types of Gas Filled Accumulators

Table 2.5 compares different operating features of various types of gas filled accumulators.

Table 2.9: Comparison of various accumulators (Gas type)

Type of accumulator	Bladder type	Diaphragm membrane	Cylinder piston	Flasked cylinder piston
Maximum operating pressure P_{max} (bar)	200	150	200	350
Volumetric efficiency (%)	60	60	90 - 96	38
Safe pressure ratio P_G/P_{max}	4	10	any	any
P_G = Pre-charge pressure temperature °C	– 15 + 65	+ 80	– 30 + 80	– 30 + 80

2.17.5 Significance of Nitrogen for Gas Filled Accumulator

Only nitrogen gas is used to charge a gas filled accumulator. Nitrogen is chemically inert, non-flammable and does not combine easily with other elements. The ingress of nitrogen into the oil through leakage is detectable as foaming in the reservoir. Reduction of nitrogen volume cause narrow limits of pump operation and its overheating. The reduced volume of nitrogen slows down the speed of the cylinders and motors.

The effectiveness of hydraulic fluid capacity of gas filled accumulators can be increased using a gas back up bottle to compensate for the loss of gas leaking into the oil-side. Fig. 2.51 shows the arrangement.

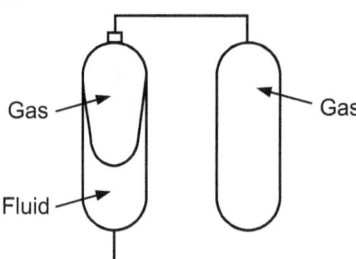

Fig. 2.51: Use of gas back-up bottle

2.17.6 Applications of Hydraulic Accumulators (May 07, 09, 12; Dec. 09)

The various applications of hydraulic accumulators are:
- Supply of fluid.
- Damping of pump discharge pulsations.
- Damping of pressure surge.
- Leakage compensation.
- Compensation for thermal expansion.
- Standby/emergency source of power.
- Counter balancing.
- Vehicle suspension, power braking of automobiles.

(a) Supply of Fluid: This is the most frequent application, to supply flow rate of fluid over a short period of time. The pump of low discharge capacity can be used, to charge the accumulator over a long period of time. Stored fluid is discharged into the system to cater to the high flow rate demanded by the system. During the period when the accumulator is fully charged and there is no demand from the system the pump is unloaded or switched off.

(b) Damping of Pump Delivery Pulsations: For most hydraulic pumps, the flow rate of discharge is pulsating with time. These pulsations can be smoothened to some extent by the piping upstream of the pump. However, when absolutely constant discharge is required say for an electrohydraulically servosystem, provision of an accumulator placed upstream of pump helps to damp down the pulsations in the flow. Yet, the complete elimination of pulsation is not possible, as seen from Fig. 2.52.

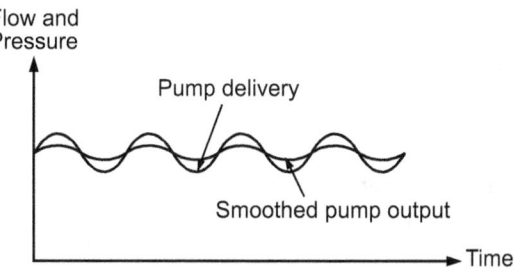

Fig. 2.52: Pump delivery pulsation damping

(c) Damping of pressure surge: Pressure surge or shock waves are caused due to sudden closure of valves. This phenomenon is known as 'water hammer' as it generates severe noise. Faster the valve closure, severe is the pressure surge.

The pressure generated by rapid valve closure is given by

$$\Delta p = \rho a \Delta V \qquad \ldots (2.10)$$

where Δp = Pressure rise

ρ = Density of fluid kg/m³

$a = \left(\dfrac{\beta}{\rho}\right)^{1/2}$ = Sonic velocity through fluid

ΔV = Change in velocity

β = Bulk modulus

For example, a pressure surge of about 45 bar results when a fluid flow at a velocity of 4 m/s is suddenly stopped. This surge in addition to the system pressure can damage the system components, produce sudden vibrations of hydraulic hose, piping etc. An accumulator fitted closed to the valve for absorbing pressure transient helps in partial damping. Fig. 2.53 shows the arrangement.

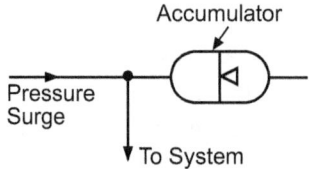

Fig. 2.53: Pressure surge damping

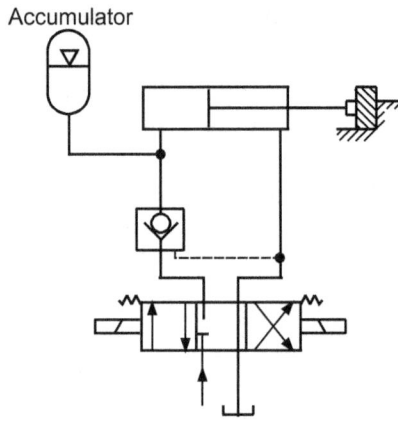

(d) Leakage Compensation: In a system including a pump unloader valve, a small leakage results in a pressure drop and chatter of unloader valve. In such situations, an accumulator is useful to make up the leakage. In hydraulic clamping, leakage reduces the clamping force. An accumulator compensates the leakage and maintains the clamping force. Fig. 2.54 shows the typical circuit.

Fig. 2.54: Leakage compensation

(e) Compensation for Thermal Expansion: The fluid undergoes volume change when its temperature changes. If this volume change is continued in a closed system, the pressure increases. The change of volume of the fluid in a closed system has to be stored in the accumulator. See Fig. 2.55. The change of volume ΔV due to temperature change Δt is given by

$$\Delta V = k_V \, V \, \Delta t \qquad \ldots (2.11)$$

where
- k_V = Coefficient of volumetric expansion of fluid
- V = Initial volume of fluid
- Δt = Change of temperature

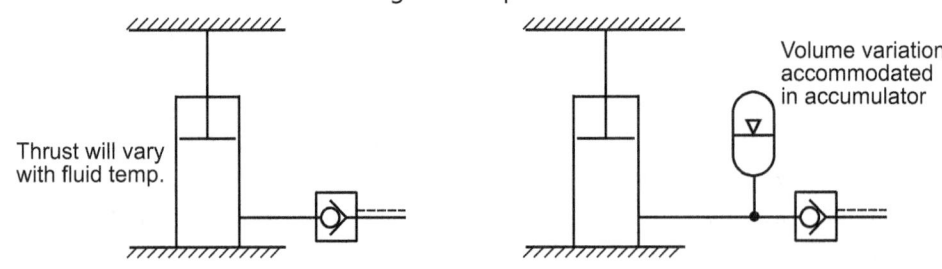

Fig. 2.55: Thermal expansion compensation

(f) Standby/Emergency Source of Power: In the event of pump failure, the hydraulic energy stored in the accumulator can be made available to complete the cycle of the circuit. Such a usage of the application is restricted to applications where power failure could result in a grave situation e.g. landing gear of an air-craft.

(g) Counter Balancing: An accumulator and hydraulic cylinder can be arranged in a closed loop to counter balance the heavy mass. The displacement volume of the cylinder and degree of under balance/over balance dictate the quantity of fluid storage required. In practice, the accumulator volume is provided to be double the counterbalance cylinder displacement, with a gas backup bottle of five times the accumulator capacity. Fig. 2.56 shows the typical circuit.

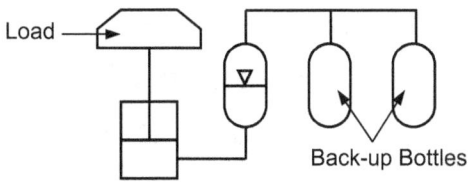

Fig. 2.56: Counterbalancing

(h) Vehicle suspension, power steering of automobiles: A typical hydraulic circuit using accumulator for a vehicle suspension system is shown in Fig. 2.57. The system is popular as Citroen system. An accumulator is provided in a strut for each wheel to absorb the shock while the main accumulator supplies additional pressure-fluid for providing fast response.

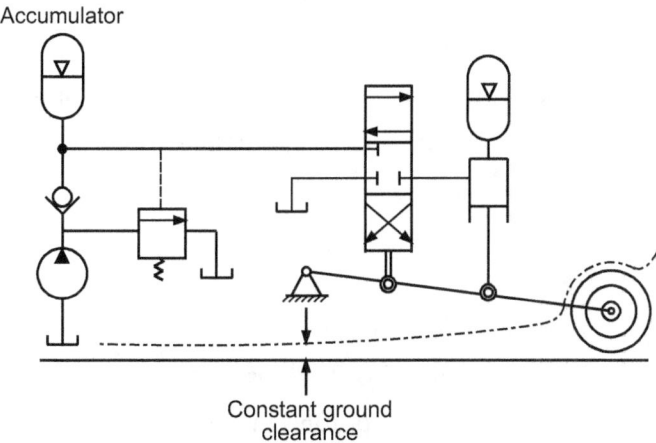

Fig. 2.57: Vehicle suspension system

Fig. 2.58 shows the use of accumulator in a power steering of a mobile equipment. The accumulator supplies pressure-oil in the event of the pump failure.

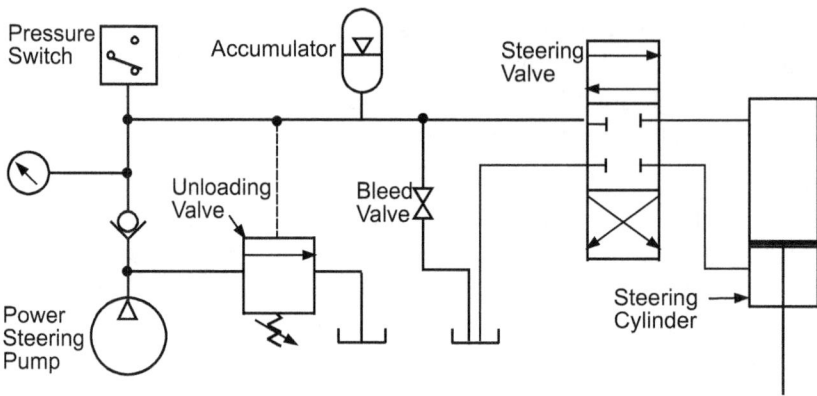

Fig. 2.58: Accumulator in a power steering circuit of an automobile

2.17.7 Calculation of Demand Volume of an Accumulator

The demand volume ΔV of an accumulator is the volume of oil which must be discharged into the system during the peak demand period. The stored gas supplies the necessary energy.

The gas precharge pressure is usually 1/3 of the system maximum pressure. A lower pre-charge pressure results in greater compression ratio and larger size of the accumulator.

If the system pressure is to be maintained constant within 5%-10% limit, the accumulator gas volume at system pressure should be large compared to the oil volume to supply large discharge of oil without excessive pressure drop. Smaller the gas volume, the larger the volume of oil discharged with rapid pressure drop.

Demand volume, $\quad \Delta V = V_{LP} - V_{HP}$ ... (2.12)

Following nomenclature shall be used for calculation of demand volume.

System:
- P_{LP} = Lowest operating pressure
- P_{HP} = Maximum operating pressure
- x = Ratio $\dfrac{P_{HP} - P_{LP}}{P_{HP}}$
- ΔV = Demand volume, m³
- Q = Pump capacity, litres/cycle
- s = Stroke of piston, cm
- d = Diameter of piston, cm
- N = Piston stroke/cycle

Accumulator:
- P_P = Pre-charge pressure, kPa
- V_P = Gas pre-charge, litre

V_{LP} = Gas volume at low pressure, litre

V_{HP} = Gas volume at high pressure

V_{Acc} = Total volume of accumulator, litre

The expansion and compression of gas can be either isothermal, adiabatic or polytropic. In practice, index for polytropic process is taken as 1.25.

Thus
$$p_{HP} V_{HP}^n = p_{LP} V_{LP}^n \qquad \ldots (2.13)$$

where n = 1 for isothermal and 1.4 - 1.7 for adiabatic process.

Now,
$$\frac{p_{HP} - p_{LP}}{p_{HP}} = x \qquad \therefore \frac{p_{LP}}{p_{HP}} = 1 - x \qquad \ldots (2.14)$$

$$\therefore \frac{V_{HP}}{V_{LP}} = \frac{V_{HP}}{(V_{HP} + \Delta V)} = (1-x)^{1/n} \qquad \text{(From 2.12)} \qquad \ldots (2.15)$$

$$\therefore V_{HP} = \left[\frac{\left(\frac{p_{LP}}{p_{HP}}\right)^{1/n}}{1 - \left(\frac{p_{LP}}{p_{HP}}\right)^{1-n}} \right] \times \Delta V = m\, \Delta V \qquad \ldots (2.16)$$

Further accumulator volume = gas volume + oil volume. It is necessary to specify the desired volume ratio of the gas to oil before estimation of the combined volume. The gas volume is specified as a multiple of oil volume at the fully charged condition. A common value for industrial application is 3 : 1.

$$\therefore V_{Acc} = 1.33\, V_{HP}$$

The pre-charge volume V_P can be calculated as explained in the Greer manual

$$V_P = \frac{\Delta V\, (p_{LP}/p_P)^{1/n}}{1 - \left(\frac{p_{LP}}{p_{HP}}\right)^{1/n}} \qquad \ldots (2.17)$$

Overall demand volume is the sum of demands from all components in the system. It can be expressed graphically as volume-cycle vs time graph.

The summation includes all working cylinders and system pump and is expressed as:

$$V = \frac{\pi}{4}\, [d_1^2\, s_1\, N_1\, \ldots\ldots\, d_n^2\, s_n\, N_n] - Q \qquad \ldots (2.18)$$

where
d = Diameter of each piston
s = Stroke length
N = Strokes per accumulator cycle
Q = Pump delivery per cycle.

2.17.8 Comparison of Various Types of Gas Filled Accumulators

The following table 2.10 compares various operating parameters.

Table 2.10

Type of accumulator	Maximum operating pressure, 'bar'	Volumetric efficiency, %	Safe pressure ratio, p_a/p_{max}	Temperature °C
Bladder type	200	60	4	– 15 + 65
Diaphragm membrane	150	60	10	+ 80
Cylinder piston	200	90 - 96	any	– 30 + 80
Flasked cylinder piston	350	38	any	– 30 + 80

p_a = precharge gas pressure

2.17.9 Efficiency of an Accumulator Circuit

Let Q = Pump discharge, m³/s

p_1 = minimum system pressure, kPa

p_2 = maximum system pressure, kPa

∴ Power input P_{in} = $Q \times$ Average pressure

$$= Q \times \frac{p_1 + p_2}{2} \text{ kJ/s}$$

The output power $P_{out} = Q \times p$ which assumes that flow control and load value of the pump flow rate are equal.

∴ Efficiency 'η' = $\dfrac{P_{out}}{P_{in}} = \dfrac{Q \times p_1}{Q\left(\dfrac{p_1 + p_2}{2}\right)} = \dfrac{2 p_1}{p_1 + p_2}$

In practice, the circuit efficiency upto 70% is maintained.

2.18 INTENSIFIER

The hydraulic intensifier is analogous to an electrical transformer. It is a device for increasing the pressure of water for supplying to the machines which is needed during their working period. These machines work intermittently. The only difference between an intensifier and an electrical transformer is that the transformer supplies continuous current at stepped up voltage while the intensifier supplies high pressure water intermittently.

The use of an intensifier with a low pressure pump thus can meet the demand of the intermittent high pressure liquid. Hence, the cost of high pressure pump is saved with a saving in operating cost.

2.18.1 Hydraulic Intensifier

Intensifier (or booster) function is to get a high pressure output from a low pressure input. The input source may be hydraulic or pneumatic. Output may be a fixed quantity of fluid per stroke or a continuous type of delivery. Fig. 2.59 shows a hydraulic intensifier. It is basically, a large diameter piston powered from the input source and it drives a small diameter piston. Low pressure fluid is received on the large diameter. Force corresponding to the product of pressure and area is developed and is available on a small piston. Since the small piston on other side has less area, pressure obtained is multiplied. Fluid at high pressure is thus forced out by a small diameter piston. Pressure intensification is directly proportional to the ratio of the piston areas.

Since force on both the pistons is same

$$F = P_1 A_1 = P_2 A_2$$

where,
P_1 = Input pressure
A_1 = Low pressure piston area
$= \left(\frac{\pi}{4} D^2\right)$

where,
D = Diameter of large piston
P_2 = Output pressure
A_2 = High pressure piston area
$= (\pi/4\, d^2)$ where d = Diameter of small piston

$$\therefore \quad P_2 = \frac{P_1 A_1}{A_2}$$

$$= \frac{P_1 (\pi/4\, D^2)}{(\pi/4\, d^2)} = P_1 \times \left(\frac{D}{d}\right)^2$$

Thus pressure intensification is proportional to the square of ratio of diameters. This is a single short type of intensifier. The amount of fluid delivered per operation is relative to the quantity of input fluid and is inversely proportional to the ratio of piston areas.

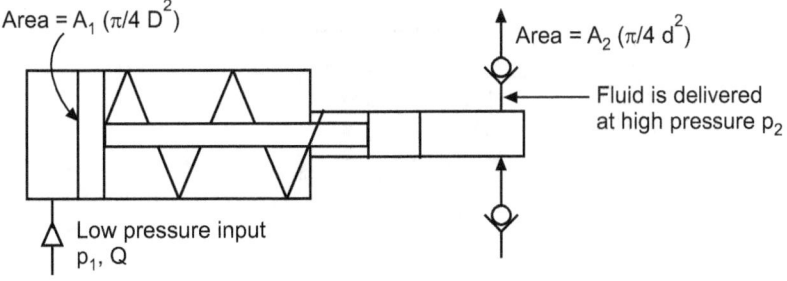

Fig. 2.59

Quantity delivered per stroke is

$$Q\left(\frac{A_2}{A_1}\right) = Q \times \frac{\frac{\pi}{4} d^2}{\frac{\pi}{4} D^2}$$

$$= Q \times \left(\frac{d}{D}\right)^2 \qquad \text{where, } Q = \text{Input flow per stroke}$$

Efficiency about 80 should be satisfactory. The performance is affected by friction and internal leakage.

In pneumatically operated intensifiers, pressure of 2000 bar can be obtained from a 7 bar air supply.

(a) Electrically Operated Fluid Power Intensifier:

In Fig. 2.60 a circuit using an intensifier is shown. Low pressure piston area is 10 times higher than high pressure piston area. A pressure of 34,475 kPa is achieved at delivery of intensifier from the input system pressure of 3448 kPa. Fluid delivery rate is reduced to 1/10.

In the neutral position of 4/3 solenoid operated valve, low pressure fluid is connected to the tank. Position (1) of D.C. valve intensifier piston is retracted. (Moves to right). When the limit switch is pressed, the cylinder is fully charged and is ready for forward stroke. High pressure reverse flow is blocked by a check valve D. When the limit switch is pressed, valve R is piloted open and piston side fluid of low pressure piston is drained to the tank. This reduces the resistance in retraction stroke.

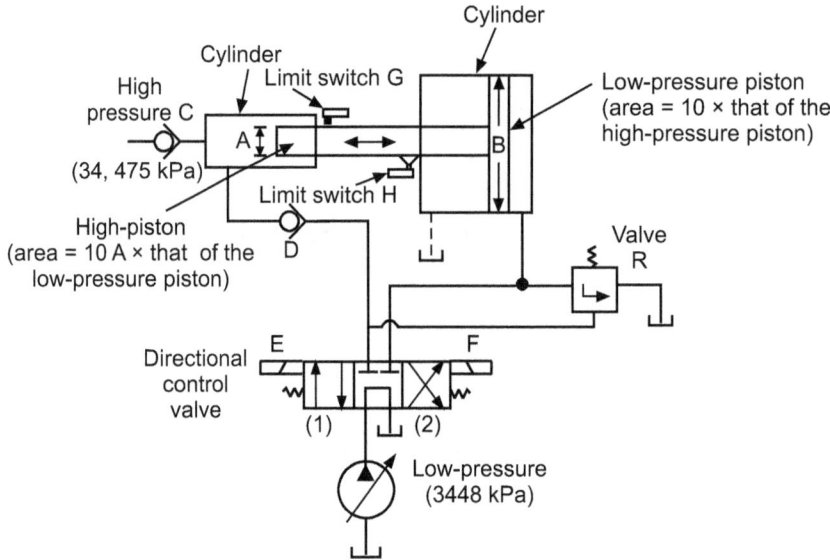

Fig. 2.60: Electrically operated fluid-power intensifier

HYDRAULICS AND PNEUMATICS — PUMPS

(b) Automatic Reciprocating Pressure Intensifier:

The circuit shown in Fig. 2.61 gives a continuous high pressure pumping of pulsating flow. A double acting intensifier is used. Cam valves E and F are both mechanically and pilot signal actuated.

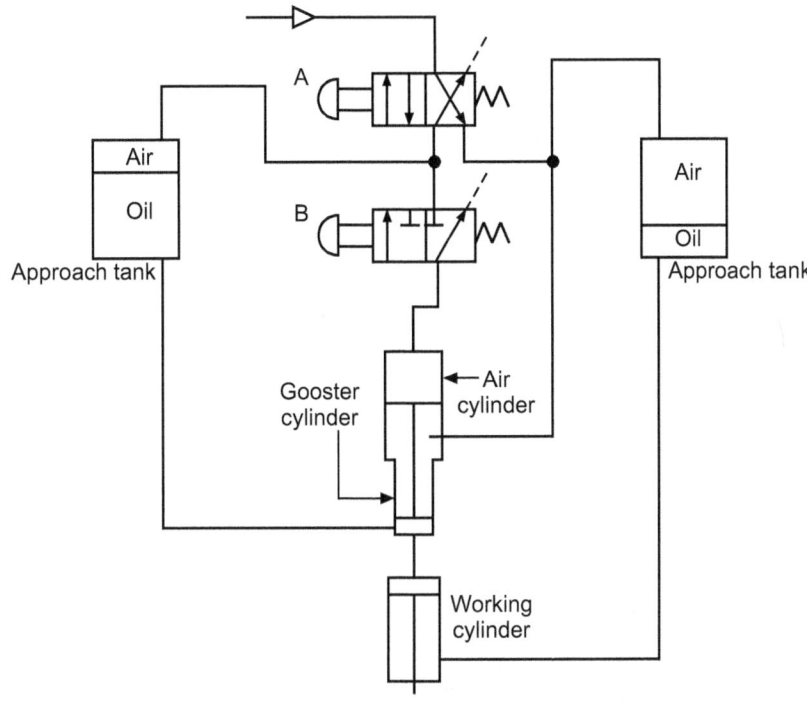

Fig. 2.61

(c) Air Over Oil Intensifier:

Shop floor air source over oil is supplied to increase the system pressure. Control flexibility is obtained. They are also used for eliminating pumps and other components to save costs. The intermittent single stroke have low volume applications e.g. bench presses, rivetting machines or bending, broaching, cutting, crimping, forming. In Fig. 2.62 a typical air oil intensifier is shown. The cylinder travels substantial distance at low pressure, and then a short distance at high pressure for completing the operation on the work. Valve A is used to extend and retract the working cylinder at shop air pressure. Valve B applies shop air pressure to head end of the air cylinder to drive the booster cylinder at high hydraulic pressure.

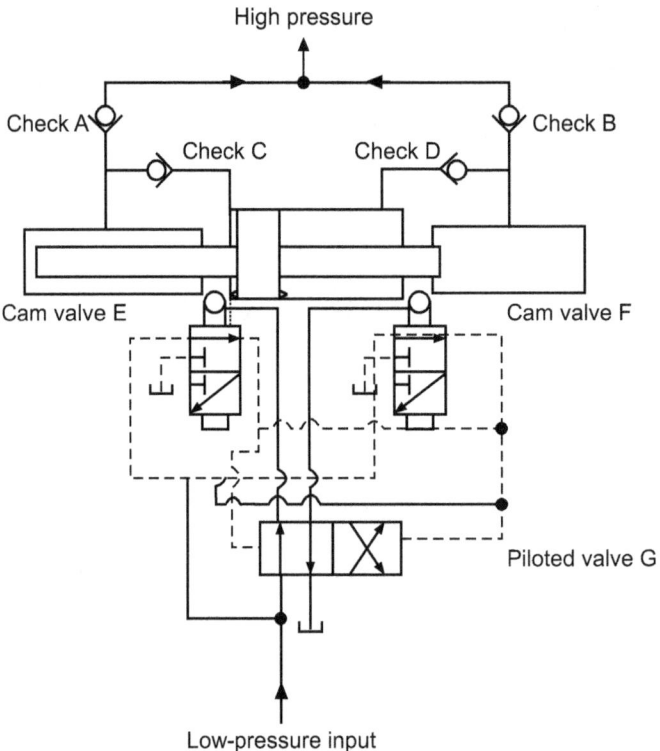

Fig. 2.62: Double pressure booster system with air-oil tank return

Step I: Valve A is actuated

The air is directed to approach the tank. Oil of approach tank is forced through the booster cylinder to the head end of the working cylinder. This is a low pressure approach stroke.

Step II: Valve B is actuated

The air is admitted to the head end of the air cylinder and it intensifies the pressure in the booster cylinder oil, and thus high pressure short stroke of the working cylinder takes place.

Step III: Return stroke: Release valve B

The air cylinder is rented valve A is released and the shop air is directed to the return tank and also to the rod end of the air cylinder. This forces the oil of the return tank to the rod end of the working cylinder. It returns CAP end oil of the booster cylinder is directed to approach the tank.

2.18.2 Construction of an Intensifier

Fig. 2.63 shows the construction of an intensifier. It consists of a fixed ram, a fixed cylinder and a sliding cylinder. The sliding cylinder slides over a fixed ram and inside the fixed cylinder.

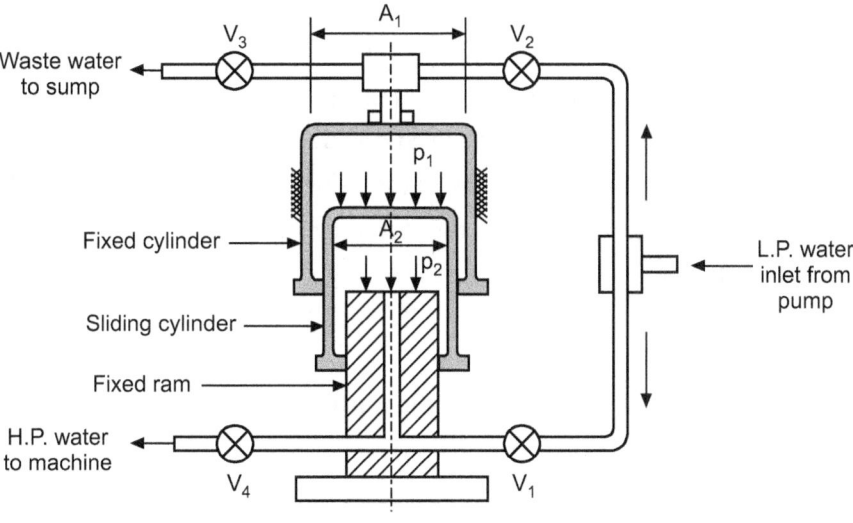

Fig. 2.63: Intensifier

The low pressure water supply is connected to the fixed ram and the fixed cylinder. The high pressure water is taken out from the fixed ram, while the waste water is discharged from the fixed cylinder.

The packing and seals are provided to prevent the leakage of water. The valves provided are manually operated. However, a multi-direction control valve operated through a servo motor can also be incorporated. The collar provided on the sliding cylinder and fixed cylinder helps to limit the travel of the sliding cylinder.

2.18.3 Principle of Operation

Let the sliding cylinder be at the b.d.c. position. The fixed cylinder is full with water. Open the valves 'V_1' and 'V_3' and keep the valves 'V_2' and 'V_4' closed. The supply water at low pressure now enters the space over the fixed ram and inside the sliding cylinder through valve 'V_1'. It forces the sliding cylinder to rise with a force '$p \times A_2$' kN. The water above the sliding cylinder is now discharged through the valve 'V_3' with a pressure of $\dfrac{p \times A_2}{A_1}$ kPa.

After the sliding cylinder reaches t.d.c. position, open the valves 'V_2' and 'V_4' and close the valves 'V_1' and 'V_3'. Now, the low pressure water from the pump is admitted above the sliding cylinder, inside a fixed cylinder through the valve 'V_2'. This forces the sliding cylinder to go downwards with a force '$p \times A_1$' kN. The descent of the sliding cylinder forces the water inside it with a high pressure of $p \times \dfrac{A_1}{A_2}$ kPa through the valve to the machine.

It is thus seen that the intensifier discharges high pressure water only during the downward stroke of the sliding cylinder. Thus, the supply of high pressure water is intermitttent. A continuous supply of high pressure water can be obtained by using two identical intensifiers working out of phase with a phase difference of 180°.

Let
p = Pressure of supply water from the pump, kPa
A_1 = Inside area of the fixed cylinder, m².
A_2 = Area of the fixed mm (or inside area of the sliding cylinder), m²
l = Stroke length of the sliding cylinder, m

Neglecting friction, for the upward stroke of the sliding cylinder,

Vertically Upward Force on the cylinder

$$= p \times A_2 \text{ kN}$$

P_w = pressure of the waste water

$$= p \times \frac{A_2}{A_1} \text{ kPa} \qquad \ldots (2.19)$$

As $A_1 >> A_2$, the pressure of the waste water, 'P_w' is quite low, even less than the supply pressure 'p'.

Also,

Q_ω = Quantity of the water wasted per cycle

$$= A_1 \times l \text{ m}^3/\text{cycle} \qquad \ldots (2.20)$$

Now, for the downward stroke at the sliding cylinder, vertically downward force on the sliding cylinder
$$= p \times A_1 \text{ kN}$$

P_h = Pressure of water discharged to the machine

$$= p \times \frac{A_1}{A_2} \text{ kPa} \qquad \ldots (2.21)$$

But, as $A_1 >> A_2$, the pressure of the water supplied to the machine 'P_h' is high.

Further, Q_h = Quantity of high pressure water discharged/cycle

$$= A_2 \times l \text{ m}^3/\text{cycle} \qquad \ldots (2.22)$$

However, the comparison of equations (2.20) and (2.22) reveals that the quantity of water wasted 'Q_w' at low pressure is much greater than the quantity of water discharged 'Q_h' at high pressure.

The ratio of these quantities of water is

$$\frac{Q_w}{Q_h} = \frac{A_1}{A_2} \qquad \ldots (2.23 \text{ a})$$

The ratio of the pressures of the water discharged is

$$\frac{P_h}{P_w} = \frac{A_1}{A_2} \qquad \text{(neglecting Friction)} \ldots (2.23 \text{ b})$$

HYDRAULICS AND PNEUMATICS — PUMPS

It may be noted here that the ratio of pressures 'P_h/P_w' is affected by the friction, the ratio of the quantities 'Q_w/Q_h' remains unaffected by the friction. This fact is illustrated later in the solved problem example.

The hydraulic intensifiers are extensively used to supply high pressure water required intermittently by the hydraulic systems like presses, cranes, lifts, etc.

SOLVED EXAMPLES

Example 2.17: *What size accumulator is necessary to supply 500 cc of fluid in a hydraulic system of maximum pressure of 200 bars which drops to 100 bar minimum? Assuming N_2 gas pre-charged of 66 bar, find adiabatic and isothermal solution.* **(May 2001)**

Solution: A gas charged accumulator can be shown schematically as follows:

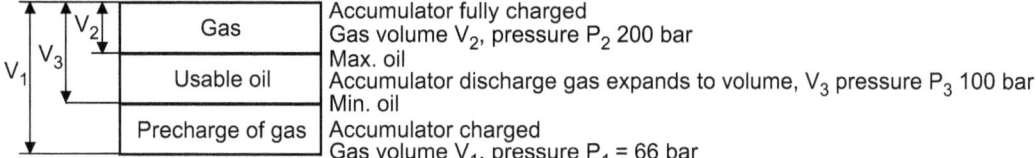

Accumulator fully charged
Gas volume V_2, pressure P_2 200 bar
Max. oil
Accumulator discharge gas expands to volume, V_3 pressure P_3 100 bar
Min. oil
Accumulator charged
Gas volume V_1, pressure P_1 = 66 bar

Fig. 2.64

The expansion of gas from fully charged to fully discharged condition and comparison of the gas from precharged to charged condition can be isothermal or adiabatic.

1. For isothermal condition

$$V_3 - V_2 = \text{Volume of usable oil}$$
$$= 0.005 \text{ m}^3$$
$$V_3 = V_2 + 0.005$$

Now, by applying the relationship,

$$P_2 V_2 = P_3 V_3$$

$$V_2 = \frac{P_3}{P_2} \times V_3 = \left[\frac{100 + 1.013}{200 + 1.013}\right] \times [V_2 + 0.005]$$

$$= 0.5025 V_2 + 0.002512$$

$$\therefore \quad V_2 = 0.00505 \text{ m}^3$$

Now, by using the relationship,

$$P_1 V_1 = P_2 V_2$$

$$V_1 = \frac{P_2}{P_1} \times V_2 = \left[\frac{200 + 1.013}{60 + 1.013}\right] \times 0.00505$$

Unit II | 2.85

$$= \frac{201.013}{67.013} \times 15151 \text{ cc}$$

= Precharge volume or accumulator's capacity

2. For adiabatic condition:

$$P_2 V_2^{1.4} = P_3 V_3^{1.4}$$

$$\therefore V_2 = V_3 \times \left(\frac{P_1}{P_2}\right)^{1/1.4}$$

$$= (V_2 + 0.005) \left(\frac{101.013}{201.013}\right)^{0.714}$$

$$= 0.6118 V_2 + 0.003059$$

$$\therefore V_2 = 0.00788 \text{ m}^3$$

Now, using the same relationship,

$$P_1 V_1^{1.4} = P_2 V_2^{1.4}$$

$$V_1 = 0.00788 \left(\frac{201.013}{67.013}\right)^{0.714}$$

$$\therefore V_{1\text{ adiabatic}} = 0.01726 \text{ m}^3 = 17260 \text{ cc}$$

= Accumulators capacity

Example 2.18: *What size of accumulator is necessary to supply 4917 cm³ of fluid into a hydraulic system of maximum operating pressure of 207 bar, which drops to minimum 103.5 bar? Assuming a Nitrogen gas pre-charge of accumulator is 67 bar, obtain both isothermal and adiabatic solutions.* **(May 2002)**

Solution: A gas charged accumulator can be shown schematically as follows:

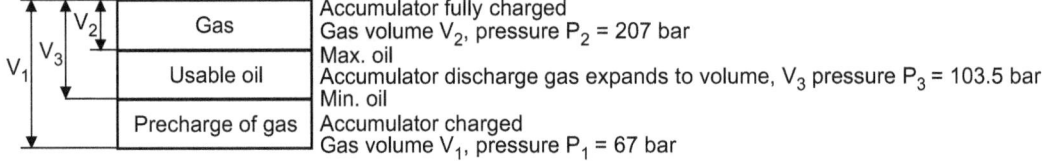

Fig. 2.65

The expansion of the gas from fully discharged condition and compression of the gas from precharged to fully charged condition can be isothermal or adiabatic.

I. For isothermal condition:

$$V_3 - V_2 = \text{Volume of usable oil}$$

$$= 0.004917 \text{ m}^3$$

HYDRAULICS AND PNEUMATICS PUMPS

$\therefore$ $\quad V_3 = V_2 + 0.004917$

Applying relationship

$$P_2 V_2 = P_3 V_3$$

$$V_2 = \frac{P_3}{P_2} \times V_3$$

$$= \left[\frac{103.5 + 1.013}{207 + 1.013}\right] [V_2 + 0.004917]$$

$$= 0.5024 V_2 + 0.00247$$

$\therefore$ $\quad V_2 = 0.00496 \text{ m}^3$

Use the relationship, $\quad P_1 V_1 = P_2 V_2$

$$V_1 = \frac{P_2}{P_1} \times V_2 = \left[\frac{207 + 1.013}{67 + 1.013}\right] \times 0.00496$$

$\therefore$ $\quad V_1 = 0.01518 \text{ m}^3 = 1518 \text{ cc}$

$\quad = $ Precharge volume or accumulators capacity

II. For adiabatic condition:

$$P_2 V_2^{1.4} = P_3 V_3^{1.4}$$

$$V_2 = V_3 \left[\frac{P_3}{P_2}\right]^{1/1.4}$$

$$= (V_2 + 0.004917) \left[\frac{104.513}{208.013}\right]^{0.714}$$

$$= 0.0117 V_2 + 0.003007$$

$\therefore$ $\quad V_2 = 0.007740 \text{ m}^3$

$$P_1 V_1^{1.4} = 0.007746 \left(\frac{208.013}{68.013}\right)^{0.714}$$

$\therefore$ $\quad V_1 = 0.0172 \text{ m}^3 = 1720 \text{ cc}$

$\quad = $ Accumulator's capacity

Example 2.19: *A gas charged accumulator supplies energy to a system with 15 litres of oil within the pressure range of 125 to 175 bar. If the accumulator has precharged pressure of 90 bar, size the accumulator for (i) isothermal, (ii) adiabatic pressures.* **(May 2003)**

Solution: Precharge pressure = P_1 = 90 bar.

Corresponding volume of the accumulator = V_1 when it contains only gas.

Maximum pressure = P_3 = 175 bar, at this pressure accumulator contains maximum oil of 15 litres and remaining volume (i.e. balance) is gas.

The balance volume of gas = $V_3 = (V_1 - 15)$.

Part A: Considering isothermal condition

$$P_1 V_1 = P_3 V_3$$
$$90 \times V_1 = 175 \times (V_1 - 15)$$
$$90 V_1 = 175 V_1 - 2625$$
$$V_1 = \frac{2625}{86} = 30.88 \text{ lit}$$

∴ Volume of accumulator assuming isothermal conditions = 30.88 lit.

Part B: Considering adiabatic condition

$$P_1 V_1^\gamma = P_3 V_3^\gamma$$
$$90 (V_1)^\gamma = 175 (V_1 - 15)^\gamma$$

Assume value of $\gamma = 1.25$.

$$90 (V_1)^{1.25} = 175 (V_1 - 15)^{1.25}$$
$$\frac{90}{175} = \left(\frac{V_1 - 15}{V_1}\right)^{1.25}$$
$$\frac{V_1 - 15}{V_1} = \left(\frac{90}{175}\right)^{1/125}$$

∴ $V_1 - 15 = 0.587 V_1$

∴ $V_1 = 36.36$ lit

∴ Volume of accumulator assuming adiabatic conditions = 36.36 lit.

Example 2.20: *For a certain hydraulic press, the following data is available:*

Diameter of cylinder = 18 cm
Diameter of the plunger = 2.5 cm
Stroke of the plunger = 30 cm
Weight to be lifted = 2000 kg
Height of the lift = 1.5 m
Time taken for lifting = 1.5 min.
Determine:
(a) Force required to lift the load
(b) Volume of water to be pumped
(c) Number of strokes required
(d) Power of the motor to drive the plunger

Solution:

Force required × Area of cylinder = Load on plunger × Area of plunger

$$\therefore \quad \text{Force required} = \frac{2000 \times 9.81 \times \pi/4 \times (0.025)^2}{\pi/4 \times 0.18^2} \text{ N}$$

$$= \mathbf{378.47 \text{ N}} \quad \text{... Ans.}$$

Volume of water to be admitted per stroke

$$= \frac{\pi}{4} \times D_P^2 \times L \text{ m}^3$$

$$= \frac{\pi}{4} \times (0.025)^2 \times 0.3 \text{ m}^3/\text{stroke}$$

Total volume of water to be pumped into cylinder

$$= \frac{\pi}{4} \times 0.15^2 \times 1.5 \text{ m}^3$$

$$= \mathbf{26.50721} \quad \text{... Ans.}$$

$$\therefore \quad \text{Number of strokes required} = \frac{26.50721}{1.473} = \mathbf{180} \quad \text{... Ans.}$$

and, Power of the motor $= \dfrac{200 \times 9.81 \times 1.5}{1000 \times 1.5 \times 60}$ kW

$$= \mathbf{0.327 \text{ kW}} \quad \text{... Ans.}$$

Example 2.21: *An accumulator having a cylinder diameter of 25 cms is connected to a pipe line. If the accumulator is loaded with 50 tons and its lift is 5 m in 200 seconds, calculate the power developed to the pipe line. The (what is connected?) connected to the pipe line supplying water to the accumulator has a discharge of 800 l.p.m. The loss due to packing friction is 5% during the descent of the plunger.*

Solution:

$$\text{Pressure of water during descent} = \frac{\text{Effective load}}{\text{Area of plunger}}$$

$$p = \frac{50 \times 1000 \times 0.95 \times 9.81}{\pi/4 \times (0.25)^2} \text{ Pa}$$

$$= 9492.76 \text{ kPa}$$

$$\text{Pressure head} = \frac{p}{eg} \text{ m}$$

$$= 967.66 \text{ m}$$

Hence, work done by the accumulator due to pump work

$$= \dot{m} \times g \times \text{head N-m}$$

$$= \frac{800 \times 9.81}{60} \times 967.66 \text{ Watts}$$

$$= 12650 \text{ watts}$$

and, Work done by the accumulator during its discharge

$$= \frac{50 \times 10^3 \times 9.81 \times 0.95 \times 5}{200} \text{ N-m/s}$$

$$= 11637.5 \text{ watts}$$

∴ Total work added to the pipe line = Work supplied by the accumulator
+ Work supplied by the pump

$$= 138207.67 \text{ W}$$

Therefore, power delivered to the pipe line = **138.208 kW** ...Ans.

Example 2.22: *An accumulator has a ram diameter of 0.3 m and lift 6 m. It is loaded with 800 kN of total weight. The packing friction is 5 % of the load on the ram. Find the power delivered to the main if the ram descends steadily through its full stroke in 3 minutes while the pump delivers 30 l/s through the accumulator.*

Solution: Pressure of the accumulator $= \dfrac{\text{Net Load}}{\text{Area}}$

$$= \frac{800 \times 0.95}{\pi/4 \times 0.3} \text{ kN/m}^2$$

$$p = 10751.8 \text{ kPa}$$

∴ Pressure of water supplied by accumulator

$$= \frac{p}{\varrho g}$$

$$h = \frac{10751.8 \times 10^3}{10^3 \times 9.81} = 1096 \text{ m of water}$$

∴ Work supplied by accumulator $= \dot{m} \times g \times h$
$= 30 \times 9.81 \times 1096 \text{ W}$
$= 322554 \text{ W}$

Also, work supplied due to discharging of the accumulator

$$= \frac{\text{Net load} \times \text{Stroke length}}{\text{Time of descent}} \text{ W}$$

$$= \frac{800 \times 0.95 \times 10^3 \times 6}{180} \text{ W}$$

$$= 25333.33 \text{ W}$$

∴ Total power delivered to the main = 322554 + 25333.33 = 347887.35 W
= **347.887 kW**

HYDRAULICS AND PNEUMATICS   PUMPS

Example 2.23: *A hydraulic press has a ram of 15 cm diameter. It is served from an intensifier. The intensifier receives supply water under a head of 30 m through a pipe of 8 cm diameter and 150 m long. The coefficient of pipe friction is 0.005. The press exerts a force of 30 tons. The intensifier ram and plunger diameters are 10 cm and 100 cm respectively. The packing friction amounts to 2% of the pressure on the ram and the plunger. Calculate the velocity of the press ram.*

Solution:

$$\text{The ram pressure} = \frac{\text{Net force}}{0.98 \times \pi/4 \times 0.15^2}$$

$$= \frac{30 \times 10^3 \times 9.81}{0.98 \times \pi/4 \times 0.15^2}$$

$$= 169.938 \text{ bar}$$

This is also the pressure on the intensifier ram.

∴ Pressure on the piston side of intensifier

$$= 169.938 \times 0.98 \times 0.98 \times \left(\frac{d}{D}\right)^2$$

$$= 169.938 \times (0.98)^2 \times \left(\frac{10}{100}\right)^2 \text{ bar}$$

$$= 1.6321 \text{ bar}$$

$$\text{Pressure at head intensifier} = \frac{1.632 \times 10^5}{10^3 \times 9.81} \text{ m of water} = 16.637 \text{ m}$$

∴ Head lost in pipe friction $= 30 - 16.637$ m

$$= 13.363 \text{ m of water}$$

∴ $$13.363 = \frac{4 \times 0.005 \times 150 \times v^2}{2 \times 9.81 \times 0.08}$$

∴ v = Velocity in supply pipe = 2.644 m/s

Now, Flow rate through pipe = Flow rate through press

$$\frac{\pi}{4} \times (0.08)^2 v = \frac{\pi}{4} \times \left(\frac{100}{100}\right)^2 \times v'$$

∴ $$v' = v \left(\frac{8}{100}\right)^2 \qquad \text{... (i)}$$

Also, $$v' \times \frac{\pi}{4} \times \left(\frac{10}{100}\right)^2 = v_p \times \frac{\pi}{4} \times \left(\frac{15}{100}\right)^2$$

Here, v_p = velocity of press ram

∴ $$v' = v_p \times \left(\frac{15}{100}\right)^2 \qquad \text{... (ii)}$$

Equations (i) and (ii)

$$v\left(\frac{8}{100}\right)^2 = v_p \times \left(\frac{15}{100}\right)^2$$

$$\therefore \quad v_p = 2.644 \times \frac{64}{10^4} \times \frac{100}{225}$$

$$= 0.00752 \text{ m/s} = \textbf{7.52 cm/s} \quad \text{... Ans.}$$

Example 2.24: Calculate the accumulator volume of a bladder type accumulator having a gas ratio of 3: 1 at fully charged condition. The index of polytropic expansion is 1.25. The system demand volume is 6 litre. The permissible pressure drop is 5% (x = 0.05).

Solution:

$$\left(\frac{V_{HP}}{V_{HP} + 6}\right) = (1 - 0.05)^{1/1.25} = 0.96$$

$$\therefore \quad V_{HP} = 0.96 (V_{HP} + 6) = 144 \text{ litres}$$

$$\therefore \quad V_{Acc} = 144 + \frac{144}{3} = \textbf{192 litres} \quad \text{... Ans.}$$

Example 2.25: An accumulator has a ram 0.3 m and 6 m lift and is loaded with 800 kN total load. If the packing friction is equivalent to 5 percent of the load on the ram, determine the power being delivered to the machine, if the ram falls steadily through its full range in 90 seconds and if at the same time the pumps are delivering 30 litres per second through the accumulator. **(May 2009)**

Solution:

$$\text{Pressure of the accumulator} = \frac{\text{Net load}}{\text{Area}} = \frac{800 \times 0.95}{\pi/4 \times (0.3)^2}$$

$$P = \textbf{10751.8 kPa} \quad \text{... Ans.}$$

∴ Pressure of water supplied by accumulator

$$= \frac{P}{\rho \cdot g} = \frac{10751.8}{10^3 \times 9.81}$$

$$h = \textbf{1096 m of water} \quad \text{... Ans.}$$

∴ Work supplied by accumulator

$$= \dot{m} \, gh = 30 \times 9.81 \times 1096$$

$$= \textbf{322554 W} \quad \text{... Ans.}$$

Also, work supplied due to discharging of the accumulator

$$= \frac{\text{Net load} \times \text{Stroke length}}{\text{Time of descent}}$$

$$= \frac{800 \times 0.95 \times 10^3 \times 6}{180}$$

$$= \textbf{25333.33 N} \quad \text{... Ans.}$$

∴ Total power delivered to the main
$$= 322554 + 25333.33$$
$$= 347887.35 \text{ W} = \mathbf{347.887 \text{ kW}} \quad \ldots \text{Ans.}$$

Example 2.26: *A gas charged accumulator supplies energy to a system with 6.7 litres of oil within the pressure range of 150 bar to 110 bar. The accumulator has the pre-charge pressure of 85 bar. What should be the size of the accumulator, if the oil is to be supplied (i) in about 5 seconds and (ii) in about 5 minutes time?* **(Dec. 2007)**

Solution: Precharge pressure = P_1 = 85 bar

Corresponding volume of the accumulator = V_1 when it contains only gas.

Maximum pressure = P_3 = 150 bar, at this pressure accumulator contains maximum oil of 6.7 litres and remaining volume (i.e. balance) is gas.

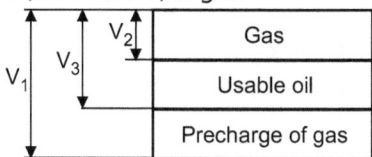

Fig. 2.66

The balance volume of gas = $V_3 = (V_1 - 6.7)$

Considering adiabatic condition with $\gamma = 1.25$

(i) In about 5 seconds:

$$P_1 V_1^\gamma = P_2 V_2^\gamma$$

$$85 (V_1)^\gamma = 150 \times \left(V_1 - \frac{6.7}{5}\right)^\gamma$$

∴ $$85 (V_1)^{1.25} = 150 \times (V_1 - 1.34)^{1.25}$$

∴ $$\frac{85}{150} = \left(\frac{V_1 - 1.34}{V_1}\right)^{1.25}$$

∴ $$\frac{V_1 - 1.34}{V_1} = \left(\frac{85}{150}\right)^{1/1.25}$$

∴ $$V_1 - 1.34 = 0.4917 \times V_1$$

∴ $$0.508\, V_1 = 1.34$$

∴ $$V_1 = 3.144 \text{ lit/sec}$$

Capacity of accumulator = **15.72 litres**

(ii) In about 5 minutes:

Similarly for 300 sec

Capacity of accumulator = **943.2 litres**

HYDRAULICS AND PNEUMATICS — PUMPS

Example 2.27: *The circuit has been designed to crush a car body into bale size using a 152 mm diameter hydraulic cylinder. The hydraulic cylinder is to extend 2.54 m during a period of 10 s. The time between crushing strokes is 5 min. The following accumulator gas absolute pressures are given:*

P_1 = Gas precharge pressure 84 bar (abs)

P_2 = Gas charge pressure when pump is turned on 210 bar (abs) = Pressure relief valve setting

P_3 = Minimum pressure required to actuate load 126 bar (abs)

Calculate: (i) The required size of the accumulator.

(ii) What are the pump hydraulic kW power and the flow requirements with and without accumulator?

(Dec. 2008)

Solution: Given data: P_1 = 84 bar d = 152 mm

P_2 = 210 bar l = 2.54 m

P_3 = 126 bar

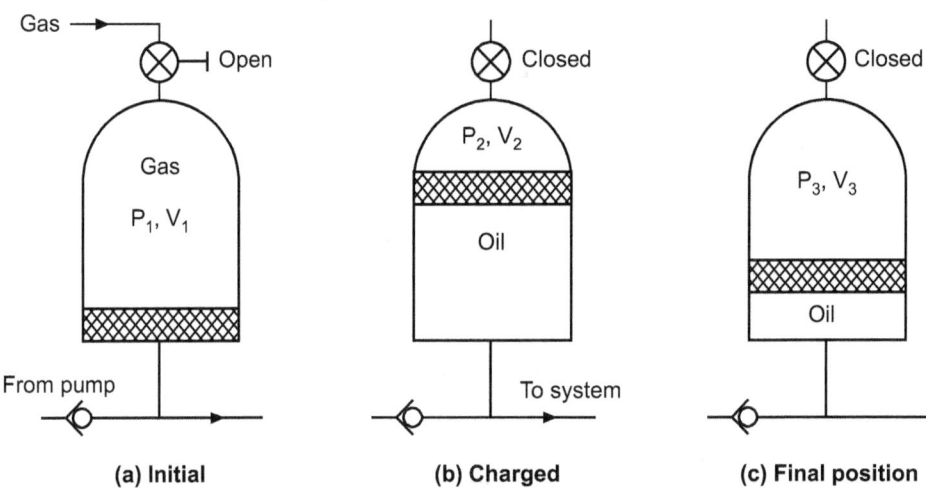

Fig. 2.67

Considering isothermal compression of gas,

$$P_1 V_1 = P_2 V_2 = P_3 V_3$$

where V_1 = Required accumulator size

and $V_{\text{hyd. cylinder}} = V_3 - V_2$

We have, $P_3 V_3 = P_2 V_2$

$\therefore \quad V_3 = \dfrac{P_2 V_2}{P_3} = \dfrac{210 \times V_2}{126} = 1.67 \, V_2$ ... (i)

Now, $V_{\text{hyd. cylinder}} = \frac{\pi}{4} d^2 l = \frac{\pi}{4}(0.152)^2 \times 2.54$

$$= 0.0461 \text{ m}^3 = V_3 - V_2 \qquad \ldots \text{(ii)}$$

Solving equations (i) and (ii), we get,

$$V_2 = 0.0688 \text{ m}^3$$

and $V_3 = 0.155 \text{ m}^3$

$\therefore \qquad V_1 = \frac{P_2 V_2}{P_1} = \frac{210 \times 0.0688}{84} = 0.172 \text{ m}^3$

$$= \mathbf{172 \text{ litres}} \qquad \ldots \textbf{Ans.}$$

With accumulator: Pump charges accumulator twice in 5 minutes. Neglecting the diameter of the rod of the hydraulic cylinder,

Flow rate of pump,

$$Q_{\text{pump}} = \frac{2(V_3 - V_2)}{30}$$

$$Q_{\text{pump}} = \frac{2(46.1)}{300} = \mathbf{0.307 \text{ litres/sec}} \qquad \ldots \textbf{Ans.}$$

Power of pump,

$$kW_{\text{pump}} = P_2 \times Q_{\text{pump}}$$

$$= \frac{(210 \times 10^5)(0.307 \times 10^{-3})}{1000}$$

$$= \mathbf{6.45 \text{ kW}} \qquad \ldots \textbf{Ans.}$$

Without accumulator: Pump extends cylinder in 10 sec.

Flow rate of pump, $Q_{\text{pump}} = \frac{46.1}{10} = \mathbf{4.61 \text{ litres/sec}} \qquad \ldots \textbf{Ans.}$

Power of pump,

$$kW_{\text{pump}} = \frac{(126 \times 10^5)(461 \times 10^{-5})}{1000}$$

$$= \mathbf{58.1 \text{ kW}} \qquad \ldots \textbf{Ans.}$$

Thus, power and flow requirement by pump is more without accumulator.

Example 2.28: *What size of accumulator is necessary to supply 10000 cm^3 of fluid in a hydraulic system of maximum pressure of 200 bar to 100 bar minimum. Assuming N_2 gas pre-charged pressure of 80 bar. Find adiabatic and isothermal solution.* **(May 2010)**

Solution: V_1 = Volume of accumulator, cm^3

V_2 = Volume of gas at high pressure, cm³
P_2 = Maximum pressure, bar
P = Minimum pressure, bar
P_1 = Pre-charged pressure, bar

$V_1 = ?$, $V_2 = ?$, $P_1 = 80$ bar, $P_2 = 200$ bar, $P = 100$ bar

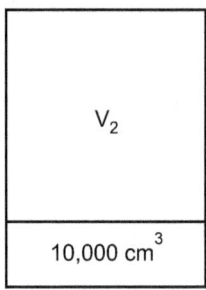

Fig. 2.68

Let V_1 be the volume of gas occupied in the accumulator at pre-charged 80 bar pressure.

Let V_2 be the volume of gas occupied in the accumulator at 200 bar and that time 10,000 cm³ of oil has also occupied in the accumulator.

$$V_1 = V_2 + 10000 \text{ cm}^3$$
$$V_2 = V_1 - 10000$$

(a) Adiabatic process: $P_1 V_1^\gamma = P_2 V_2^\gamma$

$$\gamma = 1.25$$

$$80 \times V_1^\gamma = 200 \times (V_1 - 10000)^\gamma$$

$$\frac{80}{200} = \left(\frac{V_1 - 10000}{V_1}\right)^\gamma$$

$$0.4 = \left(\frac{V_1 - 10000}{V_1}\right)^{1.25}$$

$$\frac{V_1 - 10000}{V_1} = (0.4)^{\frac{1}{1.25}}$$

$$\frac{V_1 - 10000}{V_1} = (0.4)^{0.8}$$

$$\frac{V_1 - 10000}{V_1} = 0.4804$$

$$V_1 - 10000 = 0.4804\, V_1$$
$$V_1 - 0.4804\, V_1 = 10000$$
$$0.5195\, V_1 = 10000$$
$$V_1 = 19249.27 \text{ cm}^3$$

Size of accumulator = 19249.27 cm³

(b) Isothermal process:

$$P_1 V_1 = P_2 V_2$$
$$80 \times V_1 = 200 \times (V_1 - 10000)$$
$$\frac{80}{200} = \frac{V_1 - 10000}{V_1}$$
$$0.4 = \frac{V_1 - 10000}{V_1}$$
$$V_1 - 10000 = 0.4\, V_1$$
$$V_1 - 0.4\, V_1 = 10000$$
$$0.6\, V_1 = 10000$$
$$V_1 = 16666.66 \text{ cm}^3$$

Size of accumulator = 16666.66 cm³

EXERCISE

1. List out various methods of varying swash plate angle in case of axial pumps. Explain any one method with a neat sketch. **(Dec. 02, May 01)**
2. What are the different causes of pump failures in a hydraulic system? **(May 01)**
3. Differentiate between: (a) External gear pump Vs Internal gear pump. **(May 01)**
   (b) Positive Vs Non-positive displacement pump. **(May 01, Dec. 01)**
4. Draw neat sketches of the following and explain their construction and working.
   (a) Radial plunger pump.
   (b) Axial plunger pump. **(Dec. 01)**
5. Draw the pressure versus efficiency characteristics of a gear pump at two different viscosity valves. **(Dec. 01)**
6. Classify the pumps used in hydraulic system. **(May 02, Dec. 04)**
7. Sketch and explain construction, working and performance of parallel piston pump. **(May 02)**
8. Compare fixed displacement and variable displacement pumps. **(May 02, Dec. 04)**

9. Sketch and explain difference between balanced and unbalanced vane pump. **(Dec. 02)**
10. Define various efficiencies of positive displacement pumps. **(Dec. 02)**
11. What do you mean by variable displacement pump? **(May 04)**
12. What are the advantages of gear pump? **(May 04)**
13. Comment on the relative comparison in performance among gear, vane and piston pump. **(May 04)**
14. What are the functions of reservoirs? Draw a neat sketch of standard reservoir showing its internal, external features. **(May 01)**
15. Write short notes on: (i) Heat exchanger in hydraulic system. **(Dec. 02, 03)**
    (ii) Hydraulic reservoir.
16. What is the function of the breather assembly in the hydraulic reservoir. **(May 04)**
17. Explain the following terms in relation with filter
    (a) Beta rating, (b) Absolute rating. **(May 01)**
18. Differentiate between (a) Strainers and filters, (b) full flow filters and bypass filters. **(May 02, Dec. 03)**
19. Explain what is the rating of filters? Why should they be rated? **(May 02, Dec. 03)**
20. State the types and sources of contaminants in hydraulic systems. **(Dec. 03, 02)**
21. What is a 'bypass filter'? State its advantages and disadvantages. **(Dec. 02)**
22. What do you mean by B20 = 50? Find beta efficiency. **(May 03)**
23. Write a short note on: Contamination in hydraulic system. **(May 03)**
24. Explain following terms in relation with filter (i) Beta rating, (ii) full flow filter. **(May 04)**
25. With a neat sketch explain the working of pressure intensifier and list applications. **(May 02)**
26. Write short notes on:
    (i) Gas charged accumulator. **(May 02, Dec. 02)**
    (ii) Applications of accumulator in hydraulic circuit. **(Dec. 03)**
    (iii) Applications of accumulator and intensifier. **(Dec. 04)**
27. Explain the applications of accumulator as:
    (a) A power saving device
    (b) A hydraulic shack absorber device.
    (c) A leakage compensator. **(Dec. 03, 04)**

28. Enumerate the different types of accumulators and explain any one of the accumulator. **(May 04)**

29. An axial piston pump consists of nine pistons each of diameter 12.7 mm and stroke 19.5 mm. It runs at 2000 r.p.m. Determine the theoretical flow rate in litre/min.

30. A vane pump has a volumetric displacement of 114.71 cc. It has a rotor diameter of 6.35 cm, a cam ring diameter of 8.89 cm and a vane width of 5.08 cm. Calculate the eccentricity. **(Ans. 9.42 mm)**

31. Estimate the offset angle for an axial piston pump delivering 135 litre/min. at 3000 r.p.m. The pump has nine pistons each of diameter 15.875 mm placed on a pitch circle diameter of 12.7 cm.

32. An axial piston pump has an offset angle of 9.5°. It has nine pistons each of 15.9 mm diameter placed on a pitch circle diameter of 127 mm. Calculate the theoretical flow rate of this pump running at 3000 r.p.m. **(Ans. 1.9 litre/s)**

33. Estimate the theoretical volumetric displacement of a pump per revolution having a volumetric efficiency of 96%. The pump delivers 29 l.p.m. of oil while running at 1000 r.p.m.

34. Calculate the volumetric efficiency of a positive displacement pump having mechanical efficiency of 95.65% and an overall efficiency of 88%. **(Ans. 92%)**

35. A gear pump has 82.55 mm outer diameter, 57.15 mm inside diameter and 25.4 mm width. It runs at 1800 r.p.m. If its volumetric efficiency is 86.1%, determine the actual flow rate of the pump. **(Ans. 1.83 litre/s)**

36. A pump has an overall efficiency of 88%, and a volumetric efficiency of 92%. It consumes 8 kW power. Calculate: (i) mechanical efficiency, (ii) frictional power.

    (Ans. $\eta_{mech.}$ = 96%, frictional power = 0.96 kW)

37. A pump delivers 40 l.p.m. of oil at a pressure of 10 MPa. It has an overall efficiency of 90%. Calculate the power required to operate the pump. **(Ans. 7.41 kW)**

38. A pump has a theoretical displacement of 98.34 cc/rev. It delivers 1.5144 litres/s at 1000 r.p.m. and 68.94 bar. If the torque input of prime mover is 124.3 N-m, find: (a) overall efficiency of pump, (b) theoretical torque required to operate the pump.

    (Ans. (a) η_o = 80.2% (b) theoretical torque = 108.3 N-m)

39. A pump delivers 1.0 litre/s of oil when operating at 140 bar. What is its hydraulic power? Also find power-rating of an electric motor to drive this pump if its overall efficiency is 85%. **(Ans. hydraulic power = 14 kW, Motor-rating = 16.47 kW)**

40. A pump having theoretical displacement volume of 24.585 cc/rev., discharges 0.631 litre/s at a pressure of 137.88 bar. If it has overall efficiency of 90% determine the: (i) capacity of prime mover, (ii) speed. **(Ans. (i) 9.667 kW, (ii) 1540 r.p.m.)**

41. What size of accumulator is necessary to supply 4917 cm³ of fluid in a hydraulic system of maximum operating pressure of 207 bar, which drops to minimum 103.5 bar? Assuming nitrogen gas pre-charge of accumulator is 67 bar, obtain both isothermal and adiabatic solutions.

42. An accumulator has a ram of 20 cm diameter and 6 cm lift. The packing friction amounts to 3 % of the load on the ram. The accumulator discharges fully in 2 minutes. The accumulator is loaded with a total load of 60 tonnes. If the pump discharges 0.02 m³/s through an accumulator, when the ram is falling, find the power delivered. **(Ans. 392.5 kW)**

43. What size of accumulator is necessary to supply 5000 cc of a fluid in a hydraulic system of maximum operating pressure of 200 bar which drops to 100 bar minimum? Assume nitrogen gas pre-charge of 66 bar. Find adiabatic and isothermal solution. **(Ans. V_{isoth} = 15151 cc, V_{adia} = 16250 cc)**

Unit III

HYDRAULIC ACTUATORS

3.1 INTRODUCTION

Pumps add energy to hydraulic fluid for transmission to the point of application. Pumps receive mechanical power input from the prime mover and impart hydraulic energy to fluid. The actuators perform just the opposite role. They convert the hydraulic energy of the fluid into mechanical power to serve the application.

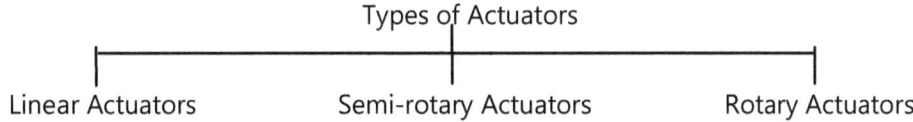

Detail Classification of Hydraulic Actuators:

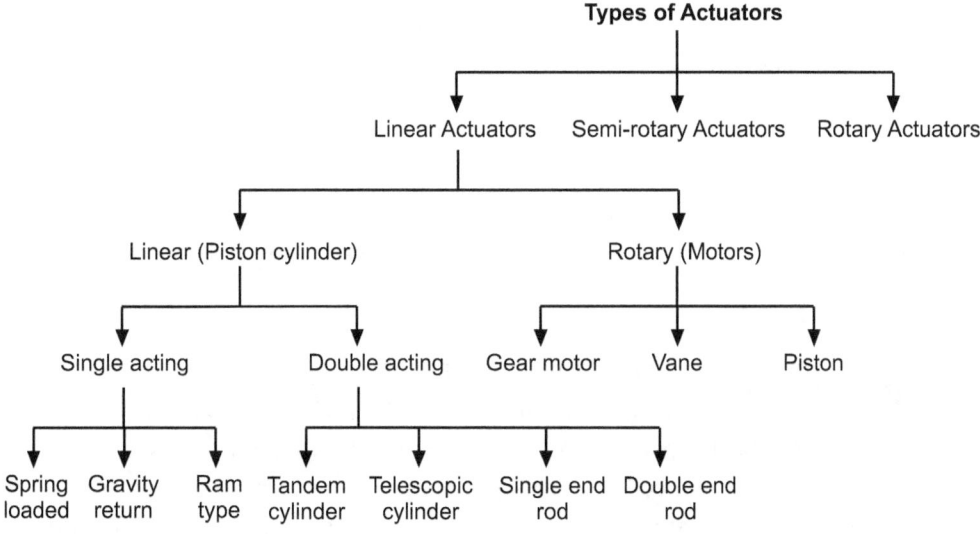

- **Linear Actuators:** These are essentially cylinder-piston systems which extend and retract during the operating cycle.
- **Semi-Rotary Actuators:** These actuators are also known as **limited rotation motors** or oscillation fluid motors. These actuators produce limited rotation or oscillatory motion.

- **Rotary Actuators:** These are also known as hydraulic motors. These actuators can be of fixed or variable displacement.

Hydrostatic transmission systems have a pump driving a motor. The hydrostatic transmission has several advantages, like stepless variation of speed, in-built overload protection, bi-directional rotation, dynamic braking and high power-to-weight ratio. These systems are extensively used in material handling equipment, agricultural equipment, earth moving machinery, machine tools, automobiles, loco-traction etc.

3.2 Rotary Actuators (Hydraulic Motors)

These actuators provide rotational motion. Rotary actuators are commonly addressed as hydraulic motors. The hydraulic motor converts hydraulic energy of the oil into rotary mechanical energy, to drive the load.

The construction of hydraulic motors is more or less similar to hydraulic pumps. In a pump, the pump element pushes the oil thereby imparting hydraulic energy whereas in a hydraulic motor, the hydraulic energy of the oil causes the element to rotate.

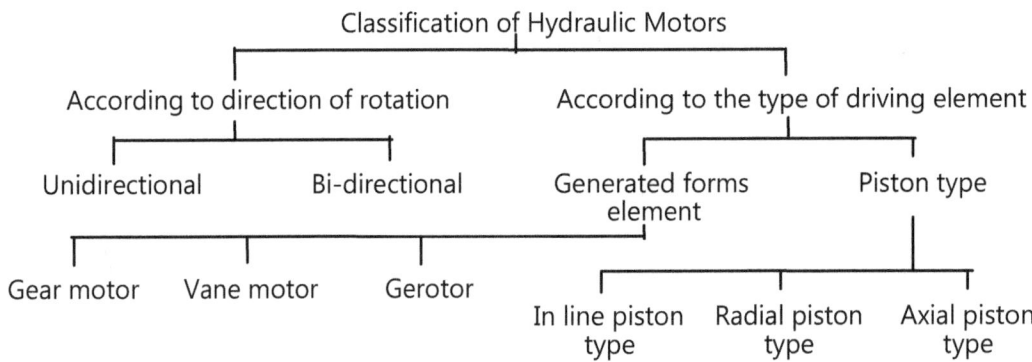

3.3 Vane Motors

Vane motors have identical construction to that of balanced vane pumps except that in vane motors, vanes are loaded by a coil or a leaf spring. In a vane motor, the imbalance is caused by the difference in the vane area exposed to hydraulic oil pressure, owing to the eccentricity between the rotor and the housing. The unequal area of the vanes exposed to oil pressure, develops a torque about the motor shaft. The output torque produced varies directly with oil pressure and vane area.

The high pressure on the inlet side and low pressure on the discharge side of a motor generates side thrust. To eliminate side thrust, the inner contour of the ring is made cam shaped instead of circular. This establishes a pressure balance.

The vane motors develop torques upto 1600 N-m with speeds above 100 r.p.m. A vane motor is a positive displacement unit. Fig. 3.1 shows a simple vane motor.

The rotational unit of a vane motor, known as cartridge assembly, consists of vanes, rotor and cam ring placed between two port plates. The cartridge is easy for servicing and replacement. For torque augmentation, a cartridge with the same outer diameter with larger exposed area of the vane can be substituted in place of the original.

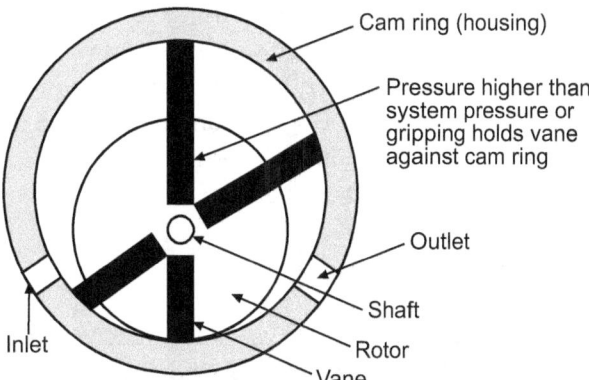

Fig. 3.1: Simple vane type motor

In vane motors, unlike in a vane pump, centrifugal force is not used for the radial travel of vanes and for seating between the cam ring and vane tip.

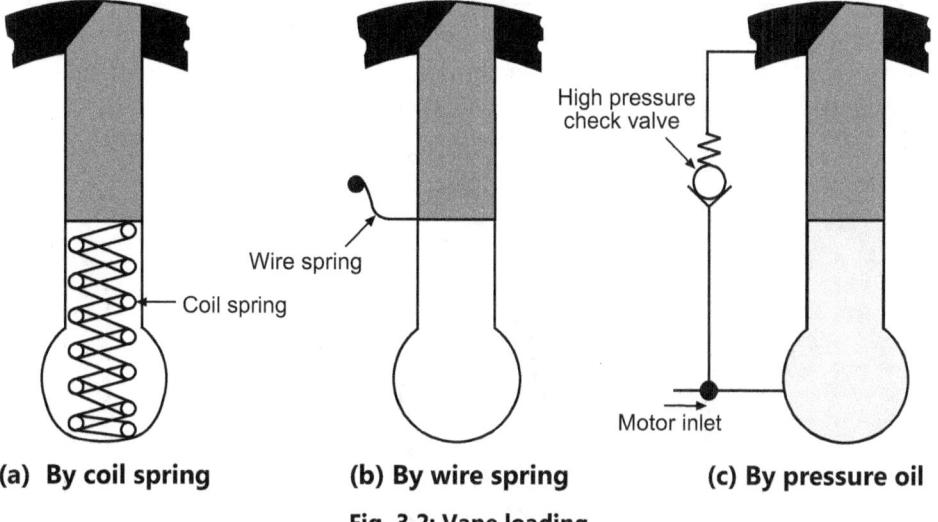

(a) By coil spring   **(b) By wire spring**   **(c) By pressure oil**

Fig. 3.2: Vane loading

For extending vanes, the common methods used are (a) spring loading of vanes and (b) applying hydraulic pressure from the underside of the vanes (Refer Fig. 3.2). Spring loading can be of coil spring type or of a small wire spring. The wire spring is attached to a post and moves with the vane as it travels in and out of the slot.

In case of vanes loaded with hydraulic oil pressure, the fluid is allowed to enter the vane chamber only after the vane is fully extended and a positive seal is ensured.

A balanced vane motor is shown in Fig. 3.3. In this motor, rotor housing vane is concentrically placed allowing two inlet and two outlet ports opposite to each other to be created. This arrangement provides a hydraulic balance and eliminates side thrust on the rotor.

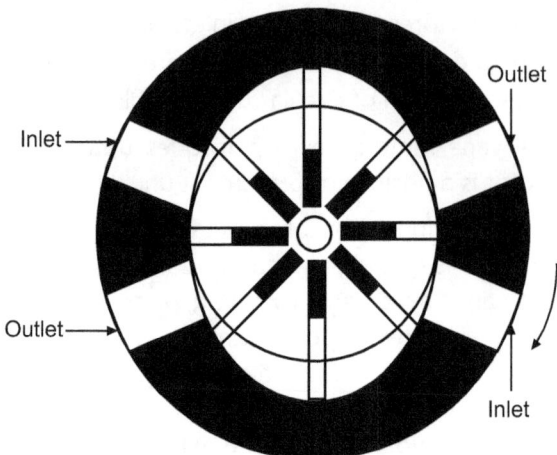

Fig. 3.3: Balanced vane motor

As the fluid chambers are of fixed capacity, the output of these motors cannot be varied contrary to the eccentrically placed rotor, permitting variable chamber size by change of eccentricity.

3.4 Gear Motors

Gear motors have generally of fixed displacement motors. The construction of gear motors is similar to that of gear pumps. The gear motor includes pressure loaded side plates for control of internal leakage and to achieve good volumetric efficiency.

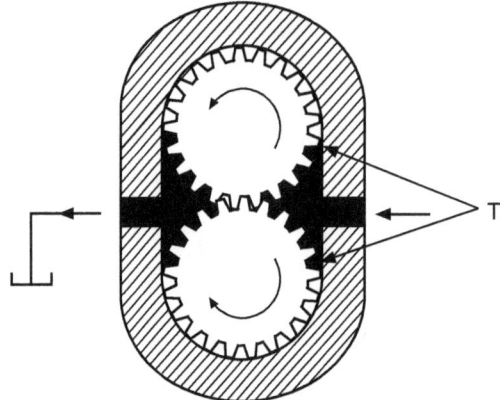

Fig. 3.4: Generated form of hydraulic motor

Fig. 3.4 illustrates a gear motor. The torque developed is a function of the force exerted by oil pressure on one tooth. The fluctuation of torque generated can be smoothened out by using a large number of teeth. The volumetric displacement however decreases with increase in the number of teeth, with low output power for a given size.

For gear motors, minimum recommended speed lies between 400 r.p.m. and 1000 r.p.m. Lower speeds can be obtained by coupling a gear motor through a reduction gear. External gear motors can be uni-directional or bi-directional. Uni-directional gear motor should not be reversed as it may damage shaft seals and internal seals.

Gear motors are preferred for high speed applications upto 4000 r.p.m., and low torque requirement. Their output power is limited to about 10 kW.

Internal Gear Motors:

These motors consist of an internal gear and an external gear.

The Gerotor type internal gear motor gives an output torque with low pulsations. These motors are suitable for slow speed.

A typical 'orbit' motor is shown in Fig. 3.5. It consists of an outer fixed ring and the rotor orbits within the fixed ring. The gerotor motor gives high torque output with low speed than a conventional gear motor. The smooth speed range spans 10-2000 r.p.m. and torques upto 300 N-m. The gerotor motors with internal reduction gear box are available, operating below 1 r.p.m. with torque beyond 4 kN-m.

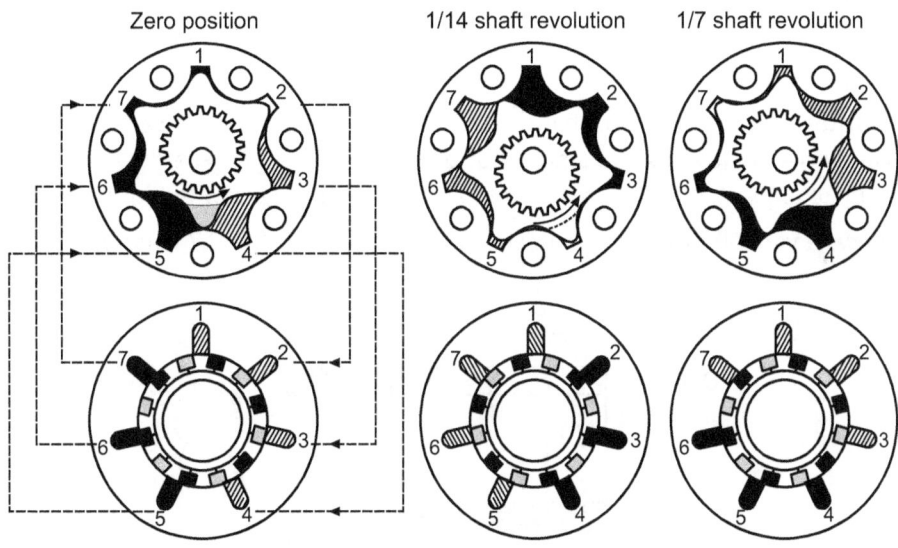

Fig. 3.5: Orbit motor

The speed of all gear motors can be controlled only by regulating the fluid flow rate supplied to the motor.

3.5 PISTON MOTORS

These motors are positive displacement type. The output torque is produced by application of oil pressure on the pistons. Axial piston motors and radial piston motors are widely used for distinct applications like.

Axial piston motors - For medium to high pressure and moderate power range

Radial piston motors - For high pressures and high power.

3.5.1 Axial Piston Motors (May 12)

These are similar to the axial piston pump-shown in Unit 2. Units which can work like a pump or a motor are available. However, units with seated valves cannot have reversal of their function.

The fluid pressure forces the piston outwards and a reaction force is set up against the fixed swash plate which produces a tangential force causing the piston block and output shaft to rotate. After the piston reaches its extreme outward stroke, the flow path is connected to the outlet part by the kidney port plate. The fluid is now forced out of the cylinder as the piston returns, driven by the swash plate reaction.

Axial piston motors with bent axis design are similar to the bent axis piston pump shown in Unit 2. The alignment between the output shaft and the cylinder block is maintained by a universal joint.

The change of direction of rotation of the cylinder block and output shaft is possible by change of direction of flow of oil.

The axial piston motors are available in both fixed and variable displacement mode. The swash plate angle 'θ' governs the amount of displacement and hence the flow rate. Greator the swash plate angle, higher is the flow rate and lower the speed with higher torque.

Fig. 3.6 shows a variable displacement axial piston motor and Fig. 3.7 illustrates the bent axis piston motor.

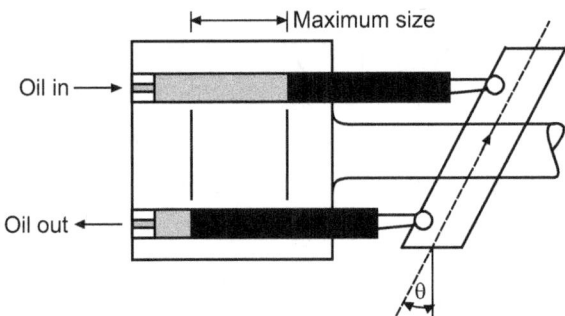

Fig. 3.6: Variable displacement axial piston motor

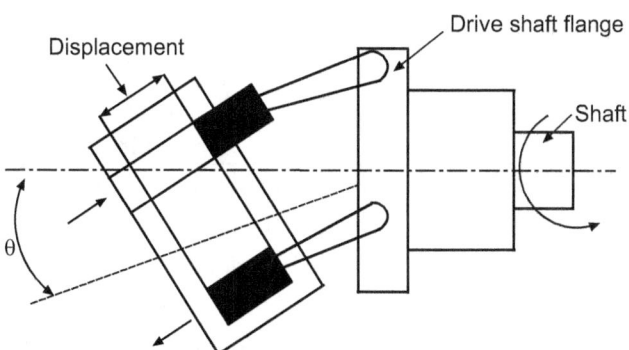

Fig. 3.7: Bent axis piston motor

3.5.2 Radial Piston Motors

These motors provide very high and uniform torque at low speeds. The radial piston motors have several design variations such as cam operated, multi-lobe cam operated etc.

Radial piston motors produce linear motion which is then converted into rotary motion through cams mounted on the output shaft. These motors have 5 - 10 cylinders with output torque upto 21.7 kN-m and speed upto 450 r.p.m.

Fig. 3.8 shows a radial piston multi-lobe cam motor. The motor shown in the figure is used as a wheel motor. The pistons are housed in a stationary cylinder housing and connected to rollers which bear on the cam ring. The rotary valve distributes oil from the inlet to each cylinder in sequence. As the oil pressure builds against the load resistance, it causes the pistons to be displaced outwards, forcing the rollers against the cam ring and outer casing of the motor rotates. At the end of the piston stroke, oil escapes through the outlet at low pressure. The torque developed by such motors is used to drive wheels of vehicles like tractors.

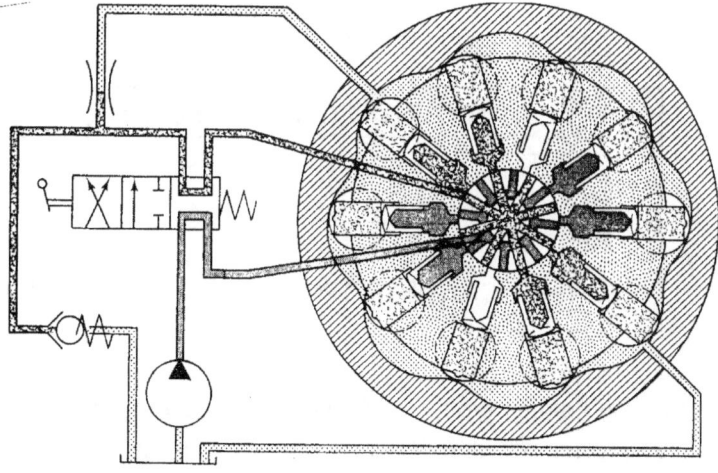

Fig. 3.8: Radial piston multi-lobe cam motor

Table 3.1: Summarizes characteristics of various rotary actuators (motors)

Motor type	Typical maximum operating pressure (bar)	Operating speech (rev/min)	Typical maximum torques (Nm)
Gear	200 to a maximum of 300	Minimum smooth speed 400 Maximum 6000	500 Nm
Vane	140 – 200	Minimum 100 Maximum 4000	100 – 16000
Gerotor	100 – 200	Minimum 10 Maximum 5000	2400 Nm
Cam rotor	175	Minimum 50 Maximum 4000	2500
Axial piston (swashplate) fixed displacement variable	400 400	Minimum 50 Maximum 4000 Minimum 50 Maximum 4000	2500 2500
Axial piston (bent axis) Fixed displacement variable	350 350	Minimum 50 Maximum 8500 Minimum 50 Maximum 8500	10 000 10 000
Radial piston	450	Minimum 1 or less Maximum 2000	150 000
Wheel motors	450	180 – 1500 (usually in the 200-400 range)	1000 - 32000

3.6 SEMI-ROTARY (OR LIMITED ROTATION) ACTUATORS

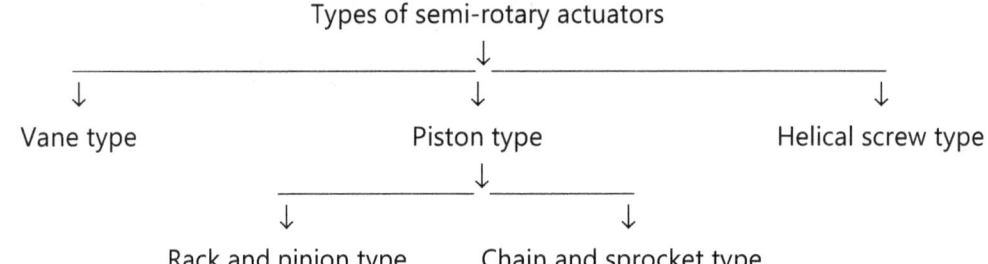

A semi-rotary or limited rotation hydraulic actuator provides rotary output motion only over a finite angle. These actuators generate high instantaneous torque in either direction and need small space and single mounting. Most of these actuators provide an angle of rotation limited to 360°.

3.6.1 Vane Type Semi-Rotary Actuators

It consists of one or two vanes mounted on the output shaft. The shaft rotates when hydraulic oil pressure is applied to one side of the vanes. Vanes rotate and are stopped by a stationary barrier attached to the housing.

A single vane type actuator produces limited rotation upto 320° and a double vane type upto 150°.

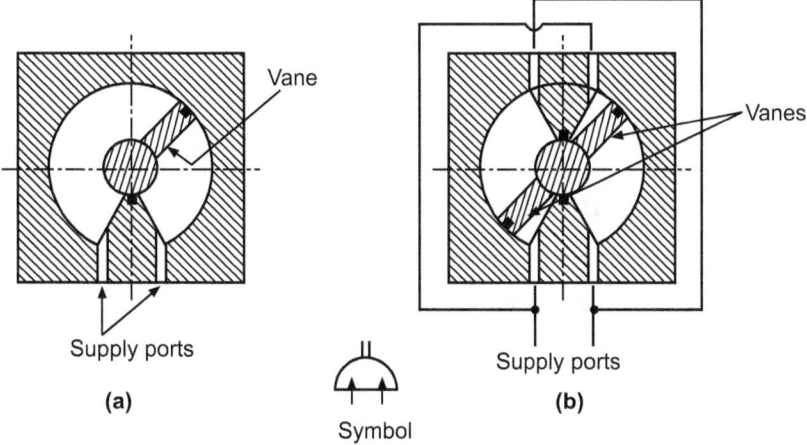

Fig. 3.9: Single (left) and double (right) vane semi-rotary actuators

Fig. 3.9 (a) and 3.9 (b) show a single vane type and double vane type semi-rotary actuator.

Some internal oil leakage always occurs past the vane. The leakage increases with increase of oil pressure and decrease in the viscosity of oil. Internal leakage affects smooth speed control of the actuator. The choice of hydraulic fluid and the operating pressure is to be made based on the manufacturer's guidelines. The maximum torque obtainable is about 40 kN-m from a single vane type and 80 kN-m from a double vane type actuator.

Analysis of a single vane semi-rotary actuators :

Let R_R = outer radius of rotor, m

R_v = outer radius of vane, m

L = width of vane, m

p = hydraulic pressure of oil, kPa

F = hydraulic force exerted on vane, kN

A = surface area of vane exposed to oil, m^2

T = Torque developed, kN-m

Now $\quad F = p \times A$ kN

$\quad = p \times (R_V - R_R)$ L kN

and Torque, $T = F \times$ Mean radius of vane

$\therefore \quad T = p \times (R_V - R_R) L \times \dfrac{(R_V + R_R)}{2}$ kN-m

$\quad = \dfrac{pL}{2} (R_V^2 - R_R^2)$ kN-m

Further volumetric displacement 'v_D' is given by

$\quad v_D = \pi (R_V^2 - R_R^2)$ L m³/rev.

hence Torque, $T = p \times V_D$ kN-m

$\quad = p \times \pi (R_V^2 - R_R^2) L$ kN-m

3.6.2 Piston Type Semi-Rotary Actuator

These actuators use piston cylinder arrangement to produce limited rotation.

Rack and pinion type semi-rotary actuator :

Fig. 3.10 shows a typical Rack and Pinion type semi-rotary actuator.

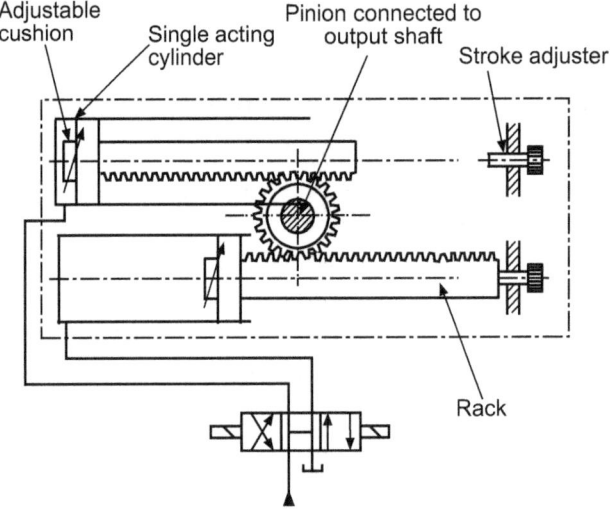

Fig. 3.10: Rack and pinion semi-rotary

In this actuator, a hydraulic piston-cylinder produces linear motion which is converted into a limited rotational motion by a rack and pinion. The angle of rotation is dependent upon the stroke of the piston and rack and the pitch circle diameter of the pinion. Internal stops are often provided for small precise adjustment of start and finish of the stroke. For controlled deceleration, cushions can also be incorporated.

This actuator can provide several rotations using double acting cylinder. This actuator can provide an output torque over 800 kN-m at a pressure of 210 bar.

3.6.3 Chain and Sprocket Actuator

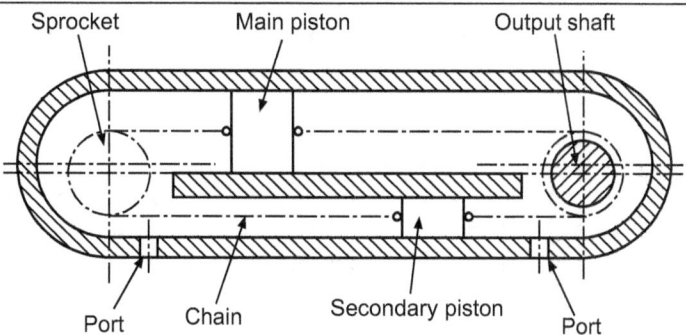

Fig. 3.11: Chain and sprocket actuator

This actuator consists of an endless chain and sprocket. It is suitable for applications requiring multi-revolutions. A typical chain and sprocket actuator is shown in Fig. 3.11. The chain is connected to two pistons of different diameters. These pistons in their respective bores separate the unit into two halves; pressure applied on one side of the pistons generates motion due to difference in area of two pistons.

3.6.4 Helical Screw Actuator

This actuator (Refer Fig. 3.12) consists of a cylinder housing a piston. The piston is constrained to have only linear travel, and not rotation, by the guide rods. The piston and the piston rod constrains a helical groove or spline and mesh together like a nut and screw. As the piston is actuated under the hydraulic thrust due to oil pressure, it causes the piston rod to rotate in one direction. The reversal of piston travel alters the direction of rotation of the rod. It has been found to be difficult to provide a hydraulic seal between the piston and the rod. As such, the arrangement is suitable for low pressure applications only. Angular rotation beyond 360° is also possible.

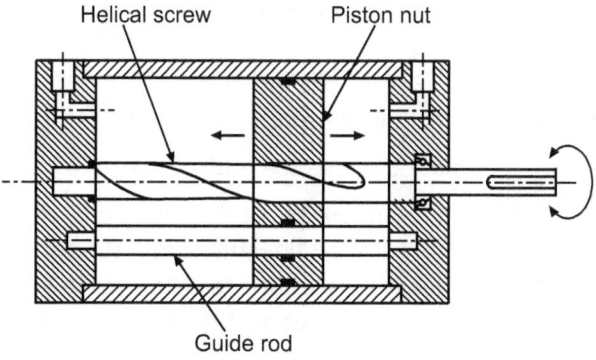

Fig. 3.12: Helical screw actuators

3.6.5 Control of Semi-Rotary Actuators

Semi-Rotary Actuators are widely used to move an element through a restricted angle e.g. operating large butterfly valves in a pipeline, for bending and forming tubes and bars.

The control of speed, torque and direction of rotation is possible by valves. The angular travel can be limited by using external or internal mechanical stops.

3.7 Deceleration Type Flow Control Valve

It is essentially a throttle valve. The throttle opening is controlled by a roller or roller lever. It can be NO or NC type valve. It controls flow rate to control acceleration or deceleration. A typical deceleration valve is shown in Fig. 3.13.

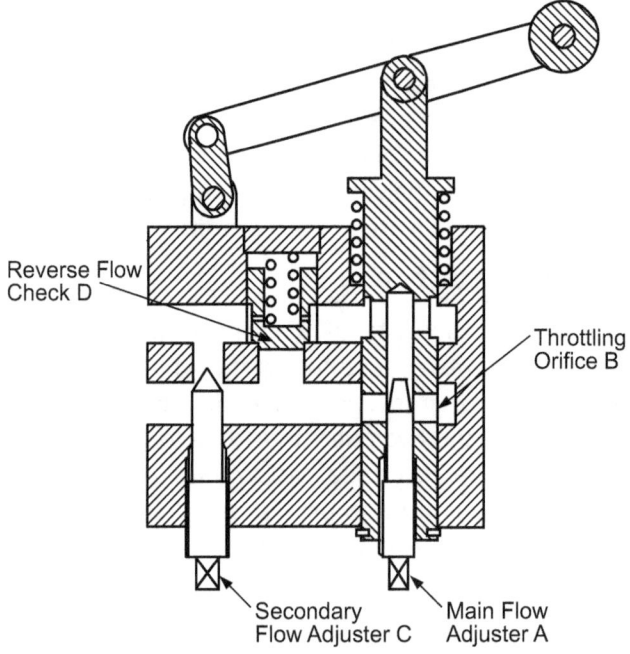

Fig. 3.13: Deceleration type flow control valve

A circuit using deceleration valve to control retardation of a piston is shown in Fig. 3.14.

This valve is used to retard a cylinder towards the end of its stroke.

During the earlier part of retardation, speed is mainly regulated by restrictor 'A' metering the outflow from the cylinder, permitting a small flow through restrictor 'C'. As the cam actuates the roller, the main spool 'B' gradually closes the main flow path. Restrictor 'C' controls the final part of the stroke. When the piston retracts, flow by-passes the deceleration valve through check valve 'D'.

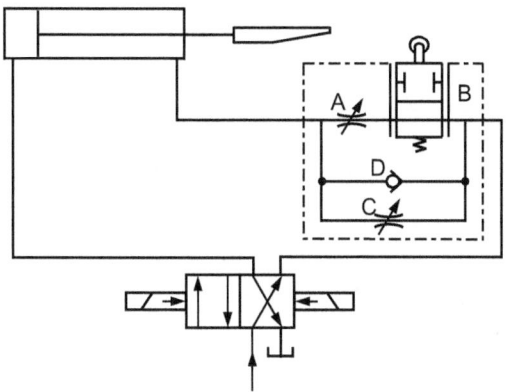

Fig. 3.14: Deceleration control of a piston

These valves are mostly recommended for high flow rate applications above 15 l.p.m.

3.8 LINEAR ACTUATORS (HYDRAULIC CYLINDERS) (May 12)

These actuators convert hydraulic energy into linear mechanical force and linear motion. The linear actuator usually consists of a piston and a piston rod, a plunger or a ram moving to and fro within a cylinder.

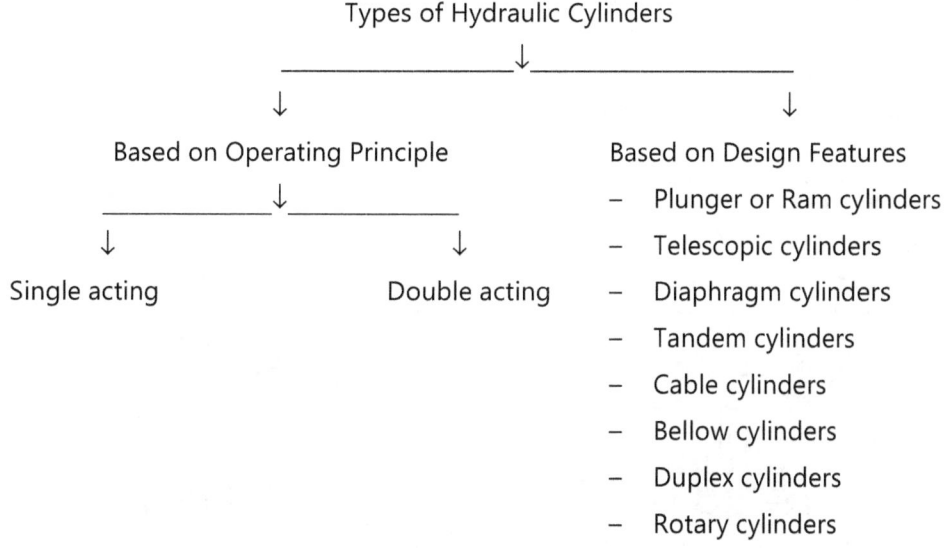

Single acting cylinder: In single acting cylinders (Refer Fig. 3.15), oil pressure acts on only one side of the piston during extension or retraction. When the oil pressure is cut off, the piston returns to its normal position by a spring or by an external load. The later type of cylinders are installed vertical to avail the force of gravity.

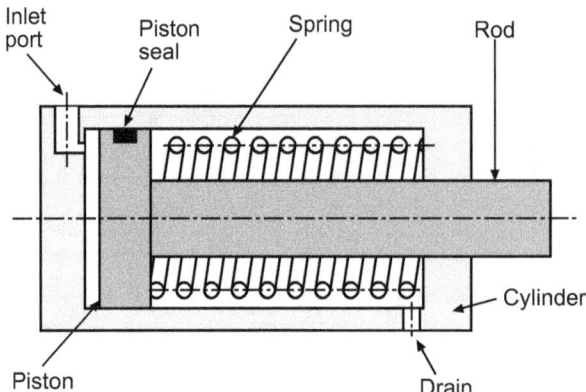

Fig. 3.15: Single acting spring return cylinder

In a spring return type cylinder, the spring may be inside or outside the cylinder. The spring index is dependent upon the load, operating speed etc. The actuators are suitable for small stroke lengths only.

Double Acting Cylinder: Double acting cylinders are operated by application of oil pressure on both sides of the piston. These actuators are extensively used for various applications.

Double acting cylinders (Fig. 3.16) can be single rod ended or double rod ended type. For a given oil supply pressure, a single rod ended cylinder exerts greater force during extension than during retraction. The double rod ended cylinder exerts equal forces in either directions.

Ram Cylinder: Ram cylinders have piston and piston-rod of equal diameter. These are usually mounted vertical to avail retraction by the external load and gravity e.g. lifting jack in an automobile service station.

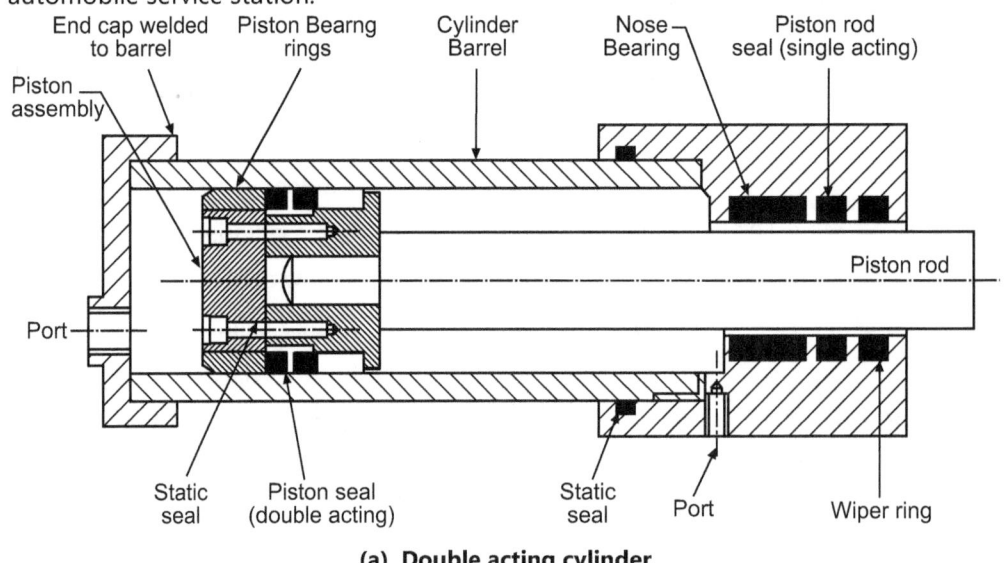

(a) Double acting cylinder

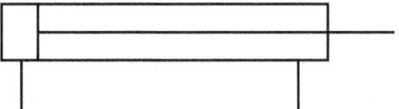

(b) Symbol of double acting cylinder

Fig. 3.16

Telescopic Cylinder (Dec. 11): These cylinders provide long forward stroke of cylinders in a short retracted envelope. It consists of multiple cylinders moving inside each other under the action of fluid pressure. This enables cylinders to provide a large working stroke as compared to a standard cylinder. A nesting of four to five cylinders can be made. The cylinder with the largest area gives the greatest force at a given pressure and moves out first, the next largest moves out at a slightly higher pressure and so on. Thus, the maximum load occurs when the cylinder is collapsed. As far as the design of this cylinder is concerned in the external position, the load is function of the cylinder of the smallest cylinder. It is schematically shown in Fig. 3.17. These are used in cranes, dumpers, fork lift trucks etc.

Fig. 3.17

Rodless Cylinder: This type of cylinder consists of installation space by eliminating the piston rod. In this type of construction, the piston is connected to the output load either by a lug protruding through a slot in a cylinder wall or magnetic force. The slotted arrangement saves the installation space by extending the piston through a slot in the sides of the cylinder, rather than using a piston rod that extends through the end of the cylinder. The mounting length is reduced from twice the stroke length to the actual cylinder dimensions just slightly more than the stroke length. The slot is sealed with a sparing steel strip, which is threaded through the piston assembly.

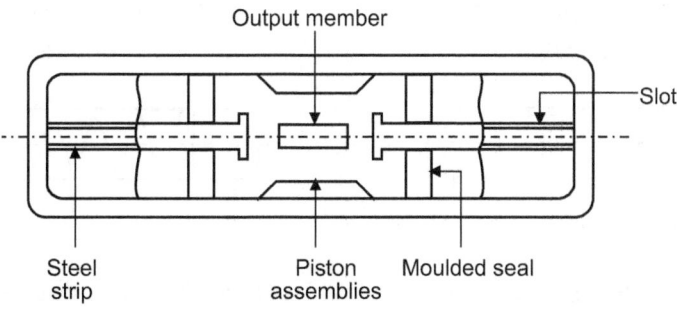

Fig. 3.18

The slotted arrangement in cylinders are used for pneumatic service and not for hydraulic. (Refer Fig. 3.18). In case of magnetic cylinders, there is no direct coupling done between the internal piston and external yoke. But they are coupled magnetically. When the piston is driven with a hydraulic pressure, the magnetic force transfers the working force from the piston to the yoke, moving the yoke along the cylinder tube. As no rod extends from these cylinders this arrangement demands less mounting space than conventional cylinders.

Diaphragm Cylinders: These are single acting, spring return type. The diaphragm may be of rolling type. They have very low break-out friction and almost no leakage past the piston. They are used in pneumatic applications.

Tandem Cylinders : In these cylinders, two cylinders are placed in line with pistons connected to a common piston rod for force multiplication in a compact space. They require more linear space. **(Dec. 11)**

Cable Cylinders: These are double acting type and are suitable for long strokes and medium forces. The load is connected to the cable running over pulleys at the ends of a tube barrel.

Bellow Cylinders: They use metallic bellows having a linear spring rate. The spring rate and the pressure decide the extension and contraction. These are used in servo-control systems.

Duplex Cylinders: These are used for multiple position operation.

The various cylinders are symbolically represented in Fig. 3.19 (a), (b), (c) and (d).

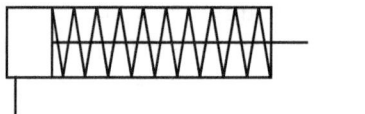

(a) Single acting spring return single rod ended

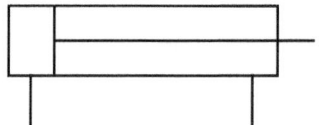

(b) Double acting single rod ended

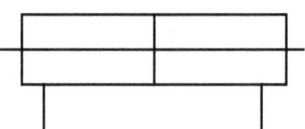

(c) Double acting double rod ended

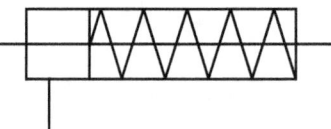

(d) Single acting double rod ended spring return

Fig. 3.19: Various types of cylinders

HYDRAULICS AND PNEUMATICS — HYDRAULIC ACTUATORS

3.9 Constructional Features

A double acting hydraulic cylinder consists of the following components as shown in Fig. 3.16.

- (a) Cylinder barrel
- (b) Piston assembly
- (c) End cap
- (d) Piston seal
- (e) Static seal
- (f) Nose bearing
- (g) Piston rod seal
- (h) Piston rod
- (i) Wiper ring
- (j) Ports

The cylinder barrel is made of hard drawn seamless tubes of aluminium alloys or steel and piston of aluminium alloy casting. Many a times, barrels are made of C.I. or mechanite, brass or bronze.

Piston rods may be of steel, carburised, hardened, ground and polished. It has a hardness of 60 - 65 HRC.

Bush is made of bronze, cylinder head cover is made of spheroidal C.I. or mechanite casting. Seals are of elastomer material, fabric material or leather.

The hydraulic cylinder manufacture requires close tolerances, precision finish and fine polish to ensure leakage control. The wall thickness of the cylinder is based upon the operating pressure of oil.

3.10 Mountings of Hydraulic Cylinders (May 07, 08, 11)

Various types of cylinder mountings are used in practice. The cylinder mountings are classified as -

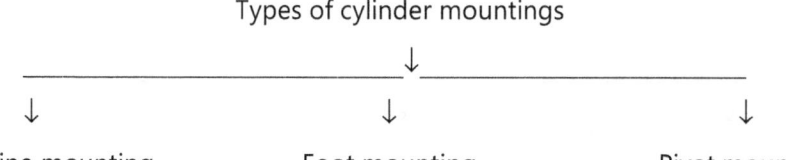

Centre Line Mounting: In this mounting, the cylinder is supported along its centre line. The mounting bolts are thus subjected to shear or simple stress. This mounting needs accurate alignment. Misalignment is not tolerable.

Foot Mounting: This mounting of cylinder introduces torque under loaded condition. The cylinder may rotate or bend about its mounting bolt when loaded. The stress level on the cylinder is higher as compared to the centre line mounting.

Pivot Mounting: Many applications need rotational freedom for a cylinder as it reciprocates. The pivot mounting can be of Clevis type or trunnion type. This mounting permits rotational freedom in one plane. Provision of universal joints at the pivots allows greater degrees of rotational freedom. Fig. 3.20 shows various types of mountings.

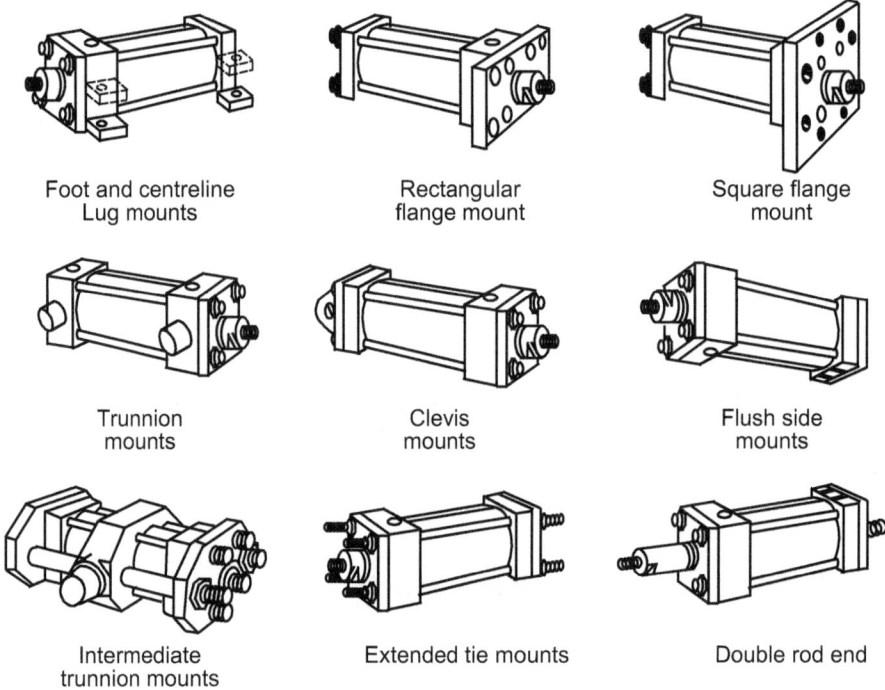

Fig. 3.20: Types of cylinder mountings

3.11 METHODS OF INSTALLATION

The cylinders may be installed using various mechanical linkages. These linkages transform a linear motion into an oscillatory motion or rotary motion. Linkage also enables to increase or decrease the effective leverage and stroke of the piston.

Cylinders are often subject to side loads due to misalignment. Perfect alignment is seldom possible. Fig. 3.21 illustrates typical mechanical linkages for installation.

The illustration however is by no means conclusive and the variety is limited by the ingenuity of the designer.

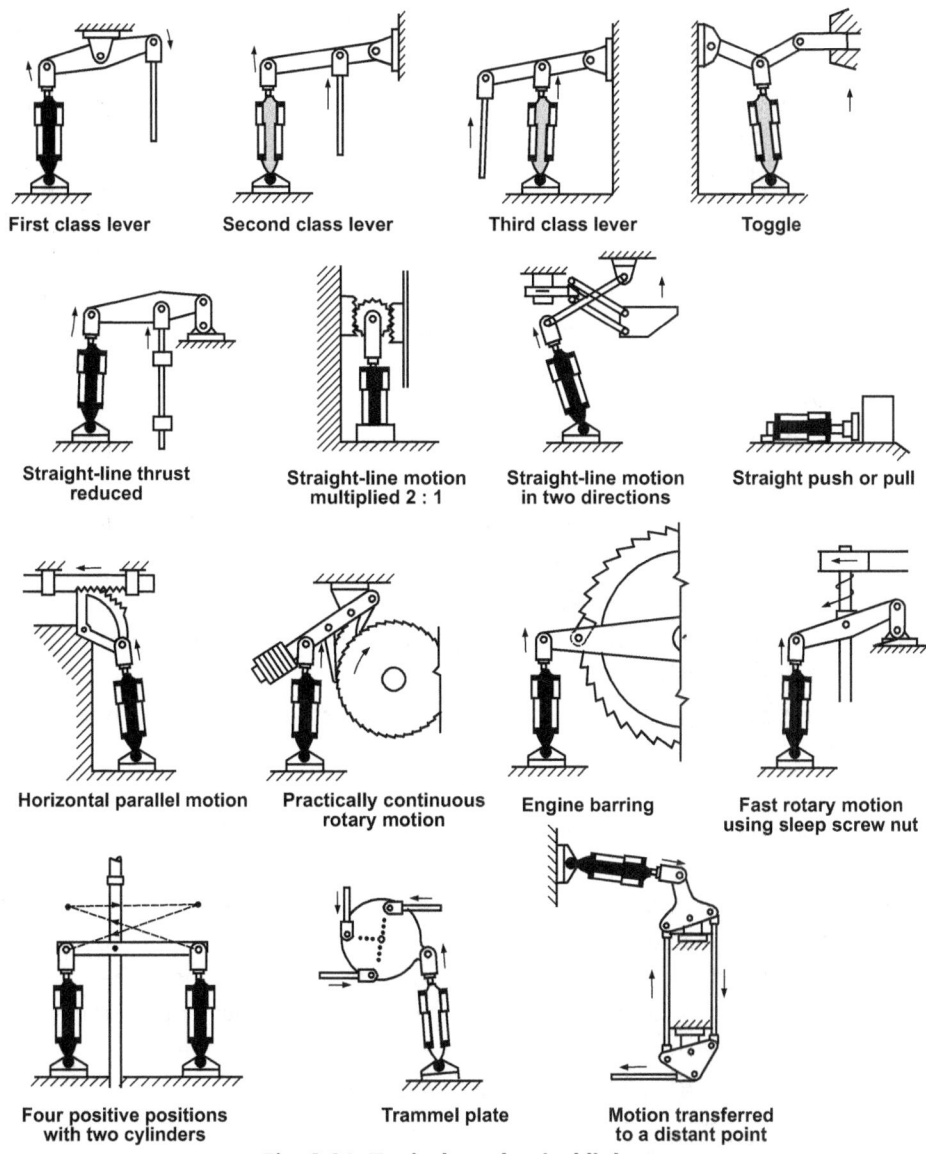

Fig. 3.21: Typical mechanical linkages

The illustration however is by no means conclusive and the variety is limited by the ingenuity of the designer.

3.12 Estimation of Cylinder Force, Acceleration and Losses

Design Considerations for Hydraulic Four Cylinders : (May 2007)

Hydraulic cylinders are designed for their anticipated use. They are rated for their maximum pressure valve. Depending upon the general characteristics required for specific application fields, following special purpose cylinders are manufactured.

(i) Steel Mills and General Heavy Equipments: Fabricated from steel plates with heavy duty thick-wall steel tubing, oversize piston rods, heavy duty packing is designed for quick easy change and is extremely rugged.

Pressure is in excess of 140 bar.

(ii) Agricultural Cylinders: Medium to light duty offers throw away type with non-replaceable packings. Seasonal activities are considered while designing. They have relatively short service life. The pressure rating is 137.9 bar.

(iii) Machine Tool Cylinders: Precise construction designed for long service life. Easy seal and packing replacement. Rugged construction, good maintenance can be expected.

Pneumatic and light duty hydraulic cylinder usually function at 68.95 bar or less. Many machine tool cylinders are rated at 137.9 bar.

(iv) Marine Application Cylinders: Rust-proof construction, oversize piston rods, fail safe structures. Pressure rating is excess of 137.9 bar.

(v) Aircraft cylinders: Maximum strength with light weight materials. Critical design to get maximum power to weight ratio.

Other considerations in Hydraulic Cylinder Design:

- To avoid bending under load, heavy duty piston rods are often designed to be equal to one-half the area of the piston.
- The retraction speed of the cylinder can also be increased by using bigger diameter piston rods.
- The available space may limit the size of fluid power cylinder. Hence to prove the same force, the decrease in area due to large rod diameter is compensated by increasing the pressure.

The cylinder is expected to provide maximum thrust. The system pressure is obtained from the total load to be sustained by the piston rod. The main losses in the operation of the cylinder are due to friction between the piston and cylinder, seals friction. The total frictional losses are restricted upto 5% to 8% of the theoretical force to achieve optimum efficiency. In case of a double acting cylinder, the back pressure is also to be considered.

Fig. 3.22 shows the kinematics (Force analysis) of a hydraulic cylinder.

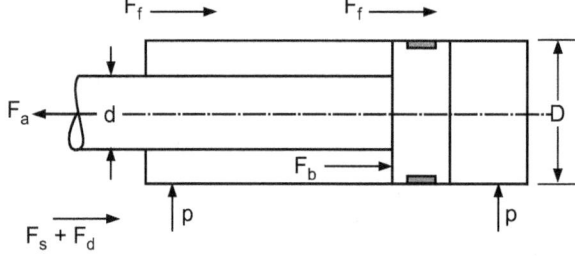

Fig. 3.22: Force analysis of a hydraulic cylinder

Let F_a = Active force on piston, kN
F_b = Back pressure force, kN
F_f = Friction force, kN
F_s = Static force, kN
F_d = Dynamic force, kN
p = Pressure of oil, kPa
D = Diameter of piston, m
d = Diameter of piston rod, m

$$F_a = F_s + F_d, \text{ kN}$$

where, F_a = Maximum force to be produced, kN
F_s = Static force due to load, friction force due to external elements F_r, rod seal, piston seal and back pressure, kN
F_d = Dynamic force for accelerating the mass, kN

The system pressure 'p' is obtained from 'F_a'. During steady travel, however, 'F_a' is equal to 'F_s'.

It is difficult to set the body in motion than to keep it moving. Therefore, static or break-out friction of a piston is always greater than the running friction. The coefficient of friction for a hydraulic cylinder 'μ' is 0.15 to 0.20.

From the very beginning of the piston travel, it is desirable to obtain maximum useful work. In other words, the piston should accelerate quickly. The acceleration is influenced by size and rigidity of the cylinder, compressibility of oil, stick-slip effect of piston seal, defects in the assembly etc. The piston should attain its normal speed within 0.5 to 1.0 second.

The piston rod is subjected to buckling as the piston extends and tensile load as the piston retracts. The effect of back pressure can be ignored if the ratio of piston area to annular area is 1.33 or less.

3.12.1 Estimation of Friction Force and Cylinder Losses

A major cylinder loss is on account of seal and packing friction. Frictional losses are governed by :

- Coefficient of friction between the seal surface and mating surface.
- Area of sealing surface
- Pre-load of seals
- Surface finish of mating components
- Operating pressure of oil.

Let
- F_r = Frictional resistance force, kN
- A_c = Circumferential area of seal = $\pi l D$ m²
- l = Length of seal surface, m
- D = Internal diameter of cylinder, m
- p = Oil pressure, kPa
- μ = Coefficient of friction (0.2 > μ > 0.1)
- F_p = Total pre-load force, kN

Then, $F_r = F_p + \mu p A_c$ kN

The pre-load force on the seal is obtained from a pressure of 0.5 to 1.0 bar/ring. The number of rings adopted lie between 2 and 4. At higher speed, usually two rings are used. For higher pressure and low speed, many rings are used.

3.12.2 Effective Useful Cylinder Force

Out of the total theoretical force of $\frac{\pi}{4} D^2 p$ kN, it is desirable that the effective useful force available should be about $0.7 D^2 p$ kN i.e. cylinder losses should be limited to 2% to 8%.

3.12.3 Estimation of Pressure Drop in Cylinder

In case of a double acting cylinder, the total pressure drop Δp is given by

$$\Delta p = \Delta p_l \left(1 + \frac{1}{r}\right) \text{ kPa}$$

where, Δp = Total pressure drop, kPa
Δp_l = Pressure drop in inlet (supply) line, kPa

$$r = \frac{A_1}{A_2} = \frac{\text{Area of piston}}{\text{Annular area}}$$

3.12.4 Determination of Piston Rod Diameter and Length

In case of equal velocities of extending and retraction of piston, the piston rod diameter 'd' is given by

d = 0.2 D to 0.3 D

where D = diameter of piston

In all other cases, d = 0.5 D to 0.7 D

For better rigidity and easy installation, the ratio of stroke length to diameter 'D' of cylinder is limited upto 20 or less. High pressure cylinders adopt short stroke length. The oil supply pressure is decided by the force 'F' necessary during accelerating period.

3.12.5 Loading on the Piston Rod

The piston rod is subjected to buckling load and friction force during extending of piston. While during retracting, the piston rod is subjected to tensile load, 'F_t'

$$F_t = W + \sum F_r + F_d \quad kN$$

where, F_t = Total tensile load on piston rod, kN

W = External load to be actuated

$\sum F_r$ = Total frictional force, kN

F_d = Dynamic piston force, kN

3.12.6 Determination of Cylinder Forces

The forces in a hydraulic cylinder are dependent upon (a) External load to be moved (b) Required acceleration and retardation (c) Coefficient of break-away or static friction (d) Coefficient of sliding friction.

3.12.7 Estimation of Flow Velocities

Flow velocity is determined based on the following considerations:

1. Pipe line location e.g. suction line or discharge (pressure line)
2. Type of pump
3. Surface finish
4. Viscosity of oil
5. Pipe diameter
6. Oil pressure

For highly viscous oils, velocity of 6 m/s to 7 m/s is adopted while in case of low or medium viscosity oils, velocity of 3 m/s to 4 m/s is recommended.

Further for pipe line diameter between 12 mm and 50 mm, flow velocities are 3 m/s to 3.5 m/s while for pipe line diameter exceeding 50 mm, velocity lies between 3.5 m/s to 4.0 m/s.

For high pressure delivery lines of pump, flow velocity of 3 m/s and for suction line, velocity of 1 m/s is usually satisfactory.

Similarly, velocity of piston during extending (forward)

$$v_f = \frac{Q_p}{\pi/4 \; D^2} \; m/s \quad \text{where} \quad Q_p = \text{Flow rate of pump, } m^3/s$$

and velocity of piston during retraction

$$V_r = V_f \left(1 - \frac{d^2}{D^2}\right) \text{ m/s}$$

For very low velocities of piston say 0.01 m/min. to 0.015 m/min. the operation of the cylinder is highly unstable. As such, low velocities are not desirable.

In case of extreme variation of piston velocity say e.g. 200: 1 and very long stroke length, rotary actuators are recommended over the linear actuators for better rigidity.

3.12.8 Design of Piston Rod

In a hydraulic cylinder assembly, the piston rod is a highly stressed component. It is subjected to buckling thus developing bending, tensile and compressive stresses. Piston rods are made of high tensile material, with fine surface finish, hardened and chromium plated. Sometimes, stainless steel is also used for piston rods.

The cross section area of the piston rod is calculated based on whether it is a stressed rod (short column) or a long column. If its 'l/d' ratio exceeds 10, the piston rod is treated as a long column under compression, subjected to buckling.

For piston rods with $l/d < 10$, the cross-sectional area is determined as follows:

$$F = \sigma \times a \text{ kN}$$

where, F = Tensile or compressive load, kN

σ = Permissible stress, kPa

a = Area of cross-section of piston-rod, m²

And for piston rod with $l/d > 10$, behaving like a long column, subjected to buckling, the piston rod diameter is obtained from the critical load using the Euler's formula given below:

$$F_c = \frac{\pi^2 E I}{l_k^2} \text{ kN}$$

where, F_c = Critical buckling load, N

l_k = Free buckling length, m

E = Modulus of elasticity ($2.1 \times 9.81 \times 10^{10}$ Pa for steel)

I = Moment of inertia, m⁴

The type of end fixing of cylinder governs the moment of inertia and maximum permissible stress for avoiding buckling.

$$\text{Moment of inertia 'I'} = \frac{\pi d^4}{64} \text{ m}^4$$

And the maximum permissible load on the piston rod 'F' to avoid buckling is given by

$$F = \frac{F_c}{S} \text{ kN}$$

where, S = Factor of safety (5 for general cylinders and 3 for cylinders with guided trunnion or centre trunnion)

The cylinder load is determined considering the type of fixing, from the Euler's rule.

Maximum load on the piston rod = $F = \dfrac{\pi^2 E I}{S \times l_e^2}$ kN

∴ Critical or equivalent column length

$$l_e = \pi \sqrt{\dfrac{E I}{F S}} \text{ m}$$

Fig. 3.23 shows crippling load based on Euler's rule for various types of end fixing.

Euler's cases and crippling load				
I	II	III	IV	
Load = $\dfrac{\pi^2 EI}{4 l^2}$	$\dfrac{\pi^2 EI}{4 l^2}$	$\dfrac{\pi^2 EI}{l^2}$	$\dfrac{4 \pi^2 EI}{l^2}$	
$l_c = 2l$	$l_c = 1$	$l_c = \dfrac{1}{\sqrt{2}}$	$l_c = \dfrac{l_c}{2}$	$l_c = \dfrac{3}{2} 1$
One end free, one end fixed or trunnion at end	Two ends pivoted and guided	One end guided and pivoted, other end fixed	Two ends fixed and guided	Trunnion centre

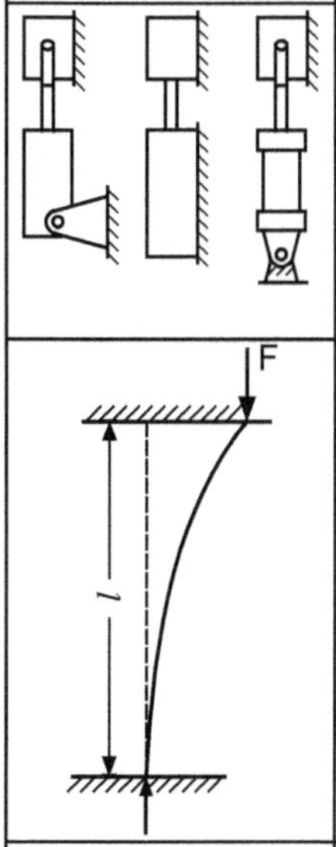

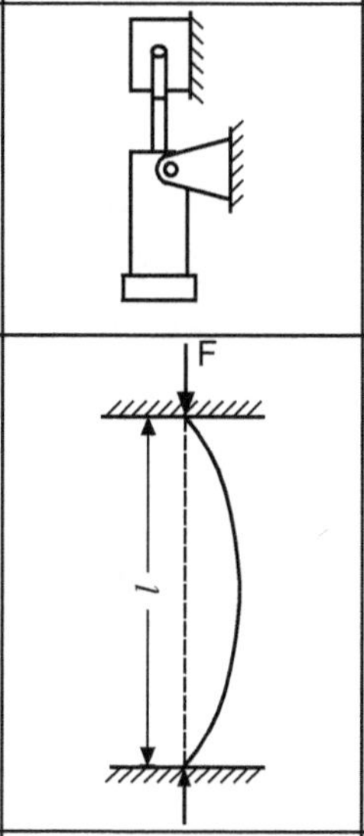

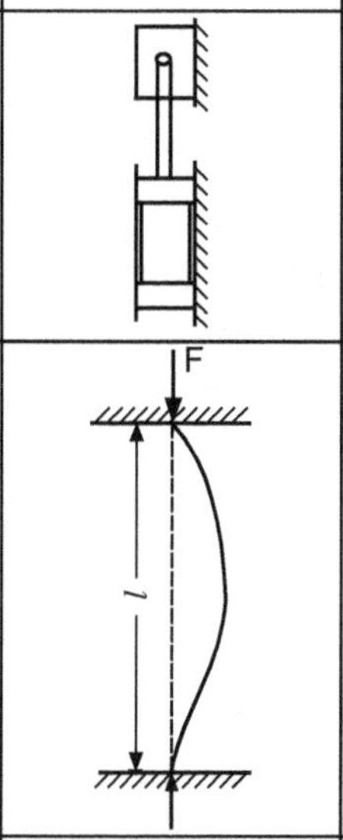

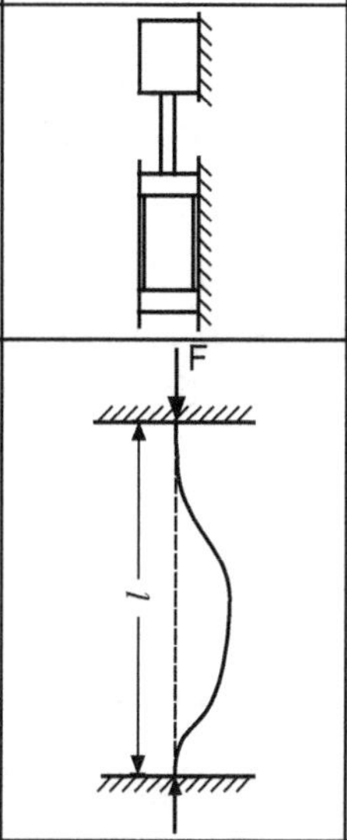

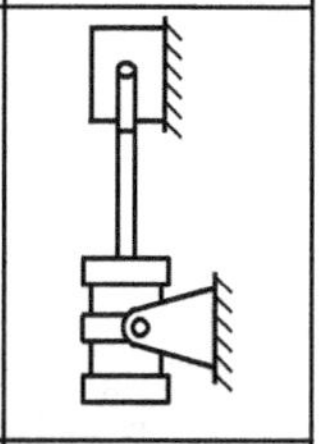

Fig. 3.23: Crippling load based on Euler's rule

3.12.9 Maximum Piston-speeds

The maximum speed of piston depends upon the rate of inflow and outflow of oil and the ability of the piston to sustain shock loads when the cylinder covers stop the piston. When only a part of the piston stroke is used, cushion is not useful to decelerate the load. In such situations external cushioning is necessary particularly for heavy loads and precision position control.

Table 3.2 gives the recommended piston speeds for different types of cylinders.

Table 3.2: Recommended piston speeds

Sr. No.	Type of cylinder	Recommended piston speed m/min.
1.	Uncushioned cylinder	8.0
2.	Cushioned cylinder	12.0
3.	High speed or externally cushioned cylinder	45.0

3.13 EFFICIENCY OF CYLINDER

The overall efficiency of a hydraulic cylinder is influenced by frictional losses. The total frictional losses can be limited within 2% and 8% of the theoretical force using close or precision tolerance, precision alignment of components. Poor design and workmanship results in excessive frictional losses. Efficiency of a hydraulic cylinder is given by

$$\eta_{cyl.} = 1 - \frac{\sum F_r}{F_s}$$

where $\sum F_r$ = Total frictional force, kN

F_s = Static force, kN

The expected efficiency of various hydraulic cylinders are:

1. For normal cylinders, $\eta_{cyl.}$ = 0.94 to 0.95
2. For telescopic cylinders, $\eta_{cyl.}$ = 0.88 to 0.90

The efficiency of a hydraulic cylinder is also found to vary with the diameter of the piston as seen from Table 3.3 below.

Table 3.3: Piston diameter and cylinder efficiency

Sr. No.	Diameter of piston, mm	Efficiency of cylinder, %
1.	20 to 50	80 – 85
2.	50 to 120	85 – 90
3.	Above 120	90 – 95

3.14 DETERMINATION OF CYLINDER WALL THICKNESS

Due to high operating pressures, careful design of cylinder wall thickness is necessary. Incorrect wall thickness often leads to safety problems and operational difficulties. When hydraulic cylinders are considered as thin cylinders having diameter thickness ratio greater than 10 : 1 the thickness 't' is obtained using normal Barlow formula given below:

Referring to Fig. 3.24.

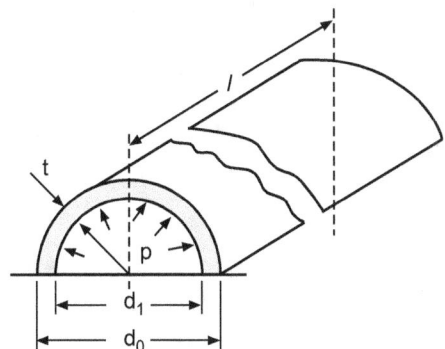

Fig. 3.24: Hydraulic cylinder-wall thickness

The internal oil pressure in a hydraulic cylinder produces hoop stress. The choice of material and wall thickness of cylinder are so made so as to ensure safety against the hoop stress.

Let σ = Hoop stress, kPa
 p = Pressure of oil, kPa
 d_o = Outer diameter of cylinder, m
 d_i = Inner diameter of cylinder, m
 t = Thickness of wall, m

Then as per Barlow formula,

$$\sigma = p \left(\frac{d_o^2 + d_i^2}{d_o^2 - d_i^2} \right) \text{ kPa}$$

when 't' $< \frac{1}{20}$ of diameter, $d_o \approx d_i$, hence $\sigma = p \frac{d_o}{2t}$.

The tensile strength of the material and the factor of safety limit provide the maximum hoop stress.

A factor of safety of 4 : 1 is necessary for continuous severe application while it can be 2 : 1 or 3 : 1 when shock loads are absent and the frequency of occurrence of maximum pressure is low. For precise and reliable estimation of wall thickness, additional allowances for material tolerance, decarburization, corrosion, thinning of material in drawing are necessary.

All these allowances can be accommodated by choosing a liberal factor of safety. The JIC standard recommends the factor of safety based on operating pressure as shown in the Table 3.4.

Table 3.4: Operating pressure and factor of safety (as per JIC standard)

Sr. No.	Operating pressure 'bar'	Factor of safety
1.	Upto 70	8 : 1
2.	70 to 110	6 : 1
3.	Above 110	4 : 1

For extremely high operating pressures, the hydraulic cylinder is treated as a thick walled cylinder. The wall thickness 't' is obtained using the following formula.

$$t = \frac{d_o}{2} \left\{ \sqrt{\frac{\sigma + p}{\sigma - p}} - 1 \right\} \text{ m}$$

However, due to non-uniform stress distribution in a thick walled cylinder, the wall thickness is determined from the modified formula given below.

$$\sigma = \frac{d_o^2 - 2t + 2t^2}{2t(d_o - t)} \times p \text{ kPa}$$

where σ = hoop stress, kPa
 p = operating pressure, kPa
 t = cylinder wall thickness, m
 d_o = outer diameter of cylinder, m

3.15 PERMISSIBLE OPERATING TEMPERATURE

Maximum operating temperature is usually limited to 80°C to avoid deterioration of elastomer seals. Above 50°C, the mineral oil deterioration starts. Some applications justify heat shielding of cylinders from external heat sources. The operating temperature range can be increased by using metal seals instead of elastomer seals.

3.16 DETERMINATION OF SPEED OF A DOUBLE ACTING CYLINDER

Refer to Fig. 3.25.

 Let D = Diameter of piston, m
 d = Diameter of piston rod, m
 A = Area on full bore side, m²
 a = Area of piston rod, m²

Q_E = Flow rate into full bore side of cylinder during extending, m³/s
q_E = Flow rate from annulus end of cylinder during extending, m³/s
V = Extend velocity of piston, m/s
v = Retract velocity of piston, m/s
p_1 = Pressure of oil at full bore end, kPa
p_2 = Pressure of oil at annulus end, kPa

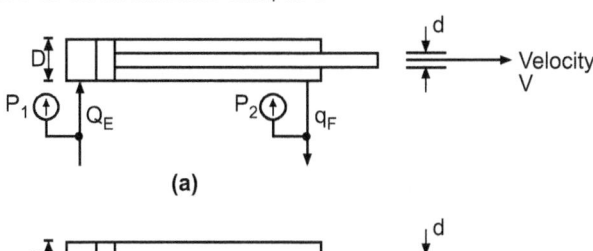

(a)

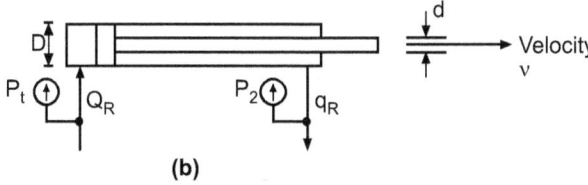

(b)

Fig. 3.25: Double acting cylinder

Full bore area $\quad A = \dfrac{\pi}{4} D^2 \; m^2$

Annulus area $\quad (A - a) = \dfrac{\pi}{4} (D^2 - d^2) \; m^2$

(I) When the piston rod is extending:

$$\text{Piston velocity } v = \frac{Q_E}{A} = \frac{q_E}{(A - a)} \; m/s$$

$$\therefore \quad q_E = Q_E \times \frac{(A - a)}{A} \; m^3/s$$

Therefore, during the extension of piston rod, the flow rate of oil entering the cylinder 'Q_E' exceeds the flow rate of oil leaving the cylinder 'q_E'

(II) When the piston rod is retracting:

Let $\quad q_R$ = Flow rate of oil entering the annulus end of the cylinder, m³/s
$\quad Q_R$ = Flow rate of oil leaving the full bore end of the cylinder

Then piston velocity $\quad v = \dfrac{q_R}{(A - a)} = \dfrac{Q_R}{A} \; m/s$

$$\therefore \quad Q_R = q_R \times \frac{A}{(A - a)}$$

It is thus clear that as the piston rod retracts, the flow rate of oil leaving the cylinder Q_R is greater than the flow rate of oil 'q_R' entering the cylinder.

3.17 DETERMINATION OF CYLINDER THRUST

The cylinder thrust comprises of two components viz static thrust and dynamic thrust.
The static thrust is obtained as the product of pressure and area.
The net thrust during extend

$$= p_1 \left(\frac{\pi}{4} D^2\right) - p_2 \left(\frac{\pi}{4} D^2 - \frac{\pi}{4} d^2\right) \text{ kN}$$

$$= \frac{\pi}{4} \left[p_1 D^2 - p_2 (D^2 - d^2)\right] \text{ kN}$$

Similarly, the net thrust during retract

$$= \frac{\pi}{4} \left[p_2 (D^2 - d^2) - p_1 D^2\right] \text{ kN}$$

The dynamic thrust is due to load inertia, seal friction, load friction etc.

Dynamic thrust can be approximately taken as 0.9 times the static thrust.

The seal friction depends upon the type of seal material, its shape and cylinder design. The break out pressure for seal friction is usually assumed as 5 bar. During motion of the piston, it reduces. Higher cylinder bores are found to reduce the pressure required to overcome seal friction.

3.18 ACCELERATION AND DECELERATION OF CYLINDER LOADS

Acceleration: It can be found from the equations of motion

Let u = Initial velocity, m/s
 v = Velocity after time 't' second, m/s
 s = Distance travelled during time 't' seconds, m
 a = Acceleration during time 't', m/s²

The three basic equations of motion are

$$v = u + at \text{ m/s}$$
$$v^2 = u^2 + 2as$$
$$s = ut + \frac{1}{2} at^2, \text{ m}$$

Also, $$s = \frac{1}{2}(u + v) t, \text{ m}$$

Further force 'F' = mass × acceleration,

and Force 'P' required for overcoming friction is given by

$$P = \mu \times W_1 \text{ N} \quad \text{where} \quad W = \text{load N}$$

Deceleration: For deceleration, cushions are fitted to the cylinder and piston.

3.19 CYLINDER CUSHIONING (A METHOD OF ACHIEVE PISTON DECELERATION TOWARDS THE END OF STROKE) (May 09, 12; Dec. 11)

For absorbing the kinetic energy of the load during deceleration, cylinders are fitted with cushions. Fig. 3.26 shows a typical cushioning arrangement.

The piston is provided with a spike or spear and the piston rod with a sleeve. The spike breaks the main flow path of the oil leaving the cylinder. Oil, thus has to find an alternative path to the reservoir which meters out the outflow of oil during the last part of the stroke. A check valve is provided for bypassing the cushion restriction for the return stroke.

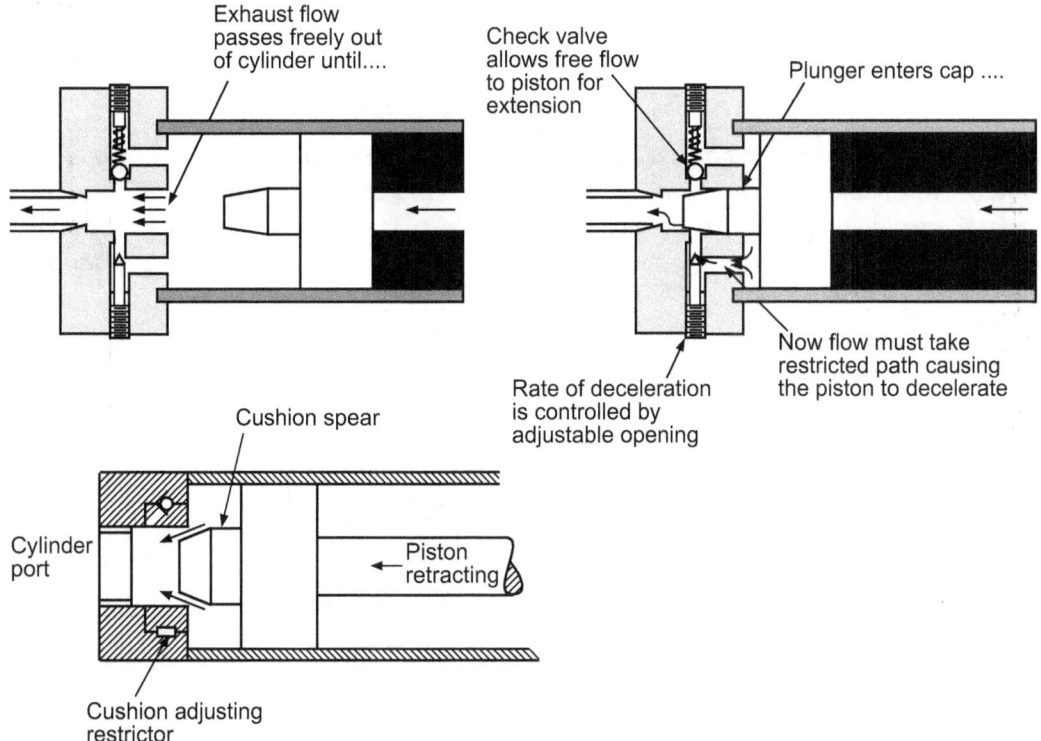

Fig. 3.26: Cylinder cushion arrangement

Extremely high pressures are likely to develop within a cylinder cushion during deceleration. The cushioning device sets up a back pressure for decelerating the load.

The variation of pressure in cushion for various positions of the cushion spike in the cushion is shown in Fig. 3.27.

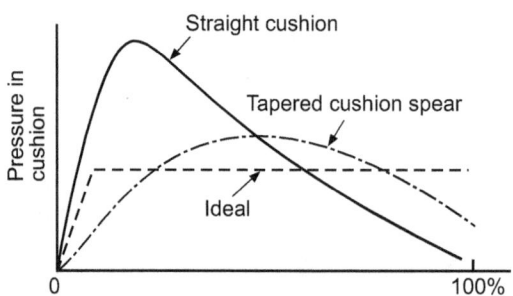

Fig. 3.27: Pressure variation in cushion

Ideally, the back pressure set-up by the cushion should be constant over the complete cushioning length for a progressive load deceleration. However in practice, the cushion pressure is much higher, as the spike enters the cushion. Cushioning performance can be improved to same extent by using a tapered or stepped cushion spike.

[Note : Refer Article 4.11.3 from Unit 4 for use of valve in case of deceleration control of a piston**]**

SOLVED EXAMPLES

Example 3.1: A double acting cylinder is looked up in the circuit as shown in Fig. 3.28 (a). The relief valve setting is 105 bar. The piston area is 130 cm² and rod area is 50 cm². If the pump flow rate is 0.0016 m³/sec, find the cylinder speed and load carrying capacity for (i) Extending stroke, (ii) Retracting stroke. **(May 2003)**

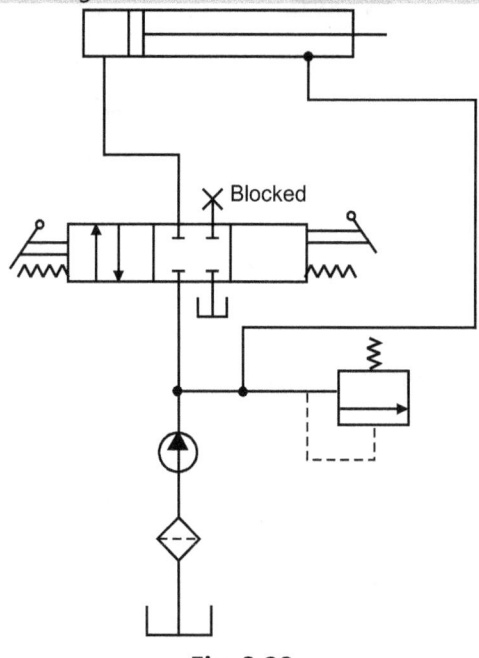

Fig. 3.28

Solution: Given data:

$$\text{Piston area} = 130 \text{ cm}^2 = A = 130 \times 10^{-4} \text{ m}^2$$
$$\text{Rod area} = 50 \text{ cm}^2 = a = 50 \times 10^{-4} \text{ m}^2$$
$$\text{Pump flow rate} = 0.0016 \text{ m}^3/\text{sec} = 1.6 \times 10^{-3} \text{ m}^3/\text{sec}$$
$$\text{Relief valve setting} = 105 \text{ bar} = 105 \times 10^5 \text{ Pa}$$

Part A: In case of extending stroke: During extending stroke, the oil goes to both the sides of the piston simultaneously.

∴ Force acting on the rod end side of the cylinder

$$= (105 \times 10^5) \times (100 - 50) \times 10^{-4} = 84000 \text{ N}$$

Now, force acting on the piston rod of the cylinder = $P \times A$

$$= (150 \times 10^5) \times (130 \times 10^{-4}) = 1,36,500 \text{ Nm}$$

∴ Net force on the piston during extending stroke

$$F = 136500 - 84000 = 52500 \text{ N}$$

Considering of step during extending stroke.

Let 'v' be the forward velocity.

The oil gain to the piston end = [The pump discharge Q_1] + [Oil returned from the rod end Q_2]

∴ $\quad Q_1 = 1.6 \times 10^{-3} \text{ m}^3/\text{sec}$

∴ $\quad Q_2 = v(A - a)$

∴ $\quad Q_2 = v(130 - 50) \times 10^{-4}$

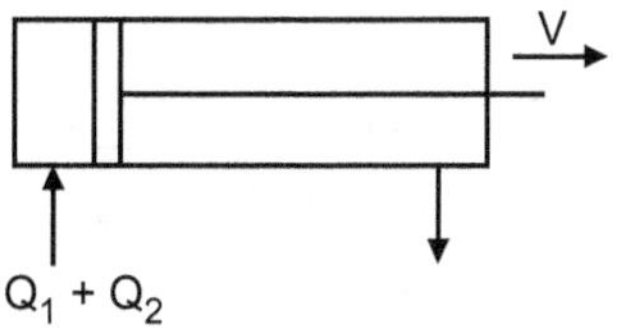

Fig. 3.29

Extending velocity 'v' is given by formula,

$$v = \frac{Q_1 + Q_2}{A}$$

$$= \frac{[v(130 - 50) \times 10^{-4}] + [1.6 \times 10^{-3}]}{130 \times 10^{-4}}$$

∴ $\quad 130 \times 10^{-4}) v = (80 \times 10^{-4}) v + 1.6 \times 10^{-3}$

∴ $\quad (130 - 80) \times 10^{-4}) v = 1.6 \times 10^{-3}$

∴ $\quad v = \frac{1.6 \times 10^{-3}}{50 \times 10^{-4}}$

∴ Velocity during extending stroke = 0.32 m/sec.

Part B: In case of retracting stroke: Load capacity calculated as

$$= \text{(Pressure setting)} \times \text{Annulus area}$$
$$= (105 \times 10^5) \times (130 - 50 \times 10^{-4})$$
$$= 84{,}000 \text{ N}$$

Now, retracting velocity of piston $= \dfrac{Q_1}{(A-a)} = \dfrac{1.6 \times 10^{-3}}{(130-50) \times 10^{-4}}$

∴ Velocity of piston during retracting stroke = 0.2 m/sec.

Example 3.2: *A hydraulic cylinder has a piston diameter of 70 mm and a piston rod diameter of 50 mm connected to a regenerative circuit where the pump flow rate is 25 lit/min and the working pressure is 100 bar. Show that both the forward and return speeds are almost equal.*

Solution: After considering the data given in the Example Fig. 3.30 explains the regenerative circuit.

Consider, v_E = velocity during extraction, v_R = Velocity during retraction

The ratio of extension velocity to retraction velocity is given by

$$\frac{v_E}{v_R} = \frac{\text{Area (blank - rod)}}{\text{Area (rod)}} = \frac{A_B - A_R}{A_R} = \frac{A_B}{A_R} - 1 = \frac{\pi/4\,(D^2)}{\pi/4\,(d^2)} - 1$$

$$= \left(\frac{D}{d}\right)^2 - 1 = \left(\frac{70}{50}\right)^2 - 1 = 1.96 - 1 = 0.96 \approx 1$$

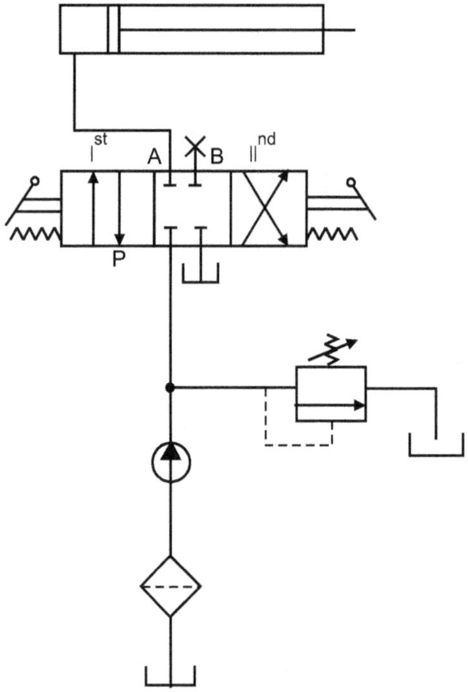

Fig. 3.30

Example 3.3: *A mass of 2000 kg is to be accelerated horizontally upto a velocity of 1 m/s from rest over a distance of 50 mm. The coefficient of friction between the load and the guide is 0.16. Calculate the bore of the cylinder required to accelerate the load if the maximum allowable pressure at the full bore end is 100 bar. Assume the back pressure at the annulus end of the cylinder as zero and seal friction to be equivalent to a pressure drop of 5 bar.*

(May 2001)

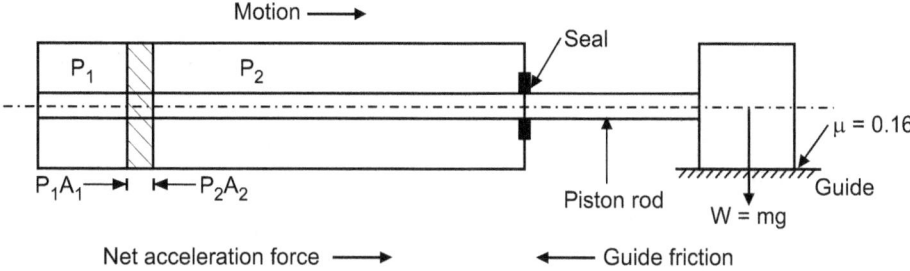

Fig. 3.31

To calculate the cylinder dimensions, first we should know the forces acting on the piston.

∴ Net forces in the direction of motion = $P_1 A_1 - P_2 A_2 - \mu W$.

Where, back pressure = 0 bar and sealing force is accounted by considering a reduction in the pressure P_1 by 5 bar.

∴ Net force = $(95 \times 10^5) A_1 - 0 - [0.16 (2000 \times 9.81)]$

∴ Net force = $(95 \times 10^5) A_1 - 3139.2$ ... (1)

Now, Newton's equation of motion can be used to calculate the acceleration, and the equation is

$$v^2 = u^2 = 2as$$

where, v = Final velocity, u = Initial velocity, s = Distance and a = Acceleration.

∴ u = 0 m/s, v = 1 m/s, s = 50 mm

∴ Acceleration = $a = \dfrac{1 \times 1000}{(2 \times 59)} = 10 \text{ m/s}^2$

The force required to accelerate the load is given by

$$F = m \times a = 2000 \times 10 \text{ N} = 20{,}000 \text{ N}$$

and the force necessary to overcome load friction is

$$P = \mu \times 2000 \times 9.81 = (0.16 \times 2000 \times 9.81)$$

∴ P = 3139.2 N

Hence, total force required to accelerate the load to overcome friction is (F + P)

HYDRAULICS AND PNEUMATICS · HYDRAULIC ACTUATORS

$$= 23139.2 \text{ N}$$

The pressure available = Maximum permissible pressure − Seal back way pressure

$$= 100 - 5 = 95 \text{ bar}$$

$$\therefore \quad 23139.2 = \left(\frac{\pi}{4} \times D^2\right) \times (95 \times 10^5)$$

$$\therefore \quad D = \mathbf{55.68 \text{ mm}}$$

Example 3.4: *A hydrostatic transmission operating at 105 bar pressure has the following characteristics:*

Pump	Motor
$V_D = 100 \text{ cm}^3$	$V_D = ?$
η_v	$\eta_v = 94\%$
η_m	$\eta_m = 92\%$
$N = 1000 \text{ rpm}$	$N = 600 \text{ rpm}$

Determine: (i) Displacement of motor, (ii) Motor output torque. **(May 2004)**

Solution: **Part A: Pump calculations:**

$$\text{Pump volumetric efficiency} = \frac{\text{Pump delivery}}{(\text{Displacement of pump}) \times (\text{Speed})}$$

Now, pump delivery $= \eta_v \times V_D \times N$

$$= \frac{0.85 \times 100 \times 1000}{60} = 1416.67 \text{ cm}^3/\text{sec}$$

Part B: Motor calculations:

Actual flow rate = Pump delivery

$$= 1416.67 \text{ cm}^3/\text{sec}$$

$$\text{Theoretical flow rate } (Q_t) = \frac{\text{Displacement of motor } (V_D) \times \text{Speed } (N)}{60}$$

$$\text{Motor volumetric efficiency } (\eta_v) = \frac{\text{Theoretical flow rate } (Q_t)}{\text{Actual flow rate } (Q_a)}$$

$$Q_t = \eta_v \times Q_a$$

$$\frac{V_D \times N}{60} = \eta_v \times Q_a$$

$$\therefore \quad V_D = \frac{\eta_v \times Q_a \times 60}{N} = \frac{0.94 \times 1416.67 \times 60}{600}$$

$$= 133.167 \text{ cm}^3$$

Displacement of motor $(V_D) = 133.167 \text{ cm}^3$.

Now, Mechanical efficiency of motor $(\eta_m) = \dfrac{\text{Actual torque of motor } (\tau_a)}{\text{Theoretical torque } (\tau_t)}$

$$\therefore \quad \tau_a = \eta_m \times \tau_t$$

$$= 0.92 \times \frac{\text{Pressure (P)} \times \text{Displacement } (V_D)}{2\pi}$$

$$= \frac{0.92 \times (105 \times 10^5) \times (133.17 \times 10^{-6})}{2\pi}$$

$\therefore$ Motor output torque $= \tau_a = 204.84$ N-m

***

Example 3.5: *A hydraulic cylinder supports a load of 2000 N and its operating acceleration is 10 m/s². Calculate the breakway load and force required to bring the hydraulic cylinder to its operating force and speed.*

Solution: Assuming static coefficient of friction as 0.16 and dynamic coefficient of friction as 0.14

$\therefore \quad$ Breaking load $= 2000 \times 0.16 = 320$ N

$\quad\quad\quad$ Dynamic load $= 2000 \times 0.14 = 280$ N

$\therefore \quad$ Accelerating force $= \dfrac{2000}{9.81} \times \dfrac{10}{100}$ (Assuming acceleration to be 10 cm/s²)

$$= 20.387 \text{ N}$$

Therefore, total load (force) to take the load table to speed

$$= 280 + 20.387$$

$$= \mathbf{300.387 \text{ N}}$$

***

Example 3.6: *A cylinder has to operate a vertical load of 3000 N. If the operating acceleration is 20 cm/s, calculate its running force.*

Solution:

$\quad\quad\quad F =$ Load encountered by cylinder

$$= \frac{3000}{9.81} \times \frac{30}{100} + 3000$$

$$= \mathbf{3891.743 \text{ N}}$$

Example 3.7: *Repeat the above example when a speed of 30 m/min. is to be reached in 1.50 cm of piston travel.*

Solution:

$$\text{Velocity} = 30 \text{ m/min.}$$
$$v = 0.5 \text{ m/s}$$

Now

$$v^2 = 2as \qquad \text{since initial velocity } u = 0 \text{ m/s}$$

$$\therefore \quad a = \frac{v^2}{2s} = \frac{0.5 \times 0.5}{2 \times \frac{1.5}{100}} = 8.3 \text{ m/s}^2$$

$$\therefore \quad F = \text{Force encountered by cylinder}$$

$$= \frac{3000}{9.81} \times 8.3 + 3000$$

$$= \mathbf{5538.22 \text{ N}}$$

Example 3.8: *A cylinder is required to carry a load of 2000 kg. The load is to move along a horizontal surface with a speed of 20 m/min. and it has to attain this speed and also stopped within 10 mm travel. Determine the pressure. Assume μ = 0.15, cylinder diameter = 50 mm.*

Solution:

$$\text{Acceleration, } a = \frac{v^2}{2s}$$

$$\therefore \quad a = \left(\frac{20}{60}\right)^2 \times \frac{1}{2 \times 0.010} = 22.22 \text{ N/m}^2$$

Now

$$F = m \times a + m \times \mu$$

$$= 2000 \times 22.22 + 2000 \times 0.15 \times 9.81 \text{ N}$$

$$= 47383 \text{ N}$$

$$\text{Pressure} = \frac{F}{\frac{\pi}{4} \times 0.05^2} \text{ Pa}$$

$$= \mathbf{241.32 \text{ bar}}$$

This pressure provides the required force.

During deceleration, Force $F = 47383 - 2943 = 44440$ N

$$\therefore \quad \text{Pressure} = \frac{44440}{\frac{\pi}{4} \times 0.05^2} \text{ Pa} = \mathbf{226.33 \text{ bar}}$$

A surge pressure of (241.32 + 226.33) bar results for which the cylinder wall thickness should be designed.

Example 3.9: Following data refer to a hydraulic cylinder:
  Tensile strength of cylinder material = 7000 bar
  Cylinder diameter = 50 mm
  Operating pressure of system = 200 bar
  Factor of safety = 4 : 1
Determine the wall thickness of the cylinder.

Solution: Working stress $\sigma = \dfrac{7000}{\text{Factor of safety}}$

∴ $\sigma = 1750$ bar

Now $\sigma = p\left(\dfrac{d_o^2 + d_i^2}{d_o^2 - d_i^2}\right)$ Here σ = Hoop stress = Working stress

$$1750 = 200\left(\dfrac{d_o^2 + 0.05^2}{d_o^2 - 0.05^2}\right)$$

∴ $d_o = 5.608$ cm   ∴ $t = \dfrac{d_o - d_i}{2} = 3.04$ mm

Example 3.10: A hydraulic cylinder has a bore of 20 cm and a piston rod diameter of 14 cm. If the extend speed of the piston is 6 m/min, determine:
  (i) Flow rate of oil entering/s
  (ii) Flow rate of oil leaving from the annulus during extend
  (iii) Speed of retracting using same flow rate as in (i)
  (iv) Flow rate from the full bore end on retract.

Solution: (i) The flow rate of oil entering during extend at 6 m/min.

$$Q_E = \dfrac{\pi}{4} \times \left(\dfrac{20}{100}\right)^2 \times \dfrac{6}{60} \text{ m}^3/\text{s}$$

$$= 3.1416 \text{ litres/s}$$

$$= \mathbf{188.496 \text{ litres/min.}}$$

(ii) Flow rate of oil leaving from the annulus during extend

$$q_E = \dfrac{\pi}{4}(D^2 - d^2) \times \text{Velocity}$$

$$= 0.7854\,(0.2^2 - 0.14^2) \times \dfrac{6}{60} \text{ m}^3/\text{s}$$

$$= \mathbf{96.133\ l/min.}$$

(iii) During retracting, using same flow rate Q_E,

$$\text{Retract velocity of piston} = \frac{Q_E}{\frac{\pi}{4}(D^2 - d^2)} = \frac{188.496 \times 10^{-3}}{0.7854(0.2^2 - 0.14^2)}$$

$$= \mathbf{11.765 \text{ m/min.}}$$

(iv) Flow rate from the full bore end on retract

$$Q_R = \frac{\pi}{4} \times D^2 \times \text{Velocity during retract}$$

$$= \frac{\pi}{4} \times 0.2^2 \times \frac{11.765}{1} \times 10^3 \text{ l/min.}$$

$$= \mathbf{369.61 \text{ l/min.}}$$

Example 3.11: *If the maximum pressure applied to the cylinder in example 3.10 is 150 bar, calculate :*

   (i) Dynamic thrust during extend

   (ii) Dynamic thrust during retract

   Assume that the dynamic thrust = 0.9 × Static thrust.

Solution: (i)   Full bore area $= \frac{\pi}{4} \times 0.2^2$

$$A = 0.0314 \text{ m}^2$$

∴ Dynamic thrust during extend $= 0.9 \times p \times A$ kN

$$= 0.9 \times 150 \times 10^2 \times 0.0314 \text{ kN} = 423.9 \text{ kN}$$

(ii)   Annulus area $= \frac{\pi}{4}(D^2 - d^2)$

$$(A - a) = \frac{\pi}{4}(0.2^2 - 0.14^2) = 0.016 \text{ m}^2$$

Dynamic thrust during retract $= 0.9 \times p \times (A - a)$

$$= 0.9 \times 150 \times 10^2 \times 0.016$$

$$= \mathbf{216 \text{ kN}}$$

Example 3.12: *A hydraulic cylinder has a bore of 20 cm and a piston rod diameter of 14 cm, connected regeneratively as shown in Fig. 3.32:*

   (i) If the flow rate of 188.486 litres/min is used, calculate the extend speed.

   (ii) If the maximum system pressure is 150 bar, calculate the dynamic extend thrust.

Solution: Refer Fig. 3.32.

HYDRAULICS AND PNEUMATICS — HYDRAULIC ACTUATORS

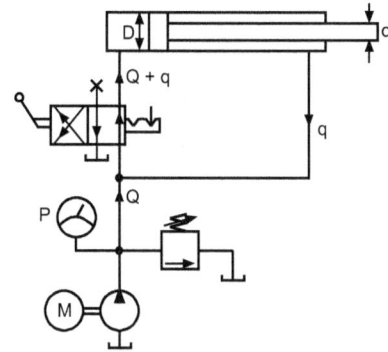

Fig. 3.32

(i) Piston rod area $= \frac{\pi}{4} \times 0.14^2$

$a = 0.0154 \text{ m}^2$

Extend speed $= \dfrac{\text{Flow rate}}{a} = \dfrac{188.486 \times 10^{-3}}{0.0154} = 12.2 \text{ m/min.}$

This is greater compared to 6 m/min speed when connected conventionally as in Example 3.10.

(ii) For a regenerative circuit,

Dynamic thrust during extend $= 0.9 \times p \times a = 0.9 \times 150 \times 10^2 \times 0.0154$

$= \mathbf{207.9 \text{ kN}}$

This is less compared with a dynamic forward thrust of 423.6 kN in Example 3.7.

As the area of the annulus is almost equal to that of the rod, the regenerative extend and conventional retract thrusts and speeds are almost same.

Example 3.13: *A mass of 1000 kg is to be accelerated horizontally upto a velocity of 1 m/s from rest over a distance of 50 mm. The coefficient of friction between the load and the guide is 0.12.*

Calculate the bore of the cylinder required to accelerate this load if the maximum permissible pressure at the full bore end is 120 bar. Assume seal friction to be equivalent to a pressure drop of 5 bar. Neglect the back pressure at the annulus end of the cylinder.

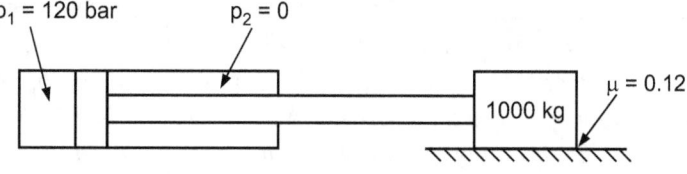

Fig. 3.33

Solution: u = 0, v = 1 m/s
s = 0.05 m, μ = 0.12

Now,
$$v^2 = u^2 + 2as$$
$$1^2 = 0 + 2a \times 0.05$$
∴ a = 10 m/s²

Force required to accelerate load, 'F' is given by
$$F = m \times a = 1000 \times 10 \text{ N} = 10,000 \text{ N}$$

And force 'P' necessary to overcome load friction is
$$P = \mu \times 1000 \times 9.81 \text{ N} = 1177.2 \text{ N}$$

Hence the total force required to accelerate the load and to overcome friction is (F + P)
$$= 11177.2 \text{ N}$$

The pressure available = Max. permissible pressure
 − Seal breakaway pressure
= 120 − 5 = 115 bar

∴ $11177.2 = \dfrac{\pi}{4} \times D^2 \times 115 \times 10^5$

∴ D = **35.178 mm**

Example 3.14: *A hydraulic motor has a volumetric displacement of 75 cc/rev. If its pressure rating is 70 bar and it receives 38 litres of oil/min. from a pump, calculate the (i) speed, (ii) torque output capacity, (iii) power output.*

Solution: Data: Q = 38 l.p.m., p = 70 bar, V_D = 75 cc/rev.

∴ Speed $= \dfrac{Q}{V_D} = \dfrac{38}{75 \times 10^{-3}} = 506.67$ r.p.m.

Torque output $T = \dfrac{V_D \times p}{6.28}$ N-m $= \dfrac{75 \times 10^{-6} \times 70 \times 10^5}{6.28}$

= **83.6 N-m**

Power output 'p' = T × w × 10⁻³ kW

$= \dfrac{83.6 \times 2\pi \times 506.67}{60} \times 10^{-3}$ kW

= **4.4356 kW**

Example 3.15: *A hydraulic motor has a displacement of 164 cc/rev. and operates with a pressure of 70 bar. It runs at 2000 r.p.m. If the actual oil flow rate consumed by the motor is 360 l.p.m. and the actual torque output delivered by the motor is 170 N-m, determine the (i) volumetric efficiency, (ii) Mechanical efficiency, (iii) Overall efficiency.*

(May 2002, Dec. 2002, Dec. 2003)

Solution: Data: V_D = 164 cc/rev., p = 70 bar, N = 1000 r.p.m.,

Q_a = 360 l.p.m., T_a = 170 N-m

Theoretical flow rate $\quad 'Q_t' = V_D \times N$

$\therefore \quad Q_t = 164 \times 10^{-3} \times 2000$ l.p.m. = 328 l.p.m.

$\therefore$ Volumetric efficiency $\quad '\eta_v' = \dfrac{Q_t}{Q_a} \times 100$

$$\eta_v = \dfrac{328}{360} \times 100 = \textbf{91.11\%}$$

Now, Theoretical torque $\quad 'T_t' = \dfrac{V_D \times p}{6.28}$

$$T_t = \dfrac{164 \times 10^{-3} \times 70 \times 10^5}{6.28} = 182.8 \text{ N-m}$$

Hence Mechanical efficiency $= \dfrac{T_a}{T_t} \times 100 = \dfrac{170}{182.8} \times 100 = \textbf{93.0\%}$

Similarly overall efficiency $\quad \eta_o = \eta_m \times \eta_v$

$$= 0.9111 \times 0.93 \times 100$$

$$= \textbf{84.73\%}$$

Actual power output $\quad 'P_a' = T_a \times w$

$$= 170 \times 10^{-3} \times \dfrac{2\pi \times 2000}{60} \text{ kW}$$

$$= \textbf{35.61 kW}$$

Example 3.16: *Show that in a cylinder having a piston diameter of 70 mm and rod = 50 mm connected in regenerative circuit and pump flow is 251 lit./min. at working pressure of 100 bar, forward and return speeds are almost equal.*

Solution:

Area of cylinder (Piston side) $= \dfrac{\pi}{4} \times (0.07)^2$

$$= 3.84 \times 10^{-3} \text{ m}^2$$

and area of annulus $= \dfrac{\pi}{4}(0.07^2 - 0.05^2) = 3.14 \times 10^{-4} \text{ m}^2$

Force developed for forward motion

$$F_f = 100 \times (3.84 \times 10^{-3})$$

HYDRAULICS AND PNEUMATICS — HYDRAULIC ACTUATORS

$$= 0.0314 \times 10^5 = 3.84 \times 10^4 \text{ N}$$

Force for retraction, $F_r = 100 \times (3.14 \times 10^{-4}) \times 10^5$

$$= 3.14 \times 10^3 \text{ N}$$

Velocity of piston if (no regeneration) in forward stroke is

$$\frac{Q}{A} = \frac{25 \text{ lit./min.}}{(3.84 \times 10^{-3})} = 101 \text{ mm/sec.}$$

and in backward stroke $= \dfrac{25}{(3.14 \times 10^{-4} \text{ m}^2)} = 220$ mm/sec.

In regenerative circuit,

$$\text{forward stroke velocity} = \frac{\text{Pump supply}}{\text{rod area}}$$

$$= \frac{25 \text{ lit./min.}}{\frac{\pi}{4}(0.5)^2} = 212 \text{ mm/sec.} = 21.2 \text{ cm/sec.}$$

and Return speed $= \dfrac{25}{(3.14 \times 10^{-4} \text{ m}^2)} = 220$ mm/sec. $= 22.0$ cm/sec.

Thus the forward stroke velocity is almost equal to the return speed..

Example 3.17: *A 10000 N weight is to be lowered by a vertical cylinder as shown in Fig. 3.34. The cylinder has a 75 mm diameter piston and a 50 mm diameter rod. The weight is to decelerate from 100 m/min to a stop in 0.5 second. Determine the required pressure in the rod end of the cylinder during the deceleration motion.* **(Dec. 2008)**

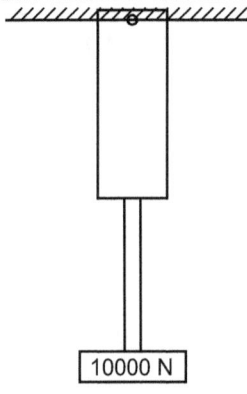

Fig. 3.34

Solution: Acceleration of cylinder,

$$a = \frac{V_2 - V_1}{t} = \frac{0 - (100/60)}{0.5} = -3.33 \text{ m/s}^2$$

The force required at the rod end side is,

$$F_r = W - \frac{W}{g} \times a = 10000 - \frac{10000}{9.81} \times 3.33 = 6602 \text{ N}$$

The required pressure in the rod end side,

$$P_r = \frac{F_r}{A_r} = \frac{F_r}{\frac{\pi}{4}(D^2 - d^2)} = \frac{6602}{\frac{\pi}{4}[(0.075)^2 - (0.05)^2]}$$

$$= \mathbf{26.89 \text{ bar}}$$

EXERCISE

1. Write a note on rotary actuators.
2. What is the need and role played by actuators in hydraulic systems.
3. List various actuators to obtain linear and rotary motions.
4. What are the applications of hydraulic motors? Discuss with suitable examples.
5. Write note on Swash plate motor.
6. Explain various hydraulic motor efficiencies.
7. Name four different types of cylinder mountings with sketches.
   (May 01, Dec. 02, 04, May 04)
8. What are the variables to determine the wall thickness and a factor of safety for a conductor for a particular operating pressure. **(Dec. 01)**
9. Explain the terms: volumetric, mechanical, overall efficiencies of hydraulic motor.
   (Dec. 01)
10. Write notes on:
    (a) Telescopic cylinder
    (b) Rodless cylinder
    (c) Hydraulic cylinder mountings
    (d) Swatch plate motor
    (e) Cushioning of cylinder
    (f) Balanced vane motor
    (g) Selection of motors.
11. Draw typical operating characteristics of hydraulic motors. **(Dec. 02)**
12. Explain the working of a radial piston motor. **(May 03)**

13. What is cushioning in a cylinder and how are cylinders are rated? **(May 03)**
14. What do you mean by Tandem cylinder and Telescopic cylinder? What are their applications? **(May 03)**
15. Write a short note on: Balanced vane motor. **(May 03, Dec. 04)**
16. What are the efficiencies of hydraulic motors? **(Dec. 03)**
17. What do you mean by stop tubes and tie rod spacers in hydraulic motors?
18. Write down expression for various efficiencies of motor. **(May 04)**
19. What is rod-wiper in cylinder? **(May 04)**
20. Explain with a neat sketch the construction and working of a typical hydraulic cylinder. **(May 04)**
21. What are the different causes of pump failures in hydraulic system? Explain. **(Dec. 04)**
22. What are the design considerations for hydraulic cylinders? **(Dec. 04)**
23. A hydraulic cylinder has a piston diameter of 70 mm and a piston rod diameter of 50 mm connected to a regenerative circuit where the pump flow rate is 25 lit/min and the working pressure is 100 bar. Show that both the forward and return speeds are almost equal.
24. A hydraulic motor has a displacement of 164 cm^3 and operates with a pressure of 70 bar and a speed of 2000 RPM. If the actual flow rate consumed by the motor is 0.006 m^3/s and the actual torque delivered by the motor is 170 Nm, find the overall efficiency and the actual power delivered by the motor.

Unit IV

INDUSTRIAL CIRCUITS

4.1 NECESSITY OF FLUID CONTROL

"Control" is one of the most important considerations in any fluid power system. The pump present in the system generates the flow of fluid which is to be fed to the cylinder and other actuators. This fluid power is controlled primarily through the use of control devices called "valves". Basically, valves are expected to control the direction of flow, pressure of flowing fluid, quantity of fluid flowing and other intended functions.

4.1.1 Need of Direction Control

In a hydraulic circuit, the hydraulic machine, the actuators make motions [Linear actuators – To and fro motions and rotary actuators – rotary motions] to operate the load. Hence, the directions of oil feeding the cylinder or motor needs to be controlled (i.e. reversed). This need of direction control of the fluid path is accomplished primarily by direction control valves viz. two-way, three-way, four-way direction control valves.

4.1.2 Need of Pressure Control

In a hydraulic system, as per demand, the oil pressure is required to be increased or decreased. Also, sometimes the system is required to be protected against over pressure, which may occur due to gradual buildup as fluid demand decreases or due to sudden surge as valves open or close. This may produce, an instantaneous increase in pressure as much as four times the normal system pressure. These abnormalities of fluid pressure need to be controlled and it is done by pressure control valves, viz. pressure relief, pressure reducing, sequence, unloading and counter balance.

4.1.3 Need of Flow Control

In many industrial hydraulic system applications, the speed of the operations are required to be changed as per the requirement. Hence, correspondingly the speed of the actuators needs to be altered. This ultimately demands control of fluid flow rate flowing through these actuators. This task is accomplished by the use of flow control valves viz. proportional flow and pressure control valve, non-compensated flow control valve, temperature compensated flow control valves.

In this unit, direction, pressure and flow control valves are discussed.

4.2 PRESSURE CONTROL VALVES

In a hydraulic circuit, a pressure control valve has the following functions:
1. Restricting maximum pressure in a system thereby ensuring safety e.g. relief valve.
2. Reducing / regulating pressure in certain sections of the circuit. e.g. pressure reducing valves.
3. Unloading system pressure e.g. unloader valves.
4. Providing pressure control for sequential operation of actuators in a circuit. e.g. sequencing valve.
5. Any other function accomplished by pressure control.

4.2.1 Types of Pressure Control Valves

Based on a specific function accomplished by a pressure control valve, they can be classified as:

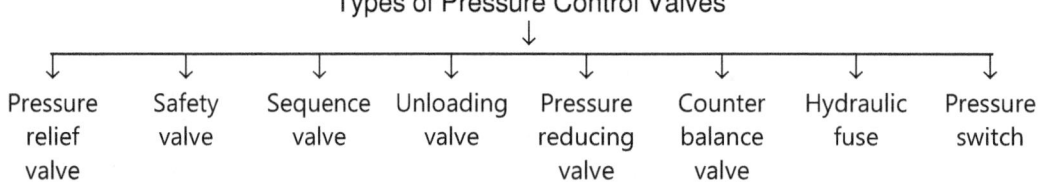

Construction and working of each valve is explained hereafter.

4.2.2 Pressure Relief Valves (May 09, 10, Dec. 11, May 12)

Every hydraulic system needs a pressure relief valve. It is a NC (normally closed) valve located between the pressure line and the oil reservoir. Its function is to limit the pressure in a system within a pre-set maximum limit by diverting partial or full flow of the pump discharge to the reservoir, whenever a pre-set pressure is reached.

A simple spring loaded pressure control valve as shown in Fig. 4.1 is often used as a pressure relief valve.

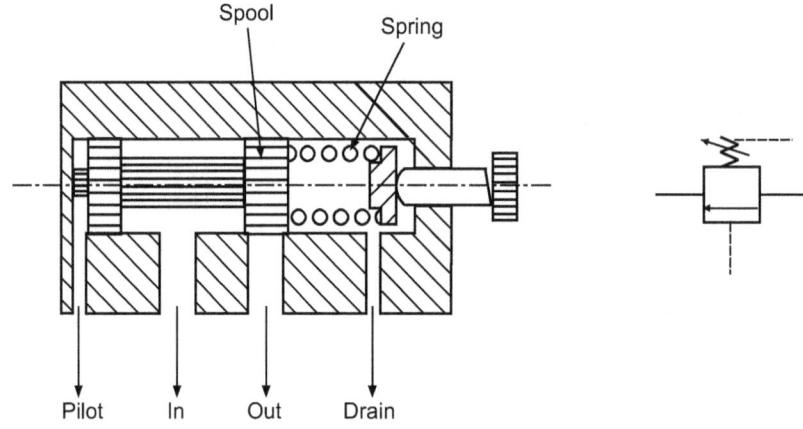

Fig. 4.1: Spring loaded pressure relief valve

When this valve is closed, inlet and outlet ports are isolated by a spool. Hydraulic sealing is ensured using fine clearance between the spool and its housing. However at high system pressure, sealing becomes less effective, permitting leakage. Often the spool proppet is replaced by a conical poppet or a ball. This is found to be quite effective at high pressure.

Fig. 4.2 shows a conical poppet type pressure relief valve.

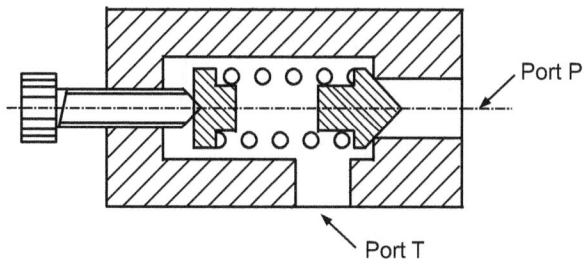

Fig. 4.2: Conical poppet type pressure relief valve

In this valve, oil pressure at port 'P' acts on the exposed surface of the conical poppet. The oil generated force is opposed by the spring force. When the pressure at port 'P' exceeds the pre-set limit, this force overcomes the spring force, lifting the conical poppet off its seat allowing the oil to flow to the tank port 'T'. Thus the system pressure is relieved.

The conical poppet or ball type valve are found to have quick response to pressure surge, commonly 25 ms. In case of systems having varying pressure-flow characteristic, the poppet or ball tries to hammer on the seat resulting in relief valve chatter, seat damage and greater leakage.

The valve chatter or whine can be eliminated using a guided piston type pressure relief valve (Fig. 4.3).

This valve provides quiet, noiseless operation but is suitable for low system pressure upto 100 bar, under constant flow characteristic. It has a high pressure over-ride characteristic.

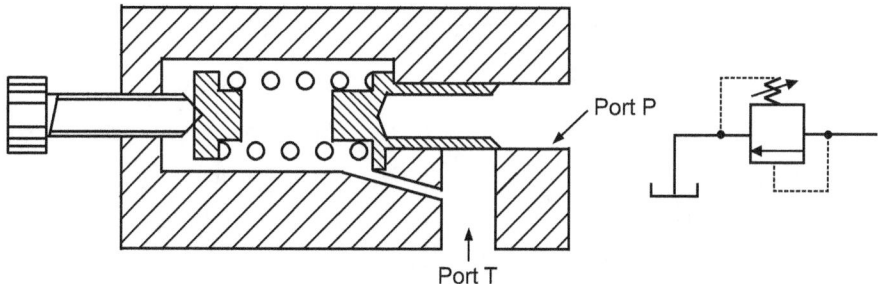

Fig. 4.3: Guided piston type pressure relief valve

The pressure override is defined as the difference between cracking pressure (or opening pressure) and the pressure drop across the valve when it is permitting maximum rated flow at a given valve setting.

Differential piston/poppet type pressure relief valve: This valve is shown in Fig. 4.4.

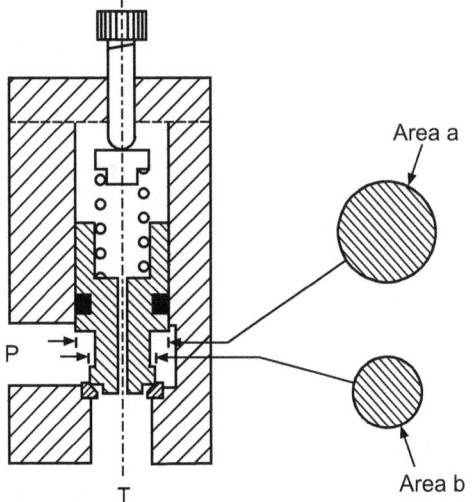

Fig. 4.4: Differential piston type pressure relief valve

This valve is suitable for pressures upto 350 bar. Oil pressure acts on differential areas between the poppet and the seat. The force required to lift the poppet = Pressure × (a − b). As the valve opens, a small poppet movement opens a large flow area. This in turn reduces the pressure over-ride. The reset pressure is required to be lower than the opening pressure.

4.2.3 Pressure Control Valve Characteristic

The pressure at which the valve first opens is known as cracking pressure. As the flow through the valve increases, the pressure drop across the valve increases. The difference between the full flow pressure and initial pressure may be undesirable to other system components. It also results in a wastage of power as the fluid is lost through the valve before attaining a maximum set pressure. Fig. 4.5 illustrates the pressure-flow characteristic for a simple relief valve.

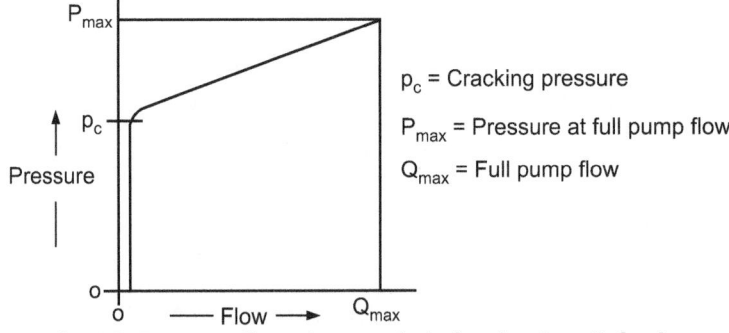

Fig. 4.5: Pressure-flow characteristic for simple relief valve

The poppet must provide sufficient opening to allow full pump flow. The pressure 'p_{max}' at full pump flow is considerably higher than the cracking pressure. The pressure setting of the relief valve represents the pressure at full pump flow through the valve. Fig. 4.6 shows the opening and closing characteristic of a pressure relief valve.

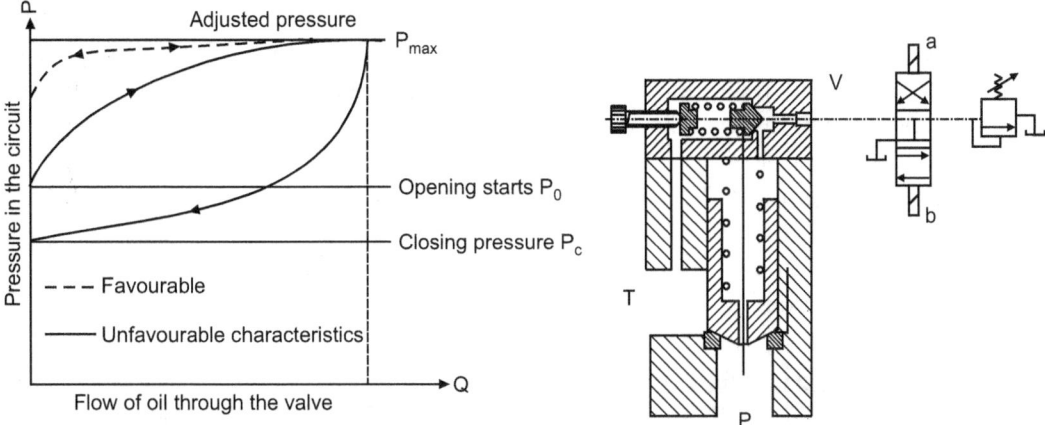

Fig. 4.6: Opening and closing characteristic of a pressure relief valve

It is evident from the graph that opening (cracking) and closing pressures of the pressure relief valve are different, the closing pressure is lower than the cracking pressure. This feature is not desirable considering the safety of the system. The desirable opening and closing characteristics are shown by the dotted line.

4.2.4 Pilot Operated Relief Valve (Dec. 07, May 08, May 12)

Fig. 4.7 shows a pilot operated pressure relief valve. It is a two-stage valve giving good pressure regulation over a wide range of flow. Its main spool is controlled by in-built direct acting relief valve. A small hole or jet in the spool or through the housing communicates the pressure to the pilot relief valve.

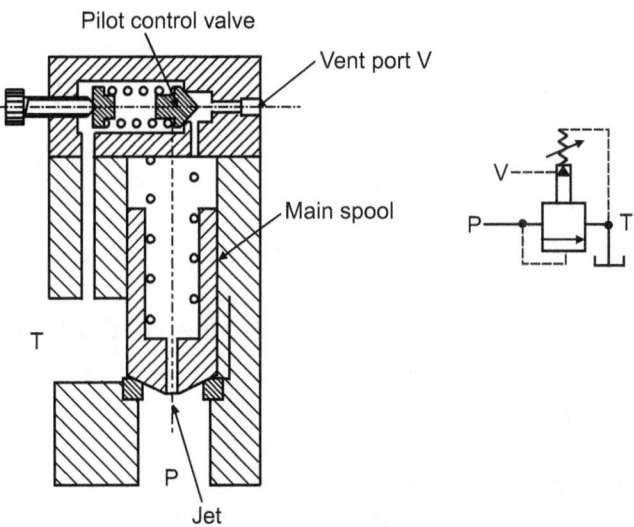

Fig. 4.7: Pilot operated pressure relief valve

Unit IV | 4.5

When the valve is closed, the main spool is in the hydraulic balance (i.e. pressure at inlet port acts under the piston and also top) retained onto its seat by a light spring. Increase of inlet pressure opens the control valve, and drains oil behind the piston. And the main spool opens under hydraulic imbalance, due to pressure drop across the jet. The spool valve lifts compressing the spring, relieving the flow to the tank preventing a further rise in pressure. The small flow passing through the control section is also returned to tank through internal drain.

A separate pilot or vent port 'V' is kept plugged during normal operation and can be used for remote operation.

Thus this valve (also known as compound relief valve) increases pressure sensitivity by reducing pressure override.

4.2.5 Dual Pressure Relief Valves

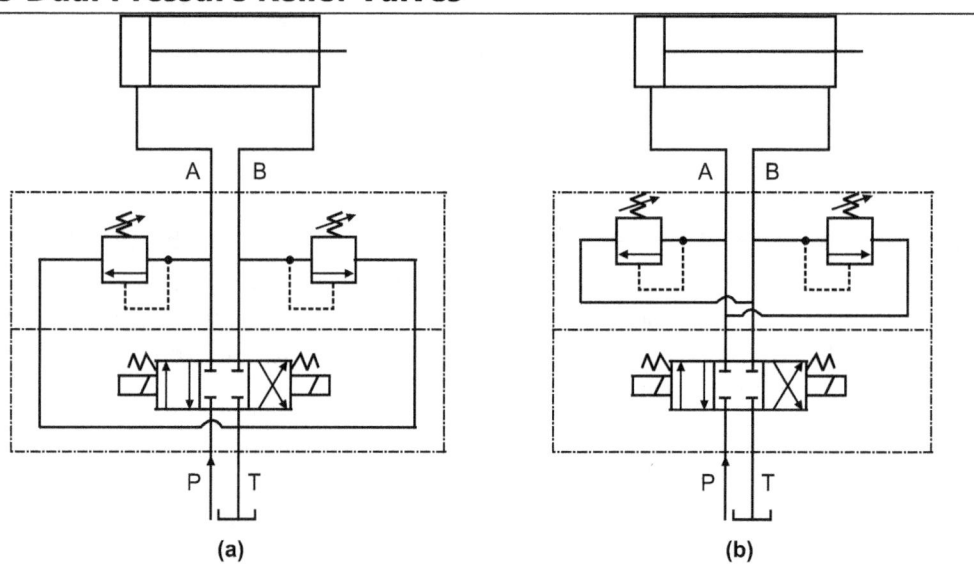

Fig. 4.8: Dual pressure relief valves

Often pressure relief valves are necessary in pairs to relieve the pressure on either side of a double acting actuator. The pressure can be relieved to a tank or the opposite (cross line relief) service valve as shown in Fig. 4.8.

4.2.6 Selection of Relief Valve and Choice of Pressure Setting

The selection of correct type of pressure relief valve and pressure setting at which the valve should crack open requires careful thought.

The factors influencing type of pressure relief valve are listed below:
1. Pressure override characteristic and nature of flow i.e. whether steady or varying.
2. Reset pressure or pressure at which the valve should close.
3. Response time.

Direct acting valve has high pressure over-ride characteristic and is suitable for unvarying flow systems. Two stage valves offer good pressure regulation covering wide range of flow with low pressure over-ride and narrow gap between cracking pressure and resetting pressure. Direct acting valves give fast response time. Poppet valves tolerate contaminated fluids and have less leakage.

A thumb rule for pressure setting suggests 10% to 20% higher pressure above the maximum working pressure of system in case of a main pressure relief valve based on its type, its location in a circuit and the pressure losses of the system. In case of multiple pressure relief valves used in a circuit, the controls pressures should not be set too close with each other to avoid hunting.

4.3 SAFETY VALVES

The safety valve in a hydraulic circuit is basically a poppet type 2-way valve. It releases the fluid to a tank whenever the system pressure exceeds the pressure setting of the valve. Thus, this valve ensures safety of piping and components from excessive pressure.

4.4 PRESSURE SEQUENCING VALVES   (May 07, 08, 10, 11, 12; Dec. 09)

This valve senses a change in fluid pressure in a system and generates a hydraulic signal (whenever the set pressure is reached. This valve may be NO or NC valve. It changes its state when the set pressure is reached in the system. This valve is used to assign priority hydraulic pressure in one system before the other system operates.

The salient feature of this valve is the provision of a separate drain connection from spring chamber. This is necessary as a high pressure is likely to develop in the output port during normal working.

This valve can as well be used as a relief valve in a circuit having a possibility of excessive back pressure in the return line. A separate drained pilot provides insensitivity to the return line back pressure.

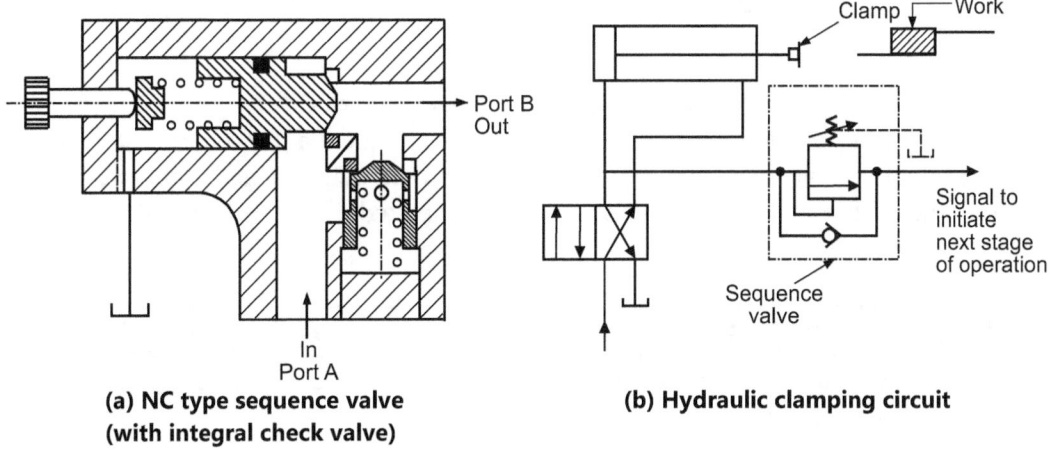

(a) NC type sequence valve (with integral check valve)

(b) Hydraulic clamping circuit

Fig. 4.9

A NC type sequence valve with a built-in reverse flow check valve is shown in Fig. 4.9 (a) while Fig. 4.9 (b) shows a typical hydraulic clamping circuit using this valve. The sequence valve does not allow the 'next' operation unless a component is clamped. After the components connected to port A have reached the adjusted pressure of the sequence valve, it passes the fluid through port B to do additional work in a different portion of the system.

Yet another most common application of a sequence valve is sequencing of cylinder movements as shown in Fig. 4.10. For one position of the D.C. valve, when the oil is supplied to cylinder A, it will extend first followed by cylinder B. The flow to cylinder B is through sequence valve S_1 which will open when the pressure at the full bore end of cylinder A has attained a certain value. In the second position of the d.c. valve, cylinder B will retract before cylinder A. For this to happen the sequence valve S_2 is provided.

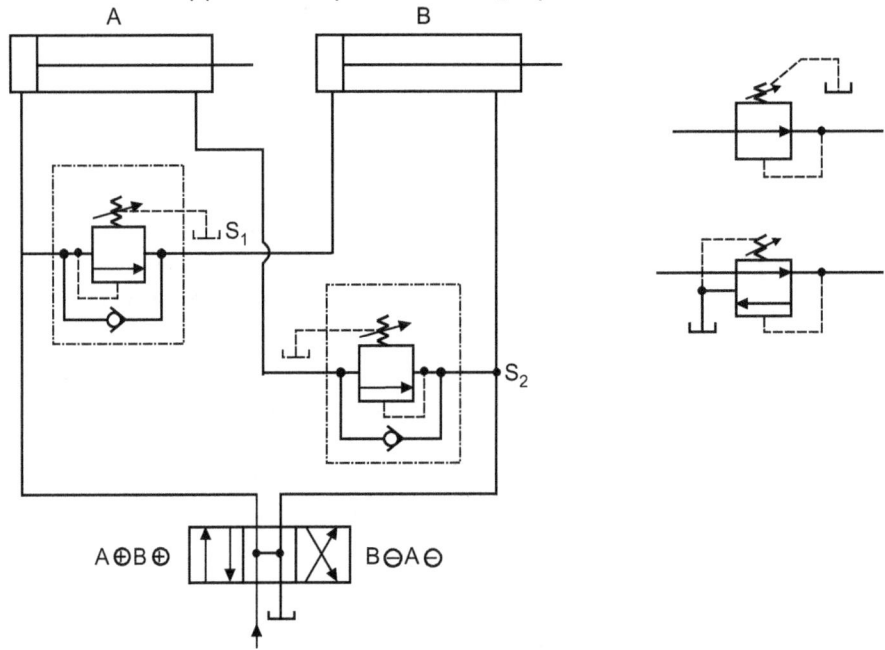

Fig. 4.10: Cylinder sequencing circuit (May 12)

Whenever pressure sensing is used to control cylinder sequential movements, it should be specifically noted that when a particular pre-set pressure is reached, sequencing valve operates irrespective of whether the pistons have completed or reached a particular position in their strokes.

4.5 UNLOADED VALVES (May 08, 09, 11, 12)

A pressure control valve can be used as an unloader valve in two ways (i) by pressure release or venting (ii) by pilot pressure.

This valve is used to allow a pump to build-up pressure to a pre-set value and then to allow it to discharge to the tank almost at zero pressure so long as a pilot pressure is maintained on the valve from a remote source. Thus the pump is unloaded and develops minimum hydraulic power output. (Power = Pressure × Flow rate)

Fig. 4.11 (a) shows relief valve unloading by venting while Fig. 4.11 (b) shows relief valve unloading by pilot pressure signal.

Referring to Fig. 4.11 (a), relief valve can be unloaded by connecting vent port 'v' to the tank. Venting makes the main spool to be unbalanced and opens at low pressure by-passing pump flow from 'P' to 'T'. The flow through the vent is quite small, though the main flow may be very large.

The direct acting unloader valve is shown in Fig. 4.11 (b). So long as the force due to pilot pressure force exceeds that of the control spring, the relief valve opens fully permitting main flow from the pump to go to the tank at low pressure.

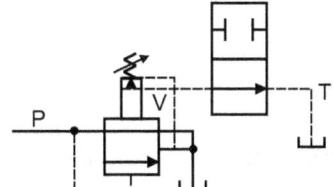   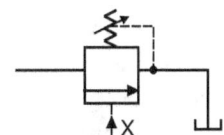

(a) Relief valve unloading by venting   (b) Relief valve unloading by pilot pressure

Fig. 4.11

The opening of the vent port 'V' releasing pressure and causing the main spool to open, is independent of control spring setting, in case of unloading by venting.

Whereas in unloading by pilot pressure, the force due to remote pilot pressure opens the spool against the spring setting.

Uses of Unloader Valves:

These valves are used in circuits using two pumps providing a large flow at low pressure and one of the pumps is required to be unloaded during a specific period of working cycle requiring a low flow of oil at high pressure. This helps to protect the system from undesirable heat generation and consequent oil heating.

4.6 PRESSURE REDUCING VALVES   (Dec. 07, May 10, May 12)

The main function of this valve is to restrict the pressure in a port of circuit to a lower value than that required in the rest of the circuit.

It is a 'NO' type valve which throttles or closes to maintain a constant low pressure in a replaced line. Direct acting pressure reducing valves for flow rates upto 45 l.p.m. and pressures upto 210 bar are available with or without a built-in reverse flow check valve.

A typical direct acting pressure reducing valve is shown in Fig. 4.12.

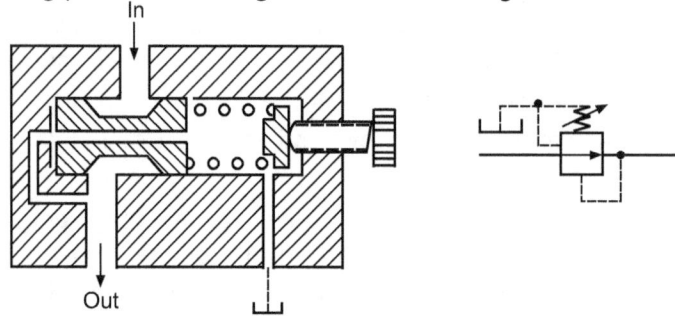

Fig. 4.12: Direct-acting pressure-reducing valve

The valve is maintained open by a spring. Pressure sensed by the outlet port is communicated to the spring loaded spool. Whenever the pressure in the secondary circuit rises, the valve tends to close against the spring pressure. The valve is prevented from complete closing by flows through a small bleed hole in the spool to the spring chamber. This avoids pressure build-up in the downstream of the circuit.

Pressure reducing valves with pilot operation are used for large flow rates and offer better pressure-flow characteristic.

The throttling effect of pressure reducing valve always generates considerable heat. The effects of heat generation have to be duly accounted while using these valves.

4.7 COUNTER BALANCE VALVES (May 08, 10, 12; Dec. 10)

A counter balance valve is essentially a pressure relief valve used in a circuit to set up a back pressure. This valve is used to 'counter balance' a load.

Fig. 4.13 (a) shows the counter balance valve and Fig. 4.13 (b) shows its typical application for counter balancing a load.

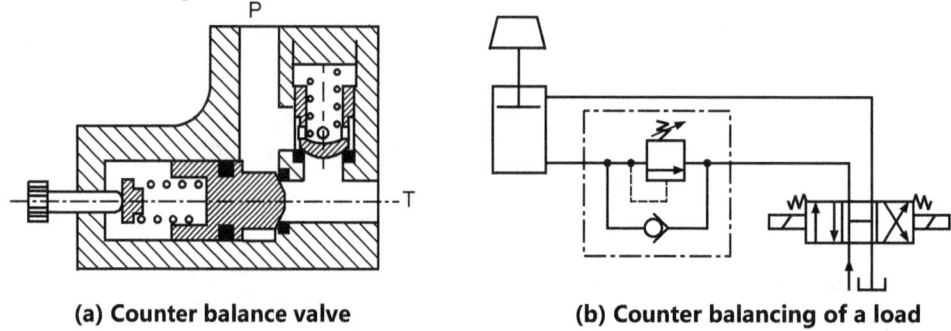

(a) Counter balance valve　　　　(b) Counter balancing of a load

Fig. 4.13

As seen from the circuit shown in Fig. 4.13 (b), the valve creates a back pressure to prevent the load coming down as a 'free fall under gravity. The counter balance pressure set is usually 1.3 times that induced due to load.

A check valve provided in the circuit allows free flow in the reverse direction, to bypass the counter balance valve during the ascent of load. Usually the check valve is integral with the counter balance valve. During counter balancing, the back pressure at 'T' should be kept to a minimum.

Over-Centre Valve:

The counter balance valve has a drawback that it reduces the available force. As an illustration, refer to press circuit shown in Fig. 4.14 (a). Here, the counter balance valve is used to counteract the load of press tools when they are closing. During pressing/forming operation, a part of possible pressing force is lost in overcoming the back pressure set-up by the counter balance valve. This drawback of loss of available force using a counterbalance valve can be eliminated by using a remote pilot operation shown in Fig. 4.14 (b).

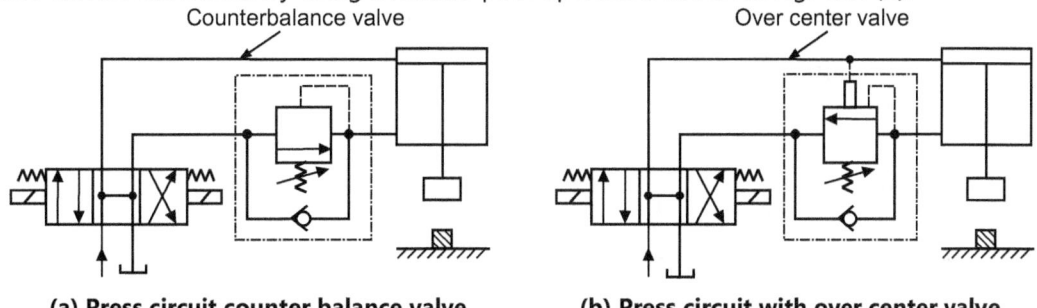

(a) Press circuit counter balance valve   **(b) Press circuit with over center valve**

Fig. 4.14

This remotely operated counter balance valve is shown in Fig. 4.15. It is also known a 'Over center' valve or Brake valve.

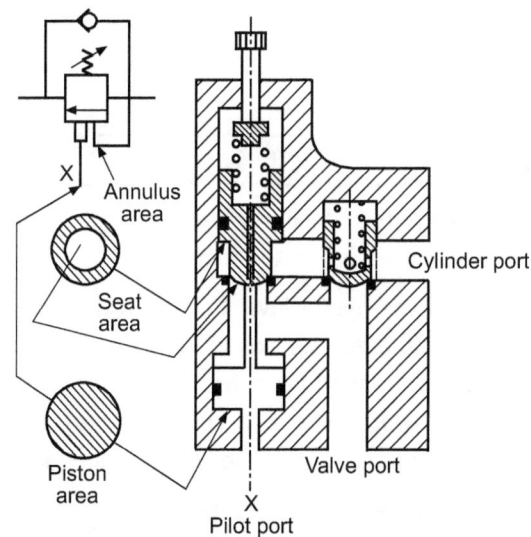

Fig. 4.15: Over center or brake valve

A low pressure in the pilot section switches on the valve open, releasing back pressure from the cylinder annulus side. When the piston tries to run away, pilot pressure is destroyed and the counter balance section returns into the circuit.

During forming / pressing operation, the valve is piloted open releasing the back pressure and all the pressure on the full bore side is thus made available for pressing.

The over-center valve is also used as a hydrostatic transmission motor circuit as a 'braking valve' as shown in Fig. 4.16. The over center valve serves to:

1. To hold the load in neutral (inclining) position.
2. To control speed of descend of winch.
3. To gradually brake the motor to halt on change over from 'descent' to 'neutral'.

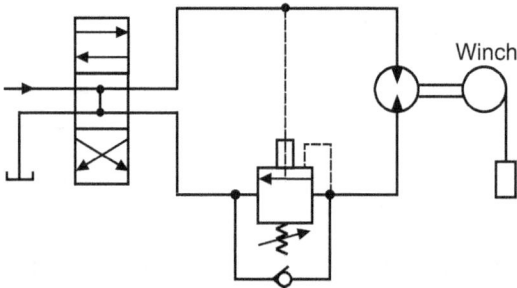

Fig. 4.16: Over center valve as a braking valve for a winch control

The ratio of pilot pressure to direct pressure necessary to open the valve ranges between 2: 1 to 10: 1 depending upon the application. Twin units for control of motors in both directions are also available.

4.8 Hydraulic Fuse

It is a safety device which is not automatically reset. It consists of a pre-stressed disk in the valve which holds the fluid under pressure in the fuse.

When the fluid pressure reaches the preset level for which the disk is pre-stressed, the disk ruptures thereby releasing the fluid to the low pressure port. In this way, the piping or components to which the fuse is attached is protected from excessive pressure by adopting a suitable disk. When the disk ruptures, the circuit is out of operation till the cause of excessive pressure built-up is rectified and a new disk is replaced in the fuse.

Hydraulic fuses offer excellent protection for hydraulic jacks and similar devices in circuits exposed to excessive pressure. Fig. 4.17 shows a typical hydraulic fuse.

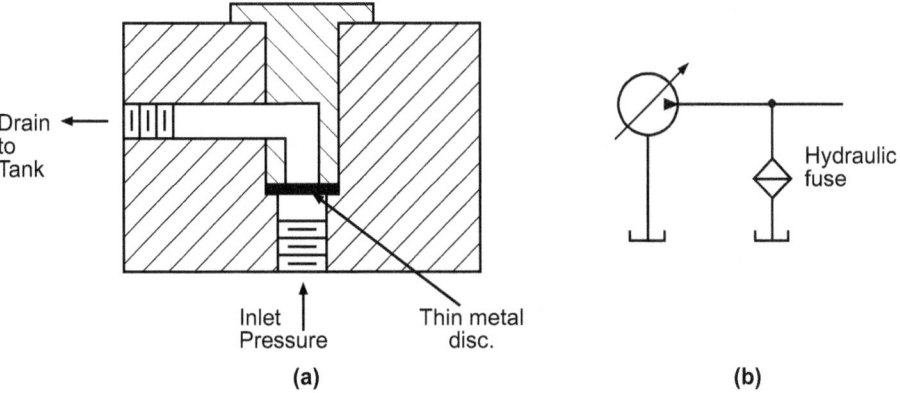

Fig. 4.17: Hydraulic fuse (Schematic and graphic symbols)

SOLVED EXAMPLES

Example 4.1: *A piston of 50 mm diameter is to support a load of 20 kN. Estimate the pressure setting required for a counter balance valve.*

Solution: Load induced pressure 'p' is given by

$$p = \frac{20 \times 10^3}{\frac{\pi}{4} \times 0.05^2} \text{ Pa} = 101.86 \text{ bar}$$

Pressure setting required for the counter balance valve

$$= 1.3 \times 101.86 = \mathbf{132.42 \text{ bar}} \quad \text{... Ans.}$$

Example 4.2: *A hydraulic press has a capacity of 200 kN and has tools weighing 10 kN. It has a piston diameter of 80 mm and piston rod diameter of 60 mm. Determine the: (i) pressure setting of counter-balance valve (ii) oil supply pressure required to provide the rated capacity.*

Solution: Full bore area $= \frac{\pi}{4} \times 0.08^2 = 0.005 \text{ m}^2$

Annulus area $= \frac{\pi}{4} (0.08^2 - 0.06^2) = 0.0028 \text{ m}^2$

∴ Pressure at annulus side to balance tool weight

$$= \frac{10 \times 10^3}{0.0028} \text{ Pa} = 35.71 \text{ bar}$$

∴ Recommended counter balance valve setting

$$= 1.3 \times 35.71 = \mathbf{46.43 \text{ bar}} \quad \text{... Ans.}$$

Now, pressure at full bore side of cylinder to overcome counterbalance

$$= 46.43 \times \frac{\text{Annulus area}}{\text{Full bore area}} = 26 \text{ bar}$$

Hence oil supply pressure required to provide 200 kN pressing force

$$= \frac{200 \times 10^3 \times 10^{-5} + 26}{0.005} \text{ bar} = \textbf{426 bar} \qquad \text{... Ans.}$$

Example 4.3: *A pressure relief valve has a pressure setting of 125 bar. Compute the power loss across this valve if it returns all flow back to the tank from 15 LPM pump.* **(Dec. 2003)**

Solution: Pressure drop is $= (125)$ bar $= \Delta P$

and Discharge $= \left(\dfrac{15 \times 10^{-3}}{60}\right)$ m³/sec $= Q$

We have the relationship as,

$$\text{Power loss across the valve} = Q \cdot \Delta P = \left(\frac{15 \times 10^{-3}}{60}\right) \times (125 \times 10^5)$$

$\therefore$ Power loss $= 3.125$ kW

Example 4.4: *A pressure relief valve has a pressure setting of 140 bars. Compute the power loss across this valve if it returns all the flow back to the tank from 1.62 litres per second pump.* **(May 2004)**

Solution: Pressure drop $= \Delta P = 140$ bar

Discharge $= Q = 1.62 \times 10^{-3}$ m³/sec

Power loss across the valve $= Q \cdot \Delta P$

$= (1.62 \times 10^{-3}) \times (140 \times 10^5) = 22680$ watt

$\therefore$ Power loss $= 22.68$ kW

Example 4.5: *Consider the application in Example 4.2 but using over-center valve with pilot input ratio 2 : 1 set at 46.43 bar to balance the tool weight, instead of using a counterbalance valve. Calculate the oil supply pressure required to provide the rated capacity.*

Solution: Pressure on pilot required to open the valve

$$= \frac{46.43}{2} = 23.225 \text{ bar}$$

This is the pressure at full bore side to descend the tooling.

Therefore, oil supply pressure required to provide a pressing force of 200 kN

$$= \frac{(200 - 10)}{0.005} \times 10^{-3} \times 10^{-5} \text{ bar}$$

$= 380$ bar (as against 426 bar pressure required using counterbalance valve) ... **Ans.**

Example 4.6: *A primary part of a certain hydraulic circuit is operating at 210 bar. A secondary circuit supplied from a primary circuit through a pressure reducing valve requires a constant flow of 40 l.p.m. at 150 bar. Calculate the loss of power over the pressure reducing valve.*

Solution: Pressure loss $= \Delta p \times Q$ kW $= (210 - 150) \times 10^2 \times \dfrac{40 \times 10^{-3}}{60}$

$= 4$ **kW** ... **Ans.**

This loss of power over the pressure reducing valve generates heat which may not be easily dissipated by natural cooling. A separate heat exchange would be necessary. The operating cost of the heat exchanger has to be weighed against the alternative of using two separate pumps in the circuits.

Example 4.7: *A pressure relief valve has a pressure setting of 80 bar. Determine the loss of power across this valve if all flow from pump, 50 l.p.m. is returned back to the tank.*

Solution: Loss of power $= \dfrac{\Delta p \times Q}{1}$ kW

$= 80 \times 10^2 \times \dfrac{90 \times 10^{-3}}{60} = 12$ **kW** ... **Ans.**

Example 4.8: *The pump of Example 4.5 is unloaded using an unloaded valve. If the discharge pressure from the pump during unloading is 2 bar, calculate the loss of power.*

Solution: Loss of power $= \Delta p \times Q$

$= \dfrac{2 \times 10^2 \times 90 \times 10^{-3}}{60}$

$= 0.30$ **kW** ... **Ans.**

The reduction in loss of power due to use of unloader valve can be noticed.

4.9 FLOW CONTROL VALVES

In a hydraulic circuit, flow control valves serve the following functions:
1. Regulation of fluid flow rate to actuators
2. Speed control of actuators.
3. Control of power output from actuators
4. Distribution of available flow from the pump to various branches of a hydraulic circuit.

The flow control is achieved by varying the area of the orifice. The flow characteristics of an orifice has a significant role in designing the hydraulic control devices.

The flow across the orifice is usually turbulent. The flow control valves enable stepless control of the speed of a hydraulic motor.

Based on the relation between flow and pressure, the flow control valves are broadly divided into two categories as flows.

Classification of flow control valves

↓ ↓

Flow restrictor or throttle valves (Pressure dependent) | Pressure independent flow control valves

4.9.1 Basic Principle of a Flow Control

The flow rate 'Q' and linear velocity of piston 'V_p' are interrelated as follows:

$$V_p = \frac{Q}{A_p} \text{ cm/min.}$$

where Q = Flow rate, cm³/min.
       A_p = Area of piston, cm².

Similarly, rotational speed 'n' of a hydraulic motor is given by

$$n = \frac{Q}{V_m} \text{ rev/min.}$$

where Q = Flow rate, cm³/min.
       V_m = Volumetric capacity of motor, cm³/rev.

It is thus evident that linear velocity 'V_p' or rotational speed 'H' directly varies with flow rate 'Q'. A throttle valve is used for a simple regulation and is pressure dependent.

When constant speed is to be maintained independent of pressure drop, a pressure compensated flow control valve is necessary.

4.9.2 Flow Phenomena Across a Throttling Aperture

When a fluid flows across a throat of a venturi, the fluid accelerates accompanied by a pressure drop. Fig. 4.18 (a) and (b) show two types of throats, one long and the other short, both of fixed type.

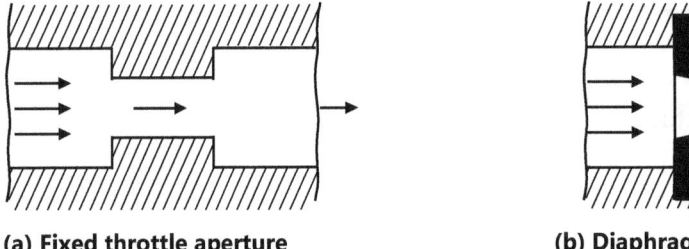

(a) Fixed throttle aperture   (b) Diaphragm throttle

Fig. 4.18

As per Hagen-Poiseuille's law, the pressure drop governing laminar flow through a small pipe diameter is given by,

$$\Delta p = \frac{8 \mu l}{r^2} v$$

where μ = Dynamic viscosity, kgf-s/m²
l = Length of flow path, cm
r = Radius of flow path, cm
v = Velocity of flow, cm/s

or $\quad \Delta p = \dfrac{32\,\mu l\, v}{d^2}$; $\qquad$ hence $d = 2r$ cm

Further,
$\quad \mu = \upsilon \times \rho$
where, υ = Kinematic viscosity, m²/s
ρ = Density of fluid, kg-s²/cm⁴

And Reynold's number, $R_e = \dfrac{\mu \times D_w}{\upsilon}$ $\qquad$ for circular cross section

Here $\quad R_e$ = Reynold's number
D_w = Wetted flow perimeter, cm

Also, $\quad \lambda = \dfrac{64}{R_e} = $ Laminar coefficient of friction at constant temperature

$= \dfrac{64}{\dfrac{v\,D_w}{\upsilon}} = \dfrac{64\,\upsilon}{v D_w}$

$= \dfrac{75}{R_e}$ $\qquad$ for laminar non-isothermal condition

Similarly, for turbulent flow,

$$\lambda = \dfrac{0.3164}{R_e^{0.25}}$$

$\therefore \quad \Delta p = \dfrac{32\, l\, \mu\, v}{D_w^2} = \dfrac{64\, l\, \upsilon\, \rho\, v}{2\, D_w^2}$

$= \dfrac{\lambda\, l\, \rho\, v^2}{2\, D_w}$

$\Delta p = \lambda \dfrac{l}{D_w} \times \dfrac{\rho}{2}\, v^2$

But $\quad A = \dfrac{\pi}{4} \times d^2$; $d^2 = \dfrac{4A}{\pi} = \dfrac{4A}{C}$

where, C = circumference = πd, cm

$\therefore \quad D_w = \dfrac{4A}{C}$

4.9.3 Coefficient of Resistance 'ξ'
(Signifies Energy Loss in Bends, Tees, Valves etc.)

$$\xi = \lambda \frac{1}{D_w}$$

$\therefore \quad \Delta p = \lambda \frac{1}{D_w} \times \frac{\rho}{2} v^2$

$$= \xi \frac{\rho}{2} v^2$$

where, $\quad \xi$ = Coefficient of local hydraulic loss in a bend, tee, valve, contraction or expansion.

$\therefore \quad$ Flow velocity, $v = \sqrt{\dfrac{\Delta p}{\xi \times \dfrac{\rho}{2}}}$

Equation of continuity for a steady flow of an incompressible fluid gives,

$$Q = A_1 v_1 = A_2 v_2$$

$\therefore \quad Q = Av = A \times \sqrt{\dfrac{\Delta p}{\xi \times \dfrac{\rho}{2}}}$

Also $\quad \gamma$ = Specific Weight = ρg

$\therefore \quad \rho = \dfrac{\gamma}{g}$

$\therefore \quad Q = A \sqrt{\dfrac{\Delta p \times 2g}{\gamma}}$

The above equation applies to laminar or turbulent flow upto a limiting area of cross-section. The Reynold number designates the type of flow, whether laminar or turbulent. The friction characteristics are determined by the coefficient of friction (laminar) λ, while flow through bends, tees is obtained by the coefficient of resistance 'ξ'.

$$\xi = \lambda \frac{1}{D_w} = \frac{64}{R_e} \times \frac{1}{D_w} = \frac{64 \times \upsilon \times l}{v \times D_w^2}$$

$$= \frac{64 \, v \, l}{v \, D_w^2}$$

From the above equation, it is seen that, coefficient of resistance 'ξ' depends upon
(a) Velocity of flow, v
(b) Kinematic viscosity, υ

(c) Throttle length, 'l'
(d) Wetted hydraulic diameter 'D_W'
(e) Form of throttle
(f) Reynold's number 'R_e'

Similarly, the flow rate through a diaphragm or an aperture is given by

$$Q = \alpha A \sqrt{\frac{\Delta p \times 2g}{\gamma}}$$

where Q = Flow rate
A = Area of aperture
Δp = Pressure drop across aperture
g = Gravitational acceleration
γ = Specific weight of fluid
α = Dimensionless coefficient to account for non-uniform velocity distribution based on form factor

4.9.4 Determination of Flow Rate

The flow rate 'Q' is given by

$$Q = \alpha A \sqrt{\frac{2g \times \Delta p}{\gamma}} \; cm^3/s$$

where γ = specific weight of oil

(0.855 at 20°C and 0.869 for oil having 'υ' = 33 cSt at 50°C)

From the above, it is seen that, the flow rate 'Q' depends upon the

(a) pressure drop, area of cross-section and throttle form
(b) specific weight, density of oil
(c) coefficient of resistance.

Thus, for flow rate to be constant, the pressure drop 'Δp' must be constant. As the effect of change in temperature on the density of most of the hydraulic oils is negligible, the change of temperature on oil has little influence on the flow rate 'Q'.

But change of temperature, changes the kinematic viscosity which in turn changes the coefficient of resistance.

4.9.5 Forms of Throttle

The form of throttle of a valve is selected considering the effect of temperature or viscosity of an oil on the flow rate 'Q'. As explained earlier, the flow rate through a valve is influenced by: (a) viscosity of oil, (b) friction, (c) length of throttle passage and cross-section of the throttling area.

The design of a throttle needs clear understanding of the effect of the following factors:
(i) coefficient of friction
(ii) oil viscosity
(iii) wetted perimeter of contraction
(iv) flow rate.

The throttle form is selected so as to provide the greatest hydraulic diameter. Wetted diameter of throttle form, 'D_w' is given by

$$D_w = \frac{4A}{C}$$

where A = area of orifice i.e. throttle aperture
C = perimeter of the orifice

The ratio 'C/A' is termed as form quotient. It should be as low as possible.

For a given area of cross-section of various throttle forms, Table 4.1 compares form quotient and wetted diameter 'D_W'.

Table 4.1: Comparison of various forms of throttle

Sr. No.	Throttle form	Area of cross-section 'A' mm²	Perimeter 'C' mm	Form quotient C/A	Wetted diameter 'D_m' mm
1.	Circular 6 mm diameter	28.27	18.85	0.667	5.999
2.	Square side a = 5.317 mm	28.27	21.27	0.7522	5.317
3.	Rectangular 4 mm × 7.0685 mm	28.27	22.137	0.7829	5.109
4.	Equilateral triangle of side a = 8.08 mm	28.27	24.242	0.8574	4.665

It is seen from the above table that a circular form having the least form quotient of all forms, is ideal. The next best choice of form is a polygonal.

The choice of a specific throttle form is based on its ability to retain the shape during its operation. A circular form when used at the end is found to result in a blind point. A square form is found to be difficult to maintain due to the change of area. A triangular shape is preferable owing to the ease of manufacture.

Fig. 4.19 (a) shows four types of throttle form and Fig. 4.19 (b) shows their characteristics, 'A/A_{max}' plotted against 'h/h_{max}'. It is evident that curve 'b' is preferred to other curves.

(A) Fixed or Constant Throttle:

A fixed or constant throttle is shown in Fig. 4.18 (a). For this circular form throttle, following characteristics are noteworthy.

(i) Throttle form is preferable.

(ii) It has less wetted perimeter.

(iii) Flow rate 'Q' depends upon the viscosity due to the length of the throttle.

Diaphragm orifice is shown in Fig. 4.18 (b). It is a good throttle form with less wetted perimeter. But the flow rate 'Q' is independent of viscosity due to small length of the throttle.

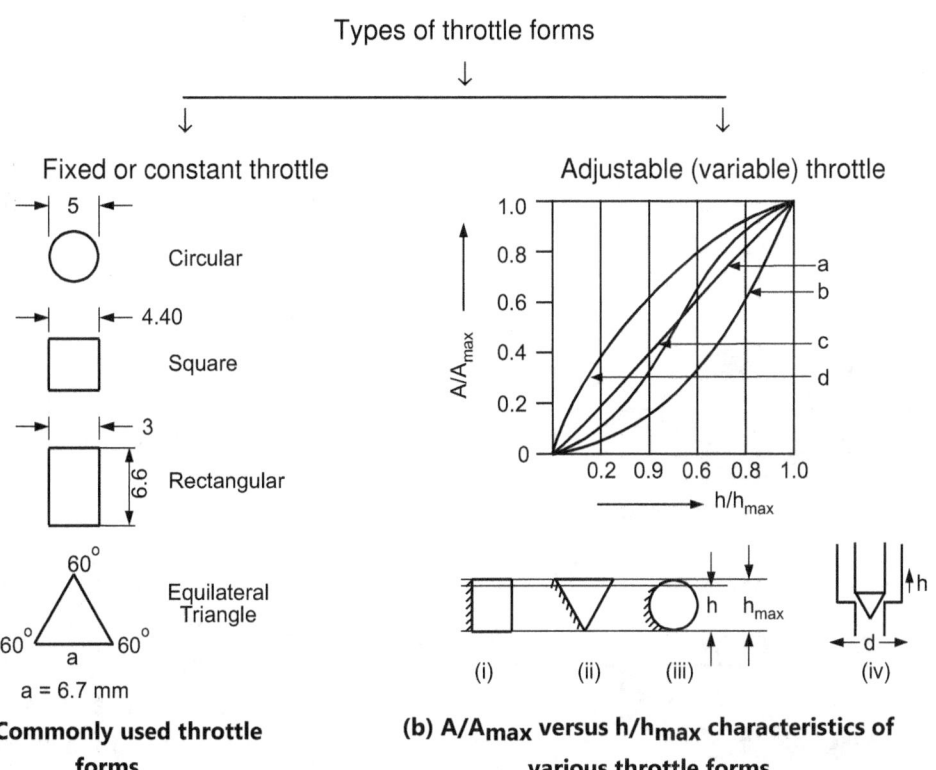

(a) Commonly used throttle forms

(b) A/A$_{max}$ versus h/h$_{max}$ characteristics of various throttle forms

Fig. 4.19

(B) Adjustable Throttle:

Various types of throttle having adjustable area are available. Table 3.4 illustrates various types of adjustable throttles, their flow area determination and characteristics.

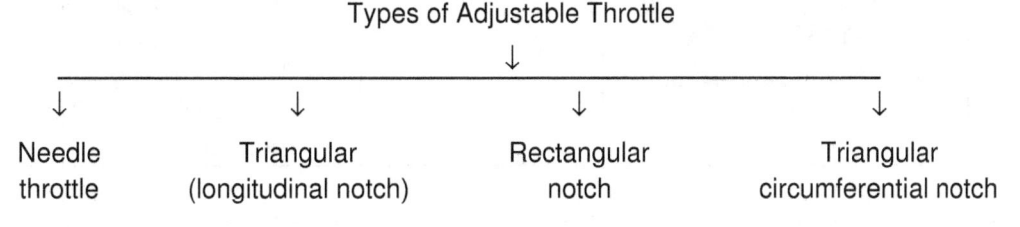

Table 4.2: Types of adjustable throttle and their characteristics

Sr. No.	Type of Adjustable Throttle	Equation of flow area	Characteristics
1.	Needle Throttle Fig. 4.20 (a): Needle throttle	Flow area $= \left\{d - \dfrac{h}{\sin \alpha}\right\} \dfrac{\pi h}{\sin \alpha}$	(a) Small throttle length. (b) Greater wetted perimeter (c) Negligible influence of viscosity (d) Small variation of 'h' produces large change of area of flow. (e) Range of flow path due to change of area is bad.
2.	Triangular (longitudinal) notch Fig. 4.20 (b): Linear triangular notch	Flow area $= \dfrac{h^2}{\sin^2 \alpha} \times \tan \beta/2$	(a) Relatively small throttle length. (b) Small wetted perimeter. (c) Less influence of viscosity. (d) Range of flow path due to area change somewhat better.
3.	Rectangular notch Fig. 4.20 (c): Rectangular notch	Flow area $= \dfrac{h}{\sin \alpha} \times b$	(a) Smaller throttle length. (b) Relatively smaller wetted perimeter. (c) Less influence of viscosity. (d) Good form for a small oil flow.
4.	Triangular circumferential notch Fig. 4.20 (d): Throttle form	Flow area $= a^2 \tan \beta/2$	(a) Longer throttle length. (b) Viscosity influences pressure drop and flow rate. (c) Not so good form of throttle as response to flow control is good between 90° to 180° of rotation of notch.

4.9.6 Performance of Throttle Valve

In a throttle valve, change of area of flow path results in a flow control. The flow rate depends upon pressure drop between the two ports. For a given opening of valve, and a given pressure drop, the flow rate changes with the change of inlet pressure. The change in pressure is influenced by load resistance, velocity of flow cannot be maintained constant in a normal throttle valve. The flow rate is affected by load resistance.

The l/d ratio influences the flow rate 'Q' and pressure drop 'Δp' as listed below.

(a) With large 'l/d' ratio: Flow rate 'Q' and pressure drop 'Δp' depends upon viscosity of oil.

(b) With small 'l/d' ratio: Flow rate 'Q' and pressure drop 'Δp' are independent of viscosity of oil. It is thus evident that the speed of hydraulic actuator also changes when oil flows through a throttle valve.

Fig. 4.21 shows change of velocity of cylinder with a change of load resistance.

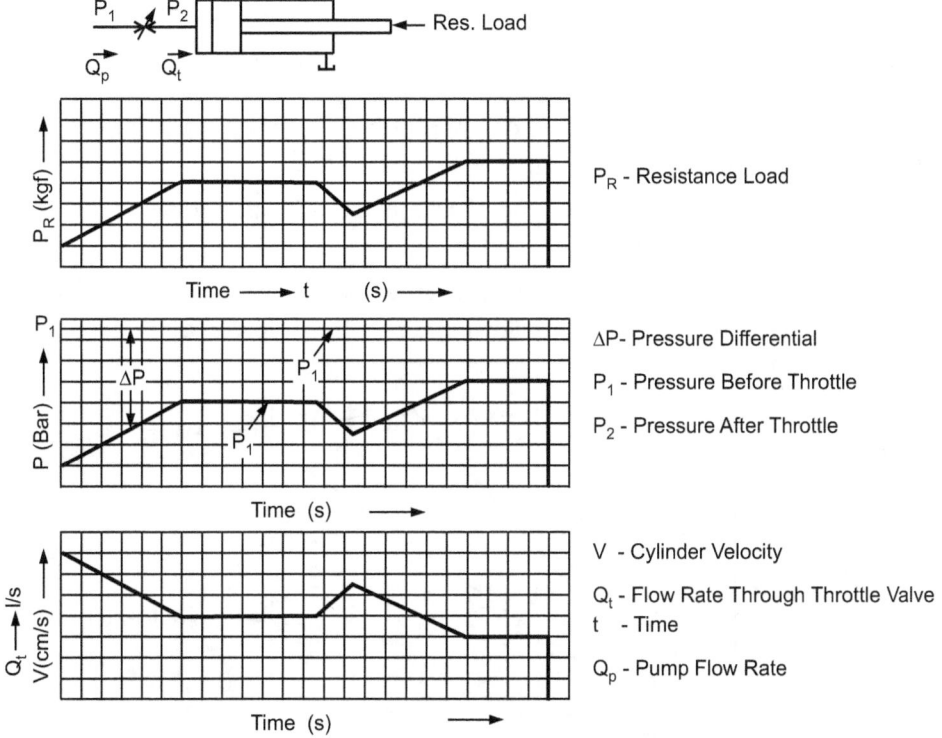

Fig. 4.21: Variation of cylinder velocity with change of load resistance

For a constant load resistance, only a throttle valve can provide a constant speed of cylinder. Often, the throttle valve has a built-in non-return valve.

4.10 ESTIMATION OF FLOW RATE THROUGH AN ORIFICE

As explained earlier

$$\Delta p = \frac{\xi \rho_a}{2} \left(\frac{Q_o}{A_o}\right)^2$$

and

$$Q_o = A_o \sqrt{\frac{2 \Delta p}{\xi \rho_o}}$$

For a given pressure drop,

$$Q = (11 A_a \sqrt{\Delta p}) 10^{-3}$$

where
- A_o = Area of orifice, mm²
- Q = Flow rate, l.p.s.
- Δp = Pressure drop, bar

Due to small diameter of orifices, it is necessary to provide oil filter on the upstream side. In a needle valve, the orifice is of an annular obstruction type and is sensitive to oil contamination.

For an accurate speed control, a pressure compensated flow control valve is necessary which maintains a constant pressure drop to provide a constant flow.

The relationship between flow rate and position of adjusting device can be linear, logarithmic or a specially contoured curve.

The characteristics of a simple needle valve are shown in Fig. 4.22. The simple needle valve usually incorporates a non-return valve allowing a regulated flow in one direction and free flow in the reverse direction.

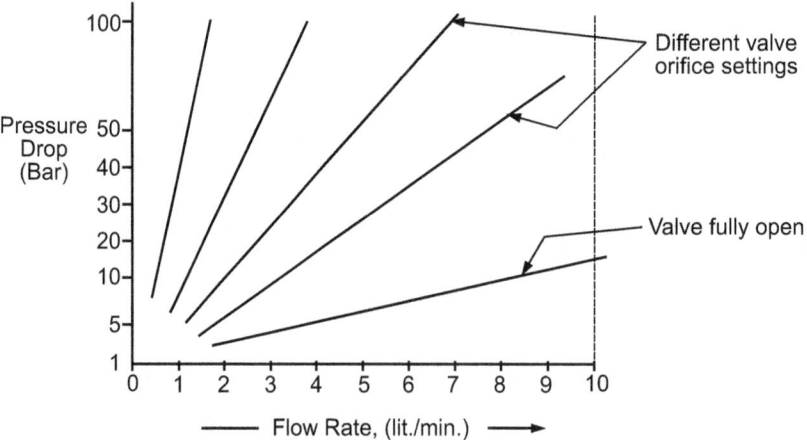

Fig. 4.22: Characteristics of a simple needle valve

4.11 Types Of Flow Control Valves (May 07, Dec. 07)

Flow control valves are further classified as follows

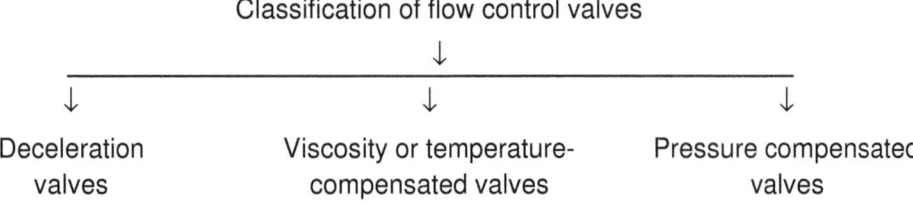

4.11.1 Pressure Compensated Flow Control Valve (May 08, 10, 11)

Fig. 4.23 shows a typical two port pressure compensated flow control valve. A pressure-compensating spool in a flow control valve maintains a constant pressure drop across the orifice independent of variations in supply pressure and load pressure.

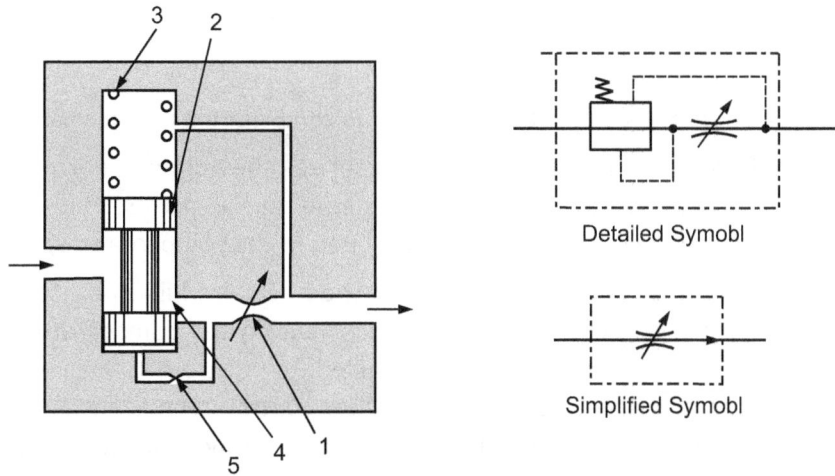

Fig. 4.23: Two port pressure compensated flow control valve

The valve consists of an adjustable metering orifice (1), a compensating spool (2), compensator spring (3), compensating orifice (4), and a damping orifice (5).

The flow rate is set by an adjustable metering orifice (1) which may also be viscosity compensated. In the non-operating position, the compensating spool is fully open by the compensator spring. Soon after the flow commences, pressure drop occurs across the valve. Upstream pressure of the metering orifice tends to close the valve but it is opposed by the spring pressure and the downstream pressure of the metering orifice. The compensator spool assumes an equilibrium position with a resultant pressure drop over the compensating orifice formed by the partially closed spool.

An increase in supply pressure tries to close the spool and greater pressure drop across the compensating orifice balances the increase in supply pressure.

If the load pressure increases, the compensating orifice opens, maintaining the pressure drop over the metering orifice at a preset value. This pressure drop is usually 3 bar to 6 bar depending upon the size of the metering orifice. The total pressure drop across the valve depends upon the difference between supply pressure and load pressure. But for proper functioning of the valve, a minimum total pressure loss of 5 - 12 bar is normally desirable. Fig. 4.24 shows the performance characteristics.

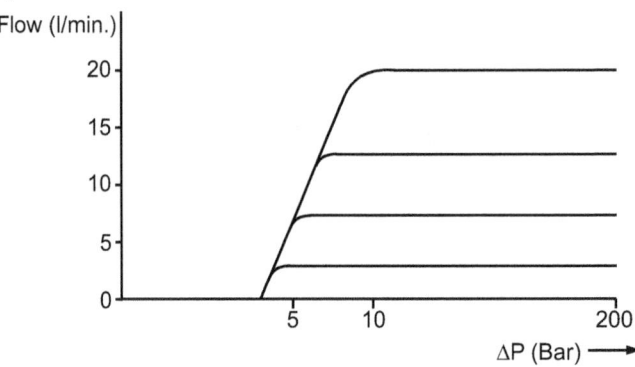

Fig. 4.24: Characteristics of a two port pressure compensated flow control valve

When pressure fluctuates, the damping orifice stabilizes the compensator and hunting is prevented. When the circuit starts up, a flow surge usually occurs. This flow surge is eliminated by a stroke limiter or anti-lunge device fitted to the compensator spool.

During no flow period, the pressure compensating spool remains fully open. Soon after flow commences, pressure drop across the valve results causing the compensator to jump or lunge. The travel of compensating spool is limited to a stroke limiter, essentially an adjustable end-stop. Each time the setting of a flow control valve is changed, the stroke limiter has to be adjusted. The stroke limiter is used to position the compensating spool somewhere near its expected final position. However, large pressure variations can hardly be corrected.

This valve should be used when precise speed control at fluctuating supply pressure or load pressure is required. The minimum regulated stable flow from such a valve is about 0.1 l.p.m. The precision flow control valve circuitry needs careful filtration of oil, better than 10 μm absolute, for efficient control and longer life of the valve. Smaller the flow to be controlled, finer filtration is necessary.

Various valve actuations like hand knot, locatable hand knob, lever operated, D.C. motor control are available.

It should be noted that use of a flow control valve in a circuit is always accompanied by some pressure drop and resultant heat generation.

4.11.2 Temperature or Viscosity Compensated Flow Control Valves

Viscosity of a hydraulic oil is greatly influenced by its temperature therefore, temperature or viscosity compensation is necessary for flow control valves.

Effect of viscosity can easily be eliminated by using a sharp-edged orifice in which flow is independent of viscosity.

Viscosity-temperature compensation is often provided by using two adjacent flat plates serving as adjustable aperture of orifice. One plate is fixed while the other is movable. The movable plate having a 'V' notch is rotated relative to the fixed plate. This causes masking or unmasking of the orifice opening. This design gives a sharp edged orifice making the flow almost independent of viscosity and temperature especially at higher flow rates. However, at low flow rates below 0.5 l.p.m., such a valve performs satisfactorily with low viscosity oils. The flow through such valves is load sensitive. Addition of a pressure compensating spool rectifies the load responsive flow characteristics. A check valve is usually provided to permit unobstructed flow in the reverse direction.

Some designs provide temperature compensation by using such a material for the orifice adjusting mechanisms, having a high coefficient of thermal expansion with the increase of oil temperature, a spindle in the mechanism elongates thereby reducing the opening of the control orifice.

4.11.3 Deceleration Type Flow Control Valve

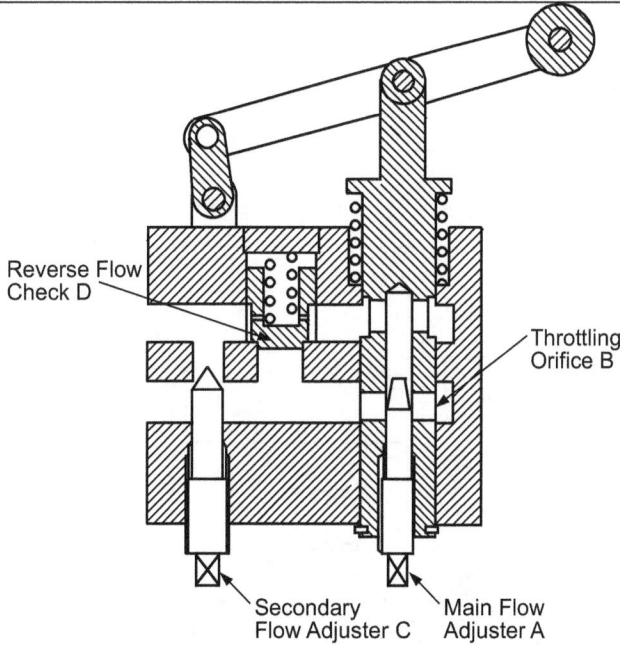

Fig. 4.25: Deceleration type flow control valve

It is essentially a throttle valve. The throttle opening is controlled by a roller or roller lever. It can be NO or NC type valve. It controls flow rate to control acceleration or deceleration. A typical deceleration valve is shown in Fig. 4.25.

A circuit using deceleration valve to control retardation of a piston is shown in Fig. 4.26.

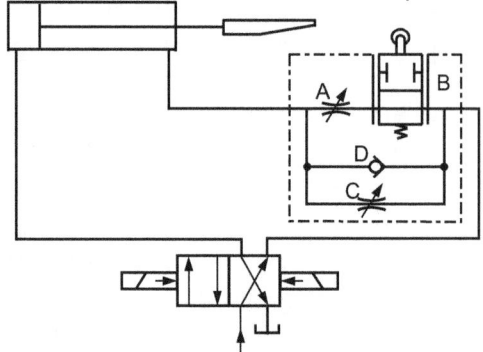

Fig. 4.26: Deceleration control of a piston

This valve is used to retard a cylinder towards the end of its stroke.

During the earlier part of retardation, speed is mainly regulated by restrictor 'A' metering the outflow from the cylinder, permitting a small flow through restrictor 'C'. As the cam actuates the roller, the main spool 'B' gradually closes the main flow path. Restrictor 'C' controls the final part of the stroke. When the piston retracts, flow by-passes the deceleration valve through check valve 'D'.

These valves are mostly recommended for high flow rate applications above 15 l.p.m.

4.12 REGERATIVE CIRCUIT OF A HYDRAULIC CYLINDER

Fig. 4.27 shows a hydraulic cylinder connected in a regenerative circuit. In this case, the oil pressure on both sides of the piston is same. However, as the full bore area is greater than the annulus area, a net force results and causes the piston rod to extend.

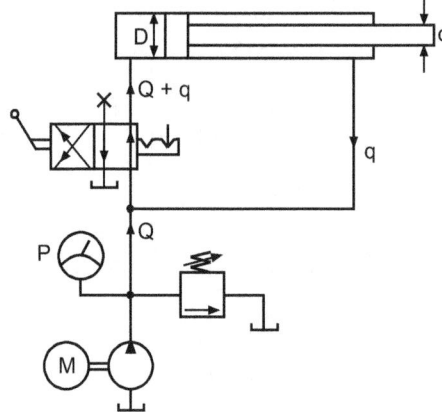

Fig. 4.27 : Regenerative circuit of a hydraulic cylinder

The flow 'q' from the annulus end combines with the pump flow 'Q' and enters the full bore of the cylinder.

Let v = Velocity of extend, m/s

Considering annulus end, we have

$$q = \frac{\pi}{4}(D^2 - d^2)\, v\ m^3/s$$

and for full bore end

$$Q + q = \frac{\pi}{4} D^2 v\ m^3/s$$

Therefore

$$Q = \frac{\pi}{4} \times d^2 v\ m^3/s$$

$$\therefore v = \frac{4Q}{\pi d^2}\ m/s$$

Thus when the cylinder extends regeneratively, the pump flow is effectively filling the volume vacated by the piston rod. The nett forward thrust is given by

$$\text{Forward thrust} = p \times \frac{\pi}{4} D^2 - p \times \frac{\pi}{4}(D^2 - d^2)$$

$$= p \times \frac{\pi}{4} \times d^2$$

When the direction control valve is operated to next position, the cylinder retracts as the annulus end of cylinder receives the flow from the pump delivery and the outflow from the full bore end is returned to tank.

$$\text{Piston retract velocity} = \frac{Q}{\frac{\pi}{4}(D^2 - d^2)}$$

and the retract thrust $= p \times \frac{\pi}{4}(D^2 - d^2)$.

4.13 INDUSTRIAL HYDRAULIC CIRCUITS

The function and principle of operation of the various components used in hydraulic systems have already been discussed in the earlier chapters.

In this article, several hydraulic circuits have been discussed. The functional and operational requirement of each application has been briefly explained and the corresponding hydraulic circuit has been shown. The reader should study the circuit, understand and justify the role of each component and correlate the inter-relationship of various components included in the circuit.

4.14 Control of a Single Acting Sprin Return Hydraulic Cylinder (Simple Reciprocating Circuit)

Functional and Operational Requirement: A single acting spring return hydraulic cylinder is to be provided with a forward and retract control. The piston is to operate continuously without any incline or hold in between extreme positions.

The hydraulic circuit meeting the above requirements is shown in Fig. 4.28.

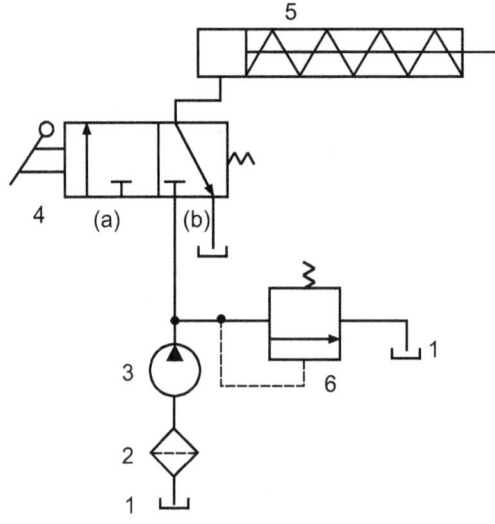

Fig. 4.28: Control of a single acting hydraulic cylinder

Working of the circuit:

A Hydraulic tank is drawn from tank (1) through the filter (2) by a positive displacement pump (3) and is directed to the single acting cylinder (5) through a 3/2 direction control valve (4). The direction control valve (D.C. valve) shown is a two position (a, b), three way, manually operated spring offset valve. In the position shown (b) which is the spring offset mode, the pump flow goes to the tank via pressure relief valve (6). The flow from the blank end of the cylinder is directed to the tank on return of the piston due to spring return force, through the D.C. valve. Thus theflow from pump is blocked in the D.C. valve, leading to a rise in the pressure. When the pressure exceeds the setting of the pressure relief valve, the valve opens and the flow is directed to tank. When the D.C. valve is manually actuated into its left envelope flow path configuration (b), pump flow is directed to the blank end of the cylinder and the piston extends compressing the spring. At full extension pump flow goes through the relief valve. Deactivation of the D.C. valve allows the cylinder to retract and the D.C. valve shifts to the spring offset mode.

4.15 CONTROL OF DOUBLE ACTING HYDRAULIC CYLINDER

Functional and Operational Requirements:

A double acting hydraulic cylinder is to be provided with a forward and return control. Provision of 'inching' or 'hold' of piston in any intermediate position is necessary. The speed of piston during forward and retract is to be the same. The actuation is to be manual.

The suitable hydraulic circuit fulfilling these requirements is shown in the Fig. 4.29.

Working:

- **Step 1:** When the D.C. valve (4) is at its centre position i.e. position (b) which is spring centred position (tandem design), the cylinder is locked. Because the blank end and rod end side flow is blocked (A, B). Pump flow is unloaded to the tank at atmospheric pressure.

- **Step 2:** In the left position (a) of the D.C. valve pump, port P gets connected to A and the tank port T to B. The cylinder extends against the load and stops at the end. The rod end side flow is directed to the tank. The pump flow is directed to the tank via the pressure relief valve.

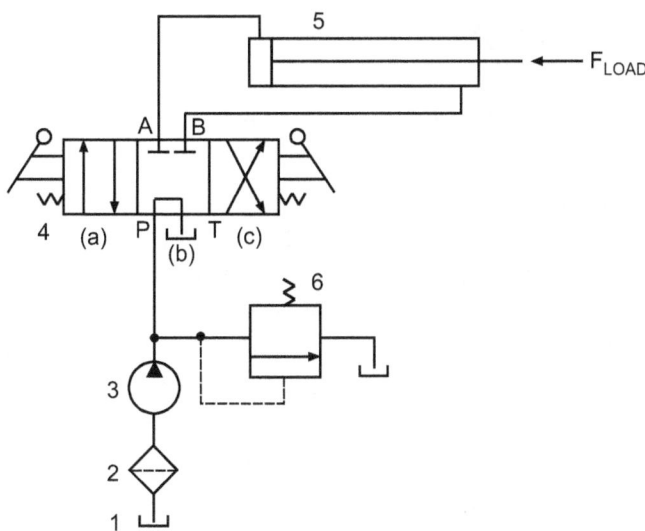

Fig. 4.29: Control of a double acting hydraulic cylinder

- **Step 3:** In the right position (c) the pump port (P) gets connected to port B and the pressured oil is admitted to the rod side of the cylinder. The cylinder thus retracts while the blank end oil is directed to the tank because port A is connected to port T i.e. tank.

4.16 REGENERATIVE CIRCUIT FOR FAST EXTENDING OF A DOUBLE ACTING CYLINDER (Dec. 07, 10; May 11)

A double acting cylinder is to be actuated such that it has a fast extend speed, intermediate 'hold' facility, and manual actuation.

These requirements can be met using a regenerative circuit. One of the ports of a 4-ways 3 position valve should be blocked, as seen from the hydraulic circuit shown in Fig. 4.30.

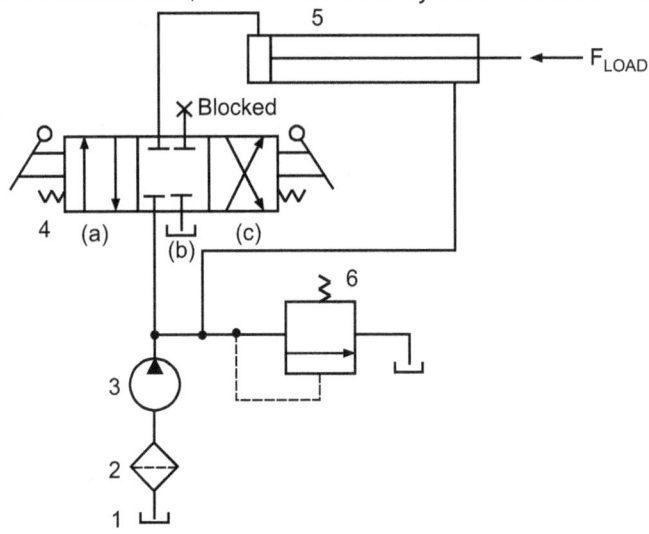

Fig. 4.30: Regenerative circuit for fast extend speed

Working:

- **Step 1:** This is known as the regenerative circuit and is used to increase the extending speed of the double acting hydraulic cylinder. One port of the D.C. valve (4) is blocked. Connection to the rod end side of the cylinder is given to the pipe from the pump.

- **Step 2:** The extension of cylinder occurs when the D.C. valve is shifted to left position (a). The speed of extension is greater than that of a regular double acting cylinder because the flow from the rod end, regenerates with pump flow to provide total flow rate.

$$Q_T = Q_P + Q_R$$
$$Q_T = \text{Total flow rate}$$
$$Q_P = \text{Pump flow}$$
$$Q_R = \text{Flow from rod end}$$

The velocity of extension of piston is

$$V_{Port} = \frac{Q_P}{A_r} \qquad \text{where} \quad A_r = \text{Rod area}$$

The rod area being small, large extending speed is provided.
The load carrying capacity of the regenerative cylinder is given by
$$F_{load} = P\,A_r \qquad \text{where } P = \text{pressure}, \quad A_r = \text{Piston rod area}$$

4.17 Speed Control

Speed control of Hydraulic Cylinder: Speed control of a hydraulic cylinder is accomplished using a flow control valve. A flow control valve regulate the speed of the cylinder by controlling the flow rate to and of the actuator.

There are three types of speed control :
- Meter- in circuit (Primary control)
- Meter-out circuit (Secondary control)
- Bleed - off circuit (By pass control)

1. Meter–in Circuit:

In this type of speed control, the flow control valve is placed between the pump and the actuator. Thereby, it controls the amount of fluid going into the actuator. Fig 4.31 shows meter-in circuit.

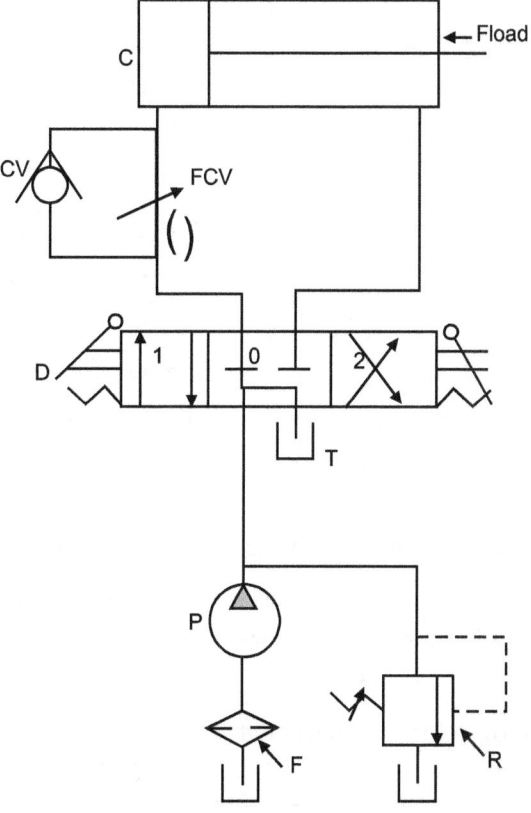

Fig. 4.31: Meter–in circuit.

C = Double acting cylinder ; P = Pump ; T = Tank ; F = Filter
R = Relief Valve; CV = Check Valve ; FCV = Flow Control Valve
D = 3-position, 4 way , Tandem center, Manually operated, Spring Centered DCV.

When the directional control valve is actuated to the 1st position, oil flows through the flow control valve to extend the cylinder. The extending speed of the cylinder depends on the setting (percent of full opening position) of the flow control valve. When the directional control valve is actuated to the 2nd position, the cylinder retracts as oil flows from the cylinder to the oil tank through the check valve as well as the flow control valve.

Analysis of Extending Speed Control:

During the extension stroke, if the flow control valve is fully open, all the flow from the pump goes to the cylinder to produce maximum cylinder speed. As the flow control valve is partially closed its pressure drop increases. This causes an increase in pressure p_1. Continued closing of the flow control valve ultimately results in pressure p_1 reaching and exceeding the cracking pressure of the pressure relief valve (PRV). The result is a slower cylinder speed since part of the pump flow goes back to the oil tank through the PRV setting and the amount of pump flow that is not desired by the cylinder flows through the PRV. An analysis to determine the extending speed is given as follows:

The flow rate to the cylinder equals pump flow rate minus the flow rate through the PRV.

$$Q_{cyl} = Q_{pump} - Q_{PRV}$$

The flow rate through the flow control valve (FCV) is governed by

$$Q_{FCV} = C_V \sqrt{\Delta P} / S_g = C_V \sqrt{(p_1 - p_2)} / S_g$$

Where,
ΔP = pressure drop across FCV
C_V = capacity coefficient of FCV
S_g = specific gravity of oil
Pressure p_1 = p_{PRV} = Relief valve pressure setting

Also, pressure $p_3 = 0$ (ignoring small frictional pressure drop in drain line from rod end of cylinder to oil tank).

Pressure p_2 can be obtained by summing forces on the hydraulic cylinder.

$$p_2 A_{piston} = F_{load} \text{ or } p_2 = F_{load}/A_{piston} \qquad ...(a)$$

Finally, the extending speed of the cylinder is found.

$$V_{cyl} = C_{cyl} / A_{piston} = Q_{FCV} / A_{piston} \qquad ...(b)$$

Using equations (a) and (b) yields the final result.

$$V_{el} = \frac{C_V}{A_{piston}} \sqrt{\frac{P_{PRV} - F_{load} / A_{piston}}{S_g}} \qquad ...(1)$$

As can be seen by Equation 1, by varying the setting of the flow control system and thus the value of C_V, the desired extending speed of the cylinder can be achieved.

2. Meter – out Circuit :

In this type of speed control, the flow control valve is placed between the actuator and the tank. Thereby, it controls the amount of fluid going out of the actuator. Fig. 4.32 shows a meter-out circuit.

Meter-in systems are used primarily when the external load opposes the direction of motion of the hydraulic cylinder. An example of the opposite situation is the case of a weight pulling downward on the piston rod of a vertical cylinder. In this case the weight would suddenly drop by pulling the piston rod down if a meter-in system is used even if the flow control valve is completely closed. Thus, the meter-out system is generally preferred over the meter-in type.

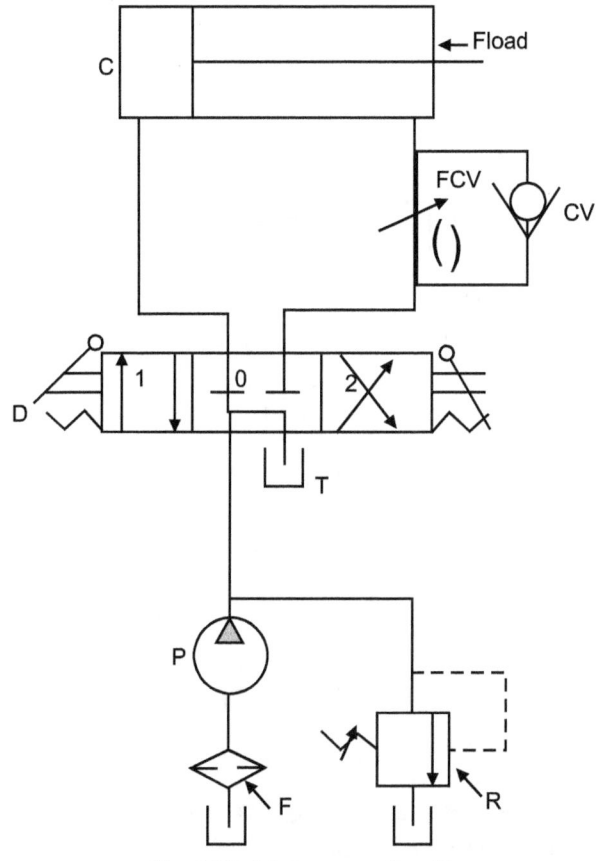

Fig. 4.32: Meter–out Circuit.

C = Double acting cylinder; P = Pump ; T = Tank; F = Filter

R = Relief Valve; CV = Check Valve ; FCV = Flow control Valve

D = 3-position, 4 way, Tandem center, Manually operated and Spring Centered DCV

One drawback of a meter-out system is the possibility of excessive pressure buildup in the rod end of the cylinder while it is extending. This is due to the magnitude of back pressure that the flow control valve can create depending on its nearness to being fully closed as well as the size of the external load and the piston-to-rod area ratio of the cylinder. In addition an excessive pressure buildup in the rod end of the cylinder results in a large pressure drop across the flow control valve. This produce the undesirable effect of a high heat generation rate with a resulting increase in oil temperature.

3. Bleed–off Circuit :

In this type of speed control, the flow control valve is placed between the pressure line and return line . Thereby, it controls the fluid by bleeding off the excess not needed by the working cylinder. Fig 4.33 shows the bleed-off circuit.

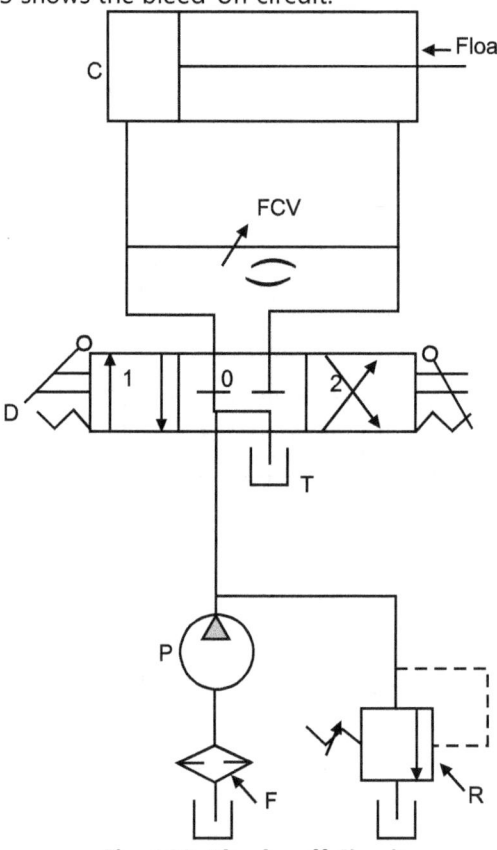

Fig. 4.33: Bleed – off Circuit
C = Double acting cylinder; P = Pump ; T = Tank; F = Filter
R = Relief Valve; FCV = Flow control Valve
D =3-position, 4 way, Tandem center, Manually operated, Spring Centered DCV

This type of flow control is much more efficient than the inlet restricting type for meter-in, because the bypass feature allows fluid to be exhausted to the tank at just slightly higher

HYDRAULICS AND PNEUMATICS — INDUSTRIAL CIRCUITS

pressure than that necessary to do the work. With the meter-in type, pump delivery not used would discharge over the main relief valve at maximum pressure.

4.18 SEQUENCING CIRCUIT

One can find the application of this circuit in manufacturing process circuit. Consider if two cylinders are used during manufacturing process, then the sequence may be for example, one of the cylinder the clamping cylinder C1 could extend and clamp a workpiece. Then the second cylinder C2, the punching cylinder extends to punch a hole in the workpiece. The right cylinder then retracts the punch, and then the left cylinder retracts to declamp the workpiece for removal. Obviously these machining operations must occur in the proper sequence as established by the sequence valves in the circuit.

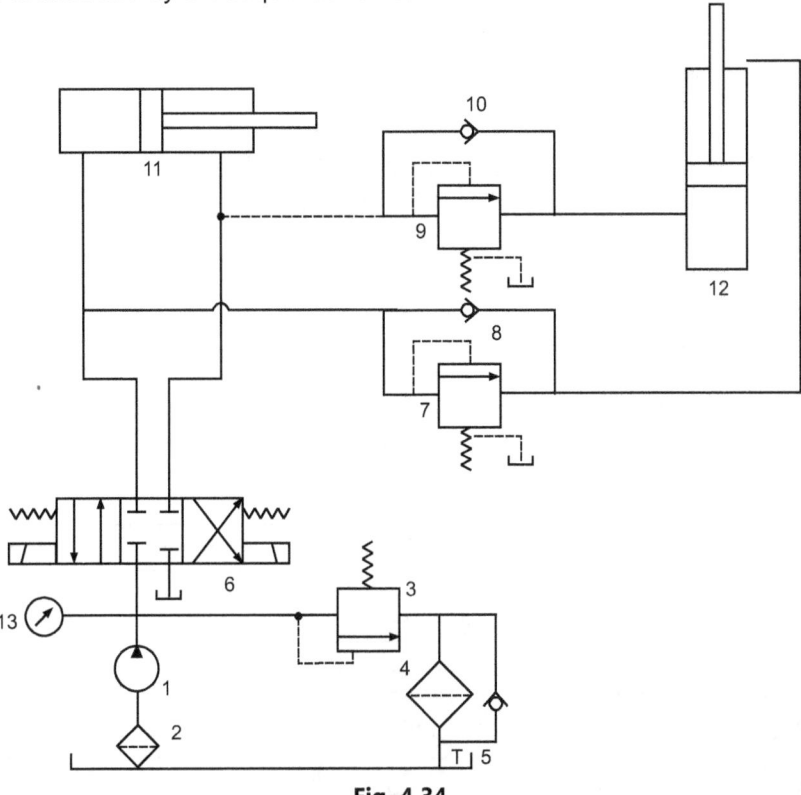

Fig. 4.34

A sequence valve causes operations in a hydraulic circuit sequentially. Fig. 4.34 is an example where two sequence valves are used to control the sequence of operations of two double-acting cylinders 11 and 12.

For central position of DCV (6): Both the cylinders (11) and (12) are stopped in the given position.

For left position of DCV (6): By actuating the left solenoid, the oil from the pump (1) passes through the blind end of the cylinder (11), after completion of the extension stroke of the cylinder (11), the pressure in the blind goes on rising which gives a pilot signal to the sequence valve (7) and valve (7) opens and allows the oil to flow through the rod end of the cylinder (12), getting retraction of the cylinder (12).

For the left position of DCV (6), first there is extension stroke of cylinder (11), then retraction of cylinder (12).

For right position of DCV (6): By actuating the right solenoid, the oil from the pump enters first in the rod end of cylinder (11) and does a complete retraction of the cylinder (11). Then the pressure goes on building at the rod end side of the cylinder (11) which opens the sequence valve (9) allowing the oil to end in the blind end of cylinder (12 causing the cylinder (12) to extend.

Thus, for the right position of DCV (6), first retraction of cylinder (11) then extension of cylinder (12) takes place.

4.19 Hydraulic Circuit For Synchronization Of Cylinders

An interesting application requires synchronized operation of identical hydraulic cylinders. The loads on these identical cylinders must necessarily be equal to achieve exact synchronization.

Many times, the loads may not be exactly equal. In such a case, the cylinder with low load would operate first as it needs somewhat low pressure. Only after this cylinder has reached its end of stroke, the pressure further builds up to the level.

In practice, two cylinders are seldom identical. Even packing friction will be different. Fig. 4.35 shows two cylinders connected in parallel to a pump. However, they will not operate in synchronization.

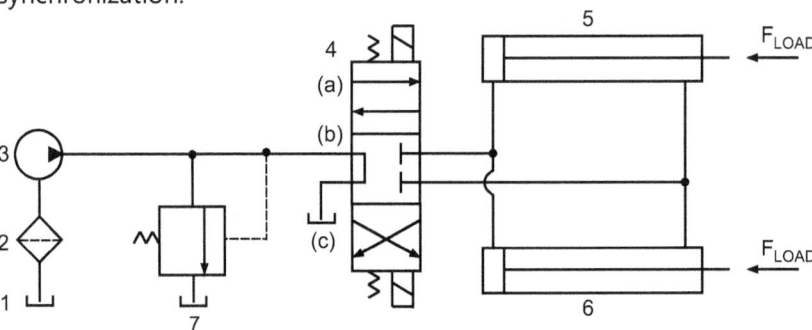

Fig. 4.35: Cylinders hooked in parallel will not operate in synchronization

For true synchronized operation, the cylinders have to be connected in series as shown in Fig. 4.36. Also it is necessary to fulfill the condition $A_{p_2} = (A_{p_1} - A_{r_1})$ and the pump delivery pressure should be $p_1 = \dfrac{F_1 + F_2}{A_{p_1}}$.

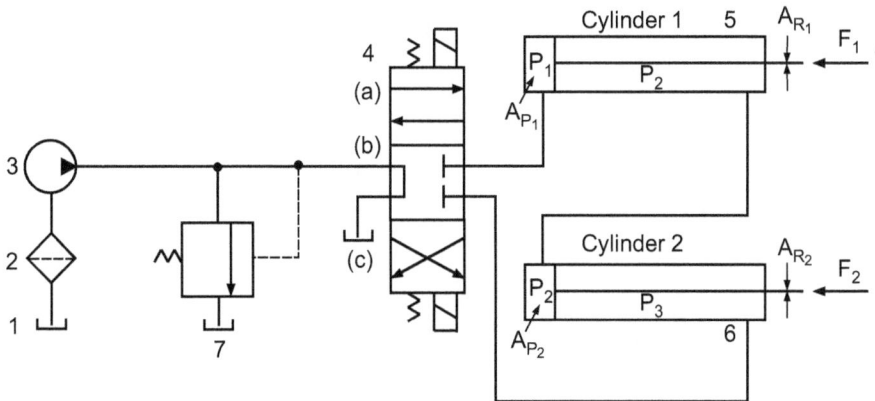

Fig. 4.36: Cylinders hooked in series will operate in synchronization

Working:
- **Step 1:** In position (a) of the D.C. valve (4), oil from pump is admitted in the first cylinder (5). The fluid from the rod end of the cylinder (1) is delivered to the blank end of the second cylinder (6). So both cylinders extend simultaneously, since after the return stroke of both cylinders oil is present on the rod side of both cylinders. The pump must be capable of delivering a pressure equal to that required for cylinder 1 by itself to overcome the loads acting on both cylinders.

4.19.1 Synchronizing with Flow Control Valves

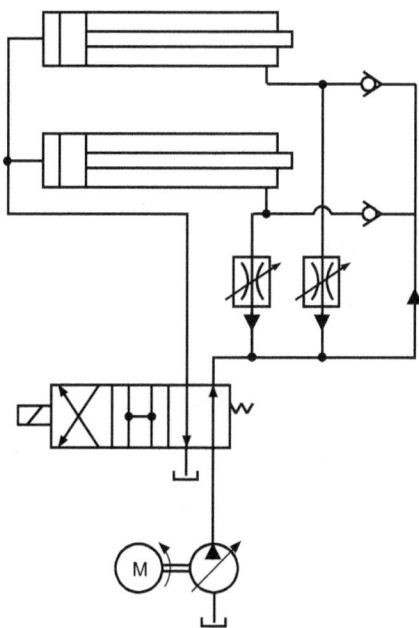

Fig. 4.37: Synchronization with compensated flow-control valves

In the circuit shown two flow control valves are used. They can be set independently and equal volumes of fluid to or from each cylinder can be obtained which should result in simultaneous movement of the two cylinders.

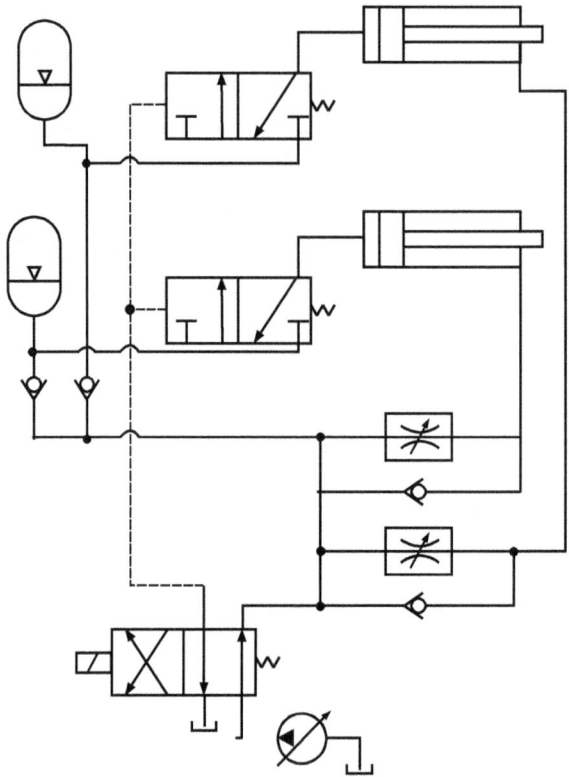

Fig. 4.38: Synchronization with flow control valves and accumulators

The circuit shows how accurate the synchronization of movement to the right is provided by use of accumulators and flow regulators. (Refer Fig. 4.38)

4.19.2 Synchronizing with Flow Dividing Motors

The circuit shows two hydraulic motors each delivering fluid to the cylinder. Motors are mechanically coupled and are of identical size, rotate at the same speed and therefore will deliver equal volumes.

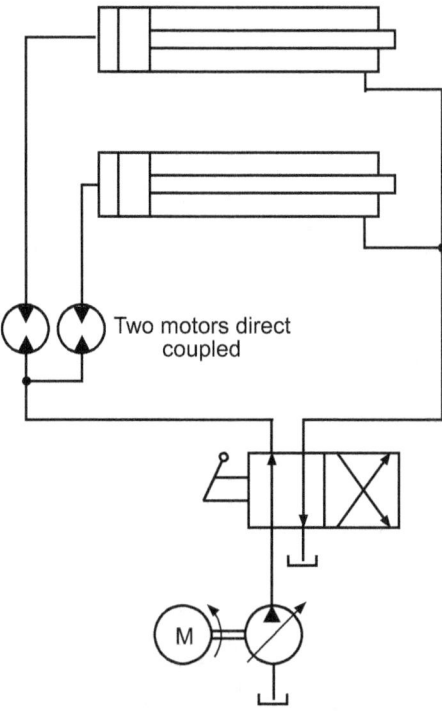

Fig. 4.39: Synchronization with flow dividing motor assembly

4.20 Transverse And Feed

(A) Transverse and Feed Circuit

For achieving different feeds in systems we can use a circuit as shown in Fig. 4.40.

The circuit uses a solenoid controlled 4/3 DC valve with spring center. The 2 solenoids are controlled by the 2 limit switches.

When the actuator energizes the first limit switch, the DC valve will be in first position and hence the cylinder will move in the forward direction. The initial speed of the cylinder is fast and after the 2/2 roller operated de-acceleration valve is actuated the speed of the actuator is controlled by the flow control valve as much as required.

When the forward stroke is completed the second limit switch will actuate the 4/3 DC valve for the reverse stroke of the cylinder. The reverse stroke is fast. The circuit can be automated.

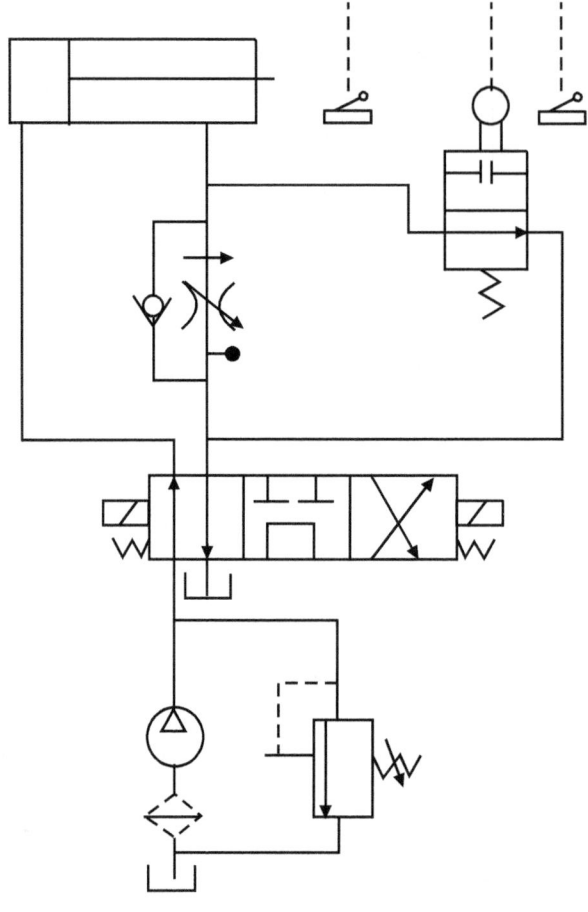

Fig. 4.40

(B) Actuator Locking Circuit

For certain applications the actuator has to be locked in a particular position of the direction control valve. This means that the actuator should not move in that position of direction control valve. Such a circuit is shown in the Fig. 4.41. Here 2 pilot operated check valves are used to lock the actuator.

For the forward stroke of the cylinder, the flow will flow to the piston end of the cylinder. Pressure builds up and the check valve in the return line of cylinder will open and fluid will be allowed to flow to the tank through the direction control valve.

In the same way for return stroke the other check valve will allow the return flow.

If the cylinder tries to move due to some external force it will be prevented by the check valves in both directions.

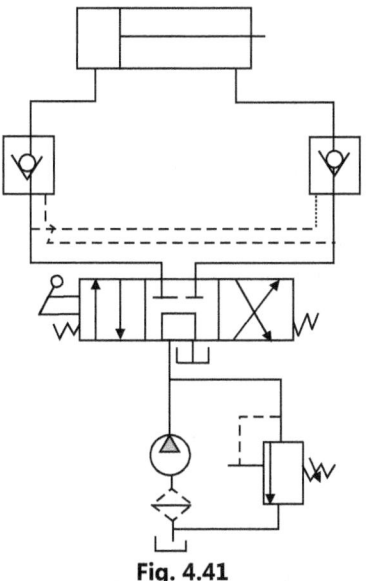

Fig. 4.41

4.21 Circuit For Riveting Machine

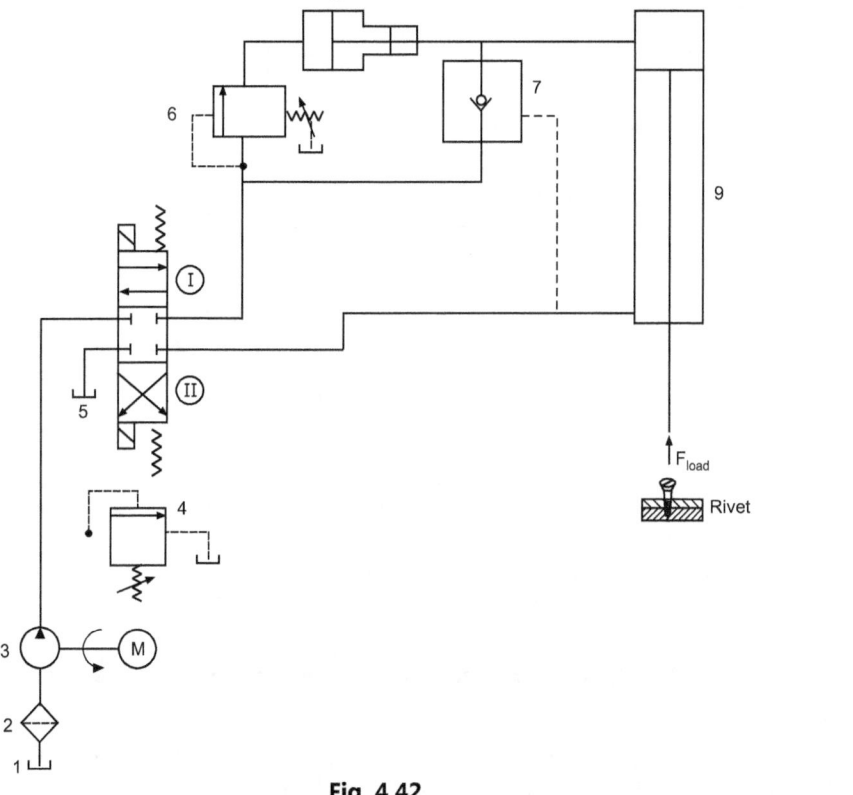

Fig. 4.42

(1) Oil reservoir, (2) Oil filter, (3) Hydraulic pump, (4) Pressure relief valve,
(5) 4/3, solenoid operated, centrally closed, DCV, (6) Sequence valve,
(7) Pilot operated check valve, (8) Pressure intensifier, (9) Double acting cylinder.

In normal position of valve (5), there is no movement. For (I) position of valve (5), oil flows through the check valve (7) to the blind end of cylinder (9), when load on the cylinder increases during riveting process, the pressure in the line increases which gives signal to sequence valve (6). This valve (6) gives oil to the intensifier, and the intensifier supplies pressurized oil to the blind end side during actual reveting.

For position (II) of valve (5), the fluid power enters to the rod end side of cylinder (9) for return upward motion.

4.22 Hydraulic Circuit For Automatic Reciprocation Of A Hydraulic Cylinder

Some applications require continuous reciprocation of a hydraulic cylinder, automatically. This is achieved by using a two sequence valve. Each valve senses completion of stroke by build-up of pressure check valve and its pilot line prevents the change of status of the four way valve until the stroke of a particular cylinder is complete. This circuit is shown in Fig. 4.43.

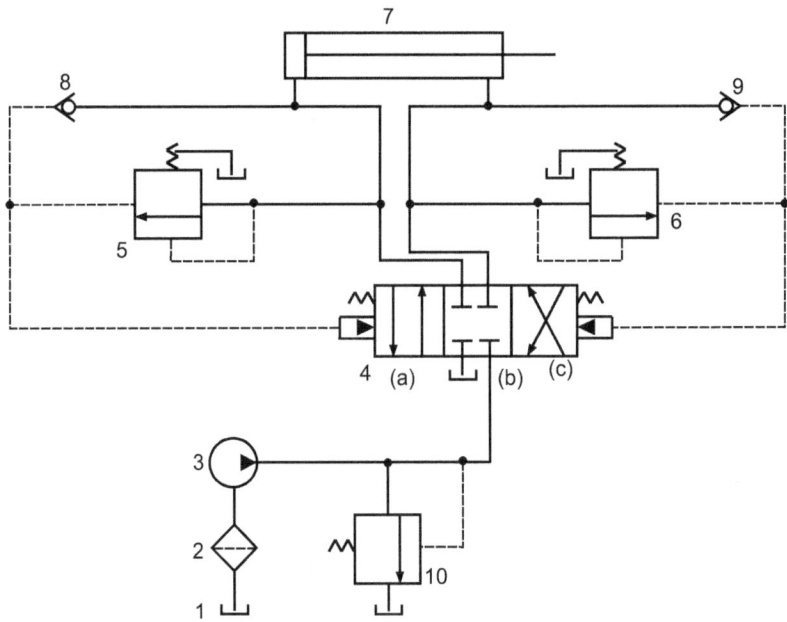

Fig. 4.43: Hydraulic circuit for automatic reciprocation of a cylinder

Automatic continuous reciprocation of a hydraulic cylinder can also be accomplished by using 4/2 direction control valve, without using a sequencing valve. The double acting double ended rod cylinder actuates the limit switches at the completion of each stroke. The limit switches in turn may operate a solenoid controlled direction control valve to a new position. The limit switches can be in the form of mechanical latches which may actuate the direction control valve through linkage to take on a new position.

Working:

- **Step 1:** At the centre position (b) of the D.C. valve (4) the cylinder is locked. The circuit produces continuous reciprocation of the cylinder by using two sequence valves.

- **Step 2:** When the cylinder extends fully, pressure is built up This is for position (c) of the D.C. valve (4). The sequence valve (5) opens and provides a pilot signal to the D.C. valve (4), and hence its position (a) is achieved.

- **Step 3:** In position (a) of the D.C. valve (4), the pressurized oil is supplied to the rod end side and hence the cylinder retracts fully. Again with the built up of pressure, the sequence valve (6) is opened and provides a pilot signal to the D.C. valve (4) to change its position to get new position (c). Each check valve and c the orresponding pilot line prevents shifting of the four way D.C. valve until a particular stroke of the cylinder has been completed.

4.23 Hydraulic Circuit With Fail – Safe Feature

Many critical applications like high capacity presses, jacks etc. require their hydraulic circuit to be totally fail-safe to ensure safety to the operator or damage to the equipment. Such circuits prevent accidental fall and overloading of the system. A typical fail-safe circuit is shown in Fig. 4.44.

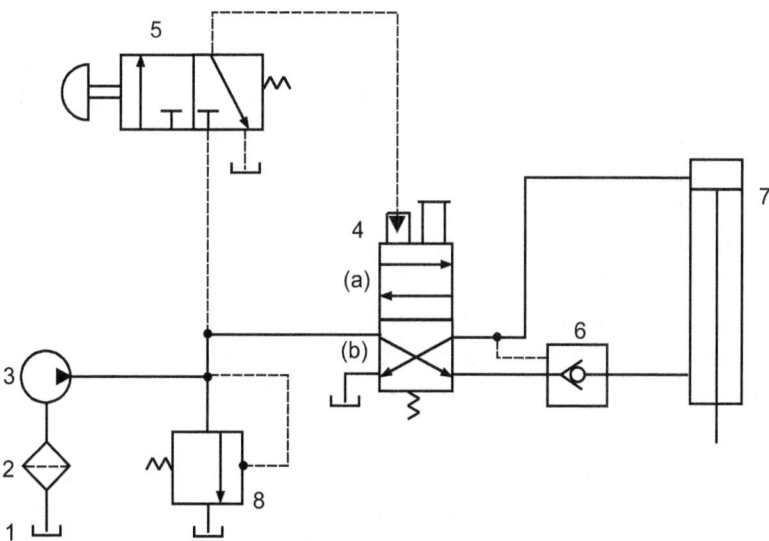

Fig. 4.44: Typical fail-safe circuit

Working of circuit:

Circuit prevents the cylinder from accidentally falling in the event of a hydraulic line breakage or if a manual override on pilot operated D.C. valve is pressed while the pump is not operating.

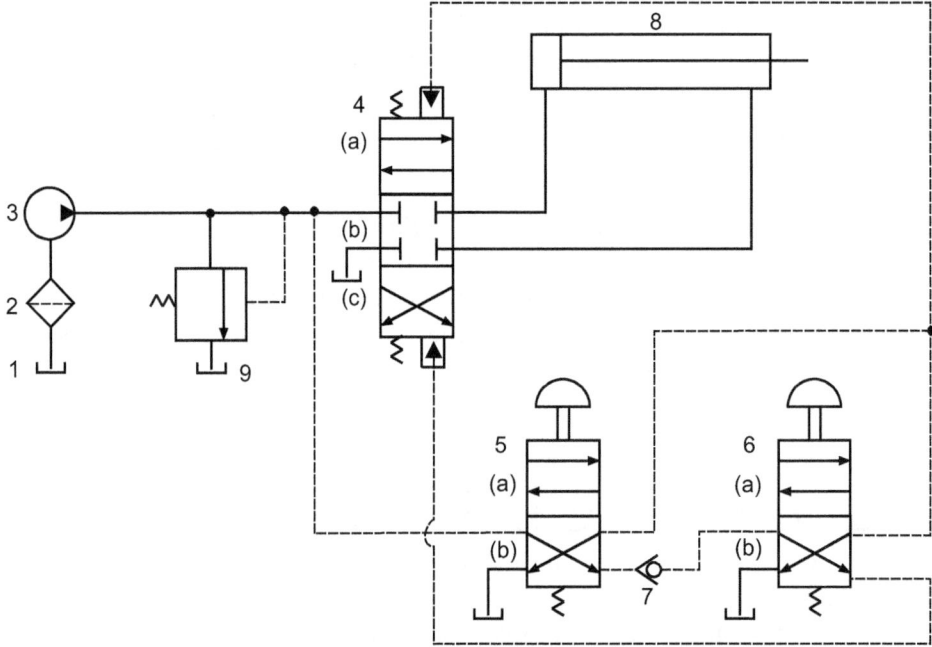

Fig. 4.45: Both hands operated safety circuit

The D.C. valve (4) is operated by receiving the pilot signal from the push button valve (5). This gives position (a) of the D.C. valve (4), where pressurized oil is admitted in the blank end of cylinder. Due to the pressure rise, the pilot operated check valve opens and allows the rod end side oil to tank through it and the piston moves down. Releasing the push button valve (5) takes it to the spring offset position and because of no signal from it, the D.C. valve (4) will have (b) position. In this position oil is admitted to the rod end side though check valve piston is lifted upwards. Thus it is ensured that piston will come down only when there is pressure on the top and the pilot operated check valve is open.

The circuit shown in Fig. 4.45 incorporates safety to the operator from accidental injury. The operator has to use both hands to press both push button valves. Further, retraction is possible only when both push button valves are released.

Working of circuit:

Push button valves (5) and (6) are required to be depressed or released simultaneously in order to move the cylinder. If only valve (5) is pressed, position 5 (a) and 6 (b) is available. Pressured oil will flow through 5 (a), 6 (b) to the tank. So no pilot signal is available for actuation of the D.C. valve (4) and it remains in spring centred centre position. The same thing occurs if (5) is not pressed and (6) is pressed. When both valves (5) and (6) are pressed pilot signal is given to the main D.C. valve (4) and position 4 (a) is achieved that extends cylinder. On releasing the two button valves 5 and 6 simultaneously a pilot signal is given from the opposite side to the main d.c. valve (4) to get 4 (c) position, and hence the cylinder (8) retracts. While main D.C. valve (4) is piloted from one side, the other side is drained through push button valves (5) and (6) to tank correspondingly.

4.24 Hydraulic Circuit Using Counter Balance Valve

A vertically mounted cylinder is required to be held in the upward position while allowing the pump to idle. e.g. a hydraulic jack raising a car in a service station is required to be maintained in the raised position till the car is serviced.

The possibility of load coming down under the action of gravity is to be avoided. This requirement can be met by use of a counterbalance valve and an open centred direction control valve. (Refer Fig. 4.46).

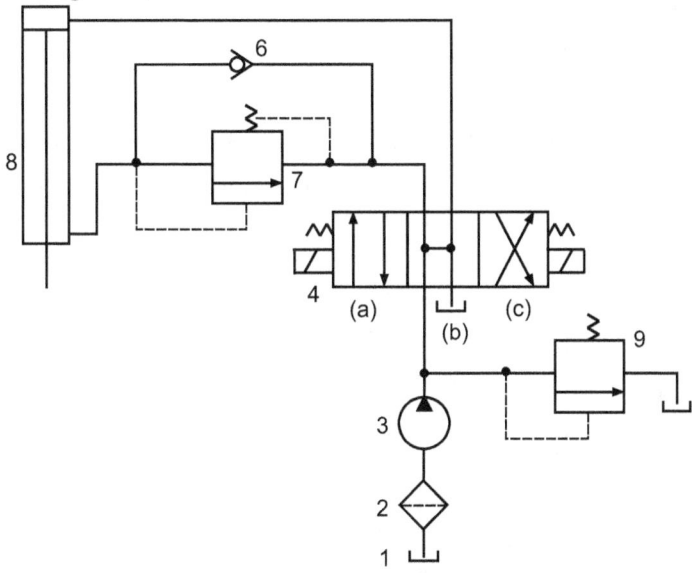

Fig. 4.46: Hydraulic circuit using a counterbalance valve

Working:

The counterbalance valve (7) is set to open,t slightly above the pressure required to hold the piston (8) up. This permits the cylinder to be forced downward when the pressure is applied on the top. This is the corresponding position (c) of the D.C. valve (4). In the (a) position of D.C. valve (4), oil flows through check valve (6) to the rod end of cylinder and lifts it. At centre position of the D.C. valve (4) pump is unloaded to the tank while the piston is held locked by the counter balance valve (7) preventing the flow to the tank by becoming closed. (pilot operated)

4.25 Hydraulic Circuit For Hydraulic Press

(A) Punching Operation Using Intensifier

A punching operation can be served using only one low pressure high flow pump, a sequence valve and a pilot operated check valve. This thus eliminates the need of high pressure low flow pump. Very high pressure needed during actual punching operation is provided by intensifier operating on a low pressure pump.

A pilot check valve instead of a regular check valve allows retraction.
(Refer Fig. 4.47).

Working:

Step 1: When pressure in the cylinder (6) reaches the sequence valve (8) pressure setting, the intensifier (7) starts to operate.

Step 2: High pressure output of intensifier closes the pilot check valve (5) and pressurizes the blank end of cylinder to perform punching operation. This happens for position (c) of D.C. valve (4).

Step 3: In the (a) position of D.C. valve (4) cylinder is retracted and pilot, check valve opens due to high pressure in the line and return flow of blank end of piston is permitted through check valve to tank.

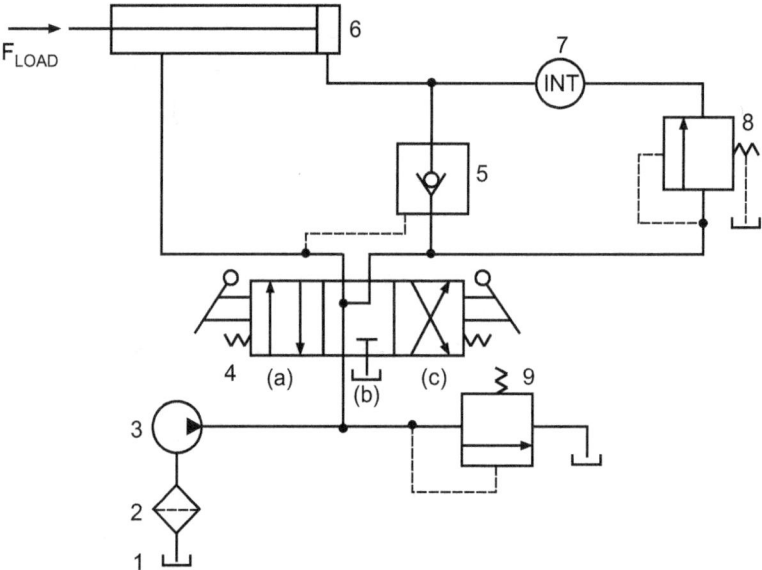

Fig. 4.47: Hydraulic circuit using intensifier for a punching operation

(B) Punching Operation Using Double Pumps:

A punching operation comprises of a rapid long travel of punch head requiring high flow with very low pressure while needs high pressure low flow rate during short travel of punching. Again during retracting after punching, it needs low pressure with large flow rate.

Such an application can as well be accomplished with use of a single high pressure high flow pump which has high initial cost and greater operating cost.

Alternatively, two pumps one pump of high pressure low flow capacity while the other of low pressure high flow rating can be incorporated.

A typical hydraulic circuit using double pump and manual control and provision of 'inching' is shown in Fig. 4.48.

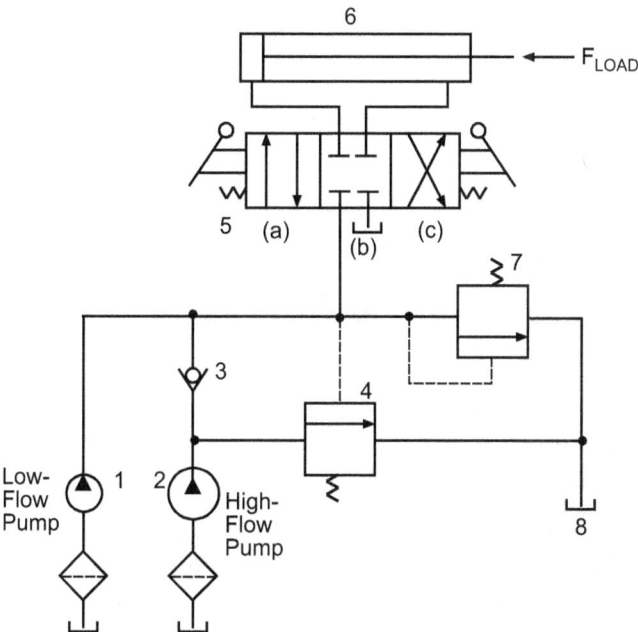

Fig. 4.48: Double pump hydraulic circuit for a punching operation

Working :

- **Step 1:** At time of punching flow is from high flow, low pressure pump (2) – check valve (3), D.C. valve position 5 (a). Increased pressure opens the unloading valve (4) and unloads low pressure pump (2), because high flow is not required. Punching is obtained by pressure from pump (1).

- **Step 2:** For rapid extension of ram over a large distance, low pressure pump with high flow requirement (2) is used.

- **Step 3:** Check valve protects low pressure pump (2) from high pressure, which occurs during punching.

4.26 Hydraulic Circuit For Unloading Of Pump (May 12)

At times, it is required to unload the pump at the end of extending and retraction strokes and also in the spring-centred position of the direction control valve.

A hydraulic circuit using an unloading valve and a check valve is shown in Fig. 4.49.

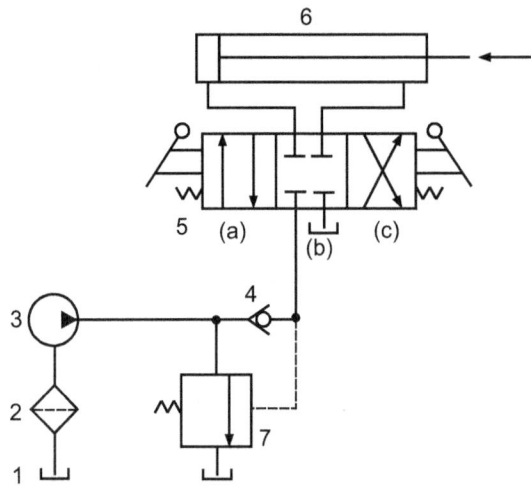

Fig. 4.49: Hydraulic circuit for unloading of a pump

Working:

- **Step 1:** Valve (7) is an unloading valve. It opens when the cylinder reaches the end of the extension stroke, because the check valve (4) keeps high pressure oil in the pilot line (shown dotted) of the unloading valve.
- **Step 2:** The D.C. valve (5) position is shifted to (c). Cylinder retracts. Pressure drops, in the pilot line of the unloading valve and the valve is closed.
- **Step 3:** On full retraction unloading valve again opens as in step 1 and unloads the pump.
- Thus at both end positions of the piston and at the centre position of the D.C. valve, the pump is unloaded through the unloading valve.

4.27 Hydraulic Circuit For Braking Of Hydraulic Motor (May 12)

Whenever a hydraulic motor is used in a circuit, it is necessary to know the type of load on the motor. A load may be some machine with large inertia. Whenever a motor is to be stopped, the large inertia of load generates a flywheel effect on the motor, making it work like a pump.

In such an eventuality, the circuit design should provide fluid to the motor while it is acting like a pump to avoid ingress of air in it. Also the fluid discharged from the motor must be returned to the tank directly or through a relief valve. Thus rapid stopping of motor is possible without any damage to the system. Fig. 4.50 shows a circuit incorporating these features.

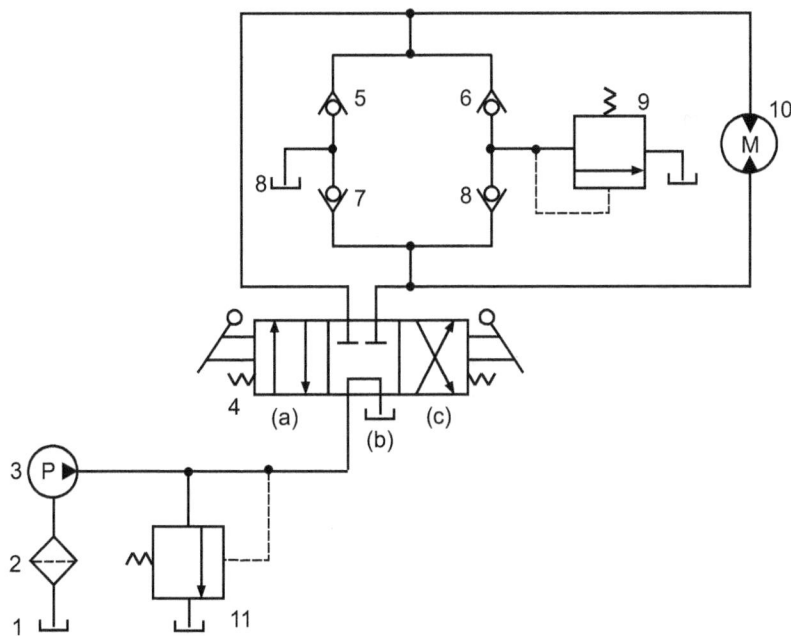

Fig. 4.50: Hydraulic circuit for braking of motor

Working of circuit (Motor braking and replenishing circuit):

- **Step 1:** Motor (10) is bidirectional motor. It rotates in two directions corresponding to positions (a) and (b) of the D.C. valve (4). To stop the motor quickly (braking) the flow from the motor is directed to the tank by a pair of check valves (6) and (8) and pressure relief valve (9). To avoid the motor working as a pump and taking air in is avoided by admitting oil from tank (8) through check valves (5) and (7) to the motor.

SOLVED EXAMPLES

Example 4.9 : A double acting cylinder is to be used to transfer parts from a magazine. The cylinder is to fully extend when a push button is operated and then retract automatically. Full extension is conformed by a roller lever valve. The cylinder is to continues forward movement even if the push button is released before full extension is reached. The cylinder speed is to be adjustable in both the directions of motion. Draw suitable circuit fulfilling above requirements and label the components.

(May 2003)

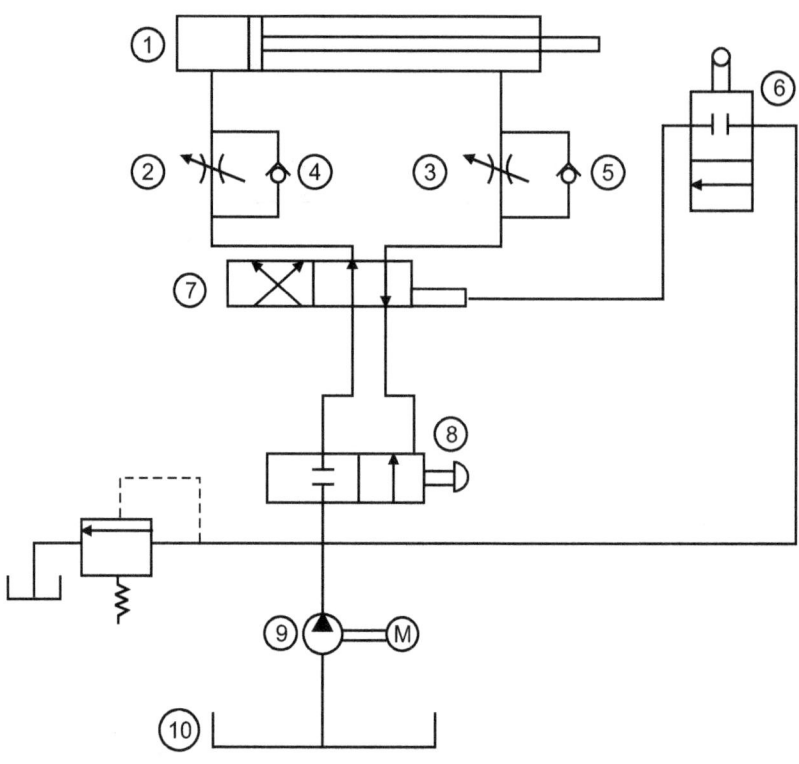

Fig. 4.51

1 = cylinder, 2 and 3 = flow control valve, 4 and 5 = non return valves,

6 = roller operated directional control valve,

7 = pilot operated directional control valve

8 = manually operated push button type directional control valve,

9 = pump and motor, 10 = reservoir

Example 4.10 : Draw an open circuit that uses double end rod hydraulic cylinder to extend and retract a large workpiece with equal velocity and equal force in both the direction. Lock the cylinder in centre position.

Solution :

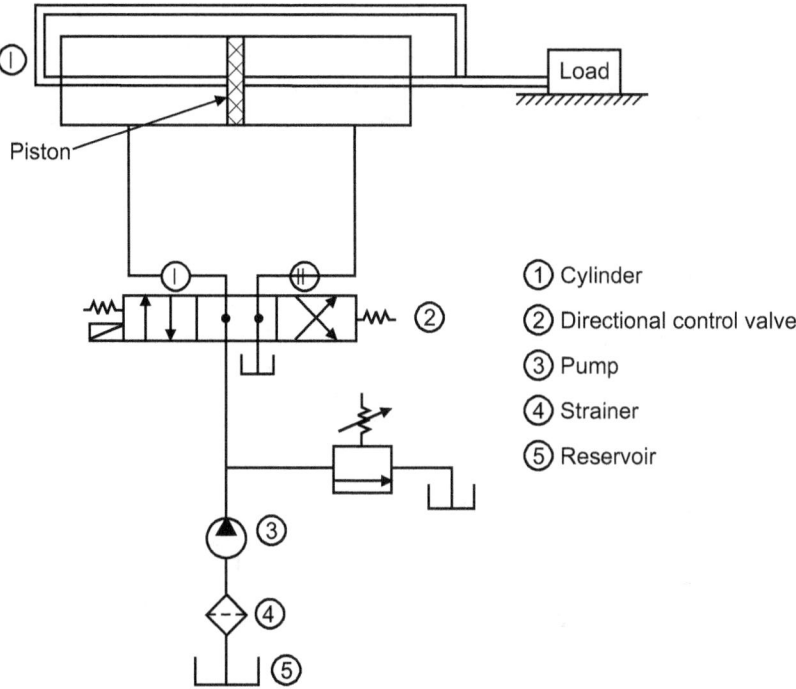

Fig. 4.52

To fulfill the requirements given in the problem above circuit shown in Fig. 4.52 is suggested. It consists of use of double end rod cylinder, whose two ends are jointed together to move a heavy load.

Step 1 : The pump (3) sucks the oil from reservoir (5) through the strainer (4) and supplies it to the left side of the cylinder (1) while the right side is connected to exhaust when directional control valve (DCV) (2) is I^{st} position. This causes the load to be moved towards the right.

Step 2 : As the DCV (2) shifts to position (II) then the supply and exhaust sides are interchanged. This will cause reversed movement of cylinder piston (i.e. in left side). As the rod diameter and oil admitted at some pressure on both the sides, the load will be moved with constant velocity and force.

In case of open centre position of DCV (2), both the sides of the cylinder are connected to exhaust and the pump discharge passes back to the reservoir, thus looking the cylinder in the centre.

Example 4.11 : *Draw circuit for following conditions.*

The combined actuation of a manually actuated valve and roller lever valve advances a forming tool on an edge folding device. The forming tool is driven by a double acting cylinder. For rapid forward travel, the circuit uses a quick exhaust valve. The retracting speed is to be adjustable. If either of two valves are released, the tool returns to its initial position. Explain the above circuit.   ***(Dec. 2003)***

Solution :

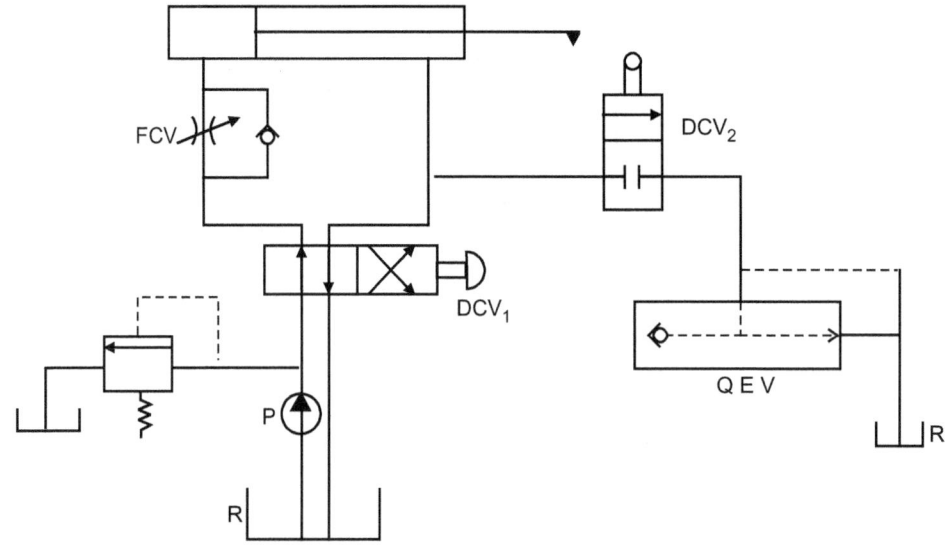

FCV = Flow control valve,
DCV$_1$ = Manually actuated directional control valve
DCV$_2$ = Roller operated directional control valve
QEV = Quick exhaust valve
P   = Pump
R   = Reservoir

Fig. 4.53

As the requirements given in the problem hydraulic circuit is suggested which is shown in Fig. 4.53.

Step 1 : When DCV$_2$ is get actuated then oil flows through the check valve to the piston end of the cylinder. And the return oil from the rod end of the cylinder goes through DCV$_2$ to the quick exhaust valve. QEV will drain the oil quickly to the tank. This results in to the rapid forward travels.

Step 2 : In this step oil goes directly to the rod end of the cylinder and oil from piston and end returns through the FCV. This is retracting stroke. Thus using the meter out configuration of the FCV, the retracting speed can be adjusted.

Example 4.12 : Draw and explain hydraulic circuit using double acting cylinder to fulfill the conditions.

(i) Velocity control - in the both directions.

(ii) Velocity control - the cylinder rod to extend two times factor than its retraction.

(Dec. 2003, Dec. 2002)

Solution :

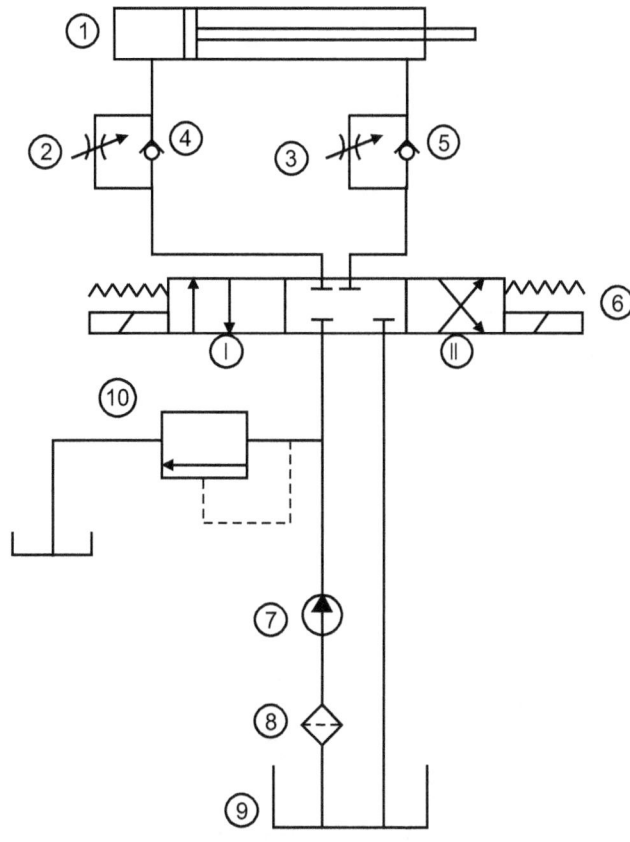

(1) = Cylinder
2 and 3 = Flow control valves (FCV)
4 and 5 = Non return valves (NRV)
6 = 4/3 directional control valves (DCV)
7 = Pump
8 = Strainer
9 = Reservoir

Fig. 4.54

To fulfill the requirements given in the problem; hydraulic circuit is suggested which is shown in Fig. 4.55. It consist of pump (3) which sucks the oil from reservoir and supplies to cylinder (1) through DCV and FCVs. In this circuit, velocity control can be done by controlling the flow of the oil entering and flowing out of the cylinder and this is done by FCVs.

Step 1 : Now consider DCV is in its Ist position. Hence, it makes the oil to flow to the piston end of the cylinder (1) through FCV(2), while the rod end of the oil flows freely back to the oil reservoir and thus achieving the velocity control in the extension stroke.

Step 2 : When DCV get shifted to position (II) then oil supply and exhaust sides are interchanged. Hence, oil get admitted to the rod end of the cylinder through the FCV (3) while the oil from piston end flow freely back to the reservoir giving 'velocity control' in the retraction stroke.

And to get cylinder rod extension two times faster than retraction, the opening of the FCV(2) may be kept almost twice that of the FCV (3).

Example 4.13 : *Draw a circuit for a milling machine for the following movements. Three cylinders are to be used :*

  (i)   Cylinder A for bed movement in X direction.

  (ii) Cylinder B for bed movement in Y direction.

  (iii) Cylinder C for tool movement.

  For feed / speed control, use a standard manifold.   **(May 2009)**

Solution :

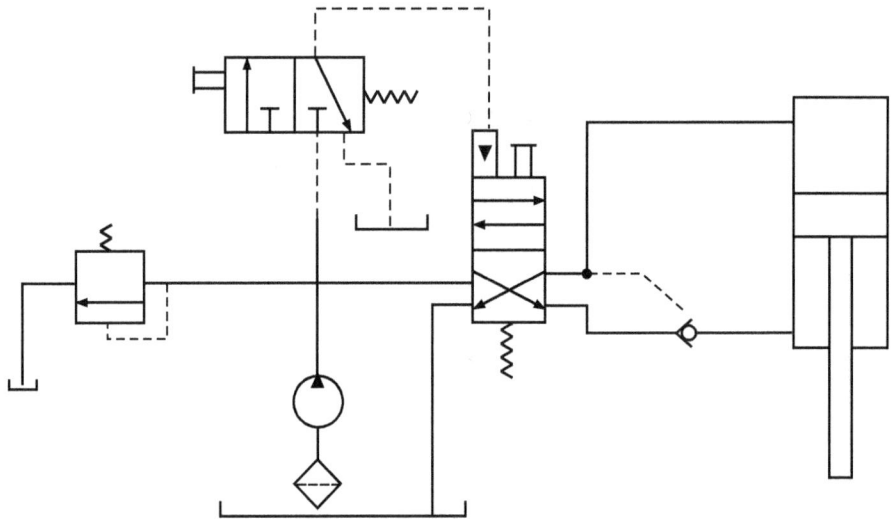

Fig. 4.55: Circuit for milling machine

HYDRAULICS AND PNEUMATICS   INDUSTRIAL CIRCUITS

Example 4.14 : *Draw a circuit for the following condition : The piston rod of a cylinder A is to advance only if a workpiece is inserted in the workpiece retainer, a guard has been lowered and operator presses the push button valve. Upon the release of the push button or if the guard is no longer in the lower position, the cylinder 'A' is to retract to the initial position.* **(Dec. 2008)**

Solution :

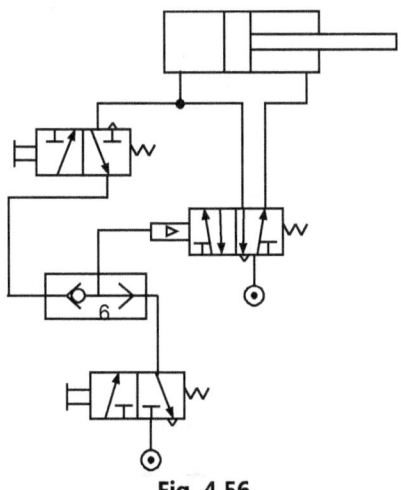

Fig. 4.56

Example 4.15 : *A regenerative circuit for hydraulic output using an additional 3/2 pilot operated DCV is shown in Fig. 4.57.. The view shows the initial fast movement of the piston during extending as there is no external load on the cylinder. Draw the views of the circuit during the following stages :*

(i) When the full load acts on the cylinder.
(ii) The cylinder is retracting.

Comment on the speed of piston during extension and retraction strokes.   **(May 2010)**

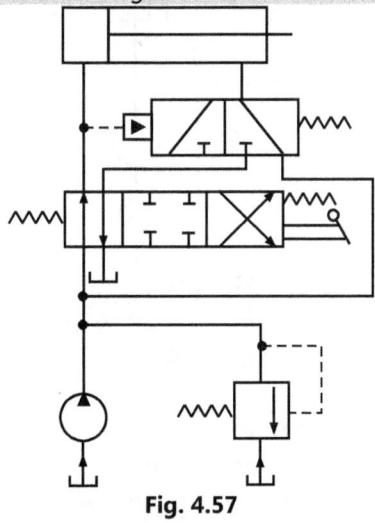

Fig. 4.57

Solution : **(i) When the full load acts on the cylinder :**

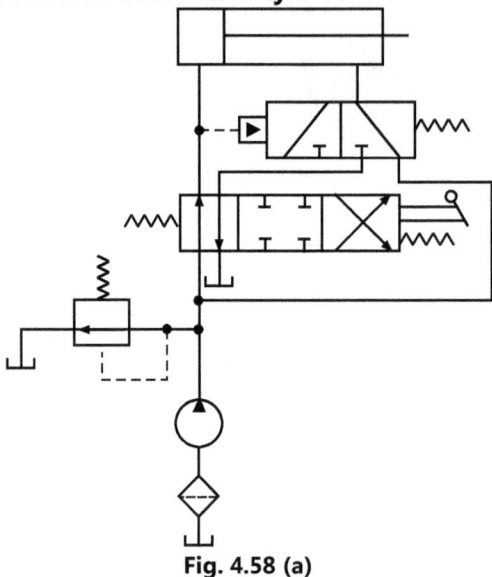

Fig. 4.58 (a)

(b) The cylinder is retracting :

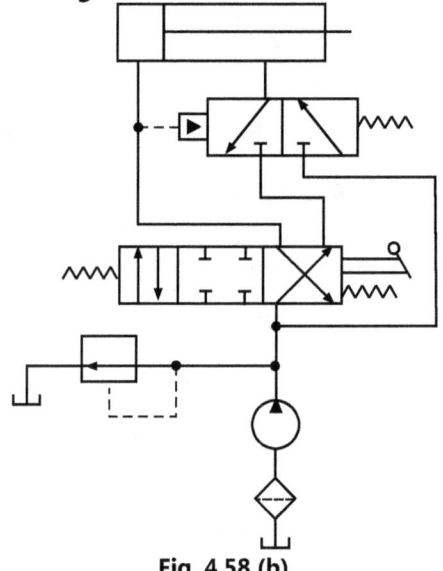

Fig. 4.58 (b)

Example 4.16 : *Study the circuit shown in Fig. 4.59. A and B are push buttons for energizing solenoids 'X' and 'Y'. Make suitable assumptions, if required, and answer the following questions :*
  (i)   Label all components of the circuit.
  (ii) Describe the operation of each cylinder with sequential details.
  (iii) Indicate difference between the valves numbered 7 and 8.

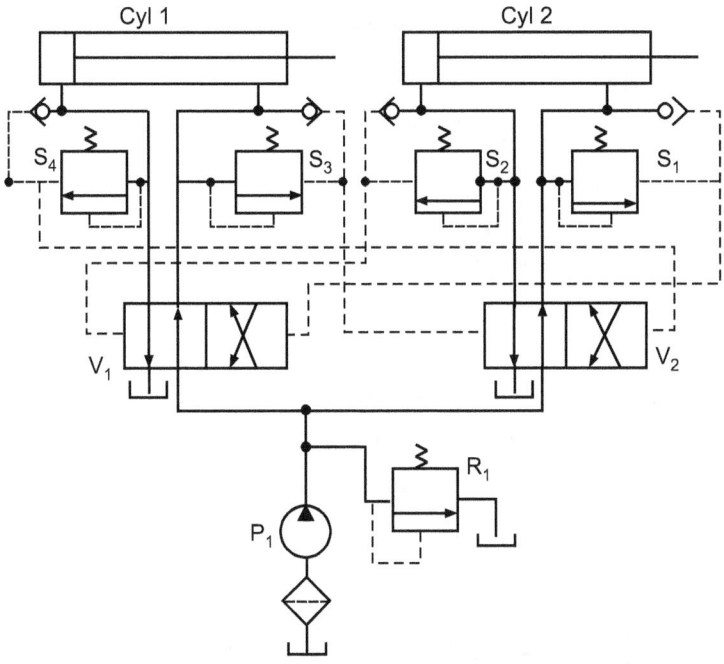

Fig. 4.59

Example 4.17 : *Draw and explain circuit for reveting machine.* **(Dec. 2008)**

Solution : Circuit for riveting machine :

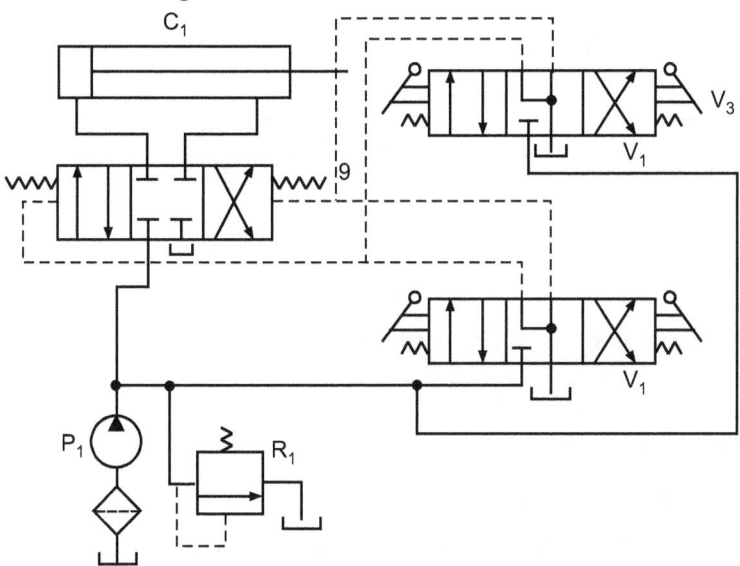

Fig. 4.60

(1) Oil reservoir, (2) Oil filter, (3) Hydraulic pump, (4) Pressure relief valve, (5) 4/3, solenoid operated, centrally closed, DCV, (6) Sequence valve, (7) Pilot operated check valve, (8) Pressure intensifier, (9) Double acting cylinder.

In normal position of valve (5), there is no movement. For (I) position of valve (5), oil flows through check valve (7) to the blind end of cylinder (9), when load on the cylinder increases during riveting process, the pressure in the line increases which gives signal to sequence valve (6). This valve (6) gives oil to intensifier, and intensifier supplies pressurized oil to blind end side during actual reveting.

For position (II) of valve (5), the fluid power enter to rod end side of cylinder (9) for return upward motion.

Example 4.18 : *Analyze the circuit shown in Fig. 4.61.* **(Dec. 2008)**

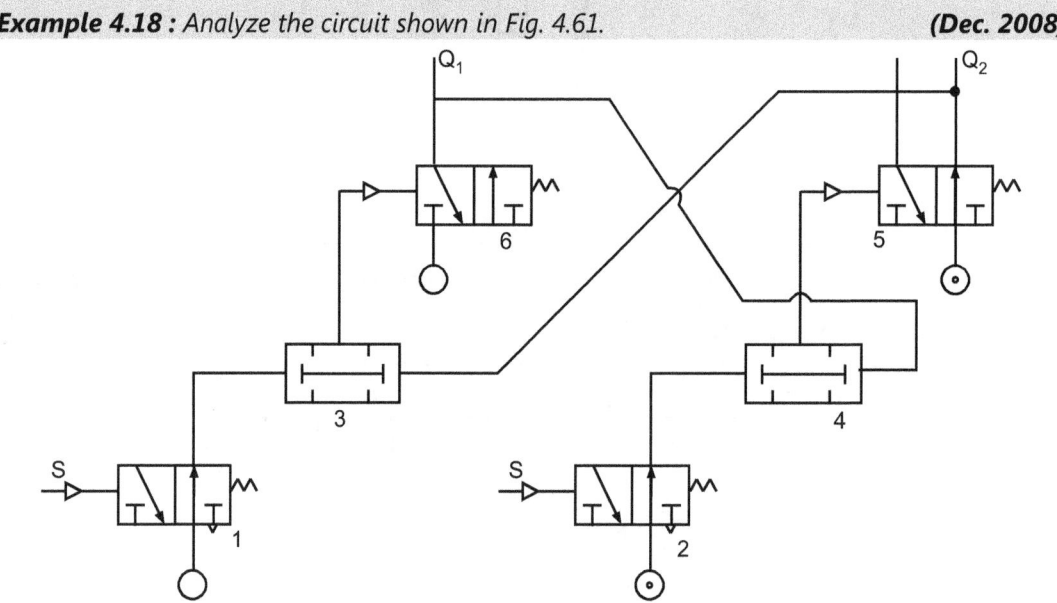

Fig. 4.61

Solution : Identification of circuit components :

- (1), (2) and (3) - Pumps
- (4), (5) and (8) - Relief valves
- (6) and (7) - Check valves
- (9) - 4/3, centrally closed pilot and solenoid activated DVC
- (10) - Double acting hydraulic cylinder

HYDRAULICS AND PNEUMATICS INDUSTRIAL CIRCUITS

Example 4.19 : *Analyze the circuit shown in Fig. 4.62.* **(Dec. 2007)**

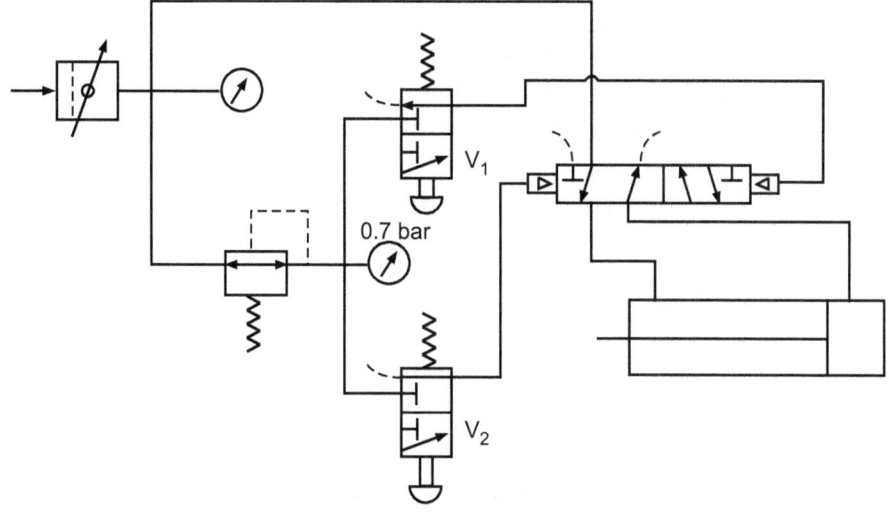

Fig. 4.62

Solution : Analysis of given circuit :

List of components :

(1) Pump
(2) Filter/strainer
(3) Vented manifold
(4) Pressure gauge
(5) Pressure relief valve
(6) 4/3, centrally closed, solenoid and pilot operated DCV
(7) 4/3, centrally closed, solenoid operated DCV
(8) Pressure gauge
(9) and (10) Pressure compensated FCV's
(11) Pressure reducing valve
(12) Check valve
(13) and (14) Pilot operated check valve
(15) and (16) Double acting cylinders

The given circuit is **"Pressure based sequence circuit"**.

When we actuate left position of both DCV's (6) and (7), the oil first flows through pressure reducing valve (11) into the blind end of cylinder (16) which gives extended stroke of cylinder (16). The pressure at blind end of (16) goes on rising, giving pilot signal to valve (11) and valve (11) closes.

The pressure goes on increasing in delivery pipe of pump, which opens the pressure compensated FCV (9) and oil enters in blind end of cylinder (15) and pilot line of check valve (14) which allows oil from rod end to the tank through pressure compensated flow control valve (10) for controlling speed of cylinder (15) depending upon pressure towards rod end.

For right hand position of DCV's (6) and (7), oil flows through FCV (10) and into the rod end of cylinder (16) which retract fast for cylinder (16) and slow retraction of cylinder (15) because of FCV (9).

For middle position of DCV's (6) and (7), cylinder (15) and (16) are locked.

Example 4.20 : *Analyze the circuit shown in Fig. 4.63.* **(Dec. 2007)**

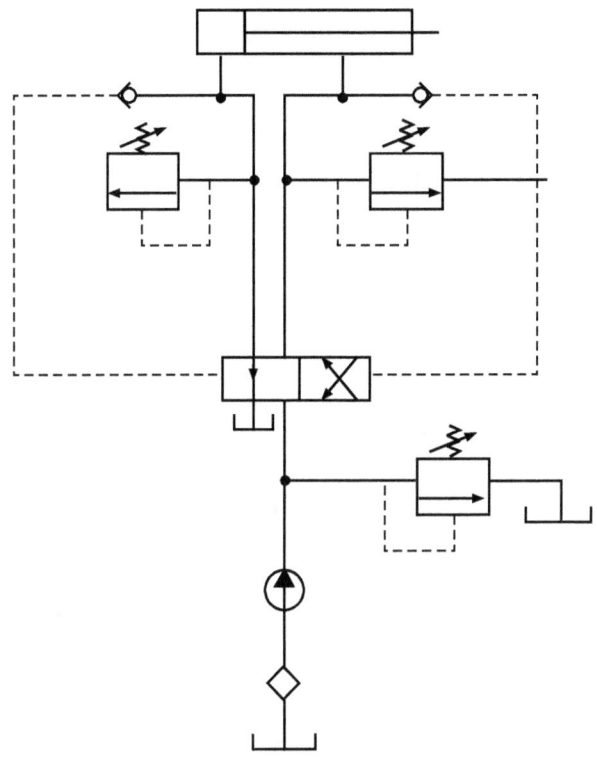

Fig. 4.63

Solution : The given circuit is **"Sequence circuit"**.

Analysis of given circuit :

For central position of DCV (6) : Both the cylinders (11) and (12) are stopped in the given position.

For left position of DCV (6) : By actuating left solenoid, the oil from pump (1) passes through the blind end of cylinder (11), after completion of extension stroke of cylinder (11), the pressure in blind and go on rising which gives pilot signal to sequence valve (7) and valve (7) opens and allows oil to flow through rod end of cylinder (12), getting retraction of cylinder (12).

For this left position of DCV (6), first extension stroke of cylinder (11), then retraction of cylinder (12).

For right position of DCV (6) : By actuating right solenoid, the oil from pump enters first in rod end of cylinder (11), does complete retraction of cylinder (11) then pressure goes on building at rod end side of cylinder (11) which opens the sequence valve (9) which allows oil to end in blind end of cylinder (12), does the cylinder (12) to extend.

Thus, for this right position of DCV (6), first retraction of cylinder (11) then extension of cylinder (12) takes place.

Example 4.21 : *Analyze the circuit shown in Fig. 4.64.* **(May 2007)**

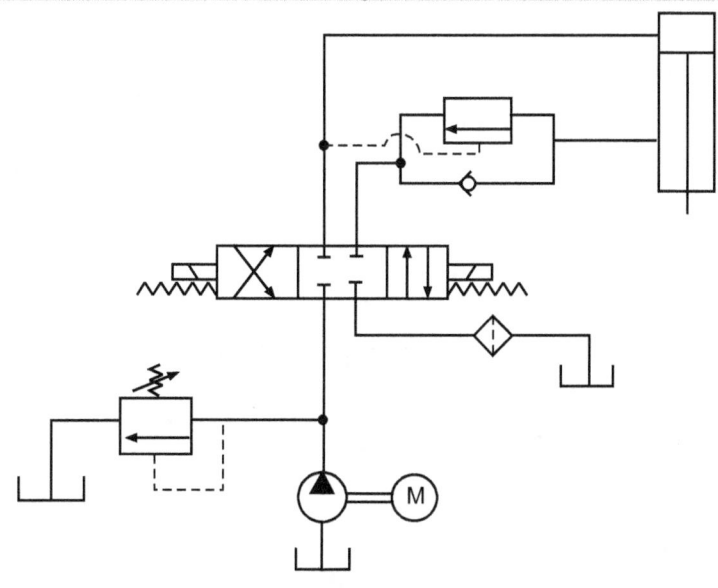

Fig. 4.64

Solution : Circuit analysis : Keeping DCV (6) in the same position and actuating left position of DCV (10). The oil from pump passes through FCV (9), then passes through check valve (11), enters in the blind end of cylinder (13) at the same time, the pump pressure gives pilot signal to check valve (12) to open to allow the fluid from rod end to the tank through return filter (14).

The speed of forward motion of cylinder (13) can be controlled by varying the flow of FCV (9).

If we shift right position of DCV (10), the oil flows through check valve (12), then into rod end of cylinder (13). Again backward motion of cylinder can be controlled by FCV (9).

Changing the position of DCV (6) towards left position and also left position of DCV (10), the fluid passes through FCV (7) as well as through FCV (9), check valve (11) towards the blind end of cylinder (13) and vice versa for the right position of DCV (10).

For backward motion, shift right position of DCV (6), oil passes through check valve (12) and pilot signal to check valve (11). For central position of DCV (10), the cylinder is locked. This type of system used in lifts, elevators, hoist, etc.

Example 4.22 : *Analyze the circuit diagram in Fig. 4.65.*   *(May 2007)*

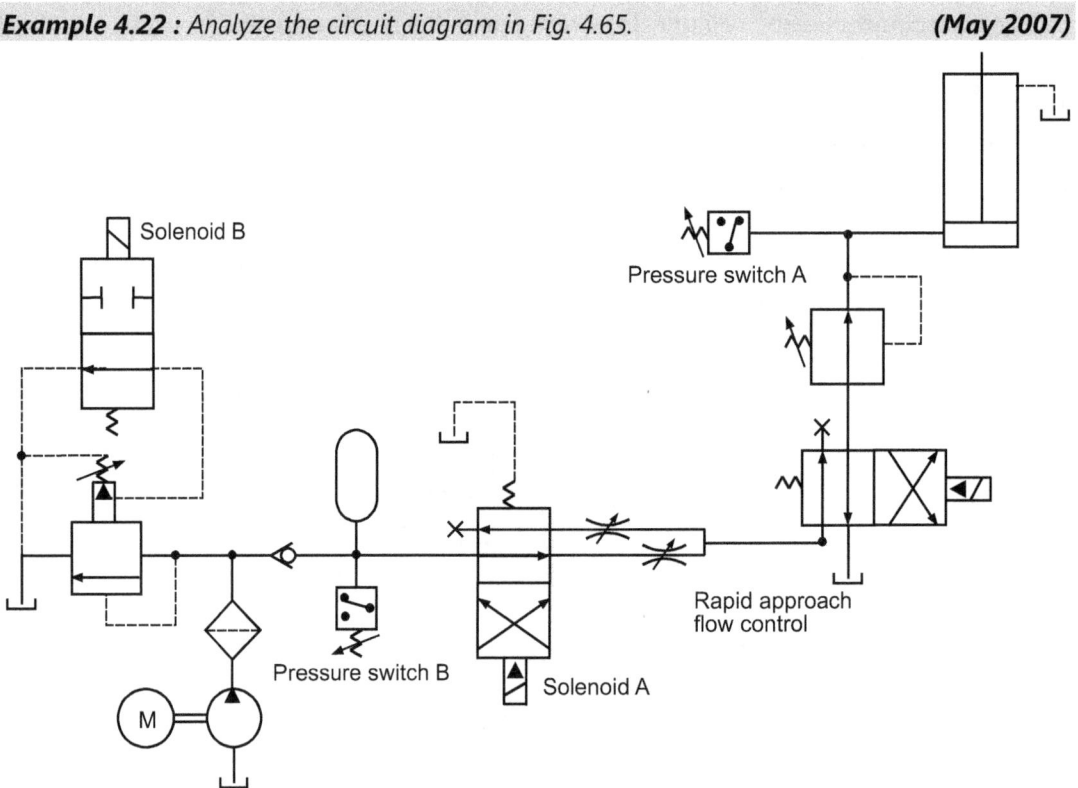

Fig. 4.65

Solution : Circuit analysis : Keeping central position of DCV (5), and giving electric signal to DCV (9), the oil will flow through DCV (9), then into the blind end of cylinders (10 a) and (10 b). If electric signal is released for DCV (9), the two cylinders (10 a) and (10 b) are in retraction motion because of spring and the oil returns to the tank.

Giving either electric or pilot signal to DCV (5) for actuating its left side position the oil enters towards left side of hydraulic motor (6) giving clockwise rotation of motor, but the outflow of oil from motor will not pass through check valve (8), but it should flow through

PCV (7) by getting pressure signal from pressure line. By this, it can control the runaway load.

By shifting to right position of DCV (5), the oil enters through check back (8) and passes through right side of motor (6) for getting anticlockwise direction for lifting the load. For centre position of DCV (5), there is no clockwise motion for motor.

If the system pressure goes beyond set pressure, the relief valve '4' will open and allow oil to return to the tank.

***Example 4.23**: A double acting cylinder is to be operated continuously to and from. Draw a hydraulic circuit without solenoid valves and explain the operation.* **(Dec. 2010)**

Solution :

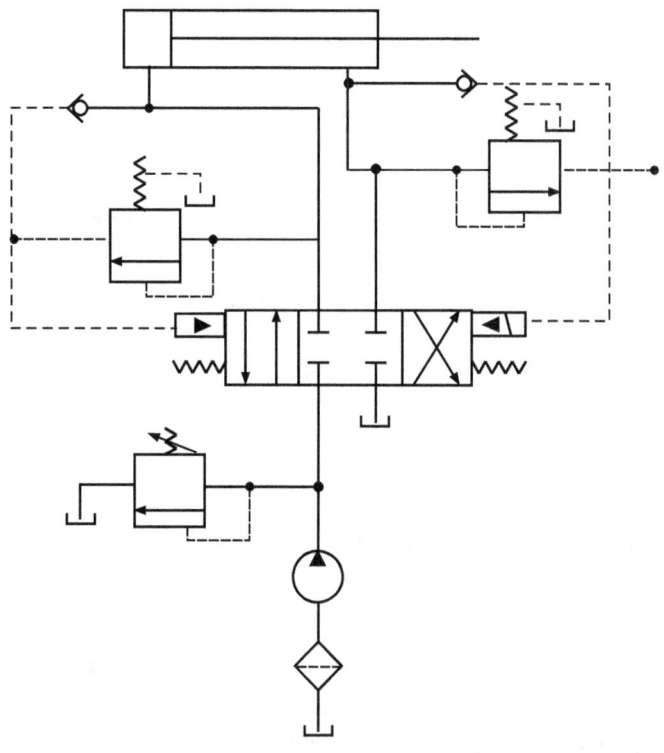

Fig. 4.66

Two sequence valves are used. When DCV is operated in its left envelope, supply will be given to the cylinder, piston rod will extend at the end of extension stroke, sequence valve will operate and pilot pressure will be at on DCV which will shift the position of DCV to the right envelope, retraction of piston rod will happen at the end of retraction sequence valve will operate and pilot pressure will act on DCV which will shift the DCV to left envelopes.

Example 4.24 : *Analyze the circuit shown in Fig. 4.67.* **(Dec. 2009)**

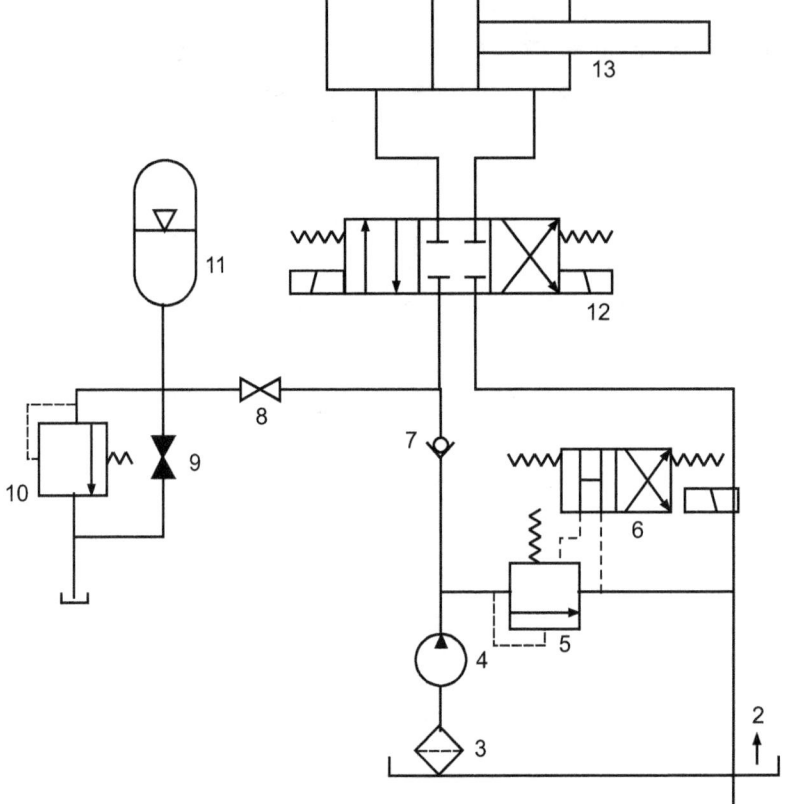

Fig. 4.67

Solution : List of components in the given circuit :
- (1) Oil reservoir,
- (2) Vented manifold,
- (3) Filter / strainer,
- (4) Pump,
- (5) Pilot operated relief valve,
- (6) 4/2 solenoid operated DCV,
- (7) Check valve,
- (8) and (9) On/Off valve / shut off valve,
- (10) Direct operated relief valve,
- (11) Gas loaded accumulator,
- (12) 4/3, centrally closed, solenoid operated DCV,
- (13) Double acting cylinder.

Circuit operation : In normal position of DCV (12), the pump flow will be diverted to tank through relief valve (5).

When valve (12) is actuated by solenoid signal to left side we get left position of valve (12). In this position, oil flow through cylinder blind end and also through shut off valve (8), which enters into accumulator (11). We can use this stored oil under pressure in accumulator for keeping pressure in blind end. We can open valve (5) by giving pilot signal which reduces / unloads pump. Due to this check valve (7) will be closed and it will not allow oil to flow back to pump. But cylinder will hold the same pressure due to accumulator which saves the energy consumed by pump.

Example 4.25 : *Analyze the circuit shown in Fig. 4.68.* **(Dec. 2009)**

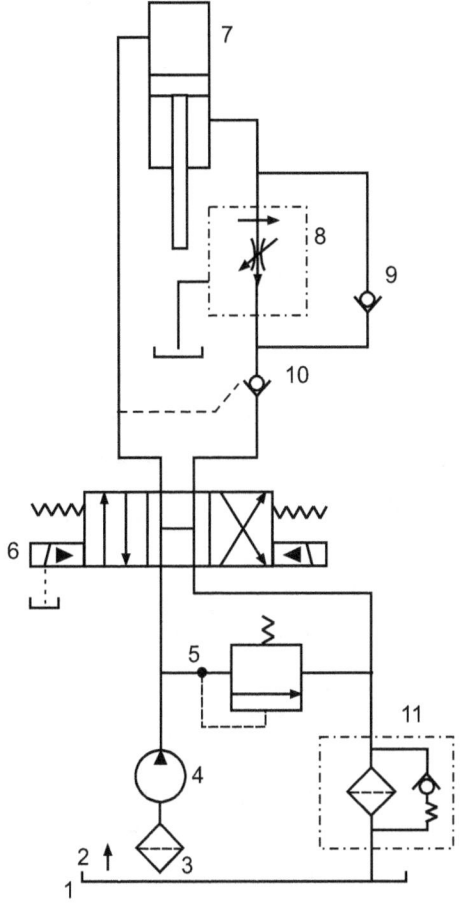

Fig. 4.68

Solution : List of components in the given circuit :

- (1) Oil reservoir, (2) Vented manifold,
- (3) Filter / strainer, (4) Hydraulic pump,
- (5) Relief valve, (6) 4/3, open centre, pilot and solenoid DCV,
- (7) Double acting cylinder, (8) Pressure compensated FCV,
- (9) Direct operated check valve, (10) Pilot operated check valve,
- (11) Return filter.

Circuit operation : In normal position (central position) of DCV (6), there is no movement of cylinder (7). When we actuate valve (6) by given solenoid and pilot signal to the left side, we get left position, in which pump flow enters into blind end of cylinder (7). The cylinder starts moving downward and the oil from rod end side will pass through the valve (8) and there is no flow through (9) then the flow passes through (1) when it gets pilot signal when pressure from blind end side of cylinder (7). Therefore cylinder (7) gradually lowers down.

The right side position of valve (6) will give upward motion of cylinder (7) where oil enters through valve (10), valve (9) and valve (8) enters into rod end side of cylinder (7). Which raises the cylinder upward and oil from blind end side enters into return filter and to the tank.

Example 4.26 : *Design the hydraulic circuit for the following operations : The circuit is required for press operation. An accumulator will supply the necessary flow once the power is shut off by pressure switch at the end of advance stroke. Locate the pressure relief valve, check valve and other essential components of the circuit. Describe the operation of the circuit. Indicate the function of the accumulator during the operation.* **(May 2010)**

Solution :

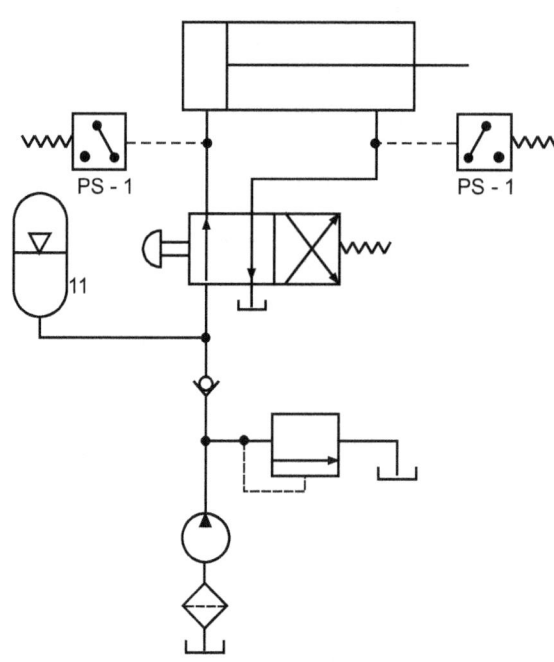

Fig. 4.69

Supply from the pump given to the DCV and then through DCV it has given to the cylinder. When DCV is operated in its left envelope, then extension of piston rod will start at the end of rapid extension pressure switch 1 will operate and it will switch off the pump for the next operation energy will be released by the accumulator.

Example 4.27 : *A circuit for clamping and punching operation is shown in Fig. 4.70 incorporated in the circuit to get an increased pressure at a punch cylinder. Explain the operation of the circuit.* **(May 2010)**

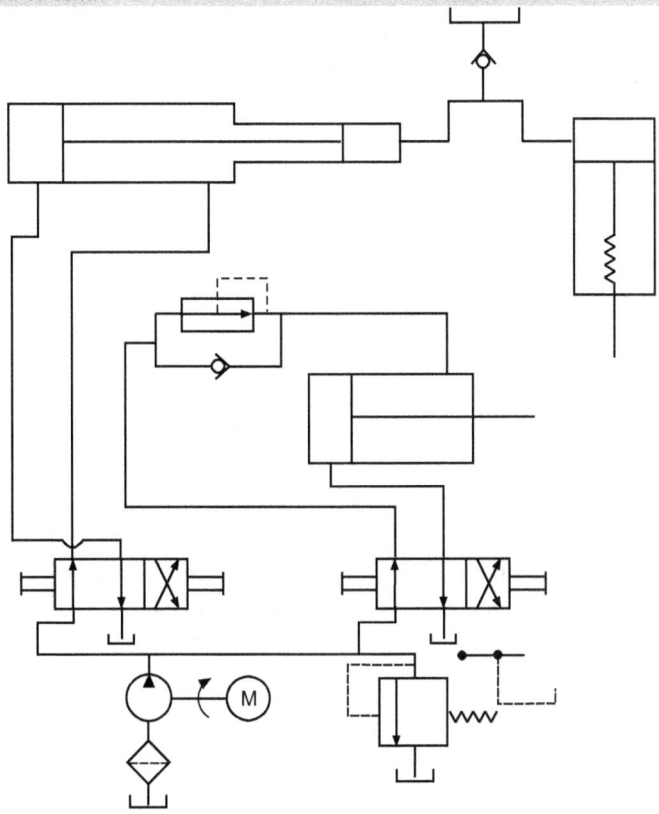

Fig. 4.70

Solution : DCV (1) - Associated with intensifier and punching cylinder.
DCV (2) - Associated with clamping cylinder.
Supply from the pump is given to DCV (1) and DCV (2) then through DCV (1) it has given to the intensifier. Intensifier gets released.
Flow of fluid from DCV (2) has given to clamping cylinder, i.e. on the rod end side, which will retract the piston and it will unclamp the workpiece. Supply to the clamping cylinder has given through pressure reducing valve which will apply only desired pressure on the workpiece while clamping.
When DCV (2) has actuated to the right envelope, supply will be given to the blank end of the cylinder. Piston rod will extend and it will clamp the workpiece.
Similarly when DCV (2) gets actuated, fluid will be forced to the intensifier and intensified pressure will be given to the punching cylinder and punching operation gets completed.
By actuating DCV (1) and then DCV (2) cycle will repeat.

EXERCISE

1. Classify the flow control valves and state their uses.
2. What are proportional control valves?
3. Describe servo control and cartridge valves.
4. Describe the pressure compensated flow control valve.
5. What is the necessity of pressure and temperature compensation in flow control valves?
6. What are the advantages of modular valves?
7. Explain with a sketch how a pressure compensated flow control valve works. Name one application of this valve.
8. Explain the pilot operated check valve and unloading valve.
9. State the use of direction control valves.
10. How are d.c. valves are designated?
11. Describe the construction of a sliding spool operated and poppet operated valve.
12. Explain the functioning of direction control valve actuated by limit switch operated solenoids.
13. Compare the characteristics of tandem centre close centre, and open centre direction control valves. What are their typical applications?
14. Explain with a neat sketch, how a solenoid operated direction control valve works.
15. With a neat sketch explain the working of a sequence valve.
16. Explain with a sketch, how a solenoid actuates a direction control valve.
17. What is 'open centre' and 'closed centre' designs of DCV? Under what circumstances they are used? Show with symbols, different centre flow paths and various methods of actuation of DCV's.
18. What is the purpose of using solenoid controlled pilot operated d.c. valves? Explain typical 4 ways, pilot operated d.c. valve.
19. Draw standard symbols for the following
    (i) Quick exhaust valve, (ii) Variable delivery vane pump, (iii) Pressure reducing valve, (iv) 3-position,4-wayDCV. **(Dec. 2001)**
20. Draw standard symbols for the following (any six):
    (i) Pressure reducing valve, (ii) Variable delivery vane pump, (iii) Silencer, (iv) Quick acting coupling, (v) Air dryer, (vi) Filter with water separator, (vii) Pressure intensifier, (viii) Cylinder with cushioning adjustable at one end. **(Dec. 2003)**
21. Draw symbols of the following:
    (i) Heat exchanger, (ii) Sequence valve, (iii) Hydraulic pilot control, (iv) Solenoid control operated by an air pilot, (v) Pressure intensifier, (vi) Double acting cylinder, double end rod. **(May 2004)**
23. Draw standard symbols for:
    (i) Pressure intensifier, (ii) Quick acting coupling, (iii) Air dryer,
    (iv) Variable delivery vane pump, (v) Silencer, (vi) FRL unit. **(Dec. 2004)**

23. Write short notes on:
    (i) Direct and pilot operated pressure relief valve. **(May 02, 04, Dec. 02, 04)**
    (ii) Counter balance valve. **(May 02)**
    (iii) Sequence valve. **(May 03)**
    (iv) Unloading valve. **(Dec. 02, 03, May 03)**
    (v) Relief valve. **(Dec. 02)**
24. Explain/ Discuss / Write a short note on:
    (i) Speed control using Meter in circuit (ii) Speed control using Meter out circuit
    (iii) Speed control using Bleed off circuit (v) Sequencing circuit
    (v) Synchronization circuit (vi) Transverse and feed circuit
    (vii) Circuit for riveting machine (viii) Automatic reciprocating circuit
    (ix) Fail safe circuit (x) Counter balance circuit
    (xi) Actuator locking circuit (xii) Circuit for hydraulic press
    (xiii) Unloading circuit. (xiv) Motor breaking circuit.
25. Sketch a typical sequencing circuit and explain its working. What is the difference between sequence valve and a pressure relief valve? **(Dec. 02)**
26. Explain with a neat sketch the working of a counter balance valve and draw a typical circuit showing its application. **(May 03, 04)**
27. Explain the difference between direct and pilot operated pressure relief valve. **(Dec. 03)**
28. Draw a pressure compensated flow control valve and explain its working. **(Dec. 01, 03)**
29. State the advantages and disadvantages of a meter-in-circuit. **(Dec. 01)**
30. Explain with a neat sketch how a pressure compensated flow control valve works. Name one application of this valve. **(May 02, 04)**
31. Write short notes on: Meter in and Meter out circuits. **(Dec. 03)**
32. Explain the different types of flow controlling methods. **(Dec. 04)**
33. Draw a neat sketch and explain the working of
    (i) Pilot operated check valve.
    (ii) Unloading valve. **(Dec. 01, May 03)**
    (iii) Pressure reducing valve. **(Dec. 01, May 01)**
    (iv) Direct and pilot operated press.
    (e) 5-way, 2-way position DCV. **(Dec. 01)**
34. What is a function of a shuttle valve? Draw a simple sketch and symbol and explain its working. State its applications. **(Dec. 02, 03)**
35. What is pilot operated check valve? Draw a simple circuit to illustrate its typical use and explain. **(Dec. 02)**
36. What is open centre and 'closed centre' valve position of a directional control valve? Sketch the different valve positions for the same. What are their typical applications? **(Dec. 02)**

37. What is the tandem and float type valve position of directional control valve? Sketch different valve positions for the same. What are their typical applications?
(May 03)
38. Draw a neat sketch and working of (1) pilot operated check valve, (2) 5-way, 2-way position DCV. **(Dec. 01)**
39. Explain with a neat sketch a float type directional control valve and draw a circuit showing its applications. **(May 04)**
40. Write a short note on: open centre directional control valve. **(Dec. 04)**
41. Explain solenoid operated directional control valve. **(Dec. 04)**
41. Describe a compound relief valve.
42. Write a note on simple relief valve.
43. Explain the functioning of a relief valve.
44. Explain pilot operated relief valve.
45. Write a note on direct and pilot operated pressure relief valve.
46. Write a note on counterbalance valve.
47. Analyse the circuit shown in Fig. 4.71.

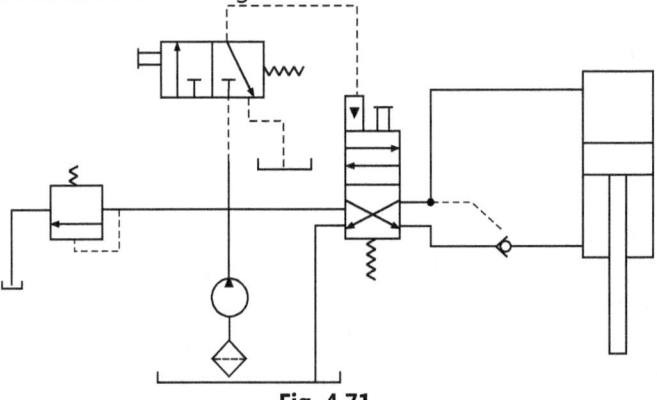

Fig. 4.71

48. Analyse the circuit in Fig. 4.72.

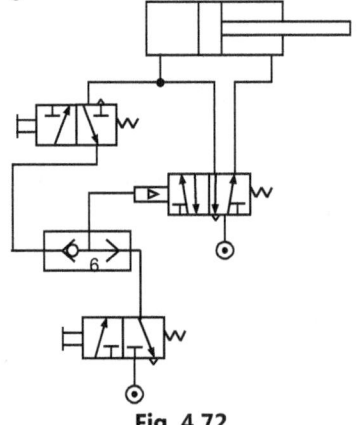

Fig. 4.72

49. Analyse the circuit shown in Fig. 4.73.

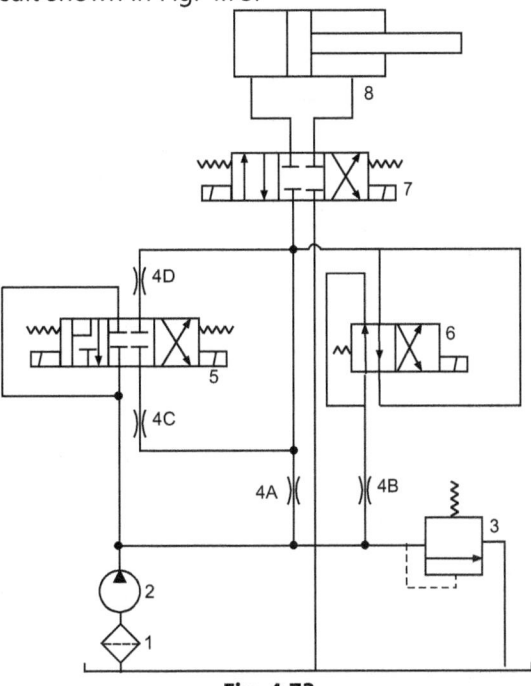

Fig. 4.73

50. For the circuit shown in Fig. 4.74, give the sequence of operations of cylinder 1 and 2 when the pump is turned on. Assume both cylinders are initially fully retracted. (Identify the components and explain the mode of their operation).

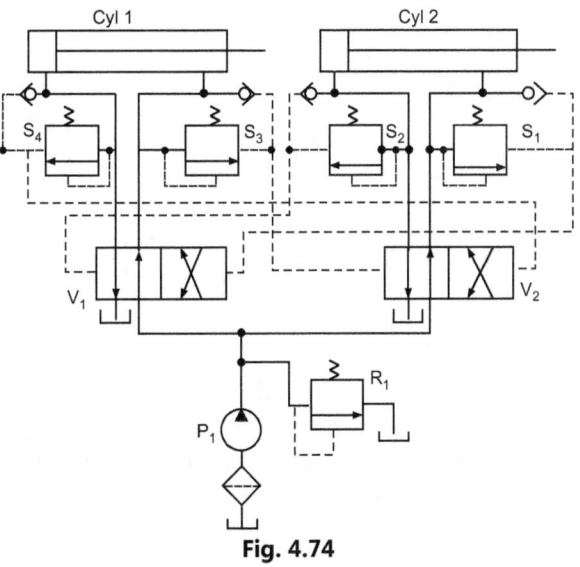

Fig. 4.74

51. What safety features does the circuit of Fig. 4.75 possess in addition to the pressure relief valve? (Identify the components and explain the mode of their operation).

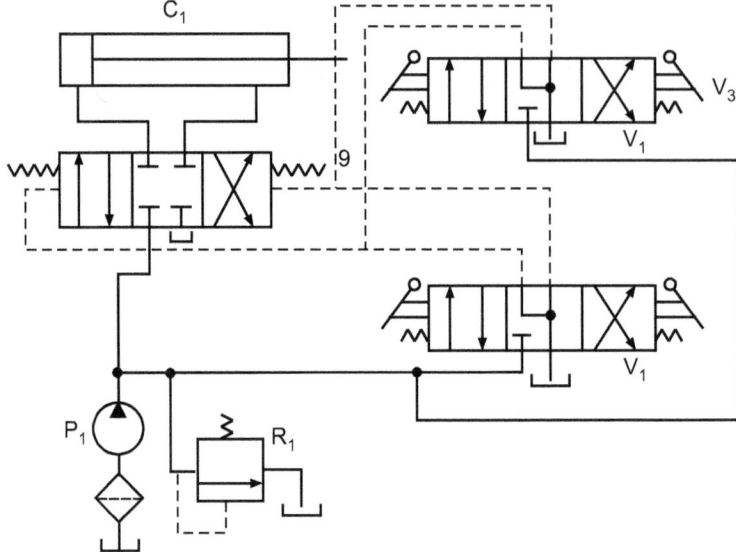

Fig. 4.75

52. Analyse following circuit.

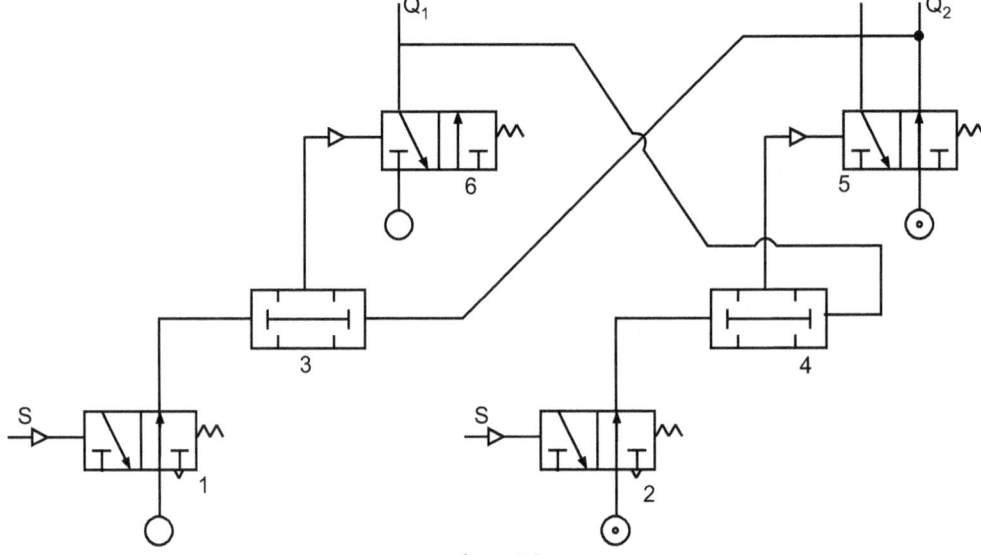

Fig. 4.76

53. Draw a circuit, using ANS graphic symbol, in which the sequence operation of two cylinders in forward and retarding stroke is achieved. Explain the circuit. **(Dec. 2001)**
54. Analyze the following circuit and label the components. **(May 2005)**

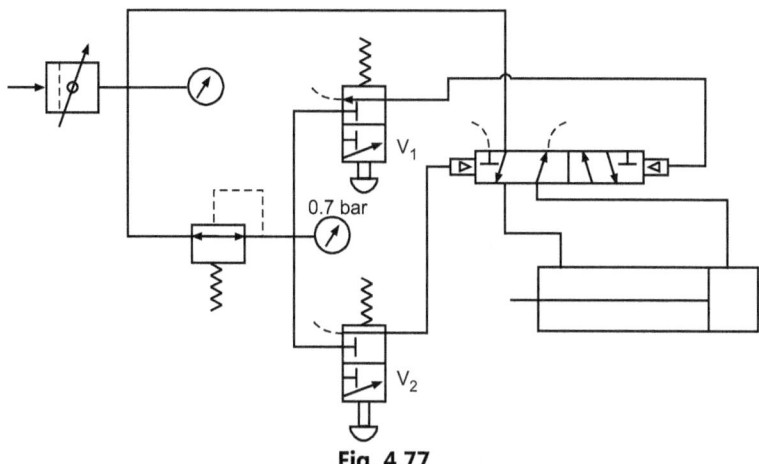

Fig. 4.77

55. Draw and explain the hydraulic circuit of a system having a double acting cylinder which has a rapid approach speed, then slow feed motion and at the end of the stroke the cylinder retracts rapidly. **(May 2002)**
56. Sketch the typical sequencing circuit and explain its working. **(Dec. 2002)**
57. Identify different components and explain the workings of the following circuit given in Fig. 4.78. **(May 01)**

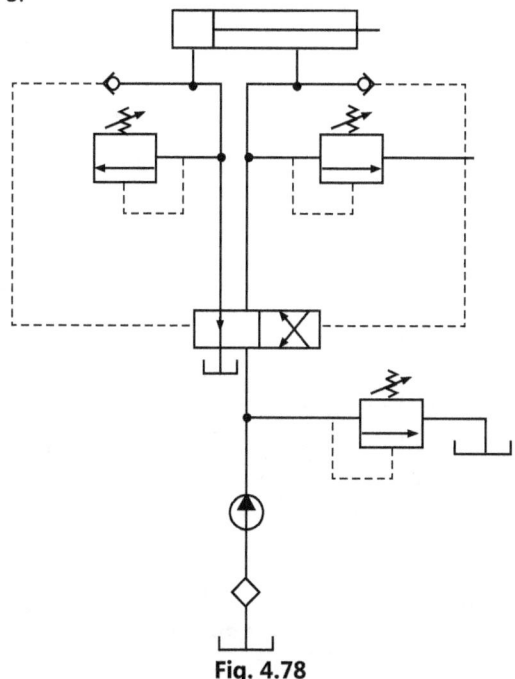

Fig. 4.78

58. Analyse the circuit shown in Fig. 4.79. Identify the components and explain the working of the circuit. **(Dec. 01)**

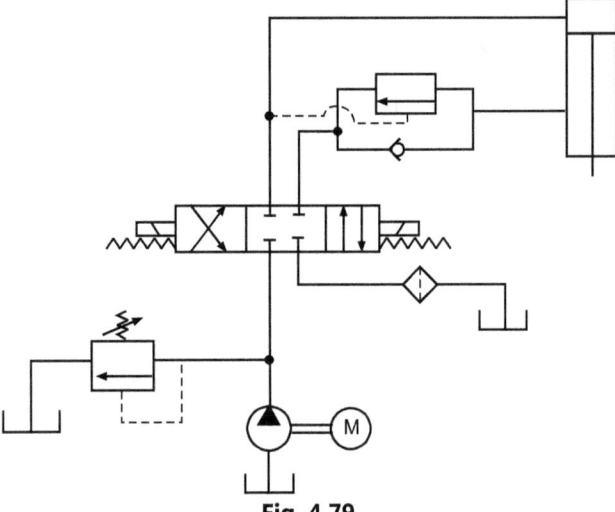

Fig. 4.79

59. Analyse the circuit shown in Fig. 4.80. Identify the components and explain the working of the circuit.

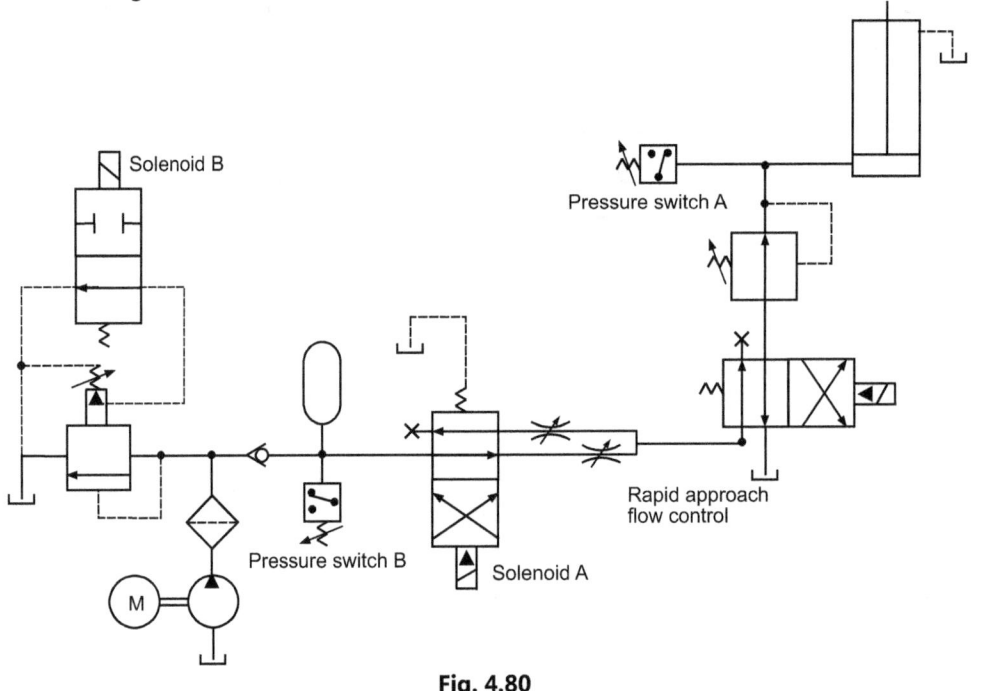

Fig. 4.80

Unit V

PNEUMATICS

5.1 INTRODUCTION (May 11)

Pneumatic systems make use of compressed air for obtaining power required for performing various tasks. Greek word pneumos means '*breath*.' Extensive use of pneumatics started only after the industrial revolution. Earlier it was used in mines for ventilation and for pumping water. Use of compressed air for a rock drill was first done in mid nineteenth century. Discovery of electricity led to the development of compressed air systems powered by small local compressor plants. Earlier the job was done with centralised compressor stations. Most of the modern industrial systems operate at pressures of 5 to 7 bar. Now-a-days there is increasing and effective use of pneumatics for mechanisation and automation, essentially low cost automation systems.

5.2 PRINCIPLES OF PNEUMATICS

(a) Pressure = $\dfrac{\text{Force}}{\text{Area}}$ (N/m²)

N/m^2 is known as Pascal (Pa).

In pneumatics a larger unit is needed. It is bar.

$$1 \text{ bar} = 10^5 \text{ Pascal}$$

and 1 mega Pascal = 10^6 Pa = 10 bar

(b) **Atmospheric pressure:** The pressure on the surface of the earth caused by weight of air is atmospheric pressure. This varies with time and place to place.

Atmospheric pressure = 1 bar = 10^5 N/m²

(i) The pressure measured above the atmospheric pressure is known as 'gauge pressure'.

(ii) Pressure measured above absolute vacuum is 'absolute pressure'.

∴ Absolute pressure = Gauge pressure + Atmospheric pressure

Note:

Unless a pressure is stated or referred to as absolute, it is customary to assume it is 'gauge pressure'.

(c) **Flow rate of air:** Air is compressible. Its volume varies with pressure and temperature. Quantity of air is expressed at atmospheric pressure (1 bar) and at temperature 20°C, as a standard. So while stating flow rate, associated pressure and temperature must be stated.

5.2.1 Properties of Air

Though air is a mixture of 78% nitrogen, 21% oxygen (by volume) with water vapour and dirt, it is considered as a perfect gas for calculation purposes.

Following data of physical constants is important:

1. Molecular weight = 28.96 kg/kmol
2. Density of air at 15°C and 1 bar = 1.21 kg/m³
3. Boiling point at 1 bar = – 191 to – 194°C
4. Freezing point at 1 bar = – 212 to – 216°C
5. Gas constant = 286.9 J/kgK

Relative Humidity is the ratio of water present in the atmosphere to water content in the saturated air at same temperature. Using Dalton's law of partial pressure, we get, pressure of a mixture of gases

= Partial pressure of air + Partial pressure of water vapour

Table 5.1 gives mass of water in kg per 100 m³ of free saturated air.

Table 5.1: Mass of water (kg) per 100 m³ of free saturated air

Temperature (°C)	Pressure [bar (gauge)]				
	0	2	4	6	8
0	0.48	0.17	0.10	0.07	0.05
20	1.73	0.576	0.346	0.247	0.192
40	5.10	1.70	1.02	0.728	0.567
60	12.95	4.32	2.59	1.85	1.44
80	29.04	9.68	5.81	4.15	3.23
100	56.00	19.33	11.76	8.40	6.53
120	0	36.73	22.04	15.74	12.24
140	0	0	37.74	29.96	20.97

5.2.2 The Gas Laws

Air is compressed by a compressor to increase pressure. This pressurized air through an actuator performs work. Hence, it is necessary to study the laws of compression and expansion of air.

Air, here is treated as perfect gas and in all calculations absolute values of pressure and temperature are used.

1. **Boyle's Law:** Volume of a perfect gas varies inversely with the absolute pressure P, while temperature and mass remain constant.

$$PV = \text{Constant}$$

2. **Charle's Law:** Volume varies directly with the absolute temperature, while mass and pressure remain constant.

$$\frac{V}{T} = \text{Constant}$$

3. **Characteristic Gas Equation:**

$$PV = mRT$$

where m = Mass of Has

R = The characteristic gas constant for a particular gas

For a given gas,

$$\frac{P_1 V_1}{T_1} = \frac{P_2 V_2}{T_2}$$ Since for given mass of gas, mR is constant.

P_1, V_1, T_1 are the initial conditions while P_2, V_2, T_2 are the final conditions of change.

4. **Expansion, Compression of Gases and Their Types :** Expansion or compression of gas indicates change in its volume.

5.2.3 Types of Expansion and Compression

(a) **Isothermal compression** means compression at constant temperature. ($P_1 V_1 = P_2 V_2$)

(b) **Adiabatic or Isontropic:** There is no flow of heat energy into or out of the gas during expansion or compression.

Process governing equation

$$PV^\gamma = \text{Constant}$$

where $\quad \gamma = \dfrac{C_p}{C_v} \quad$ where, $\quad C_p$ = Specific heat at constant pressure

C_v = Specific heat at constant volume

[For air C_p = 1.005 kJ/kg.K

C_v = 0.718 kJ/kg·K

$\gamma = \dfrac{C_p}{C_v}$ = 1.4 for air]

(c) Polytropic: Lies between isothermal and adiabatic. This is the most common type of volume change.

Law : PV^n = constant

n = polytropic index

n = 1 to 1.4 for all types of volume changes

In pneumatics most compressions/expansions are neither isothermal (slow change) nor adiabatic (rapid change). It is polytropic.

5.2.4 Expansion of Air

Area under P - V diagram represents the work done either by the gas or on the gas for any of the above processes.

(1) Consider a piston being driven forward at constant pressure P with compressed air fed to the cylinder.

A = area of piston, F = force exerted by cylinder. The PV diagram in Fig. 5.1 shows work done at constant pressure.

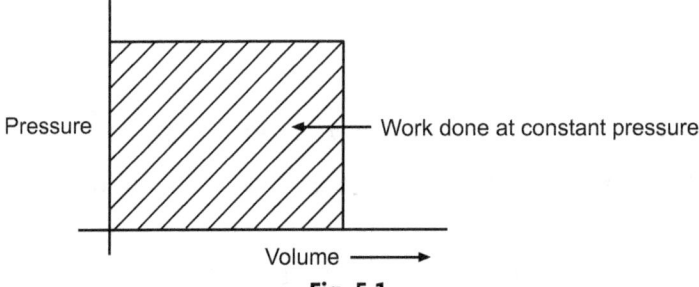

Fig. 5.1

Area under the curve = $P \times V$ = work done

When the piston moves through distance L, the total work done at constant pressure and by expansion of air is given in Fig. 5.2.

Total work done in this process = Area A + Area B

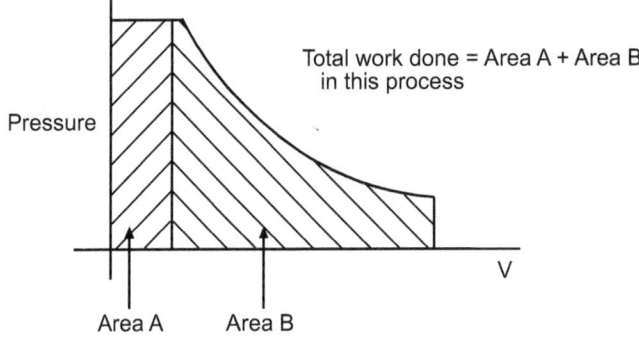

Fig. 5.2

5.2.5 Compression of Air

Fig. 5.3 shows a schematic representation of a single acting piston type compressor. Air is taken in and then compressed by the piston to increase its pressure. Work done in compression will depend on the type of compression.

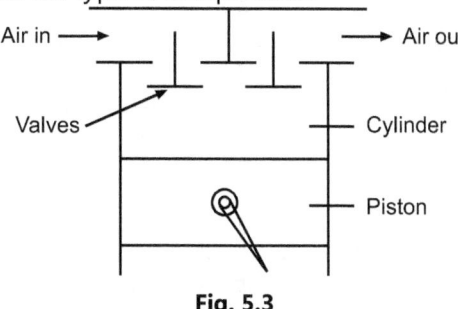

Fig. 5.3

Fig. 5.4 shows polytropic compression.

Initial pressure of air is P_1 and fills the volume V_1 swept by the piston inside cylinder. It is compressed polytropically to delivery pressure P_2 and volume reduces to V_2.

Work done during this process is area under the curve in Fig. 5.4.

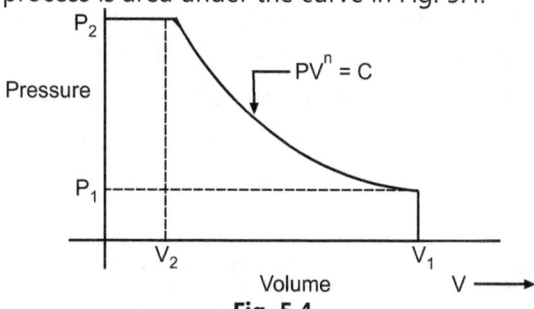

Fig. 5.4

$$\text{Work done} = \int_{V_2}^{V_1} P\, dV + P_2 V_2 - P_1 V_1 \qquad \ldots (5.1)$$

$$PV^n = C \quad \text{or} \quad P = CV^{-n}$$

$$\therefore \quad \text{Work done} = \int_{V_2}^{V_1} CV^{-n}\, dV + P_2 V_2 - P_1 V_1$$

$$= \left[\frac{1}{1-n} CV^{(1-n)}\right]_{V_2}^{V_1} + P_2 V_2 - P_1 V_1$$

$$= \frac{CV_1^{(1-n)} - CV_2^{(1-n)}}{1-n} + P_2 V_2 - P_1 V_1$$

∴ Work done is this process = $\frac{n}{n-1}(P_2V_2 - P_1V_1)$

For isothermal compression the equation for work done (5.1) above is as follows:

Here, $n = 1$ ∴ $PV = \text{constant} = C$ ∴ $P = \frac{C}{V}$

∴ Work done i.e equation (5.1) becomes

$$= C \int_{V_2}^{V_1} \frac{dV}{V} = C \log\left(\frac{V_1}{V_2}\right) = P_1 V_1 \log\left(\frac{P_2}{P_1}\right)$$

5.3 BASIC PNEUMATIC SYSTEM

A basic pneumatic system consists of compressed air (an air compressor plant), control valves, pipings, pneumatic cylinder or air motor and auxiliary appliances like drier, filter regulator-lubricator etc.

The air is compressed in an air compressor driven by an electrical motor or I.C. engine, to required high pressure. It is then passed through a drier for separation of moisture and through the F.R.L. unit for filtration, pressure regulation and addition of lubricating oil. The filtered air with regulated pressure and lubricated oil added is then transported to the cylinder or air motor through piping and control valves. The pipe lines are designed to carry designated flow rate of air with minimum pressure drop. The valves enable the control of flow rate, direction and pressure relief to ensure the designed and safe performance of the pneumatic circuit.

5.3.1 Flow through Pipes and Pressure Drop

Air that leaves the compressor is hot and heat is liberated in the air receiver, heat exchanger or after coolers. As the air flows through pipes, system pressure varies because of the expansion taking place. Continuous change in temperature of air makes calculations complex.

Neglecting the temperature changes, pressure drop (losses) is calculated by formula

$$P = \frac{f \times L \times Q^2}{d^5 \times P_m}$$

where, P = Pressure drop (bar)
   f = Friction factor
   L = Length of pipe (m)
   Q = Volume of free air flowing, lit/sec.
   d = Internal diameter of pipe, mm
   P_m = Average absolute pressure over the pipe length (bar)

5.4 Compressor Plant Layout (May 09, 12)

Fig. 5.5 (a) and 5.5 (b) show various components in the compressor plant system. The various important components shown are :

1. Two stage double acting air compressor
2. Air receiver
3. After cooler
4. Accumulator
5. Service unit
6. Pipings connecting these components.

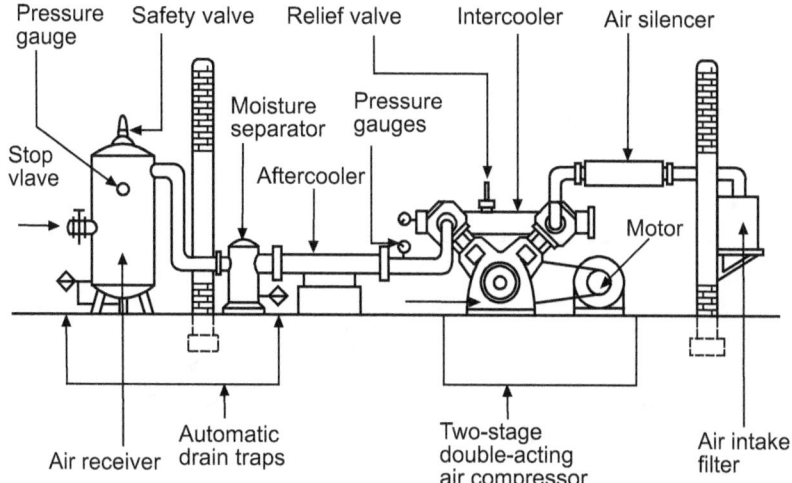

(a) Compressor installation upto receiver

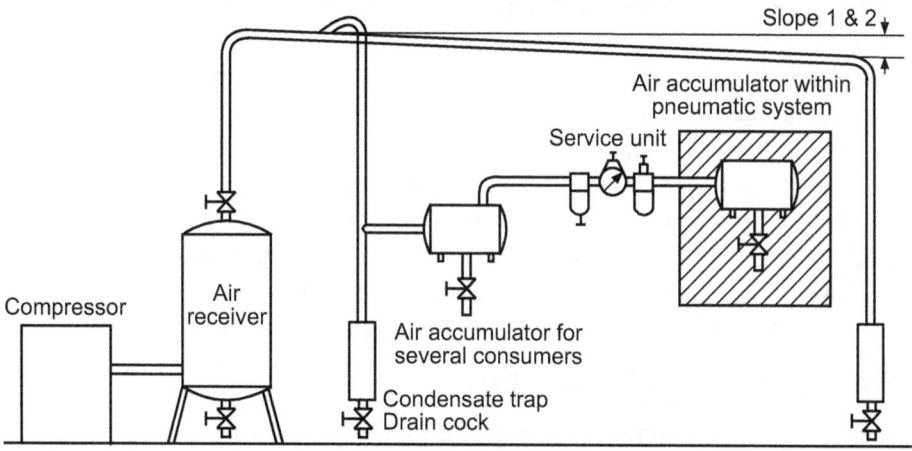

(b) Compressor installation after receiver

Fig. 5.5

Location of the compressor should be as near as possible to the point where air is used. This reduces the length of pipes used. Intake air to compressor must be cool, clean and dry. This increases efficiency and reduces cost incurred for conditioning of air. The noise created by the compressor is significant and while locating the compressor care has to be taken that noise does not cause nuisance. Air receivers and air accumulators have one common function of equalizing pressure fluctuations in the overall air distribution system. They also separate moisture condensing out of compressed air. Air receivers are installed downstream of the compressor.

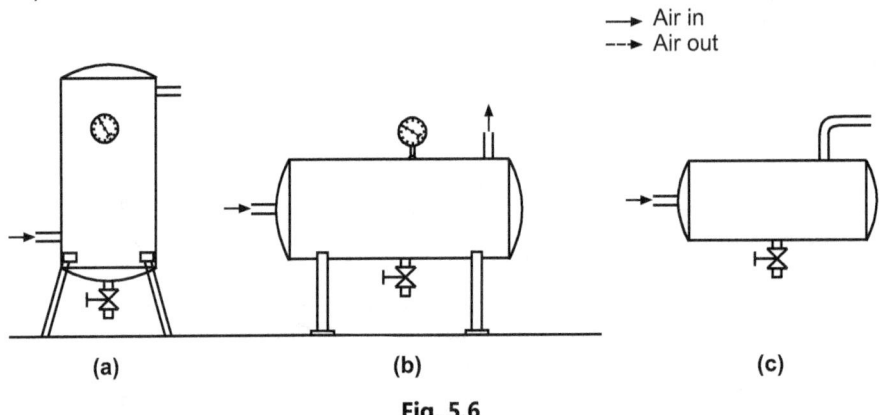

Fig. 5.6

They receive compressed air from the compressor. Air flow coming in pulses from a compressor is then balanced. Receivers are also storage reservoirs for overall mains. They also cool the air and help separating condensate before air is distributed further. In large compressor systems, intercooler is mounted between the compressor and air receiver. Use of intercooler removes the condensate before air enters the receiver. Air accumulators are also receivers. They are installed at intermediate locations to equalise pressure variations within the system, so as to ensure that operating pressure is as constant as possible for all consumers. For each shop served by a compressor, such accumulators should be provided. Use of such accumulators is to compensate for pressure drop in long lines and thus flow velocity in the piping can be maintained at the required level. When large volumes of air are consumed in short periods (intermittent peak loads) during work in the system, for meeting this demand accumulators are needed. If they are not provided, air pressure in pipe lines will reduce at that instant and that will result in abnormally high velocities in the air main, excessive cooling of piping and air in it and thus condensation will increase. Air receivers and accumulators can be mounted vertically or horizontally as shown in Fig. 5.6.

5.4.1 Piping and Line Installation

Pipes used to convey air may be constructed of rubber, plastic or metal. From receiver, air is conveyed further to the points where it is used, through pipe lines known as **air mains**. It is a permanently installed system of interconnected steel pipes with welded joints.

Considerations for design of pipe mains:

Internal diameter of the pipes is decided by

- (a) Flow velocity of air permitted.
- (b) Pressure drop permissible.
- (c) Working pressure required in the system
- (d) Number of restrictions of flow in pipes
- (e) Length of piping.

Table 5.2 : Flow resistance of valves and pipe fittings converted to equivalent piping length

Valve or Fittings	Equivalent pipe length in metres							
	Pipe internal diameter in millimetres							
	25	40	50	80	100	125	150
Seated valve	6	10	15	25	30	50	60
Streamlined valve	3	5	7	10	15	20	25
Sluice valve	0.3	0.5	0.7	1	1.5	2	2.5
Pipe elbow	1.5	2.5	3.5	5	7	10	15
Pipe elbow	1	2	2.5	4	6	7.5	10
Pipe elbow, r = d	0.3	0.5	0.6	1	1.5	2	2.5
Pipe elbow, r = 2d	0.15	0.25	0.3	0.5	0.8	1	1.5
Hose coupling, pipe tee	2	3	4	7	10	15	20
Reducer	0.5	0.7	1	2	2.5	3.5	4

Recommended velocity of flow of air in mains is 6 to 10 m/sec. Pressure drop and flow velocity are related. Rough inside walls of pipes and number of valves or fittings influence the pressure drop. Higher the velocity higher is the pressure drop upto the take-off connection in a pipe. Pressure drop should not exceed 0.1 bar, from distribution leg to connected user. Another guideline in this regard is pressure drop should not exceed 5% of the working pressure in the system.

Variety of empirical formulae have been used by engineers to calculate the pressure drop. One of the popular formula is,

$$\Delta P = \frac{1.6 \times 10^3 \times Q^{1.85} \times L}{d^5 \times P_1}$$

where, ΔP = Drop in pressure (Pa)

L = Length of pipeline (m)

Q = Volume of free air (m³/s)
d = Internal diameter of pipe (m)
P_1 = Absolute pressure of air at entrance of pipe (Pa)

Another formula known as Harris formula, which is also being used is,

$$\Delta P = \frac{C \cdot L}{r} \cdot \frac{Q^2}{d^5}$$

where, ΔP = Pressure drop (psi)
C = An empirical coefficient [= 0.31, for steep pipes]
Q = Cubic feet of free air per second
d = Internal of pipe (feet)

In the industry, various nomograms are used to find out the pressure drop and select the appropriate pipe diameter. One such nomogram is shown in Fig. 5.7

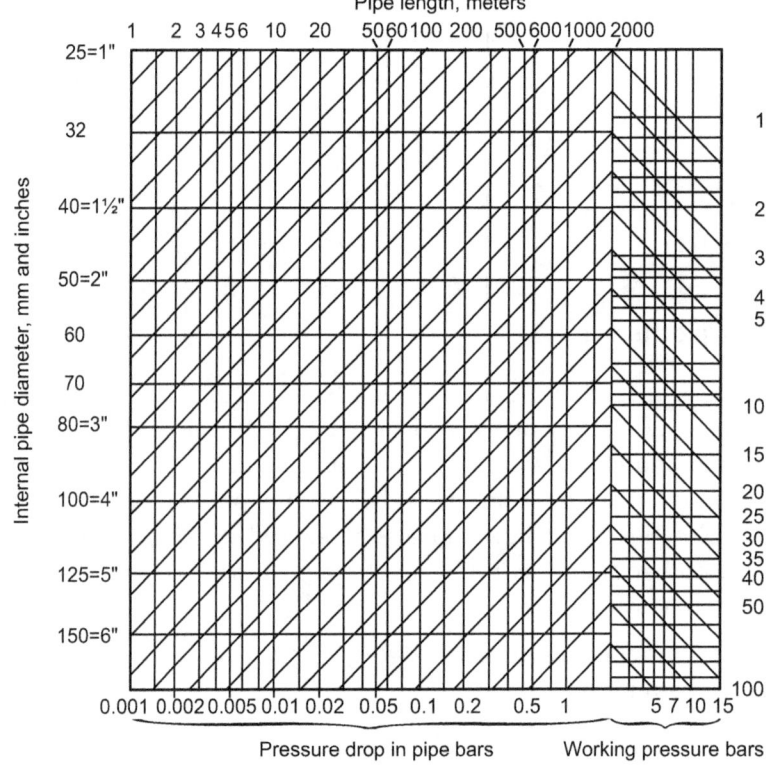

Fig. 5.7: Nomogram

Flow restrictions are caused by bends, tees and valves installed. Such restrictions are converted into equivalent pipe lengths for calculation of diameter of the mains. Table 5.2

gives the data of pressure drop converted into such equivalent piping length. For using the nomogram, data required to be known is flow rate of air, working pressure, overall pipe length and permissible pressure drop.

5.4.2 Installation of Pipings

Pipe lines must not be installed inside walls or brickwork so that it is accessible from all sides. This is needed for inspection for finding leakages. Fig. 5.8 shows the connection between the main line and branch line. Horizontal runs of air pipe should slow downwards 1 to 2% in the direction of flow to allow any condensate to run to the drain point. Refer Fig. 5.5. User point must not be directly attached to vertical mains. In Fig. 5.8 horizontal line of mains runs further horizontally and the branch is taken upwards by bends to avoid ingress of condensate and then the vertical line is installed. From this vertical line the consumer takes air. Thus condensate precipitated in the main will collect at the lowest point branch line where it can be drained off. Vessel valves for collecting and draining condensate from the system must be arranged at the lowest points of the piping main. Branch line as shown in Fig. 5.8 has an inner radius of bend (r = 2 D).

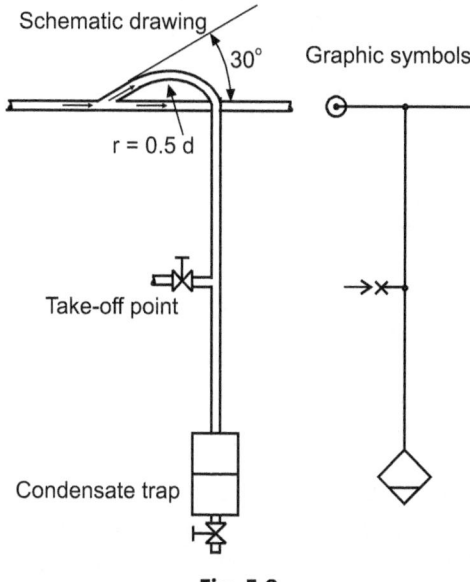

Fig. 5.8

Fig. 5.9 shows a typical ring main system that serves a complete shop or factory. The air main takes the shape of a ring in such a case. Interm accumulator or reservoir is needed. Ring main gives two flow route to every take off point. Inside diameter of ring main pipe should be two third of diameter of branch line. This helps in achieving balanced air supply with reduced pressure fluctuations.

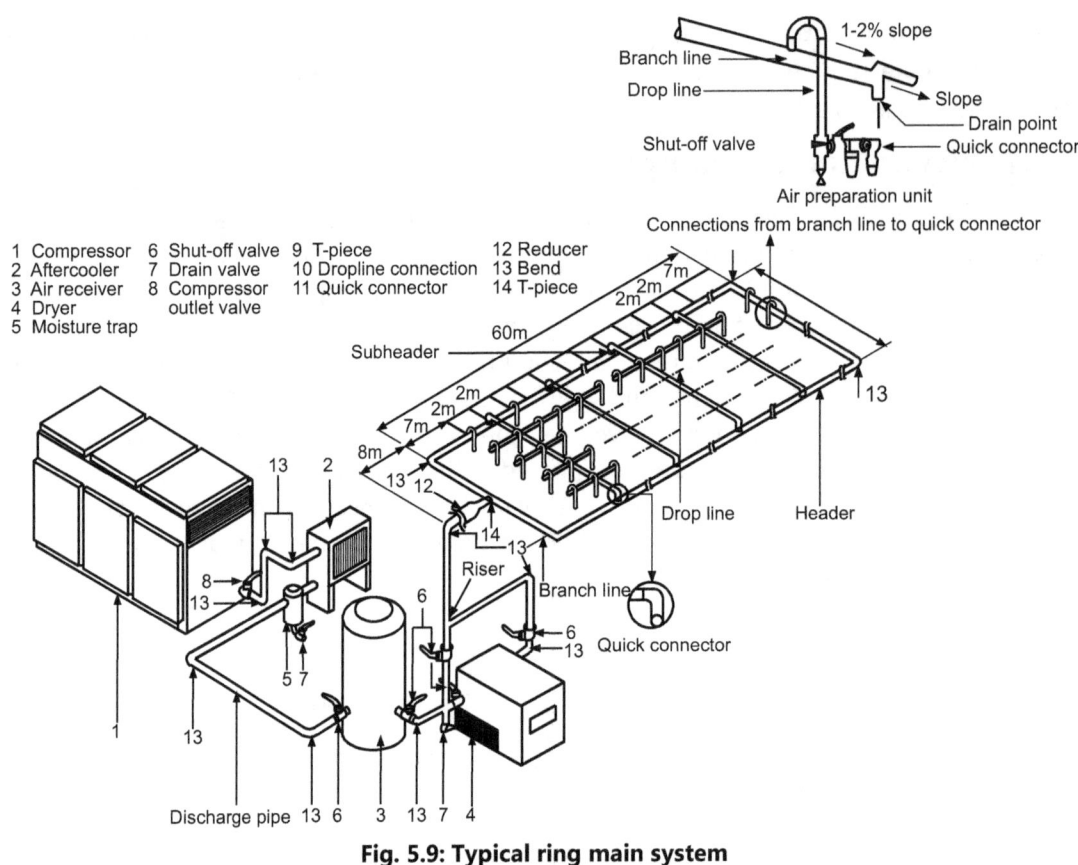

Fig. 5.9: Typical ring main system

SOLVED EXAMPLES

Example 5.1: *Convert 5 bar absolute to gauge pressure.*

Solution: Absolute pressure   = Gauge pressure + Atmospheric pressure

                           5 bar = Gauge pressure + 1 bar

∴   Gauge pressure = **4 bar**   ... Ans.

Example 5.2: *A compressor delivers 400 m³ of free air per hour at a pressure of 6 bar gauge and a temperature of 40°C. Atmospheric air at compressor intake has a relative humidity of 80 per cent and a temperature of 20°C. Determine the amount of water that has to be extracted from the compressor plant per hour.*

Solution: Refer to Table 5.1 of this chapter.

At 20°C and 0 (bar) gauge pressure, 100 m³ of free saturated air contains 1.73 kg of water. Output of a compressor may be given as so many units of free air delivered (f.14.d.). Humidity is 80%.

So at outlet of air from compressor,

Water content in air = 1.384 kg per 100 m³ of (f.14.d). Air at the compressor plant will be saturated. Water content per 100 m³ f.14.d. at 6 bar gauge and 40°C is 0.728 kg.

Since 500 m³ of free air is delivered, water content of air entering the compressor
$$= 5 \times 1.384 = 6.92 \text{ kg}$$
and water content of air leaving the compressor
$$= 5 \times 0.728 = 3.64 \text{ kg}$$
Thus, amount of water to be extracted from the compressor plant per hour is
$$6.92 - 3.64 = \textbf{3.28 kg or (3.28 litres)} \qquad \text{... Ans.}$$

Example 5.3: *A compressor delivers 4 m³ of free air per minute at a pressure of 7 bar gauge. Assuming that the compression follows the law $PV^{1.3}$ = constant, determine the theoretical work done.*

Solution:

Work done $= \dfrac{n}{n-1}(P_2V_2 - P_1V_1)$

Here,
$n = 1.3$
$P_1 =$ Atmospheric pressure = 1 bar abs.
$V_1 = 4$ m³/min.
$P_2 = 7$ bar = 8 bar absolute

∴ Work done $= \dfrac{1.3}{(1.3-1)}\left[(8) \times V_2 - (1) \times 3\right]$

Here V_2 is unknown.

But $P_1V_1^{1.3} = P_2V_2^{1.3}$

∴ $V_2 = V_1 \times \left(\dfrac{P_1}{P_2}\right)^{1/1.3} = 4 \times \left(\dfrac{1}{8}\right)^{1/1.3} = 0.807$ m³/min.

∴ Work done $= \dfrac{1.3}{0.3}[8 \times (0.807) - 3] \times 10^5$ N/m² $\times \dfrac{m^3}{min}$

$= 14.97$ N·m/min $\times 10^5 = 0.2$ N·m/sec. $\times 10^5$
$= 0.2$ (watt) $\times 10^5$

∴ Work done $= 20 \times 10^3$ watt = **20 kW** ... Ans.

Example 4.4: *Find the pressure drop given*

Pipe length = 100 m
Bore diameter of pipe = 50 mm
Flow rate of air = 100 lit./sec.
Mean pressure in pipe = 5 bar gauge.
$f = 500$

Solution: Pressure drop, $P = \dfrac{fLQ^2}{d^5 P_m}$

$= \dfrac{500 \times 100 \times 100^2}{(50)^5 \times 6}$ [Mean pressure $P_m = 5 + 1$ bar abs.]

= **0.27 bar**

Pressure drop means loss of energy. We can increase the pipe diameter to reduce the pressure drop but the cost will also increase. The size of pipings is decided taking into account the future needs also. Air mains having a small diameter will result in high air velocity that prevents water separation. Maximum velocity of flow in the supply main should be limited to 9 m/sec. or better less than it.

5.5 INTRODUCTION TO COMPRESSORS

Air compressors are the source of power to pneumatic system. They play an important role in performance of the system. There are two main types of compressors.

(i) Positive Displacement Compressors: These compressors increase pressure of air having definite volume by reducing the volume in the closed chamber.

(ii) Turbo or Dynamic Compressors: These use rotating members like impellers and impart velocity and pressure to the flow of air. Air pressure is developed as a result of dynamic effect such as centrifugal force.

5.6 CLASSIFICATION OF COMPRESSORS   (May 2008)

```
                          Air compressors
                                ↓
            ┌───────────────────┴───────────────────┐
            ↓                                       ↓
    Positive displacement                        Dynamic
            ↓                                       ↓
    ┌───────┴───────┐                ┌──────────────┼──────────────┐
    ↓               ↓                ↓              ↓              ↓
Reciprocating   Rotary            Axial        Centrifugal      Ejector
compressors   compressors
    ↓               ↓
┌───┼───┐    ┌──────┼──────┬──────┬──────┐
↓   ↓   ↓    ↓      ↓      ↓      ↓      ↓
Diaphragm Piston Labyrinth Sliding Lobe Liquid Screw  Twin
                          vane         ring  (mono) screw
```

Unit 5 | 5.14

5.6.1 Single Acting Compressors

In this type, the air is compressed in the space on one side of the piston. For each revolution of the crankshaft one compression stroke takes place per stage.

5.6.2 Double Acting Compressors

Here the compression takes place on both sides of piston giving two stokes per revolution of the crankshaft.

Air compressors are specified in terms of their capacity to deliver free air and pressure of compressed air at the final discharge point.

5.7 Reciprocating Compressors

These units use piston and cylinder arrangement for compressing the air. Single stage compressors are suitable for discharge pressures upto 7 bar. For higher pressures than 7 bar, multistage compressors are recommended. In single stage compressors, entire compression of air takes place in single step i.e. single stroke of the piston. For maximum compressor efficiency it is desirable to cool air during compression. So in multistage compressors, the entire compression takes place in two or more distinct steps or stages. These stages are done in separate cylinders in reciprocating type compressors. Considerable saving in power consumption is achieved by this. In two stage compressors initial compression takes place in the first or 'Low Pressure'. Air out from this stage is passed through the intercooler to reduce the temperature. This provides cool air for final compression in the 'High Pressure' cylinder. Having more number of stages, the resulting compression approaches the isothermal process and becomes more efficient. To achieve 7 bar output pressure two stages while for 17 bar three stages would be economically justified.

5.7.1 Construction

In Fig. 5.10 a two-stage reciprocating air compressor is shown. The compressor has a body made of cast iron or aluminium. At the base, an oil tank is present. Two cylinders and pistons are arranged in a 'V' shape. There is an intercooler between two cylinders. For obtaining the reciprocating motion of the piston, crankshaft and connecting rod are used like that of an I.C. engine.

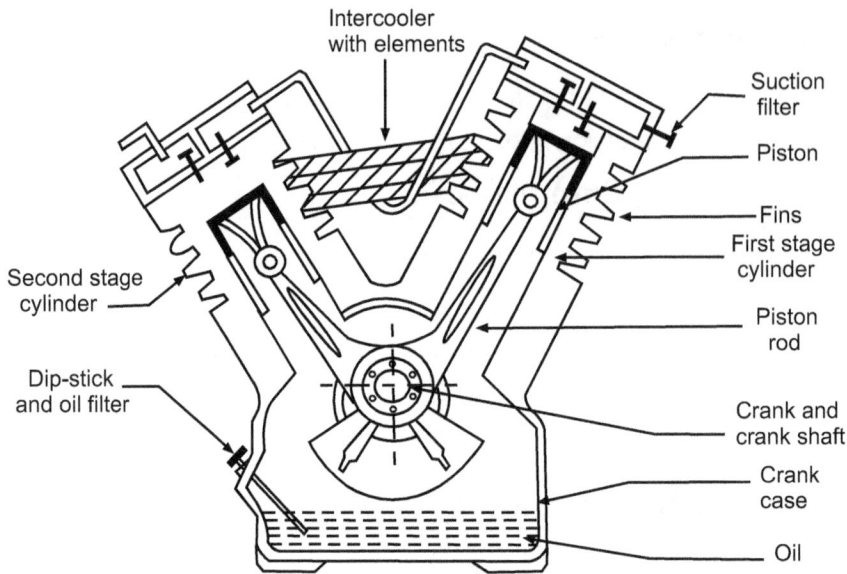

Fig. 5.10: Two-stage reciprocating air compressor

Working:

With the start of the electric motor, the crank rotates and the piston in the first stage cylinder start reciprocating. It sucks air through the suction filter and inlet valve. Then the compression stroke starts. At the end of first stage compression, air enters the second stage cylinder through the intercooler. The air is further compressed and then fed to the receiver through the condenser through the outlet valve. Refer Fig. 5.11.

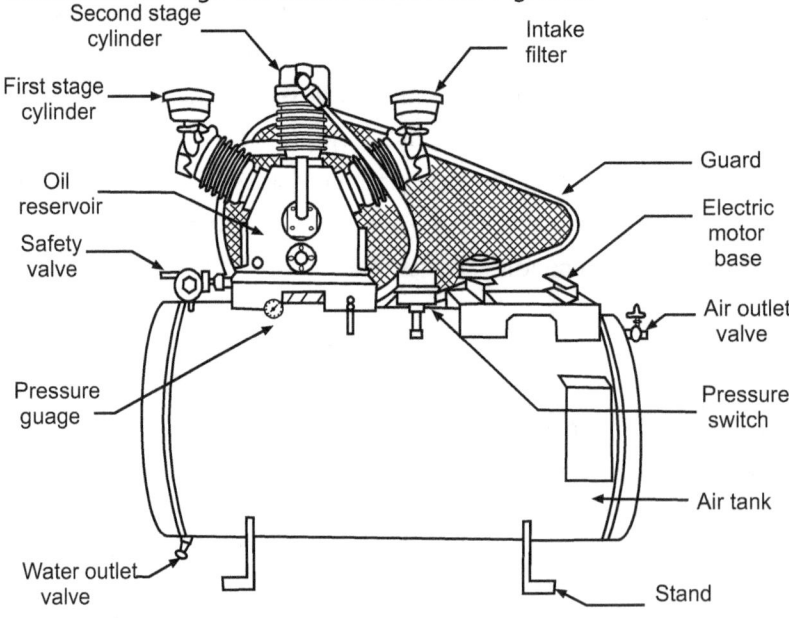

Fig. 5.11: Reciprocating air compressor

Various external parts of this compressor are shown in Fig. 5.10. Note and study the various parts and the air tank or receiver. The pressure switch is connected to the electric motor. When the desired pressure in the receiver is achieved it stops the motor and hence the compressor stops. The safety valve opens in case the pressure in the receiver exceeds the set pressure.

The drain valve drains the condensate produced at the condenser and receiver. Cooling of air is obtained by having fins on the cylinders and fan in air cooled compressor, that is the one type shown in Fig. 5.11. In water cooled compressors, water is circulated through jackets to cool cylinders and also for intercooler.

Air cooled compressors are convenient for colder ambient and low delivery pressures. Water cooling is suggested for hot ambient and where heat dissipation from compressor to the surrounding cannot be tolerated.

5.8 P-V Diagram for the Compressor

In Fig. 5.12 P-V diagram for two-stage compressor with an intercooler is shown. The ideal diagrams for adiabatic compression (1) isothermal compression (2) and actual compression that is of polytropic (3) nature are shown in the Fig. 5.12 In the first stage, we see the pressure is increased from suction pressure P_1 to P_i i.e. intercooler pressure polytropically. In the second stage pressure from intercooler pressure is further increased to delivery pressure (P_2) polytropically. The saving in compressor input power is shown by the shaded area. This saving will vary if the intercooler pressure is variable.

Here, $$P_i = \sqrt{P_1 \times P_2}$$

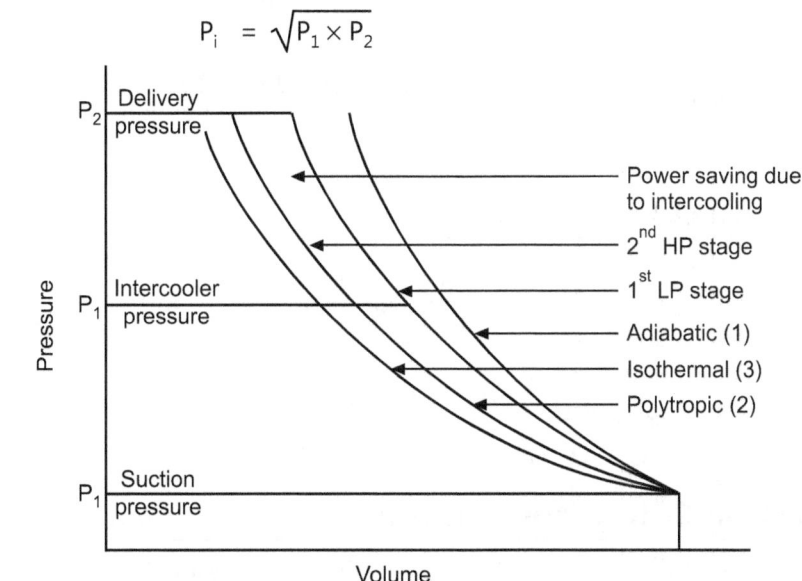

Fig. 5.12: P-V diagram for a two-stage compressor with intercooling

HYDRAULICS AND PNEUMATICS — PNEUMATICS

5.8.1 Work Done in One Cycle of Compression

$$W = \frac{n}{n-1} P_1 V_1 \left[\left(\frac{P_2}{P_1}\right)^{\frac{n-1}{n}} - 1 \right]$$

where,
P_1 = Initial pressure (abs)
P_2 = Final pressure (abs)
V_1 = Initial volume
V_2 = Volume at end of compression
n = Index for polytropic conditions

Usually $n = 1.4$

5.8.2 Volumetric Efficiency of Compressor

$$\eta_{vol.} = \frac{\text{Weight of free air delivered per min.}}{\text{Weight of air equivalent to swept volume at inlet conditions}}$$

$$= \frac{\text{Volume of air delivered per min at N.T.P.}}{\text{Swept volume of LP cylinders per minute}}$$

Volumetric efficiency depends upon the weight of air entering compressor, air temperature and pressure at the inlet. A lower inlet temperature is desirable and it means higher weight of air entering the compressor per cycle. Efficiency also depends upon the clearance volume at the ends of the cylinders, internal leakage of compressor; speed of compressor.

$$\text{Overall isothermal efficiency} = \frac{\text{Isothermal work done per min.}}{\text{Actual work done per min.}}$$

This value varies between 60 to 80%.

5.8.3 Mean Effective Pressure

$$MEP = \frac{n}{n-1} \times P_1 \left[\log_e \left(\frac{P_2}{P_1}\right)^{\frac{n-1}{n}} - 1 \right]$$

Power for single stage compressor $= (M.E.P.) \times V_1$

For two-stage compressor power $= 2 \times (M.E.P.) \times V_1$

5.8.4 Selection Criteria for Compressors (Dec. 2007)

The important criteria to be considered while selecting compressors for a pneumatic system are listed below.

(i) Pressure: The operating pressure of the system has to be determined and while deciding the compressor pressure, the length of the lines has to be considered. If long lines are involved, then to cater for the losses in the pipe lines, a higher pressure rating of the filter has to be selected. If a few devices out of several ones make use of high pressures, then it is advisable to have a separate high pressure compressor exclusively for those devices alone. If considerable amount of low pressure air is required, then it is better to install a low pressure compressor.

(ii) Capacity: It means the volume of air required. The capacity selected should be large enough to cater for the operation of all devices at a time. If the equipments are used intermittently then depending upon the nature of the devices the capacity required at any one time has to be estimated. In this, experience of similar plants and advise of manufacturers have to be considered.

(iii) Compressor Configuration and Cylinder Geometry: This will further involve the following such as

(a) Type of Compressor: Reciprocating, vane type, screw type, etc.
- Vertical,
- Horizontal.

(b) Arrangement of Cylinders:
- Vertical in line,
- V type,
- Horizontal and vertical,
- Horizontal opposed,
- Horizontal duplex.

5.9 ROTARY VANE COMPRESSOR

The rotary sliding vane type compressors can produce a pressure ratio upto eight per stage. They have a good performance efficiency over a wide range of pressure and flow rate. Since their discharge is free of pulsation, a receiver can be eliminated. An illustrative diagram of a vane compressor is shown in Fig. 5.13.

It consists of a rotor enclosed in a casing. The rotor is eccentrically placed with respect to the casing and it has radial slots. Sliding vanes are inserted in these slots. The vanes slide in and out of the rotor. As the rotor rotates at high speed, centrifugal force throws each vane outwards. Thus, the outer tip of each vane maintains a constant with the circumference of the casing. Vanes can also be loaded with springs. Oil is injected into the casing which lubricates the bearings, gears, provides cooling of air while it is being compressed and seals all clearances to check air leakage from high pressure to low pressure.

The lubricating oil passes with the air discharged into the receiver and is separated through filters. During the operation of the compressor, oil gets heated. It is continuously cooled in an oil cooler. A low viscosity oil like SAE-10 grade is usually used.

The compressor is compact sized, light weight and can be run at high speed air discharge temperature is low. It needs little maintenance and low cost foundation.

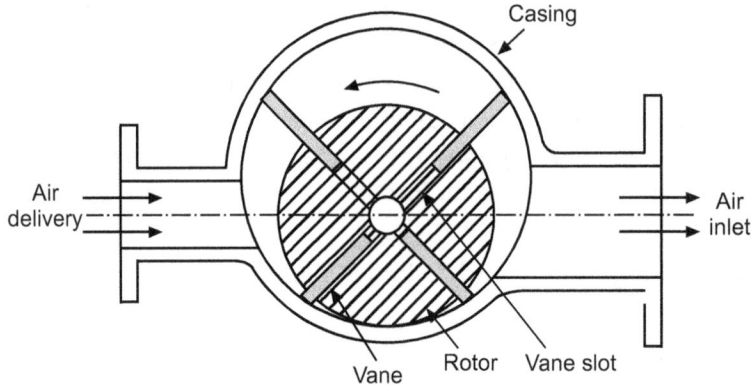

Fig. 5.13: Rotary vane type air compressor

5.10 Liquid Ring Compressor

The principle of operation of this compressor is similar to the vane type compressor. In addition, it uses water or other low viscosity liquids for compressing the gas trapped between the blades and the casing. The metal contact between the blades and casing is avoided, hence there no lubrication and wear at the contact points. These compressors are suitable for a wide range of flow, radial and pressure ratios upto five. Arrangement for maintaining constant liquid level is necessary. The maximum pressure is limited to about 6 bar and the maximum speed is restricted by the cavitation erosion of components. Fig. 5.14 shows the arrangement of a liquid ring compressor.

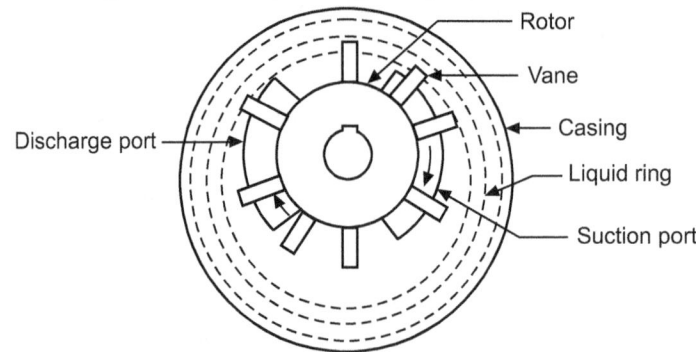

Fig. 5.14: Liquid ring compressor

5.11 Lobe Compressor

A twin lobe compressor is shown in Fig. 5.14 while a screw lobe type compressor is shown in Fig. 5.15.

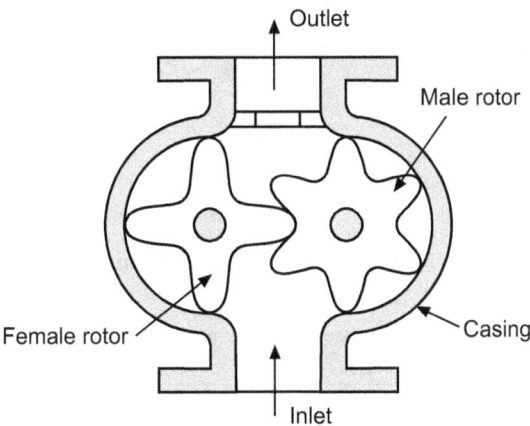

Fig. 5.15: Screw lobe compressor

Two lobes are housed in a casing. Air is progressively compressed continuously while the lobes rotate. There is no reduction of air volume. They generate low discharge pressure. There is no internal compression but the lobes discharge air towards the discharge opening against the system back pressure. The clearance between the lobes is maintained by timing the gears. Hence, no internal lubrication is needed. Compression ratio is upto 1.7 for a single stage. A screw lobe compressor is a refined version of the lobe type compressor.

5.12 Screw Compressor

It consists of a male and female rotor screws. These are driven by a gear train placed outside the housing. They run at high speed, necessitating the provision of suction and discharge silencers and other measures to reduce the noise level. Air delivered is oil-free. Sometimes, oil is injected for cooling and sealing clearances. The design of the helix of the male and female rotor is such, as to allow complete filling of interlobe space before remeshing. The re-engagement of male and female rotor reduces the volume of air continuously. The delivery of air is smooth and free of pulsations. Male and female rotors are often uneven such as from 4 to 6 or 5 to 7. This allows the female rotor to have a larger root diameter for greater strength. The rotors and the casing do not have a direct contact and lubrication is not needed. (Fig. 5.16)

Often the screw compressors are cooled by liquid (oil) to dissipate the heat generated. The coolant oil is injected into the interlobe space. The air delivered is cool, clean and pulsation free. Due to few moving parts, maintenance is less. Its installation is simple and does not need foundation due to absence of vibrations.

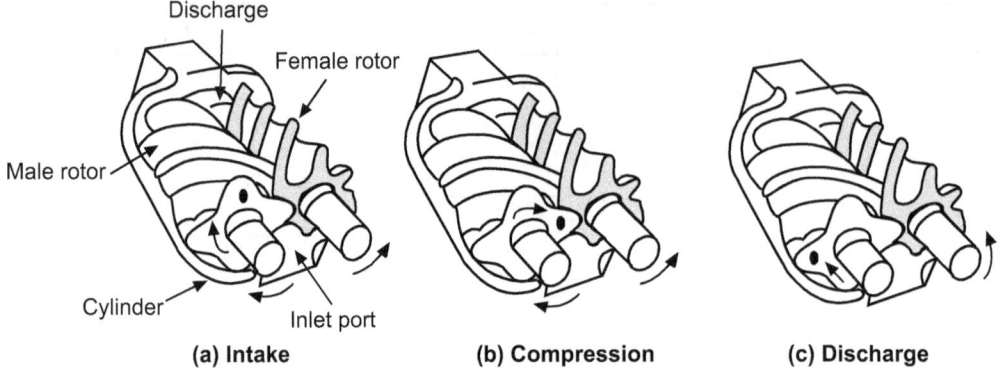

(a) Intake (b) Compression (c) Discharge

Fig. 5.16: Working details of screw compressor's cycle

5.13 Centrifugal Compressors

These are dynamic compressors. These are driven at very high speed. It consists of a rotor (impellar) fit.

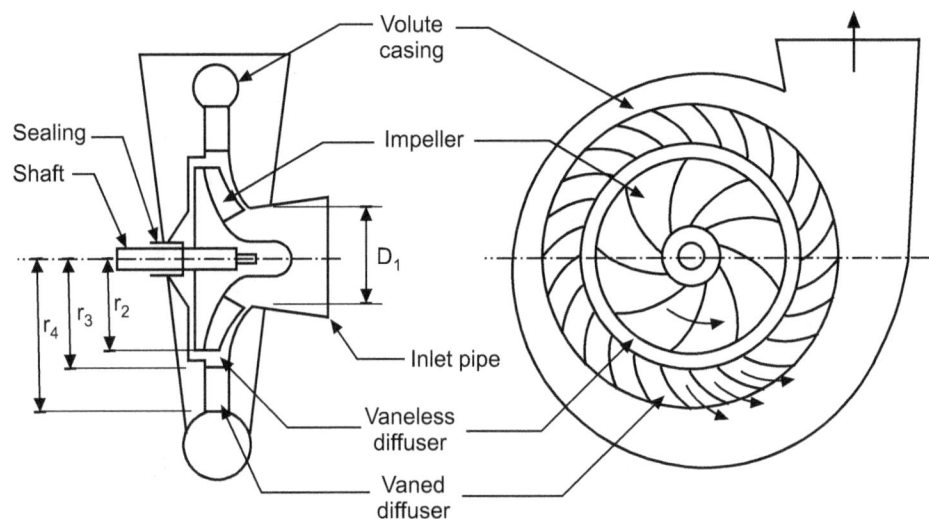

Fig. 5.17: Centrifugal air compressor

5.14 Air Receiver

Air receiver is essential with reciprocating compressors and is desirable with other compressors. It evens out the flow pulsations, provides interim storage space for compressed air and allows the air to cool and to dry when moisture in it condenses. The volume of the air receiver should be large enough and is estimated as follows:

$$\text{Receiver volume} = \frac{Q \times P_a}{P_d} \text{ m}^3$$

where, Q = Volume of air delivered by the compressor, m³/min.
(assuming volumetric efficiency of 100%)

P_d = Discharge pressure, bar absolute

P_a = Atmospheric pressure, bar absolute

The receiver volume is influenced by the delivery volume of the compressor, air consumption by the application piping network, type and setting of ON / OFF regulation and allowable pressure difference in pipings.

When ON / OFF regulation is provided for the compressor, the receiver volume can be determined by

$$\text{Receiver volume} = \frac{15\,Q \times P}{\Delta P \times N} \text{ m}^3$$

where, Q = Delivery volume N m³/min.

P = Intake pressure, bar absolute.

ΔP = Pressure difference (cut-in, cut-off setting differential), bar

N = Switching cycle/hr of compressor running

An empirical rule suggests that the receiver volume should be about 1/10 of f.a.d. per minute to 1/6 of f.a.d. per minute for a small compressor.

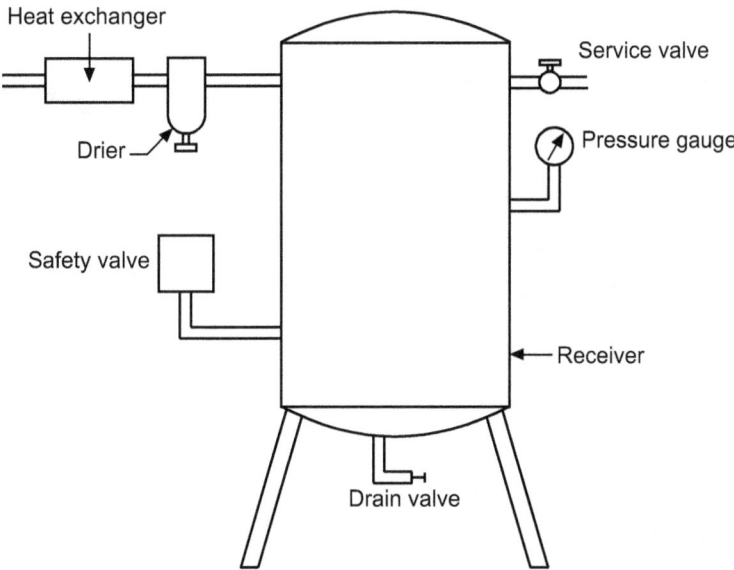

Fig. 5.18: Air receiver

The receiver is fabricated out of steel plates and is basically a pressure vessel and attracts the safety of testing requirements as per the factories act. A safety valve is necessary to release the excess pressure of air stored. A pressure gauge to indicate the pressure of air in the receiver and a drain valve at its bottom to flush out the condensed moisture and accumulated lubricating oil are provided. A typical compressed air receiver is shown in Fig. 5.18.

5.15 FACTORS INFLUENCING SELECTION OF AIR COMPRESSORS

The selection of an air compressor for an application is governed by several factors which are briefly discussed below:

(a) Pressure: The discharge pressure of air from the compressor should be decided first considering the needs of the cylinder, air motor and pressure drop in the circuit. Most of the pneumatic systems and tools are designed for a pressure of 6 - 7 bar. A normal compressor should meet this requirement. A specific section of the pneumatic circuit requiring air at high pressure can be supplied with air by a separate high pressure compressor while any low pressure requirement can be met by availing a reducing valve. For huge air flow rates at pressures below 2 bar, a turbo blower or low pressure rotary compressor may be used.

The maximum pressure ratio obtainable from various types of air compressors are tabulated in the table.

Table 5.3

Sr. No.	Type of Compressor	Maximum Pressure Ratio
1.	Piston	10.0
2.	Vane	8.0
3.	Liquid piston ring	5.5
4.	Diaphragm	5.0
5.	Screw	3.0
6.	Lobe	2.0

(b) Flow Rate or Capacity: The volume of air required per minute is also an important factor deciding the selection. The precise estimation of air required is quite difficult. The capacity should be adequate enough to supply air to all devices operating simultaneously.

In many other plants, various pneumatic tools operate intermittently. Here, the maximum instantaneous demand of the compressed air has to be ascertained first.

SOLVED EXAMPLES

Example 5.5: *A compressor has an output of 70 cm²/sec and the system requires 95 cm³/sec for 30 seconds. The initial working pressure is 7 bar. The pressure drop cannot drop below 5.5 bar. What receiver size is needed ? How long will it take to recharge the receiver if the demand decreases to 28 cm³/sec.* **(May 2002)**

Solution: The air receiver capacity is given by formula,

$$V = \frac{1.0147\, t\, (Q_r - Q_c)}{P_{max} - P_{min}}$$

where, V = Receiver size (m³)

t = Time for which the receiver can supply the required amount of air, (min) = 0.5 min.

Q_r = Consumption rate of pneumatic system, (m³/min) = 95 m³/min

Q_c = Output flow rate of compressor, (m³/min) = 70 m³/min

P_{max} = Maximum pressure in receiver, (bar) = 7 bar

P_{min} = Minimum pressure in receiver, (bar) = 5.5 bar

∴ $$V = \frac{1.0147 \times 0.5 \times (95 - 70)}{7 - 5.5}$$

∴ $V = 3.044 \times 10^{-4}$ m³ = 304.42 m³

When the receiver is empty, the compressor will immediately start charging it.

∴ Net amount of air available for charging

$= 70 - 28 = 42$ cm³/s

And, the time required for charging the receiver

∴ $t = \dfrac{304.4}{42} = 7.2476$ sec

Example 5.6: *Following data refers to a compressor.*

1. *Delivery of air = 10 m³/min at 7 bar*
2. *Systems average demand of air = 7 m³/min*
3. *Allowed fluctuation of delivery pressure from 7 to 6 bar.*
4. *Receiver capacity 5 m³.*

Determine the total time the compressor is working per hour.

Solution: (1) $\dfrac{P_1 V_1}{T_1} = \dfrac{P_2 V_2}{T_2}$ [For 7 bar gauge pressure]

P_1 = 1 bar abs., P_2 = (7 + 1) bar abs., V_1 = ? unknown, V_2 = 5 m³, $T_1 = T_2$

∴ $V_2 = \dfrac{8 \times 5}{1} = 40$ m³

(2) $\dfrac{P_3 V_3}{T_3} = \dfrac{P_4 V_4}{T_4}$ [For 6 bar gauge]

∴ $V_4 = \dfrac{P_3 V_3}{P_4} = \dfrac{7 \times 5}{1} = 35$ m³

The compressor starts at 6 bar receiver pressure and has 40 m³ air and stops at 7 bar receiver pressure and has 35 m³ air. The delivery of compressor is 10 m³/min. The system demand is 7 m³/min. So 3 m³/min is required to charge the receiver.

$$\text{Charging time} = \dfrac{(40-35)\ m^3}{3\ m^3/min}$$

$$= \dfrac{5}{3} = 1.66\ min$$

$$\text{Discharge time} = \dfrac{\text{Air available from receiver}}{\text{Air required/min by system}}$$

$$= \dfrac{5}{7} = 0.71\ min.$$

Total time between the compressor going on load is

1.66 + 0.71 = **2.37 min.**

It means 25.3 starts per hour. Since this is high the receiver size may be increased to 6 m³.

Example 5.7 : A pneumatic main ring supplies a plant with an average demand of 20 m³/min f.a.d. The minimum working pressure at the receiver is 5 bar gauge. The air compressor has a rated delivery of 35 m³/min f.a.d. at a working pressure of 7 bar gauge. The control system switches the compressor off load when the receiver pressure reaches 7 bar gauge rising, back on load when receiver pressure is 5 bar gas falling. If the maximum allowable number of starts per hour of the compressor is 20, determine the suitable receiver capacity.

Solution: Number of starts per hour of compressor = 20.

So minimum time between starts = $\dfrac{60}{20}$ min. = 3 min.

System air demand = 20 m³/min.

∴ In 3 minutes the system demand = 3 × 20 = 60 m³

Compressor delivery = 35 m³/min.

So the time the compressor must run to meet the demand of 60 m³ for $\frac{60}{35}$ = 1.714 min.

So running time of compressor = 1.714 min.

and non-running time of compressor = 3 – 1.714 = 1.286 min.

So in 1.286 min. the receiver has to supply air required by system. During this pressure in the receiver falls from 7 bar to 5 bar gauge.

Volume of air supplied during this time from the receiver = 1.286 × 20 = 25.72 m³ f.a.d   ... (1)

Let V be the receiver's actual volume capacity:

Volume of air at 7 bar = 8 V m³

Volume of air at 5 bar = 6 V m³

So volume of air available from receiver to system when pressure drop from 7 bar to 5 bar

$$= 8V - 6V = 2V \text{ m}^3 \qquad ...(2)$$

Equating Equations (1) and (2),   2 V = 25.72

∴   V = 12.86 m³

Thus volume required of the receiver = 12.86 m³

Select 13 m³ receiver. ... Ans.

Example 5.8: A double acting pneumatic cylinder has the following data:

Bore = 100 mm

Rod diameter = 32 mm

Stroke = 300 mm

Pressure = 6 bar gauge both for extension and retraction.

If the cylinder makes 25 cycles per min, calculate the air consumption.

Solution: Extension volume = $\frac{\pi}{4} \times (100)^2 \times 300$

= 2.355 litres

Retract volume = $\frac{\pi}{4} \times (100^2 - 32^2) \times 300$

= 2.114 litres

Total volume of air per cycle = 2.355 + 2.114 = 4.469 litres.

Volume of compressed air per min. (for 25 cycles)

$$= 4.469 \times 25 = 111.7 \text{ lit./min.}$$

Volume of air at atmospheric pressure is required to be calculated.

$$\frac{P_1 V_1}{T_1} = \frac{P_2 V_2}{T_2}$$

$$T_1 = T_2 \quad \therefore \quad P_1 V_1 = P_2 V_2$$

$$\therefore \quad (1) \times V_1 = (6 + 1) \text{ bar} \times (111.7) \text{ lit./min.}$$

$$\therefore \quad V_1 = \mathbf{782 \text{ lit./min. f.a.d.}} \qquad \text{... Ans.}$$

Example 5.9: *Air demand of plant = 15 m³/min f.a.d.*

Compressor = 35 m³/min f.a.d. at 7 bar gauge.

Receiver size = 13 m³

Switching pressures = 7 bar × 5 bar gauge.

Calculate charge time.

Solution: (1) Volume of air stored in receiver at 7 bar

$$\left(\frac{13 \times 8}{1}\right) = 104 \text{ m}^3 \text{ f.a.d.}$$

(2) Volume of air stored in receiver at 5 bar

$$\left(\frac{13 \times 6}{1}\right) = 78 \text{ m}^3 \text{ f.a.d.}$$

(3) Volume of air from receiver to system when pressure falls from 7 bar to 5 bar

$$104 - 78 = 26 \text{ m}^3 \text{ f.a.d.}$$

(4) System demand is 15 m³/min f.a.d.

So the receiver can supply stored air to the system for

$$\frac{26}{15} = 1.734 \text{ minutes}$$

(5) Volume of air entering the receiver when charging is done

$$= (\text{Compressor output} - \text{System demand})$$

$$= 35 - 15 = 20 \text{ m}^3 \text{ f.a.d.}$$

So charging time $= \dfrac{\text{Volume of air supplied to system by receiver}}{\text{Volume entering receiver}}$

$$= \frac{26}{20} = 1.3 \text{ min.}$$

$$\text{Cycle time for receiver} = \text{Charge time} + \text{Discharge time}$$
$$= 1.3 + 1.734$$
$$= 3.03 \text{ min.}$$
$$\text{Number of starts per hour} = \frac{60}{3.03} = 19.9 \approx \mathbf{20 \text{ starts.}} \qquad \text{... Ans.}$$

5.16 COMPARISON OF PNEUMATIC AND HYDRAULIC SYSTEMS

(May 07, 12; Dec. 11)

In what follows hereafter, is a comparison of the salient features of the hydraulic and pneumatic systems.

Sr. No.	Parameter	Hydraulic System	Pneumatic System
1.	Suitability for fluctuating load	Resistant to fluctuating load	Not resistant to fluctuating load
2.	Operating speed	Limited speed	Very high speed possible
3.	Suitability for feed movement in machine tools	Very suitable	Unsuitable
4.	Operating pressure	From low to very high pressure	Generally 6 bar gauge
5.	Operating fluid	Oil	Air
6.	Change of operating fluid	Oil change required as per schedule	Does not arise
7.	Source of power	Hydraulic pump	Air compressor
8.	Rigidity of system	Good	Poor
9.	Operating cost	Moderate	High
10.	Stroke control of cylinder	Very precise stroke control attainable	Stroke control easy but fluctuations unavoidable
11.	Maintenance	Skilled	Simple
12.	Downtime in overhaul	Longer downtime	Short downtime
13.	Cavitation	Major problem to be tackled carefully	No such problem
14.	Cost of overhaul	Moderate to high	Low

Cont....

15.	Weight to pressure ratio	Small	Large
16.	Necessity of cylinder cushioning	Recommended	Not needed
17.	Response to leakage of operating fluid	Highly sensitive to leakage as system performance is affected due to leakage	Leakage does not influence the system performance too much
18.	Lubrication	Usually operating fluid serves as a lubricant	Separate lubrication is required
19.	Manufacturing/Machining	Precise machining, close tolerances and superior surface finish necessary to control leakage	Less precision
20.	Initial cost	High	Low
21.	Influence of temperature change	System performance affected significantly due to temperature variations	Temperature variations do not affect the system performance significantly
22.	Space requirement	Less due to compact size	More
23.	Internal heat generation	Considerable heat generation	Small heat generation

5.16.1 Introduction to Air Treatment

An atmospheric air cannot be used directly for pneumatic system. We have to give treatment to the sucked atmospheric air. The reasons for this treatment and the types of treatment given to the air before its use for pneumatic system applications are discussed below :

Air treatment before its use for Pneumatic System:

The air we breathe from our atmosphere contains moisture in the form of water vapour; people often refer the amount of moisture in the air as levels of 'humidity'. Humidity levels are a percentage of the saturation of air with water.

The maximum amount of water saturation in air varies greatly with temperature; hotter air can hold much more moisture than cold air. Due to the change in air pressure when compressing air its ability to hold moisture is seriously reduced, so some of the moisture content that was previously in the air will simply condense out of it when the air is compressed. This is why drainage systems and dryers are an important part of compressor systems.

If the water was allowed to travel out of the compressor into the pneumatic components that it was powering then this could cause big problems, for example, ceasing valves and actuators.

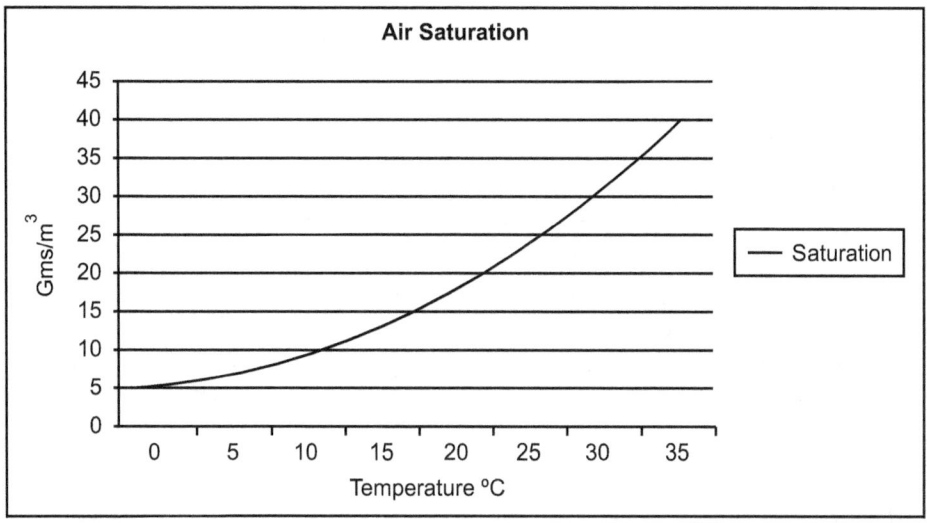

$$\text{Relatively Humidity} = \frac{\text{Mass of water vapour present}}{\text{Mass of water needed to saturate it}} \times 100$$

Graph

Stages of Air Treatment :

Filters :

Compressed air requires filtration and drying before it leaves for pneumatic components, atmospheric air carries many particles of debris and moisture that unless filtered out can block valves or cause increased wear. Compressors usually filter air before it is compressed, this is mainly to remove relatively large particles which could damage the compressor. A fine grade filter used after it is compressed helps filter the small particles which could clog or damage the pneumatic components that are used in pneumatic system set ups.

Air Dryers :

Before air can be used the excess moisture has to be removed, where well dried air is not a requirement all that may be needed is a basic intercooler followed by a separator unit; this is where the condensed water collects and is drained off.

Refrigeration Units :

The dew point can be lowered even further by cooling the air with a refrigeration unit which cools the air even further to around 0°C helping more moisture collect in the separator tank. This cold air is then routed through a separate section of the initial heat exchanger to help cool the warm air which is flowing through from the compressor. This system of drying is suitable for most systems as air is dried out well.

Deliquescent Dryer :

Where completely dry air is a necessary then a chemical dryer should be used, the chemicals can remove moisture in two ways.

(1) A chemical agent called a desiccant is used, this chemical agent collects water vapour and holds it while it eventually turns itself into a liquid once so much vapour has been collected and runs to the bottom of the unit where it is drained off. This chemical agent needs to be replaced quite regularly.

Absorption Dryer :

(2) Within an absorption dryer a material called silicone dioxide or copper sulphate is used, this process works by attracting moisture to the sharp edges of these granular materials. Once these materials become saturated they are dried by passing heat through them, this process cannot be carried out while it is still drying incoming air so they are usually set up with 2 of these moisture collectors which can be swapped over instantly, this allows one collector to collect the moisture while the remaining collector is left to dry itself out.

5.17 SERVICE UNIT OR F-R-L UNIT (Dec. 08)

Before pneumatic components one finds this unit installed in the pneumatic system. F-R-L unit is 'Filter-Regulator-Lubricator' unit. These three units together are also called *service unit*. The unit provides clean, pure air, at required constant pressure, having lubricating properties.

5.17.1 Air Filter

Air filter in FRL unit performs the following functions:

- To prevent entry of all impurities and removal of solid contaminants from air.
- To condensate and remove water from air.
- To arrest fine particles.

5.17.2 Construction and Working of Air Filter (May 12)

Fig. 5.19 shows a section view of air filter used in pneumatic system. It contains a filter bowl, that is transparent and made of plastic. For pressure exceeding 10 bars, this bowl may be made of brass. Air enters in the filter chamber of bowl from air in the connection shown. The entering air is set in rotation by guide slots or a baffling system shown in Fig. 5.19. The air flow velocity is increased. Air cools due to the centrifugal action, residual water vapour is separated from the air stream, condensate and other removed impurities, collect at the bottom of chamber. This must be drained off periodically. If not removed, air leaving the filter would again entrain droplets of moisture and the filter is of no use. Together with the guide bar, filter element is placed. The element shown in Fig. 5.19 is 5 micron cellulose felt, reusable, surface type element.

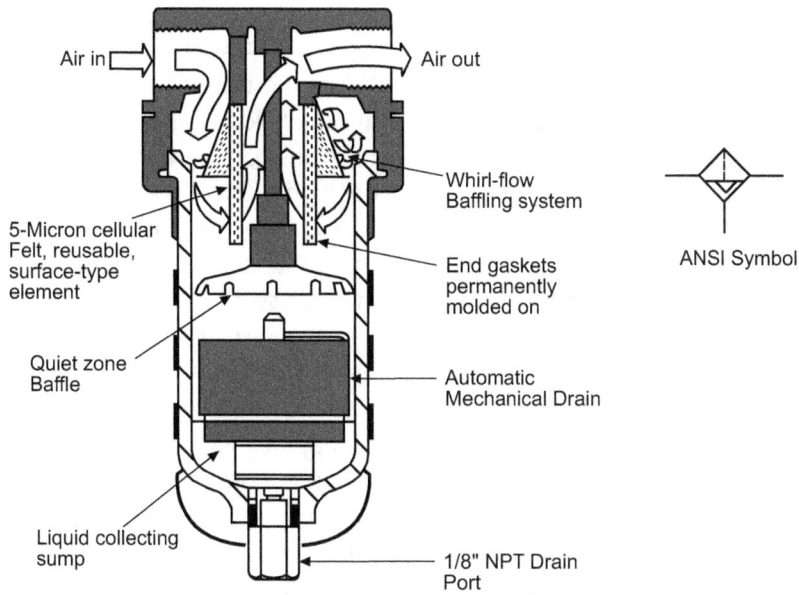

Fig. 5.19: Operation of air filter

Air before going out of the filter unit passes through this element and then goes out as shown in the Fig.. Entrained solids larger than the mesh width of the filter element are retained. The element becomes clogged by accumulation of dirt after use. Regular cleaning or replacement is essential. The filter element shown in the Fig. is for critical applications, filter element having mesh size 0.02 to 0.05 may be used. For selection of the filter, the rating must be considered. The flow capacity and pressure rating should be considered. Fig. 5.20 gives pressure drop characteristics of pneumatic filters at different pressures and flow.

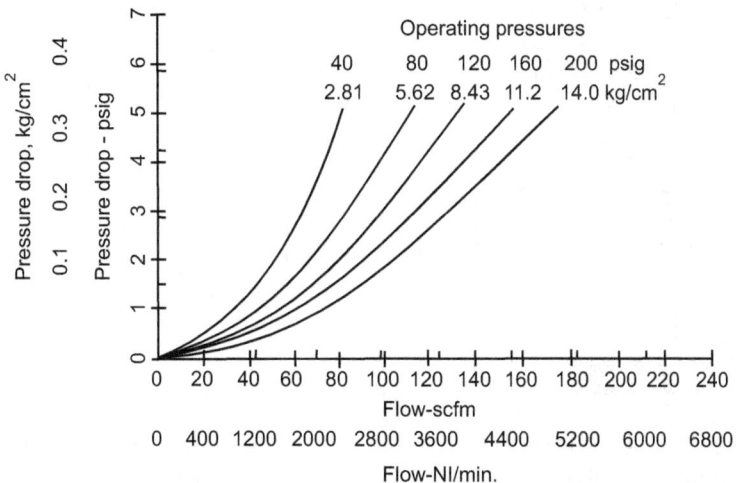

Fig. 5.20

5.17.3 Pressure Regulator (May 07, Dec. 09, May 11)

This is similar to the pressure reducing type of valve. The duty of a pressure regulator is to decrease or increase flow so that pressure on the outlet side i.e. pressure at user points like valves, actuators remains constant. In the air, mains pressure fluctuates and also air consumption varies. The inlet pressure must be higher than the operating pressure. In Fig. 5.21 a diaphragm is shown. It controls and regulates outlet pressure. Diaphragm is loaded by an outlet pressure on one side while the other side is loaded by a spring. Spring force can be adjusted by a screw. The desired outlet pressure is set by this screw. When the outlet pressure increases, the diaphragm moves against the spring. Attached to the diaphragm on other side of the spring is a valve seat, that controls the flow of inlet compressed air. With the diaphragm moving against the spring, the flow across the valve seat is restricted and reduced, and at the end it may be stopped. Thus outlet pressure is controlled via the flow rate through the valve. Air is consumed next and if the outlet pressure drops the valve opens by spring force. Outlet pressure is thus regulated as set by repeated opening and closing of the valve seat. To prevent flutter of the valve, a dash pot or damping spring is provided above the valve plate, as shown in Fig. 5.21. The type of regulator shown in the figure is a vented type. The excess pressure is released to the atmosphere through a vent port so that the newly adjusted outlet pressure is obtained quickly. This type of regulator may be used only when non-precision regulation is required. Pressure and flow relationship of such regulators is given by Fig. 5.22.

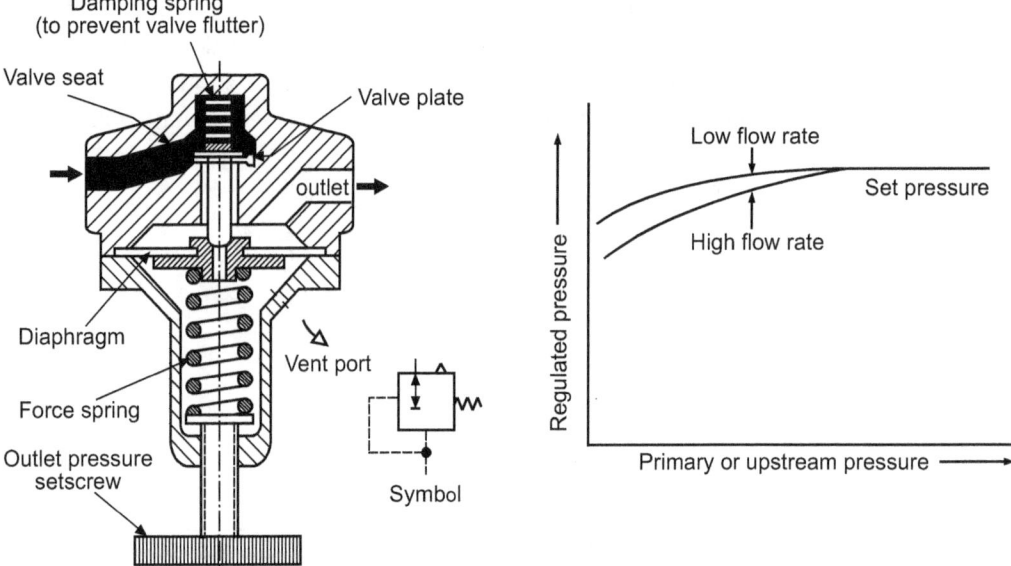

Fig. 5.21: Section through pressure regulator (reducing valve)

Fig. 5.22: Typical pressure regular performance curves

5.17.4 Lubricator (May 08)

Air from compressor is passed through a filter unit, then through regulator and finally through a lubricator. Many components in the pneumatic system like valves, cylinders and motors, require lubrication. Lubricator injects very fine particles or droplets of clean oil into the air stream.

(a) Fog Type Lubricator: (May 12)

This type is shown in Fig. 5.23. Air enters from one end passes through a narrow opening. Air velocity increases and the pressure drops. As an effect, oil is drawn up from the reservoir through a siphon tube. The oil then enters the sight feed dome where oil flow is controlled by a metering screw. Oil drips at the prescribed amount into the air flow path. Thus, atomised spray of oil with air is formed. Particle size of oil droplets in fog is about 2 microns. Such a lubricator can provide lubrication up to a pipe run lengths of 10 m. They should be used one per appliance in the system.

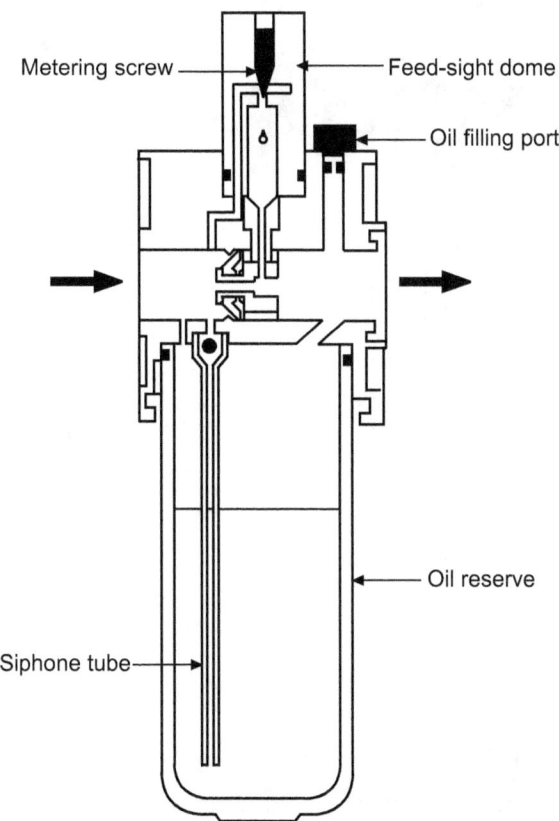

Fig. 5.23: General arrangement of an oil fog lubricator

(b) Oil Mist (or Micro Fog) Lubricator:

This type is shown in Fig. 5.24. Air is allowed to enter into the oil reservoir. Air takes along with it oil flow to the sight dome through a metering needle valve and then through the atomising jet and back into the upper part of the bowl. Oil particles larger than about 2 micron size fall down and return to the oil of the reservoir. Small particles of oil remaining air borne can be carried out of the lubricator and through long distances without separating out.

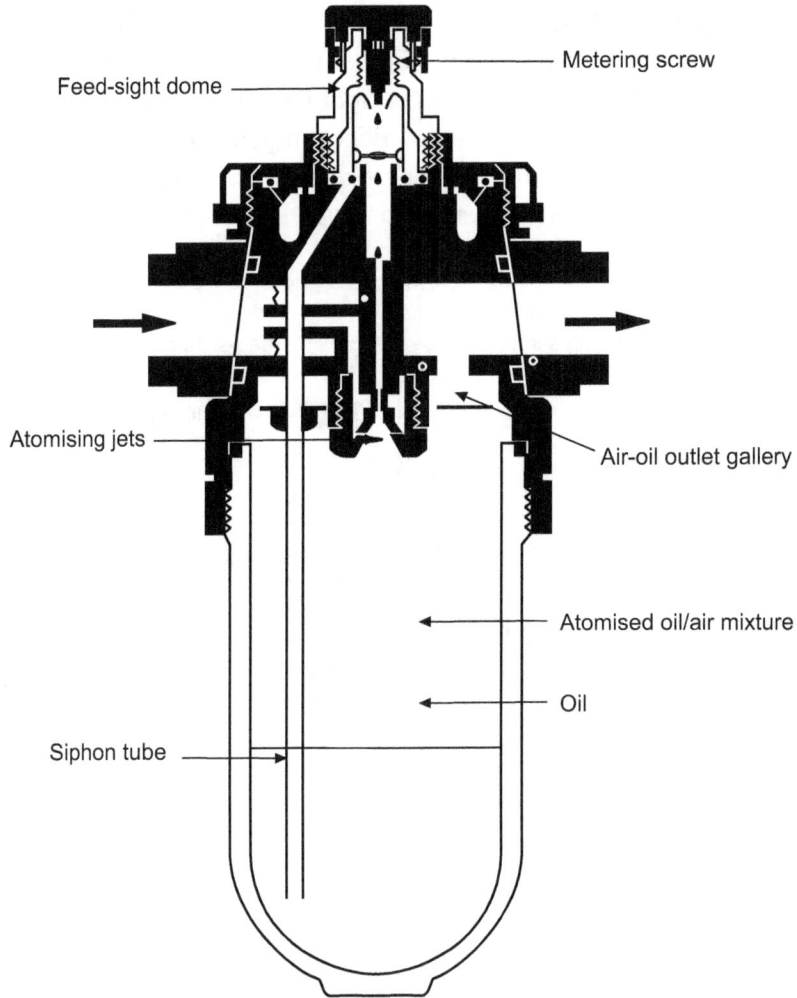

Fig. 5.24: General arrangement of a oil micro-fog lubricator

At any given pressure, a minimum flow rate of air is required through the lubricator for its operation. Manufacturer's data must be referred to. The oil used also must be compatible with the system components. Good quality hydraulic oils may be used. Thin mineral oil may also be used. Viscosity ratings are 2 - 5° Engler at 20°C or 10 – 50° centistokes or SAE 10.

Position of the lubricator should be as near as possible to the unit it is servicing. Correct quantity of oil into the components is a necessity. Over and above lubrication should be avoided. For air pressure of about 6 bar, 3.125 mm system may require 3 to 4 drops of oil per minute to produce effective oil-air mist. The three separate units i.e. filter, regulator and lubricator of service unit are joined together (combined into single unit) by two double male couplings. Recently, the filter and regulator are combined into one single unit and a lubricator unit is separate. A combined F.R.L unit is shown in Fig. 5.25. Such a unit must be selected to suit the given parameters of flow and pressure. Table 5.4 gives the approximate pressure and flow ranges and line connections.

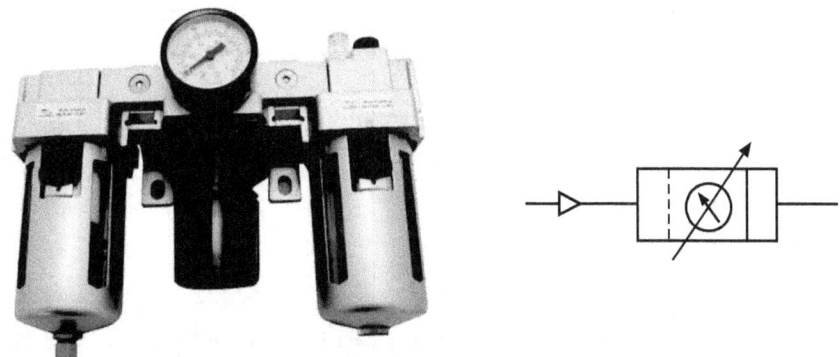

Fig. 5.25: Combination of filter, regulator, lubricator unit

Table 5.4: Duty range of combined service units as a function of line connector size. The sizes listed are normally adequate for pneumatic applications

Line Connection	Range of Flow Rate litres/min	Oil Reservoir Capacity cm^3	Pressure Range Bars
1/3"	50 – 80	16	0 – 7
1/4"	50 – 400	42	0 – 10
3/8"	100 – 1000	137	0 – 10
1/2"	150 – 2000	137	0 – 10

5.18 Drying of Compressed Air

Air from the atmosphere contains varying amount of moisture depending on the atmospheric conditions at that place or time.

Amount of water vapour in the air depends on relative humidity of air.

$$\text{Relative humidity (RH)} = \frac{\text{Amount of water actually present in air}}{\text{Amount of water present in saturated air}} \times 100$$

Table 5.5: Amount of water condensate in g/m³ of air at various temperature and RH values

Temp. °C	% Relative Humidity (RH)									
	10	20	30	40	50	60	70	80	90	100
−12	0.179	0.354	0.533	0.709	0.888	1.066	1.250	1.421	1.600	1.780
0	0.483	0.965	1.451	1.933	2.426	2.906	3.387	3.867	4.348	4.830
10	0.934	1.865	2.790	3.730	4.670	5.606	6.520	7.460	8.400	9.337
15	1.313	2.617	3.816	5.063	6.386	7.795	9.029	10.158	11.631	17.957
21	1.826	3.661	5.469	7.300	9.131	11.946	12.793	14.600	16.431	18.698
27	2.494	4.980	7.516	10.069	12.521	15.012	17.582	20.024	22.757	25.634
32	3.307	6.614	10.061	13.548	16.835	20.276	23.486	27.004	30.451	33.721
35	3.936	7.872	11.808	15.744	19.681	23.617	27.554	31.489	35.426	39.248
37.8	4.531	9.039	13.571	18.102	22.611	27.141	31.673	36.181	39.900	45.248
43.3	6.018	12.037	18.056	24.075	30.094	36.112	42.131	48.150	54.160	60.371
49	7.895	15.790	23.686	31.580	39.476	47.370	55.267	63.166	78.910	78.928
55	10.161	20.322	30.583	40.650	50.805	61.200	71.127	81.300	91.504	101.656

Table 5.5 shows water vapour content per m³ of air under varying temperature and % RH values. Ambient conditions, at sea level pressure, 21°C and 60% RH at compressor intake, give us water vapour = 11.946 gm/m³.

If we assume 37.8°C as the temperature of compressed air in a receiver, the maximum water vapour capacity (i.e. 100 RH) for 1 m³ of air is 45.25 gm.

1. **Dew Point:**

The temperature at which air is fully saturated with moisture (i.e. 100% humidity) is the dew point. Cooling below dew point will cause condensation of the water vapour. Lower the dew point, the less moisture the air is able to absorb or hold. e.g. 1 m³ air has 17 grams of water at 20°C and at −10°C water vapour = 2.1 grams. The capacity of holding water in air is a function of volume and temperature. It does not depend on pressure. But for comparison of performance of drying systems, working pressure of systems is considered.

2. **Pressure Dew Point:**

Temperature representing the dew point at the respective operating pressure is the pressure dew point. This is absolute humidity of compressed air referred to dew point (relative humidity of air). This means that compressed air of a given volume and given pressure dew point contains an amount of water vapour corresponding to the dew point of air. If this compressed air is expanded to atmospheric pressure, it will contain the same water as was in compressed state. But with change in volume, the pressure reduces, and the dew point also changes. This dew point is determined by calculation and is referred to as atmospheric dew point.

For example, we saw saturated compressed air at the receiver at 37.8°C which is pressure dew point, air was holding 45.25 gm of water per m³. If this air in receiver is brought to atmospheric pressure, each m³ of air at atmospheric pressure will contain $\frac{45.25}{6.9}$ = 6.7 gm of water vapour. (with 6.9 bar compression ratio).

[**Note:** Compression ratio = $\frac{6 \text{ kg/cm}^2 \text{ (g)} + 1.013}{1.013}$ = 6.9 (sec.) means 6.9 m³ of free air is to be injected to produce 1 m³ of compressed air at 6 kg/cm² (g) pressure].

Thus 6.7 gm represents saturation (100% RH at about 5°C) and this is the equivalent atmospheric dew point. Fig. 5.26 gives nomogram to convert pressure dew point to atmospheric dew point.

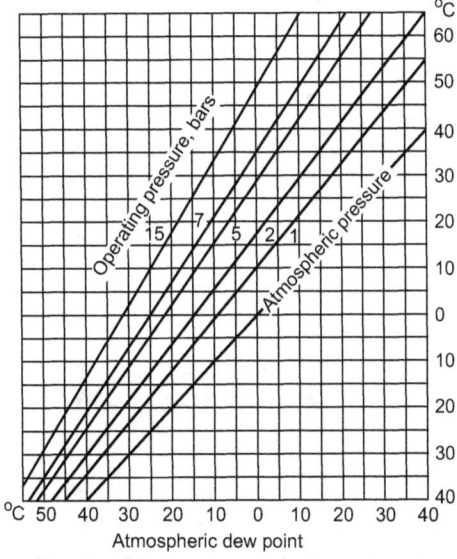

Fig. 5.26: Nomogram to convert pressure dew point into atmospheric dew point

When air passes through the cooler, air receiver, collecting points in piping and filter service unit, the moisture gets separated in all these locations. But compressed air will always contain as much water vapour as it is capable of holding, at the lowest temperature assumed by air on its passage from the compressor to the consumption point. Low residual moisture content of air will not cause any hazards to standard pneumatic control and operating components. In case of specialised applications e.g. spray painting complex low pressure control systems, pharmaceutical and chemical and food industry, pneumatic conveyor systems etc. compressed air comes directly into contact with the process medium.

In these cases the moisture in the system is not tolerated. It then becomes necessary to provide additional means of dehydrating and filtering the compressed air. Air drying is achieved by drying the air at high pressure and then reducing the pressure by expanding the air, so lowering the dew point.

Hence, to safeguard the pneumatic components from the corrosive effects of water and rust, air dryers are to be installed at suitable points in the pressure air line. Coolers are placed just after the air compressor to help remove the major part of the water. To remove in the line further, the following methods may be used.

Compressed air could be either passed through a refrigerator or may be heated by a burner/furnace or may be passed through various types of industrial desiccants or fine filters may be used to arrest submicron size of liquid contaminants.

3. Drying of Air is Accomplished by Following Three Methods:

(i) Absorption Drying: Fig. 5.27 shows schematic diagram of absorption drying. In this method, water from air combines with chemical reagents (desiccant). Air passes through a bed of salts. Water vapour combines with salt to form a solution which is drained off.

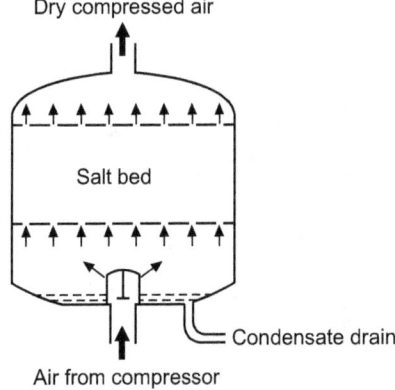

Fig. 5.27: Diagrammatic representation of drying by absorption. Air passes through a bed of salt, whereby water vapour combines with salt to form a solution which is drained off. This method entails continuous salt consumption

The desiccants are deliquescent (melt away) absorbents which are based on sodium chloride i.e. salts. In one type of absorption dryer about 13 kg of water may be removed by using 1 kg of salt. Regular replenishment of salt in the absorber is necessary. A filter is necessary on the outlet of the dryer. This will remove entrained salt dust from the air. Inlet temperature of air to be dried should be lower than 30°C. By this method, a pressure dew point below (0°C) can be obtained.

(ii) Adsorption Drying: In this method, adsorbent materials, usually called 'gel' (e.g. silica gel) is used for capturing moisture. These materials are pink in colour and on taking up moisture change their colour to blue. Adsorption means deposition of a substance on a solid surface. Schematically adsorption drying is represented in Fig. 5.28. Adsorbent materials are regenerated by heating that removes air from them and thus can be reused again.

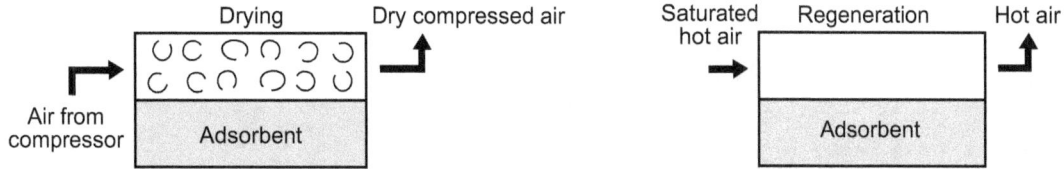

Fig. 5.28: Diagrammatic representation of drying by adsorption

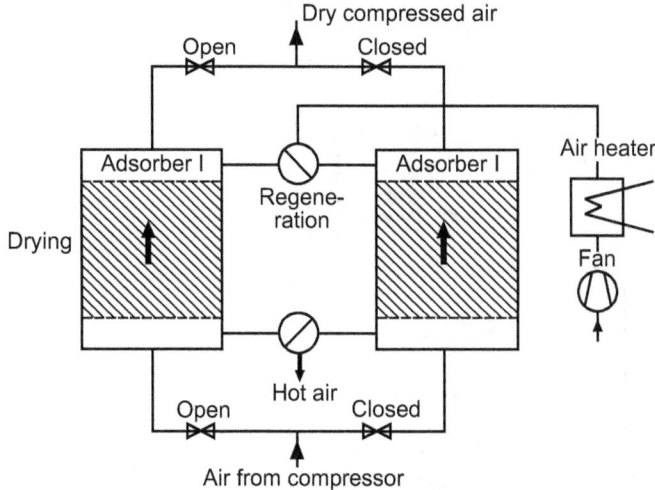

Fig. 5.29: Flow sheet for drying by adsorption with hot-air regeneration of adsorbent. Two adsorbers operate alternately on a drying and regeneration cycle to permit continuous working

A typical set up of pair unit of adsorption dryer is shown in Fig. 5.29. It consists of two pressure chambers filled with a water adsorbing chemical. The air to be dried is passed through one chamber and moisture is removed. In the other chamber, spent chemical is regenerated by either heating or passing hot dry air over it.

It is necessary to fit a micro filter on the dryer outlet. These dryers can attain pressure dew point down to − 90°C.

(iii) Refrigeration drying: The capacity of air to absorb moisture reduces with reduction of the dew point. This principle is applied in drying of air by refrigeration. The compressed air is cooled to a temperature between 1.7 and 5°C. The equipment required for this is shown in Fig. 5.30. It consists of a refrigerating unit and a heat exchanger.

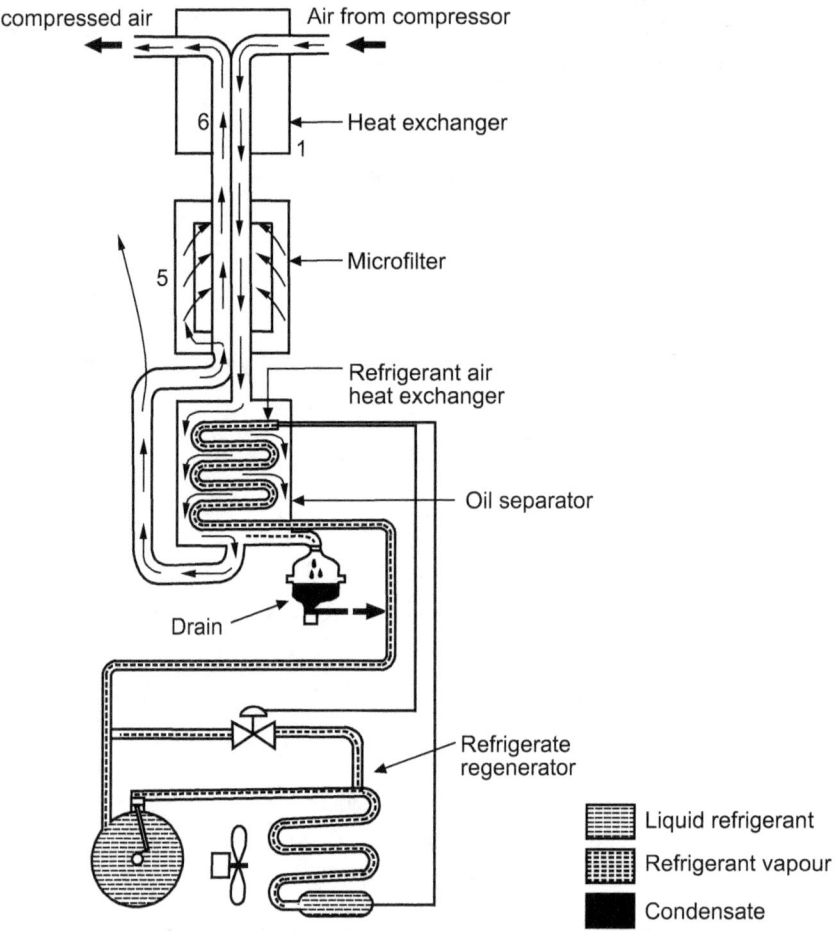

Fig. 5.30: Flow sheet for drying by refrigerator

Pressure dew point to which air is to be cooled is decided and air is cooled to that temperature. It causes excess water vapour to condense out. This depends on the difference between inlet temperature and set dew point. This is achieved by passing air over refrigerant as shown in Fig. 5.30. Air after cooling is filtered. This removes solid entrants and oil vapour present. 80 to 90% of oil is separated in this system of refrigeration dryer. Finally cold air is allowed to pass through the heat exchanger. Air entering the heat exchanger is still moist. But here it is precooled while dry outlet air is rewarmed a certain degree. Drying by refrigeration is only suitable for pressure dew point over 0°C. Refrigeration drying is least expensive of the above other mentioned drying processes. Cost of drying compressed air is above 10 to 20% of the cost of compressing the air.

(iv) Oil-free compressed air: For applications requiring air, free from oil the following schemes may be used. (1) Non-lubricated compressor, (2) Drying by refrigeration with removal of 80% of oil, (3) Oil separating filters.

Ultrafilters now-a-days are capable of removing oil and water down to the size of 0.01 microns.

5.19 After Cooler

After cooler is installed (shown in Fig. 5.31) immediately, downstream of a compressor, it removes most of the moisture from the compressed air. It also cools the air, reducing its temperature to a convenient level. This is the first stage cooling and separation of moisture from air. Air then enters the drying devices as explained earlier.

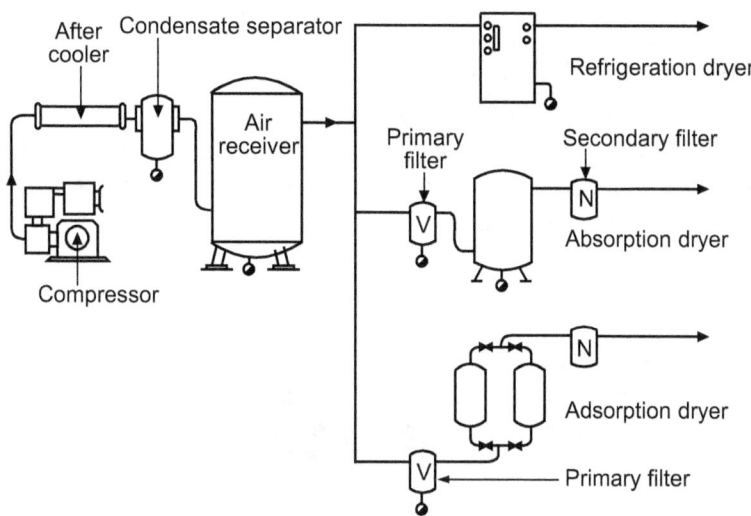

Fig. 5.31: Installation of compressor unit with downstream air dryer (optional). Air receiver may be downstream of dryer in alternative arrangement

Fig. 5.32 shows the after cooler. It is a heat exchanger using water. Water is circulated at high velocity and turbulence. Heat transfer from hot air to cold water takes place. After passing through the tubes, the cooled air enters the moisture separating chamber to trap water.

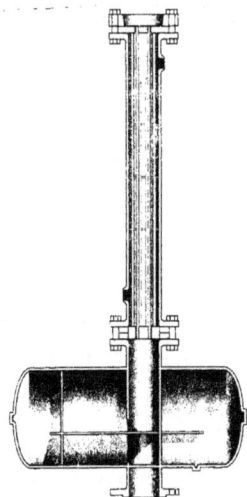

Fig. 5.32: After cooler

5.20 MUFFLER (PNEUMATIC SILENCER)

Air exhausts to atmosphere rapidly in operating pneumatic system. It makes noise which is high intensity sound energy. Continuous exposure to this can cause hearing loss or pain. Noise also causes fatigue and hence low production rate. Silencers are fitted at each pneumatic exhaust port to reduce the noise levels. Fig. 5.33.

Fig. 5.33: Pneumatic silencers

Warning signals of systems may not be noticed if the sound level is high and it may cause accidents.

5.21 PRESSURE REGULATING VALVE

Pressure of air flowing through the valve or pressure in the system is controlled by these valves. Fig. 5.34 (a) and (b) show pressure relief valve, sequence valve, pressure reducing valve. The function of the pressure relief or limiting valve is to prevent the pressure in the system from rising above a permissible maximum. The function of a sequence valve is to allow flow to the outlet only when the pressure upstream of it builds up to a predetermined value. Only then the valve will open to permit flow. Pressure reducing valves are pressure regulators that ensure constant downstream pressure is maintained. Any change in the downstream pressure actuators diaphragm to open or close valve opening (Regulator in F.R.L. unit).

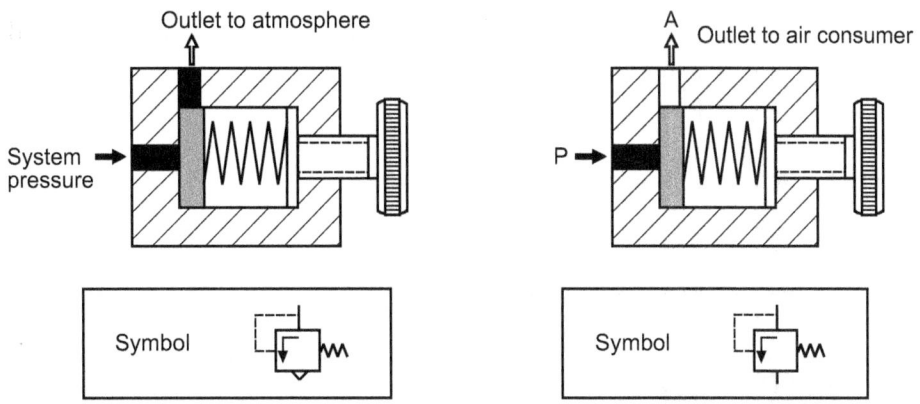

(a) Functional diagram of pressure limiting (b) Functional diagram of sequence valve

Fig. 5.34

SOLVED EXAMPLES

Example 5.10: *Find the amount of condensate per shift in a plant, if air is compressed to 6 kg/cm² (gauge) receiver pressure.*

Solution: Refer Table 5.5

Initial conditions: Air at sea level 21°C and 60% RH.

1 m³ of air has 11.946 grams of water vapour.

Compression ratio reveals how many m³ of ambient air is to be injected to produce 1 m³ of compressed air at that pressure.

$$\text{Compression ratio} = \frac{6 + 1.013}{1.013} = 6.923 \approx 6.9$$

That means 6.9 m³ of free air is required. From the table each m³ of air contains at 60% RH and 21°C, 11.946 gram of moisture.

Hence, amount of water in 6.9 m³ is

$$6.9 \times 11.946 = 82.43 \text{ gm of water.}$$

Let us assume 37.8°C temperature of compressed air receiver.

From the table, 1 m³ of air at 37.8°C and 100% (RH) is only = 45.250 gm.

This means difference (82.43 − 45.250) = 37.18 gm gets separated and condensed and removed.

Therefore, there will be $\dfrac{37.18}{6.9}$ = 5.38 gm of liquid for each m³ of ambient air.

Assume the flow rate of compressor to be 0.25 m³/min per kW of power and 75% efficiency.

$$\text{Flow} = 25 \times 0.75 = 18.75 \text{ m}^3/\text{min}$$

With 8 hours shift,

$$\text{Amount of water per shift} = 8 \times 18.75 \times 60 \text{ g/shift}$$
$$= 48420.0 \text{ gm/shift}$$
$$\approx 48.42 \text{ lit.}$$

5.22 PNEUMATIC VALVES

Valves are devices to regulate, start, stop, change direction, pressure; flow rate of air under pressure delivered by compressor. Function of a valve, mode of operation of a valve and connection size that determines the flow size of a valve, are important areas of study in the study of valves. Valves control the output and it is essential to achieve this control with minimum efforts.

Valves for pneumatic control are classified as:

1. Direction control valves
2. Non-return valves
3. Pressure control valves
4. Flow control valves.

5.23 DIRECTION CONTROL VALVES

These are used to start, stop and control the direction of air flow. They are classified according to :

(a) The number of connection ports in the body e.g. 2, 3, 4 or 5. Alternatively, it is the number of paths, the air is allowed to take directional control (d.c.). Valves are termed as two way, three way, or multiway. Inlet connection is to the compressor (P), outlet is given to the actuator (air consumer) (A, B, C) and exhaust connections (R.S.T.) to the atmosphere. Even though a valve contains many exhaust ports they are considered as only one way or one connection. Control lines are indicated by Z, Y, X ....

(b) The number of positions which the spool can be located at:

The normal position is the original operating position assumed by the moving parts of the valve after the valve has been installed in the system, the air supply and electrical power has been turned on and the position at which the designed operating program starts.

In Fig. 5.35 letter 'O' shows the neutral position whereas the other operating positions are shown by letters 'a', 'b', 'c' etc.

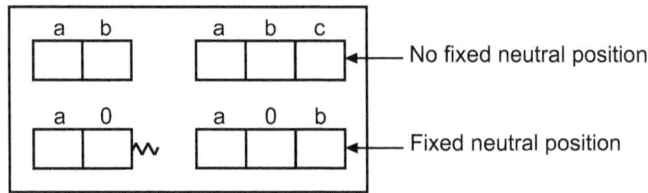

Fig. 5.35

A four connection / two position valve is designated as 4/2 way valve.

Direct actuation		Remote actuation	
Manual	**Mechanical**	**Pneumatic**	**Electrical**
⊢▭▭	⊣▭▭〜	▷▭▭〜	▭▭〜
⊣▭▭〜	⊣▭▭〜	(throttle pilot)	▷▭▭〜
⊨▭▭〜	⊙▭▭〜	▷▭▭◁	▷▭▭◁
⊣▭▭〜	⊙▭▭〜	◁▭▭▷	
▭▭	⊿▭▭〜		
⊢▭▭〜	⊿▭▭〜		
⊣▭▭			

Fig. 5.36: Types of actuation available for directional valves

(c) The method of valve actuation: **(May 07, 08)**

The mode of actuation is important. It decides whether the valve is incorporated into the pneumatic control loop as the control signal input, the controller or the final control element. Valve actuating devices can be identified by lower case letters a, b, c etc. according to the associated operating position. Fig. 5.36 shows valves operated by manual mechanical, remote pneumatic and electrical means. Actuation of valves may be direct or remote.

(d) The connection or port size that governs the air flow rate through the valve.

(e) Nature of the internal valve mechanism. Valves use sliding spool, poppet / diaphragm, rotary spool or disc or slide for actuation.

5.23.1 Poppet and Ball Seat Valves and Sliding Spool Valves

From the view point of design, d.c. valves are divided into two groups: lifting (poppet) valves and sliding (piston or rotary) valves.

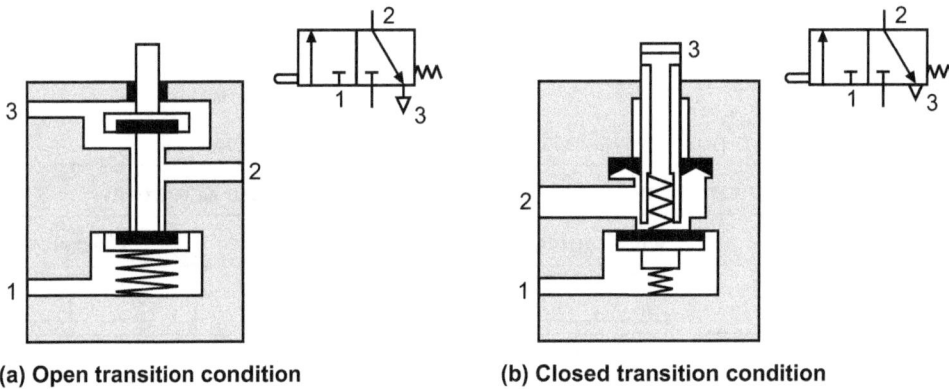

(a) Open transition condition   (b) Closed transition condition

Fig. 5.37: Poppet valves with open and closed transition conditions

1. **Seat Valves:** The flow through the poppet valve is opened or closed by a plate, disc, ball or plug with a flexible gasket. These valves show quick response. A small lift of the plunger opens up a full valve flow area (Fig. 5.37).

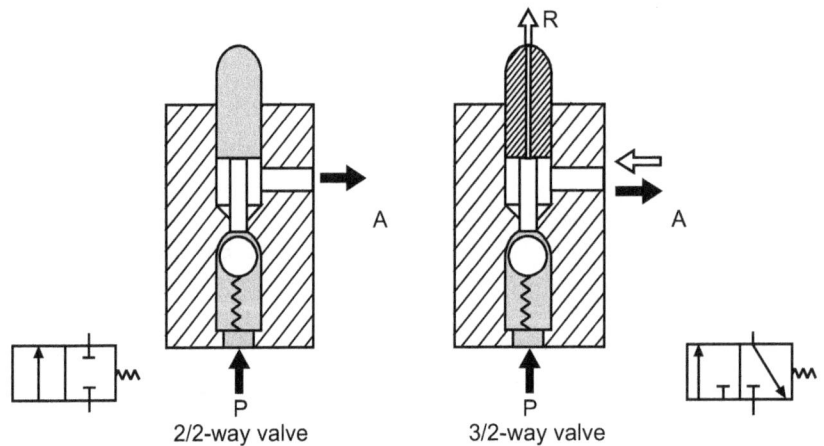

Fig. 5.38: 2/2 way valve and 3/2 way valve, ball, seat type

In Fig. 5.38 the ball seat valve is shown. They are inexpensive but do not ensure perfect sealing. Disc seat valve shown in Fig. 5.39 (a) and (b) are 3/2 way valves. These designs do not have exhaust overlap. (Exhaust overlap means inlet air gets connected to the exhaust port during operation, this is undesirable). So no leakage loss is present.

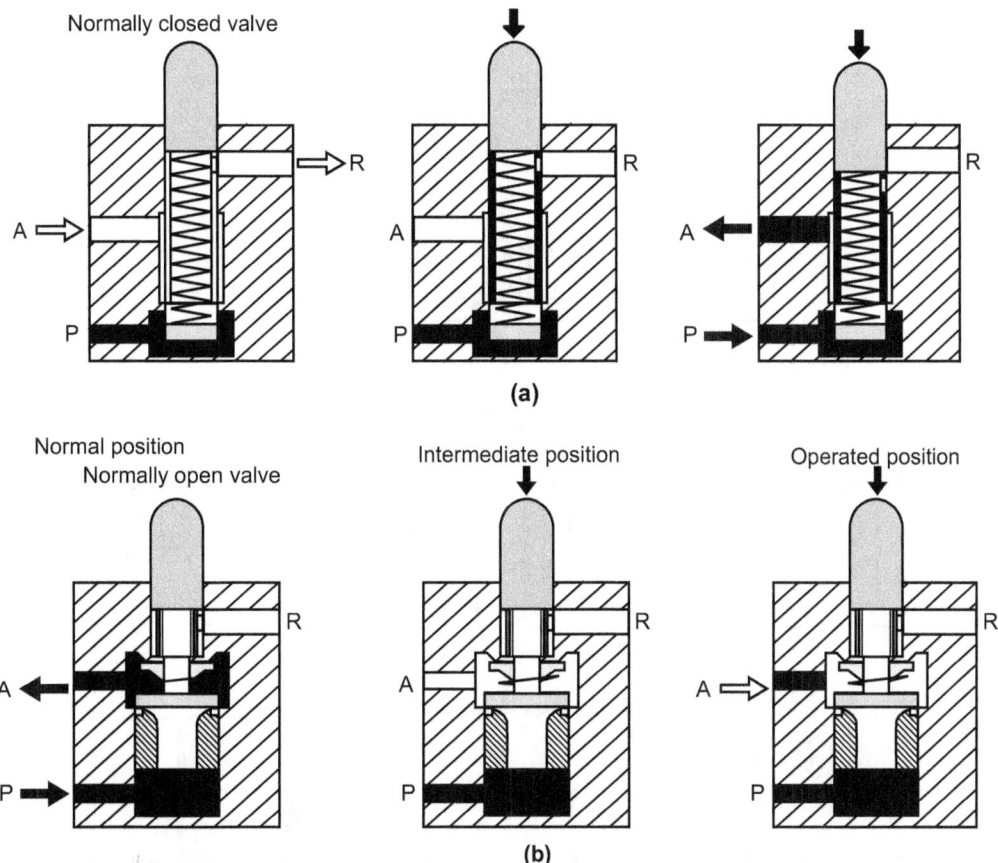

Fig. 5.39: 3/2 way valves of disc-seat type working with how exhaust overlap

2. **Sliding Valves:** According to the design, these are piston or spool valves, piston slide valves and rotary valves.

In Fig. 5.40 the commonly used piston or spool valve is illustrated. The control element is a pilot piston or spool. It longitudinally moves and alternately loads and unloads the cylinder ports. The spool is precisely fitted in the bore. In pneumatic valves, clearance between the spool and bore should be less than 0.002 to 0.004 mm. Otherwise excessive leakage will take place. Fig. 5.41 and Fig. 5.42 show the seal on the spool and the seal on the bore of body. An 'O' ring is used for sealing.

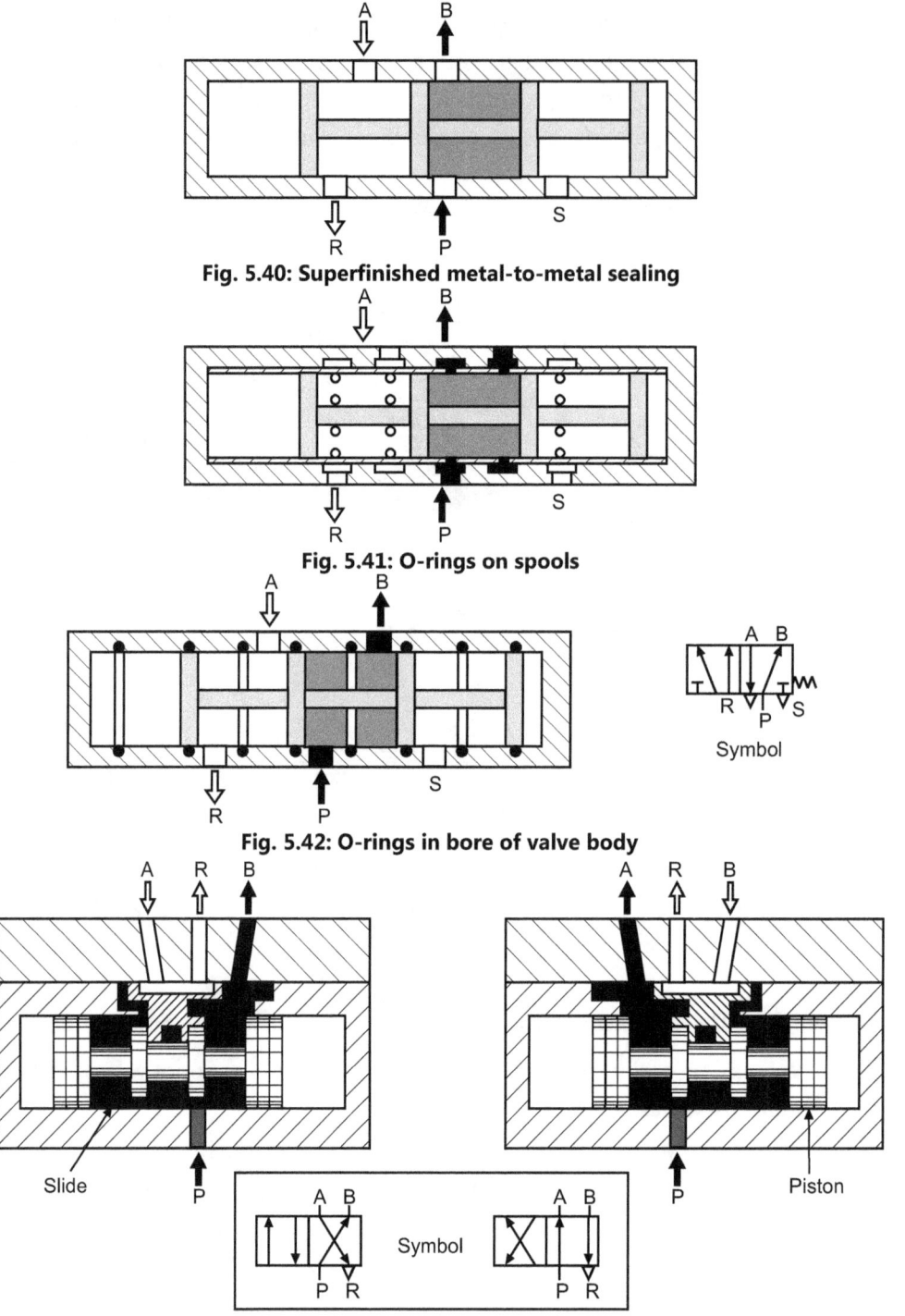

Fig. 5.40: Superfinished metal-to-metal sealing

Fig. 5.41: O-rings on spools

Fig. 5.42: O-rings in bore of valve body

Fig. 5.43: 4/2 way piston slide valve shown in both operating positions

Piston slide valves are shown in Fig. 5.43. The pistons are attached to another additional slide. The additional slide controls the flow through the ports.

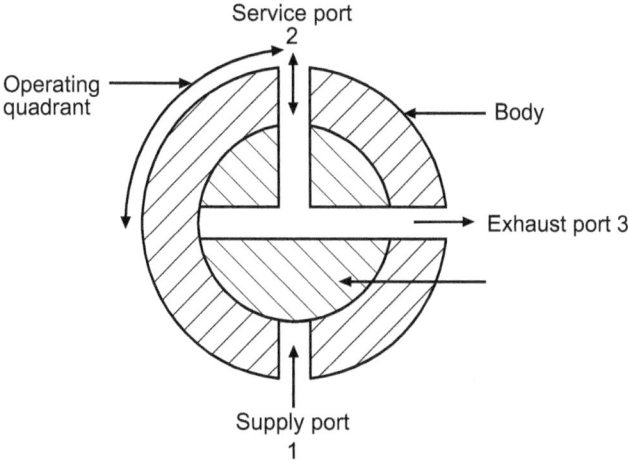

Fig. 5.44 (a): Section through a rotary spool valve

Rotary valves Fig. 5.44 (a) and (b) are hand or foot operated. These are 3/3 or 4/3 way valves. All lines are closed in the mid position of the valve. This helps the piston rod of controlled cylinder to be halted at any point of its stroke. But this position cannot be precisely obtained since air is compressible and the position also will vary depending on the load.

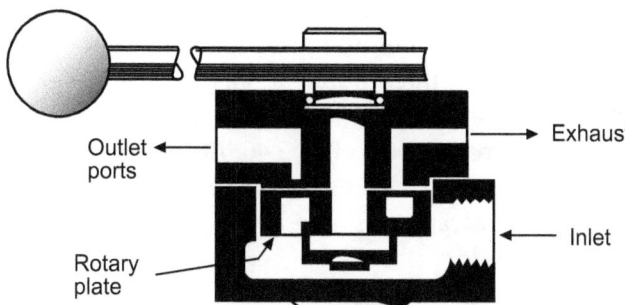

Fig. 5.44 (b): Section through a rotary plate valve

3. **Two-way, Three-Way, Four-Way Valves:** (i) Two-way valves are used in pneumatic controls where a pure straightway function is required. Air from actuators is not exhausted to the atmosphere through this valve. Fig. 5.45 shows a two-way valve using poppet.

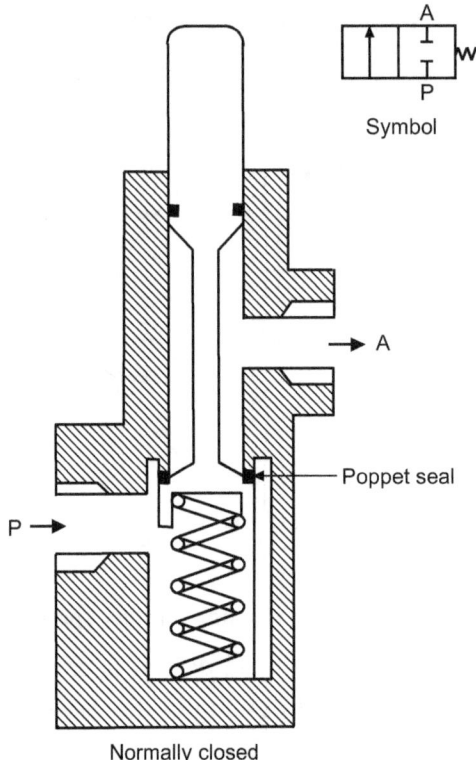

Fig. 5.45: Typical 2-port, 2-position poppet direction control valve (Normally closed)

(ii) A three-way valve is used when after performing an operating stroke, the air from cylinder has to be exhausted before a new cycle can start. Such a valve is shown in Fig. 5.46 (a) and (b). It has three ports: air inlet (P), air outlet to consumer (A), and third connection to the air exhaust (R). In both cases of normally open and normally closed type of 3/2 valves shown in Fig. 5.46. At the exhaust position, air inlet (P) is closed and the outlet line (A) is vented to the atmosphere through the exhaust port (R), allowing the air to escape. A single acting cylinder control is achieved by such type of 3/2 valve. **(Dec. 07)**

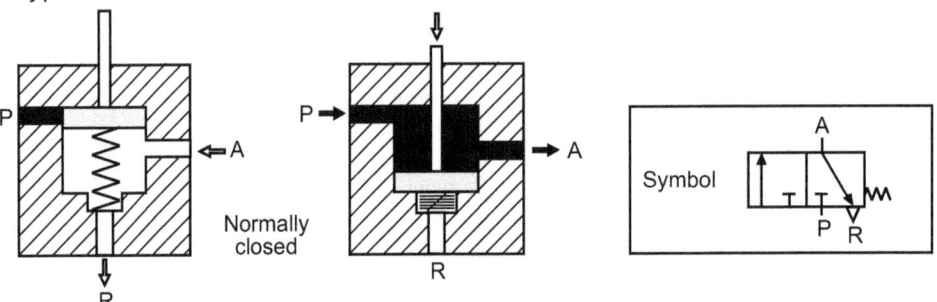

Fig. 5.46 (a): Normally closed three-way valve

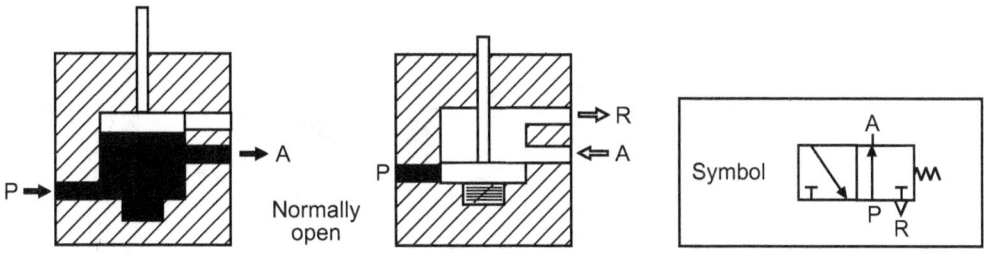

Fig. 5.46 (b): Functional diagram of three-way valve normally open type

(iii) For control of double acting cylinder a four-way valve is needed. Fig. 5.47 shows 4/2 valves where ports A and B are connected outlets, P is the inlet and R, S are the exhaust. In one position, pressure port P gets connected to the outlet port A while port B gets connected to the atmosphere through port R.

In the second position, the pressure port P gets connected to the outlet B by sliding of the spool of the valve and thus air is exhausted to atmosphere through outlet A. A 4/2 seat type valve is shown in Fig. 5.48.

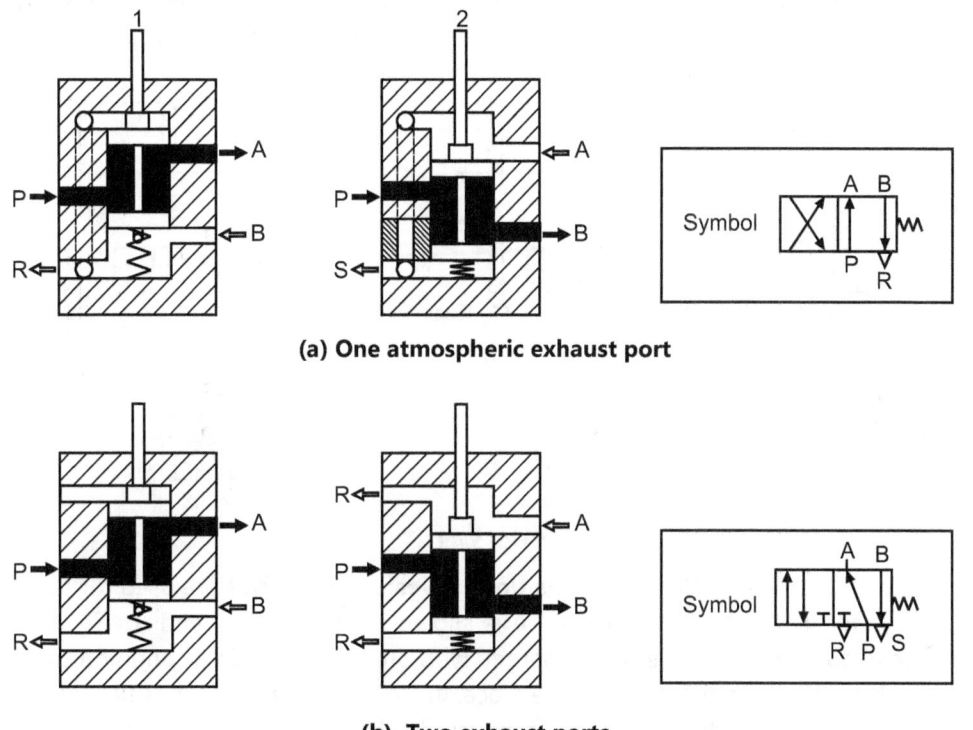

(a) One atmospheric exhaust port

(b) Two exhaust ports

Fig. 5.47: Functional diagram of four-way valve

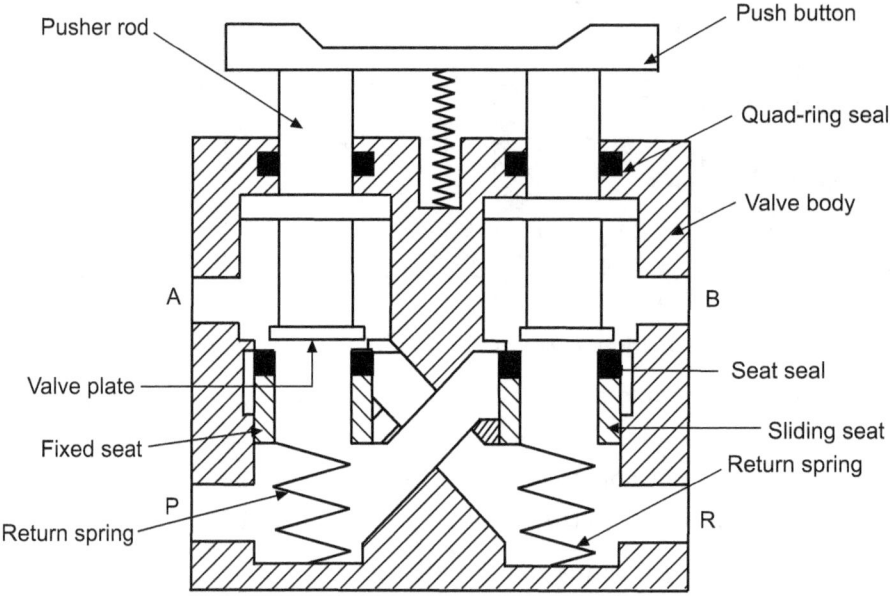

Fig. 5.48: 4/2 direction control valve seat type

(iv) 4 port-3 position valves (4/3 valve): These are disc type valves for robust manual operation. Inching of a double acting cylinder may be performed with these valves. Such a valve is shown in Fig. 5.49.

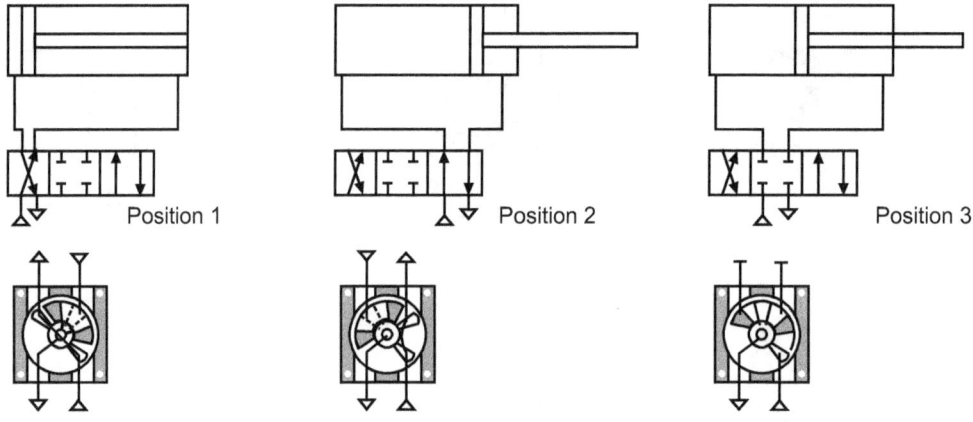

Fig. 5.49

(v) 5 port, 2 position/5 port, 3 position valves: These valves are used for controlling cylinder and motors. Such a valve is shown in Fig. 5.50 (a) and (b). In the centre position, the cylinder remains charged with pressurised air in a condition that allows inching in either direction to take place. In Fig. 5.51, the centre position of 5/3 valve causes the cylinder to be pre-exhausted allowing the cylinder to be manually moved.

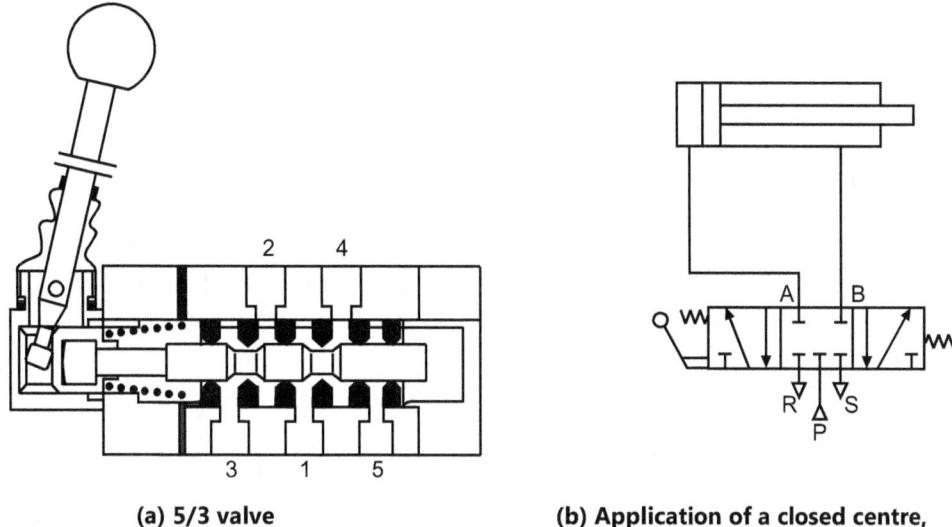

(a) 5/3 valve

(b) Application of a closed centre, 5-port, 3-position direction control valve

Fig. 5.50

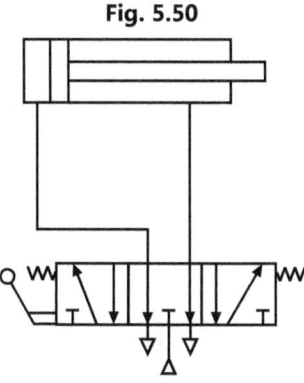

Fig. 5.51: Another application of an open centre, 5-port, 3-position direction control valve

4. **Direct Actuation and Pilot Actuation of Valve:** In the direct actuation, the actuator is directly mounted on the valve. The actuator may be either manual or mechanical. In Fig. 5.52, various manual actuators, for actuating valves are shown. The neutral position is automatically obtained, the valve actuates and remains open as long as the push button is depressed [Fig. 5.52 (a)]. The 4/2 valve, shown in Fig. 5.52 (b) is actuated by the lever and remains there until the lever is turned to another position. A foot operated valve shown in Fig. 5.53, actuates the valve until the pedal is held down. When the pedal is released, the valve returns to the neutral position.

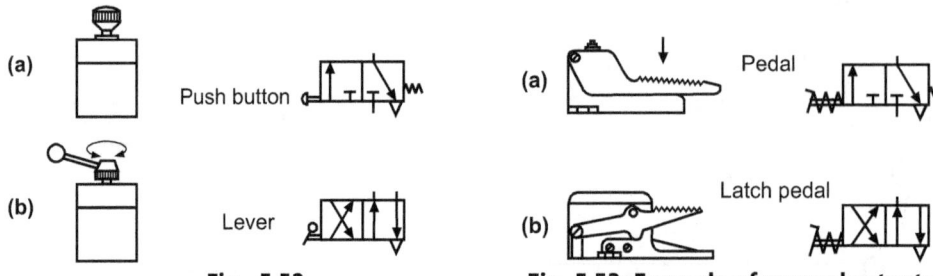

Fig. 5.52   **Fig. 5.53: Example of manual actuator**

In many applications, valves are required to be actuated by mechanical means. i.e. cams on the piston rod of a cylinder, a cam-plate, slide of machine are the mechanical actuators for directional control valves as shown in Fig. 5.54.

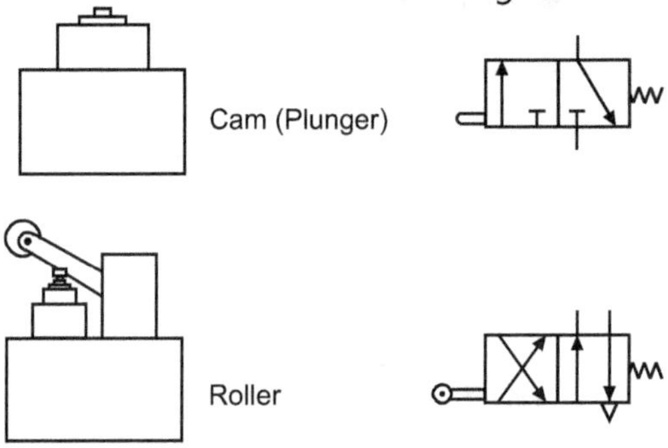

Fig. 5.54

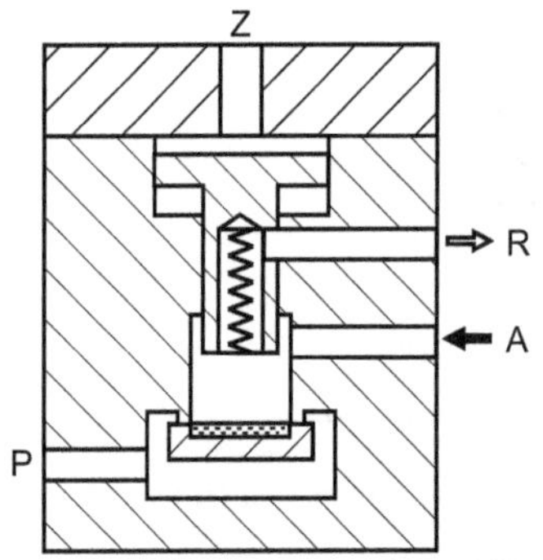

Fig. 5.55: (a) Shows neutral position 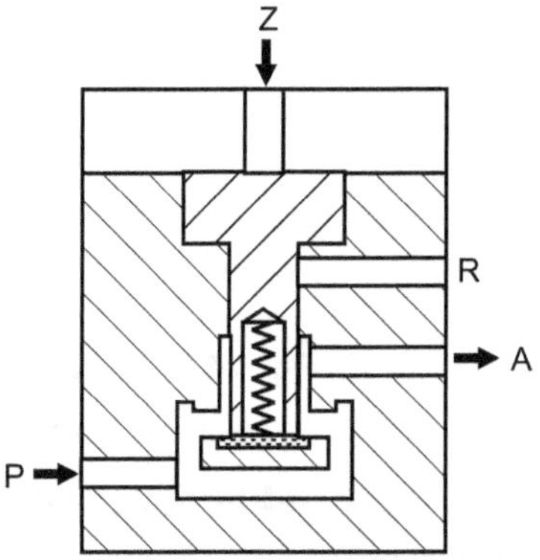   **Fig. 5.55: (b) Operated position**

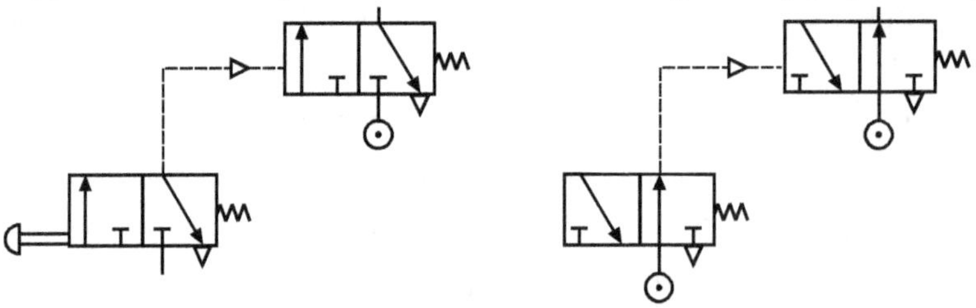

Fig. 5.55: (c) 3/2 disc seat valve pilot operated at Z port

In remotely actuated valves, the actuating element, that initiates operation of the valve, is located at a distance from the valve, that is actuated. In Fig. 5.55, pressure operated valves and valves operated by release of pressure, are shown. Valves having automatic spring that return to the neutral position, must be pressure-operated. In Fig. 5.55 (c), a 3/2 valve shown is at neutral position. It comes into two operated position with air-pressure loading at point Z. In this position, the pressure port is connected to the outlet port. While in the neutral position, the pressure-port is blocked and the outlet port A is connected to the exhaust.

5. **Pulse Load Valves:** These valves are shown in Fig. 5.56. They may be pressure or bleed operated. They require air signal for a short duration to effect operation. The valve will then remain at the operated position, until a counter signal is received.

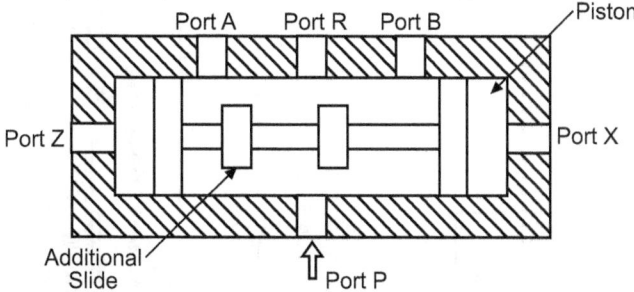

Fig. 5.56: A 4/2 valve (piston slide) having pilot signals at Z and Y

(a) **Pressure Operation:** Pilot signal at y will connect P to B and remains there. For connecting P to A a pilot signal from the port Z is required.

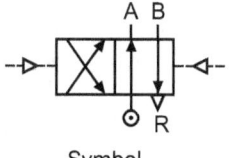

Symbol

(b) **Bleed Operation:** The same functioning is achieved by connecting pilot ports z and y alternatively to the exhaust instead of pressurised air.

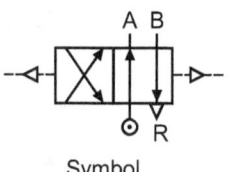

Symbol

6. **Pilot-operated 3/2 Solenoid Valve:** (May 07)

In this type of valve, actuation of pilot valve is done by electrical means i.e. solenoid. Solenoid is an electromagnet i.e when current is supplied a magnetic force is developed. Due to this force the pilot valve moving element actuates. This is shown in Fig. 5.57.

The present position i.e. neutral position is obtained due to spring when no signal is given to the solenoid. In this condition the pressure port is blocked and outlet A is connected to the exhaust. When a pilot valve solenoid actuates the plunger gets lifted connecting the pressure port P to outlet A. This happens because of opening of the main valve seat by movement of seat against the spring due to compressed air pressure acting on top of the valve seat for moving against the spring. When the solenoid current is switched off, the valve returns to the original neutral position. Thus electrical actuating force needed to operate the pilot valve can be very small, in such a valve, the actual operation of the main valve being accomplished with the operating pressure of the system.

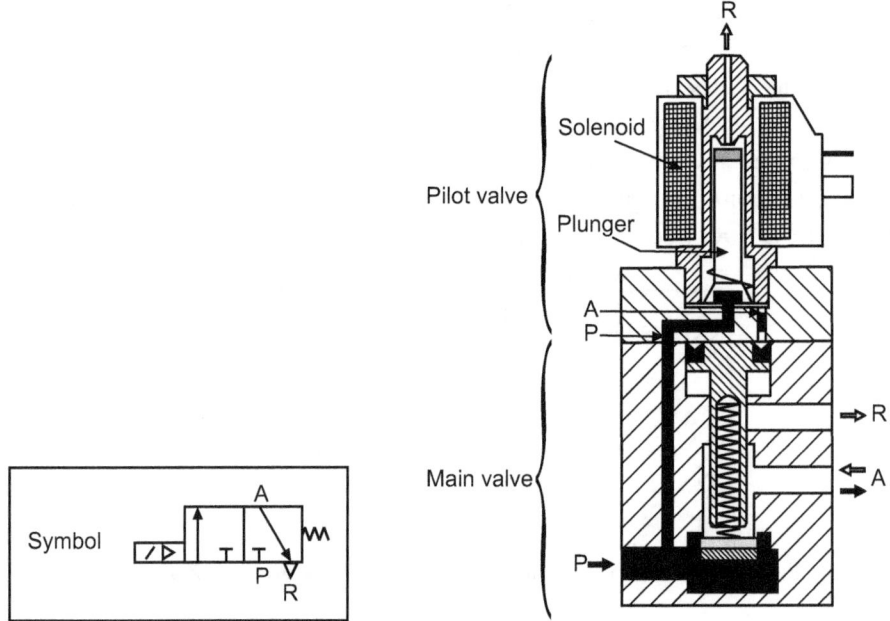

Fig. 5.57: Functional diagram of pilot controlled 3/2 way solenoid valve

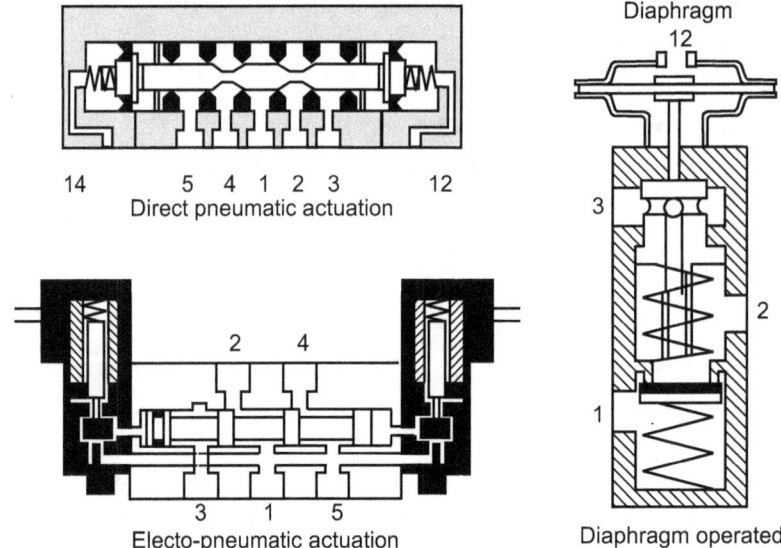

Fig. 5.58 (a): A selection of pneumatic valve actuators

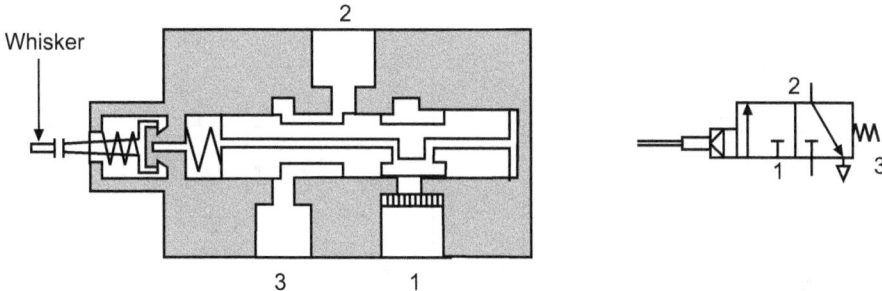

Fig. 5.58 (b): Whisker-actuated valve operation

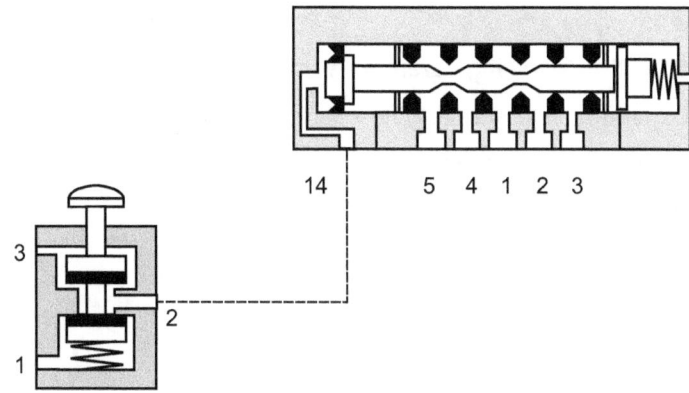

Fig. 5.58 (c): Direct pilot operation from a remote signal valve

In the discussions so far we have seen manual actuation, mechanical actuation and pilot operation of direction control valves. Other methods are diaphragm, direct pneumatic, direct hydraulic, direct electrical and electromagnetic actuation. Fig. 5.58 (a), (b) and (c) illustrate some of these methods.

Special Design: Time Delay Valve: (May 2008, Dec. 2008)

Refer to Fig. 5.59. This design provides time delay function. Compressed air enters at point 'Z', passes through a throttle valve and goes into the reservoir. A certain pressure is achieved in the reservoir after sometime, when air fills the reservoir and this time depends on the setting of the throttle valve. When a given pressure level is obtained, the main valve actuates and the pressure port 'P' gets connected to the outlet port 'A'. The time taken for pressurisation of the reservoir is adjustable and constitutes the delay between the reception of actuating signal and actual operation of the valve. For the valve to return back to its neutral position, air from the reservoir, quickly passes through the relief port in the throttle valve to the exhaust side. This allows the valve to return the normal position, because of the return force of the spring.

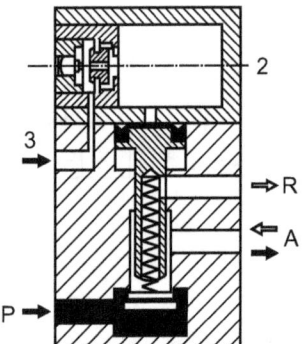 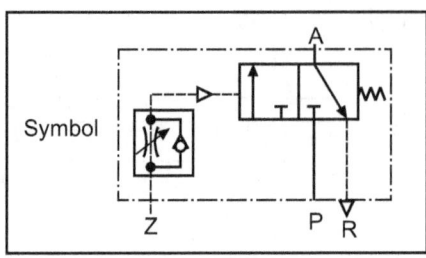

Fig. 5.59: Functional diagram of 3/2 way time delay valve, normally closed type

Valve Specification:

For selection of valves the following parameters should be studied :

1. Maximum operating pressure and flow rate required
2. Minimum and maximum operating temperature
3. Rate of cycling
4. Response time
5. Method of operation
6. Manifold and mounting requirements

Table 5.6 gives the approximate flow rates through different valves.

Table 5.6: Approximate air flow rates through a range of valves

Metric	Normal bore (mm)	Flow (l/min)
M5	2 – 2.7	60 – 185
M10 × 1	3 – 4	140 – 400
M18 × 1.5	8 – 9	3800 – 2000
M22 × 1.5	12 – 13	1800 – 4500
M26 × 1.5	19 – 20	4000 – 9000

Valve Performance:

For comparing valve performances, the following standard factors and tests should be considered.

(1) Nominal flow rate (Q_n) for a given entry and exit conditions (lit/min.). Fig. 5.60 shows a chart for a valve. From these graphs, actual flow at a particular inlet and outlet pressure can be found out.

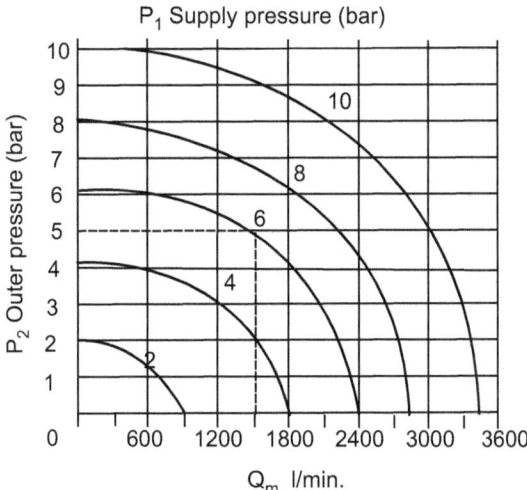

Fig. 5.60: Nominal flow rates for a given valve over a given pressure drop range

(2) Flow factors C_v and k_v:

$$Q = 6.844\, C_v \sqrt{[\Delta P\, (P_{S+1}) - \Delta P]}$$

where
- Q = Air flow (lit/sec. of free air at 12.8°C)
- C_v = Flow factor for valve
- ΔP = Pressure drop across the valve (bar)
- P_S = Supply pressure at the valve inlet (bar)

A metric version of C_v flow factor is k_v flow factor and is the flow of air in lit/min with $\Delta P = 1$ bar.

$$k_v = 14.28\, C_v$$

(3) Conductance

$$C = \frac{Q}{P_1}$$

$\begin{pmatrix} \text{where } Q \text{ is flow rate, } P_1 \text{ is inlet pressure} \\ \text{when air velocity reaches sonic} \\ \text{conditions at } + 20°C \end{pmatrix}$

(4) Critical pressure ratio

$$b = \frac{P_2}{P_1}$$

$\begin{pmatrix} P_2 = \text{outlet pressure} \\ P_1 = \text{inlet pressure as above} \end{pmatrix}$

b is between 0.25 and 0.5. In an ideal orifice having no flow restrictions, b is 0.528.

5.24 NON-RETURN VALVES

These valves permit flow of air in one direction only. The other direction is blocked for air flow at all times. The following non-return valves are used in pneumatic systems.

(i) Check valve, (ii) Shuttle valve, (iii) Restrictor check valve, (iv) Quick exhaust valves, (v) Two pressure valves.

(1) Check valve is illustrated in Fig. 5.61. On achieving the required force to lift a poppet against the spring, air flows in the free flow direction. Check valves are installed where different components need to be isolated so as to avoid mutual interference or for safety purposes.

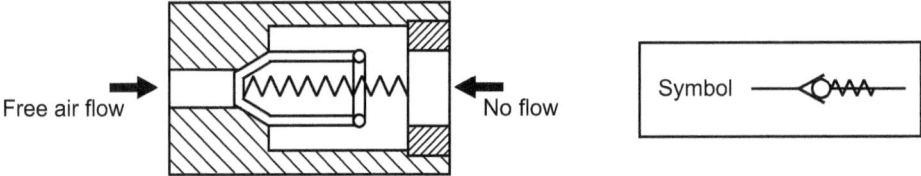

Fig. 5.61: Functional diagram of non-return valve (check valve)

(2) Shuttle Valve (May 08, 12, 09; Dec. 11): This is a double check valve. In Fig. 5.62, two inlets and one outlet are shown. The first position P_1 is loaded by air while P_2 is connected to the exhaust. Hence flow is from P_1 to outlet A and in the other one flow is from P_2 to A. Fig. 5.63 shows the use of a shuttle valve. In the circuit shown, movement of a single acting cylinder is controlled by two different valves but by using only one, at a time.

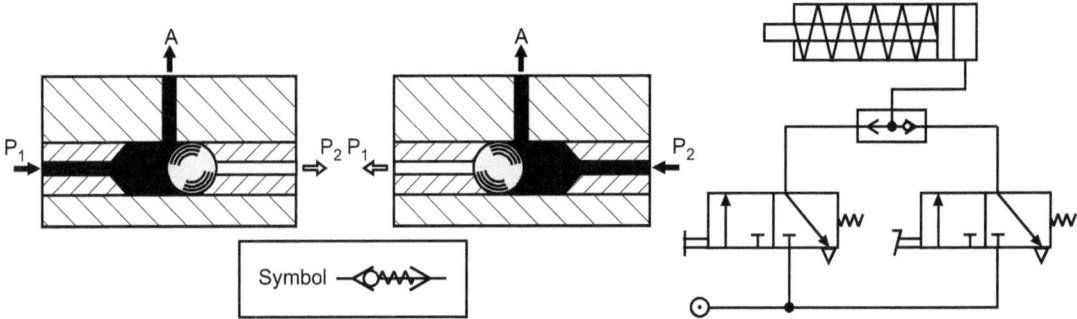

Fig. 5.62: Functional diagram of shuttle valve

Fig. 5.63: Cylinder control by shuttle valve from two positions (hand or foot)

(3) Restrictor Check Valve: (also known as speed control valve)

They are a combination of check valve and flow control valve. Fig. 5.64 shows the construction of these valves. In the free flow direction, the check valve permits the flow. But in the other direction flow can be controlled by adjustable throttle to change the speed of pneumatic cylinders.

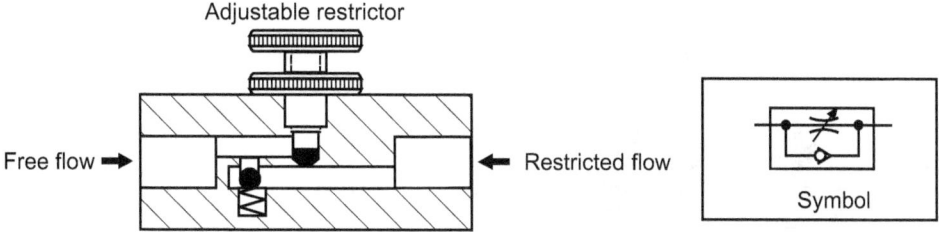

Fig. 5.64: Functional diagram of restrictor check valve

(4) Quick Exhaust Valve: Use of these valves is to increase the piston speed in the cylinder.

(Dec. 11, May 12)

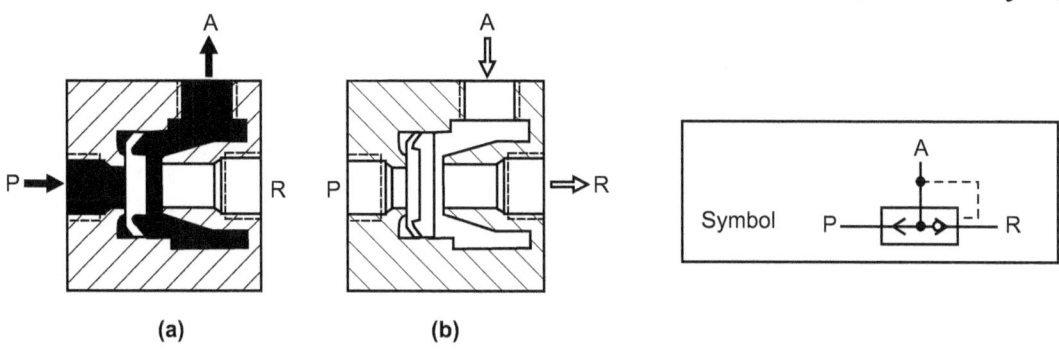

Fig. 5.65: Functional diagram of quick exhaust valve

(a) Air flow from P to A (from control valve to cylinder), (b) Exhausting of inlet line P effects direct exhaust to atmosphere from A through R

Refer Fig. 5.65 for working of the valve. In the position (a) shown, air acts on the cup seal and the seal closes the exhaust port. The pressure port gets connected to the outlet port A. When the port of the control valve is exhausted, exhaust air from the outlet port pushes the lips of the cup seal. The cup seal blocks the pressure port P and the exhaust air flows from A to R gaining rapid direct access to the atmosphere instead of having to take a path through the control valve. Obviously this valve is placed directly on the cylinder port.

(5) Two-Pressure Valves: Refer to Fig. 5.66. These are used for safety and interlocking purpose. There are two inlets P_1 and P_2 and one outlet A. To get any pressure port connected to outlet A, an equal pressure signal from both P_1 and P_2 is required at the same time. Otherwise for all other conditions, the pressure port remains blocked and the valve will remain in exhausted condition.

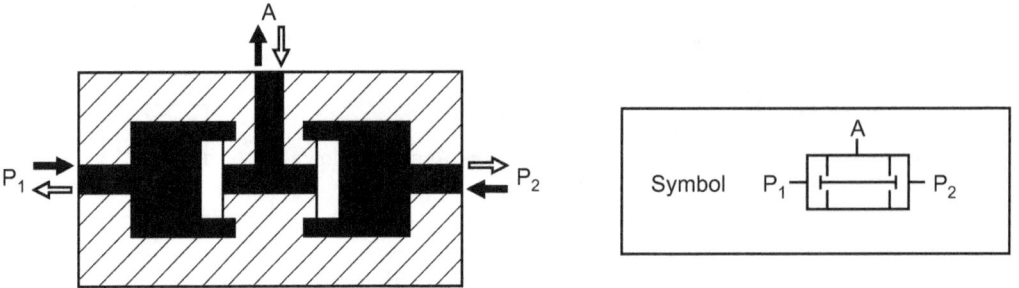

Fig. 5.66 : Functional diagram of two-pressure valve

5.25 Speed Control Valves

Control of speed of an actuator needs the use of some form of flow regulator. In cylinder circuits, the flow regulator is unidirectional. The flow is controlled in one direction and free flow occurs in the opposite direction. A typical unidirectional flow control valve is shown in Fig. 5.67.

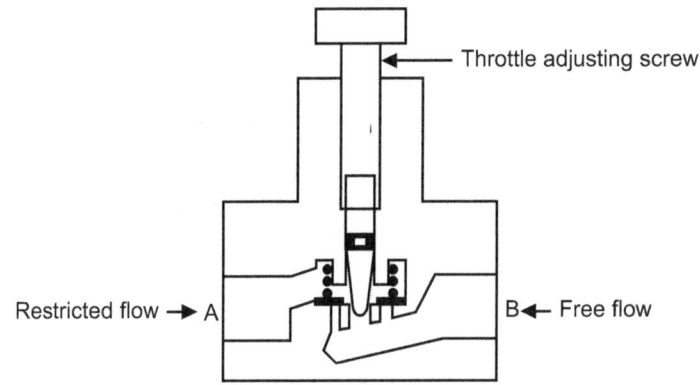

Fig. 5.67: Typical unidirectional flow control valve

Thus flow control valve regulates the rate of air flow.

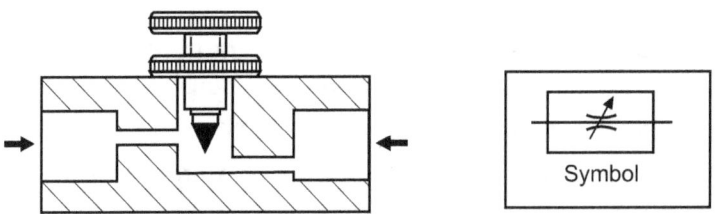

Fig. 5.68: Restriction valve: Flow in both directions

In Fig. 5.68 shown, the air flow passing through the valve is maintained at set volume per unit of time. The flow is restricted in both directions. Adjustment of the restrictor is manual.

Restrictor check valves described earlier are used in pneumatic systems as flow control values.

5.26 Pneumatic Actuators

Pneumatic actuators convert energy of compressed air into mechanical work.

There are three types of actuators: (1) Linear, (2) Rotary, (3) Semi-rotary.

5.27 Pneumatic Cylinders

The purpose of the cylinder is to generate straight line motions. There are forward and backward strokes which supply forces and thrust required for motion to be carried out. The cylinders can be of single rod, double rod (through rod), or rodless tape. They can be single acting or double acting.

5.27.1 Single Acting Single Rod Cylinders

The design of this type is illustrated in Fig. 5.69. Note the rear end and front end terms used to identify the ends. The piston inside the cylinder is extended by air supply to the rear end.

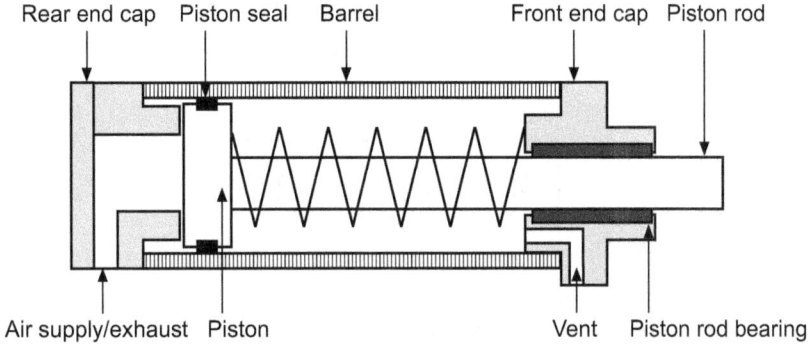

Fig. 5.69: General arrangement of a single-acting cylinder

For retraction, rear end is exhausted and the piston returns due to the force of the spring. A single acting cylinder is only capable of performing and operating motion in one direction. The spring return cylinders are limited in their stroke by the length of the return spring. (max. stroke = 100 mm approx.)

The double acting type cylinder has the following advantages over the single acting cylinder :

1. Low price.
2. Simple, compact pipe work.
3. On supply failure takes the initial at rest position.

A true piston type cylinder is shown in Fig. 5.70. This is an assembly of tubular cylinder housing, front and rear end covers (i.e. caps), piston and piston rod, seal and guide bushes. The cylinder is manufactured from drawn steel pipes. The bore is superfinished by honing or other processes. End covers are made from Aluminium casting, machined to get the required shape. The cup shaped packing or seal is most commonly used. The rod return spring is designed to provide sufficient force to return the piston back with the required speed. Friction between the surfaces (cylinder and piston) must be considered. Normally, the spring force is approximately 10 to 15% of the available piston thrust with 6 bar compressed air. Single acting cylinders require about half of the air volume than that of double acting cylinders.

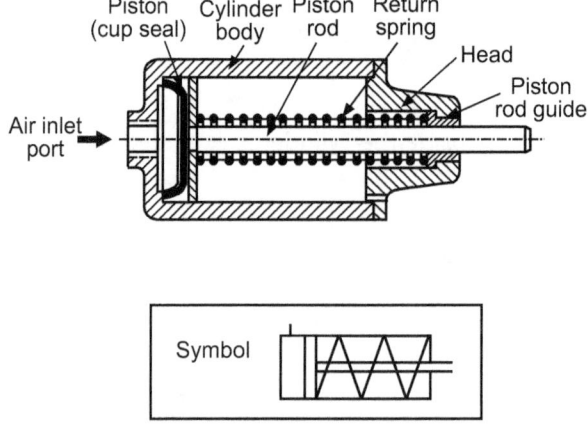

Fig. 5.70: Single acting cylinder, cast body

5.27.2 Diaphragm Cylinders

This is a simplest design of a single acting cylinder. The piston is replaced by diaphragm of hard rubber or plastic or metal. The operating stem is the piston rod. Only short strokes can be obtained upto a maximum of 50 mm. They are suitable for clamping operations. Fig. 5.71 and Fig. 5.72 shows a diagram and working of rolling diaphragm cylinders.

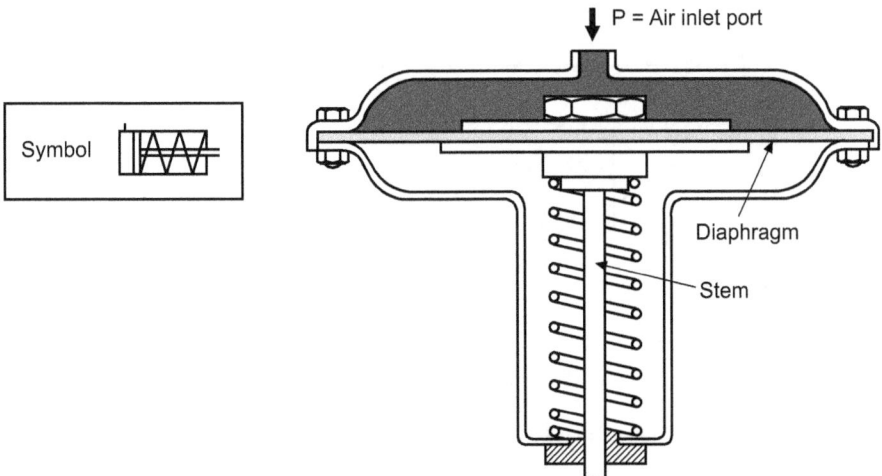

Fig. 5.71: Section through spring-return diaphragm cylinder

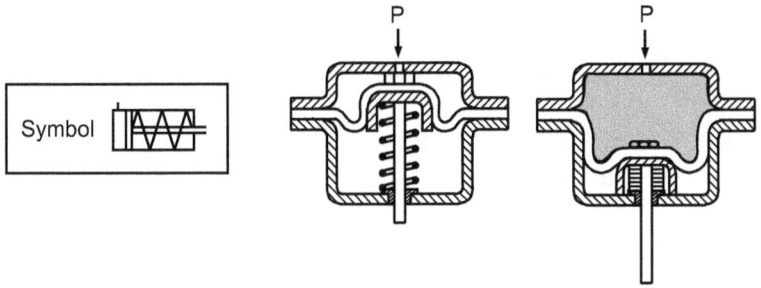

Fig. 5.72: Working principle of rolling diaphragm cylinder

5.27.3 Double Acting Cylinders

Application of double acting cylinders is in the situation where reciprocating motion with moderate forces in either direction is required. For the same supply pressure, force exerted while extending is greater than that while retraction. And retraction speed will be faster than extension speed for the same supply conditions. This happens because on the rear end side, a full diameter of the piston and hence the bore is available while on the rod side, the available area is full bore area minus rod area i.e. annulus area.

Double acting cylinders are always piston type. They have two inlets, one on either side of the piston.

Fig. 5.73 shows a cross section through a double acting cylinder. In the head of the assembly, the piston rod is sealed by grooved packing ring and guided by a bushing. A wiper ring (seal) is also fitted at the front end so that no dirt can enter the cylinder.

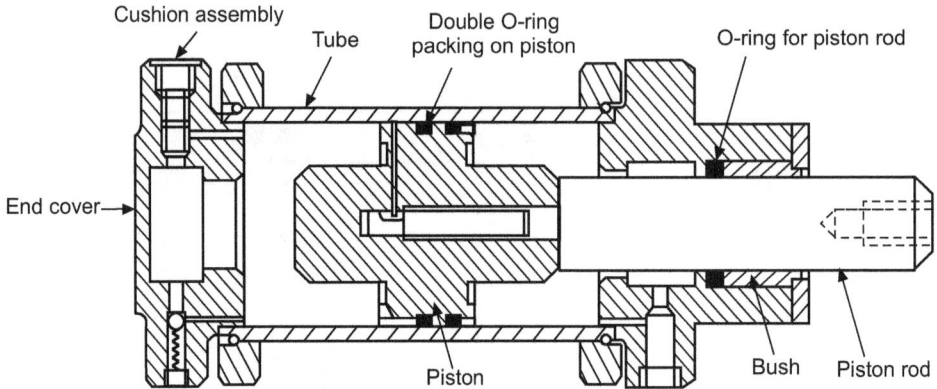

Fig. 5.73: Double acting cylinder

5.27.4 Special Type Cylinders

Special duty cylinders are designed for non-standard conditions of service or application.

1. Tandem Cylinders:

Refer to Fig. 5.74. There are number of cylinders arranged in series. Two double acting cylinders are arranged in line - in one cylinder body. Power produced by the two is added. This power is supplied for extending the piston rod. Tandem cylinders are used where a small diameter of assembly is required.

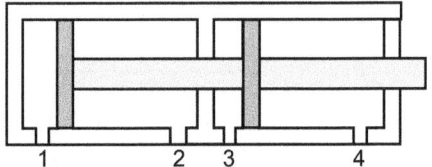

Fig. 5.74: General arrangement of a tandem cylinder

2. Rotary Cylinders:

The reciprocating linear motion of a piston is converted to rotary motion. A rack is cut on the piston rod and gear is attached to it. Usually smaller than 360°, the rotary motion is used in application. Refer Fig. 5.75.

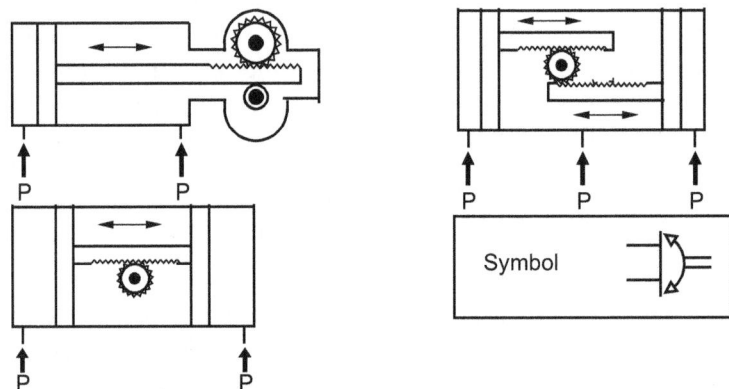

Fig. 5.75: Rotary cylinder

3. Opposed Thrust or Duplex Cylinders:

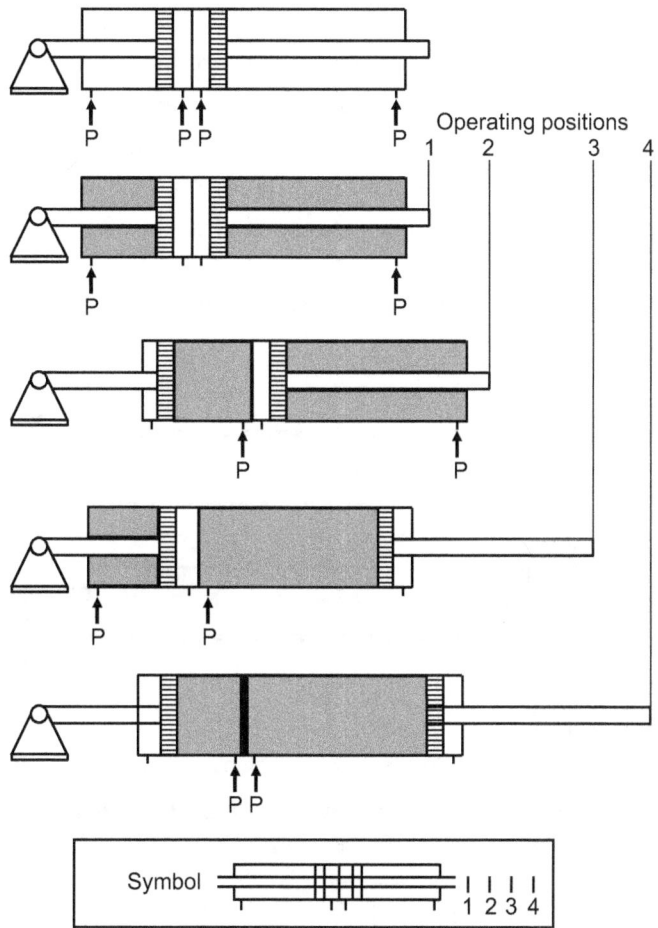

Fig. 5.76: Opposed thrust piston, example illustrated is four position type

They are also known as multiposition cylinders. In Fig. 5.76, two cylinders are arranged so that their pistons and rods are in opposite arrangement. There are four ports for supply of compressed air. This results in four different positions of the cylinder. The supply of air, the ports and the corresponding cylinder and piston rod positions achieved are shown in the figure, along with the symbol.

4. Impact Cylinders:

These special cylinders are used for applications like stamping, punching, cutting riveting, beading, embossing etc. Such a cylinder is shown in Fig. 5.77 (a) and (b). This cylinder derives power from the expansion of compressed air accelerating the piston rod and tooling to high velocity before it makes a stroke on the work. In this, high energies are involved. So the piston, piston rod are heavier and stronger than the standard double acting cylinder. The cylinder has a pressurising chamber. The piston does not move unless a certain pressure in this chamber is obtained. On obtaining this pressure the chamber seat will open, resulting in higher pressure acting suddenly on the piston to produce a powerful impact stroke. Depending on the pressure, piston velocities of order of 360 m/min can be obtained. Kinetic energy obtainable is 500 N/m. Maximum energy is attained after about 7 mm of piston travel.

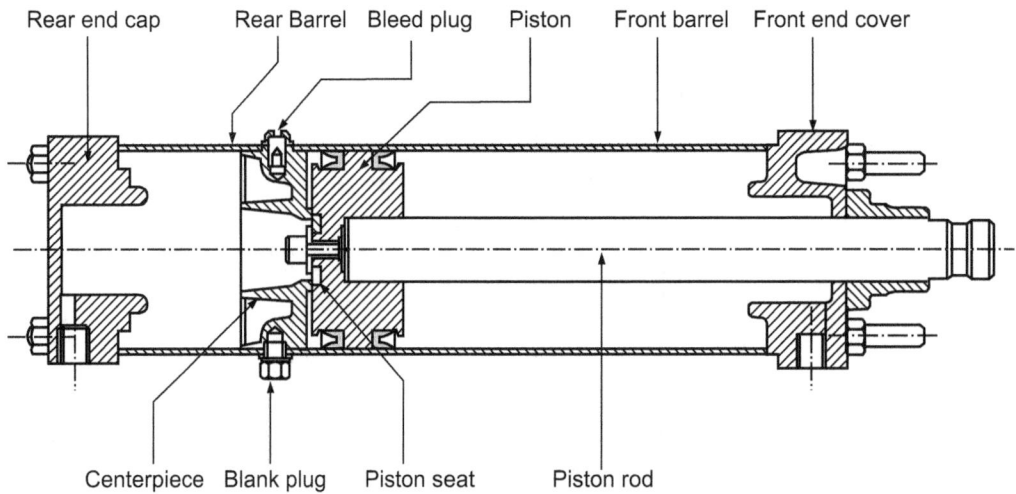

(a) General arrangement of an impact cylinder

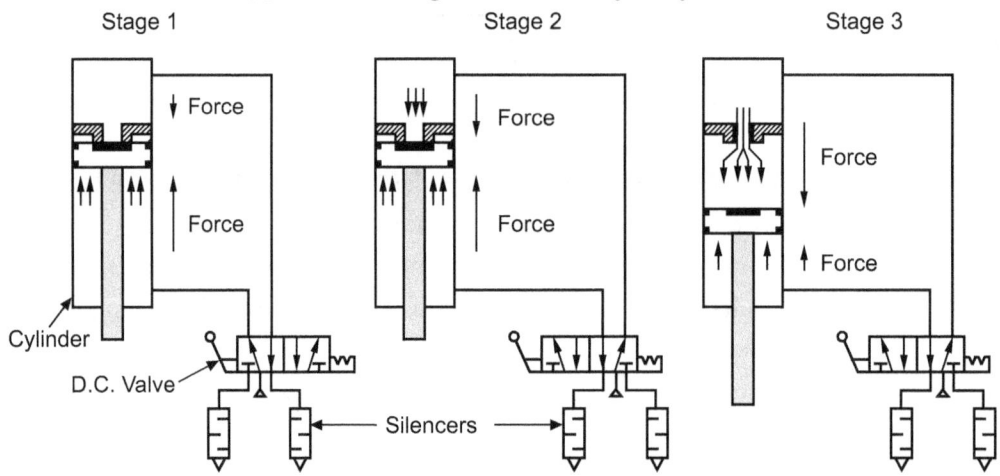

(b) Sequence of operations of an impact cylinder cycle

Fig. 5.77

5. **Double rod or Through rod cylinders:**

   Refer Fig. 5.78. This design provides equal thrusts and equal speeds in either direction.

   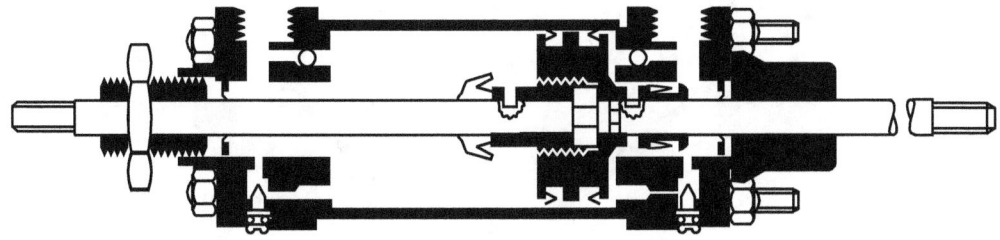

   Fig. 5.78: General arrangement of a through or double rod cylinder

6. **Rodless Cylinders:**

There are three types of rodless cylinders:

   (a) Magnetic,

   (b) Band cylinders,

   (c) Slot type cylinders.

They are shown in Fig. 5.79 (a), (b), and (c). The magnetic rodless cylinder has a series of magnets in both the piston and carriage. The piston moves in a polished S.S. cylinder. The stainless cylinder on the outside becomes a slide for carrier. They are available upto 40 mm diameter and at operating speed of 3 m/sec.

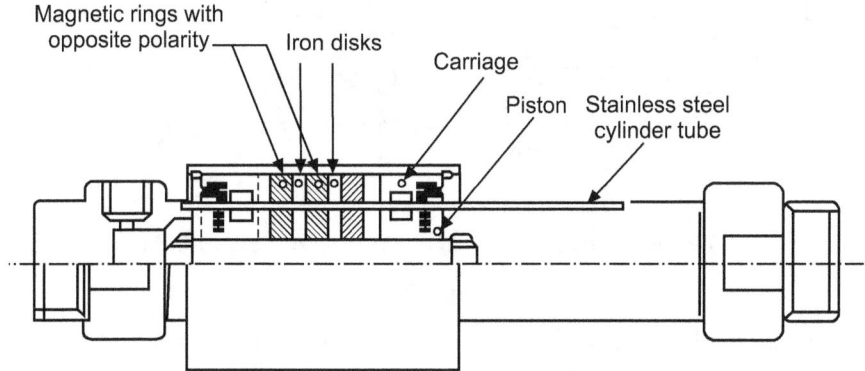

(a) Typical rodless cylinder with magnetic coupling between piston and carriage

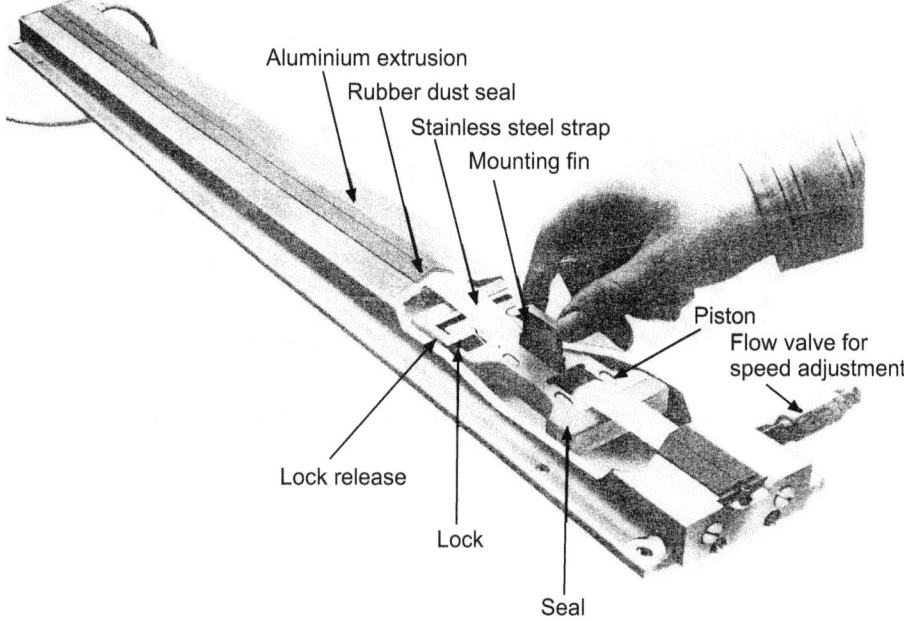

(b) Rodless pneumatic cylinder has a fin to carry the load. A stainless strap seals in the compressed air when forced against the slot in the extrusion

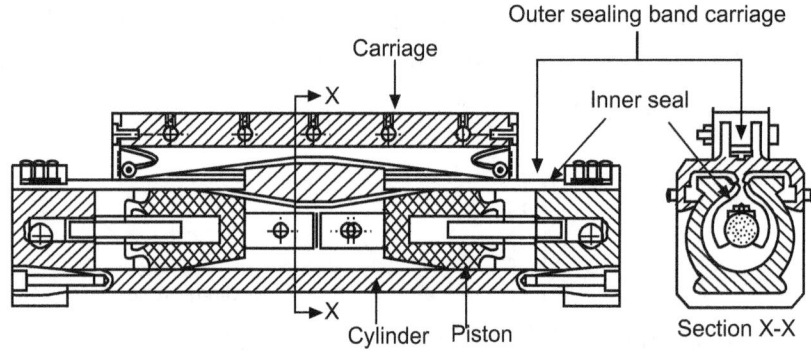

(c) General arrangement of a slot type rodless cylinder

Fig. 5.79

Band cylinders use a cable or band to connect both sides of the piston to the carriage. They are available upto 63 mm diameter, 7 m stroke and speed of 2 m.

Slot type cylinders are used for sliding doors in railway carriages and buses.

5.27.5 Cushioning of Standard Double Acting Cylinder

A moving mass of piston gains kinetic energy. This energy must be dissipated at the end of stroke. If not, it will cause damage to the piston, and the end caps. For cylinders above 25 mm bore, adjustable cushioning is provided, while below 25 mm fixed elastomeric sleeve or buffer is attached to the end caps.

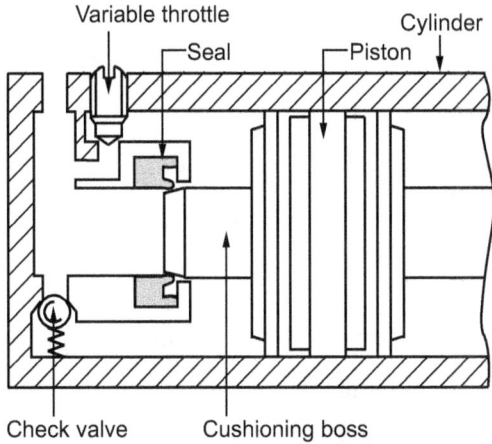

Fig. 5.80: General arrangement of the internal cushioning of a cylinder

Fig. 5.80 shows internal cushioning of a cylinder. When the piston comes near the end of stroke, the tapered boss enters the main outlet port. It creates initial restriction to air flowing out, and thus by increasing opposing a pressure reduces speed of piston. As the piston moves further, the boss enters in the outlet bore. Air now has to pass through the throttle to the exhaust, that induces higher back pressure to further retard the piston.

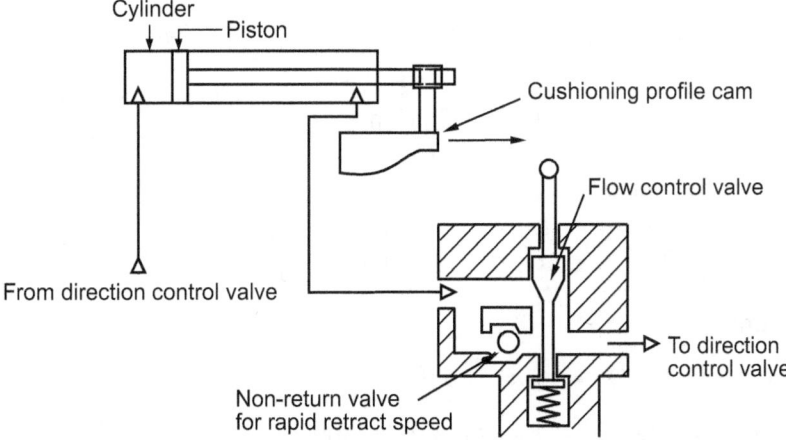

Fig. 5.81: General arrangement of the external cushioning of a cylinder

In certain applications (e.g. for heavy loads) external cushioning is required because internal cushioning is ineffective.

External cushioning is shown in Fig. 5.81. This uses a restrictor valve. The piston rod is connected to a template. (Profile cam). As the piston comes to the end of the stroke, the flow control valve is actuated by the cam and flow of air from the rod side is throttled. Hence the speed of piston reduces. For return in a normal way the piston, the check valves allow free flow to the rod end side.

5.27.6 Cylinder Sizing

The thrust developed by the cylinder is a function of:

(a) Piston diameter,

(b) Operating air pressure,

(c) Static frictional resistance (break away moment of the piston).

Static thrust of a pneumatic cylinder for double acting cylinders

$$F_{ext} = P \times A$$

$$F_{ext} = \text{Extension force (N)}$$

$$P = \text{Static pressure (N/m}^2\text{)}$$

$$A = \text{Cross-section area of full bore size}$$

$$= \frac{\pi}{4} \times D^2 \qquad \text{where } D = \text{Diameter of bore}$$

$$\text{Retraction pull force, } F_{ret} = \frac{\pi (D^2 - d^2)}{4} \times P \qquad \text{where } d = \text{Diameter of rod}$$

$$F_{actual} = P \times A \times \text{Efficiency} \qquad \begin{bmatrix} \text{Efficiency is taken} = 94 \text{ to } 98 \\ \text{for pressure between 4 to 7 bar} \end{bmatrix}$$

For single acting cylinders

$$\text{Thrust } F = \left[\frac{\pi}{4} \times D^2 \times P \right] - f \qquad \text{where } f = \text{Spring force (N)}$$

Air consumption:

Single acting cylinder $Q = S \times n \times q$ (lit./min.)

Double acting cylinder $Q = 2 (S \times n \times q)$ (lit./min.)

where, Q = Air consumption lit/min.

q = Air consumption per centimeter of piston stroke
(Tables are available for this)

S = Piston stroke in centimeter

n = Number of cycles per minute

Alternatively, air consumption at a given operating pressure, piston diameter and stroke is calculated as :

Compression ratio × Piston area × stroke

where Compression ratio $= \dfrac{1.033 + \text{Operating pressure in bar}}{1.033}$

Piston velocity: Normal piston velocity for standard design cylinders is approximately between 6 to 9 m/min.

Example 5.11: *A pneumatic cylinder is required to move 200 kg weight, 600 mm up on a 60° incline. Coefficient of friction = 0.15, load velocity is 0.6 m/s and distance travelled = 30 mm. Max. pressure at piston = 56 bar gauge. Determine actuator size and air consumption if the cylinder operates at speed = 15 cycles/min. Assume internal frictional resistance and other losses = 10 % of total force available.*

Solution: Let us decide the total force that opposes the motion of load.

$$\sin 60 = \dfrac{F_1}{mg}$$

∴ Force $F_1 = 200 \times 9.81 \times 0.866$

$= 1699$ N ... (1)

Frictional force $= mg \cos 60 \times (\mu)$

$= 200 \times 9.81 \times 0.5 \times 0.15$

$= 147$ N ... (2)

F_a = Acceleration force = Mass × Acceleration

We have $v^2 = u^2 + 2as$

$\therefore$ As $u = 0$, $\dfrac{v^2}{2s} = a$

$\therefore$ Mass × Acceleration $= m \times \dfrac{v^2}{2s}$

$$= \dfrac{200 \times 0.6^2}{2 \times 0.003}$$

$$= 1200 \text{ N} \qquad \ldots (3)$$

$\therefore$ Total force $= (1) + (2) + (3)$

$$= 3046 \text{ N}$$

Internal friction is 10% of total force $= 304.6$ N

Total resistance force (R) $= 3350.6$ N

Piston diameter $= \sqrt{\dfrac{4 \times (R)}{\pi \times P}}$

$$= \sqrt{\dfrac{4 \times 3350.6}{\pi \times 5 \times 10^5}}$$

$$= 85 \text{ m}$$

From standard tables, we select 100 mm diameter cylinder.

Air consumption $= Q = \pi \times \left(\dfrac{2D^2 - d^2}{4}\right) \times L \times n \times \left(\dfrac{P_1 - P_0}{P_0}\right)$

$$= \pi \times \left[\dfrac{2 \times 0.1^2 - 0.025^2}{4}\right] \times 0.8 \times 15 \times \left(\dfrac{5-1}{1}\right)$$

$$= 0.73 \text{ m}^3/\text{min}$$

$$= 12.17 \text{ lit./sec.}$$

Cylinder Mounting: Different ways by which cylinders are mounted are illustrated in Fig. 5.82. The method of mounting depends on the type of operation carried out and nature of the load. For loads following a straight line, rigid mounting is used while where load is required to turn in a plane, Clevis mounting may be used. Consideration must be given to bending loads on the piston rod when long strokes are performed. The supported length of The piston rod should be approx. 20% of the length of the stroke.

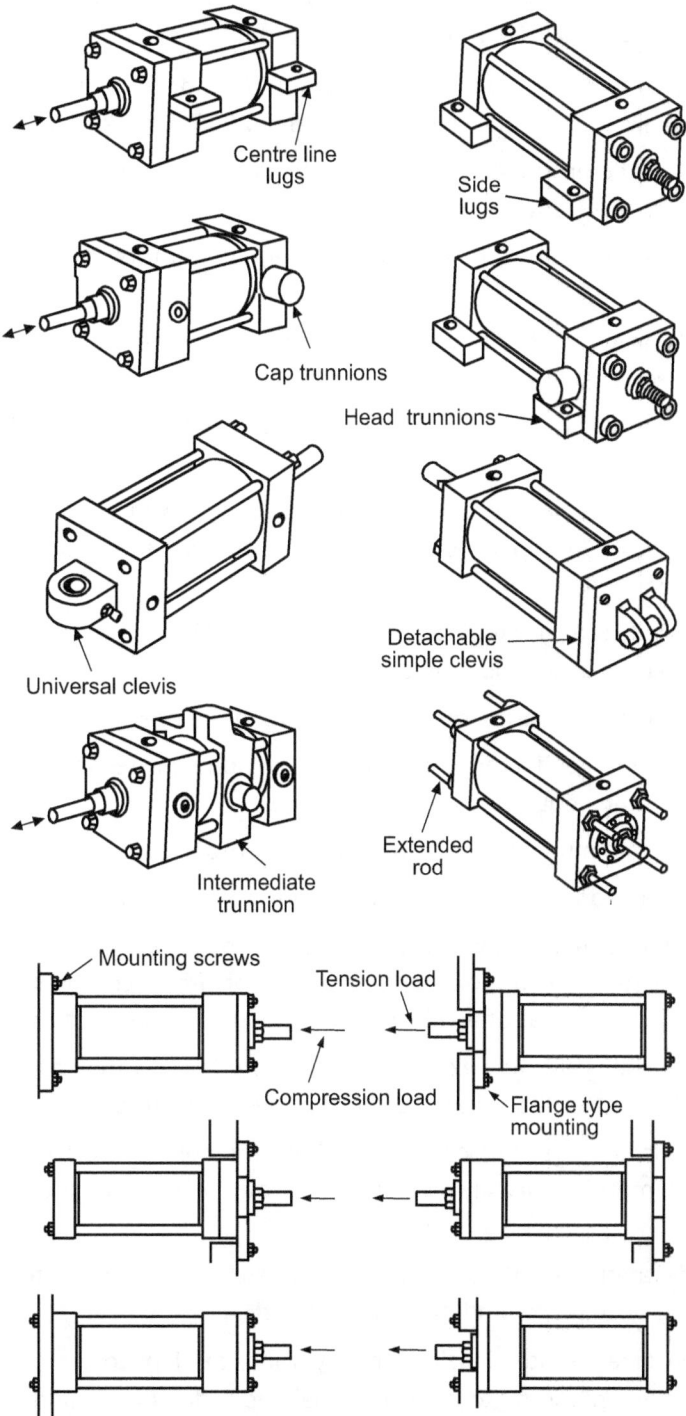

Fig. 5.82: Cylinder mounting arrangements

5.28 PNEUMATIC MOTORS (Rotary Actuators)

Rotary motion and torque is obtained by using pneumatic motors. The power range available is upto 25 kW. **(Dec. 2007, May 2009, Dec. 2009, May 2011, May 12)**

Air motors are used to produce continuous rotary power from a compressed air system. They offer a number of advantages over electric motors:

- Because they do not require electrical power, air motors can be used in volatile atmospheres.
- They generally have a higher power density, so a smaller air motor can deliver the same power as its electric counterpart.
- Unlike electric motors, many air motors can operate without the need for auxiliary speed reducers.
- Overloads that exceed stall torque, generally cause no harm to air motors. With electric motors, overloads can trip circuit breakers, so an operator must reset them before restarting the equipment.
- Air motor speed can be regulated through simple flow-control valves instead of expensive and complicated electronic speed controls.
- Air motor torque can be varied simply by regulating the pressure.
- Air motors do not need magnetic starters, overload protection, or a host of other support components required by electric motors.
- Air motors generate much less heat than electric motors.

Further, electric motors do possess some advantages over air motors:

- If no convenient source of compressed air exists for an application, the cost of an air motor and its associated support equipment (motor-driven compressor, controls, filters, valves, etc.) will exceed that of an electric motor and its support equipment.
- Air motors consume relatively expensive compressed air, so the cost of operating them will probably be greater than that of operating electric motors.
- Even though electronic speed controls escalate the cost of electric motor drives, they control speed more accurately (within ± 1% of the desired speed) than air motor controls do.
- Air motors operated directly from a plant air system are susceptible to speed and torque variations if the system flow and pressure fluctuate.

Common designs of air motors include rotary vane, axial piston, radial piston, gerotor, turbine, V-type and diaphragm. Rotary vane, axial and radial-piston and gerotor air motors are most commonly used for industrial applications. These designs operate with highest efficiency and longevity from lubricated air. Ofcourse, specific designs are available for applications where lubricated air proves undesirable. Turbine motors are used where very high speed but low starting torque are required. V-type diaphragm air motors are used primarily for special applications and will not be covered here.

5.28.1 Vane Motors

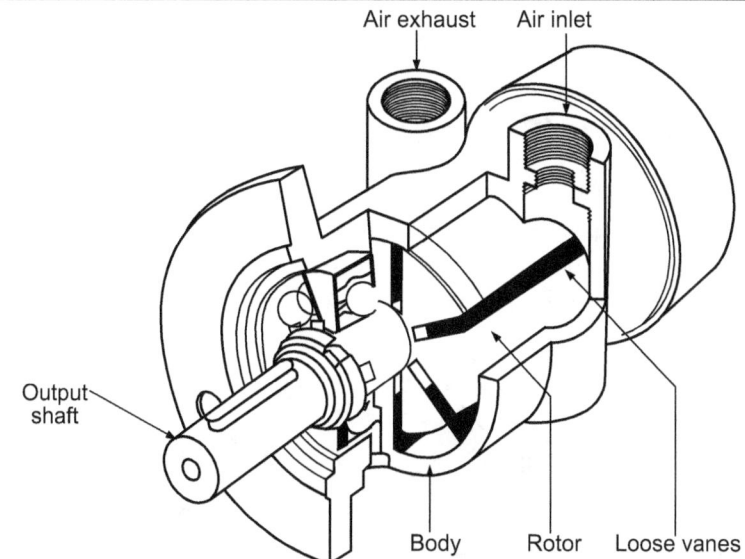

(a) General arrangement of a vane motor

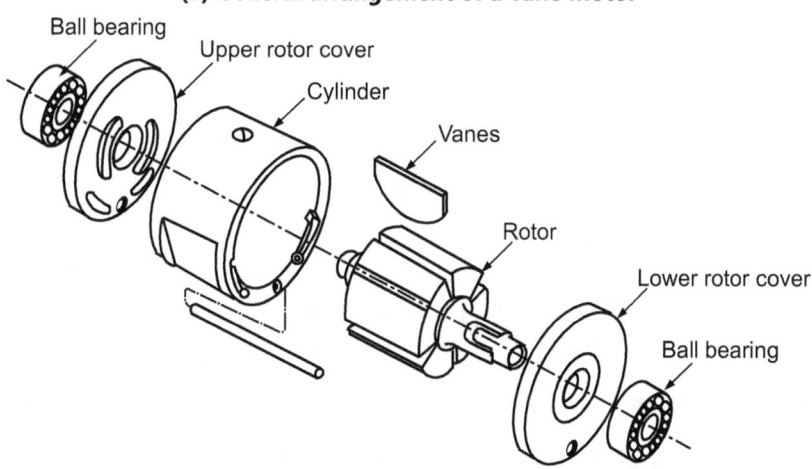

(b) Exploded view of vane motor

Fig. 5.83

Refer Fig. 5.83 (a) and (b). They are under the category of displacement motors and are widely used. They are compact having versatile construction, power upto 5 kW with speeds from 200 to over 30,000 revolution/min. The rotor is placed in the body. The rotor has slots in which vanes are provided. The rotor rotates eccentrically in the chamber formed by the cylinder and end plates. A crescent shaped chamber is formed while the rotor rotates. Vanes move freely in and out of the slots in the rotor. Compressed air is admitted through the inlet into the compartment at a point where its volume is enlarging. Compressed air forces the vanes and hence a torque or turning moment results. The speed of the motor determines the delivery of motor. For high speeds the vanes used are thinner and longer to reduce the vane force.

5.28.2 Piston Motors (Radial and Axial)

For larger output power, piston motors are used instead of vane motors. They are available with 2000 to 5000 r.p.m. speeds. Fig. 5.84 shows a schematic representation of the radial piston motors. Volumetric efficiency is high and speed control is easier. Reversal of motor is easier and is accomplished by reversing the air flow.

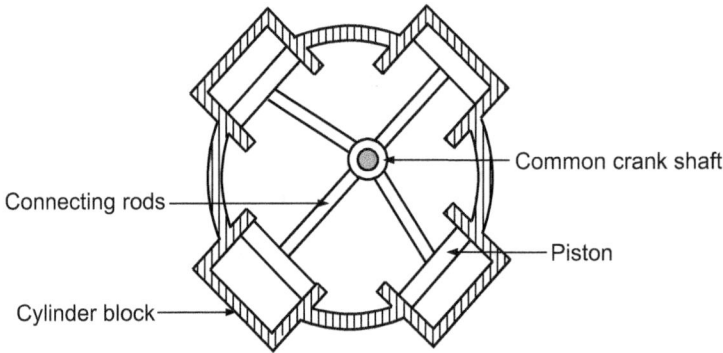

Fig. 5.84: General arrangement of a radial piston motor

Compared to vane motors these motors are bulky and have complex construction.

Axial piston motors (e.g. Swash plate type) lie between vane motors and radial piston motors. They are smaller but produce higher torque. The important advantage of this motor is, change in speed is possible without change in air supply by varying angle of swash plate. Decreasing the angle of the swash plate increases speed but reduces the torque.

5.28.3 Gear Motors

These motors are categorised in dynamic type motors. The mating gears are of three types, straight, helical or double helical. These are pure displacement motors and do not use the expansive properties of compressed air. Gear motors are used in heavy industrial applications requiring power capacities to the rate of 300 kW. The gear motors have low volumetric efficiency.

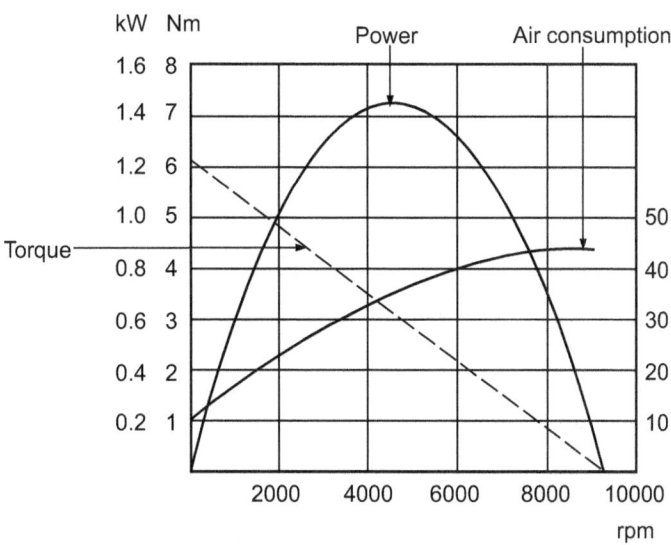

Fig. 5.85: Typical pneumatic motor characteristics

Fig. 5.85 shows characteristics of pneumatic motors. Note the straight line graph of the torque-speed characteristic. Maximum power output of these motors occur at approximately half the maximum no-load speed. For any pneumatic motor, the torque depends on the input pressure and speed on the quantity of air flowing.

5.28.4 Air Motor Efficiencies (Dec. 11)

Fluid power is defined as F.P. = QΔp

Q is the flow rate in m^3/s and Δp is the difference between the inlet and outlet pressures in N/m^2.

The output power is the shaft power given by the formula S.P. = 2πNT = ωT.

N is the speed in rev/s, T is the shaft torque in Nm and ω is the shaft speed in radian/s.

The output power is reduced because of friction and internal slippage of fluid. This gives the overall efficiency for the motor and this is defined as follows :

$$\text{Overall efficiency} = \eta_o = \text{Output/Input} = \text{Shaft power/Fluid power}$$

It must be remembered that in the case of gas as the working fluid, the volume depends upon the pressure.

Speed-Flow Relationship :

The basic relationship between flow rate and speed is, flow rate = Q = $K_q \times$ Speed

where K_q is the nominal displacement of the motor usually expressed in units of cm^3/rev.

Torque-pressure relationship :

In fluid power, shaft speed is normally given in rev/min or rev/s. The formula for shaft power is given by the well-known formula SP = $2\pi NT$. If the motor is 100% efficient, the shaft power is equal to the fluid power, so equating we get the following :

$$2\pi NT = Q \Delta p$$

Rearrange to make T the subject.

$$T = (Q/N) \Delta p/2\pi \quad T = K_q \Delta p/2\pi$$

Δp is the difference in pressure between the inlet and outlet of the motor. K_q is the nominal displacement in m^3/s.

In control theory it is more usual to use radians/s for shaft speed in which case :

$$\omega T = Q \Delta p$$

Rearrange to make T the subject.

$$T = (Q/\omega) \Delta p, \quad T = K_q \Delta p$$

K_q is the nominal displacement in m^3/radian.

The operating characteristics of an ideal motor may be summed up by the two equations

$$\text{Flow rate} = K_q N \qquad T = K_q \Delta p$$

Volumetric efficiency :

It is possible for hydraulic fluid to slip forward from the high pressure port to the low pressure port through the clearance gaps around the working elements without doing anything to rotate the shaft. This is called internal slippage and it results in a flow rate larger than the theoretical.

$$\text{Actual flow rate} = \text{Ideal flow rate} + \text{Slippage}$$

The volumetric efficiency of the motor is defined as

$$\eta_v = \text{Ideal flow rate / Actual flow rate}$$

5.29 BASIC PNEUMATIC CIRCUITS

Complex pneumatic circuits used for various industrial applications involve many cylinders for actuation of components, safety and other important operations. It is desirable that control of one cylinder is clearly understood. The various methods for performing the same task should be studied.

5.29.1 Control of Single Acting Cylinder

The extension and retraction of a single acting cylinder can be achieved by using a 3/2 valve. In Fig. 5.86 (a), the control is achieved using normally closed 3/2 valve. Here, we note that in the symbol of 3/2 direction control valve (A), the valve has three ways or ports. The two positions shown in the symbol are designated as (0) and (1). The position '0' is the neutral position that is obtained when valve is not actuated by the manual lever shown. This position is obtained because of the spring shown in the symbol. In this position, the pressure port is blocked and the piston side of cylinder is connected to an exhaust. This is normal neutral position hence the valve is normally closed type. When the lever of this valve is operated, the position (1) will be obtained. In this position compressed air supply port gets connected to the piston side (full bore side or rear end side) and air acts on the full area of the piston causing the piston to move against the spring compressing it. This is known as extension stroke of the cylinder. This position is shown in Fig. 5.86 (b). The piston remains extended till the d.c. valve position is again shifted. When the valve is brought back to normal or at rest position '0', the rear end side of air is exhausted to the atmosphere and due to the spring force, the piston returns rapidly to the rest position.

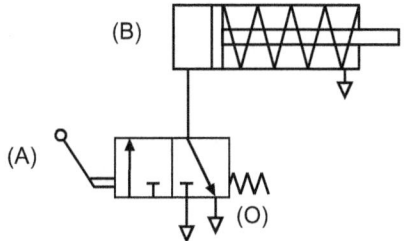 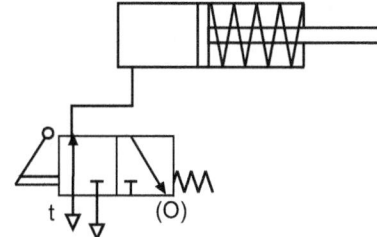

(a) Valve unoperated rod retracted (b) Valve operated rod extended

Fig. 5.86: Control of a single-acting cylinder by NC valve

The same function can be obtained by using 3/2 d.c. valve of normally open type. Here in Fig. 5.87 we see that at neutral position '0' (At rest) compressed air is supplied to the piston side and the piston is in extended condition. When the d.c. valve is shifted to second position (1), air from the piston side is exhausted and due to the spring force, the return stroke of the piston will take place.

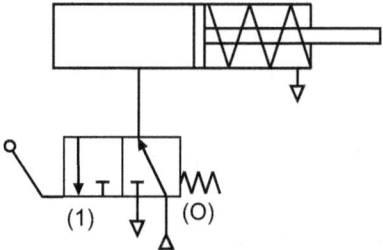

Fig. 5.87: Control of a single-acting cylinder, by NO valve

5.30 CONTROL OF DOUBLE ACTING CYLINDERS

In Fig. 5.88, the extension and retraction of cylinder is achieved by using two 3/2 valves, whereas the same function is obtained by using a one 5/2 valve in Fig. 5.89 and one 5/3 valve in Fig. 5.90.

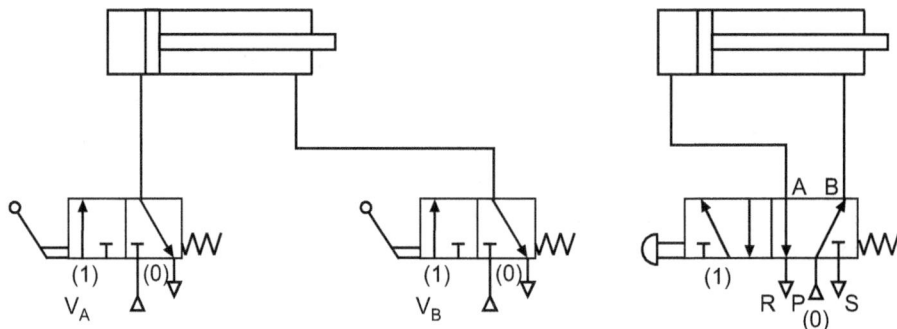

Fig. 5.88: Control of a double-acting cylinder, with individual 3-port valves

Fig. 5.89: Control of a double-acting cylinder with one 5-port, 2-position valve

In Fig. 5.88 two 3/2 valves are indicated by V_A and V_B. Both are shown in their normal neutral position. In this position, the piston side and rod side air is exhausted to the atmosphere. So the piston is free to move in any direction. Extension stroke of cylinder can be obtained by shifting the valve V_A to position (1) and air is admitted to the piston side. Since the rod side air is exhausted through V_B position (0), extension of the piston is allowed. For the return stroke valve V_B must be operated to get position (1) and valve V_A is operated back to position (0). Then only return stroke will be permitted. When both valves V_A and V_B are in position (1), there will be constant compressed air pressure on both sides of the piston. A larger force is applied on the full bore area side as it has larger area than the other rod side (annular area is available). If friction and load permit, the cylinder will try to extend in this case.

The above scheme is used for special cylinder applications of long strokes. Valves may be placed near to each port. This reduces piping runs and thus air consumption.

In Fig. 5.89 when one 5/2 d.c. valve is used, in the neutral position (0), cylinder has completed retraction. Port B is connected to pressure port P causing retraction while piston side air is exhausted to the atmosphere from ports A and R. When the push button is pressed position (1) is obtained and pressure port P gets connected to port A causing extension of the cylinder while the rod end side air is exhausted through ports B and S and port R remains blocked.

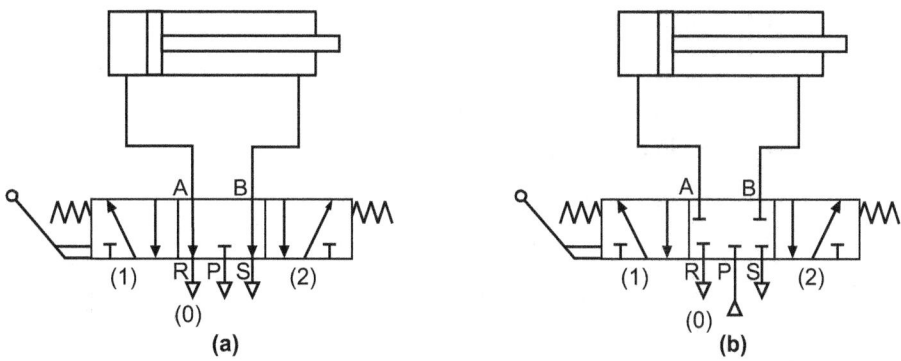

Fig. 5.90: Control of a double-acting cylinder with 5 port, 3-position valves

In Fig. 5.90 (a) and (b), two different centre position designs of 5/3 valve are shown. In Fig. 5.90 (a), both sides of the piston are exhausted to the atmosphere (open centre) and the pressure port is blocked [position (0)]. In position (1) left envelope, pressure port is connected to A and return air to port B, port S to the atmosphere, causing extension of the piston. Valve position (2) gives return stroke because P is connected to B and A to R to the atmosphere. In Fig. 5.90 (b), the centre position (0) of the valve blocks the air of the piston rod side. Extension and retraction strokes are same as in Fig. 5.90 (a).

5.31 Speed Control of Pneumatic Cylinders

The velocity of pneumatic cylinders or motors depends on the volume of air entering and leaving the cylinder. But air is a compressible fluid. Hence this volume of given mass of air changes with temperature and pressure. Temperature variation across the actuator system is

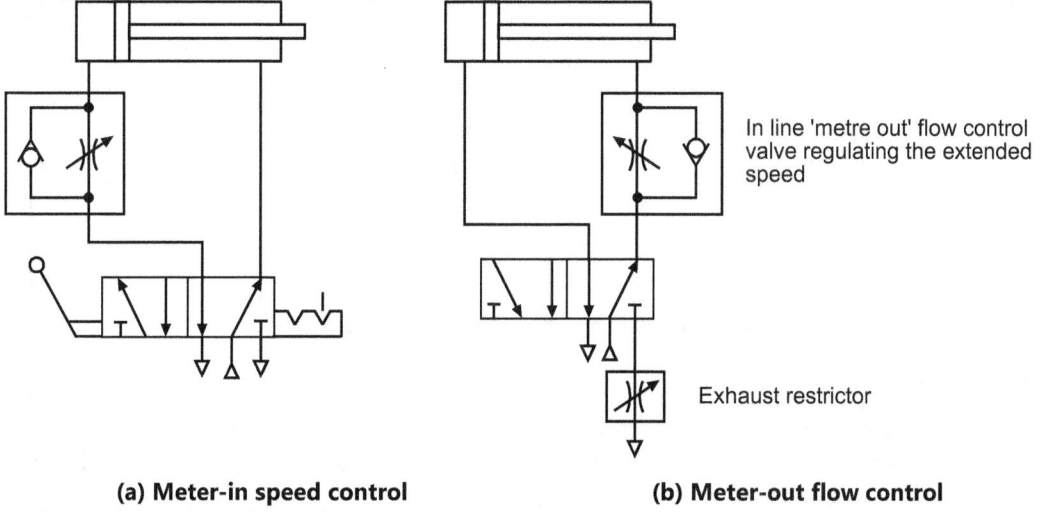

(a) Meter-in speed control   (b) Meter-out flow control

Fig. 5.91

small and its effect is neglected. The effect of pressure can vary as the load and flow rate changes. For control of speed of actuators either the quantity entering the piston side is controlled (meter in) or the quantity of air leaving the actuator is controlled (meter out). For this purpose, variable restrictor and check valve (to permit free flow in the other direction where air flow is not controlled) are used.

Meter out and meter in circuits are shown in Fig. 5.91 (a) and (b).

Air Pilot Control of Double Acting Cylinder:

Large size valves (power valves) for causing actual actuation of actuators are placed near to them. These valves may be controlled by other small pneumatic control valves (remotely placed) by providing pilot signal from these valves. Fig. 5.92 shows air pilot control of a double acting cylinder. CV_1 and CV_2 are push button control valves while PV_1 is the valve that gets actuated on receiving air signals from CV_1 and CV_2.

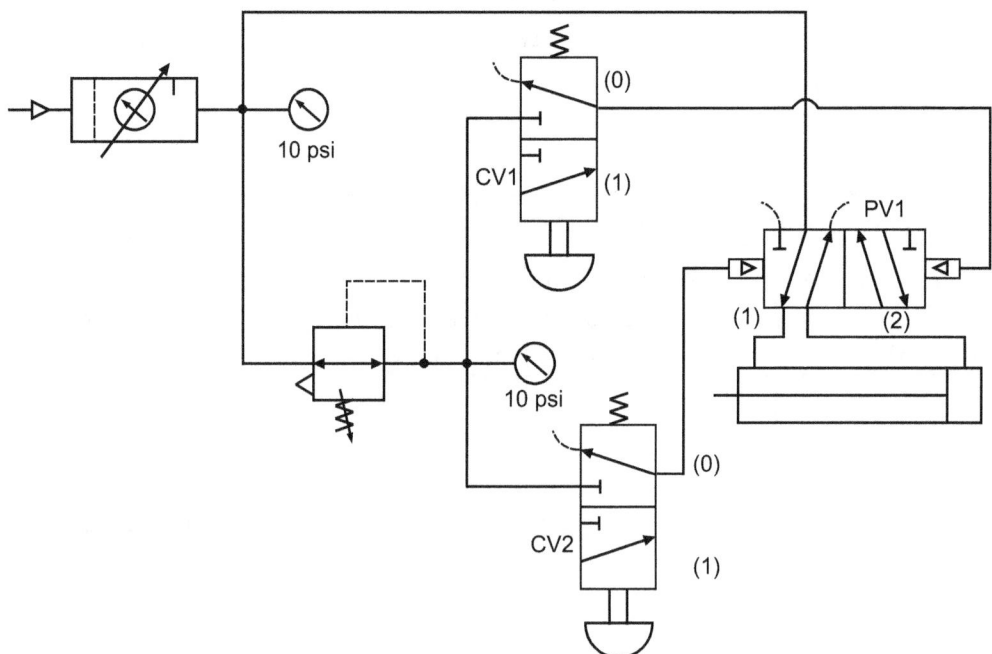

Fig. 5.92: Air pilot control of a double-acting cylinder

Working of the Circuit:

Step I: The circuit shows F.R.L. unit, pressure gauges. The system pressure is 100 psi while the control valves deliver a signal of 10 psi for the main valve PV_1 actuation. Pressing of the push button of CV_1 gives its position (1). The pilot signal to PV_1 is given and No. (2) position of PV_1 is achieved. In this position of PV_1 (5/2 D.C. valve) compressed air of 100 psi is supplied to the rod end side and the piston extends. The rod end air is exhausted to the atmosphere. This position is retained till the pilot signal from CV_2 is obtained.

Step II: Pressing CV_2 gives its position (1) and supplies a pilot signal to get No. (1) position of PV_1. In this position the cylinder retracts.

Thus high pressure air cylinder is ultimately controlled by low pressure push button valves from a place away from the cylinder.

In above circuit it must be noted that after pressing the push buttons of CV_1 and CV_2 for the respective strokes to take place, and after release of the push buttons the valves come back to initial spring offset mode (0) positions. This permits acceptance of pilot signal and activation of PV_1 so that the other side pilot signal is exhausted through CV_1 and CV_2 to the atmosphere. Also, even after CV_1 and CV_2 are released to return to their (0) positions the pilot signals once sent are memorized and accordingly performs the desired piloting function.

5.32 SAFETY CIRCUIT

Circuit Fig. 5.93 shows an arrangement for emergency air supply.

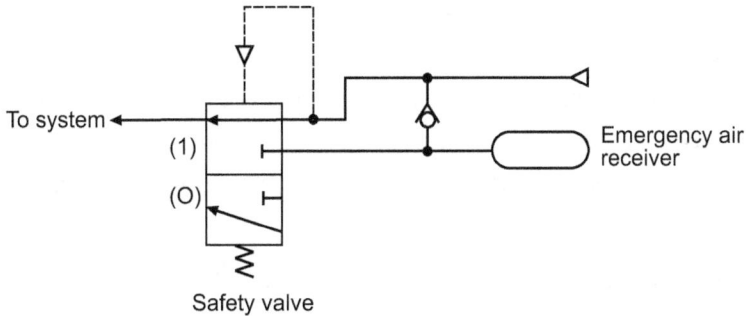

Fig. 5.93: Arrangement for emergency air supply

In the normal working cycle, compressed air is supplied through a safety valve to the system. In the event of failure of compressed air supply to system, the air stored in air receiver supplies air to system and the respective running operation can be thus completed. The safety valve will assume position (0) spring offset neutral position for supply of air to the system. This will happen because pilot signal for actuation of safety valve is now absent and the valve cannot retain its position (1) shown.

5.33 CYLINDER CYCLE TIMING SYSTEM

In Fig. 5.94 symbol (1) shows the system is pneumatic and compressed air supply is available in that line. No. (2) is the FRL unit. Valve V_2 (3) is a power valve controlled by valves 5 (V_3), (6) V_4. V_3 is operated by a push button while V_4 is the limit valve.

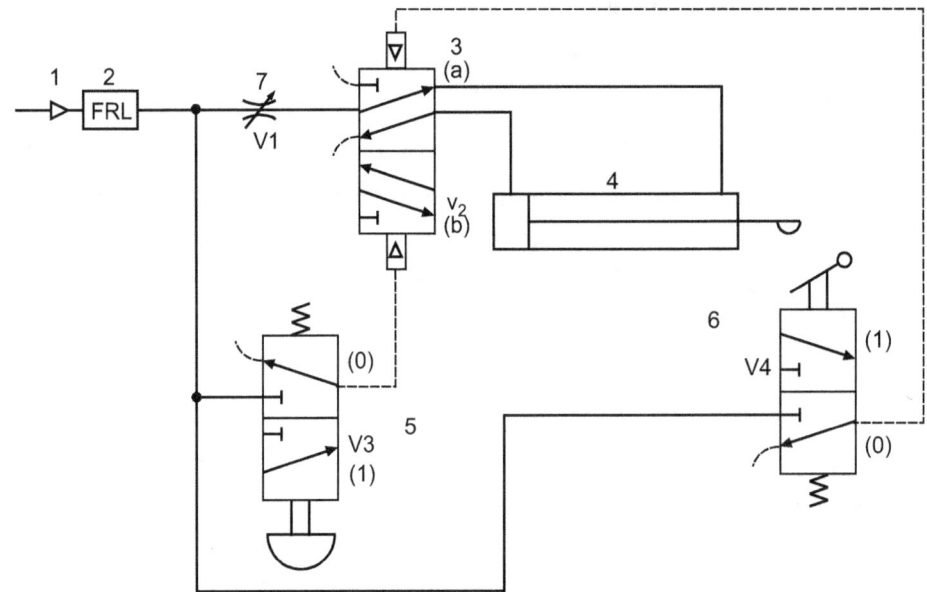

Fig. 5.94: Cylinder cycle timing system

Operation: When the push button valve V_3 is actuated, valve V_2 shifts to get position 3 (b) and the cylinder extends. When the piston rod cam actuates the limit valve (6) V_4, it shifts valve V_2 into the opposite mode to get position 3 (a) to retract the cylinder. Flow control valve V_1 (7) in the main line, controls the flow rate and thus the cylinder speed.

Two Step Speed Control:

Refer to Fig. 5.95. Note the two flow controls (7) V_3, and (8) V_4 and shuttle valve (9).

The flow control valve V_3 is set to allow greater flow rate than V_4.

- **Step I:** The cylinder is retracted. The push button valve (5) V_1 is actuated [position (1)]. Air flows through V_2 [position (a)], V_3, V_5 and the cylinder extends at high speed.

- **Step II:** Piston rod cam actuators valve (6) V_6, to get its position (1), gives position 3 (b) of valve (3) V_2 and air flow is now allowed through (8) V_4, (9) valve V_5 to the cylinder. But now the speed of extension of the cylinder is less.

- **Step III:** After the cylinder fully extends, valve 5 (V_1) is released by the operator to cause retraction of the cylinder position (0) of valve 5 (V_1).

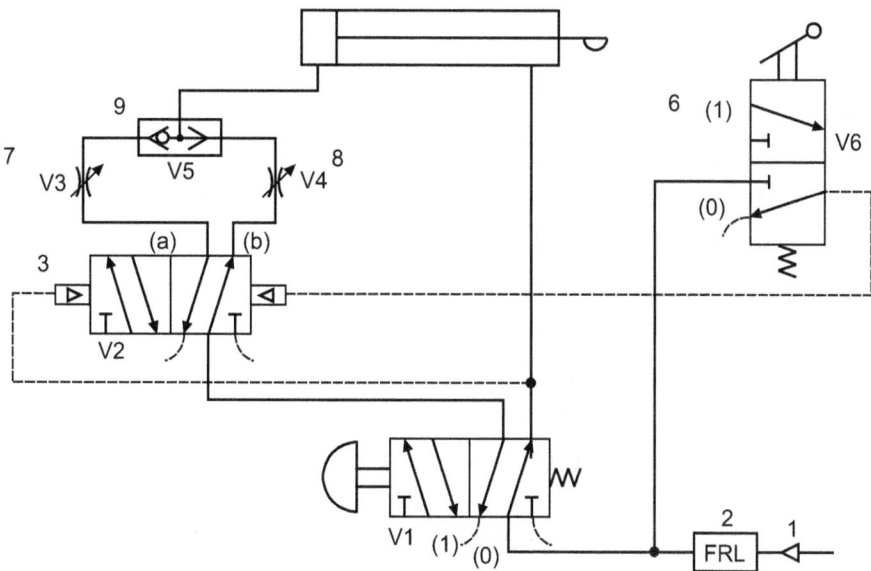

Fig. 5.95 : Two step speed control system

5.34 USE OF START-UP INTERLOCK

Refer Fig. 5.96 for the circuit.

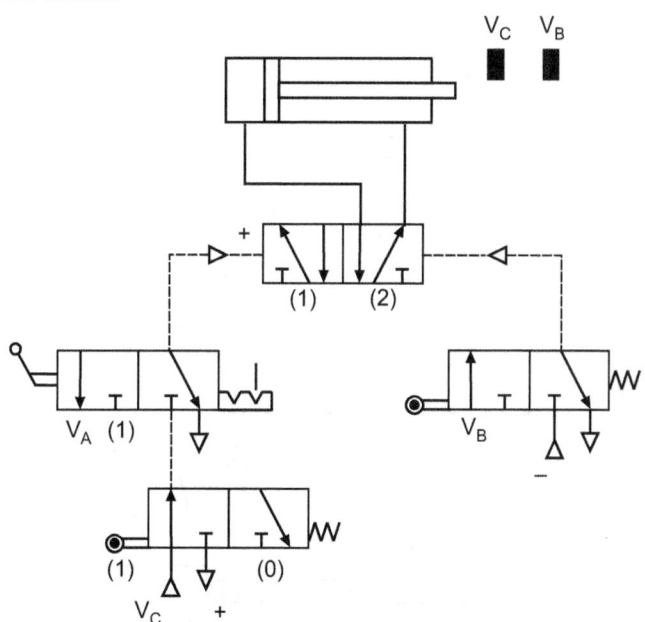

Fig. 5.96: Automatic retraction of a pneumatic cylinder with start-up interlock

- **Step I:** Actuation of valve V_A will allow the pilot signal to the main valve to obtain position (1) in which the cylinder extends. But this will happen only when the valve V_C is operated by full retraction of the piston. If V_C is not operated, it will remain in spring offset position (0) and no air supply is available for the pilot signal.
- **Step II:** With V_C actuated and V_A shifted to position (1) the pilot signal is given to main valve and extension of the cylinder takes place [Position (1) of 5/2 d.c. valve]. Valve V_B is in normal at rest position and connected to the exhaust permitting other side pilot signal of 5/2 d.c. valve to the atmosphere.
- **Step III:** On full extension piston operates valve V_B to get the pilot signal to 5/2 d.c. valve [Position (2) is obtained] and the piston retracts. If the stop/run valve V_A is held in the run condition, the cylinder will continue cycling until V_A is switched to the stop position. If V_A is in run condition and V_C is not operated, return of pilot signal of 5/2 d.c. valve is permitted through V_a and V_c to the atmosphere permitting retraction of the cylinder.

Two Handed Safety Circuit:

Refer Fig. 5.97. Push buttons of valves V_1 and V_2 must be pressed simultaneously to cause the cylinder extension. Similarly for retraction of the cylinder, both the buttons must be released simultaneously.

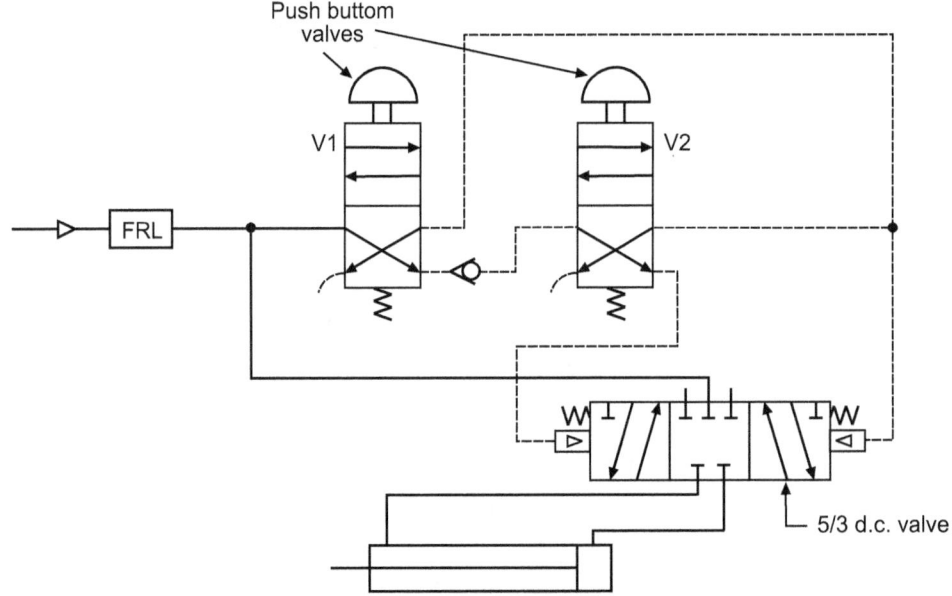

Fig. 5.97: Two-handed safety control circuit

5.35 AIR MOTOR CONTROL CIRCUIT

Refer Fig. 5.98 for the circuit.

- **Step I:** Shift hand operated pilot valve to position (1). The pilot signal is given to the main valve. Its position (1) is obtained. Air supply to the motor is given and the motor rotates. Compressed air supply to the motor is given through the FRL unit. Note that a muffler is provided to reduce the noise and eliminate air borne particles from leaving the exhaust of the air motor.

- **Step II:** When detent pilot valve is shifted to position (0), air supply of the motor is discontinued, because the spring in the power valve returns the spool to the closed position (0) and the motor stops. No braking is provided for the motor. Also there is no flow control valve for speed regulation. Check valve protects the motor against overrunning loads.

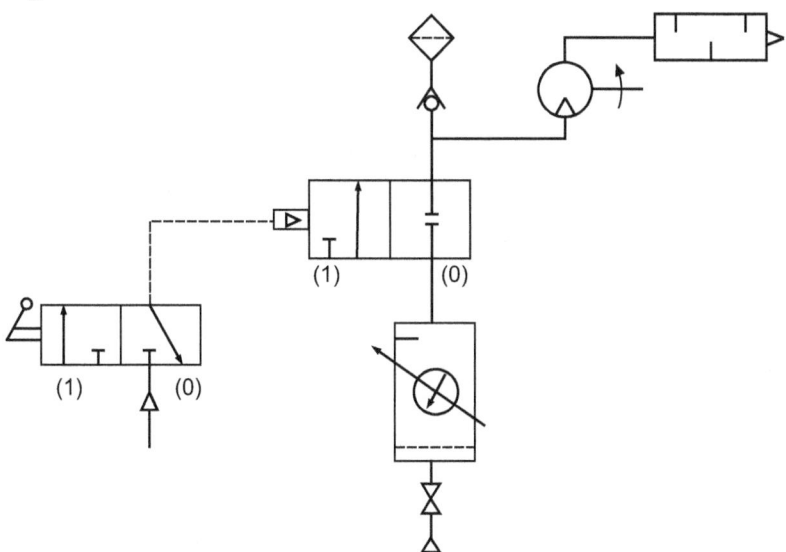

Fig. 5.98: Motor control circuit

5.36 AIR CUSHIONING OF CYLINDERS IN BOTH STROKE ENDS

Refer circuit in Fig. 5.99.

- **Step I:** In the position of valve V_1 shown, the cylinder retracts. Path $V_1 - V_2$ to rod end. Return path through V_5 to the atmosphere because V_5 would be in spring offset mode. Note the second simultaneous path of air through V_3 to V_5 for piloting when the pressure increases. V_5 is piloted and now air passes through the control valve V_7 to the atmosphere. The piston decelerates at the end of the stroke.

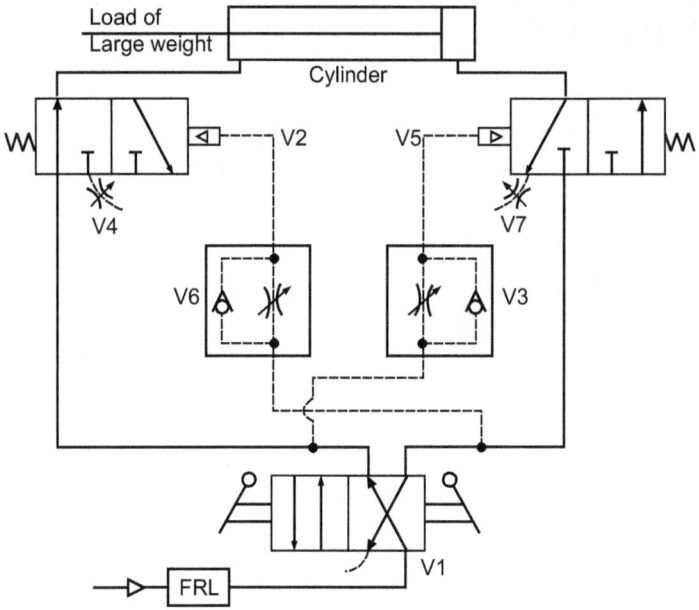

Fig. 5.99: Air cushion of a pneumatic cylinder

- **Step II:** Forward stroke: Path $V_1 - V_5$ to piston side. Rod side air to the atmosphere through V_1. When valve V_2 is piloted because of the second path $V_1 - V_6$ to V_2, exhaust air flows through the frontal valve V_4 and the piston decelerates.

5.37 SEQUENCE CIRCUITS

Pneumatic circuits perform a series of events in a prescribed order using limit valves. These are called sequence circuits.

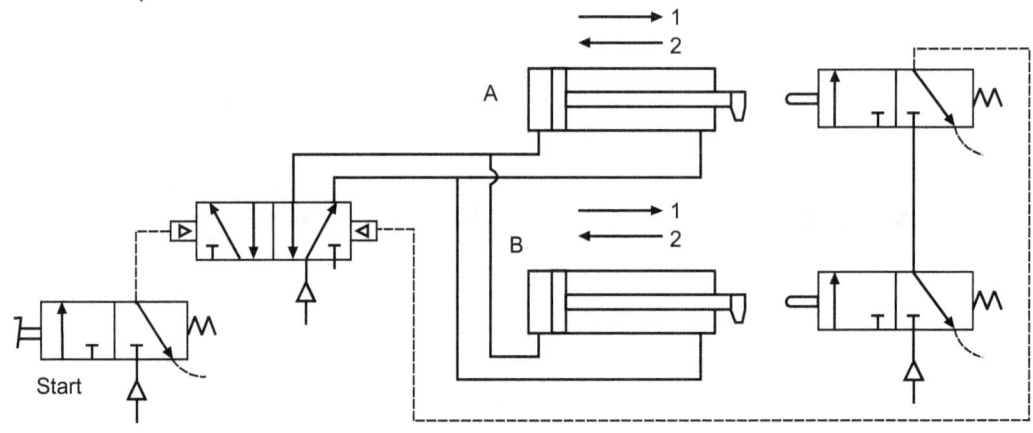

Fig. 5.100: Two double acting cylinders extending and retracting together

(A+, B+, A−, B−)

(1) Two cylinders extend and retract together (A+, B+, A−, B−). Refer to the circuit shown in Fig. (5.100). Both the cylinders start and stop to their stroke ends. If any one reaches first, it stops there till the other joins it.

Components:
  (a) Main valve 5/2 unbiased pilot operated
  (b) Sequence valves - 2 position 3 way spring returned and two such valves are plumbed in series.
  (c) One start valve: 3/2 d.c. spring offset.
  (d) Two double acting cylinders.

- **Step I:** At the start both cylinders are in fully retracted position. The start valve is actuated by depressing the pedal valve. The main valve is piloted and both cylinders receive air to the piston side and they extend. When both are fully extended they press the limit valves and only then the pilot signal is given to the main valve for retraction to take place.
- **Step II:** Retraction of cylinders occurs on actuation of the power valve and air is allowed to the rod side of both the cylinders. For this to happen the start valve foot pedal by the operator must be released.

(2) Circuit in which cylinder A extends fully, then cylinder B extends. Then cylinder A returns first and then cylinder B. (A+, B+, A−, B−). Refer to Fig. 5.101.

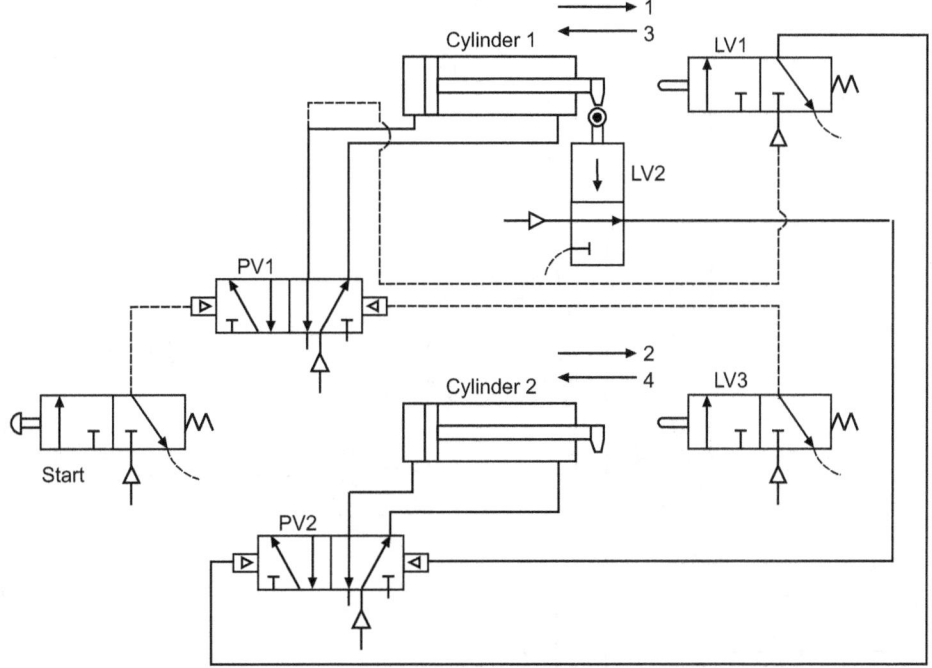

Fig. 5.101: Extending and rectracting two double-acting cylinders in sequence (A+, B+, A−, B−)

Note that the pilot pressure for limit valve 1 is taken from the line that connects to the piston side of the cylinder. This allows the limit valve 1 to shift power valve 2 only when cylinder 1 is under pressure to extend. The header is requested to trace the circuit and understand the sequence stated above.

(3) Circuit showing extending one cylinder while other retracts: A+, B− and A−, B+. Refer Fig. 5.102 for circuit. In place of two power valves, cam operated valve to cylinder 2 is provided.

Operation:

- **Step I:** Air path – 3/2 start valve pilot signal to limit valve 3 and limit valve 2 and power valve position (1). Cylinder 1 extends and cylinder 2 retracts.

- **Step II:** Full extension of cylinder 1 shifts limit valve 1, cylinder 2 on return shifts limit valve 4. Air path LV_4, LV_1, power valve to get position (2). Air path to the rod side of cylinder 1 to retract and to piston side of the cylinder 2 to cause extension.

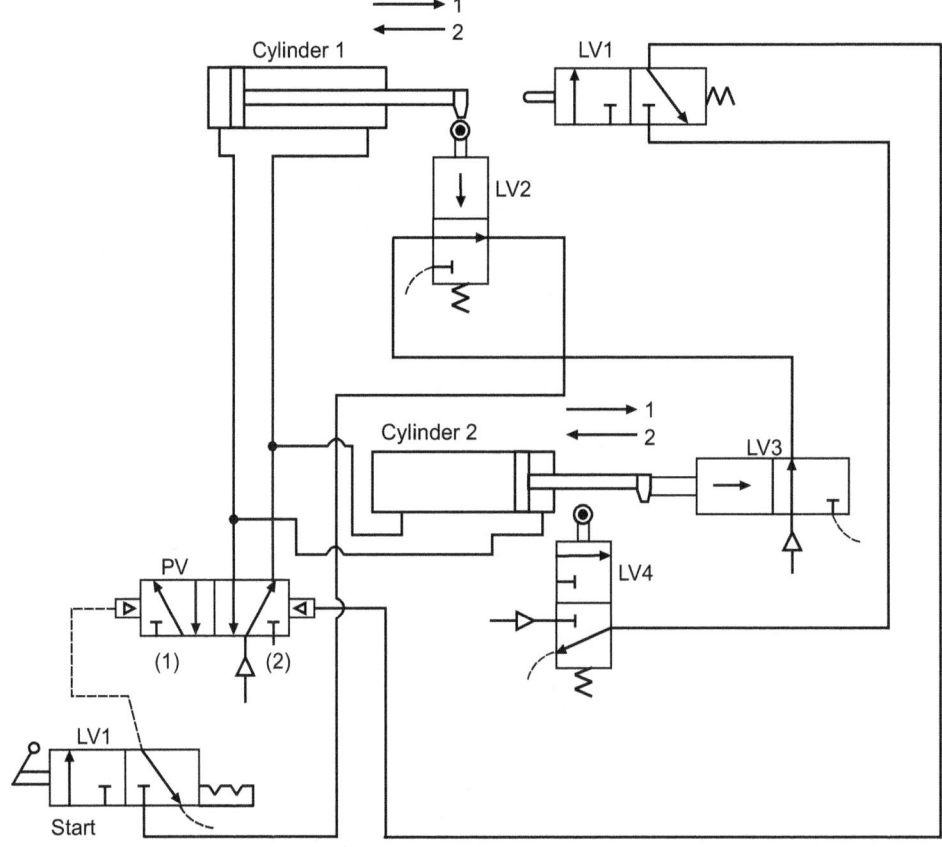

Fig. 5.102: Sequence circuit (A+, B−, A−, B+)

5.38 APPLICATIONS OF PNEUMATICS IN LOW COST AUTOMATION AND INDUSTRIAL AUTOMATION

Pneumatic control is one of the control devices used in modern industries for automation. Almost any mechanical task that we come across can be achieved pneumatically. Compressed air can be made available in plenty, survives safety in any environment and is faster than any other fluid. Air is used in variety of applications. Some of them are discussed here.

1. Rotary Transfer Machines: Transfer machines are used to perform several successive operations of the same part automatically. Each operation is performed at a specific station and a part is transferred automatically from one station to next. At each station air cylinder or actuators are used. Pneumatic systems are used in transfer mechanisms, part orientation devices in this type as well as in line type of transfer machines. Fig. 5.103 shows a rotary transfer machine.

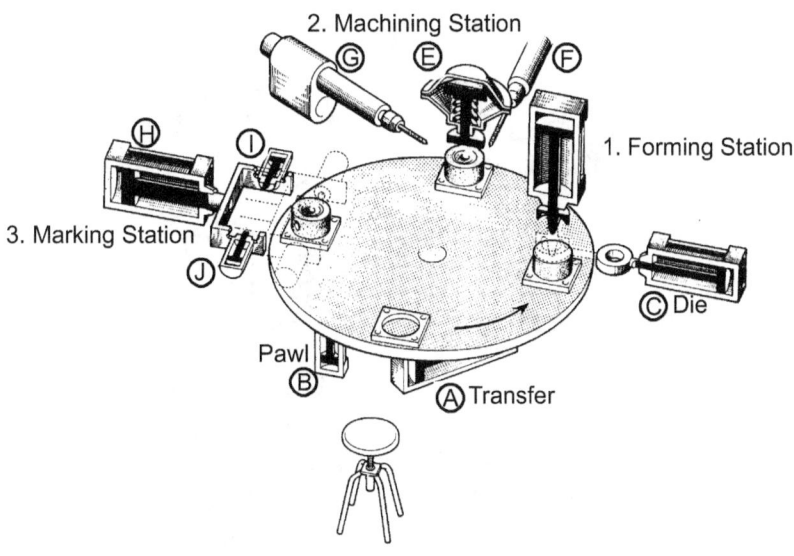

Fig. 5.103

2. Bernoulli Vacuum Lifters : Compressed air creates vacuum for the lifter assembly shown in Fig. 5.104 using multiple nozzle ejectors.

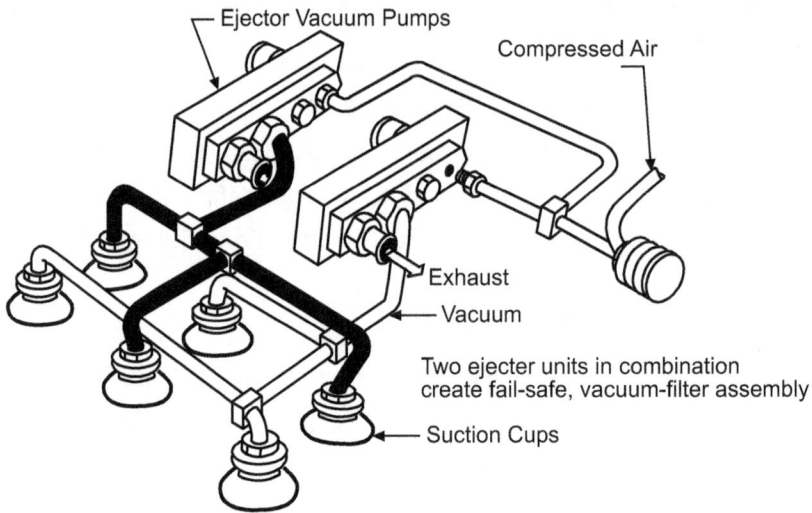

Fig. 5.104

3. Use of Pneumatics for Clamping: Single acting cylinders are commonly used for clamping applications. Various arrangements for clamping work pieces before machinery are shown in Fig. 5.105 (a).

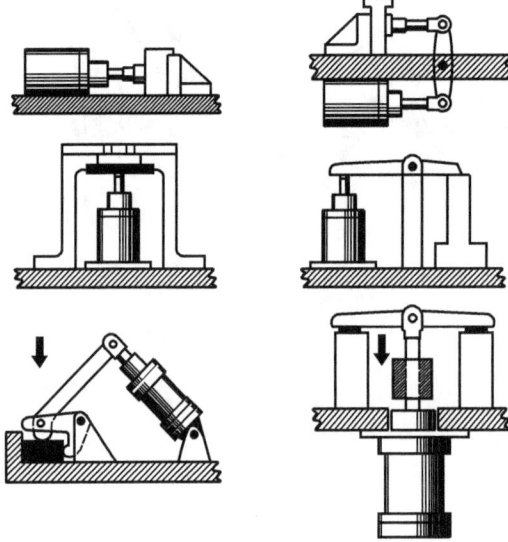

Fig. 5.105 (a)

In fixtures for clamping parts, pneumatic cylinders are used for quick operation. First some cylinders locate the work (casting) on the fixture. Only then clamping cylinders will operate and clamp the work. Fig. 5.105 (b).

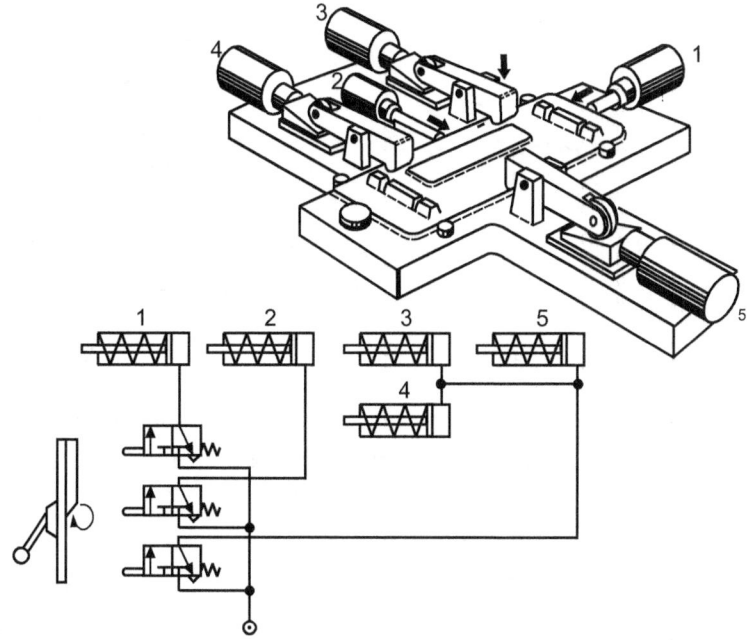

Fig. 5.105 (b)

4. **Work Feeding:** In Fig. 5.106 in magazine work pieces are kept. The cylinder on the left side is actuated where its cylinder pushes the bottommost part to feed the roller and returns back to push the next part. Workpieces are thus fed to the machine or conveyors for further work.

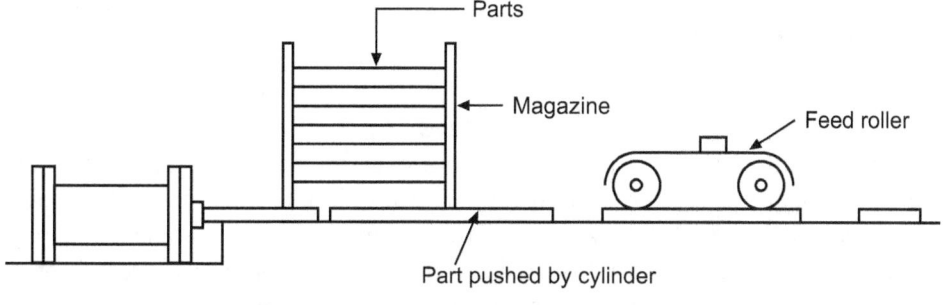

Fig. 5.106

5. Uses of pneumatic system in presses, jacks, and for forming punching operations are already discussed in the chapters.

6. **Measurement and Inspection:** The measuring head of pneumatic length measuring attachment (shown in Fig. 5.107) is swung into working position by a pneumatic positioning unit on a grinding machine.

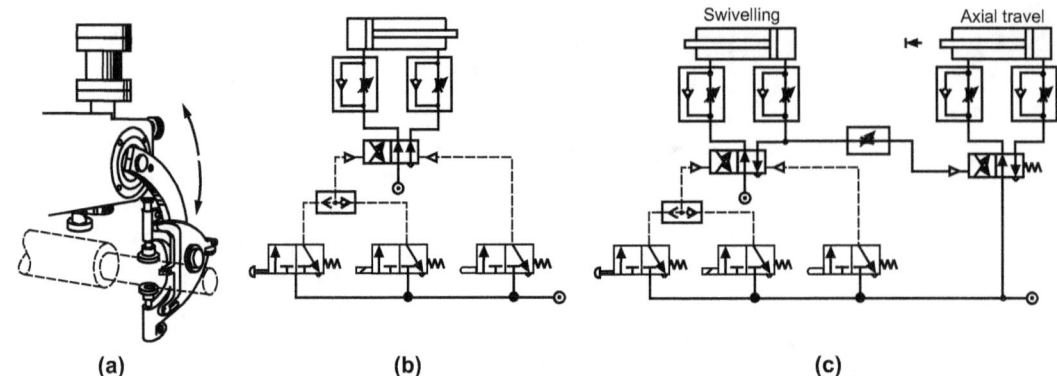

Fig. 5.107

7. Pneumatic Hand Tools: Fig. 5.108 (a) and (b) show pneumatic hand tools used in industries. For hammering, riveting, driller the tools are used. For assembly operations pneumatic screw drivers, nut runners are widely used.

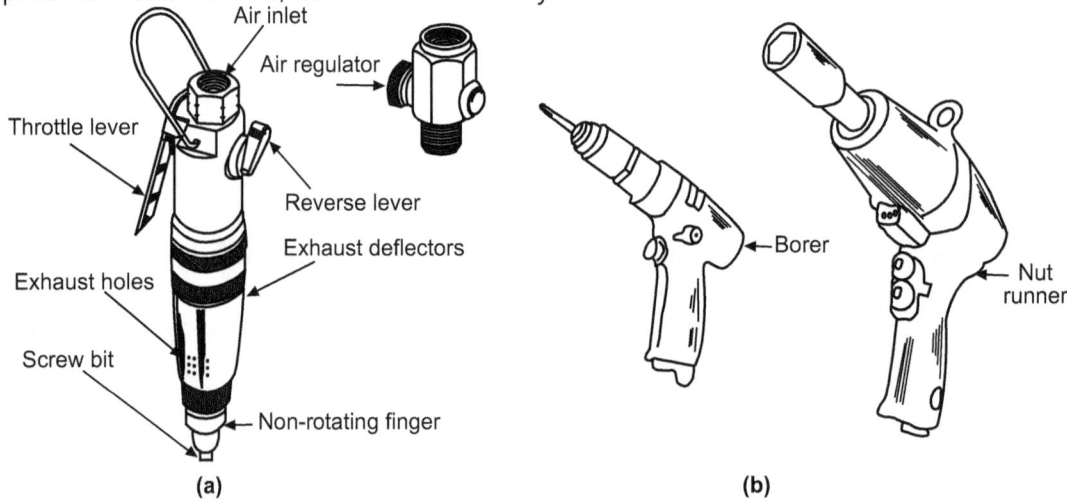

Fig. 5.108

Compressed air, though used for most common processes, is at its best in an assembly line, machine shop, foundry shop, wood and timber processing, etc. to tackle the problems of work feeding, handling and manipulating. Pneumatic power applied to industrial automations are summarised as: Material handling (e.g. lifter, hoist, cranes, etc.), food processing industry (e.g. bottling, warping, etc.), packing industry (special machines for packing different kinds of product, cartoon folding), assembly (e.g., screwing, press fitting, hammering, rivetting etc.), pressing industry (e.g. locating and clamping sheets, for light presses), foundry industry (e.g. full and semiautomatic moulding machines, fetting, tilting of furnace, opening and closing of doors, etc.), automatic machine (e.g. for holding, griping and feeding the components and other auxilliary application), printing industry (for feeding the mixing of concrete ingredients from hopper, handling etc.), agriculture and agro industries (e.g. for automatic tillers, husking, etc.), mining (e.g. for boring, shoveling, etc.)

5.39 Instructions For Selection Of Pneumatic Components

5.39.1 General Instructions for selection of Pneumatic components

1. General guidelines on the installation, use, and maintenance of Pneumatic Component (viz. Valves, FRLs (Filters, Pressure Regulators, and Lubricators), Vacuum products and related accessory components) are as follows.

2. **Fail-Safe:** Valves, FRLs, Vacuum products and their related components can and do fail without warning for many reasons. Design all systems and equipment in a fail-safe mode, so that failure of associated valves, FRLs or Vacuum products will not endanger persons or property.

3. **Relevant International Standards:** For a good guide to the application of a broad spectrum of pneumatic fluid power devices one can refer: ISO 4414 : 1998, Pneumatic Fluid Power – General Rules Relating to Systems. See www.iso.org for ordering information.

4. **Distribution:** Provide a copy of this safety guide to each person that is responsible for selection, installation, or use of Valves, FRLs or Vacuum products.

5. **User Responsibility:** Due to the wide variety of operating conditions and applications for valves, FRLs, and vacuum products of specific manufactures and its distributors do not represent or warrant that any particular valve, FRL or vacuum product is suitable for any specific end use system. This safety guide does not analyze all technical parameters that must be considered in selecting a product. The user, through its own analysis and testing, is solely responsible for:

- Making the final selection of the appropriate valve, FRL, Vacuum component, or accessory.
- Assuring that all user's performance, endurance, maintenance, safety, and warning requirements are met and that the application presents no health or safety hazards.
- Complying with all existing warning labels and / or providing all appropriate health and safety warnings on the equipment on which the valves, FRLs or Vacuum products are used; and,
- Assuring compliance with all applicable government and industry standards.

6. **Safety Devices:** Safety devices should not be removed, or defeated.

7. **Warning Labels:** Warning labels should not be removed, painted over or otherwise obscured.

8. **Additional Questions:** Call the appropriate parker technical service department if you have any questions or require any additional information.

5.39.2 Product Selection Instructions

1. **Flow Rate:** The flow rate requirements of a system are frequently the primary consideration when designing any pneumatic system. System components need to be able to provide adequate flow and pressure for the desired application.

2. **Pressure Rating:** Never exceed the rated pressure of a product. Consult product labeling, Pneumatic Division catalogs or the instruction sheets supplied for maximum pressure ratings.

3. **Temperature Rating:** Never exceed the temperature rating of a product. Excessive heat can shorten the life expectancy of a product and result in complete product failure.

4. **Environment:** Many environmental conditions can affect the integrity and suitability of a product for a given application. Pneumatic products are designed for use in general purpose industrial applications. If these products are to be used in unusual circumstances such as direct sunlight and/or corrosive or caustic environments, such use can shorten the useful life and lead to premature failure of a product.

5. **Lubrication and Compressor Carryover:** Some modern synthetic oils can and will attack nitrile seals. If there is any possibility of synthetic oils or greases migrating into the pneumatic components check for compatibility with the seal materials used. Consult the factory or product literature for materials of construction.

6. **Polycarbonate Bowls and Sight Glasses:** To avoid potential polycarbonate bowl failures:

- Do not locate polycarbonate bowls or sight glasses in areas where they could be subject to direct sunlight, impact blow, or temperatures outside of the rated range.
- Do not expose or clean polycarbonate bowls with detergents, chlorinated hydrocarbons, keytones, esters or certain alcohols.
- Do not use polycarbonate bowls or sight glasses in air systems where compressors are lubricated with fire resistant fluids such as phosphate ester and di-ester lubricants.

7. **Chemical Compatibility:** For more information on plastic component chemical compatibility refer standards published by specific manufacturer under consideration.

8. **Product Rupture:** Product rupture can cause death, serious personal injury, and property damage.

- Do not connect pressure regulators or other Pneumatic Division products to bottled gas cylinders.
- Do not exceed the maximum primary pressure rating of any pressure regulator or any system component.
- Consult product labeling or product literature for pressure rating limitations.

5.39.3 Product Assembly and Installation Instructions

1. **Component Inspection:** Prior to assembly or installation a careful examination of the valves, FRLs or vacuum products must be performed. All components must be checked for correct style, size, and catalog number. DO NOT use any component that displays any signs of nonconformance.

2. Installation Instructions: Parker published Installation Instructions must be followed for installation of Parker valves, FRLs and vacuum components. These instructions are provided with every company's product.

3. Air Supply: The air supply or control medium supplied to Valves, FRLs and Vacuum components must be moisture-free if ambient temperature can drop below freezing.

4. Fail Safe : Cylinder products can and do fail without warning for many reasons. All systems and equipment should be designed in a fail-safe mode so that if the failure of a cylinder product occurs people and property won't be endangered.

5. Distribution : Provide a free copy of this safety guide to each person responsible for selecting or using cylinder products. Do not select or use. The Company's cylinders without thoroughly reading and understanding this safety guide as well as the specific Manufacturer's / Company publications for the products considered or selected.

6. User Responsibility : Due to very wide variety of cylinder applications and cylinder operating conditions.

The specific Manufacturer/Company does not warrant that any particular cylinder is suitable for any specific application. This safety guide does not analyze all technical parameters that must be considered in selecting a product. The hydraulic and pneumatic cylinders outlined in this catalog are designed to The Company's design guidelines and do not necessarily meet the design guideline of other agencies such as American Bureau of Shipping, ASME Pressure Vessel Code etc. The user, through its own analysis and testing, is solely responsible for:

- Making the final selection of the cylinders and related accessories.
- Determining if the cylinders are required to meet specific design requirements as required by the Agency(s) or industry standards covering the design of the user's equipment.
- Assuring that the user's requirements are met, OSHA requirements are met, and safety guidelines from the applicable agencies such as but not limited to ANSI are followed and that the use presents no health or safety hazards.
- Providing all appropriate health and safety warnings on the equipment on which the cylinders are used.

5.39.4 Cylinder and Accessories Selection

1. Seals : Part of the process of selecting a cylinder is the selection of seal compounds. Before making this selection, consult the "seal information page(s)" of the publication for the series of cylinders of interest. The application of cylinders may allow fluids such as cutting fluids, wash down fluids etc. to come in contact with the external area of the cylinder. These fluids may attack the piston rod wiper and or the primary seal and must be taken into account when selecting and specifying seal compounds.

Dynamic seals will wear. The rate of wear will depend on many operating factors. Wear can be rapid if a cylinder is mis-aligned or if the cylinder has been improperly serviced. The user must take seal wear into consideration in the application of cylinders.

2. Piston Rods : Possible consequences of piston rod failure or separation of the piston rod from the piston include, but are not limited to are:

- Piston rod and or attached load thrown off at high speed.
- High velocity fluid discharge.
- Piston rod extending when pressure is applied in the piston retract mode.

Piston rods or machine members attached to the piston rod may move suddenly and without warning as a consequence of other conditions occurring to the machine such as, but not limited to:

- Unexpected detachment of the machine member from the piston rod.
- Failure of the pressurized fluid delivery system (hoses, fittings, valves, pumps, compressors) which maintain cylinder position.
- Catastrophic cylinder seal failure leading to sudden loss of pressurized fluid.
- Failure of the machine control system.

Follow the recommendations of the specific manufacturer's catalogue for selection of "Piston Rod Selection Chart and Data" in the publication for the series of cylinders of interest. The suggested piston rod diameter in these charts must be followed in order to avoid piston rod buckling.

The piston rod to piston and the stud to piston rod threaded connections are secured with an anaerobic adhesive. The strength of the adhesive decreases with increasing temperature. Cylinders which can be exposed to temperatures above +250°F (+121°C) are to be ordered with a non studded piston rod and a pinned piston to rod joint.

3. Cushions : Cushions should be considered for cylinder applications when the piston velocity is expected to be over 4 inches/second.

Cylinder cushions are normally designed to absorb the energy of a linear applied load. A rotating mass has considerably more energy than the same mass moving in a linear mode. Cushioning for a rotating mass application should be review by our engineering department.

4. Cylinder Mountings : Some cylinder mounting configurations may have certain limitations such as but not limited to minimum stroke for side or foot mounting cylinders or pressure de-ratings for certain mounts. Carefully review the catalog for these types of restrictions.

Always mount cylinders using the largest possible high tensile alloy steel socket head cap screws that can fit in the cylinder mounting holes and torque them to the manufacturer's recommendations for their size.

HYDRAULICS AND PNEUMATICS — PNEUMATICS

5. Port Fittings : Hydraulic cylinders applied with meter out or deceleration circuits are subject to intensified pressure at piston rod end.

The rod end pressure is approximately equal to: operating pressure x effective cap end area effective rod end piston area Contact your connector supplier for the pressure rating of individual connectors.

6. Cleanliness : It is an important consideration, and cylinders are shipped with the ports plugged to protect them from contaminants entering the ports. These plugs should not be removed until the piping is to be installed. Before making the connection to the cylinder ports, piping should be thoroughly cleaned to remove all chips or burrs which might have resulted from threading or flaring operations.

SOLVED EXAMPLES

Example 5.12: *Draw a circuit for the following conditions. The piston rod of a double acting cylinder is to advance when 3/2 way push button valve is actuated manually. The cylinder is to remain advanced until a second valve is actuated. The signal of the second valve can only take effect after the first valve has been released. The cylinder is to then return to the initial position. The cylinder is to remain in the initial position until a new start signal is given. The speed of the cylinder is to be adjustable in both directions. Explain the above circuit* **(May 2004)**.

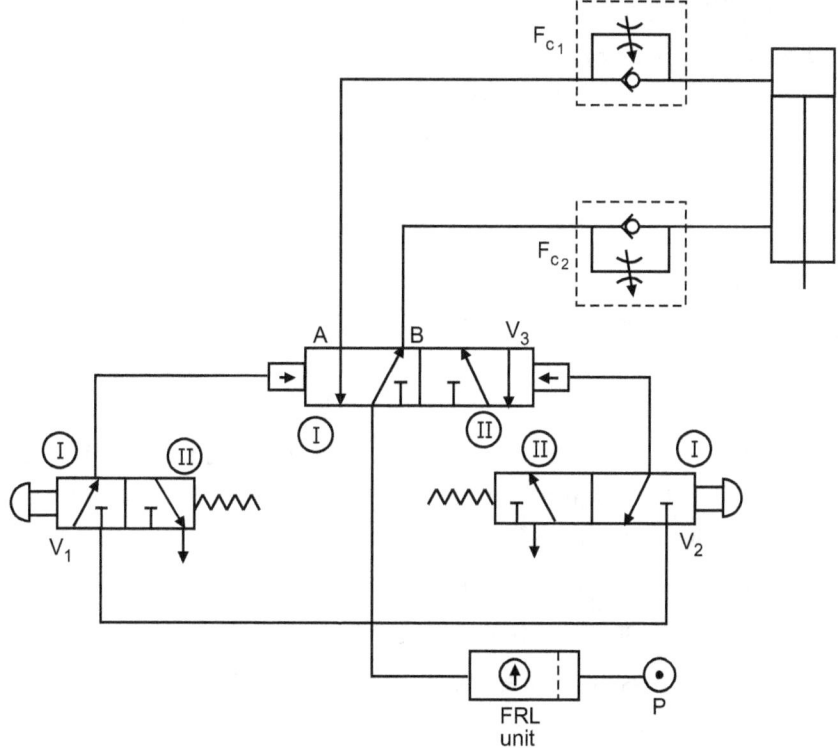

Fig. 5.109

Solution:

1. Cylinder is in retracted position.
2. Firstly actuate valve V_1, then air will pass through position (II) towards the left side of valve V_3 and it is actuated, shifted to position (II).
3. Then the air will pass through position (II) and through FC_1 and enter into the left side of the cylinder. This will give the forward motion of the rod and its speed can be adjusted by using the flow control valve FC_1.
4. During the remaining half cycle of operation till V_2 is actuated the cylinder will advance.
5. Once the signal from V_2 is obtained, at the same time V_1 valve is released. This will result into valve V_1 getting into position (I).
5. Then, air will pass through valve FC_2 to the right side of the cylinder until it gets retracted fully.
6. Again a second cycle gets started by the actuating valve V_1 while simultaneously releasing valve V_2.

Example 5.13: *A pneumatic cylinder is to be operated to and fro continuously. The cylinder returns after a delay of time, after reaching the completely extended position. The forward motion commences immediately after the cylinder is completely retracted. The continuous motion is interrupted by knob operated valve so that the cylinder completely retracts and then the continuous operation stops. Develop a pneumatic circuit for this purpose.* **(Dec. 2002)**

Solution:

- The compressed air supply is connected to the circuit through both sides of the manually operated directional control valve (DCV) (7) and the normally open 4/2 DCV (2).
- The cylinder shown is in retracted position which is operated using a pilot operated DCV (5). In this position, the piston rod actuates the 3/2 operated DCV (4), which applies pilot pressure to the valve (5) while the right side pilot is connected to the exhaust.
- Valve (5) admits compressed air on the bank end of the cylinder while the rod end is connected to the exhaust, which causes extension of the cylinder.
- At the end of the extension stroke, the piston rod actuates 3/2 roller tip operated DCV (3), which connects the air supply to the right side of the pilot valve (5) through a time delay valve (6).

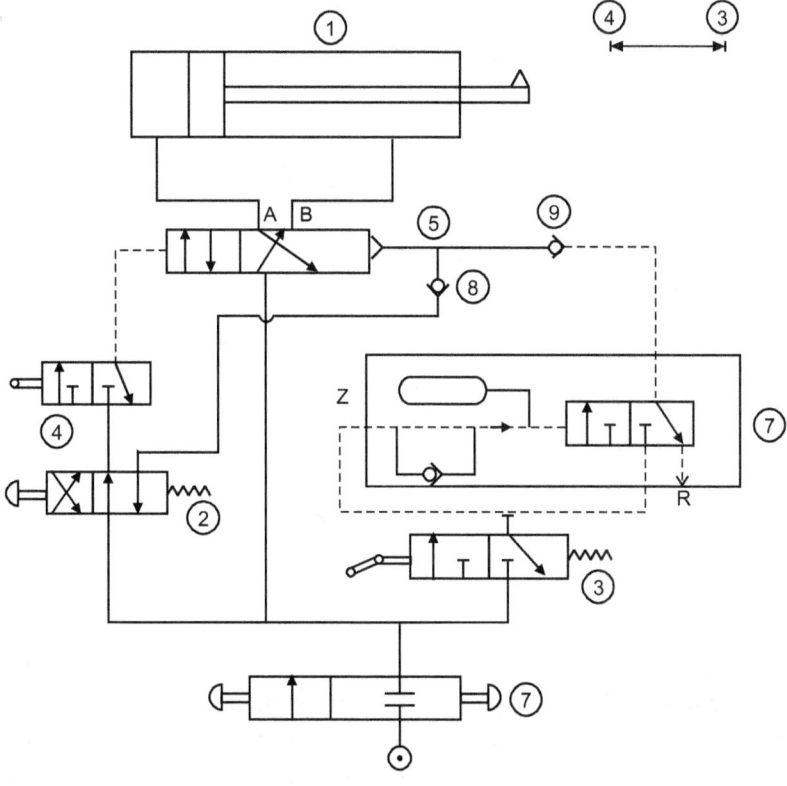

Fig. 5.110

- Due to this valve there is a time lag before which the actual supply is given to the valve (5) during which the cylinder remains in its extended position. And at the end of this time lag, valve (5) is operated due to signal from the time delay valve (6) with the left hand side pilot signal connected stroke of the cylinder and then the cycle is repeated automatically as long as valve (2) is in open position.

- With the operation of the push button of valve (2) the automatic operation of the cylinder is interrupted and the cylinder is completely retracted due to compressed air supply to the right hand side pilot of valve (5) and the left hand side is being connected to exhaust through valve (2).

- With the retraction of cylinder, valve (4) is actuated and the circuit again comes into operation with the release of push button of valve (2).

- The non-return valve (NRV) (8) prevents the connection of the time delay valve signal to the exhaust and allows compressed air pressure to the right side pilot of valve (5) when valve (2) has been actuated for interruption of the circuit.

- And NRV (9) prevents the right side pilot signal from going to the exhaust through the time delay valve (6) when valve (2) is operated for circuit interruption.

Example 5.14: Draw a typical circuit showing the control of a double acting cylinder remotely operated through the use of an air pilot operated directional control valve.

(May 2003)

Solution:

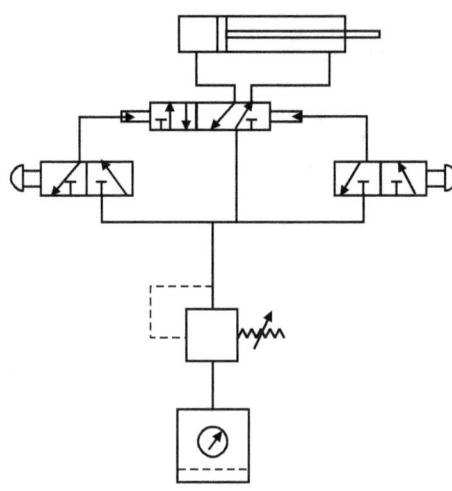

Fig. 5.111

Example 5.15: The automatic door of a bus is operated by a double acting cylinder. Both the opening and closing of the door is performed with a selector switch. The time duration for which the door is kept open, is decided by the bus driver. The speed of closing and opening the door is adjustable. Draw the pneumatic circuit. **(May 2009)**

Solution: Pneumatic circuit:

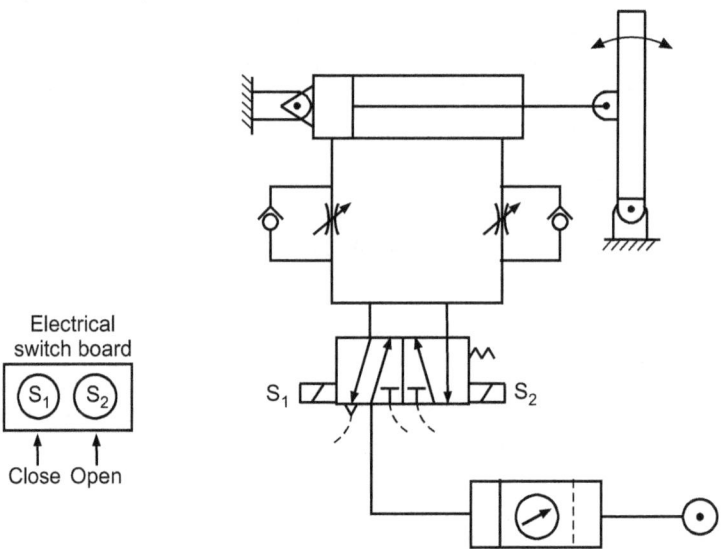

Fig. 5.112: Circuit for automatic door opening

HYDRAULICS AND PNEUMATICS

Example 5.16: *A pneumatic cylinder is needed to press fit a pin to a hole. Design a circuit diagram with a precondition that while actuating, both the hands of the operator should be engaged.* **(Dec. 2008)**

Solution: Pneumatic circuit according to given condition:

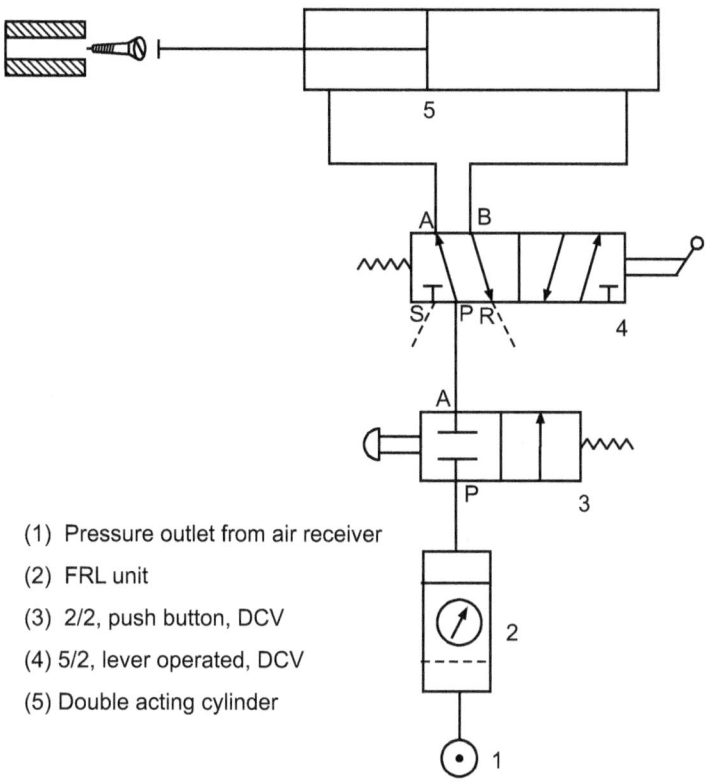

(1) Pressure outlet from air receiver
(2) FRL unit
(3) 2/2, push button, DCV
(4) 5/2, lever operated, DCV
(5) Double acting cylinder

Fig. 5.113

In normal position of valve (4) and actuated position of valve (3), we get retraction motion of cylinder (5). When we actuated valves (4) and (3), then we get forward motion of cylinder (5) which presses the pin into hole.

Example 5.17: *A pneumatic cylinder is used in a machine. The operation of the machine is such that the cylinder is to be continuously operated to and fro. Draw a pneumatic circuit which will operate the cylinder as desired. The operation of the cylinder can be stopped by pressing the knob of a 3/2 direction control valve. The cylinder should completely retract and then stop. (Make suitable assumptions if required and do not use solenoid operated valves).*

(May 2007)

Solution:

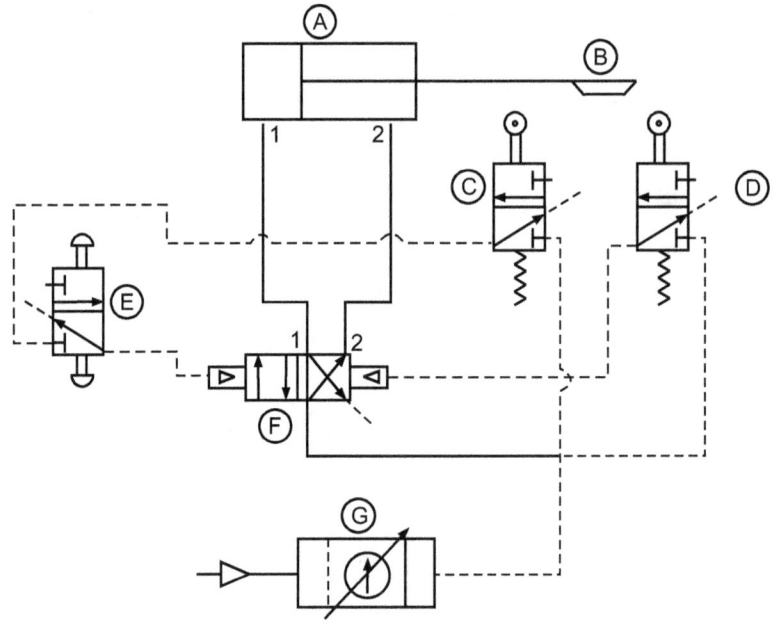

Fig. 5.114: Desired pneumatic circuit

List of components used:
- (A) Pneumatic cylinder
- (B) Cam
- (C) 3/2, roller operated, DCV (D) 3/2 roller operated DCV
- (E) 3/2, manually operated (F) 4/2, pilot operated, DCV
- (G) FRL unit (filter, regulator, lubricator)

Example 5.18: *The two pneumatic cylinders A_1 and A_2 are used in a machine. The sequence of operations is as follows:*

(i) *Cylinder A_1 advances completely after pressing the knob of a 3/2 direction control valve.*

(ii) *Cylinder A_2 advances completely.*

(iii) *Cylinder A_1 retracts.*

(iv) *Cylinder A_2 retracts.*

Develop a pneumatic circuit for this application. Do not use solenoid operated valves.

(Dec. 2009)

Solution: Pneumatic sequence circuit:

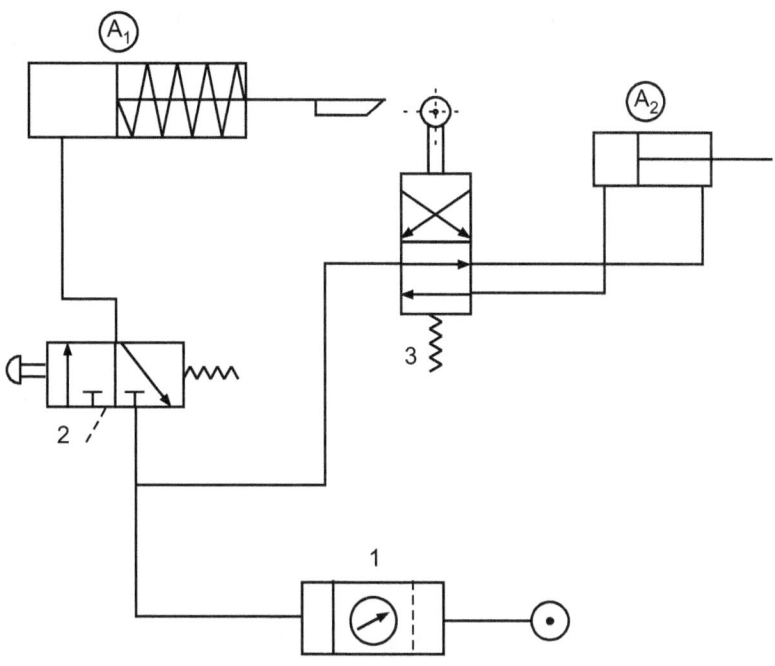

Fig. 5.115

Initially A_1 and A_2 are in retraction position. As the knob of 3/2 DCV (2) is pressed, the air enters in A_1 blind end and extends during this, can provided on rod actuates 4/2 DCV (3), air enters in blind end of A_2 which advances. When the force on the knob of 3/2 valve is released, A_1 as well as A_2 retracts.

Example 5.19: *A pneumatic cylinder is to be continuously moved to and fro. The motion is to be started by operating the knob of a direction control valve. The continuous motion is interrupted by operating knob of another direction control valve. The cylinder should stop immediately after pressing this knob. Develop a suitable pneumatic circuit for this application using standard symbols.* ***(Dec. 2009)***

Solution: Circuit according to the requirement:

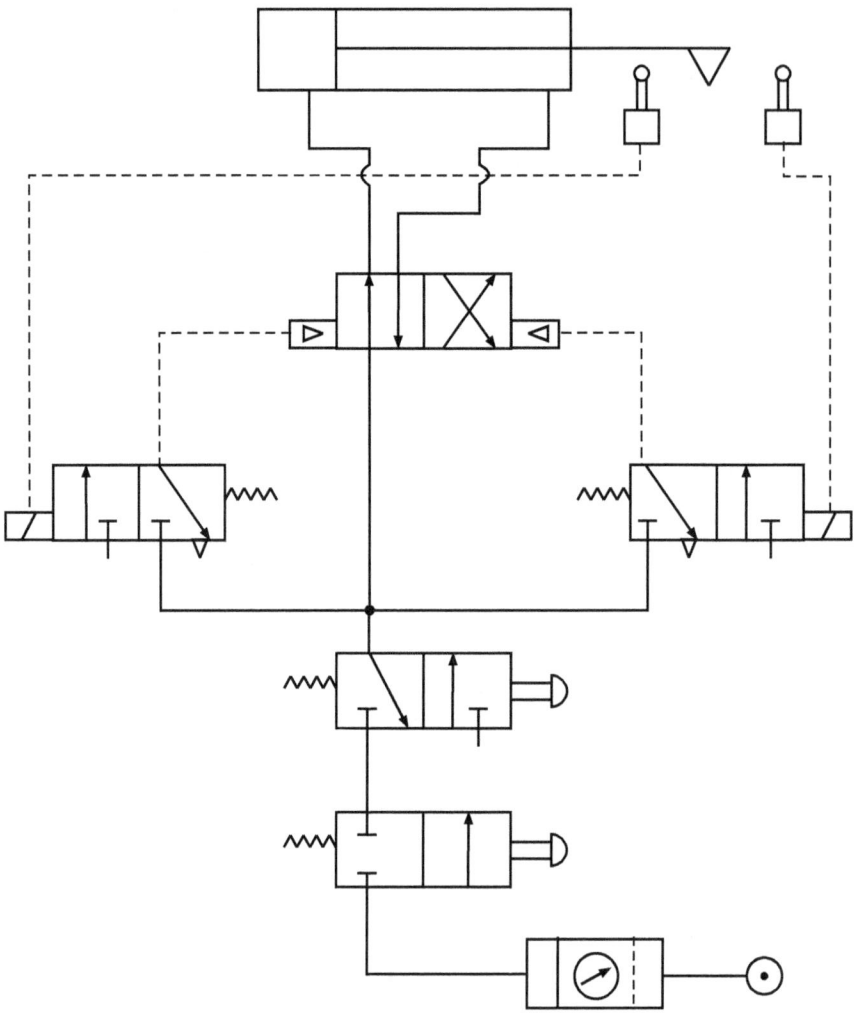

Fig. 5.116: Pneumatic circuit for automatic to and fro motion of cylinder

Example 5.20: *A carton weighing 25 kg is to be lifted through a height of 200 mm. It has to be then pushed on to a conveyor. The pushing length required is 300 mm. Compressed air is available for this facility at 5 kg/cm².*

The sequence is that the lifting cylinder should start first to lift the weight and then the pushing cylinder to push the carton. Once the carton is pushed through a distance of 300 mm, the pushing cylinder retracts and then only the lifting cylinder retracts.

Design and draw the circuit. **(May 2009)**

Solution: Pneumatic sequence circuit:

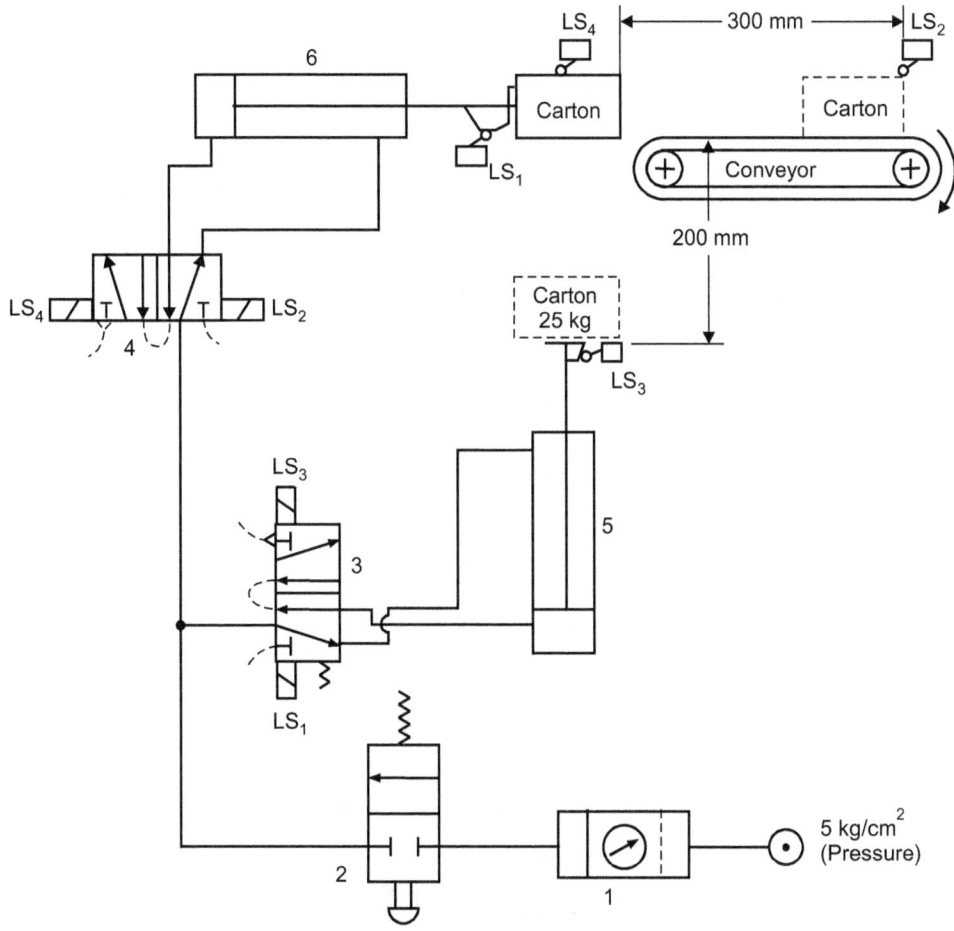

Fig. 5.117: Pneumatic circuit according to the requirement

(1) FRL unit
(2) 2/2 DCV, push button operated
(3) 5/2 solenoid operated DCV
(4) 5/2 solenoid operated DCV
(5) Double acting pneumatic cylinder
(6) Double acting pneumatic cylinder

For starting the circuit operation, first operate valve (2) by pushing button. Air enters into rod end side of cylinder (5) and cylinder (6). Both cylinders are in refraction motion. At the end of refraction motion, LS_1 and LS_3 are actuated.

For cylinder (5), Piston area $= \dfrac{\text{Force}}{\text{Pressure}} = \dfrac{25}{5}$ $\therefore \dfrac{\pi}{4} D^2 = 5 \text{ cm}^2$

$\therefore \qquad D^2 = \dfrac{5 \times 4}{\pi} = \dfrac{20}{\pi}$

∴ Piston diameter = D = 2.525 cm = 25.23 mm

and Stroke of cylinder = L = 200 mm

For cylinder (6) also same dimensions will be preferred.

Example 5.21: *Draw typical circuits of different speed regulating methods used in pneumatic circuits.* **(Dec. 2009)**

Solution: Speed control methods in pneumatics:

(1) Speed regulation of single acting cylinder:

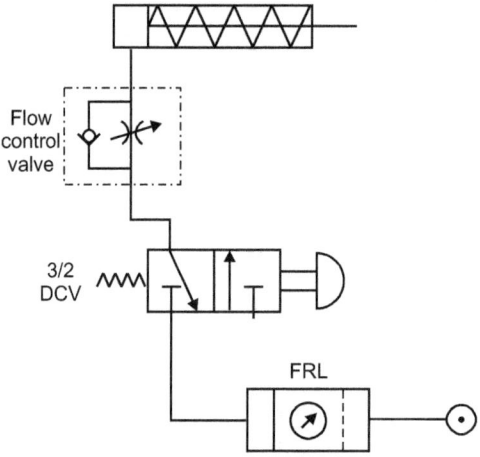

Fig. 5.118: Speed regulating circuit

(2) Speed regulation of double acting cylinder:

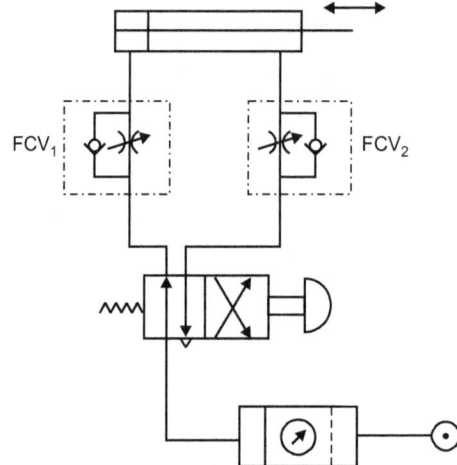

Fig. 5.119: Speed regulation of double acting cylinder

Example 5.22: Sequential operations of two pneumatic cylinders are required as follows:

(i) Cylinder 'A' extends,   (ii) Cylinder 'B' extends,

(iii) Cylinder 'B' retracts,   (iv) Cylinder 'A' retracts.

Develop a pneumatic circuit using a starting valve, pilot operated 4/2 directional control valve and cam / roller operated valves to maintain proper sequence. Do not use solenoid-operated valves. **(May 2010)**

Solution:

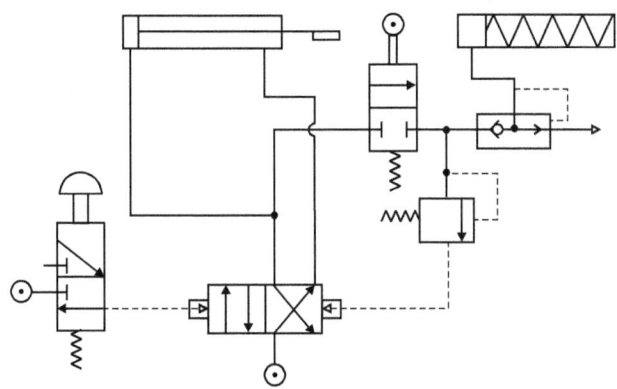

Fig. 5.120

Example 5.23: Study the pneumatic circuit shown in Fig. 5.121 and explain the operation of double acting cylinder. What happens if there is sudden built up of pressure, due to obstruction occurring in between during the advance of piston. Comment on the result. Explain the purpose of the vent item no. '6' of the circuit. **(May 2010)**

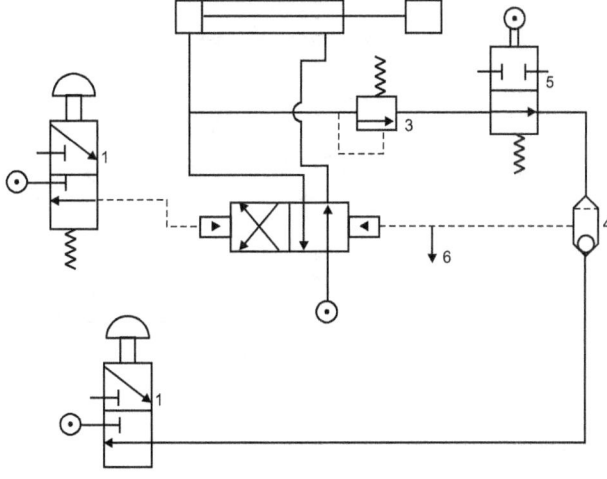

Fig. 5.121

Solution: As push button no. 1 gets pressed, the pressurized air will apply pilot pressure on the direction control valve and DCV will shift to its left envelope. Pressured air through DCV will be given to the blank side of the cylinder and extension of the piston rod will start. At the end of the extension stroke, the piston rod will push the valve no. 5 and will disconnect the line.

As push button no. 2 gets pressed, the pressurized air will apply pilot pressure on DCV and it will shift to its right envelope. Pressurized air through DCV will be given to the rod end side of the cylinder which will start the retraction of the piston. Like wise extension and retraction of double acting cylinder gets complete.

If there is sudden built-up of pressure, due to an obstruction occurring in between, during the advance of piston, then the rise of pressure will open the relief valve and through valve no. 5 it will be given to vent 6.

Vent is provided to exhaust the excess air at the time of obstruction and the air for pilot operation is also exhausted through vent numbered 6.

At full load only high pressure low flow pump will operate.

Selection of high pressure low flow pump:

$$Q = 0.33 \text{ l.p.m.} \quad P = 66 \text{ bar}$$

Selection of high flow low pressure pump:

As total flow required during extension is 1.11 l.p.m. and out of that 0.33 l.p.m. is given by a high pressure pump, the remaining should by high flow pump,

$$Q = 1.11 - 0.33 = 0.78 \text{ l.p.m.} \quad P = 9 \text{ bar}$$

Example 5.24: *Analyze the circuit as shown in Fig. 5.122.* **(Dec. 2008)**

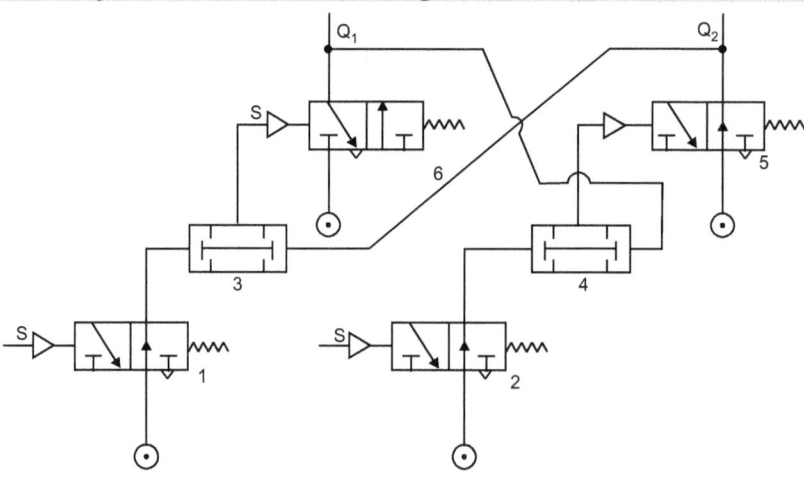

Fig. 5.122

Solution: Identification of circuit components:

(1), (6), (5) and (2) are 3/2, pilot operated DCV.

(3) and (4) are twin pressure valves ('AND' Gate).

In the given circuit twin pressure valves are used to give pilot signal for actuating valves (6) and (5).

Valve (3) compares the pressure signal from valve (1) and valve (5) and gives output as a pilot signal for valve (6). Similarly, valve (4) will compare the pressure signal from valve (2) and valve (6) and give output as pilot signal to valve (5).

5.40 Vacuum Measurement

The absence of matter. A space that contains air or gas that is at less that atmospheric pressure.

Pressure below the atmospheric pressure is referred to as vacuum pressure. The gage pressure is negative when we specify vacuum pressure. Absolute pressure, however, is certainly positive! It is possible to use, U tube manometers, Bourdon gages for the measurement of vacuum as long as it is not high vacuum. In the case of the U tube with mercury as the manometer liquid we can practically go all the way down to -760 mm mercury but there is no way of using it to measure vacuum pressures involving less than a fraction of a mm of mercury (also referred to as Torr – short for Torricelly). A U tube manometer can thus be used for rough measurement of vacuum. A Bourdon gage capable of measuring vacuum pressure will have the zero (zero gage pressure) somewhere in the middle of the dial with the pointer going below zero while measuring vacuum and the pointer going above zero while measuring pressures above the atmosphere. Again a bourdon gage can not be used for measurement of high vacuum. Now we discuss those instruments that are useful for measuring moderate and high vacuum ranging from, say 0.1 mm mercury to 10-6 mm mercury. Such low pressures (absolute pressures) are used in many applications and hence there is a need to measure such pressures.

2.40.1 McLeod Gage

McLeod gage is basically manometric method of measuring a vacuum pressure that is useful between 0.01 and 100 μm of mercury column. This range translates to absolute pressure in the range of 0.001 to 10 Pa. Note that this range will also translate to 10-8 to 10-4 bar. The principle of operation of the McLeod gage is as described below (refer Fig. 5.123).

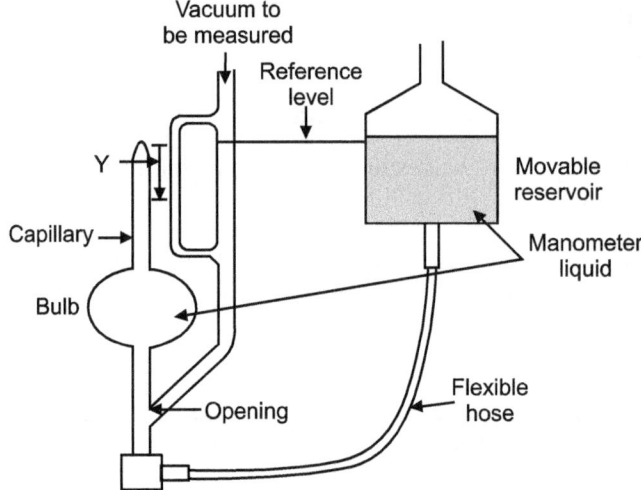

Fig. 5.123. Schematic of a McLeod gage

A known volume (V) of the gas at the vacuum pressure (p) given by the volume of the capillary, the bulb and the bottom tube up to the opening is trapped by lowering the movable reservoir down to the appropriate extent. It is then slowly raised till the level of the manometer liquid (usually mercury) in the movable reservoir is in line with the reference level marked on the stem of the forked tube. This operation compresses the trapped gas to a pressure (pc) equivalent to the head y indicated by the manometer as shown. The corresponding volume of the gas is given by the clear volume of the capillary $V_c = ay$ where a is the area of cross section of the capillary. The gage is exposed to the ambient and hence remains at the ambient temperature during this operation.

5.40.2 Pirani Gage

Another useful gage for measuring vacuum is the Pirani gage. The temperature of a heated resistance increases with a reduction of the background pressure. The rise in temperature changes its resistance just as we found in the case of RTD.

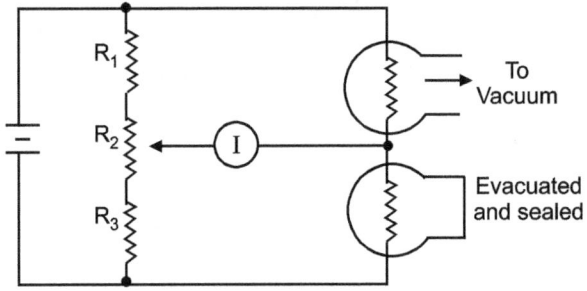

Fig. 5.124 : Schematic of a Pirani gage

As shown in Fig. 5.124 the Pirani gage consists of two resistances connected in one arm of a bridge. One of the resistors is sealed in after evacuating its container while the other is exposed to the vacuum space whose pressure is to be measured. Ambient conditions will affect both the resistors alike and hence the gage will respond to only the changes in the vacuum pressure that is being measured. The Pirani gage is calibrated such that the imbalance current of the bridge is directly related to the vacuum pressure being measured. The range of this gage is from 1 µm mercury to 1 mm mercury that corresponds to 0.1 – 100 Pa absolute pressure range.

5.40.3 Ionization Gage

Very high vacuum pressures (higher the vacuum, lower the absolute pressure) are measured using an ionization gage. Schematic of such a gage is shown in Fig. 5.125.

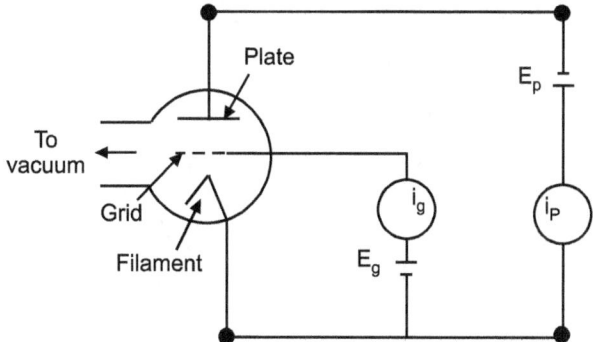

Fig. 5.125 : Schematic of a Ionization gage.

The ion gage is similar to a triode valve which was used in radio receivers built with vacuum tubes, before the advent of transistors. The gage consists of a heated cathode that emits electrons. These electrons are accelerated towards the grid, basically wire mesh, which is maintained at a potential positive with respect to the cathode. The high speed electrons suffer collisions with the molecules of the residual gas in the bulb (that is exposed to the vacuum space) and ionizes these gas molecules. The electrons move towards the grid and manifest in the form of grid current. The positive ions move towards the plate that is maintained at a potential negative with respect to the grid. These ions are neutralized at the plate and consequently we have the plate current.

5.41 Vacuum Pumps

Exactly how do we produce a vacuum? Many different kinds of vacuum pumps exist, each with their own application. The most common types of pumps are the rotary pump for reaching rough vacuum, and the diffusion pump for reaching high vacuum. These will be discussed first followed by other pumps. We can classify pumps in different ways; by their range of pressures, their means of operation, their cleanliness, their ability to pump a continuous gas flow, and their ability to pump different gases. Method of Operation Mechanical Pumps such as the rotary vane, Roots blower, and turbomolecular use rotating parts (macroscopic!) to reach vacuum.

5.41.1 Rotary Pump

Rotary vane pumps (usually called rotary pumps) take a volume of gas at a low pressure, compress it so that the pressure becomes slightly higher than atmospheric, and vent the gas to the atmosphere. They are very similar in principle to the ideal pump introduced in the previous chapter except that they are rotary. A typical rotary pump is shown in Fig. 5.126

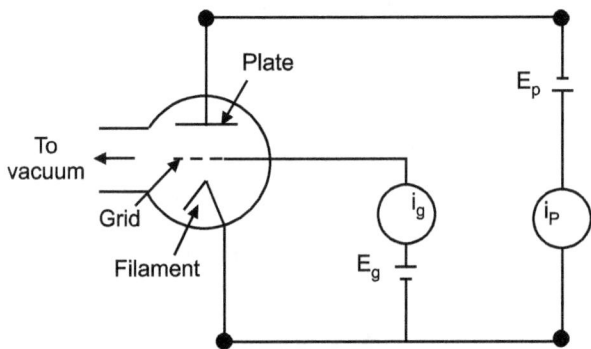

Fig. 5.126 : Rotary Mechanical Pump.

The vacuum chamber is connected to the inlet, and the pressure in region I is about the same as that of the chamber. Region I is an expanding volume. As the rotor moves it eventually traps a relatively large volume of gas at chamber pressure. In the diagram this is region II. This region is decreasing in volume. The rotor continues to move and region II is made accessible to the outlet valve (region III). Region III continues to be compressed in volume, and thus its pressure rises. Eventually the pressure exceeds atmospheric and the gas is expelled through the outlet valve and through the oil into the room. Usually the pumping speed for roughing pumps is given in L/min. Rotary pumps are available with speeds ranging from 0.25 to more than 80 L/s.

The pump is relatively cheap and mechanically sturdy. It can operate from atmospheric pressure down, and is thus used before many of the higher vacuum pumps. It is commonly referred to as a roughing pump (to get rough vacuum), a backing pump (back behind the diffusion pump), or a fore pump (before the diffusion pump).

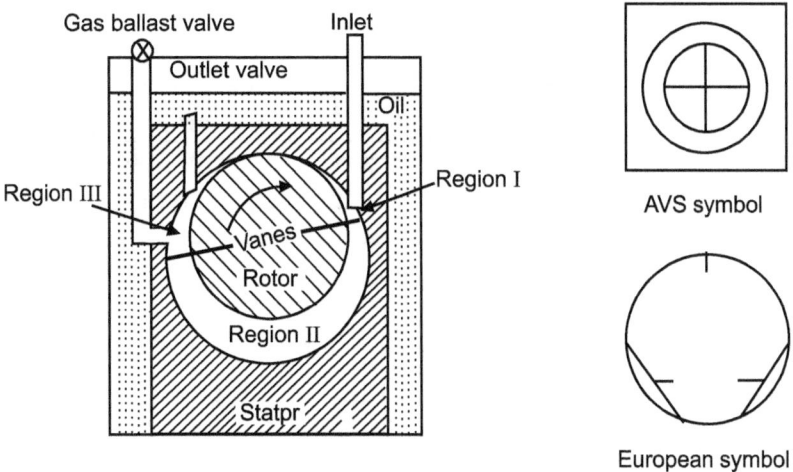

Fig. 5.127: Rotary Pump Speeds

Roughing pumps such as the rotary pump have a problem if they pump on a chamber that contains condensable vapors. The most common condensable vapor is water vapor. As the low pressure gas from the inlet is compressed, we may reach a pressure where the water vapor will condense into a liquid. When, upon compression in the pump, the partial pressure of the water vapor exceeds 32 Torr, the vapor condenses into liquid prior to the opening of the outlet valve. The liquid dilutes the oil, and may corrode the pump. For some vacuum applications there is a large vapor load such as freeze drying (water vapor), Chemical Vapor Deposition (HCl), or plasma etching (organics) and large quantities of condensable liquids are possible. To prevent the condensation in moderate vapor loads we use gas ballast. The gas ballast valve, GB, adds a small amount of dry gas such as nitrogen to region III. This reduces the amount of compression that the vapor undergoes and thus reduces the condensation problem. The ultimate pressure of the pump is not as low when we use gas ballast.

Other types of mechanical pumps are available that work on slightly different principles. These include rotary piston pumps, dry scroll pumps, and trochoid pumps. The rotary piston pump can have larger speeds, up to 500 liter/second.

Diffusion Pump (100 mT (throttled) to below 10-10 Torr)

In outline the diffusion pump is very simple refer Fig. 5.128. The pump consists of a cylinder called a "pumping stack". High purity oil at the bottom of the pump is heated and evaporates.

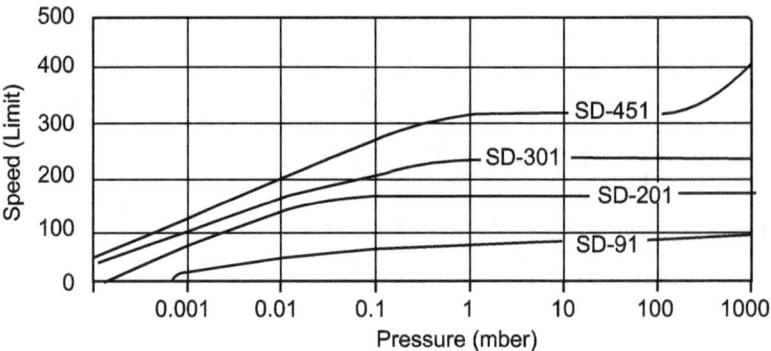

Fig. 5.128 : A Two Stage Diffusion Pump

The stack contains the oil, and when the oil leaves the stack it moves in a downward direction, colliding with gas molecules and driving them towards the bottom of the pump. At the bottom of the pump the gas pressure is high enough that a rotary pump can remove the gas to atmosphere. The oil vapor hits the sides of the pump that are cooled by water pipes, and the condensed oil runs to the bottom of the pump to be reheated.

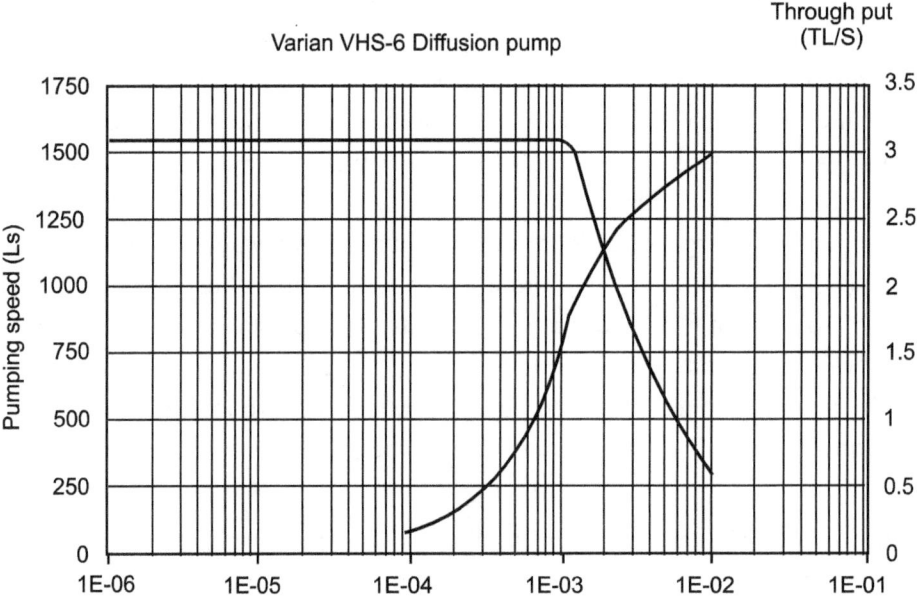

Fig. 5.129 : Speed and Throughput for Diffusion Pump

At the inlet to the diffusion pump the pressure must be low, well below 100 mTorr. At the outlet the pressure is much higher than at the inlet, typically as high as 600 mTorr. In modern pumps the working fluidis an oil, historically mercury was used. Under normal conditions the pressure at the inlet may be anywhere from 10-4 to 10-10 Torr, and the pressure at the outlet may be 1 mTorr, which means that the compression ration may be as high as 1010. The heater creates a vapor pressure of oil (or mercury) of about 1 to 3 Torr.

This heating is confined in the center of the pump, underneath the pumping stack. The oil is heated to a temperature of about 250C. At this temperature the heavy oils have reasonable high speeds of about 300 m/s. The hot vapor molecules move up the stack at high velocity where they are detected downwards by the shape of the exit nozzles in the stack.

The high-speed vapor jets shoot downwards toward the walls of the pump which are water cooled. Molecules arrive at the top of the pump randomly according to molecular flow. The vapor jets sweep the molecules down towards the ejector stage. Thus each vapor jet produces a pressure differential from above it to below it. The oil vapor condenses on the water-cooled walls and runs back to be heated again.

The vapor stream works because it imparts a preferred downward direction to the system molecules that it strikes. Because of the high temperature of the vapor, the molecules have a high average speed. In collisions between the oil vapor molecules and the system molecules both tend to move in the original direction of the oil vapor. Thus the system molecules are driven downwards where they eventually are removed by a mechanical pump.

When the inlet pressure of gas is too high the diffusion pump fails to operate. At high pressures the oil vapor will have a short mean free path and make several collisions before reaching the wall. The preferred direction of the oil vapor molecules are then lost and gas molecules will migrate backwards in the pump, from the higher pressures at the bottom of the diffusion pump towards the vacuum chamber. The gas molecules will also carry some of the oil vapor with them, contaminating the system. The critical value of inlet pressure is about 100 mTorr. Usually the critical pressure is specified at the output (foreline) because of the location of gauges. The maximum allowable foreline pressure may be in the range of 300 to 600 mTorr.

5.41.2 Other Mechanical Pumps

1. Root's Blower :

Roots blower, also called a booster pump, has highest pumping speeds but low compression ratio. It consist of two Fig.-eight rotors mounted on parallel shafts and rotating in opposite directions at speeds of about 3000 rpm. The Root's pump is a booster pump. It typically is found on a large system between a diffusion pump and a rotary pump. The rotary pump is permitted to operate in its high speed, high throughput pressure (typically above 0.1 Torr) and at the same time the diffusion pump is allowed to operate at its high speed, high throughput pressure (typically below 0.5 mTorr).

2. Turbo-Molecular Pump :

The turbomolecular pump or turbopump consists of a rotor assembly, a multi-bladed turbine which rotates at high speed (such as 50 000 rpm), which rotates in a stator assembly, a similar non-rotating turbine. A gas molecule which strikes the blades of either the rotor or stator is more likely, upon reection, to be ejected than to reenter the system. In order to produce an effective pump between 8 and 20 stages are used, half in the rotor and half in the stator.

3. Newer Mechanical Pumps :

With the growth of microelectronics and other applications requiring very clean, oil-free vacuum but with a high throughput of gas the manufacturers have begun to introduce oil-free mechanical pumps that operate from atmospheric down.

More sophisticated systems are used for most industrial applications, but the basic principle of cyclic volume removal is the same:

(a) Rotary vane pump, the most common
(b) Diaphragm pump, zero oil contamination
(c) Liquid ring high resistance to dust
(d) Piston pump, fluctuating vacuum
(e) Scroll pump, highest speed dry pump
(f) Screw pump (10 Pa)
(g) Wankel pump
(h) External vane pump
(i) Multistage Roots pump that combine several stages providing high pumping speed with better compression ratio
(j) Toepler pump
(k) Lobe pump
(l) Venturi vacuum pump (aspirator) (10 to 30 kPa)
(m) Steam ejector (vacuum depends on the number of stages, but can be very low)

Entrapment pumps may be cryopumps, which use cold temperatures to condense gases to a solid or adsorbed state, chemical pumps, which react with gases to produce a solid residue, or ionization pumps, which use strong electrical fields to ionize gases and propel the ions into a solid substrate. A cryomodule uses cryopumping viz. Ion pump, Cryopump, Sorption pump, Non-evaporative getter.

5.42 VACUUM SENSORS

In industry variety of Vacuum sensing technology are used, some of the important types are discussed below :

1. Capacitive Sensing Technology :

Capacitive sensing technology transmitters incorporate the same ceramic pressure measuring cell sensing technology found in high accuracy.

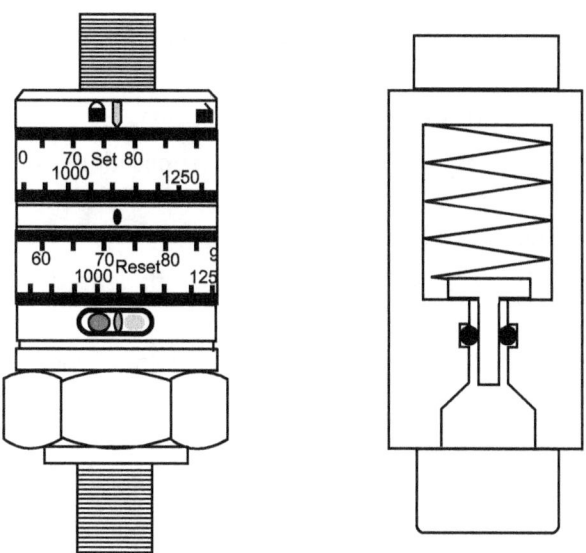

(a) Electronic pressure switch (b) Mechanical piston pressure switch

(No moving parts reduces wear and)   Piston movement can wear the sealing ring)

Fig. 5.130 : Capacitive sensing technology switches for vacuum measurement

The sensor's ceramic measuring cell is made of high purity aluminum oxide. The ceramic cell element resembles a plate capacitor with a reference electrode and measuring electrode placed 10 µm apart.

The capacitance is inversely proportional to the distance between the electrodes. If the distance changes by a small value because of an increase in pressure applied to the cell, the capacitance changes proportionately. The signal is then evaluated by a microprocessor.

Fig. 5.131

The sensor can be placed in direct contact with media, insuring reliable pressure detection in sanitary applications.

This can be used for sanitary and high temperature applications its pressure ranges from vacuum up to 363 psi.

(2) Piezoresistive sensing technology :

Such type of sensors are designed for pneumatic applications in robotics and material handling. The switches made up of these sensors precisely measure the full range of vacuum and pressure typical in these applications.

The silicon measuring cell is unaffected by liquids (e.g. condensed water) and deposits that might occur in the system.

This can be used for hydraulic and pneumatic applications where pressure ranges from vacuum up to 363 psi.

(3) Industrial Applications of Vacuum :

This is true of vacuum pumps and other vacuum components such as measuring devices and leak detectors, which are involved in many industrial applications. These include, among others, vacuum packaging of food evacuation and environment-friendly charging of refrigerators and air conditioners production of ultrapure high-strength metals evacuation of lamps and picture tubes manufacture of flat-panel displays.

Industrial vacuum applications range from mechanical handling (such as the manipulation of heavy and light items by suction pads) to the deposition of integrated electronic circuits on silicon chips. Obviously, vacuum requirements are as widely varied as the particular processes using vacuums. In the rough vacuum range from about one torr to near atmosphere, typical applications are mechanical handling, vacuum packing and forming, gas sampling, filtration, degassing of oils, concentration of aqueous solutions, impregnation of electrical components, distillation, and steel stream degassing.

At lower pressures down to about 10-4 torr, many metallurgical processes such as melting, casting, sintering, heat treatment, and brazing can derive benefit. Chemical processes such as vacuum distillation and freeze-drying also need this range of vacuum. Freeze-drying is used extensively in the pharmaceutical industry to prepare vaccines and antibiotics and to store skin and blood plasma. The food industry freeze-dries coffee mainly, although most foods can be stored without refrigeration after freeze-drying, and the technique is receiving widespread acceptance.

The pressure range down to about 10-6 torr is used for cryogenic (low-temperature) and electrical insulation. It is used in the production of lamps; television picture tubes, X-ray tubes; decorative, optical, and electrical thin-film coatings; and mass spectrometer leak detectors.

In thin-film coating, a metal or compound is evaporated under high vacuum from a source onto a base material or substrate. The base material is generally plastic for decorative coatings; glass for optical coatings; and glass ceramic, or silica for electrical coatings. Thickness of the film can vary from about 1/4 wavelength of visible light to 0.001 inches or more. In the optical field, antireflection coatings are deposited on lenses for cameras, telescopes, eyeglasses, and other optical devices, considerably reducing the amount of light reflected by the lenses and thus giving a brighter transmitted image.

To achieve vacuum high enough for thin-film coating and for other industrial uses requiring pressures down to 10-6 torr, a pumping system consisting of an oil-sealed rotary pump and a diffusion pump is used. The oil-sealed rotary pump (sometimes referred to as forepump) "roughs" the chamber down to a pressure of about 0.1 torr, after which the roughing valve is closed. The fore valve and high-vacuum baffle valve are then opened so that the chamber is evacuated by the diffusion pump and rotary pump in series.

EXERCISE

1. What are the fluids used in pneumatic systems ?
2. Why is air preferred in pneumatic systems ?
3. Compare pneumatic systems with electrical systems.
4. What are the various laws that govern compression and expansion of air ?
5. What are the advantages of pneumatic drive over hydraulic drives ?
6. Classify compressors.
7. What is the difference between single stage and double stage compressors ?
8. Describe various linear and rotary compressors.
9. A compressor has an output of 70 cm^3/s and the system requires 95 cm^3/s for 30 seconds. The initial working pressure is 7 bar. The pressure drop cannot drop below 5.5 bar. What receiver size is needed ? How long will it take to recharge the receiver if the demand decreases to 28 cm^3/s ?
10. What is the role of F.R.L. unit in pneumatic systems ?
11. Describe the various valves used in pneumatic systems.
12. Write a note on working and use of the sequence valve.
13. What is the purpose of providing a lubricator unit in pneumatic systems ?
14. Draw a neat sketch and explain the working of a typical regulator used in pneumatic installations.
15. Write short note on 'air preparation in pneumatic systems.'
16. What is the purpose of providing a quick exhaust valve in a pneumatic system ? Sketch a typical quick exhaust valve.
17. Classify different direction control valves used in pneumatics.

18. Draw a neat sketch of a typical 5-way 2-position direction control valve which is used to operate a large pneumatic cylinder.

19. Write note on Time delay valve and its application in pneumatic circuits.

20. What is a shuttle valve and two pressure valves ? Draw circuits using these valves.

21. Write notes on: (a) Pneumatic cylinders, (b) Motors.

22. Describe a vane motor with sketch.

23. What is the use of drawing pneumatic circuits ?

24. What is the position step diagram ? What is its use ?

25. Describe with an example the extensive use of pneumatics in industries.

26. Two air cylinders are used for operating a packing machine. The sequence of operations is as follows: (a) cylinder A advances (b) cylinder B advances

    (c) cylinder B returns (d) cylinder A returns

    Make additional assumptions if required and develop a pneumatic circuit for this application.

27. For the circuit of Fig. 5.132, cylinder 1 will not hold against a load while cylinder 2 is retracting. Modify the circuit by adding a pilot check valve and appropriate pipings so that cylinder 1 will hold while cylinder 2 is retracting.

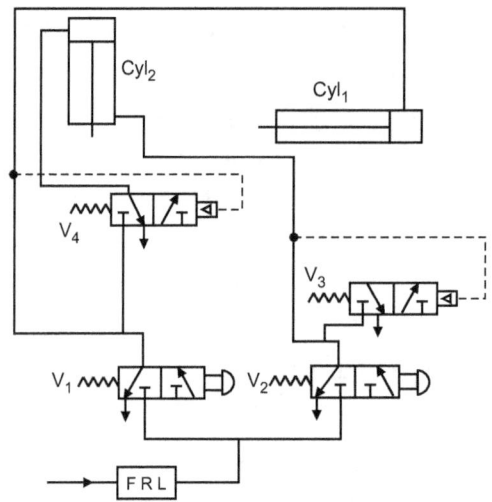

Fig. 5.132

28. What is the purpose of providing FRL unit in a pneumatic system ?   **(May 2001)**
29. What is the purpose of quick exhaust valve in a pneumatic system ?   **(May 2001)**
30. What are the different selection criteria for an air compressor ?   **(May 2001)**
31. Write short notes on:

(a) OSHA standards,

(b) Air oil intensifier, **(May 2001)**

(c) Air dryers,

(d) Use of pneumatics in low cost automation. **(May 2001)**

32. How do pneumatic actuators differ from hydraulic actuators ?

33. Explain in brief, with the help of a neat sketch and symbol, the working of 'FRL' unit used in pneumatic systems. **(May 2002, Dec. 201)**

34. Explain time delay valve and its application in pneumatic circuits. **(May 2003)**

35. Write short notes on:

(a) Sliding vane type rotary compressor, **(May 2002)**

(b) Air control valves, **(Dec. 2003)**

(c) Selection criteria for compressor, **(Dec. 2003, May 2004)**

(d) Air dryers.

36. Explain with the help of a neat sketch a time delay valve and also draw a typical circuit showing its application. **(May 2003, Dec. 2004)**

37. Draw a typical circuit showing the control of double acting cylinder, remotely operated through use of an air pilot operated directional control valve. **(May 2003)**

38. What is FRL unit ? Draw a neat sketch. **(May 2003, Dec. 2003)**

39. What are the advantages and disadvantages of pneumatic system ? **(Dec. 2003)**

40. Explain why pneumatics is used in low cost automation. **(Dec. 03, 04, May 04)**

41. Explain in brief with the help of a neat sketch the working of a lubricator unit used in pneumatic system. **(May 2004)**

42. Explain the time step travel diagram with reference to any typical circuit.**(Dec. 01, 04)**

43. What is the purpose of providing FRL unit in a pneumatic system ? **(May 2001)**

44. What is the purpose of quick exhaust valve in a pneumatic system ? **(May 2001)**

45. What are the different selection criteria for air compressors ? **(May 2001)**

46. Write short notes on:

(a) OSHA standards **(May 2001)**

(b) Air oil intensifier **(May 2001)**

(c) Air dryers **(May 2001)**

(d) Use of pneumatics in low cost automation. **(May 2001)**

47. How do pneumatic actuators differ from hydraulic actuators ? **(Dec. 2001)**

48. Explain in brief, with the help of a neat sketch and symbol, the working of 'FRL' unit used in pneumatic system. **(Dec. 2002, 01)**

49. Explain time delay valve and its application in pneumatic circuit. **(May 2002)**

50. Write short notes on:
    (a) Sliding vane type rotary compressor **(May 2002)**
    (b) Air control valves **(Dec. 2003)**
    (c) Selection criteria for compression **(Dec. 2003, 2004)**
    (d) Air dryers. **(May 2004)**

51. Explain with the help of neat sketch a time delay valve and also draw a typical circuit showing its application. **(May 2003, Dec. 2004)**

52. Draw a typical circuit showing the control of double acting cylinder remotely operated through use of an air pilot operated directional control valve. **(May 2003)**

53. What is FRL unit? Draw a neat sketch. **(May 2003, Dec. 2003)**

54. What are the advantages and disadvantages of pneumatic system? **(Dec. 2003)**

55. Explain why pneumatics is used in low cost automation. **(Dec. 2003, May 04, Dec. 04)**

56. Explain in brief with the help of a neat sketch the working of a lubricator unit used in pneumatic system. **(May 2004)**

57. Explain the time travel diagram with reference to any typical circuit. **(Dec. 01, 04)**

Unit VI

SYSTEM DESIGN

6.1 Introduction

In the earlier chapters, the constructional features and working of hydraulic circuit components are studied. A hydraulic circuit is built up by careful selection and proper assembly of several components to perform a specific function.

The hydraulic circuit design has a primary task of devising a proper circuit to provide a derived speed, sequence, power and position as necessitated by an application like machine tools, cranes, winches, hoists, brakes, lifts, press, jack. The design needs thorough understanding of the working cycle of the application, variation of energy demands over the cycle, the safety aspects desirable, expected performance level of the circuit etc. Thus, a designer has to correlate and synthesize various elements of the working cycle.

6.2 Design Considerations

The prime consideration of a hydraulic circuit design aim is to fulfill the following requirements of the circuit:

- To perform the desired function of the application.
- To achieve expected efficiency of performance.
- To provide assured safety and reliability of operation.
- To provide simplicity of maintenance, servicing and longer life.
- To provide allowance for some overload.
- To meet the above requirements in a cost effective manner.

The designer, in addition to selection of components, assesses the interaction and compatibility of various components to be connected in a circuit.

It is convenient and customary to represent a hydraulic circuit with a circuit diagram using standard symbols of each components incorporated in a circuit. In chapter number 3, the symbols of several hydraulic circuit components as per the ISO standard are tabulated.

HYDRAULICS AND PNEUMATICS — SYSTEM DESIGN

6.3 Information Required for Design

For better design of a hydraulic system, the designer should have detailed information about the exact function of the system, its relationship with other units or processes and energy demand variation in the cycle. In general, the designer must have sufficient information about the following:

(a) Operating Pressure: If the maximum pressure in the system is to be restricted or the designer has a choice.

(b) Actuators:
  (i) Reciprocating: For extend and retract, the required force/stroke and speed/stroke for each cylinder, also variation of speed, thrust if any, cushioning requirements, seals requirement etc.
  (ii) Semi-Rotary Actuators: Angle of rotation, speed, torque required, cushioning, seals necessary.
  (iii) Rotary Actuators: Speed, torque required, acceleration and retardation required etc.

(c) Operating Sequence: Event based or time based sequence.

(d) Type of Control: It may be manual, mechanical, hydraulic, pneumatic, electrical or a combination.

(e) Operating Conditions: Location and surrounding ambient conditions/like dusty, corrosive, fire-prone, tolerable noise level, skills of operator and maintenance facilitate available.

(f) Special Requirements:
  - Whether continuous or intermittent operation
  - Daily hours of operation
  - Special requirements of the working fluid.

6.4 Design Study

For developing a better understanding of the hydraulic circuit design, typical field applications are explained and various alternative hydraulic circuit designs are analysed.

SOLVED EXAMPLES

Example 6.1: *The following data refers to a single acting upstroking moulding press.*
  Cylinder diameter = 400 mm
  Stroke (total) = 300 mm
  Stroke used to close dies = 250 mm
  On the work piece
  Cylinder pressure to close dies = 20 bar
  Final stroke for moulding = 50 mm

Cylinder pressure during moulding = 300 bar
Number of components to be moulded/h = 60
Rapid approach = 250 mm = 5 s
Pressing over final 50 mm = 5 s
Hold under full thrust (cure time) = 25 s
Return time = 10 s
Unloading and reloading of press = 15 s
Total cycle time = 60 s

The return time is estimated based on gravity return. The final pressing time and cure (hold time) are fixed. Propose alternative hydraulic circuits and discuss their design analysis.

Solution 'A': Using pump of fixed discharge.

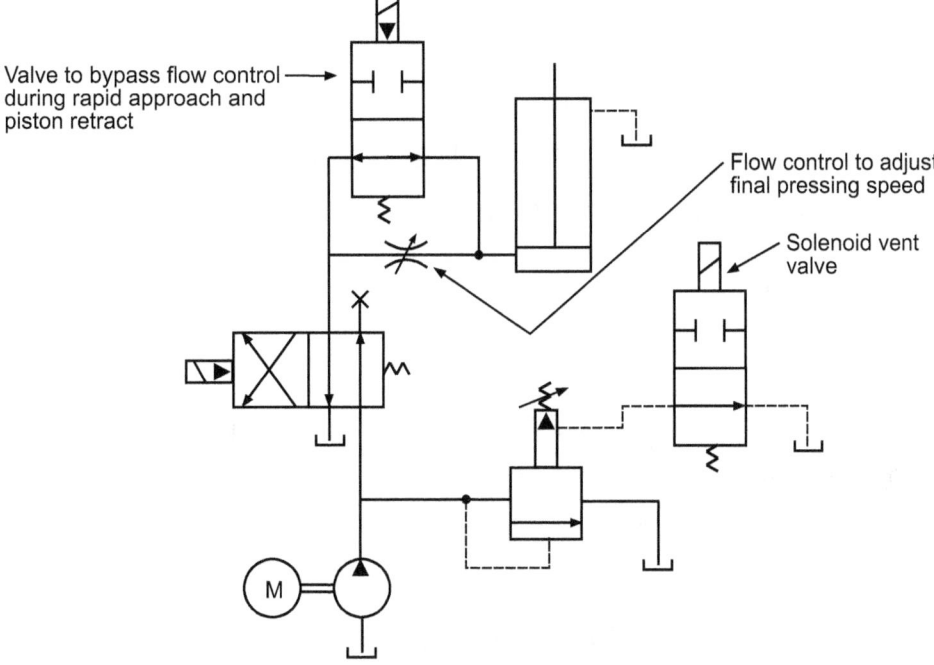

Fig. 6.1: Single fixed displacement pump circuit

The proposed circuit is shown in Fig. 6.1. It uses a pump of fixed discharge.
Thrust developed during rapid approach

$$\text{Pressure} \times \text{Area} = 20 \times 10^5 \times \frac{\pi}{4} \times 0.4^2 \times 10^{-3} \text{ kN}$$

$$= 251.33 \text{ kN}$$

And thrust developed during final mould pressing

$$= 300 \times 10^5 \times \frac{\pi}{4} \times 0.4^2 \text{ MN}$$

$$= 3.77 \text{ MN}$$

For estimation of pump capacity

(a) Estimation of flow rate required during rapid approach period:

$$\text{Area of cylinder} = \frac{\pi}{4} \times 0.4^2 = 0.126 \text{ m}^2$$

$$\text{Velocity of piston} = \frac{0.250}{5} = 0.05 \text{ m/s}$$

∴ Flow rate required = Area × Velocity

$$= 0.126 \times 0.05 \text{ m}^3/\text{s}$$

$$= 0.126 \times 0.05 \times 10^3 \times 60 \text{ litre/min.}$$

$$= 378 \text{ l.p.m.}$$

(b) Estimation of flow rate required during final pressing:

$$\text{Piston velocity} = \frac{0.05}{5} = 0.01 \text{ m/s}$$

$$\text{Flow rate required} = 0.126 \times 0.01 \text{ m}^3/\text{s}$$

$$= 0.126 \times 0.01 \times 10^3 \times 60 \text{ l.p.m.}$$

$$= 75.6 \text{ l.p.m.}$$

Therefore, the single pump must have a capacity to deliver 378 l.p.m. against a maximum system pressure of 300 bar.

Theoretical power input required for the pump

$$= Q \times p \text{ kW}$$

$$= 300 \times 10^2 \times \frac{378 \times 10^3}{60} \text{ kW}$$

$$= 189 \text{ kW}$$

During the holding (curing) time, all the pump output is discharged over the relief valve. A flow control valve provided, sets the piston speed during slow pressing. This valve is bypassed by a two position direction control valve during the period of rapid approach. Due to high flow rates, the direction control valve having two stage valves is chosen.

Now work done during rapid approach

$$= \text{Force} \times \text{Piston travel}$$
$$= 251.33 \times 10^3 \times 0.250 \text{ N-m}$$
$$= 62.83 \times 10^3 \text{ N-m}$$

And work done during actual pressing (moulding)

$$= \text{Force} \times \text{Piston travel}$$
$$= 3.77 \times 10^6 \times 0.05$$
$$= 188.5 \times 10^3 \text{ N-m}$$

Total work done in one cycle i.e. energy utilized

$$= 10^3 (62.83 + 188.5) \text{ N-m}$$
$$= 251.33 \times 10^3 \text{ N-m}$$

Further energy input to pump in one cycle consists of two quantities as given below:

(c) During rapid approach, the pump operates against a pressure of 20 bar for a period of 5 seconds,

$$\text{Energy supplied by pump} = 20 \times 10^5 \times \frac{378 \times 10^{-3}}{60} \times 5 \text{ J}$$
$$= 63.0 \times 10^3 \text{ J}$$

This is almost equal to the work done during rapid approach period.

(d) Energy supplied by the pump during the 30 seconds pressing period (i.e. pressing time + curing time)

$$= 300 \times 10^5 \times \frac{378 \times 10^{-3}}{60} \times 30 \text{ J}$$
$$= 5670 \times 10^3 \text{ J}$$

Hence, total energy supplied by the pump per cycle

$$= (5670 + 63) \, 10^3 \text{ J}$$
$$= 5733 \times 10^3 \text{ J}$$

Therefore, overall efficiency of the system

$$= \frac{\text{Total energy utilised/cycle}}{\text{Total energy supplied by pump/cycle}}$$

$$= \frac{251.33 \times 10^3}{5733 \times 10^3} \times 100 = 4.384\%$$

This is certainly a very inefficient circuit.

Solution B:

The circuit shown uses three pumps (Fig. 6.2).

1. High flow low pressure pump.
2. Low flow high pressure pump.
3. A small pump to provide pilot supply for the main D.C. valve. Main pumps are unloaded during part of the cycle.

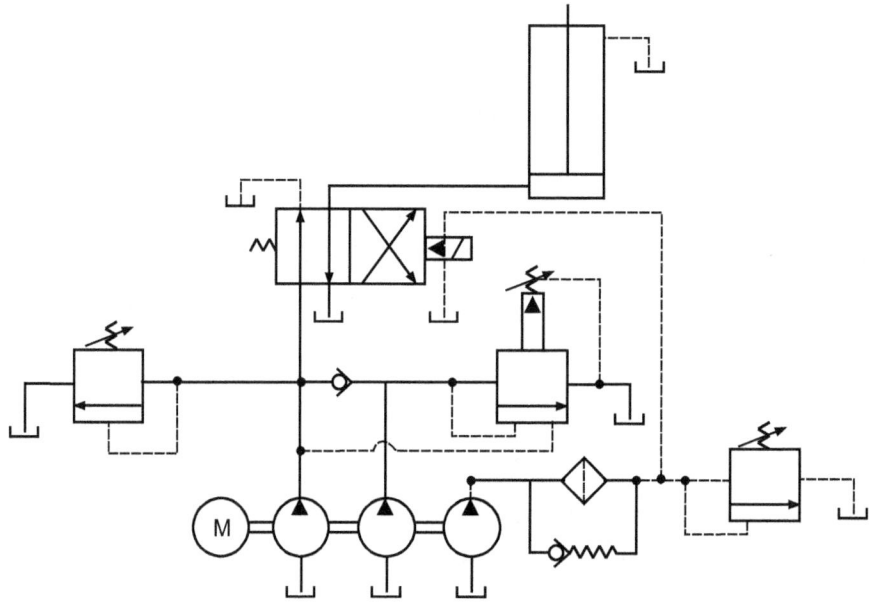

Fig. 6.2: Multi-pump circuit

Calculations:

Power for rapid approach and final pressing:

(1) Theoretical input power for final pressing is pressure × flow.

$$\text{Power for pressing} = \frac{350 \times 10^5 \times 75.6}{60 \times 10^3} \quad \text{... From solution (A) } Q = 75.6 \text{ lit./min.}$$

$$= 44.1 \text{ kW}$$

(2) Power for rapid approach:

For rapid approach flow required = 378 lit./min. (From solution A)

So for rapid approach, low pressure pump will have to deliver

$$378 - 75.6 = 302.4 \text{ lit./min.}$$

Theoretical input power for rapid approach is

$$\frac{378 \times 20 \times 10^5}{60 \times 10^3} = 12.6 \text{ kW}$$

Maximum power required in the system is 44.1 kW.

(3) Theoretical energy input during rapid approach

$$= \text{Power (watt)} \times \text{Time}$$
$$= 12.6 \times 10^3 \times 5$$
$$= 63 \times 10^3 \text{ Nm}$$

(4) Input energy during final pressing + curing

$$= 44.1 \times 10^3 \times 30$$
$$= 1323 \times 10^3 \text{ Nm}$$

Total energy input $= (63 + 1323) \times 10^3$ joule

$$= 1386 \times 10^3 \text{ joule}$$

Work done per cycle from solution (A) is

$$= 251.33 \times 10^3 \text{ joule}$$

So theoretical system efficiency is therefore

$$= \frac{251.33 \times 10^3}{1386 \times 10^3} = 0.181 \text{ i.e. } 18\%$$

Solution C:

A fixed pump with accumulator:

(1) Pump capacity $= \dfrac{\text{Swept volume of cylinder}}{\text{Total cycle time}}$

$$= \frac{\text{Area of piston} \times \text{Stroke}}{\text{Total time}}$$

$$= \frac{\pi/4 \times (0.4)^2 \times 0.3}{60}$$

$$= 0.000628 \text{ m}^3/\text{s} = 0.628 \text{ lit./sec.}$$

$$= 37.68 \text{ lit./min.}$$

Refer circuit: (Fig. 6.3)

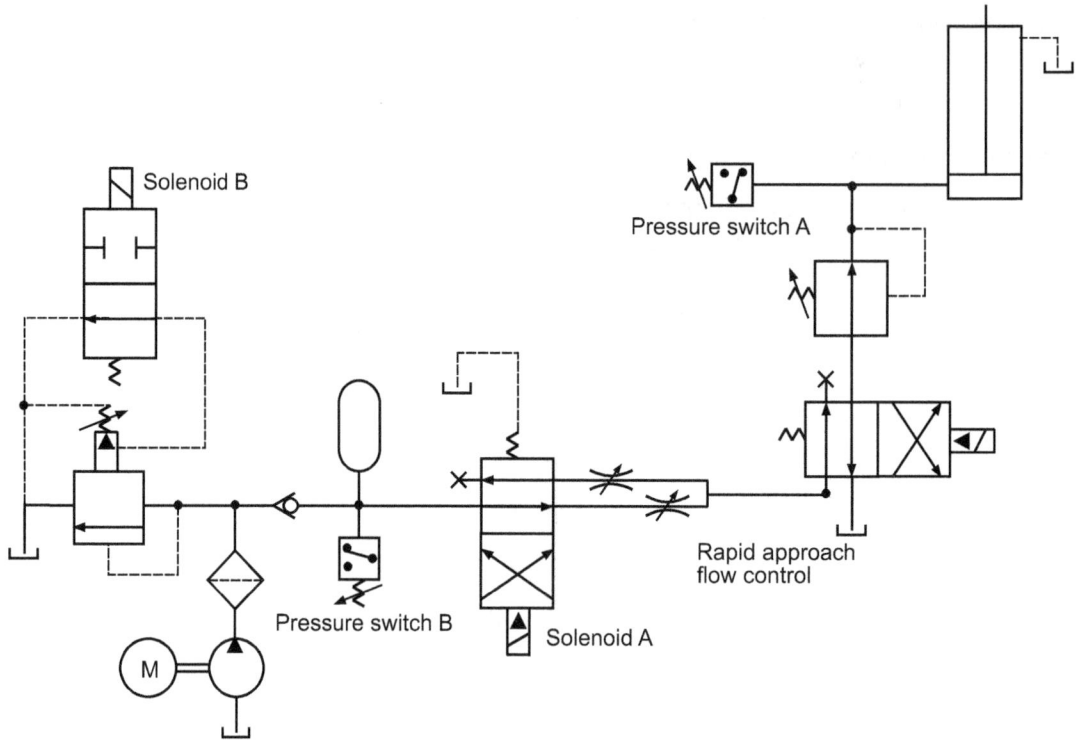

Fig. 6.3: Accumulator circuit

Assume the maximum operating pressure as 400 bar to take into account internal leakage and wear within the pump.

Accumulator gas precharge pressure

$\qquad$ = 90% of maximum pressure required at the cylinder

$\qquad$ = 0.9 × 300 = 270 bar

(2) To determine the size of accumulator:

(a) Quantity of oil delivered from accumulator during rapid approach =

[flow required by circuit − flow provided by pump for rapid approach] for 5 sec.

$$= \frac{(378 - 37.68) \times 5}{60} = 28.36 \text{ litres}$$

(b) Flow from accumulator for rapid approach + actual pressing.

$$= 28.36 + \frac{(75.6 - 37.68)}{60} \times 5 = 31.52 \text{ litres}$$

For remaining 50 seconds of the cycle, accumulator is being charged by the pump at a rate of 37.68 lit/min. The accumulator charge during this period is

$$\frac{(37.68 \times 50)}{60} = 31.4 \text{ lit.} \quad \begin{pmatrix}\text{approx. same as the quantity}\\\text{of fluid discharged per cycle}\end{pmatrix}$$

Thus, accumulator must be capable of delivering 31.52 lit. at pressure of 300 bar.

(c) Accumulator Design:

Assumption: During discharge adiabatic conditions, during charging isothermal conditions.

Let P_1, V_1 be the gas pressure and volume when precharged

P_2, V_2 gas pressure and volume when fully charged

P_3, V_3 gas pressure and volume when discharged

Assume P_1 = 90% of working pressure

$= 0.9 \times 300 = 270$ bar gauge = 271 bar absolute

$P_2 = 400$ bar gauge = 401 bar absolute

$P_3 = 300$ bar gauge = 301 bar absolute

V_1, V_2, V_3 are unknown.

The difference $(V_3 - V_2)$ is the quantity discharged by accumulator between pressure of 400×300 bar.

∴ $V_3 - V_2 = 31.52$ lit. ... (1)

For initial charge, assume isothermal compression

∴ $P_1 V_1 = P_2 V_2$

∴ $271 \times V_1 = 401 \times V_2$

∴ $V_1 = 1.48 V_2$ ... (2)

For discharge adiabatic expansion

$$\left(\frac{V_3}{V_2}\right) = \left(\frac{P_2}{P_3}\right)^{1/1.4} = \left(\frac{401}{301}\right)^{1/1.4} = (1.332)^{1/1.4} = (1.332)^{0.7142}$$

∴ $\dfrac{V_3}{V_2} = 1.22$

∴ $V_3 = 1.22 V_2$ ... (3)

From equations (1), (2) and (3), we have

$V_1 = 1.48 V_2$

$V_3 = 1.22 V_2$

and $V_3 - V_2 = 31.52$

So, $V_1 = 212.043$ lit.

Thus, the required accumulator volume = 212.04 litres.

(d) Theoretical power input in this circuit = $\dfrac{37.68}{60 \times 10^3} \times 400 \times 10^5$ = 25.12 kN

Theoretical input energy is

$25.12 \times 10^3 \times 60$ joules = 1507.2×10^3 J

Efficiency = $\dfrac{251.33 \times 10^3}{1507.2 \times 10^3}$ = 0.1667 i.e. 16.7%.

Solution D:

A constant delivery pump and intensifier. The intensifier is used for final pressing. Pressure and flow required for rapid travel and punching by fixed delivery pump are as before. (Fig. 6.4).

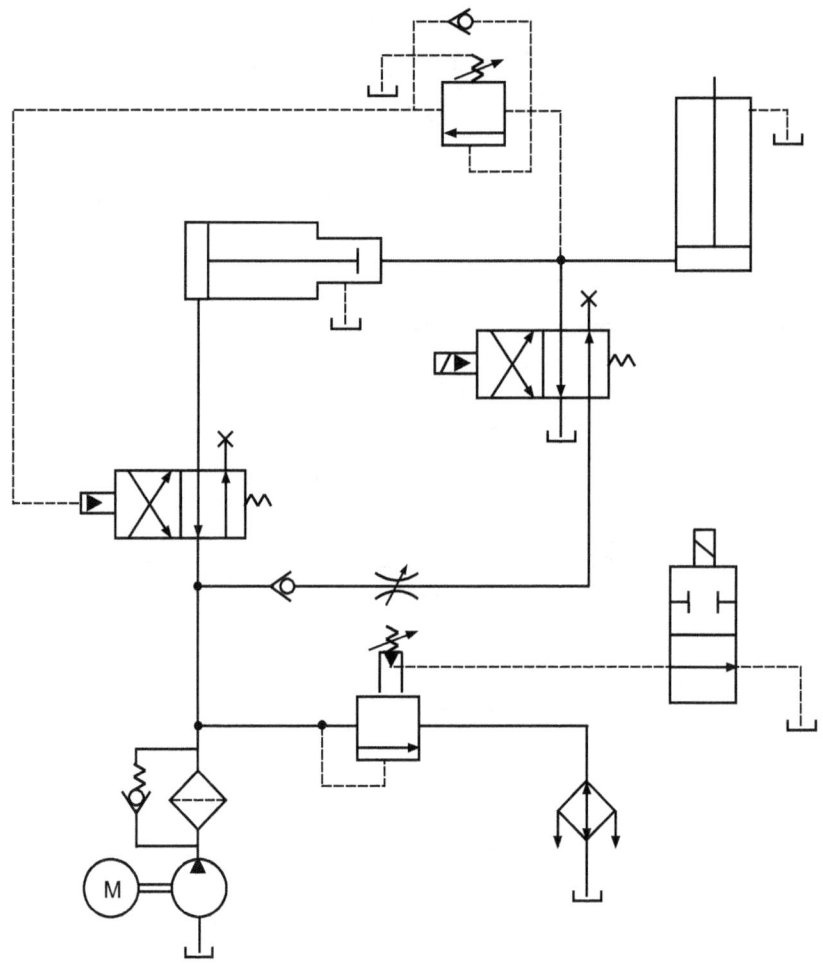

Fig. 6.4

HYDRAULICS AND PNEUMATICS　　　　　　　　　　　　　　　　SYSTEM DESIGN

i.e. $\dfrac{\text{Flow and pressure}}{\text{for rapid travel}}$ = 378 lit./min. and 20 bar

and pressure = 300 bar and flow 75.6 lit./min. for final pressing.

(a) Intensification of pressure required

$$= \frac{300}{20} \Rightarrow 15:1$$

Output side flow × Pressure = Input side flow × Pressure

$$75.6 \times 300 = Q_{input} \times 20$$

∴　　　　　　Q_{input} = 1134 lit./min.

Pump should have delivery of 1134 lit./min. against a pressure of 20 bar for final pressing and for rapid approach delivery of 378 lit./min. is required. So a flow control valve is needed to reduce the flow during rapid approach and [(1134 − 378) = 756 lit./min] flow will pass over the relief valve during rapid approach.

(b)　　　Input power = $\left(\dfrac{1134}{60 \times 10^3}\right) \times (20 \times 10^5)$

$$= 37.8 \text{ kW}$$

Energy input = $37.8 \times 10^3 \times 35$　　　$\begin{bmatrix}\text{Approach + final pressing} \\ \text{+ holding time = 35 sec.}\end{bmatrix}$

$$= 1323 \times 10^3 \text{ joules}$$

Efficiency = $\dfrac{\text{Work done by piston}}{\text{Energy input}}$

$$= \frac{251.33 \times 10^3}{1323 \times 10^3} = 0.189 \text{ i.e. } 18.9\%$$

Example 6.2: Design study of conveyor feed system. There are two screw feed conveyors and three bunker cylinders. Refer the following data for design.

　　　Bunker cylinder stroke = 0.5 m
　　　　　　Thrust = 2000 kg both to open and close bunker doors.

Bunker cylinders are such that they can be stopped and locked in any position between strokes. The closing time of bunkers = 10 sec.

Sr. No.	Data for conveyors
1.	Starting torque = 120 Nm
2.	Running torque = 900 Nm
3.	Speed range = 10 – 35 r.p.m. (variable)

There is a reduction gear box (4 : 1) between the hydraulic motor and screw conveyor. Gear efficiency 80%.

HYDRAULICS AND PNEUMATICS

SYSTEM DESIGN

Solution:

- **Step 1:** A centralised hydraulic system using multi pump system is suggested.
- Since, no system pressure is given, the pressure has to be judiciously selected. In this system, actuators required are cylinders and motors. Standard hydraulic cylinders work at 210 bar continuous pressure while slow speed georotor motor or radial piston motor would need pressures of 210 bar to 450 bar. Select 210 bar as the maximum pressure in the system.
- **Step 2:** Mineral oil is selected as a fluid.
- **Step 3:** Selection of cylinder:

$$\text{Force required} = 2000 \text{ kg}$$
$$= 2000 \times 9.81$$
$$= 19620 \text{ N}$$
$$\text{Cylinder stroke} = 0.5 \text{ m}$$

To prevent buckling, let us calculate the minimum piston rod diameter.

Buckling load

$$\Rightarrow \qquad K = \frac{\pi^2 EI}{SL^2}$$

where, E = Modulus of elasticity, kg/cm²
$= 2.1 \times 10^6$ kg/cm² for steel

$J = \left(\frac{\pi d^4}{64}\right)$ cm⁴ for solid circular piston

d = Rod diameter (cm)

L = Buckling length (cm)

S = Factor of safety
$= 3.5$

Here, $K = 2000$ kg

Take $L = 2 \times 0.5$ m
$= 100$ cm

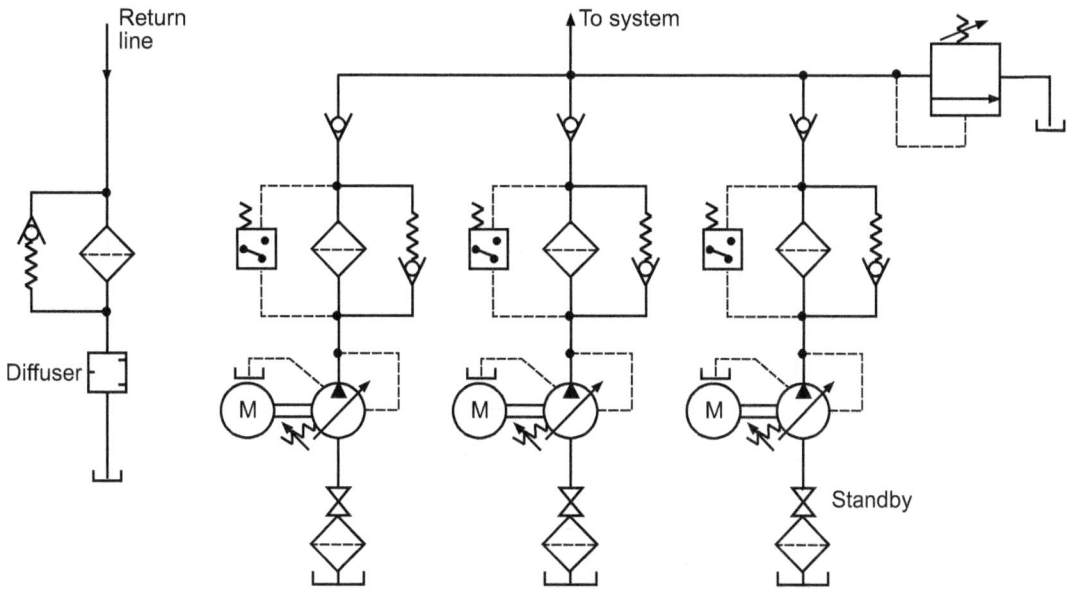

Fig. 6.5 (a): Power pack circuit

(L is taken approximately twice the stroke length)

$$\therefore \quad K = 2000 = \left(\frac{\pi^2 \times 2.1 \times 10^6}{3.5 \times 100^2}\right) \times \left(\frac{\pi d^4}{64}\right)$$

$$\therefore \quad d = 28.8 \text{ mm}$$

From the table, the next larger diameter = 36 mm

Assume 180 bar maximum pressure at the cylinder.

$$\text{Effective area} = \frac{2000 \times 9.81}{180 \times 10^5} = 1090 \text{ mm}^2$$

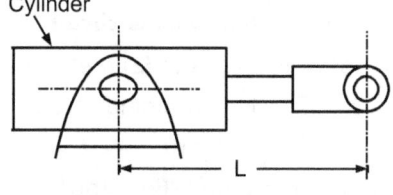

Fig. 6.5 (b)

Area with 36 mm diameter rod full bore, area needed is

$$[1090 + (\pi/4)(36)^2] = 2108 \text{ mm}^2$$

Thus, full bore diameter $\quad D = \left(\frac{2108 \times 4}{\pi}\right)^{1/2} = 51.8 \text{ mm}$

Standard cylinder available has 50 mm diameter piston with 36 diameter rod.

The pressure required to develop 2000 kg thrust on the annulus side is

$$\frac{2000 \times 9.81}{\pi/4 \, (50^2 - 36^2)} = 207 \text{ bar}$$

This pressure is too near to the maximum pressure of 210 bar. To reduce the pressure choose the next cylinder in the range. Let us consider a 63 mm diameter bore. With this there are 36 mm and 45 mm diameter rods available. If we calculate the annulus side pressure as above for both, then 36 mm rod pressure = 94 bar and 45 mm rod pressure = 129 bar. Larger rod i.e. 45 mm is selected. It makes design strong.

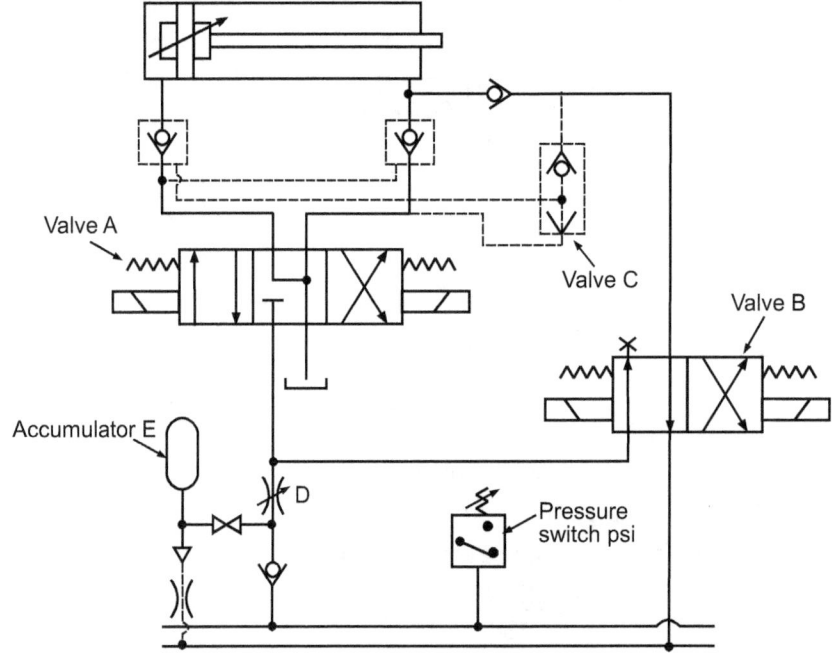

Fig. 6.5 (c): Cylinder circuit

Step 4: Design of motor: For conveyors (1) and (2) (Refer to Fig. 6.6)

    Data = Starting torque = 1200 Nm, Running torque = 900 Nm

    Speed variation = 10 – 35 r.p.m.

Referring to the motor selection catalog type M6 motor has startup torque = 1600 Nm at 207 bar and running torque of 1100 Nm at 138 bar. Thus, pressure required to produce 1200 Nm is approximately 160 bar and running torque at 10 r.p.m. speed is approximately 120 bar. So this motor is selected.

Its specification is, Displacement = 558 cc/rev.

    Maximum pressure = 240 bar

    Volumetric efficiency = 95%

HYDRAULICS AND PNEUMATICS SYSTEM DESIGN

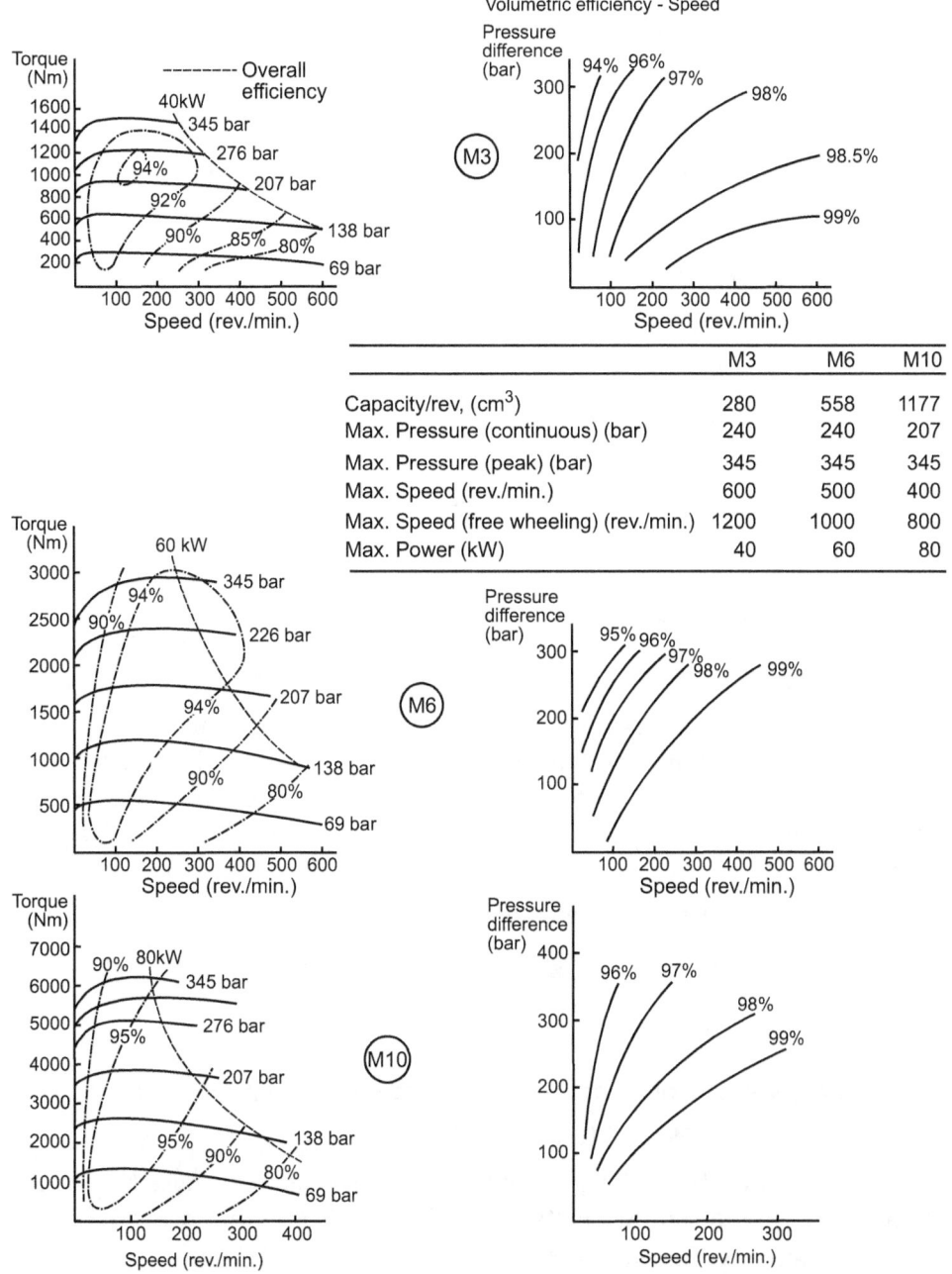

Fig. 6.6: **Typical motor performance curves and figures**

Step 5: Flow requirement for actuators

For cylinders: Cylinders are required to extend 0.5 m in 10 sec.

$$\text{Velocity} = \frac{0.5 \times 60}{10} = 3 \text{ m/min}$$

$$\text{Flow required } Q = \frac{\pi}{4} \times (63)^2 \times 10^{-6} \times 3 = 9.35 \text{ lit./min.}$$

Conveyor drives 1 and 2.

$$\text{Maximum speed} = 35 \text{ r.p.m.}$$

Motor M6

$$\text{Capacity} = 558 \text{ cc/rev.}$$
$$\text{Maximum flow required} = 35 \times 558$$
$$= 19530 \text{ cc/min.}$$
$$= 19.53 \text{ lit./min.}$$

Volumetric efficiency is 95% (given)

$$\therefore \text{ Actual maximum flow} = \frac{19.53}{0.95} = 20.5 \text{ lit./min.}$$

Step 6: Pump selection:

The use of pressure compensated axial pumps is suggested. Maximum circuit demand is 50.35 lit./min. Three pumps are selected, two working at a time at 30 lit/min. at 160 bar and third as a stand by. From Vickers System Ltd. catalogue of axial piston pumps PBV 10 series has a rated delivery of 21.2 lit./per 1000 r.p.m. i.e. 30.6 l.p.m. at 1450 r.p.m. The maximum pressure is 210 bar.

$$\text{Theoretical power input} = \text{Pressure} \times \text{Flow}$$
$$= \left(\frac{30.6}{60}\right) \times 10^3 \times (160 \times 10^5)$$
$$= 8.08 \text{ kW}$$

Circuits for power pack and conveyors 1 and 2 are shown in Fig. 6.6 (a) and 6.6 (b).

Step 7: Cylinder circuits: (Fig. 6.6 (b))

D.C. valve A with check valves (Pilot operated) enable cylinders to be locked in any position. The cylinder flow is controlled by a meter in the flow control valve. PS_1 is a safety pressure switch and in emergency it energizes the solenoid on valve A for retraction. The hydraulic fluid for cylinder emergency retract is supplied by the accumulator E. The shuttle valve C allows the pilot operated check valve on the full bore side of the cylinder to be opened by a signal from valve A or valve B.

Following the same procedure as that of the previous example of accumulator design.

Here,
P_2 = Maximum pressure in system = 161 bar
P_3 = Minimum pressure in system = 91 bar
P_1 = Precharge pressure = $0.9 P_3$ = 82 bar absolute

Volume of oil required to fully retract cylinders is $V_3 - V_2$

$$= \frac{\pi}{4}(63^2 - 36^2) \times 500 \times 3$$

$$= 3.15 \text{ lit.} \qquad \ldots (1)$$

Assume $\gamma = 1.4$ – adiabatic charge

$$P_1 V_1^\gamma = P_2 V_2^\gamma$$

$$\therefore \quad \frac{V_1}{V_2} = \left(\frac{P_2}{P_1}\right)^{1/\gamma} = (1.96)^{1/1.4} = 1.61$$

$$\therefore \quad V_1 = 1.61 V_2 \qquad \ldots (2)$$

Assume isothermal discharge

$$P_2 V_2 = P_3 V_3$$

$$161 V_2 = 91 V_3 \qquad \ldots (3)$$

$\therefore$ From equations (1), (2) and (3) V_1 = 6.6 litres.

From the manufacturer's catalogues, 7 lit. and 10 lit. models are available. So 10 lit. is selected to have some more spare capacity.

Step 8: Oil Reservoir:

Heat generated is low because of pressure compensated pumps.

Reservoir capacity = (3 to 4) × Pump flow rate
= 200 lit. should be adequate

Example 6.3: *A machine tool slide is moved by means of a hydraulic cylinder as follows:*

(a) Initially it moves through a distance of 200 mm against a load of 12 kN in about 3 sec.

(b) It is followed by a working stroke of 100 mm against an effective load of 35 kN. The feed rate during this part of the stroke is required to be between 0.5 to 1 m/min.

(c) The return stroke is as fast as possible. A meter out type of circuit is used. Draw the circuit. Select different components used in the circuit.

Solution: The resulting circuit is as follows: (Refer Fig. 6.7)

HYDRAULICS AND PNEUMATICS — SYSTEM DESIGN

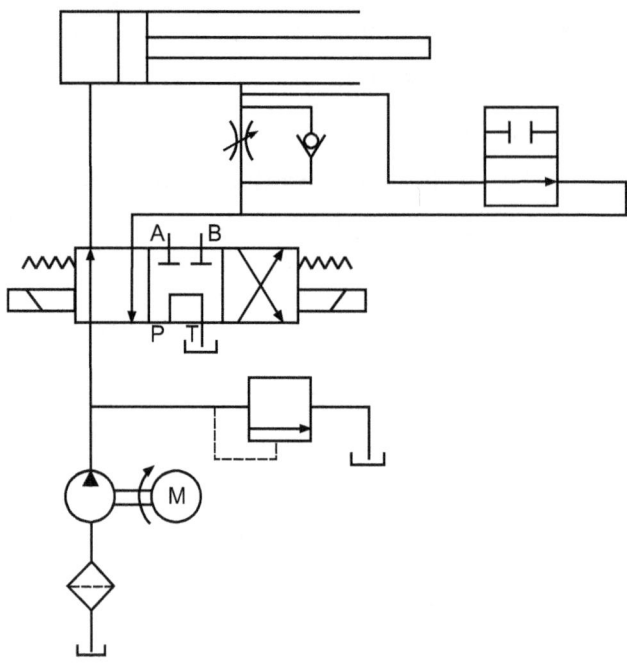

Fig. 6.7

The working of such circuit is explained earlier.

Step 1: Selection of Cylinder:

　Maximum load = 35 kN

　Feed rate = 0.5 m/min.

From the supplied data table

The reference catalogue required of system design is given below.

1. **Suction Strainer:**

Model	Flow Capacity (lpm)
S_1	38
S_2	76
S_3	152

2. **Pressure Gauge:**

Model	Range (bar)
PG_1	0 – 25
PG_2	0 – 45
PG_3	0 – 100
PG_4	0 – 160

3. Vane pump:

Model	Delivery in lpm		
	At 0 bar	At 35 bar	At 70 bar
P_1	8.5	7.1	5.3
P_2	12.9	11.4	9.5
P_3	17.6	16.1	14.3
P_4	25.1	23.8	35.6
P_5	39.0	37.5	35.6

4. Relief valve:

Model	Flow capacity (lpm)	Max. working pressure (bar)
R_1	11.4	70
R_2	19	210
R_3	30.4	70
R_4	57	105

5. Flow control valve:

Model	Working pressure (bar)	Flow range (lpm)
F_1	70	0 – 4.1
F_2	105	0 – 4.9
F_3	105	0 – 16.3
F_4	70	0 – 24.6

6. Direction control valve:

Model	Max. working pressure (bar)	Flow capacity (lpm)
D_1	350	19
D_2	210	38
D_3	210	76

7. **Check valve:**

Model	Max. working pressure (bar)	Flow capacity (lpm)
C_1	210	12.5
C_2	210	30.4
C_3	210	76

8. **Pilot operated check valve:**

Model	Max. working pressure (bar)	Flow capacity (lpm)
PO_1	210	19
PO_2	210	38
PO_3	210	76

9. **Cylinder (Maximum working pressure - 210 bar):**

Model	Bore dia (mm)	Rod dia (mm)
A_1	25	12.5
A_2	40	16
A_3	50	35
A_4	75	45
A_5	100	50

10. **Oil reservoirs:**

Model	Capacity (litres)
T_1	40
T_2	100
T_3	250
T_4	400
T_5	600

Selecting an A_5 cylinder, maximum pressure = 210 bar

   (D) Bore diameter = 100 mm

   (d) Rod diameter = 50 mm.

Stroke of cylinder = 200 mm + 100 mm = 300 mm

$$\text{Full bore area} = \frac{\pi}{4} D^2 = \frac{\pi}{4} \times (0.100)^2$$

$$= 7.85 \times 10^{-3} \text{ (m}^2)$$

and

$$\text{Annulus area} = \frac{\pi}{4} (D^2 - d^2) = \frac{\pi}{4} (0.1^2 - 0.05^2)$$

$$= 5.89 \times 10^{-3} \text{ m}^2$$

$$\text{Maximum working pressure} = \frac{\text{Load}}{\text{Area}} = \frac{35 \times 10^3}{7.85 \times 10^{-3}} = 4.45 \times 10^6 \text{ N/m}^2 = 44.56 \text{ bar.}$$

Step 2: Flow requirement Calculations:

(A) For rapid approach, i.e 200 mm distance in 3 sec.

$$\text{Velocity of piston needed} = \frac{200 \times 10^{-3}}{3} = 0.06667 \text{ m/sec.}$$

$$\text{Flow required} = \text{Area} \times \text{Velocity}$$

$$= 7.85 \times 10^{-3} \times 0.06667 \text{ m}^3/\text{sec.}$$

$$= 31.42 \text{ lit/min.}$$

(B) For working stroke: velocity = 0.5 m/min.

$$\text{Flow required} = 7.85 \times 10^{-3} \times 0.5$$

$$= 3.925 \times 10^{-3} \text{ m}^3/\text{min.}$$

$$= 3.925 \text{ lit/min.}$$

And for velocity 1 m/min. flow required = 7.854 lit/min.

This is achieved by setting of the flow control valve in the meter-out circuit.

Step 3: Selection of Pump:

The maximum flow rate required in the circuit is 31.42 lit./min. and maximum pressure is 44.56 bar. So the pump should provide the required flow against the required pressure.

Selecting the vane pump P_5 model from the given catalogue data, the pump has delivery of 35.6 lit./min at 70 bar pressure. This should satisfy our requirement.

Step 4: Flow Control Valve and Reservoir Sizing:

For achieving a speed of 0.5 m/min., the flow to be metered is

$$Q = \text{Annulus area} \times \text{Velocity}$$

$$= 5.89 \times 10^{-3} \times 0.5$$

$$= 2.945 \times 10^{-3} \text{ m}^3/\text{min.} = 2.945 \text{ lit./min.}$$

HYDRAULICS AND PNEUMATICS — SYSTEM DESIGN

For achieving a speed of 1 m/min, the flow required

$$Q = 5.89 \times 10^{-3} \times 1 = 5.9 \text{ lit./min.}$$

Hence, model F_3 having working pressure of 105 bar and flow range 0 – 16.3 lit./min. is selected.

$$\text{Displacement of cylinder} = \frac{\pi}{4} \times D^2 \times \text{Stroke}$$

$$= (7.85 \times 10^{-3}) \times (300 \times 10^{-3})$$

$$= 2.36 \times 10^{-3} \text{ m}^3$$

$$= 2.36 \text{ lit. of oil}$$

$$\text{Total oil required} = 2.36 \text{ lit.} + 2.36 \text{ lit (approx. same for in piping)}$$

$$= 4.72 \text{ lit.}$$

If we assume the velocity of oil in the suction pipe = 2 m/sec. then

$$Q = A \cdot V$$

$$\frac{31.42}{2 \times 1000 \times 60} = 0.0002618 = \text{Area of pipe}$$

∴ Diameter of pipe = 18.25 mm

Sizing of reservoir from the thumb rule formula is (3 to 4) × pump delivery per min.

∴ $\quad 3 \times 31.42 = 94.26$ lit.

Select mode T_2 having capacity 100 lit.

Example 6.4: *Two identical cylinders A and B are to be operated simultaneously. The cylinder A moves against a load of 25 kN while the cylinder B has a load of 20 kN. Both the cylinders have a stroke of 1 m. The working stroke is to be completed in about 20 seconds time. The return stroke of the cylinder B is to start only after the cylinder A is completely retracted. The return speeds are to be as fast as possible.*

Draw a circuit which will fulfil these requirements. Select the different components you have used in the circuit from the data given. Mention the ratings of the components in case it is not available in the given data.

DATA

(a) Suction strainer:

Model	Flow Capacity (lpm)
S_1	38
S_2	76
S_3	152

HYDRAULICS AND PNEUMATICS — SYSTEM DESIGN

(b) Pressure gauge:

Model	Range (bar)
PG_1	0 – 25
PG_2	0 – 40
PG_3	0 – 100
PG_4	0 – 160

(c) Vane pump:

Model	Delivery in lpm		
	At 0 bar	At 35 bar	At 70 bar
P_1	8.5	7.1	5.3
P_2	12.9	11.4	9.5
P_3	17.6	16.1	14.3
P_4	25.1	23.8	22.4
P_5	39.0	37.5	35.6

(d) Relief valve:

Model	Flow capacity (lpm)	Max. working pressure & bar
R_1	11.4	70
R_2	19.0	210
R_3	30.4	70
R_4	57.0	105

(e) Flow control valve:

Model	Working pressure (bar)	Flow range (lpm)
F_1	70	0 - 4.1
F_2	105	0 - 4.9
F_3	105	0 - 16.3
F_4	70	0 - 24.6

(f) **Directional control valve:**

Model	Max. working pressure & bar	Flow capacity (lpm)
D_1	350	19
D_2	210	38
D_3	210	76

(g) **Check valve:**

Model	Max. working Pressure & bar	Flow capacity (/pm)
C_1	210	15.2
C_2	210	30.4
C_3	210	76

(h) **Pilot operated check valve:**

Model	Max. working Pressure (bar)	Flow capacity (lpm)
PO_1	210	19
PO_2	210	38
PO_3	210	76

(i) **Cylinder (Max. working pressure 210 bar)**

Model	Bore diameter (mm)	Rod diameter (mm)
A_1	25	12.5
A_2	40	16
A_3	50	35
A_4	75	45
A_5	100	50

(j) **Oil reservoirs:**

Model	Capacity (litres)
T_1	40
T_2	100
T_3	250
T_4	400
T_5	600

Solution: (Refer Fig. 6.8)

Since, both cylinders are to be operated simultaneously and the loads on both differ, it is necessary to supply oil directly to the cylinder A and through a pressure reducing valve (1) to B. A sequence valve (2) is needed to ensure return of cylinder B, starts after full return of cylinder A. The resulting circuit is as follows:

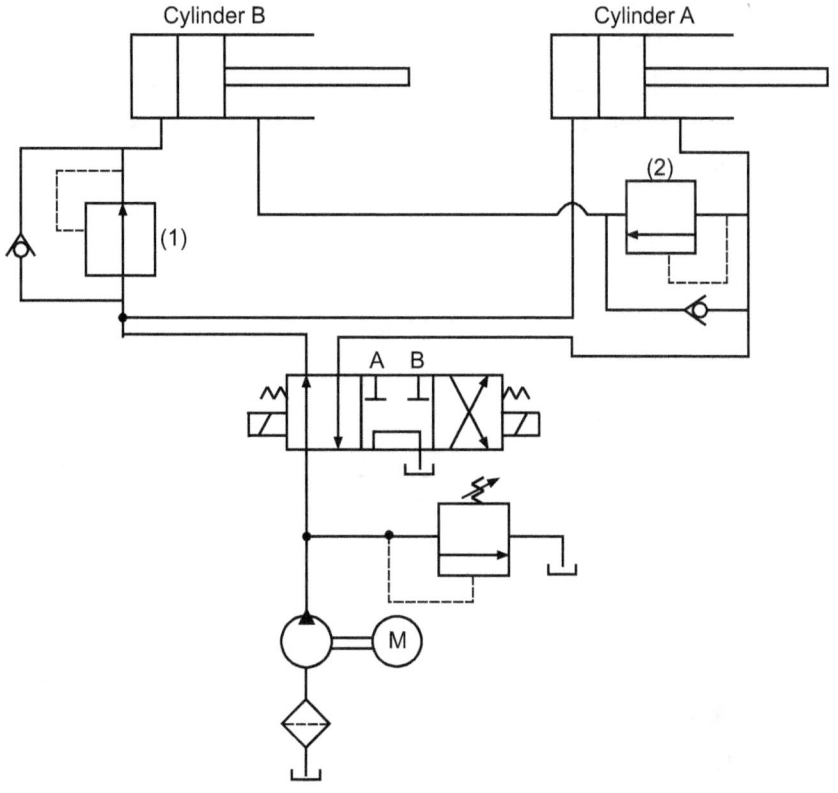

Fig. 6.8

Step 1: Selection of cylinder:

$$\text{Maximum load} = 25 \text{ kN}$$

For cylinder A : Model A_2 having bore diameter = 40 m and Rod diameter = 16 mm

$$\text{Calculating maximum pressure} = \frac{25 \times 10^3}{\pi/4 \times (0.04)^2} = 198.95 \text{ bar}$$

This is too near to the maximum working pressure of 210 bar.

So selecting a larger cylinder A_3 cylinder.

$$\text{Bore diameter} = 50 \text{ mm}$$

Rod diameter = 35 mm

$$\text{Maximum pressure} = \frac{25 \times 10^3}{\pi/4 \times (0.05)^2} = 127 \text{ bar}$$

Important Note:

The diameter of the power cylinder of the machine tool is selected in accordance with the force that the piston exerst, or with the its required speed. If the pressure in the cylinder is increased, its diameter is reduced and the pump output pipe size and size of all other hydraulic apparatus are also reduced. As a result a more compact system is obtained, that is easier to assemble and install. On the other hand, a higher pressure requires the use of more expensive pumps, higher leak proof qualities of the piping and more reliable packing and seals. The pressure in the power cylinder does not as a rule exceed approximately 45 bar and also the ratio of cylinder length l to the diameter D over 20 is not advisable.

So for cylinder A and B model A_5 with bore diameter = 100 mm and rod diameter = 50 mm is selected.

1. Maximum working pressure for cylinder A

$$= \frac{25 \times 10^3}{\pi/4 \times (0.1)^2}$$

$$= 31.83 \text{ bar}$$

2. Maximum pressure for cylinder B

$$= \frac{20 \times 10^3}{\pi/4 \times (0.1)^2} = 25.47 \text{ bar}$$

- **Step 2: Flow required:**

  1 metre stroke to be completed in 20 sec.

  $$\text{Velocity of piston} = \frac{1.0}{20} = 0.05 \text{ m/sec.}$$

  Flow required for cylinders A and B simultaneously

  $$= [\text{Area} \times \text{Velocity}] \times 2$$

  $$= \left[\frac{\pi}{4} \times (0.1)^2 \times 0.05 \times 60\right] \times 2$$

  $$= 0.0471 \text{ m}^3/\text{min}$$

  $$= 47.1 \text{ lpm}$$

- **Step 3:** P_5 model of pump having delivery 37.5 lit/min. at 35 bar is selected to suit the requirements.

HYDRAULICS AND PNEUMATICS   SYSTEM DESIGN

- **Step 4: Reservoir Capacity:**

    $\quad\quad\quad$ = 4 × pump delivery (Thumb rule)

    $\quad\quad\quad$ = 4 × 37.5 = 150 litre a select model T_3 having 250 lit. capacity

- **Step 5: Direction Control Valve Selection:** Model D_3 with flow capacity of 76 *lpm* is selected.

- **Step 6: Strainer:** Model S_2 with flow capacity 76 *lpm* is selected.

- **Step 7: Check Valve:** For the selection of check valve, maximum flow rate through one cylinder i.e. 23.5 *lpm* is to be considered. Therefore, model C_2 with capacity of 30.4 *lpm* is selected to suite the requirements. The check valves considered for this problem, C_1 and C_2 are identical even though C_2 has to pass less flow rate from the rod end of the cylinder B.

- **Step 8: Relief Valve:** Relief valve ('R' as shown in circuit) of model R_4 whose maximum allowable working pressure is of 105 bar and flow capacity of 57 *lpm* is selected. As in case of the main line obstruction, the total discharge of 47.1 *lpm* from the two cylinders can be bypassed through the relief valve opening back to the oil reservoir.

- **Step 9: Sequence Valve:** Since it is used in the circuit, its capacity may be 30 *lpm* at 35 bar working pressure.

- **Step 10: Pressure Reducing Valve:** As per the requirement, pump model P_4 is selected whose flow rate is 37.5 *lpm* at 35 bar pressure, hence inlet pressure is 37.5 bar may be still higher outlet pressure is 24.46 bar.

    $\quad\quad$ Flow capacity = 30 *lpm*

Example 6.5: *A machine has two slides 'A' and 'B' which are to be operated hydraulically. The cylinder 'A' has a load of 10 kN and stroke of 50 cm to be completed in 20 sec. The cylinder B has to overcome a load of 15 kN and has a stroke of 50 cm to be completed in 29 sec. The two cylinders are to be moved simultaneously. They are to be retracted as soon as they reach the end position. The loads during return strokes are 5 kN and 3.5 kN respectively. Individual direction control valves are provided for the two cylinders. Draw a suitable circuit to achieve these requirements. Select the different components you have used in the circuit from the given data. Mention the rating of components in case, it is not available in the given data. (Assume reasonable values of data in case, it is not provided in problem)*

Solution: (Refer Fig. 6.9)

Here, two pumps which are mounted on common shaft drive. The pumps are used for synchronisation of the cylinders. The circuit is as follows:

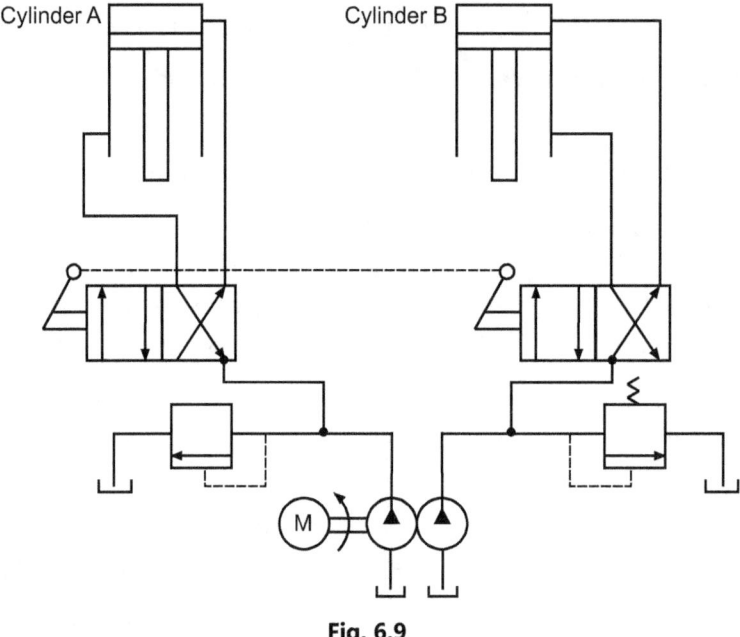

Fig. 6.9

Step 1:

Data for cylinder A	for cylinder B
Load = 10 kN	15 kN
Stroke = 50 cm	50 cm
Time = 20 sec.	29 sec.
Return stroke load = 5 kN	3.5 kN

Selection of Cylinders:

(1) **Cylinder A selection:** Selecting A_4 model

Bore = 75 mm, Rod diameter = 45 mm

Full bore area = $\frac{\pi}{4} \times (0.075)^2 = 4.417 \times 10^{-3}$ m²

Annulus area = $\frac{\pi}{4} [(0.075)^2 - (0.045)^2] = 7.068 \times 10^{-4}$ m²

Working pressure = $\frac{10 \times 10^3}{4.417 \times 10^{-3}} = 44.17 \times 10^6$

= 2263537 N/m² = 22.64 bar

(2) For cylinder B: For A_4 model as above

$$\text{Working pressure} = \frac{15 \times 10^3}{4.417 \times 10^{-3}}$$

$$= 3.395 \times 10^6 = 34 \text{ bar}$$

Step 2: Pump selection:

For cylinder A:

$$\text{Flow rate} = 4.417 \times 10^{-3} \times \frac{0.5}{20} \times 60$$

$$= 6.625 \times 10^{-3} \text{ m}^3/\text{min}$$

$$= 6.625 \text{ lit./min.}$$

and Pressure = 22.64 bar.

So from the catalogue pump P_1 at 35 bar lpm = 7.1 lit/min is selected.

For cylinder B:

$$\text{Flow} = 4.417 \times 10^{-3} \times \frac{0.5}{29} \times 60$$

$$= 4.56 \times 10^{-3} \text{ m}^3/\text{min}$$

$$= 4.56 \text{ lit/min.}$$

and Pressure = 34 bar

So the same pump P_1 is selected.

Thus here, we see that the pumps are have identical delivery. But the loads on both cylinders are not identical. Hence, one pump delivers a little more fluid than the other. Thus, we see that cylinders and pumps are identical but the loads are different. Hence cylinder A will extend fully earlier than B and when both reach the end of their extension, both direction control valve positions are shifted to achieve their retraction. Hence, 4/2 d.c. valves are selected. Model D_1 having a rating of 350 bar and flow of 19 lit/min. is selected.

Step 3: Reservoir size:

$$\text{Size} = (3 \text{ to } 4) \times \text{Pump delivery}$$

$$= 3 \times 7.1$$

$$= 21.3 \text{ litres}$$

Reservoir mode T_1 having capacity 40 lit. is selected.

Example 6.6: *In a special purpose machine, a hydraulic system is used for (i) clamping of job, (ii) moving the machine bed during machining operation. The clamping force required to be developed by each of four clamp cylinders is 1 kN. The bed is to be moved against an effective load of 10 kN. The feed rate required is between 1 m/min to 3.5 m/min. The bed movement is 100 cm. Assume a suitable sequence of operation. Draw a circuit and select the components from the data given.*

Solution:

This is typical example of a sequencing circuit. The one of this type is already explained. It is desired that the clamping cylinders clamp the job first and then the machine bed should move for performing the machine operation. Two sequence valves are required in such circuit. (Refer Fig. 6.10).

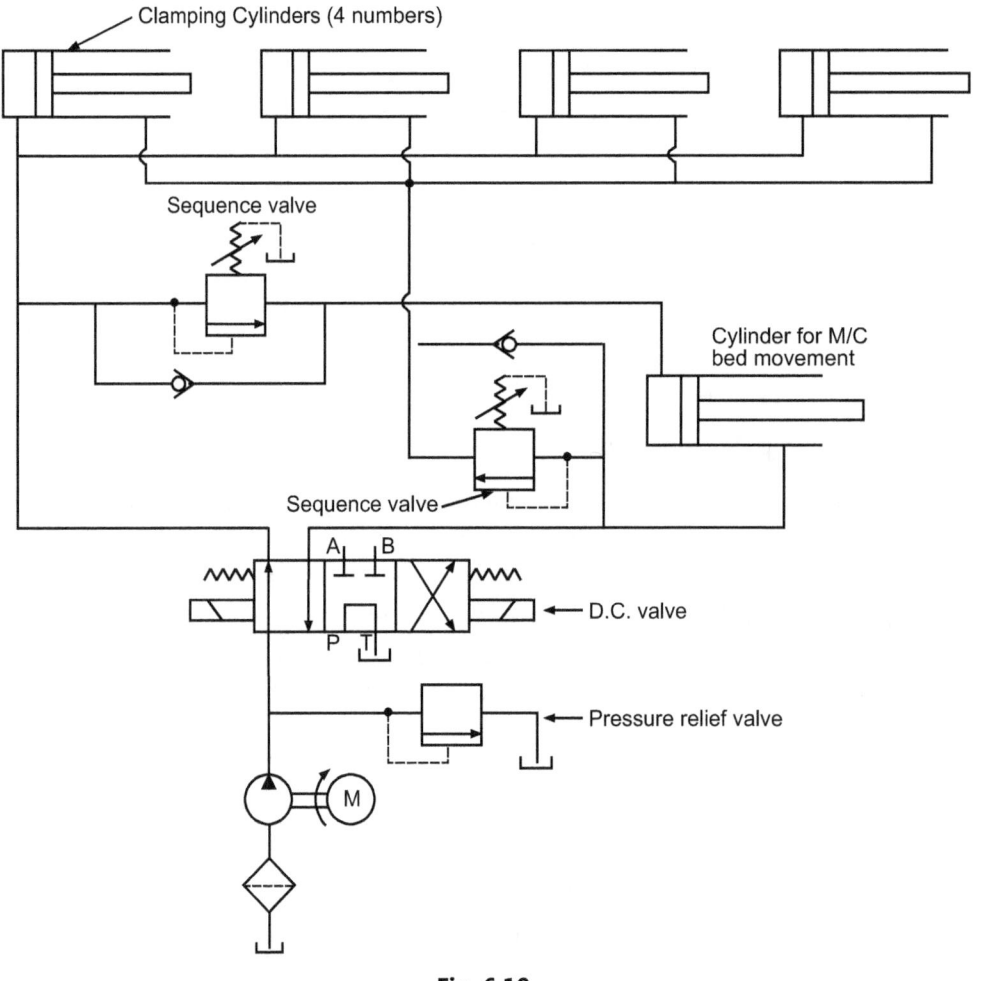

Fig. 6.10

Following the sequence of procedure given in the earlier examples, readers can calculate easily and arrive at the following answers.

(a) For clampling small size cylinders A, bore = 25 mm and rod diameter 6.5 mm are selected. Working pressure = 21 bar.
(b) For bed, larger cylinder A_3 is selected
   Bore = 50 mm,   Rod = 35 mm,   Pressure = 50 bar (approx.)
(c) Pump selected is P_2 : working pressure 70 bar and flow 9.5 lit/min.
(d) Sequence valve setting to 51 bar.
(e) Check valve C_1: 210 bar pressure 15.2 lpm.
(f) D.C. valve model D_1
(g) Oil reservoir = T_1 = 40 lit. capacity.

Example 6.7: *For the fluid power system as shown in Fig. 6.11 determine the external loads F_1 and F_2 so that each cylinder can sustain while moving in the extending direction. Take frictional pressure losses into account. The pump produces an increase of 70.5 bar from the inlet port to discharge port and a flow rate of 2.54×10^{-3} m³/s.*
The following data are applicable.
Kinematic viscosity of oil = 9.3×10^{-5} m²/s, Density of oil = 802 kg/m³   **(Dec. 2001)**
Cylinder diameter = 200 mm, Cylinder rod diameter = 100 mm
All elbows are 90° with K factor = 0.75. Pipe lengths and inside diameters are as given below.

Pipe No.	Length (m)	Diameter (mm)
1	2	40
2	10	25
3	6.5	30
4	3.5	25
5	3.5	25
6	3.5	20
7	3.5	20
8	13.5	25
9	13.5	25

If pipe diameter of pipe (4) is changed to 12.5 mm and forces F_1 and F_2 are kept same, find its effect on the performance of cylinders 1 and 2. Assume the same friction factor for pipes 4 and 5 for this purpose.

Use $\quad f = \dfrac{64}{Re} \quad$ ... For laminar flow

$\quad\quad\quad f = \dfrac{0.316}{(Re)^{1/4}} \quad$ ... For turbulent flow

where, $\quad f$ = Friction factor, Re = Reynold's number

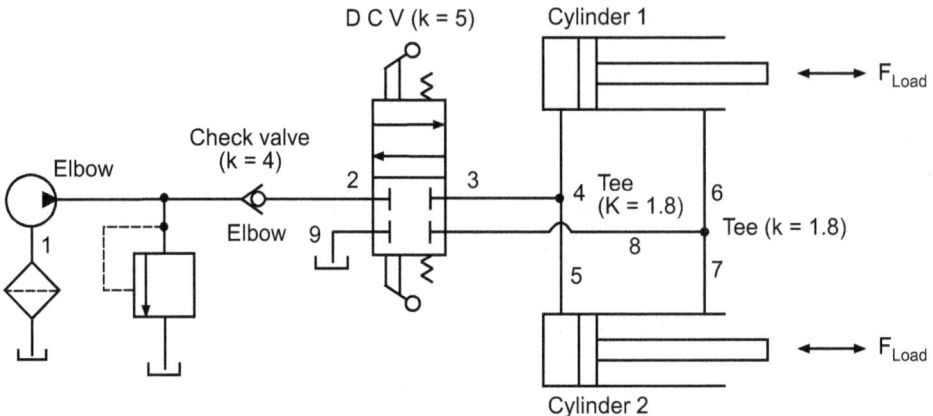

Fig. 6.11

Solution: Flow rate = 2.524×10^{-3} m³/sec

Minimum pipe diameter No. 6 = 20 min.

$$Q = A \cdot V$$

$$V = \frac{2.524 \times 10^{-3}}{\pi/4 \times (0.02)^2} = 8.034 \text{ m/s}$$

Reynold's number $Re = \frac{VD}{v} = \frac{8.034 \times 0.02}{9.3 \times 10^{-5}} = 1727$

Since, Re is < 2000, flow is laminar in all pipes. Using formulae for laminar flow and calculating head loss for each pipe. e.g. for pipe No. 1 : diameter in metre is 0.04, length = 2 m.

Velocity = 2 m/sec, $Re = \frac{VD}{v} = 860$, $f = \frac{64}{Re} = 0.0744$ and

h_f (head loss) $= \frac{FLQ^2}{12.1 \, D^5} = 0.765$

We get table.

Pipe No.	Head loss h_f
1	0.765
2	24.96
3	7.83
4 and 5	8.4
6 and 7	21.36
8 and 9	33.7

Similarly, head loss in various accessories also needs to be calculated.

(a) There are two elbows:
   First is after pipe 1 (k = 0.75)
   $$h_f = \frac{kv^2}{2g} = 0.75 \times \frac{(2)^2}{2 \times 9.81} = 0.15 \text{ m} \qquad \ldots (1)$$
   Second is after pipe 8 (k = 0.75)
   $$h_f = k\frac{V^2}{2g} = 0.75 \times \frac{(5.4)^2}{2 \times 9.81} = 1 \text{ m} \qquad \ldots (2)$$

(b) Check valve k = 4
   $$h_f = 5.39 \text{ m} \quad (v = 5.14 \text{ m/sec}) \qquad \ldots (3)$$

(c) D.C. valve k = 5 (forward line)
   $$h_f = 4.83 \text{ m} \quad \left[\text{Velocity} = \left(\frac{5.14 + 3.567}{2}\right) = 4.353 \text{ m/s}\right] \qquad \ldots (4)$$

(d) There are two Tee joints
   (i) Between pipes 3 and 4, k = 1.8, velocity = 3.5 m/sec.
   $$h_f = 1.17 \text{ m} \qquad \ldots (5)$$
   (ii) Between pipes 6, 7 and 8 (k = 1.8)
   $$h_f = 2.42 \text{ m} \qquad (\text{velocity} = 5.14 \text{ m/sec}) \ldots (6)$$

(e) D.C. valve k = 5 (Return line)
   $$h_f = 6.73 \qquad (\text{Velocity} = 5.14 \text{ m/sec}) \ldots (7)$$

So total head loss in all above accessories before oil reaches cylinder
$$= \text{head loss in 7 pipe (1) + elbow + check valve + pipe 2}$$
$$+ \text{D.C. valve (Forward) + pipe 3 + Tee + Pipe 4/5}$$
$$= 53.84 \text{ m}.$$

$$\therefore \quad \text{Drop in pressure} = \rho g h_f = \frac{802 \times 9.81 \times 53.84}{10^5} = 4.24 \text{ bar}$$

Now, pressure specified in problem to cylinder is 70.5 bar.

Actual pressure after considering drop is 70.5 − 4.24 = 66.26 bar.

Now, head loss in the pipe after cylinders i.e. head loss in (pipe 6 and 7 + Tee + pipe 8 + D.C. valve (return) + elbow + pipe 9)
$$= 21.36 + 2.47 + 33.7 + 6.73 + 1 + 33.7$$
$$= 98.96 \text{ metres}$$

So, associated pressure drop $= \rho g h_f = \dfrac{802 \times 9.81 \times 98.96}{10^5} = 7.79 \text{ bar}$

So pressure on rod end = 7.79 bar

Given data:

$$\text{Cylinder diameter} = 200 \text{ mm}$$
$$\text{Rod diameter} = 100 \text{ mm}$$

So that force can be sustained $= P_1 A_1 - P_2 A_2$

$$= \left[66.26 \times 10^5 \times \frac{\pi}{4} \times (0.2)^2\right] - \left[7.79 \times 10^5 \times \frac{\pi}{4} \times \{(0.2)^2 - (0.1)^2\}\right]$$

$$= 208161.93 \text{ newton}$$

Second Part of Problem:

Initially pipes (4) and (5) are of same diameter = 25 mm
Now pipe (4) diameter is changed to 12.5 mm

But
$$hf_4 = hf_5$$

$$\frac{Q_4^2}{d_4^5} = \frac{Q_5^2}{d_5^5}$$

$$\therefore \quad Q_5^2 = \frac{d_5^5}{d_4^5} \times Q_4^2 = \frac{25^2}{12.5^5} \times Q_4^2$$

i.e. $\quad Q_5 = 5.66 \, Q_4$

and $\quad$ Total flow $= 2.564 \times 10^3 \text{ m}^3/\text{sec} = Q_4 + Q_5$

$\therefore \quad Q_4 = 3.85 \times 10^{-4} \text{ m}^3/\text{sec}$ and $Q_5 = 2.179 \text{ m}^3/\text{sec}$.

$$Q_4 = A \cdot V$$

$$3.85 \times 10^{-4} = \frac{\pi}{4} \times (0.2)^2 \times \text{velocity}$$

$\therefore \quad$ Velocity in cylinder 1 $= 0.01225 \text{ m/sec}$

and now velocity in cylinder (2)

$$= \frac{2.179}{\frac{\pi}{4} \times (0.2)^2} = 0.0694 \text{ m/sec}.$$

Earlier both pipes were of diameter 25 mm

$$Q_4 = Q_5 = \frac{2.564 \times 10^{-3}}{2} = 1.282 \times 10^{-3} \text{ m/sec}.$$

and $\quad$ Velocity in both $= \dfrac{1.282 \times 10^{-3}}{\frac{\pi}{4} \times (0.2)^2} = 0.0408 \text{ m/s}$

So piston in cylinder (1) will be slower by

0.0408 − 0.01225 = 0.02855 m/sec.

Piston in cylinder (2) will be faster by

0.0694 − 0.0408 = 0.02855 m/sec.

Example 6.8: *A 50 kN hydraulic press has a stroke of 1 m. The main ram is required to move down with a velocity of about 5 m/min for the first 80 cm against a negligible load. The ram is slowed down to a velocity of 2 m/min for the next 12 cm against a load of 12 kN, followed by the working stroke of last 8 cm developing a maximum force of 50 kN. The cylinder is returned as quickly as possible and is to be held at the top most position.*

Draw a circuit which will fulfill these requirements. Select the different components used in the circuit from the data tables given in Example 6.4. Mention the ratings of components in case it is not available in the given data. **(Dec. 2008)**

Solution:

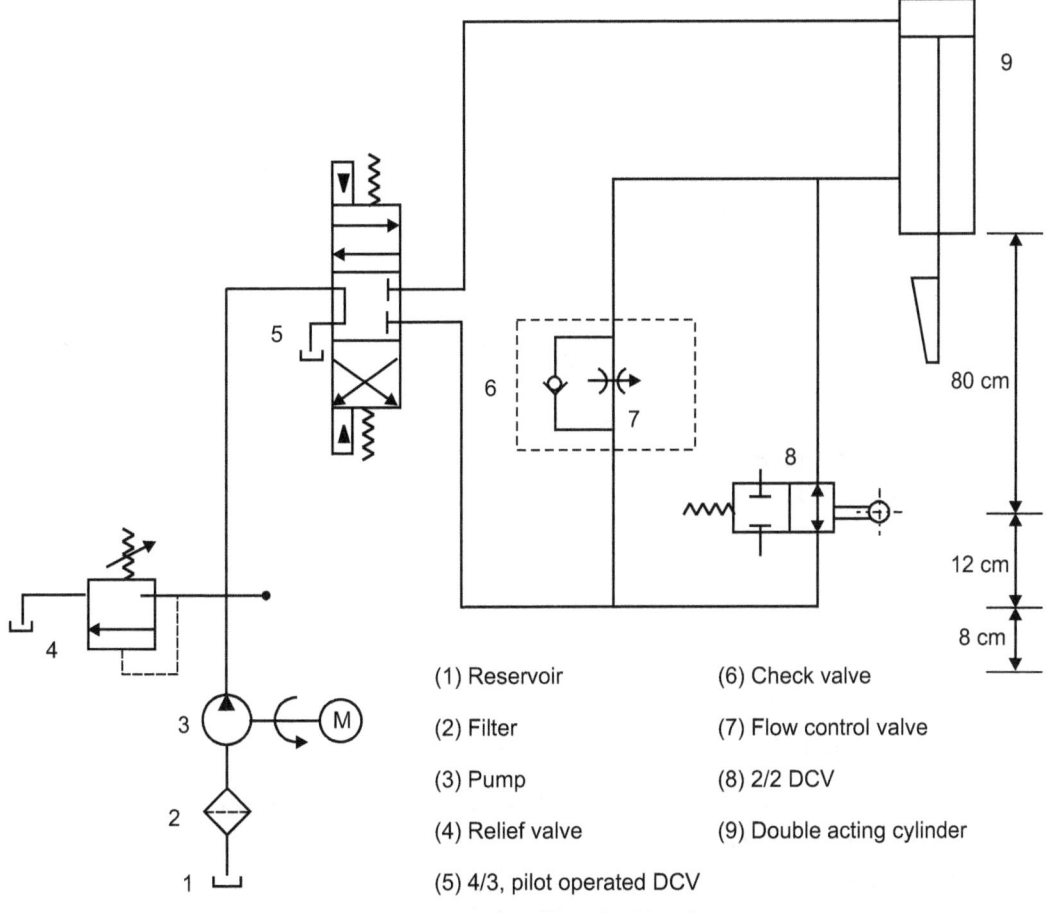

(1) Reservoir (6) Check valve
(2) Filter (7) Flow control valve
(3) Pump (8) 2/2 DCV
(4) Relief valve (9) Double acting cylinder
(5) 4/3, pilot operated DCV

Fig. 6.12: Hydraulic press circuit

Fig. 6.12 shows the hydraulic circuit for a given press working operation. The downward motion of the cylinder is controlled and upward motion is as fast as possible. Now we calculate the pressure flow requirement in the extension and retraction motion of the cylinder.

(i) Downward Motion of Cylinder:

(a) First 80 cm stroke with negligible load:

Velocity during this stroke, V_{ext} = 5 m/min

Selecting model A_5 with piston diameter = 100 mm and rod diameter = 50 mm

$$\text{Flow rate, } Q_1 = \frac{\pi}{4} D^2 \times V_{ext} = \frac{\pi}{4}(0.1)^2 \times 5 = \mathbf{39.27 \text{ lpm}}$$

$$\text{Pressure, } P_1 = \text{negligible}$$

(b) Next 12 cm stroke with 2 m/min speed against 12 kN load:

$$\text{Flow rate, } Q_2 = \frac{\pi}{4} D^2 \times V_{ext}$$

$$= \frac{\pi}{4}(0.1)^2 \times 2 = 15.7 \text{ lpm}$$

$$\text{Pressure, } P_2 = \frac{F}{\frac{\pi}{4}(D^2)} = \frac{12000}{\frac{\pi}{4}(0.1)^2} = \mathbf{15.28 \text{ bar}}$$

(c) Last 8 cm stroke with 2 m/min speed against 50 kN load:

$$\text{Flow rate} = Q_3 = Q_2 = \mathbf{15.7 \text{ lpm}}$$

$$\text{Pressure} = P_3 = \frac{50000}{\frac{\pi}{4}(0.1)^2} = \mathbf{63.66 \text{ bar}}$$

(ii) For Upward Motion of the Cylinder:

Upward motion is as fast as possible.

$$\text{Flow rate to rod end side} = Q_4 = \frac{\pi}{4}(D^2 - d^2) \times V_{ret}$$

$$\therefore \quad 39.27 \times 10^{-3} = \frac{\pi}{4}\left[(0.1)^2 - (0.05)^2\right] \times V_{ret}$$

$$\therefore \quad V_{ret} = \mathbf{6.67 \text{ m/min}}$$

$$\text{Time required for upward motion} = \frac{\text{Stroke}}{V_{ret}} = \frac{1}{6.67}$$

$$= 0.149 \text{ min} = 8.999 \text{ sec} \approx \mathbf{9 \text{ sec}}$$

(iii) Selection of Components:

(a) Reservoir (1):

Maximum flow rate required = 39.27 lpm

∴ Reservoir capacity = 3 × 39.27 = 117.81 lpm

Select model T_3 having 250 litre capacity.

(b) Filter (2):

Select model S_2 with 76 lpm capacity.

(c) Pump (3):

Maximum pressure = 63.66 bar

and Maximum flow rate = 39.27 lpm

Select a model other than given in the table with these ratings.

(d) Relief Valve (4):

Maximum pressure = 63.66 bar

and Maximum flow capacity = 39.27 lpm

Select model R_4 with pressure 105 bar and flow 57 lpm

(e) Direction Control Valve (5):

Select D_3 with 210 bar and 76 lpm.

(f) Check Valve (6):

Select C_3 with 210 bar and 76 lpm

(g) Flow Control Valve (7):

Minimum flow capacity = 15.7 Lpm

Working pressure = 63.66 bar

Select model F_3 with maximum operating pressure 105 bar and flow range 0 - 16.3 lpm.

(h) Direction Control Valve (8):

Maximum pressure = Minimum flow rate = 39.27 lpm

Select model D_3 with 210 bar and 76 lpm.

Example 6.9: *A machine tool cross slide is moved by means of a hydraulic system. The motion of the cylinder is as follows:*
(a) Initially it moves through a distance of 150 mm against a load of 15 kN in about 4 seconds.
(b) It is followed by a working stroke of another 150 mm against an effective load of 25 kN. The feed rate during this part of the stroke is required to be 1 m/min.
(c) The load during return stroke is 15 kN.
A meter-out type of circuit is used. Draw a circuit which will fulfill these requirements. Select different components used in the circuit from the data tables given in Example 6.4. Mention the ratings of the components in case it is not available in the given data. **(Dec. 2008)**

Solution:

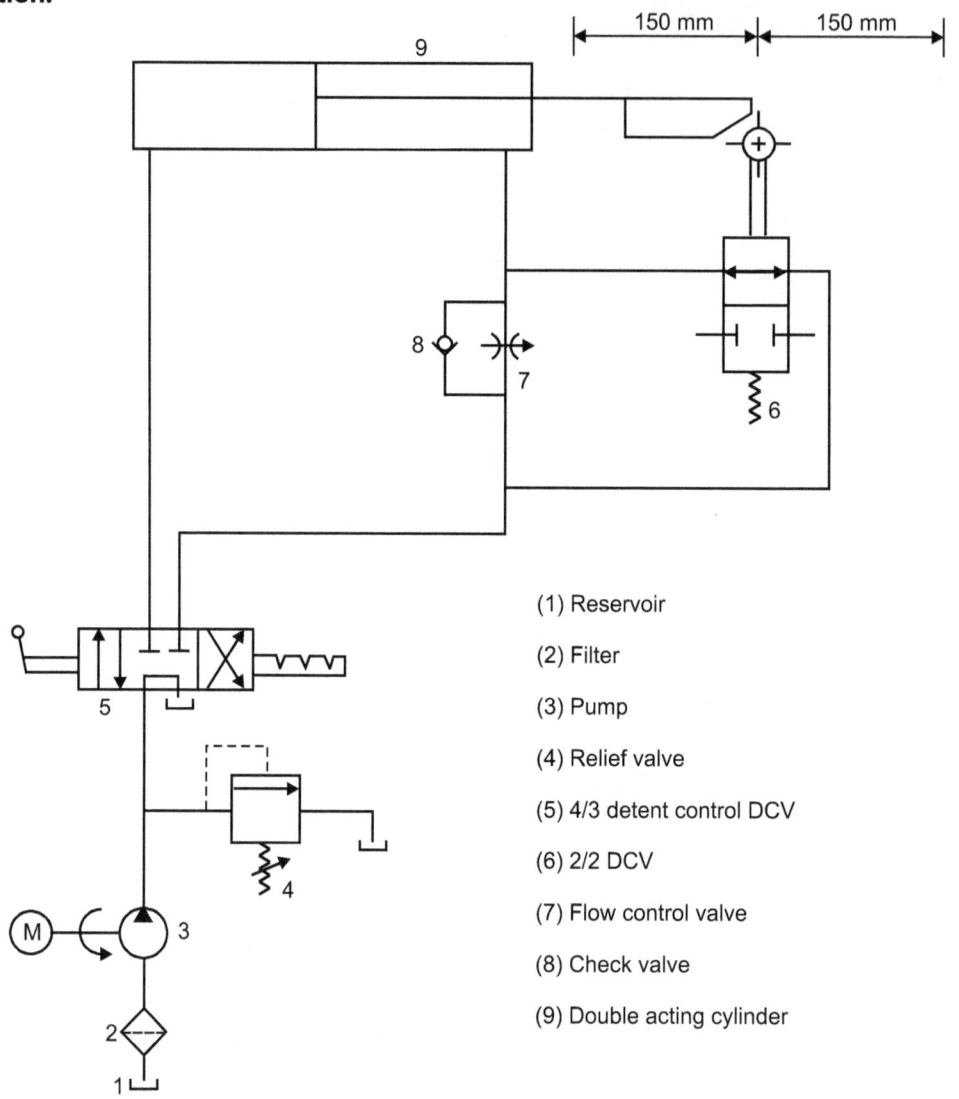

(1) Reservoir
(2) Filter
(3) Pump
(4) Relief valve
(5) 4/3 detent control DCV
(6) 2/2 DCV
(7) Flow control valve
(8) Check valve
(9) Double acting cylinder

Fig. 6.13

(i) For Forward Motion of Cylinder:

For first 150 mm, with a load of 15 kN.

$$\text{Velocity of extension} = V_{ext} = \frac{0.15}{4} = 2.25 \text{ m/min}$$

Selecting model A_4 from the table,

Bore diameter = 75 mm, Rod diameter = 45 mm

Then,

Maximum working pressure, $P_1 = \dfrac{F}{A_p}$

$= \dfrac{15000}{\dfrac{\pi}{4}(0.075)^2}$ = **33.95 bar**

Flow rate, $Q_1 = A_p \times V_{ext}$

$= \dfrac{\pi}{4}(0.075)^2 \times 2.25$ = **9.94 lpm**

For next 150 mm, with a load of 25 kN,

$V_{ext} = 1$ m/min

Pressure required, $P_2 = \dfrac{F}{A_p} = \dfrac{25000}{\dfrac{\pi}{4}(0.075)^2}$ = **56.59 bar**

Flow rate, $Q_2 = A_p \times V_{ext}$

$= \dfrac{\pi}{4}(0.075)^2 \times 1$ = **4.42 lpm**

(ii) For Return Motion:

Return motion is faster.

The flow rate to rod end side, $Q_3 = \dfrac{\pi}{4}(D^2 - d^2) \times V_{ret}$

$\therefore \quad 9.94 \times 10^{-3} = \dfrac{\pi}{4}[(0.075)^2 - (0.045)^2] \times V_{ret}$

$\therefore \quad V_{ret} = $ **3.51 m/min**

Time required for return motion $= \dfrac{\text{Stroke}}{V_{ret}} = \dfrac{300 \times 10^{-3}}{3.5} = 0.0857$ min

= **5.143 seconds**

(iii) Component Selection:

(a) **Reservoir:** Maximum flow rate needed is 9.94 lpm

$\therefore$ Reservoir capacity = 3×9.94 = 29.82 lpm

Select model T_1 with capacity 40 litres.

(b) **Suction Strainer:** Select model S_1 with flow capacity 38 lpm.

(c) **Pump:** Select P_3 with pressure 70 bar and flow capacity 14.3 lpm.

(d) **Relief Valve:** Select model R_1 with maximum working pressure 70 bar and flow capacity 11.4 lpm.

(e) **Direction Control Valve:** Select model D_1 with maximum working pressure 350 bar and 19 lpm.

(f) **Flow Control Valve:** For flow capacity 4.42 lpm select model F_2 with 105 bar and 0 - 4.9 lpm.

(g) **Check Valve:** Select model C_1 with 210 bar and 15.2 lpm.

Example 6.10: *Draw a simple hydraulic circuit which will operate a hydraulic cylinder of a machine. The load during the forward stroke is 15 kN and that during the return stroke is approximately 9.5 kN. The forward and return speeds are about 3.5 m/min and 5.5 m/min respectively. The total stroke of the cylinder is 300 mm. A provision is required to hold the cylinder anywhere in between the end positions. Select the different components from the data tables given in Example 6.4. Specify the ratings of the components in case, it is not available in the given data.*

(May 2007)

Solution:

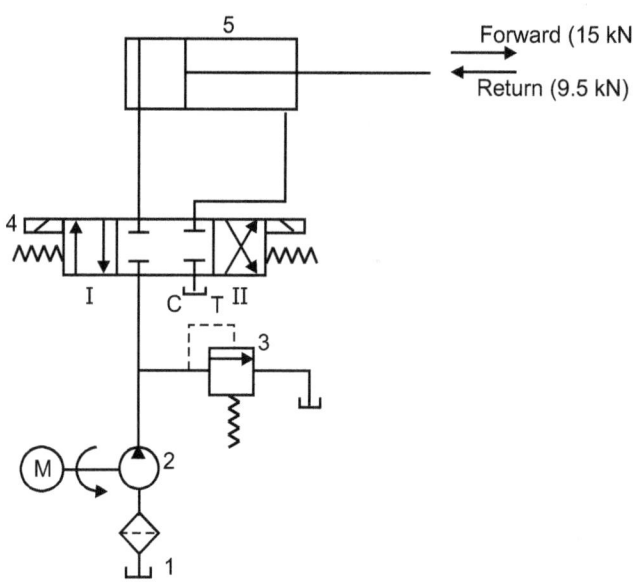

Fig. 6.14

(i) Functional Approach:

This circuit makes use of one DCV (4/3, centrally closed, solenoid operated). When DCV (4) is in 'I' position, the cylinder (5) will have forward motion with a speed of 3.5 m/min and when it is in 'II' position, cylinder (5) has a return stroke with a speed of 5.5 m/min. If we want to stop in between, keep the DCV in normal central position.

(ii) Strength Considerations:

Forward stroke: Piston moves with 3.5 m/min (0.05833 m/s) having load equal to 15 kN. From the table, selecting model 'A_5', Bore = 100 mm = 0.1 m and Rod diameter = 50 mm = 0.05 m

Pressure, $P = \dfrac{F}{A_p} = \dfrac{15000}{\dfrac{\pi}{4}(0.1)^2} = 19.098$ bar

Flow rate, $Q = A_p \times V_{ext}$

$= \dfrac{\pi}{4}(0.1)^2 \times (0.05833)$

$= 4.58 \times 10^{-4}$ m³/sec

$= 27.48$ lpm

Return motion: Return motion with 5.5 m/min speed and with 9.5 kN load.

Pressure, $P = \dfrac{F}{(A_p - A_{ir})}$

$= \dfrac{9500}{\dfrac{\pi}{4}[(0.1)^2 - (0.05)^2]}$

$= \mathbf{16.13\ bar}$

Flow rate, $Q = \dfrac{\pi}{4}[(0.1)^2 - (0.05)^2] \times \dfrac{5.5}{60}$

$= 5.39 \times 10^{-4}$ m³/sec

$= \mathbf{32.39\ lpm}$

(iii) Component Selection:

(a) **Reservoir:** By the thumb rule 2 to 3 times of the maximum flow rate

$= 32.39 \times 3 = 97.17$ lpm ≈ 100 lpm

Select model T_2 of capacity = 100 lpm.

(b) **Suction strainer:** Minimum flow rate capacity is 27.48 lpm, maximum upto infinity. Select model S_1 of capacity 38 lpm.

HYDRAULICS AND PNEUMATICS — SYSTEM DESIGN

(c) **Pump:** Minimum flow rate capacity 27.48 lpm and maximum flow of 32.39 lpm required. Select model P_5 from chart of capacity 35.6 lpm at 70 bar.

(d) **Relief valve:** Maximum working pressure 19.09 bar and flow rate 32.39 lpm.

Select model R_4, Q = 57 lpm and P = 105 bar.

(e) **DCV:** 4/3 valve.

Flow rate 32.39 lpm, pressure = 19.09 bar.

∴ Select model D_2 of capacity 38 lpm and working pressure 210 bar.

(f) **Cylinder:** Selected cylinder 'A_5' has maximum working pressure of 210 bar which is higher than the actual working pressure (10.09 bar). Thus, it is also safe.

Example 6.11: *A machine slide is moved by a cylinder. The motion required is as follows:*

(a) *Initially the cylinder moves against a load of 2.5 kN till it reaches the workpiece at a speed of about 1.5 m/min.*

(b) *The speed drops down to about 0.5 m/min as soon as the load increases to 12.5 kN.*

(c) *The return motion is against a load of 2.5 kN. A meter out circuit is used. Draw a circuit which will fulfill these requirements. Select different components you have used in the circuit from the given data. Mention ratings of the components in case it is not available in the given data.*

Use data tables given in Example 6.4. **(Dec. 2010)**

Solution:

(a) Forward Motion of Cylinder Against 2.5 kN:

$$\text{Load} = 2.5 \text{ kN}$$
$$V_{ext} = 1.5 \text{ m/min}$$

Selection of Cylinder: Selecting A_5 cylinder from the data given.

From data table corresponding to A_5 model,

Bore diameter = 100 mm = 0.1 m, Rod diameter = 50 mm = 0.05 m

Maximum pressure = 210 bar

$$\text{Bore area} = \frac{\pi}{4} D^2 = \frac{3.14}{4} \times (0.1)^2 = 7.85 \times 10^{-3} \text{ m}^2$$

$$\text{Annular area} = \frac{\pi}{4}(D^2 - d^2) = \frac{3.14}{4} \times [(0.1)^2 - (0.05)^2]$$

$$= 5.88 \times 10^{-3} \text{ m}^2$$

Maximum pressure required during extension

$$= \frac{\text{Load}}{\text{Area}} = \frac{2.5 \times 10^3}{7.85 \times 10^{-3}}$$

$$= 3.18 \times 10^5 \text{ N/m}^2 = 3.18 \text{ bar}$$

(b) Forward Motion Against 12.5 kW with 0.5 m/min Speed:

Load = 12.5 kN, V_{ext} = 0.5 m/min

Maximum working pressure required

$$= \frac{\text{Load}}{\text{Area}} = \frac{12.5 \times 10^3}{7.85 \times 10^{-3}}$$

$$= 15.92 \times 10^5 \text{ N/m}^2 = 15.92 \text{ bar}$$

Fluid flow requirement:

(i) Motion Against 2.5 kN with 1.5 m/min Velocity:

$$Q = A \times V_{ext}$$

$$= 7.85 \times 10^{-3} \times 1.5 = 0.011775 \text{ m}^3/\text{min}$$

$$= 11.775 \text{ lit/min}$$

(ii) Motion Against 12.5 kN with 0.5 m/min Velocity:

$$Q = A \times V_{ext}$$

$$= 7.85 \times 10^{-3} \times 0.5 = 3.925 \times 10^{-3} \text{ m}^3/\text{min}$$

$$= 3.925 \text{ lit/min}$$

(iii) For return Motion: Flow rate given to the rod end side,

$$Q = (A_P - A_R) \times V_{ext}$$

The maximum flow rate required during extension is 11.775 lit/min. So considering the same flow rate available for retraction, we get,

$$11.771 \times 10^{-3} = 5.88 \times 10^{-3} \times V_{ret}$$

$$V_{ret} = \frac{11.775 \times 10^{-3}}{5.88 \times 10^{-3}} = 2 \text{ m/min}$$

Selection of Components:

1. **Pump:** Maximum pressure required is 15.92 bar and maximum flow rate required is 11.775 lit/min.

   Select model P_3 gives 16.1 lit/min.

2. **Oil reservoir:** By thumb rule, 3 to 4 times the maximum flow rate required

   $$= 3 \times 11.775 = 35.52 \text{ lit/min}$$

   Select T_1 40 litres capacity.

3. **Check valve:** Select C_1. It can work at maximum pressure of 210 bar with flow capacity 15.2 lit/min.
4. **DCV:** Select D_1. It can work at maximum pressure 350 bar with flow capacity 19 lit/min.
5. **FCV:** Select F_3 having working pressure 105 bar with flow capacity 0 - 16.3.
6. **Relief valve:** Select R_2 having flow capacity 19 lit/min and maximum pressure 210 bar.
7. **Pressure gauge:** Select PG_1 having range 0 - 25 bar.
8. **Suction strainer:** Select S_1 having flow capacity 38 lit/min.

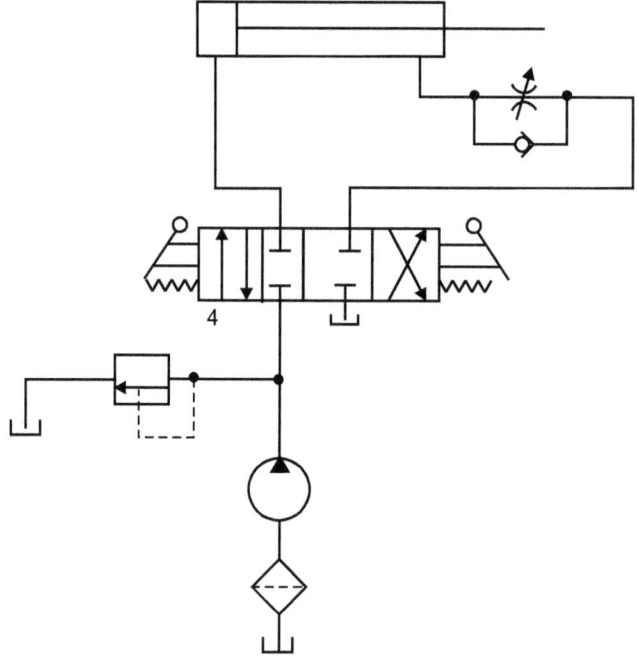

Fig. 6.15

Example 6.12: *A hydraulic cylinder used to operate a machine has the following requirements:*

(a) During the initial movement of 300 mm it has a load of 30 kN and it should complete this distance in about 6 seconds.

(b) This is followed by a slow working stroke of 100 mm against a load of 50 kN which should be completed in 3 to 6 seconds. The time required is to be adjustable.

(c) The return motion of 400 mm is against a load of 40 kN which should be completed in about 7 seconds time.

HYDRAULICS AND PNEUMATICS — SYSTEM DESIGN

Facility is required to hold the cylinder anywhere in between the entire stroke. Solenoid operated valves are used in the circuit. A meter out circuit is used.

Draw a circuit which will fulfill these requirements. Select different components you have used in the circuit from the given data tables used in Example 6.4. Mention the ratings of the components in case it is not available in the given data. **(Dec. 2009)**

Solution: The hydraulic circuit for a given example:

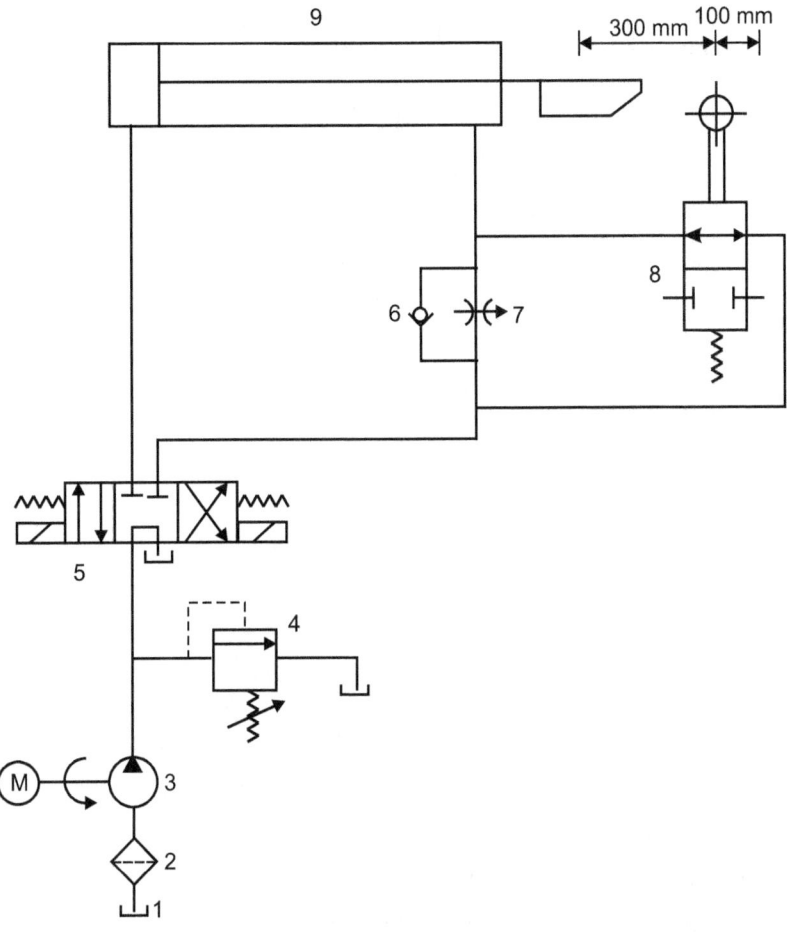

Fig. 6.16

Step 1: Selection of Cylinder:

Selecting 'A_5' cylinder from the data given having,

    Maximum pressure = 210 bar

    Bore diameter = 100 mm and rod diameter = 50 mm

Total stroke of cylinder = 300 + 100 = 400 mm

Full bore area = $\frac{\pi}{4} D^2 = \frac{\pi}{4}(0.1)^2 = 7.85 \times 10^{-3}$ m²

and Annulus area = $\frac{\pi}{4}(D^2 - d^2) = \frac{\pi}{4}\left[(0.1)^2 - (0.05)^2\right]$

= 5.89×10^{-3} m²

Maximum working pressure = $\dfrac{\text{Load}}{\text{Area}} = \dfrac{30 \times 10^3}{7.85 \times 10^{-3}}$

= 3.82×10^6 N/m²

= 38.2 bar

Step 2: Flow Requirement Calculations:

(a) For rapid approach 300 mm distance in 6 seconds:

Velocity of piston needed = $\dfrac{300 \times 10^{-3}}{6}$ = 0.05 m/sec

Flow required = $A \times V = 7.85 \times 10^{-3} \times 0.05$

= 23.55 lpm

(b) For working stroke:

Velocity = $\dfrac{0.1}{3}$ = 0.0333 m/sec

Flow required = $7.85 \times 10^{-3} \times 0.0333$ = 15.7 lpm

and for velocity = $\dfrac{0.1}{6}$ = 0.01667 m/sec

Flow required = $7.85 \times 10^{-3} \times 0.01667$ = 7.85 lpm

This is achieved by adjusting the flow control valve in meter out circuit.

Step 3: Selection of Pump:

Maximum flow rate required = 23.55 lpm

Maximum working pressure required = 38.2 bar

Selecting the vane pump of model 'P_5' from the data having

P = 70 bar and Q = 35.6 lpm.

Step 4: Flow Control Valve and Reservoir Sizing:

For achieving speed of 0.0333 m/sec, the flow to be metered is,

Q = Annulus area × Velocity

$$= 5.89 \times 10^{-3} \times 0.0333$$
$$= 11.77 \text{ lpm}.$$

and for achieving 0.01667 m/sec, the flow required is

$$Q = 5.89 \times 10^{-3} \times 0.01667$$
$$= 5.89 \text{ lpm}$$

Hence model 'F_3' having P = 105 bar and Q = 0 - 16.3 lpm.

Now, displacement of cylinder $= \frac{\pi}{4} D^2 \times$ Stroke

$$= \frac{\pi}{4} (0.1)^2 \times 400 \times 10^{-3}$$
$$= 3.14 \text{ litres of oil}$$

Total oil required = 3.14 lit + 3.14 lit (approximately for piping)
$$= 6.28 \text{ lit}$$

If we assume the velocity of oil in suction pipe = 2 m/sec.

Then $\quad Q = A \times V$

∴ $\quad$ Area of pipe $= \dfrac{23.55}{2 \times 1000 \times 60}$

∴ $\quad$ Diameter of pipe = 15.8 mm

Sizing of the reservoir from thumb rule formula is 3 to 4 times pump delivery per min.

∴ $\quad 3 \times 23.55 = 70.65$ lit.

Select model 'T_2' having capacity 100 lit.

Step 5: Selection of Relief Valve:

Selecting 'R_3' having P = 70 bar and Q = 30.4 lpm.

Step 6: Selection of DCV:

Selecting 'D_2' having P = 210 bar and Q = 38 lpm

Example 6.13: *A double acting hydraulic cylinder has a reciprocating motion. The forward motion is obtained using a regenerative circuit. The load during the forward stroke is 12 kN. The total stroke of 50 cm is to be completed in about 5 seconds. The return speed is to be as fast as possible.*

Draw a circuit to achieve above. Select different components you have used in the circuit from the given data tables used in Example 6.4. Mention the ratings of the components in case it is not available in the given data.

HYDRAULICS AND PNEUMATICS — SYSTEM DESIGN

Solution:

Hydraulic circuit according to the given condition:

System design will be started with selecting the actuator first. Now, selecting cylinder (6) with the model 'A$_4$' from the data.

Bore diameter = D = 75 mm = 0.075 m
Rod diameter = d = 45 mm = 0.045 m

Extension/forward motion:

Pressure of the blind end side of the cylinder required to take a load of 12 kN.

$$\text{Net force} = F_1 - F_2$$

$$\therefore \quad 12 = PA_p - PA_r = P(A_p - A_r)$$

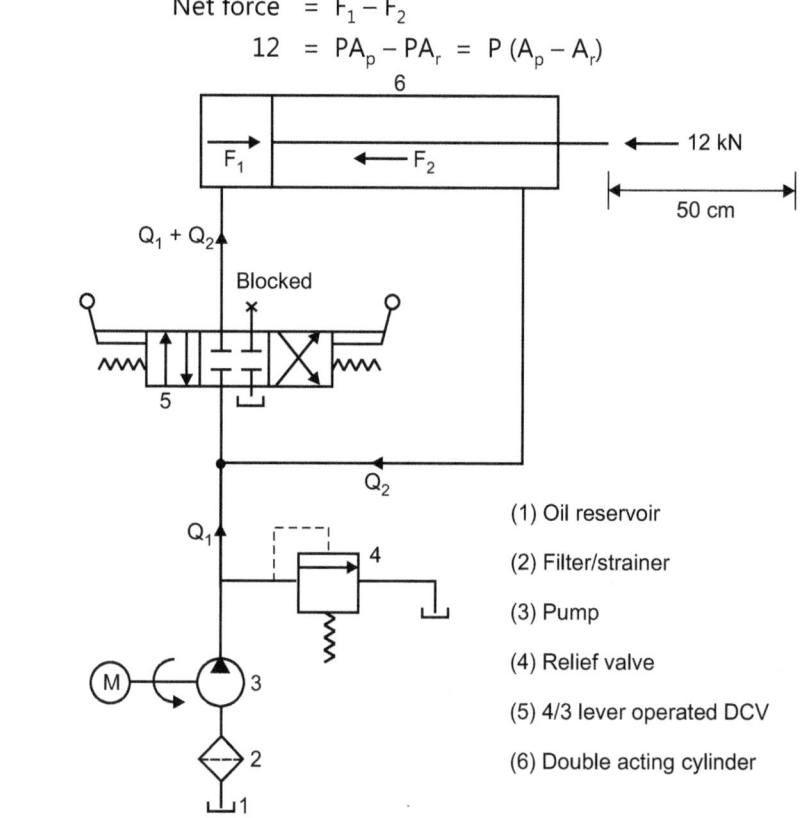

Fig. 6.17: Regenerative circuit

(1) Oil reservoir
(2) Filter/strainer
(3) Pump
(4) Relief valve
(5) 4/3 lever operated DCV
(6) Double acting cylinder

$$\therefore \quad P = \frac{12}{A_p - A_r} = \frac{12}{\frac{\pi}{4}(D^2 - d^2)}$$

$$\therefore \quad P = \frac{12}{\frac{\pi}{4}[(0.075)^2 - (0.045)^2]}$$

HYDRAULICS AND PNEUMATICS — SYSTEM DESIGN

$$\therefore \quad P = 4244.13 \text{ kN/m}^2$$
$$\therefore \quad P = 42.44 \text{ bar}$$

Now, extension velocity, $V_{ext} = \dfrac{0.50}{5} = 0.1 \text{ m/sec}$

$$V_{ext} = \dfrac{Q_1 + Q_2}{A_p}$$

$\therefore \quad 0.1 \times \dfrac{\pi}{4}(0.075)^2 = Q_1 + 0.1\left(\dfrac{\pi}{4}\left[(0.075)^2 - (0.045)^2\right]\right)$

$\therefore \quad 4.4178 \times 10^{-4} = Q_1 + 2.827 \times 10^{-4}$

$\therefore \quad Q_1 = 1.591 \times 10^{-4} \text{ m}^3/\text{sec}$

Return/Backward motion:

$$\text{Refraction speed} = V_{ret} = \dfrac{Q_1}{A_p - A_r} = \dfrac{1.591 \times 10^{-4}}{\dfrac{\pi}{4}\left[(0.075)^2 - (0.045)^2\right]}$$

$\therefore \quad V_{ret} = 0.0563 \text{ m/sec}$

Selection of components:

1. **Oil reservoir:** Maximum flow rate, $Q_1 = 1.591 \times 10^{-4}$ m³/sec = 9.54 Lpm.

   To compensate for the leakage and pipe line volumes, we consider the reservoir capacity = $3 \times 9.54 = 28.62$ lpm.

   From the data given, we select model 'T$_1$ with velocity 40 lit.

2. **Filter/strainer:** Select model 'S$_1$' with 38 lpm capacity.
3. **Pump:** Maximum pressure 42.44 bar and discharge 9.54 lpm. Selecting model 'P$_3$' with P = 30 bar and Q = 14.3 lpm.
4. **Relief valve:** Select 'R$_1$' model with P = 70 bar and Q = 11.4 lpm.
5. **Direction control valve:** Select model 'D$_1$' with P = 350 bar and 19 lpm.

EXERCISE

1. A 100 kN hydraulic press has a total stroke of 1.2 m. The initial approach is of 1 m. The speed during the next 0.2 m stroke is required to be between 1 m/min to 3 m/min. The load during return stroke is 40 kN and the speed is to be limited to 5 m/min. A provision is required to obtain uniform speed working stroke and for holding the ram at the top most position.
   Draw a circuit which will fulfill these requirements. Select different components you have used in the circuit from the data given. Mention the ratings of the components in case, it is not available in the given data.
2. A hydraulic cylinder used to operate a machine has the following requirements:
   (a) During initial movement of 35 mm it has a load of 20 kN and it should complete this distance in about 7 seconds.

(b) This is followed by a slow working stroke of 150 mm against a load of 50 kN, which should be completed in 5 to 10 seconds. The time required is to be adjustable.

(c) The return motion of 500 mm is against a load of 40 kN which should be completed in about 8 seconds.

Solenoid operated valves are used in the circuit. Draw a circuit which will fulfill these requirements. Select different components you have used in the circuit from the given data. Mention the ratings of the components in case, it is not available in the given data.

3. Construct a hydraulic circuit for a machine of following sequence requirements.
   (a) Cylinder 1 extends fully to contact the work piece. Pressure exerted by the cylinder in the work piece should be 60 bar.
   (b) Cylinder 2 extends fully.
   (c) Cylinder 2 retracts fully, while cylinder 1 should be in the extended position.
   (d) When pressure in the system drops to 25 bar, cylinder 1 retracts.
   Draw a hydraulic circuit. Select the components from the catalogue used in solved problem.

   Hint : Draw sequencing circuit and follow all steps mentioned in Example (solved) 6.4.

4. A machine tool slide is to be moved by means of hydraulic cylinder as follows :
   (a) Initially it moves through a distance of 250 mm against a load of 10 kN in 5 seconds.
   (b) It then follows a working stroke of 120 mm against an effective load of 40 kN. The feed rate required is between 0.5 to 1 m/min.
   (c) The return stroke is as fast as possible.
   A meter-out circuit is used for speed control. Draw the circuit and select different components used in circuit. **(Dec. 2011)**

   Hint : Follow steps similar to Solved Example 6.11.

5. Two similar cylinders A and B are to be operated simultaneously. The load for cylinder A is 20 kN and for B is 25 kN. Cylinders A and B has a stroke of 1 M which need to be completed in 25 seconds. The cylinder B should start retracting when cylinder A has completed its retraction. Returning of cylinders are as quickly as possible. Draw a circuit as per above requirements. Select all the components used in circuit from standard data tables. **(Dec. 2011)**

APPENDIX

However, often more common practical units are used to measure viscosity as given below:

°E - Degree Engler in Germany and Europe

RS - Redwood seconds in UK

SUS - Saybolt Universal Seconds in USA

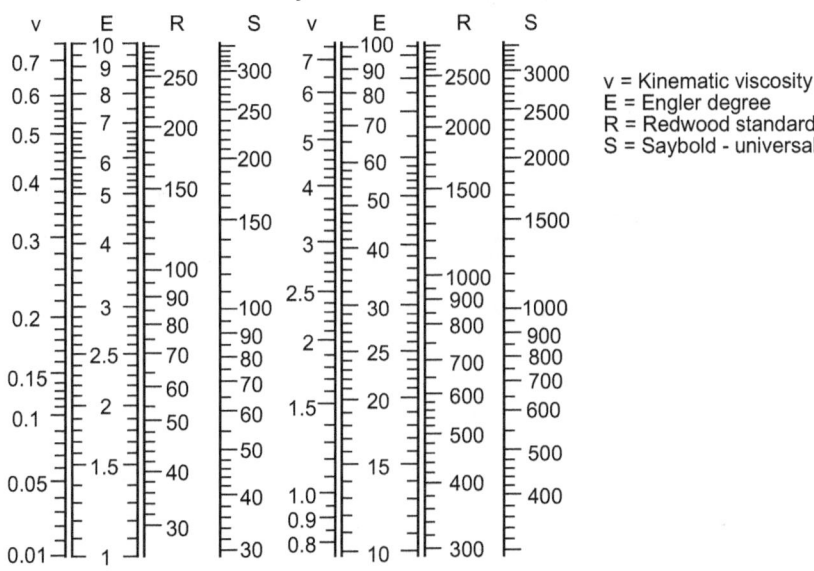

v = Kinematic viscosity
E = Engler degree
R = Redwood standard
S = Saybold - universal

Fig. 1 : Viscosity Conversion Scale from cSt to °E, SUS and RS

In each of the above case, viscosity is measured by a specially designed viscometer.

Interconversion of various units of viscosity can be more readily done using Nomograms given below in Figs. 1 and 2.

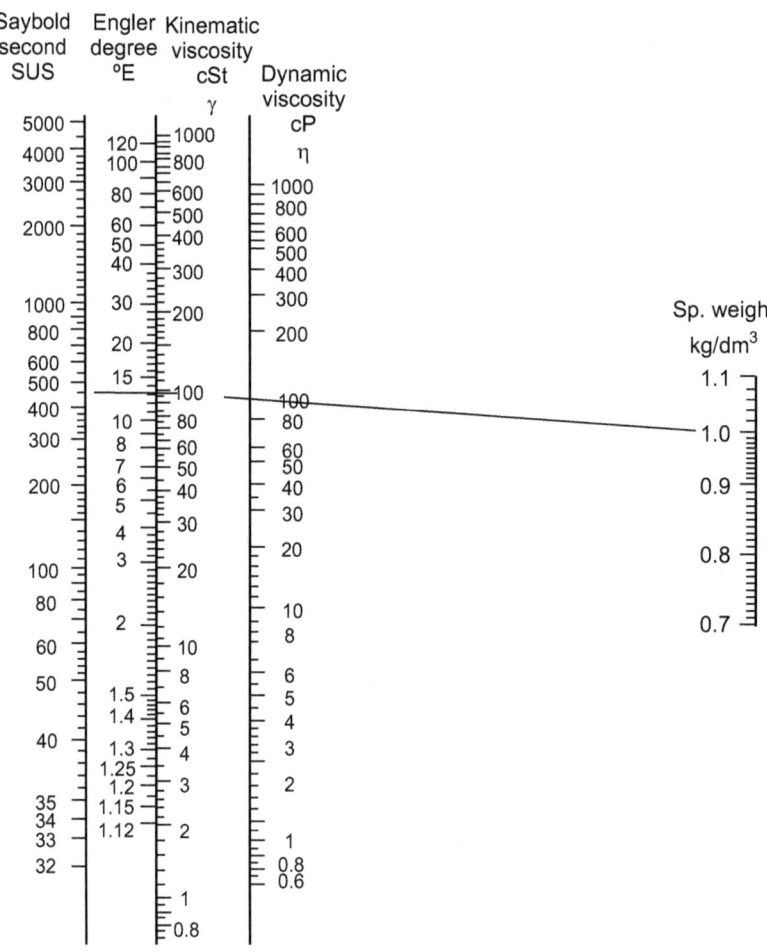

Fig. 2: Calculation of Viscosity by Using Nomograms

Table 1.1: ISO VG Classification

ISO Viscosity Grade ISO VG	Kinematic Viscosity Centistokes @ 40°C	
	Min.	Max.
2	1.98	2.42
3	2.88	3.52
5	4.14	5.06
7	6.12	7.48
10	9.0	11.0
15	13.5	16.5
22	19.8	24.2
32	28.8	35.2
46	41.4	50.6
68	61.2	74.8
100	90	110
150	135	165
220	198	242
320	288	352
460	414	506
680	612	748
1000	900	1100
1500	1350	1650

Table 1.2: Hydraulic and Circulation System Oils

Old No.	New VG No.
Servosystem 311	Servosystem 32
Servosystem 314	Servosystem 46
Servosystem 317	Servosystem 57*
	Servosystem 68
Servosystem 321	Servosystem 81*
_	Servosystem 100
Servosystem 526	Servosystem 121
_	Servosystem 150
Servosystem 533	Servosystem 176
_	Servosystem 220
Servosystem 563	Servosystem 320
Servosystem 563	Servosystem 460
Servosystem 711	Servosystem A 32
Servosystem 733	Servosystem A 176*
Servocirol 11	Servocirol 32
Servocirol 14	Servocirol 46
Servocirol 17	Servocirol 57*
_	Servocirol 68
Servocirol 21	Servocirol 81*
_	Servocirol 100
Servocirol 26	Servocirol 121*
_	Servocirol 150
Servohydrex 14	Servohydrex 32
Servohydrex 21	Servohydrex 57*

* Indicates non ISO VG product.

Before ISO classification of oils, the Indian oils corporation was marketing oils as per their own standard, under the designation of Servo System (SS) oils.

Compound	N	G	D	B	C	H	E	V	L	I	R	A	T	P	S	
Number prefix used by Parker Seal Co	Buna N or Nitrile	Buna S	Butadiene	Butyl	Chloroprene	Chlorosulfonated polyethylene	Ethylene propylene	Fluorocarbon	Fluorosilicone	Isoprene	Natural rubber	Polyacrylic	Polysulfide	Polyurethane	Silicone	Teflon®
Ozone resistance	P	P	P	GE	GE	E	E	E	E	P	P	E	E	E	E	E
Weather resistance	F	F	F	GE	E	E	E	E	E	F	F	E	E	E	E	E
Heat resistance	G	FG	F	GE	G	G	E	E	G	F	F	E	P	F	E	E
Chemical resistance	FG	FG	FG	E	FG	E	E	E	FG	FG	FG	P	G	F	GE	E
Oil resistance	E	P	P	P	FG	F	P	E	G	P	P	E	E	G	PG	G
Impermeability	G	F	F	G	G	G	GE	G	P	F	F	P	E	F	P	E
Cold resistance	G	G	E	G	FG	FG	GE	FP	GE	G	G	FG	G	F	P	E
Tear resistance	FG	FG	GE	FG	FG	G	GE	F	P	GE	GE	G	P	GE	P	E
Abrasion resistance	G	G	E	G	G	G	GE	G	P	E	E	G	P	E	P	P
Set resistance	GE	G	G	G	F	F	GE	G	GE	G	G	F	P	F	GE	P
Dynamic properties	GE	G	F	G	FG	G	G	E	P	FG	FG	P	P	P	P	E
Acid resistance	F	F	E	G	F	F	GE	GE	FG	F	F	F	F	F	FG	E
Tensile strength	GE	GE	E	G	G	G	G	E	F	G	G	G	F	E	P	E
Electrical properties	F	G	G	G	F	F	G	F	E	G	G	P	F	F	E	E
Water/steam resistance	FG	FG	FG	G	F	F	E	FG	F	FG	FG	F	F	F	F	E
Flame resistance	P	P	P	P	G	G	P	E	G	P	P	P	P	P	G	G

P - Poor; F – Fair; G – Good; E – Excellent

Teflon® is a registered trademark of E.I. Du Pont De Nemours and Co. (Inc.) Courtesy – Parker Seal Co.

Table 1.3: Cold Drawn Seamless Carbon Steel Tube for Pressure Applications (DIN 2391/C)

Outer Diameter × Wall Thickness (mm)	Approximate Weight (kg/m)	Maximum Working Pressures (bar)		
		Safety Factor 2.5: 1	Safety Factor 3.0: 1	Safety Factor 4.0: 1
6 × 1.5	0.166	703	586	441
6 × 1.0	0.123	428	359	269
8 × 1.5	0.240	496	414	310
8 × 1.0	0.173	310	255	193
10 × 3.5	0.561	1089	903	676
10 × 2.0	0.395	531	441	331
10 × 1.5	0.314	386	317	241
10 × 1.0	0.222	241	200	152
12 × 2.5	0.586	552	462	345
12 × 1.5	0.388	310	262	193
14 × 2.5	0.709	324	282	217
14 × 1.5	0.462	262	221	166
15 × 2.5	0.771	428	352	262
15 × 1.5	0.499	241	207	152
16 × 3.0	0.962	490	407	303
16 × 2.5	0.832	393	331	248
16 × 2.0	0.691	310	255	193
16 × 1.5	0.536	228	186	145
18 × 1.5	0.610	200	166	124
20 × 4.0	1.58	531	441	331
20 × 3.0	1.26	379	317	234

Table 1.3 Contd...

Outer Diameter × Wall Thickness (mm)	Approximate Weight (kg/m)	Maximum Working Pressures (bar)		
		Safety Factor 2.5: 1	Safety Factor 3.0: 1	Safety Factor 4.0: 1
20 × 2.5	1.08	303	255	193
20 × 2.0	0.888	241	200	152
20 × 1.5	0.684	179	152	110
22 × 3.0	1.41	338	283	214
22 × 2.0	1.07	221	179	138
22 × 1.5	0.758	159	138	103
25 × 4.0	2.072	394	263	210
25 × 3.0	1.63	297	248	186
25 × 2.0	1.13	193	159	117
28 × 4.0	2.37	359	297	221
28 × 3.5	2.11	310	255	193
28 × 2.5	1.57	214	179	131
28 × 2.0	1.28	166	138	103
28 × 1.0	0.666	83	69	52
30 × 4.0	2.56	332	276	207
30 × 3.0	2.00	241	200	152
35 × 5.0	2.367	242	161	121
38 × 5.0	4.07	324	269	228
38 × 4.0	3.35	255	214	159
38 × 3.0	2.59	186	159	117
40 × 6.0	5.03	379	317	234
40 × 5.0	4.32	310	255	193
42 × 3.0	2.885	201	133	101
48 × 6.0	6.21	310	255	193
65 × 8.0	11.24	303	255	186

Table 1.3 gives weight/m and maximum working pressure for different factors of safety, for various sizes of cold draw seamless carbon steel tubes as per DIN 2391/C.

One such nomogram is shown in Fig. 3.

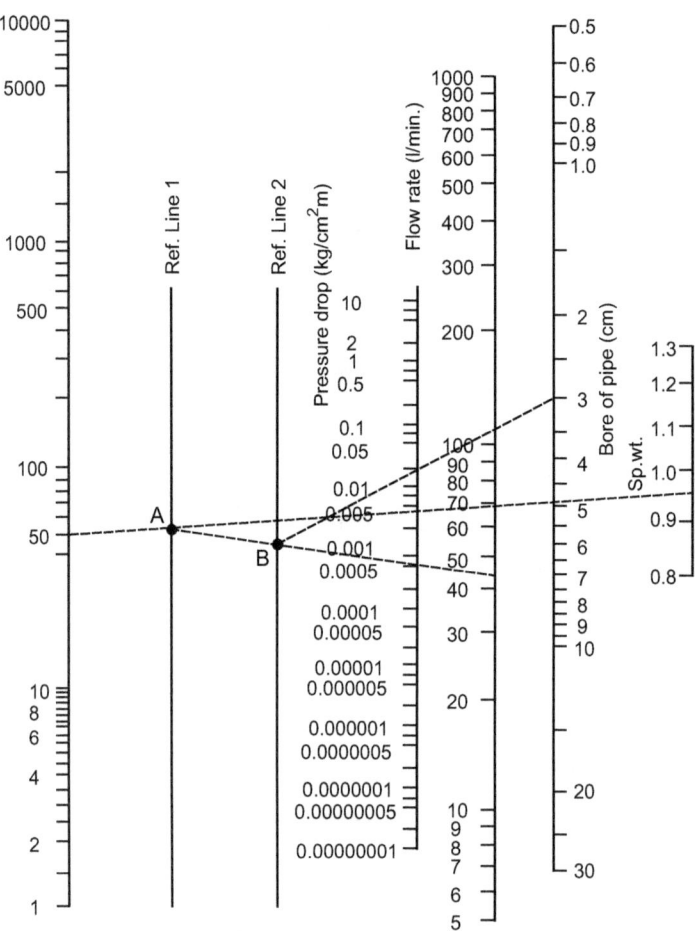

Fig. 3: Nomogram to Estimate Pressure Drop in a Straight Pipe

Table 1.4: Contamination Level for Hydraulic Fluid (particle per 100 ml) as per SAE 749D

Range of particle size in micron	Contamination class						
	0	1	2	3	4	5	6
5 - 10	2700	4600	9700	24000	32000	87000	128000
10 - 25	670	1340	2680	5360	10700	21400	42000
25 - 50	93	210	380	780	1510	3130	6500
50 - 100	16	28	56	110	225	430	1000
100	01	03	05	11	21	41	92

This standard is rarely used these days.

Table 1.5: Various Contamination Standards and Their Comparison

ISO DIS 4406 or Cetop RP 70 H	Particles per ml > 10 µm	ACFTD solids content mg/L	MIL STD 1246 A (1967)	NAS 1638 (1964)	SAE 749 D (1963)
26/23	140000	1000			
25/23	85000		1000		
23/20	14000	100	700		
21/18	4500			12	
20/18	2400		500		
20/17	2300			11	
20/16	1400	10			
19/16	1200			10	
18/15	580			9	6
17/14	280		300	8	5
16/13	140	1		7	4
15/12	70			6	3
14/12	40		200		
14/11	35			5	2
13/10	14	0.1		4	1
12/9	9			3	0
18/8	5			2	
10/8	3		100		
10/7	2.3			1	
10/6	1.4	0.01			
9/6	1.2			0	
8/5	0.6			00	
7/5	0.3		50		
6/3	0.14	0.001			
5/2	0.04		25		

Table 1.5 gives a comparison of various standards, specifying the number of particles of a certain size per 100 ml of oil.

Table 1.6: Contamination classification to specification NAS 1638

Class	Size range (μm) for number of particles per 100 ml sample				
	5 - 15	15 - 25	25 - 50	50 - 100	100 +
00	125	22	4	1	0
0	250	44	8	2	0
1	500	89	16	3	1
2	1000	178	32	6	1
3	2000	356	63	11	2
4	4000	712	126	22	4
5	8000	1425	253	45	8
6	16000	2850	506	90	16
7	32000	5700	1012	180	32
8	64000	11400	2025	360	64
9	128000	22800	4050	720	128
10	256000	45600	8100	1440	256
11	512000	91200	162000	2880	512
12	1024000	182000	324000	5760	1024

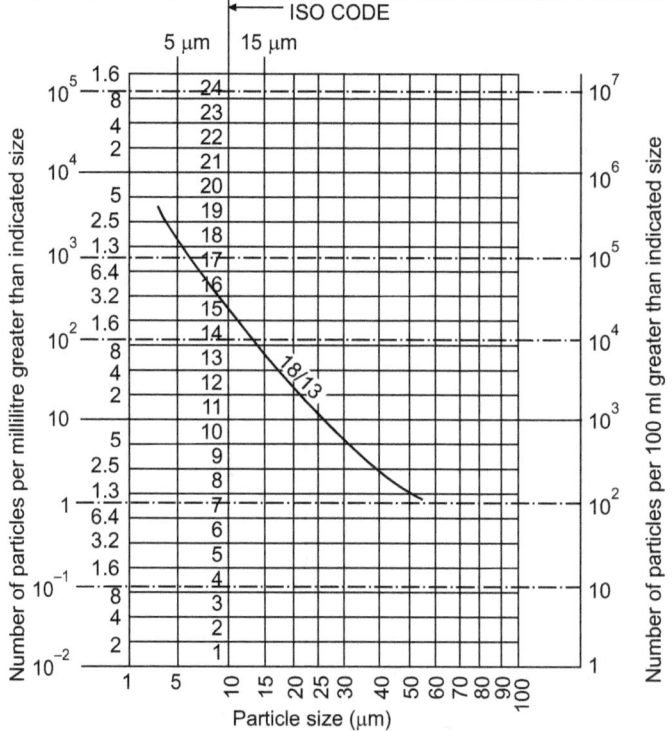

Fig. 4: ISO solid contaminant coding graphical representation

Table 1.7: Filter element, application and characteristics

Type of element	Average filtration rating	Specific points to note
Felt	25 - 50 microns	Subjects to element migration unless resin-impregnated.
Paper	Down to 10 microns	Medium dirt holding capacity, low permeability, low element strength suitable for suction/return time filter/fine filter. Subject to element migration. Disposable, low cost, low pressure drop.
Fabric	Down to 20 microns	Higher permeability than papers. Higher strength with rigid back up mesh.
Wire gauge	Down to 35 microns	Suitable for suction strainer
Wire wound	Down to 25 microns	Better mechanical strength
Wire cloth	Down to 10 microns	Expensive, high strength and free from migration
Glass fibre	Used as random layers with binding agent. Very fine filter for precision components	Fine filtering, good dirt holding capacity, good chemical resistance, absorption of particles over wide pressure drop range.
Edge type (Paper disc)	10 to 1 micron	Compatible with all fluids. High resistance to flow, clogs readily. Degrees of filtration variable with compression.
Phenolic resin impregnated paper	Fine filter, disposable low cost.	Same as above. Fluid compatibility should be a deciding factor.
Edge type (metal)	Down to 25 microns	Very strong self-supporting, suitable for high temperature, at high pressure.

Sintered woven wire cloth (Metal granular sintered together, The diameter of granules determines the filtration rating)	10 - 20 microns	High strength suitable for high temperature, complete freedom cost, low dirt capacity. Sensitive to pressure shock, high pressure drop good mechanical strength, suitable for high pressure and temperature, low dirt holding capacity. However element migration not completely eliminated under severe conditions.
Sintered porous metal (may be used as protection filter)	Down to 2 microns	Low manufacturing cost, very high strength, high pressure drop, suits low flow rates.
Sintered porous metal with woven wire reinforcement	–	Low manufacturing cost, very high strength, high pressure drop.
Sintered PTFE	5 - 25 microns	High cost, subject to element migration, strength improved with reinforcement
Sintered polythene	30 microns	Low resistance to flow and temperature above 60°C
Sintered metal felts	Down to 5 microns	High cost, but freedom from element migration. Difficult to clean. Elements usually replaced.
Membrane filter	Down to sub-micron	Low mechanical strength, poor dirt capacity, used in oil-reclamation.
Magnetic filter	Ferrous particles only	Little or no resistance to flow
Filter clothes	Down to 10 microns	May be used in air-breather.
Metal non-woven type	Stainless steel wire random layering fine and very fine.	Suits high operating temperature, high pressure drop, used for all fluids. Very expensive, limited cleaning, good fatigue properties. Good compatibility
Activated earth		Limited application in hydraulics. Used as a depth type filter.

Notes

Notes

www.ingramcontent.com/pod-product-compliance
Lightning Source LLC
Chambersburg PA
CBHW060503300426
44112CB00017B/2529